DUMBARTON OAKS STUDIES

ᴇᴄ XVII ᴊᴏ

DATED GREEK MANUSCRIPTS
OF THE THIRTEENTH
AND FOURTEENTH CENTURIES
IN THE LIBRARIES OF GREAT BRITAIN

DATED GREEK MANUSCRIPTS
OF THE
THIRTEENTH AND FOURTEENTH
CENTURIES IN THE LIBRARIES
OF GREAT BRITAIN

ALEXANDER TURYN

Dumbarton Oaks
Center for Byzantine Studies
Trustees for Harvard University
Washington, District of Columbia
1980

The Dumbarton Oaks Studies are published by the Editorial Staff at Dumbarton Oaks
under the supervision of the Senior Fellows of the Center for Byzantine Studies; Professor Peter Topping, Advisor for Byzantine Publications; Miss Julia Warner, Associate
Editor; Dr. Fanny Bonajuto, Research Associate for Publications (retired); and Mrs.
Nancy Rogers Bowen, Assistant Editor.

Distributed by
J. J. Augustin, Publisher
Locust Valley, New York 11560

Library of Congress Catalogue Card Number 80–81547; ISBN 0–88402–077–0
Printed in Germany *at* J. J. Augustin, Glückstadt

PREFACE

The book which I now submit to the scholarly world is a part of the research in dated Greek manuscripts of the thirteenth and fourteenth centuries in the libraries of Western Europe which I initiated in 1959. In the course of this investigation, I have previously published studies of MSS of this period extant in the Vatican Library (1964) and in the libraries of Italy (1972). The present volume includes all the dated MSS of the same period known to be preserved in the libraries of Great Britain.

Only MSS provided with subscriptions dated precisely to a year, or MSS supplied with similarly dated scribal notes that pertain to the time when a MS was being written, were taken into account. As an exception I added to this assemblage the Edinburgh MS written by Maximus Planudes (National Library of Scotland, MS Adv.18.7.15), although it is dated only approximately by a note on the lunar eclipse of A.D. 1290 written by Planudes. Still, I added this MS because of its famous scribe and because its writing closely resembles the handwriting of Planudes from that period. Moreover, it includes the original exemplar of the Planudean edition of Aratus' Phaenomena.

Deliberately omitted is MS London, British Museum, Additional 37002, because there is no proof at all that the subscription on the present last page (fol. 253ᵛ) of an extraneous final gathering pertains to the original body of the MS; this subscription cannot even be cogently referred to that last gathering, since the subscription and the said gathering are written in entirely different hands (on this MS, cf. *New Pal. Soc.*, Series I, pl. 52; Thompson, *Introduction*, pp. 254, 260 facsim. no. 74). Also omitted is MS Oxford, Bodleian Library, Barocci 135, written by the well-known scribe of the early fourteenth century, Manuel Pancratius, in view of the doubtful chronology of its subscription which in any case does not include an explicit year date.

Between 1959 and 1974, I examined directly all the MSS presented here, most of them several times. Furthermore, I scrutinized them additionally at home, using either partial photographic reproductions or complete reproductions on microfilm. In the descriptions and analyses of the MSS, I have observed the same rules as before. My study of MSS naturally centered on their subscriptions as the documentary evidence of their dates. They are edited diplomatically, and their facsimiles are included in the plates. The chronological, historical, geographical, prosopographical, and linguistic elements of the subscriptions were analyzed with particular attention.

From each MS at least one specimen of its book-script is presented in the plates. If there appeared to be some variation in a scribe's handwriting, more than one specimen is offered. Careful examination of the entire manuscript volumes revealed that in some cases more than one scribe participated within a MS or its original and integral parts covered by the subscription. Obviously, each scribe in such a situation must be considered a dated scribe and, accordingly, each has been represented by a specimen of his handwriting. A striking example of this is MS Oxford, Bodl. Libr., Roe 22 (of A.D. 1286), in which I detected the work of eleven scribes. Their specimens, shown in Plates **28–39**, expand our knowledge of the handwritings of that period in a most welcome manner, especially since the scripts in question are of a more natural secular character (in contrast with the conventional character of biblical MSS).

In describing the MSS I have reported their contents rather concisely only in order to indicate the nature of the texts carried by a MS, so that the reader may observe the correlation between the genre of a text and its paleographical appearance. On the whole, for a more detailed indication of the contents, the reader may turn to the descriptions of MSS given in standard catalogues, in special catalogues, or in reference books, where available (they are listed here in the bibliographical sections). Only in a few cases, when a particular situation warranted it, have I listed the contents of a MS more specifically. Thus, in the case of MS Oxford Roe 22, mentioned above, which is especially interesting as a carrier of the works of Nicetas Choniates, I considered it worthwhile to supply more exact data on the contents of the entire volume.

In the course of my work, I have benefited from the friendly assistance of many persons and institutions. All the libraries which were included in my project extended to me every facility for conducting my research and readily approved my requests for photographic reproductions. Mr. Nigel Wilson (Lincoln College, Oxford) gave me useful information on some MSS, which is acknowledged in the pertinent places in the text. Dr. R. W. Hunt, Keeper (now emeritus) of Western MSS in the Bodleian Library, Oxford, gave considerate and careful attention to my photographic needs and granted me permission to publish photographs of Bodleian MSS. Miss Ruth Barbour, formerly on the staff of the Bodleian Library, was constantly helpful in many respects. Mr. T. S. Pattie, Department of MSS, British Museum (London), answered my inquiries addressed to him by mail with unfailing kindness and helped solve some practical difficulties which arose while I was working in the Museum. Mr. R. O. MacKenna, University Librarian, Glasgow, readily supplied me with additional information on the two Hunterian MSS with which I was concerned, with exceptional helpfulness expedited the photographic arrangements, and granted me permission to publish photographs of the MSS in question. Dr. Frank Taylor, Deputy Director and Principal Keeper, John Rylands University Library, Manchester, kindly answered my queries concerning MS Rylands Gaster 1574 and gave me permission to publish photographs of that MS. Whenever I needed additional information on MSS, assistance in photographic arrangements, or other aid, the following persons were especially helpful: Mr. A. E. B. Owen, Cambridge University Library; Mr. Trevor Kaye, Trinity College Library, Cambridge; Mr. I. C. Cunningham, National Library of Scotland, Edinburgh; Mr. Charles P. Finlayson, Keeper of MSS, Edinburgh University Library; Mr. N. R. Thorp, University Library, Glasgow; Mr. T. A. J. Burnett, Department of MSS, British

Museum; Mr. H. M. T. Cobbe, Department of MSS, British Museum; Mr. E. G. W. Bill, Librarian, Lambeth Palace Library, London; Dr. Bruce Barker-Benfield, Bodleian Library, Oxford; Mr. H. J. R. Wing, Christ Church Library, Oxford; Rev. Dr. G. V. Bennett, Librarian, New College, Oxford.

My sincere thanks go to all the persons and libraries named above.

For permission to publish photographs of MSS, in addition to those authorities of the Bodleian Library at Oxford, the University Library at Glasgow, and the John Rylands University Library of Manchester mentioned previously, I wish to express my deep gratitude to the following persons and authorities of the librarie sconcerned: the Syndics of Cambridge University Library; the Master and Fellows of Trinity College, Cambridge; the Trustees of the National Library of Scotland, Edinburgh; Mr. E. R. S. Fifoot, Librarian, Edinburgh University Library; the Trustees of the British Museum and the British Library Board, London; His Grace the Archbishop of Canterbury and the Trustees of Lambeth Palace Library, London; the Governing Body of Christ Church, Oxford; the Warden and Fellows of New College, Oxford.

It should perhaps be mentioned that on 1 July 1973 the Department of MSS of the British Museum became a part of the new British Library, while remaining in the same location. Out of deference to long tradition and for obvious practical reasons, since these MSS are listed in published catalogues and in scholarly literature as belonging to the British Museum, I have continued to refer to them in this book as MSS of the British Museum.

I am under great obligation to the Research Board of the University of Illinois at Urbana, which for many years has generously supported my research project by granting funds for the acquisition of photographic reproductions needed in this connection. The University Library has always extended gracious consideration to my special needs.

I am very grateful to Professor William C. Loerke, Director of Studies, Dumbarton Oaks Center for Byzantine Studies, who most kindly accepted this book for publication in the series of Dumbarton Oaks Studies.

University of Illinois   Alexander Turyn
Urbana
September 1976

I wish to thank Miss Julia Warner, Associate Editor, for her competent advice and assistance in editorial matters, as well as Mrs. Nancy Rogers Bowen, Assistant Editor, for her conscientious proofing of the work as it progressed through the press.

In the exacting task of proofreading I was assisted substantially by Professor Elizabeth Bryson Bongie of the University of British Columbia, Vancouver. With painstaking care and attention she simultaneously read the proofs of this book at every stage, offering throughout many helpful and constructive suggestions. The responsibility for any flaws that may remain rests, of course, solely with me. Professor Bryson Bongie also compiled the General Index with great competence, thoroughness, and accuracy. I wish to record my deep gratitude to her for her important and valued collaboration.

A.T.

CONTENTS

PAGE

PREFACE vii

LIST OF PLATES xiii

INDEX OF MANUSCRIPTS xxiii

CONSECUTIVE DATES OF MANUSCRIPTS xxv

LISTS OF ABBREVIATIONS
    Bibliographical Abbreviations xxvii
    General Abbreviations and Symbols xxxii

CRITICAL NOTATION xxxii

NOTE ON GREEK PROPER NAMES xxxiii

DESCRIPTIONS AND ANALYSES OF MANUSCRIPTS . . 1

GENERAL INDEX 151

PLATES
    Specimens of Manuscript Book Texts . . . . . **1–96 A**
    Facsimiles of Subscriptions and Scribal Notes . . . **97–126**

LIST OF PLATES

All the plates are reproduced to original scale (except for Plate **118a**, for which the reduction ratio is indicated in its legend). Blank parts of margins are cut off in many reproductions. References in *italics* in parentheses are to pertinent text pages of this book.

SPECIMENS OF MANUSCRIPT BOOK TEXTS

PLATES	DATES
1. Edinburgh, University Library, MS 224 (fols. 59ᵛ–60ʳ): St. Neophytus the Recluse, Typicon of the Encleistra monastery. Written in Cyprus by the priest and notary Basilius of Paphos (*p. 5*)	A.D. 1214
2. Oxford, Bodleian Library, MS Cromwell 11 (page 230): Lessons from the New Testament. Written by the lector Michael Papadopulus of Tzemernikos in Epirus (*p. 11*)	A.D. 1225
3. Oxford, Bodl. Libr., MS Holkham Greek 64 (fol. 291ᵛ): Theophylact, archbishop of Bulgaria, Commentary on the Four Gospels. Written by the monk Gregorius (*p. 12*)	A.D. 1228
4. London, British Museum, MS Additional 27359 (fol. 126ᵛ, lower part): John Zonaras, Commentary on the Resurrectional Canons of the Octoechus (*p. 14*)	A.D. 1252
5. Oxford, Bodl. Libr., MS E. D. Clarke 8 (fol. 141ᵛ): Lectionary of the Gospels. Written by the lector Demetrius Brizopulus (presumably in Epirus) (*p. 16*)	A.D. 1253
6. London, Brit. Mus., MS Additional 40754 (fol. 25ᵛ): Lectionary of the Gospels. Written by the lector Georgius Sudarias (*p. 17*)	A.D. 1255/1256
7. Glasgow, University Library, MS Hunter 440 (page 131): Lectionary of the Gospels (*p. 20*)	A.D. 1258/1259
8a. London, Brit. Mus., MS Additional 39597 (fol. 19ᵛ): Four Gospels (*p. 21*)	A.D. 1271/1272
8b. London, Brit. Mus., MS Additional 39597 (fol. 109ʳ): Four Gospels (*p. 21*)	A.D. 1271/1272
9a. London, Brit. Mus., MS Additional 39597 (fol. 146ʳ): Four Gospels (*p. 21*)	A.D. 1271/1272
9b. London, Brit. Mus., MS Additional 39597 (fol. 157ʳ): Four Gospels (*p. 21*)	A.D. 1271/1272
10a. London, Brit. Mus., MS Additional 39597 (fol. 183ʳ): Four Gospels (*p. 22*)	A.D. 1271/1272
10b. London, Brit. Mus., MS Additional 39597 (fol. 219ᵛ): Four Gospels (*p. 22*)	A.D. 1271/1272
11. London, Brit. Mus., MS Additional 28818 (fol. 33ᵛ): Lectionary of the Gospels. Written by the priest Metaxares (*p. 23*)	A.D. 1272
12. Oxford, Bodl. Libr., MS Roe 7 (fol. 26ʳ): Euthymius Zigabenus, Commentary on the Psalms. Written by the monk Galaction (*p. 24*)	A.D. 1278/1279
13. Cambridge, University Library, MS Ii.5.44 (fol. 120ʳ): Aristotle, Eudemian Ethics. Written by the lector Nicolaus ⟨Damenus⟩ in Messina (*p. 26*)	A.D. 1279

PLATES   DATES

14. Oxford, Bodl. Libr., MS Barocci 122 (fol. 64ʳ): Euthymius Zigabenus, Commentary on the Psalms. Written by Syropulus
(*p. 27*)   A.D. 1279/1280
15. Oxford, Bodl. Libr., MS Barocci 122 (fol. 82ᵛ): Euthymius Zigabenus, Commentary on the Psalms (*p. 27*)   A.D. 1279/1280
16. Oxford, Bodl. Libr., MS Barocci 122 (fol. 140ʳ): Euthymius Zigabenus, Commentary on the Psalms. Page written partly by Syropulus, partly by another scribe (*p. 27*)   A.D. 1279/1280
17. London, Brit. Mus., MS Harley 5575 (fol. 185ʳ): Euthymius Zigabenus, Commentary on the Psalms. Written by the hieromonk
Maximus (*p. 29*)   A.D. 1281
18. Oxford, Bodl. Libr., MS Auct.E.5.8 (fol. 62ʳ): Synaxarion (Lives
of Saints) (*p. 29*)   A.D. 1281
19a. Manchester, John Rylands University Library, MS Rylands
Gaster 1574 (fols. 344ᵛ–345ʳ): St. John Climacus, Ladder of Paradise. Pages written by Ioasaph (?) (*p. 30*)   A.D. 1282
19b. Manchester, John Rylands University Library, MS Rylands
Gaster 1574 (fols. 181ᵛ–182ʳ): St. John Climacus, Ladder of Paradise (*p. 30*)   A.D. 1282
20a. Manchester, John Rylands University Library, MS Rylands
Gaster 1574 (fols. 343ᵛ–344ʳ): St. John Climacus, Ladder of Paradise (*p. 31*)   A.D. 1282
20b. Manchester, John Rylands University Library, MS Rylands
Gaster 1574 (fol. 87ʳ): St. John Climacus, Ladder of Paradise
(*p. 31*)   A.D. 1282
21. London, Brit. Mus., MS Harley 5535 (fols. 165ᵛ–166ʳ): Psalter.
Written by Andreas of Brindisi (Terra d'Otranto) (*p. 32*)   A.D. 1284
22. Oxford, Bodl. Libr., MS Roe 13 (fol. 30ʳ): ⟨Hesychius of Jeru-
salem⟩, (Third) Commentary on the Psalms. Written on Mount
Galesion (near Ephesus) (*p. 34*)   A.D. 1284/1285
23. Oxford, Bodl. Libr., MS Roe 13 (fol. 103ᵛ): St. John Chrysostom,
Expositiones in Psalmos. Written on Mount Galesion (near Ephe-
sus) (*p. 34*)   A.D. 1284/1285
24. Oxford, Bodl. Libr., MS Roe 13 (fol. 126ʳ): St. John Chrysostom,
Expositiones in Psalmos. Written on Mount Galesion (near Ephe-
sus) (*p. 35*)   A.D. 1284/1285
25. Oxford, Bodl. Libr., MS Auct.T.3.6 (fol. 12ʳ): Triodion. Written
by the priest Nilus Cucubistianus (*p. 41*)   A.D. 1285
26. London, Brit. Mus., MS Burney 20 (fol. 17ʳ): Four Gospels.
Written by the hieromonk Theophilus (*p. 43*)   A.D. 1285
27. Oxford, Bodl. Libr., MS Laud Greek 3 (fols. 132ᵛ–133ʳ): Four
Gospels. Written by Nicetas Maurones (*p. 45*)   A.D. 1285/1286
28. Oxford, Bodl. Libr., MS Roe 22 (fol. 146ᵛ): Nicetas Choniates,
Panoplia dogmatica (Thesaurus orthodoxiae). Written by the
monk Ionas (*p. 53*)   A.D. 1286
29. Oxford, Bodl. Libr., MS Roe 22 (fol. 440ᵛ): Nicetas Choniates,
History. Written by the monk Ionas (*p. 53*)   A.D. 1286
30. Oxford, Bodl. Libr., MS Roe 22 (fol. 290ᵛ): Nicetas Choniates,
Panoplia dogmatica (Thesaurus orthodoxiae). Written by the
monk Ionas (*p. 53*)   A.D. 1286
31. Oxford, Bodl. Libr., MS Roe 22 (fol. 507ʳ): St. Anastasius Sinaita,
Viae dux. Written by the monk Ionas (*p. 53*)   A.D. 1286

PLATES   DATES

32. Oxford, Bodl. Libr., MS Roe 22 (fol. 195ʳ): Nicetas Choniates,
    Panoplia dogmatica (Thesaurus orthodoxiae) (*p. 53*)   A.D. 1286

33. Oxford, Bodl. Libr., MS Roe 22 (fol. 71ʳ): Nicetas Choniates,
    Panoplia dogmatica (Thesaurus orthodoxiae) (*p. 54*)   A.D. 1286

34. Oxford, Bodl. Libr., MS Roe 22 (fol. 390ᵛ): Nicetas Choniates,
    Panoplia dogmatica (Thesaurus orthodoxiae) (*p. 54*)   A.D. 1286

35. Oxford, Bodl. Libr., MS Roe 22 (fol. 399ʳ lines 18–33):
    Nicetas Choniates, Panoplia dogmatica (Thesaurus orthodoxiae)
    (*p. 54*)   A.D. 1286

36. Oxford, Bodl. Libr., MS Roe 22 (fol. 460ᵛ, lower part): Michael
    Attaleiates, Law Treatise (with marginal excerpts from the Col-
    lectio Constitutionum Ecclesiasticarum Tripartita) (*p. 54*)   A.D. 1286

37. Oxford, Bodl. Libr., MS Roe 22 (fol. 501ᵛ): St. Anastasius Sinaita,
    Viae dux (*p. 55*)   A.D. 1286

38a. Oxford, Bodl. Libr., MS Roe 22 (fols. 227ᵛ lines 31–33, 228ʳ
     lines 1–6): Nicetas Choniates, Panoplia dogmatica (Thesaurus
     orthodoxiae) (*p. 54*)   A.D. 1286

38b. Oxford, Bodl. Libr., MS Roe 22 (fol. 534ᵛ lines 15–33): St. Ana-
     stasius Sinaita, Viae dux (*p. 55*)   A.D. 1286

39. Oxford, Bodl. Libr., MS Roe 22 (fol. 553ᵛ): St. Sophronius, patri-
    arch of Jerusalem, Synodal Epistle (*p. 55*)   A.D. 1286

40. Oxford, Bodl. Libr., MS Laud Greek 40 (fol. 113ʳ): Antiochus,
    monk of the Laura of St. Sabas, Pandectes Sacrae Scripturae.
    Written by Macarius (*p. 57*)   A.D. 1289/1290

41. Edinburgh, National Library of Scotland, MS Adv.18.7.15 (fol.
    52ᵛ): Cleomedes, Circular Theory of the Stars. Written by Maxi-
    mus Planudes, presumably in Constantinople (*p. 59*)   *circa* A.D. 1290

42. Edinburgh, National Library of Scotland, MS Adv.18.7.15 (fol.
    12ᵛ): Cleomedes, Circular Theory of the Stars. Written by an
    amanuensis of Maximus Planudes, presumably in Constantinople
    (*p. 59*)   *circa* A.D. 1290

43. London, Brit. Mus., MS Burney 21 (fol. 249ᵛ): Four Gospels.
    Written by Theodorus Hagiopetrites (*p. 61*)   A.D. 1291/1292

44. Oxford, Bodl. Libr., MS Barocci 16 (fols. 168ᵛ–169ʳ): St. John
    Climacus, Ladder of Paradise (*p. 63*)   A.D. 1294

45. Cambridge, University Library, MS Dd.9.69 (fol. 240ᵛ): Four
    Gospels. Written by Michael Mantylides (*p. 66*)   A.D. 1297

46. London, Brit. Mus., MS Additional 22506 (fol. 47ʳ): Four
    Gospels. Written by the monk and deacon Neophytus of Cyprus
    (*p. 67*)   A.D. 1304/1305

47. London, Brit. Mus., MS Additional 29714 (fol. 114ʳ): Lectionary
    of the Acts and Epistles. Written by Ignatius (*p. 69*)   A.D. 1305/1306

48. Oxford, Bodl. Libr., MS Auct.T.3.16 (fol. 45ᵛ): Synaxarion (Lives
    of Saints) of Constantinople. Written by the lector Georgius
    Saracinopulus (*p. 70*)   A.D. 1306/1307

49. Oxford, New College, MS 258 (fol. 93ʳ): Hermogenes, Rhetorical
    Writings. Written by Demetrius Triclines (or Triclinius) of Thes-
    salonica (*p. 71*)   A.D. 1308

50. London, Brit. Mus., MS Additional 38538 (fol. 114ᵛ): Acts of
    the Apostles and Epistles. Written by Ioannes (*p. 73*)   A.D. 1311/1312

51. Oxford, Bodl. Libr., MS Lyell 94 (fols. 102ᵛ–103ʳ): Theotocarion
    (*p. 74*)   A.D. 1312

PLATES   DATES

52. London, Brit. Mus., MS Arundel 523 (fol. 22ʳ): Constantine
    Manasses, Chronicle. Written in Crete by the priest Michael
    Lulludes of Ephesus (*p. 75*)   A.D. 1312/1313

53. Oxford, Bodl. Libr., MS Cromwell 22 (page 37): St. Theodore
    the Studite, Short Catecheses. Written by the hieromonk Marcus
    (*p. 78*)   A.D. 1314/1315

54. Oxford, Christ Church, MS 71 (fol. 158ʳ): St. John Climacus,
    Ladder of Paradise (*p. 79*)   A.D. 1315

55. Cambridge, Trinity College, MS B.10.16 (fol. 141ᵛ): Four Gos-
    pels. Written by the hieromonk Iacobus on Mount Sinai (*p. 81*) A.D. 1315/1316

56. London, Brit. Mus., MS Burney 22 (fol. 133ᵛ): Lectionary of the
    Gospels. Written most probably in Cyprus (*p. 82*)   A.D. 1319

57. London, Brit. Mus., MS Harley 5579 (fol. 131ʳ): St. Athanasius
    of Alexandria, Writings. Written by the lector Romanus ⟨Char-
    tophylax⟩, most probably in Cyprus (*p. 87*)   A.D. 1320/1321

58. London, Brit. Mus., MS Harley 5579 (fol. 209ᵛ): St. Athanasius
    of Alexandria, Writings. Written by the lector Romanus ⟨Char-
    tophylax⟩, most probably in Cyprus (*p. 88*)   A.D. 1320/1321

59. Oxford, Bodl. Libr., MS Gr.bibl.d.1 (fol. 167ʳ): Four Gospels
    (*p. 89*)   A.D. 1321/1322

60. London, Brit. Mus., MS Additional 11838 (fol. 69ʳ): Four Gospels.
    Written by the priest and notary Constantinus Pastil (*p. 91*) A.D. 1325/1326

61. London, Brit. Mus., MS Additional 5117 (fol. 40ᵛ): Four Gospels
    (*p. 94*)   A.D. 1326

62. London, Brit. Mus., MS Additional 5117 (fol. 158ᵛ): Four Gospels
    (*p. 95*)   A.D. 1326

63. London, Brit. Mus., MS Additional 5117 (fol. 39ᵛ): Four Gospels
    (*p. 95*)   A.D. 1326

64. London, Brit. Mus., MS Additional 5117 (fol. 60ʳ): Four Gospels
    (*p. 95*)   A.D. 1326

65. London, Brit. Mus., MS Additional 5117 (fol. 83ʳ): Hypothesis
    (end) and List of Chapters (beginning) to the Gospel of St. Mark
    (*p. 96*)   A.D. 1326

66. Oxford, Bodl. Libr., MS Auct.T.5.28 (fol. 194ʳ): St. Gregory of
    Nazianzus, Orations (*p. 97*)   A.D. 1333

67. London, Brit. Mus., MS Additional 19993 (fol. 131ᵛ): Lectionary
    of the Gospels. Written probably in Cyprus (*p. 99*)   A.D. 1334/1335

68. Oxford, Bodl. Libr., MS Laud Greek 2 (fol. 157ʳ): Psalms (*p. 100*) A.D. 1335/1336

69. Cambridge, University Library, MS Additional 3049 (fol. 78ʳ):
    George Moschampar, Capita antirrhetica contra Ioannis Becci
    dogmata et scripta. Written by Nicolaus of Clarentza (in the
    Peloponnesus) (*p. 102*)   A.D. 1336

70. Cambridge, University Library, MS Additional 3049 (fol. 63ʳ):
    George Moschampar, Capita antirrhetica contra Ioannis Becci
    dogmata et scripta. Written in the Peloponnesus (*p. 103*)   A.D. 1336

71. London, Brit. Mus., MS Additional 5468 (fol. 129ʳ): Four Gospels.
    Written by Constantinus of Adrianople (*p. 103*)   A.D. 1337

72. Oxford, Bodl. Libr., MS Selden Supra 29 (fols. 109ᵛ–110ʳ): Four
    Gospels. Written by Theodosius (*p. 105*)   A.D. 1337/1338

73. Oxford, Bodl. Libr., MS Selden Supra 9 (fol. 3ʳ): Panegyricon.
    Written by the priest and chartophylax Constantinus Magedon
    of Italy (*p. 106*)   A.D. 1340

PLATES

DATES

74. Oxford, Bodl. Libr., MS Auct.E.1.14 (fol. 81ᵛ, upper part): St. John Chrysostom, Homilies on Genesis (*p. 107*)

A.D. 1340/1341

75. Oxford, Bodl. Libr., MS Laud Greek 71 (fol. 256bᵛ): St. Augustine, De Trinitate (translated into Greek by Maximus Planudes) (*p. 107*)

A.D. 1341/1342

76. Oxford, Bodl. Libr., MS Barocci 197 (fol. 374ᵛ): St. Gregory of Nazianzus, Oration 44. Written by the hieromonk Galaction Madaraces in Constantinople (*p. 112*)

A.D. 1343

77. Oxford, Bodl. Libr., MS Barocci 156 (fol. 177ʳ): Macarius Chrysocephalus, Catena on the Gospel of St. Matthew (Book I). Written by Macarius Chrysocephalus, metropolitan of Philadelphia (*p. 114*)

A.D. 1344

78. Oxford, Bodl. Libr., MS Roe 18ᴬ (fol. 146ʳ): Theodore Balsamon, Responsa ad interrogationes Marci patriarchae Alexandrini. Written by Constantinus Sophus (*p. 115*)

A.D. 1348

79. Glasgow, University Library, MS Hunter 424 (fol. 239ʳ): Plutarch, Parallel Lives (*p. 116*)

A.D. 1348

80a. Oxford, Christ Church, MS 63 (fol. 26ᵛ, upper part): St. John Climacus, Ladder of Paradise. Written by the monk Germanus (*p. 119*)

A.D. 1355/1356

80b. Oxford, Christ Church, MS 63 (fol. 360ᵛ, upper part): St. John Climacus, Liber ad pastorem. Written by the hieromonk Gennadius (*p. 119*)

A.D. 1355/1356

81. London, Brit. Mus., MS Additional 11837 (fol. 12ʳ, upper part): New Testament. Written by the hieromonk Methodius (most probably in the monastery τῶν Ὁδηγῶν in Constantinople) (*p. 120*)

A.D. 1357

82. Oxford, Bodl. Libr., MS Laud Greek 18 (fol. 19ʳ): Proclus Diadochus, On Platonic Theology. Written by Stelianus Chumnus, probably in Constantinople (*p. 122*)

A.D. 1357/1358

83. London, Lambeth Palace, MS 1183 (page 332): Acts of the Apostles and Epistles. Written by Theophanes (most probably in the monastery τῶν Ὁδηγῶν in Constantinople) (*p. 126*)

A.D. 1358

84. Oxford, Bodl. Libr., MS Barocci 110 (fol. 186ʳ): Theodore Prodromus, Commentary on the Canons of Cosmas of Maïuma and St. John of Damascus. Written by the priest Nicetas (*p. 127*)

A.D. 1359/1360

85. London, Brit. Mus., MS Burney 50 (part I, fol. 97ᵛ): Apophthegmata Patrum. Written by Ioannes(-Ioseph) Philagrius in Crete (*p. 128*)

A.D. 1361/1362

86. London, Brit. Mus., MS Burney 50 (part I, fol. 163ʳ): Apophthegmata Patrum. Written in Crete (*p. 129*)

A.D. 1361/1362

87. Oxford, Bodl. Libr., MS Canonici Greek 93 (fol. 13ʳ, middle part): Plutarch, Parallel Lives. Written by Manuel Tzycandyles in Mistra (near Sparta) (*p. 130*)

A.D. 1362

88. London, Brit. Mus., MS Harley 5782 (fol. 147ʳ): Synaxarion (Lives of Saints). Written by the hieromonk Iacobus (*p. 131*)

A.D. 1362/1363

89. London, Brit. Mus., MS Burney 18 (fol. 10ʳ, upper part): Four Gospels. Written by Ioasaph (of the monastery τῶν Ὁδηγῶν in Constantinople) (*p. 132*)

A.D. 1366

90. London, Brit. Mus., MS Burney 18 (fol. 53ʳ): Four Gospels. Written by Ioasaph (of the monastery τῶν Ὁδηγῶν in Constantinople) (*p. 133*)

A.D. 1366

91. Oxford, Christ Church, MS 69 (fol. 44ʳ): Matthew Blastares, Syntagma. Written by Manuel Mauromates of Zichnai (in Macedonia) (*p. 136*)

A.D. 1367

PLATES   DATES

92. Oxford, Christ Church, MS 69 (fol. 154ʳ): Matthew Blastares,
    Syntagma (Appendix). Written presumably in Zichnai (in Mace-
    donia) (*p. 136*)   A.D. 1367
93. Oxford, Bodl. Libr., MS Barocci 69 (fol. 261ᵛ): Hesychius of
    Sinai, De temperantia et virtute. Written by the hieromonk
    Niphon, presumably in Crete (*p. 140*)   A.D. 1378
94. Oxford, Bodl. Libr., MS Barocci 69 (fol. 102ʳ): Nicetas Stetha-
    tus, Physicorum capitum centuria II. Written presumably in
    Crete (*p. 140*)   A.D. 1378
95. Oxford, Bodl. Libr., MS Canonici Greek 102 (fol. 30ᵛ, upper
    part): Pentecostarion. Written by the priest Constantinus Cha-
    rases in Constantinople (*p. 141*)   A.D. 1383
96. Oxford, Christ Church, MS 61 (fol. 106ʳ): Psalter. Written by
    Ioasaph (of the monastery τῶν Ὁδηγῶν in Constantinople) (p. *143*)   A.D. 1391
96A. Oxford, Bodl. Libr., MS Auct.T.inf.1.10 (fol. 10ʳ): Synaxarion
    and Menologion (Tables of New Testament lessons). From an
    addition written by Ioasaph of the monastery τῶν Ὁδηγῶν in
    Constantinople (*p. 148*)   A.D. 1391

FACSIMILES OF SUBSCRIPTIONS AND SCRIBAL NOTES

In the legends to some of these facsimiles, parentheses enclose dates or names of
scribes that are self-evident or based on internal grounds, although they are not
explicitly stated in the subscriptions or scribal notes reproduced.

PLATES   DATES

97. Edinburgh, University Library, MS 224 (fol. 83ʳ): Subscription
    by the priest and notary Basilius of Paphos (in Cyprus), preceded
    by an autographic note of St. Neophytus the Recluse (*p. 3*)   A.D. 1214
98a. Oxford, Bodl. Libr., MS Cromwell 11 (page 416): Subscription
    by the lector Michael Papadopulus of Tzemernikos in Epirus
    (*p. 8*)   A.D. 1225
98b. Oxford, Bodl. Libr., MS Holkham Greek 64 (fol. 300ᵛ): Sub-
    scription by the monk Gregorius (*p. 12*)   A.D. 1228
99a. London, Brit. Mus., MS Additional 27359 (fol. 191ᵛ): Subscrip-
    tion (*p. 14*)   June 5, A.D. 1252
99b. London, Brit. Mus., MS Additional 27359 (fol. 239ᵛ): Subscrip-
    tion (*p. 14*)   July 6, A.D. 1252
99c. Oxford, Bodl. Libr., MS E. D. Clarke 8 (fol. 196ʳ right column
    196ᵛ left column): Subscription by the lector Demetrius Bri-
    zopulus (presumably of Epirus) (*p. 15*)   A.D. 1253
100a. London, Brit. Mus., MS Additional 40754 (fol. 151ʳ): Subscrip-
    tion by the lector Georgius Sudarias (*p. 17*)   A.D. 1255/1256
100b. Glasgow, University Library, MS Hunter 440 (page 224): Sub-
    scription (*p. 20*)   A.D. 1258/1259
100c. London, Brit. Mus., MS Additional 39597 (fol. 230ᵛ): Subscrip-
    tion (*p. 21*)   A.D. 1271/1272
100d. London, Brit. Mus., MS Additional 28818 (fol. 118ʳ): Subscrip-
    tion by the priest Metaxares (*p. 23*)   A.D. 1272
101a. Oxford, Bodl. Libr., MS Roe 7 (fol. 331ᵛ): Subscription by the
    monk Galaction (*p. 23*)   A.D. 1278/1279

PLATES	DATES
101b. Cambridge, University Library, MS Ii.5.44 (fol. 143ᵛ): Subscription by the lector Nicolaus ⟨Damenus⟩ written in Messina (*p. 25*)	A.D. 1279
101c. Oxford, Bodl. Libr., MS Barocci 122 (fol. 223ᵛ): Subscription by Syropulus (*p. 27*)	A.D. 1279/1280
102a. London, Brit. Mus., MS Harley 5575 (fol. 307ʳ): Subscription by the hieromonk Maximus (*p. 28*)	A.D. 1281
102b. Oxford, Bodl. Libr., MS Auct.E.5.8 (fol. 142ᵛ): Subscription (*p. 29*)	A.D. 1281
102c. Manchester, John Rylands University Library, MS Rylands Gaster 1574 (fols. 376ᵛ–377ʳ): Subscription (written by Ioasaph?) (*p. 30*)	A.D. 1282
102d. London, Brit. Mus., MS Harley 5535 (fol. 221ᵛ): Subscription by Andreas of Brindisi (Terra d'Otranto) (*p. 31*)	May 8, A.D. 1284
102e. London, Brit. Mus., MS Harley 5535 (fol. 260ᵛ): Subscription by Andreas of Brindisi (Terra d'Otranto) (*p. 31*)	May 14, A.D. 1284
103a. Oxford, Bodl. Libr., MS Roe 13 (fol. 224ʳ): Subscription written on Mount Galesion (near Ephesus) (*p. 34*)	A.D. 1284/1285
103b. London, Brit. Mus., MS Burney 20 (fol. 288ᵛ): Subscription by the hieromonk Theophilus (*p. 43*)	A.D. 1285
104. Oxford, Bodl. Libr., MS Auct.T.3.6 (fols. 201ᵛ–202ʳ): Two subscriptions by the priest Nilus Cucubistianus (*p. 38*)	A.D. 1285
105a. Oxford, Bodl. Libr., MS Laud Greek 3 (fol. 158ʳ): Subscription by Nicetas Maurones (*p. 44*)	A.D. 1285/1286
105b. Oxford, Bodl. Libr., MS Laud Greek 40 (fol. 308ʳ): Subscription (partly cryptographic) by Macarius (*p. 56*)	A.D. 1289/1290
105c. Edinburgh, National Library of Scotland, MS Adv.18.7.15 (fol. 54ᵛ): Note on lunar eclipse in the handwriting of Maximus Planudes (*p. 57*)	A.D. 1290
106. Oxford, Bodl. Libr., MS Roe 22 (fol. 560ʳ–560ᵛ): Subscription by the monk Ionas (*p. 49*)	A.D. 1286
107a. London, Brit. Mus., MS Burney 21 (fol. 258ʳ): Subscription by Theodorus Hagiopetrites (*p. 60*)	A.D. 1291/1292
107b. Oxford, Bodl. Libr., MS Barocci 16 (fol. 283ʳ): Subscription (*p. 63*)	A.D. 1294
108. Cambridge, University Library, MS Dd.9.69 (fol. 293ʳ–293ᵛ): Subscription by Michael Mantylides (*pp. 64–66*)	A.D. 1297
109a. London, Brit. Mus., MS Additional 22506 (fol. 219ʳ): Subscription by the monk and deacon Neophytus of Cyprus (*p. 67*)	A.D. 1304/1305
109b. London, Brit. Mus., MS Additional 29714 (fol. 178ᵛ): Subscription by Ignatius (*p. 69*)	A.D. 1305/1306
109c. Oxford, Bodl. Libr., MS Auct.T.3.16 (fol. 124ᵛ): Subscription by the lector Georgius Saracinopulus (*p. 70*)	A.D. 1306/1307
110a. Oxford, New College, MS 258 (fol. 250ᵛ): Subscription by Demetrius Triclines (later Triclinius) (of Thessalonica) (*p. 71*)	A.D. 1308
110b. London, Brit. Mus., MS Additional 38538 (fol. 238ᵛ): Subscription by Ioannes (*p. 72*)	A.D. 1311/1312
110c. Oxford, Bodl. Libr., MS Lyell 94 (fol. 189ʳ): Subscription (*p. 74*)	A.D. 1312
110d. London, Brit. Mus., MS Arundel 523 (fol. 144ᵛ): Subscription by the priest Michael Lulludes of Ephesus, written in Crete (*p. 74*)	A.D. 1312/1313
111a. Oxford, Bodl. Libr., MS Cromwell 22 (page 450): Subscription (partly cryptographic) by the hieromonk Marcus (*p. 78*)	A.D. 1314/1315
111b. Oxford, Christ Church, MS 71 (fol. 342ᵛ): Subscription (*p. 78*)	A.D. 1315

PLATES   DATES

111c. Cambridge, Trinity College, MS B.10.16 (fol. 160ᵛ): Subscription
by the hieromonk Iacobus, written on Mount Sinai (*p. 80*)   A.D. 1315/1316

112a. London, Brit. Mus., MS Burney 22 (fol. 248ᵛ): Subscription
written most probably in Cyprus (*p. 82*)   A.D. 1319

112b. London, Brit. Mus., MS Harley 5579 (fol. 210ʳ): Subscription by
the lector Romanus ⟨Chartophylax⟩, written most probably in
Cyprus (*p. 84*)   A.D. 1320/1321

112c. Oxford, Bodl. Libr., MS Gr.bibl.d.1 (fol. 271ʳ): Subscription
(*p. 89*)   A.D. 1321/1322

112d. London, Brit. Mus., MS Additional 11838 (fol. 269ᵛ): Subscription by the priest and notary Constantinus Pastil (*p. 91*)   A.D. 1325/1326

113a. London, Brit. Mus., MS Additional 5117 (fol. 224ʳ): Subscription (*p. 92*)   A.D. 1326

113b. Oxford, Bodl. Libr., MS Auct.T.5.28 (fol. 263ʳ): Subscription
(*p. 97*)   A.D. 1333

113c. London, Brit. Mus., MS Additional 19993 (fol. 281ᵛ): Subscription written probably in Cyprus (*p. 98*)   A.D. 1334/1335

113d. Oxford, Bodl. Libr., MS Laud Greek 2 (fol. 201ᵛ): Subscription
(*p. 100*)   A.D. 1335/1336

113e. Glasgow, University Library, MS Hunter 424 (fol. 323ʳ): Subscription (*p. 116*)   A.D. 1348

114a. Cambridge, University Library, MS Additional 3049 (fol. 78ᵛ):
Subscription by Nicolaus of Clarentza (in the Peloponnesus)
(*p. 101*)   A.D. 1336

114b. London, Brit. Mus., MS Additional 5468 (fol. 225ᵛ): Subscription by Constantinus of Adrianople (*p. 103*)   A.D. 1337

114c. Oxford, Bodl. Libr., MS Selden Supra 29 (fol. 230ᵛ): Subscription by Theodosius (*p. 104*)   A.D. 1337/1338

114d. Oxford, Bodl. Libr., MS Selden Supra 9 (fol. 110ᵛ): Subscription
by the priest and chartophylax Constantinus Magedon of Italy
(*p. 106*)   A.D. 1340

115a. Oxford, Bodl. Libr., MS Auct.E.1.14 (fol. 296ᵛ): Subscription
(*p. 107*)   A.D. 1340/1341

115b. Oxford, Bodl. Libr., MS Laud Greek 71 (fol. 270ᵛ): Subscription
(*p. 107*)   A.D. 1341/1342

115c. Oxford, Bodl. Libr., MS Barocci 197 (fol. 374ʳ): Note on an
earthquake during the writing (written by the hieromonk Galaction Madaraces in Constantinople) (*p. 108*)   October 14, A.D. 1343

115d. Oxford, Bodl. Libr., MS Barocci 197 (fol. 380ᵛ): Note on an
earthquake during the writing, written by the hieromonk Galaction (Madaraces) in Constantinople (*p. 109*)   October 18–29, A.D. 1343

115e. Oxford, Bodl. Libr., MS Barocci 197 (fol. 425ᵛ): Note on the
time of the writing (written by the hieromonk Galaction Madaraces in Constantinople) (*p. 109*)   November 20 (A.D. 1343)

115f. Oxford, Bodl. Libr., MS Barocci 197 (fol. 426ᵛ): Note on an
earthquake during the writing (written by the hieromonk Galaction Madaraces in Constantinople) (*p. 109*)   November 20 (A.D. 1343)

116a. Oxford, Bodl. Libr., MS Barocci 197 (fol. 434ʳ): Note on the
time of the writing (written by the hieromonk Galaction Madaraces in Constantinople) (*p. 109*)   December 5 (A.D. 1343)

116b. Oxford, Bodl. Libr., MS Barocci 197 (fol. 277ᵛ): Personal reference by the scribe, hieromonk Galaction Madaraces (*p. 110*)   (A.D. 1343)

PLATES   DATES

116c. Oxford, Bodl. Libr., MS Barocci 197 (fol. 344ʳ): Personal reference by the scribe, hieromonk Galaction Madaraces (*p. 110*)   (A.D. 1343)

116d. Oxford, Bodl. Libr., MS Barocci 197 (fol. 460ʳ): Personal reference by the scribe, hieromonk Galaction Madaraces (*p. 110*)   (A.D. 1343)

116e. Oxford, Bodl. Libr., MS Barocci 197 (fol. 630ᵛ): Personal reference by the scribe, hieromonk Galaction Madaraces (*p. 110*)   (A.D. 1343)

117a. Oxford, Bodl. Libr., MS Barocci 197 (fol. 669ʳ): Transcript of the colophon of the hieromonk Galaction Madaraces (*p. 111*)
    (transcribed shortly after A.D. 1343)

117b. Oxford, Bodl. Libr., MS Barocci 156 (fol. 360ᵛ): Subscription by Macarius Chrysocephalus, metropolitan of Philadelphia (*p. 113*)   A.D. 1344

117c. Oxford, Bodl. Libr., MS Roe 18ᴮ (fol. 476ᵛ): Subscription by Constantinus Sophus (*p. 115*)   A.D. 1348

118a. Oxford, Christ Church, MS 63 (fol. 362ʳ–362ᵛ): Subscription by the hieromonk Gennadius. Reproduced at three-fourths the original measurements (*p. 118*)   A.D. 1355/1356

118b. Oxford, Christ Church, MS 63 (fol. 333ᵛ): Note by one of the scribes of the MS, the hieromonk Gennadius (*p. 118*)   (A.D. 1355/1356)

119a. London, Brit. Mus., MS Additional 11837 (fol. 464ᵛ): Subscription by the hieromonk Methodius (written most probably in the monastery τῶν Ὁδηγῶν in Constantinople) (*p. 120*)   A.D. 1357

119b. Oxford, Bodl. Libr., MS Laud Greek 18 (parts of fol. 288ᵛ): Subscription by Stelianus Chumnus, written probably in Constantinople (*p. 122*)   A.D. 1357/1358

120a. London, Lambeth Palace, MS 1183 (parts of page 472): Subscription by Theophanes (written most probably in the monastery τῶν Ὁδηγῶν in Constantinople) (*p. 125*)   A.D. 1358

120b. London, Brit. Mus., MS Burney 50 (part II, fol. 179ʳ): Subscription by Ioannes(-Ioseph) Philagrius, written in Crete (*p. 128*)   A.D. 1361/1362

120c. London, Brit. Mus., MS Burney 50 (part I, fol. 2ʳ): Invocation by Ioannes(-Ioseph) Philagrius, written in Crete (*p. 128*)   (A.D. 1361/1362)

121a. Oxford, Bodl. Libr., MS Barocci 110 (fol. 362ᵛ): Subscription by the priest Nicetas (*p. 127*)   A.D. 1359/1360

121b. London, Brit. Mus., MS Harley 5782 (fol. 241ʳ): Subscription by the hieromonk Iacobus (*p. 130*)   A.D. 1362/1363

122a. Milan, Biblioteca Ambrosiana, MS D 538 inf. (fol. 305ᵛ): Subscription by Manuel Tzycandyles, written in Mistra (near Sparta) at the conclusion of the once entire MS Oxford Canonici Greek 93 + Milan D 538 inf. (*p. 129*)   A.D. 1362

122b. London, Brit. Mus., MS Burney 18 (fol. 222ᵛ): Subscription by Ioasaph (of the monastery τῶν Ὁδηγῶν in Constantinople) (*p. 132*)   A.D. 1366

123a. Oxford, Christ Church, MS 69 (fol. 156ʳ): Subscription written presumably in Zichnai (in Macedonia) (*p. 135*)   August 14, A.D. 1367

123b. Oxford, Christ Church, MS 69 (fol. 171ʳ): Invocation by Manuel (Mauromates) of Zichnai (in Macedonia) (*p. 135*)   (after August 14, A.D. 1367)

123c. Oxford, Christ Church, MS 69 (fol. 172ʳ): Subscription by Manuel Mauromates of Zichnai (in Macedonia) (*p. 135*)   (after August 14, A.D. 1367)

124a. Oxford, Bodl. Libr., MS Barocci 69 (fol. 280ʳ): Subscription by the hieromonk Niphon, written presumably in Crete (*p. 137*)   A.D. 1378

124b. Oxford, Bodl. Libr., MS Canonici Greek 102 (fol. 70ʳ): Subscription by the priest Constantinus Charases of Constantinople (*p. 141*)   A.D. 1383

PLATES   DATES

125. Oxford, Christ Church, MS 61 (fol. 222ᵛ): Subscription by Ioasaph (of the monastery τῶν Ὁδηγῶν in Constantinople) (p. *143*)   A.D. 1391

126a. Oxford, Bodl. Libr., MS Auct.T.inf.1.10 (fol. 424ʳ): Note by Ioasaph of the monastery τῶν Ὁδηγῶν in Constantinople on the
completion of the adaptation of this MS for liturgical use (*p. 146*)   A.D. 1391

126b. Oxford, Bodl. Libr., MS Auct.T.inf.1.10 (fol. 14ᵛ): Subscription
of an addition by Ioasaph (of the monastery τῶν Ὁδηγῶν in Constantinople) (*p. 148*)   A.D. 1391

INDEX OF MANUSCRIPTS
WITH TEXT AND PLATE REFERENCES

Text pages on which a manuscript is discussed are indicated in *italic* figures. Corresponding plates are indicated in **boldface** figures. Plates **1–96A** show specimens of manuscript book texts; plates **97–126** include facsimiles of subscriptions and scribal notes.

CAMBRIDGE, TRINITY COLLEGE
MS B.10.16: cf. text pp. *79–82*, Plates **55, 111c**

CAMBRIDGE, UNIVERSITY LIBRARY
MS Additional 3049: *100–3*, **69, 70, 114a**
MS Dd.9.69: *63–66*, **45, 108**
MS Ii.5.44: *25–27*, **13, 101b**

EDINBURGH, NATIONAL LIBRARY OF SCOTLAND
MS Adv.18.7.15: *57–59*, **41, 42, 105c**

EDINBURGH, UNIVERSITY LIBRARY
MS 224: *3–7*, **1, 97**

GLASGOW, UNIVERSITY LIBRARY
MS Hunter 424: *116–18*, **79, 113e**
MS Hunter 440: *20*, **7, 100b**

LONDON, BRITISH MUSEUM
MS Additional 5117: *92–96*, **61, 62, 63, 64, 65, 113a**
MS Additional 5468: *103–4*, **71, 114b**
MS Additional 11837: *120–21*, **81, 119a**
MS Additional 11838: *91–92*, **60, 112d**
MS Additional 19993: *98–100*, **67, 113c**
MS Additional 22506: *66–69*, **46, 109a**
MS Additional 27359: *13–15*, **4, 99a, 99b**
MS Additional 28818: *23*, **11, 100d**
MS Additional 29714: *69–70*, **47, 109b**
MS Additional 38538: *72–73*, **50, 110b**
MS Additional 39597: *20–22*, **8a, 8b, 9a, 9b, 10a, 10b, 100c**
MS Additional 40754: *17–19*, **6, 100a**
MS Arundel 523: *74–78*, **52, 110d**
MS Burney 18: *131–34*, **89, 90, 122b**
MS Burney 20: *42–44*, **26, 103b**
MS Burney 21: *60–62*, **43, 107a**
MS Burney 22: *82–83*, **56, 112a**
MS Burney 50: *128–29*, **85, 86, 120b, 120c**
MS Harley 5535: *31–33*, **21, 102d, 102e**
MS Harley 5575: *28–29*, **17, 102a**
MS Harley 5579: *83–89*, **57, 58, 112b**
MS Harley 5782: *130–31*, **88, 121b**

London, Lambeth Palace
    MS 1183: *125–26*, **83**, **120a**

Manchester, John Rylands University Library
    MS Rylands Gaster 1574: *30–31*, **19a**, **19b**, **20a**, **20b**, **102c**

Oxford, Bodleian Library
    MS Auct.E.1.14: *106–7*, **74**, **115a**
    MS Auct.E.5.8: *29*, **18**, **102b**
    MS Auct.T.3.6: *38–42*, **25**, **104**
    MS Auct.T.3.16: *70–71*, **48**, **109c**
    MS Auct.T.5.28: *97*, **66**, **113b**
    MS Auct.T.inf.1.10 (addition): *146–50*, **96A**, **126a**, **126b**
    MS Barocci 16: *62–63*, **44**, **107b**
    MS Barocci 69: *137–41*, **93**, **94**, **124a**
    MS Barocci 110: *126–27*, **84**, **121a**
    MS Barocci 122: *27–28*, **14**, **15**, **16**, **101c**
    MS Barocci 156: *113–15*, **77**, **117b**
    MS Barocci 197: *108–12*, **76**, **115c–115f**, **116a–116e**, **117a**
    MS Canonici Greek 93 (+ Milan, Bibl. Ambros., MS D 538 inf.): *129–30*, **87**, **122a**
    MS Canonici Greek 102: *141–42*, **95**, **124b**
    MS E. D. Clarke 8: *15–17*, **5**, **99c**
    MS Cromwell 11: *7–11*, **2**, **98a**
    MS Cromwell 22: *78*, **53**, **111a**
    MS Gr.bibl.d.1: *89–90*, **59**, **112c**
    MS Holkham Greek 64: *11–13*, **3**, **98b**
    MS Laud Greek 2: *100*, **68**, **113d**
    MS Laud Greek 3: *44–47*, **27**, **105a**
    MS Laud Greek 18: *122–25*, **82**, **119b**
    MS Laud Greek 40: *56–57*, **40**, **105b**
    MS Laud Greek 71: *107–8*, **75**, **115b**
    MS Lyell 94: *73–74*, **51**, **110c**
    MS Roe 7: *23–25*, **12**, **101a**
    MS Roe 13: *33–38*, **22**, **23**, **24**, **103a**
    MS Roe 18: *115–16*, **78**, **117c**
    MS Roe 22: *47–56*, **28–37**, **38a**, **38b**, **39**, **106**
    MS Selden Supra 9: *105–6*, **73**, **114d**
    MS Selden Supra 29: *104–5*, **72**, **114c**

Oxford, Christ Church
    MS 61: *142–46*, **96**, **125**
    MS 63: *118–20*, **80a**, **80b**, **118a**, **118b**
    MS 69: *134–36*, **91**, **92**, **123a**, **123b**, **123c**
    MS 71: *78–79*, **54**, **111b**

Oxford, New College
    MS 258: *71–72*, **49**, **110a**

CONSECUTIVE DATES OF MANUSCRIPTS
WITH TEXT AND PLATE REFERENCES

Text pages on which a manuscript is discussed are indicated in *italic* figures. Corresponding plates are indicated in **boldface** figures.

A.D. 1214: Edinburgh, University Library, MS 224: cf. text pp. *3–7*, Plates **1, 97**
A.D. 1225: Oxford, Bodl. Libr., MS Cromwell 11: *7–11*, **2, 98a**
A.D. 1228: Oxford, Bodl. Libr., MS Holkham Greek 64: *11–13*, **3, 98b**
A.D. 1252: London, Brit. Mus., MS Additional 27359: *13–15*, **4, 99a, 99b**
A.D. 1253: Oxford, Bodl. Libr., MS E. D. Clarke 8: *15–17*, **5, 99c**
A.D. 1255/1256: London, Brit. Mus., MS Additional 40754: *17–19*, **6, 100a**
A.D. 1258/1259: Glasgow, University Library, MS Hunter 440: *20*, **7, 100b**
A.D. 1271/1272: London, Brit. Mus., MS Additional 39597: *20–22*, **8a, 8b, 9a, 9b, 10a, 10b, 100c**
A.D. 1272: London, Brit. Mus., MS Additional 28818: *23*, **11, 100d**
A.D. 1278/1279: Oxford, Bodl. Libr., MS Roe 7: *23–25*, **12, 101a**
A.D. 1279: Cambridge, University Library, MS Ii.5.44: *25–27*, **13, 101b**
A.D. 1279/1280: Oxford, Bodl. Libr., MS Barocci 122: *27–28*, **14, 15, 16, 101c**
A.D. 1281: London, Brit. Mus., MS Harley 5575: *28–29*, **17, 102a**
A.D. 1281: Oxford, Bodl. Libr., MS Auct.E.5.8: *29*, **18, 102b**
A.D. 1282: Manchester, John Rylands University Library, MS Rylands Gaster 1574: *30–31*, **19a, 19b, 20a, 20b, 102c**
A.D. 1284: London, Brit. Mus., MS Harley 5535: *31–33*, **21, 102d, 102e**
A.D. 1284/1285: Oxford, Bodl. Libr., MS Roe 13: *33–38*, **22, 23, 24, 103a**
A.D. 1285: Oxford, Bodl. Libr., MS Auct.T.3.6: *38–42*, **25, 104**
A.D. 1285: London, Brit. Mus., MS Burney 20: *42–44*, **26, 103b**
A.D. 1285/1286: Oxford, Bodl. Libr., MS Laud Greek 3: *44–47*, **27, 105a**
A.D. 1286: Oxford, Bodl. Libr., MS Roe 22: *47–56*, **28–37, 38a, 38b, 39, 106**
A.D. 1289/1290: Oxford, Bodl. Libr., MS Laud Greek 40: *56–57*, **40, 105b**
circa A.D. 1290: Edinburgh, National Library of Scotland, MS Adv.18.7.15: *57–59*, **41, 42, 105c**
A.D. 1291/1292: London, Brit. Mus., MS Burney 21: *60–62*, **43, 107a**
A.D. 1294: Oxford, Bodl. Libr., MS Barocci 16: *62–63*, **44, 107b**
A.D. 1297: Cambridge, University Library, MS Dd.9.69: *63–66*, **45, 108**
A.D. 1304/1305: London, Brit. Mus., MS Additional 22506: *66–69*, **46, 109a**
A.D. 1305/1306: London, Brit. Mus., MS Additional 29714: *69–70*, **47, 109b**
A.D. 1306/1307: Oxford, Bodl. Libr., MS Auct.T.3.16: *70–71*, **48, 109c**
A.D. 1308: Oxford, New College, MS 258: *71–72*, **49, 110a**
A.D. 1311/1312: London, Brit. Mus., MS Additional 38538: *72–73*, **50, 110b**
A.D. 1312: Oxford, Bodl. Libr., MS Lyell 94: *73–74*, **51, 110c**
A.D. 1312/1313: London, Brit. Mus., MS Arundel 523: *74–78*, **52, 110d**
A.D. 1314/1315: Oxford, Bodl. Libr., MS Cromwell 22: *78*, **53, 111a**
A.D. 1315: Oxford, Christ Church, MS 71: *78–79*, **54, 111b**
A.D. 1315/1316: Cambridge, Trinity College, MS B.10.16: *79–82*, **55, 111c**
A.D. 1319: London, Brit. Mus., MS Burney 22: *82–83*, **56, 112a**
A.D. 1320/1321: London, Brit. Mus., MS Harley 5579: *83–89*, **57, 58, 112b**
A.D. 1321/1322: Oxford, Bodl. Libr., Gr.bibl.d.1: *89–90*, **59, 112c**

A.D. 1325/1326: London, Brit. Mus., MS Additional 11838: *91–92*, **60, 112d**
A.D. 1326: London, Brit. Mus., MS Additional 5117: *92–96*, **61, 62, 63, 64, 65, 113a**
A.D. 1333: Oxford, Bodl. Libr., MS Auct.T.5.28: *97*, **66, 113b**
A.D. 1334/1335: London, Brit. Mus., MS Additional 19993: *98–100*, **67, 113c**
A.D. 1335/1336: Oxford, Bodl. Libr., MS Laud Greek 2: *100*, **68, 113d**
A.D. 1336: Cambridge, University Library, MS Additional 3049: *100–3*, **69, 70, 114a**
A.D. 1337: London, Brit. Mus., MS Additional 5468: *103–4*, **71, 114b**
A.D. 1337/1338: Oxford, Bodl. Libr., MS Selden Supra 29: *104–5*, **72, 114c**
A.D. 1340: Oxford, Bodl. Libr., MS Selden Supra 9: *105–6*, **73, 114d**
A.D. 1340/1341: Oxford, Bodl. Libr., MS Auct.E.1.14: *106–7*, **74, 115a**
A.D. 1341/1342: Oxford, Bodl. Libr., MS Laud Greek 71: *107–8*, **75, 115b**
A.D. 1343: Oxford, Bodl. Libr., MS Barocci 197: *108–12*, **76, 115c–115f, 116a–116e, 117a**
A.D. 1344: Oxford, Bodl. Libr., MS Barocci 156: *113–15*, **77, 117b**
A.D. 1348: Oxford, Bodl. Libr., MS Roe 18: *115–16*, **78, 117c**
A.D. 1348: Glasgow, University Library, MS Hunter 424: *116–18*, **79, 113e**
A.D. 1355/1356: Oxford, Christ Church, MS 63: *118–20*, **80a, 80b, 118a, 118b**
A.D. 1357: London, Brit. Mus., MS Additional 11837: *120–21*, **81, 119a**
A.D. 1357/1358: Oxford, Bodl. Libr., MS Laud Greek 18: *122–25*, **82, 119b**
A.D. 1358: London, Lambeth Palace, MS 1183: *125–26*, **83, 120a**
A.D. 1359/1360: Oxford, Bodl. Libr., MS Barocci 110: *126–27*, **84, 121a**
A.D. 1361/1362: London, Brit. Mus., MS Burney 50: *128–29*, **85, 86, 120b, 120c**
A.D. 1362: Oxford, Bodl. Libr., MS Canonici Greek 93 (+ Milan, Bibl. Ambros., MS D 538 inf.): *129–30*, **87, 122a**
A.D. 1362/1363: London, Brit. Mus., MS Harley 5782: *130–31*, **88, 121b**
A.D. 1366: London, Brit. Mus., MS Burney 18: *131–34*, **89, 90, 122b**
A.D. 1367: Oxford, Christ Church, MS 69: *134–36*, **91, 92, 123a, 123b, 123c**
A.D. 1378: Oxford, Bodl. Libr., MS Barocci 69: *137–41*, **93, 94, 124a**
A.D. 1383: Oxford, Bodl. Libr., MS Canonici Greek 102: *141–42*, **95, 124b**
A.D. 1391: Oxford, Christ Church, MS 61: *142–46*, **96, 125**
A.D. 1391: Oxford, Bodl. Libr., MS Auct.T.inf.1.10 (addition): *146–50*, **96A, 126a, 126b**

LISTS OF ABBREVIATIONS

BIBLIOGRAPHICAL ABBREVIATIONS

AbhBerl   Abhandlungen der Preussischen Akademie der Wissenschaften, Berlin

AbhLeipz   Abhandlungen der Königl. Sächsischen Gesellschaft der Wissenschaften, Leipzig

AbhMünch   Abhandlungen der Königl. Bayerischen Akademie der Wissenschaften, München

ADB   *Allgemeine Deutsche Biographie*, 56 vols. (Leipzig, 1875–1912; repr. Berlin, 1967–71)

Ahrweiler, "La région de Smyrne"   H. Ahrweiler, "L'histoire et la géographie de la région de Smyrne entre les deux occupations turques (1081–1317) particulièrement au XIIIe siècle," *Travaux et Mémoires*, 1 (1965), pp. 1–204

Aland, I   K. Aland, *Kurzgefasste Liste der griechischen Handschriften des Neuen Testaments*. I, *Gesamtübersicht*, Arbeiten zur neutestamentlichen Textforschung, 1 (Berlin, 1963)

Aland et al., *The Greek New Testament*   K. Aland, M. Black, C. M. Martini, B. M. Metzger, and A. Wikgren, eds., *The Greek New Testament*, 2nd ed. ([London, 1968])

AnalBoll   *Analecta Bollandiana*

AOC   Archives de l'Orient Chrétien

Aubineau, *Codices Chrysostomici graeci*, I   M. Aubineau, *Codices Chrysostomici graeci*. I, *Codices Britanniae et Hiberniae* (Paris, 1968)

Barbour, in *Greek Manuscripts in the Bodleian Library*   R. Barbour, in *Greek Manuscripts in the Bodleian Library. An Exhibition Held in Connection with the XIIIth International Congress of Byzantine Studies* (Oxford, 1966)

BCH   *Bulletin de Correspondance Hellénique*

BECh   *Bibliothèque de l'Ecole des Chartes*

Beck, *Kirche und theologische Literatur*   H.-G. Beck, *Kirche und theologische Literatur im byzantinischen Reich* (Munich, 1959; repr. as 2nd ed., 1977)

BEFAR   Bibliothèque des Ecoles Françaises d'Athènes et de Rome

Belting, *Das illuminierte Buch*   H. Belting, *Das illuminierte Buch in der spätbyzantinischen Gesellschaft*, Abhandlungen der Heidelberger Akademie der Wissenschaften, Philos.-hist.Kl., 1970, 1 (Heidelberg, 1970)

BGrottaf   *Bollettino della Badia greca di Grottaferrata*

*BHG*³   *Bibliotheca Hagiographica Graeca*, 3rd ed., ed. F. Halkin, 3 vols., SubsHag, 8a (Brussels, 1957)

BHG Auct.   F. Halkin, *Auctarium Bibliothecae Hagiographicae Graecae*, SubsHag, 47 (Brussels, 1969)

Bonn ed.   Corpus Scriptorum Historiae Byzantinae, ed. B. G. Niebuhr et al. (Bonn, 1828–97)

Byzantine Art an European Art   *Byzantine Art an European Art (Ninth Exhibition Held under the Auspices of the Council of Europe)*, 2nd ed. (Athens, 1964)

ByzArch   Byzantinisches Archiv

ByzF   *Byzantinische Forschungen*

BZ   *Byzantinische Zeitschrift*

Cereteli–Sobolevski, *Exempla*, I   G. Cereteli and S. Sobolevski, *Exempla Codicum Graecorum Litteris minusculis scriptorum annorumque notis instructorum*. I, *Codices Mosquenses* (Moscow, 1911)

CFHB   Corpus Fontium Historiae Byzantinae

Clark, *Greek New Testament Manuscripts in America*   K. W. Clark, *A Descriptive Catalogue of Greek New Testament Manuscripts in America* (Chicago [1937])

ClMed   Classica et Mediaevalia

Coxe, I and III   H. O. Coxe, *Catalogi codicum manuscriptorum Bibliothecae Bodleianae* pars I, *recensionem codicum graecorum continens*; pars III, *codices graecos et latinos Canonicianos complectens* (Oxford, 1853–54)

Coxe², I and III   H. O. Coxe, *Greek Manuscripts*, Bodleian Library, Quarto Catalogues, I (repr. of Coxe, I and III, cols. 1–108, with corrections, Oxford, 1969)

CR   Classical Review

DB   Dictionnaire de la Bible

Δελτ.Χριστ.᾽Αρχ.῾Ετ.   Δελτίον τῆς Χριστιανικῆς ᾽Αρχαιολογικῆς ῾Εταιρείας

Δελτ.῾Ιστ.᾽Εθν.῾Ετ.   Δελτίον τῆς ῾Ιστορικῆς καὶ ᾽Εθνολογικῆς ῾Εταιρείας τῆς ῾Ελλάδος

Demetrakos, Μέγα Λεξικόν   D. Demetrakos, Μέγα Λεξικὸν τῆς ἑλληνικῆς γλώσσης, ed. I. S. Zerbos, 9 vols. (Athens, 1933–[50])

DenkWien   Denkschriften der kaiserlichen Akademie der Wissenschaften, Wien

Dieterich, *Untersuchungen*   K. Dieterich, *Untersuchungen zur Geschichte der griechischen Sprache von der hellenistischen Zeit bis zum 10. Jahrhundert n. Chr.*, ByzArch, 1 (Leipzig, 1898; repr. Hildesheim–New York, 1970)

DNB   Dictionary of National Biography, I–IX, ed. L. Stephen and S. Lee; X–XXII, ed. S. Lee (London, 1908–9)

von Dobschütz, *Eberhard Nestle's Einführung*   E. von Dobschütz, *Eberhard Nestle's Einführung in das Griechische Neue Testament*, 4th ed. (Göttingen, 1923)

Dölger, *Regesten*   F. Dölger, *Regesten der Kaiserurkunden des oströmischen Reiches von 565–1453*, 5 vols. (Munich–Berlin, 1924–65)

DOP   Dumbarton Oaks Papers

DOS   Dumbarton Oaks Studies

DTC   Dictionnaire de Théologie Catholique

Du Cange, *Glossarium graecitatis*   C. Du Fresne Du Cange, *Glossarium ad Scriptores mediae et infimae graecitatis*, 2 vols. (Lyons, 1688; repr. Wroclaw, 1891, Graz, 1958)

Ehrhard, *Überlieferung und Bestand*, I, II, III,1, and III,2   A. Ehrhard, *Überlieferung und Bestand der hagiographischen und homiletischen Literatur der griechischen Kirche.* I, *Die Überlieferung*, in TU, 50 (1937), 51 (1938), 52,1 (1943), and 52,2 (1952)

Eleutheroudakes, ᾽Εγκυκλ.Λεξ.   K. Eleutheroudakes, ed., ᾽Εγκυκλοπαιδικὸν Λεξικόν, 12 vols. (Athens [1927–31])

EO   Echos d'Orient

᾽Επ.῾Ετ.Βυζ.Σπ.   ᾽Επετηρὶς ῾Εταιρείας Βυζαντινῶν Σπουδῶν

᾽Επ.Μεσ.᾽Αρχ.   ᾽Επετηρὶς τοῦ Μεσαιωνικοῦ ᾽Αρχείου

Εὐαγγέλιον (1880)   Θεῖον καὶ ἱερὸν Εὐαγγέλιον (Rome, 1880)

Εὐαγγέλιον (1968)   Θεῖον καὶ ἱερὸν Εὐαγγέλιον, ἔκδοσις ᾽Αποστολικῆς Διακονίας ([Athens], 1968)

Fletcher, *English Book Collectors*   W. Y. Fletcher, *English Book Collectors*, The English Bookman's Library, III (London, 1902)

Follieri, *Codices*   H. Follieri, *Codices graeci Bibliothecae Vaticanae selecti*, Exempla scripturarum, fasc. IV (Vatican City, 1969)

Forshall, *Catalogue*, I,1 and I,2   J. Forshall, *Catalogue of Manuscripts in the British Museum.* N.S. I, pt. 1, *The Arundel Manuscripts*; pt. 2, *The Burney Manuscripts* ([London], 1834–40)

Frati, *Dizionario bio-bibliografico*   C. Frati, *Dizionario bio-bibliografico dei bibliotecari e bibliofili italiani dal sec. XIV al XIX*, Biblioteca di bibliografia italiana, XIII (Florence, 1933)

Gardthausen, *Griechische Palaeographie*   V. Gardthausen, *Griechische Palaeographie*, 2nd ed., 2 vols. (Leipzig, 1911–13)
GBA   Gazette des Beaux-Arts
GCS   Die griechischen christlichen Schriftsteller der ersten drei Jahrhunderte (1897–)
Gregory, I, II, and III   C. R. Gregory, *Textkritik des Neuen Testamentes*, 3 vols. with continuous pagination (Leipzig, 1900–9; repr. 1976)
Grumel, *Chronologie*   V. Grumel, *La chronologie* (Paris, 1958)

Hatch, *Facsimiles and Descriptions*   W. H. P. Hatch, *Facsimiles and Descriptions of Minuscule Manuscripts of the New Testament* (Cambridge, Mass., 1951)
Ἑλλ.Φιλολ.Σύλλ.   Ὁ ἐν Κωνσταντινουπόλει Ἑλληνικὸς Φιλολογικὸς Σύλλογος
HJ   Historisches Jahrbuch

Indice Barocci   Indice de libri greci antichissimi scritti a penna, Che si trouano nella Libraria, che fù del Q. Illustriss. Sig. Giacomo Barocci, Nobile Veneto (Venice, 1617)
IRAIK   Izvěstija Russkago Arheologičeskago Instituta v Konstantinopolě

Jannaris, *Historical Greek Grammar*   A. N. Jannaris, *An Historical Greek Grammar Chiefly of the Attic Dialect as Written and Spoken from Classical Antiquity down to the Present Time* (London, 1897; repr. Hildesheim, 1968)
JIAN   Journal International d'Archéologie Numismatique
JÖB   Jahrbuch der Österreichischen Byzantinistik
JÖBG   Jahrbuch der Österreichischen Byzantinischen Gesellschaft
JPh   Journal of Philology
JSav   Journal des Savants
JThS   Journal of Theological Studies
JWarb   Journal of the Warburg and Courtauld Institutes

Komines, Πίνακες   A. D. Komines, Πίνακες χρονολογημένων Πατμιακῶν κωδίκων (Athens, 1968)
Komines–Naoumides, *Facsimiles*   A. D. Komines and M. Naoumides, trans., *Facsimiles of Dated Patmian Codices* (Athens, 1970)
Κρ.Χρον.   Κρητικὰ Χρονικά
Krumbacher   K. Krumbacher, *Geschichte der byzantinischen Litteratur*, 2nd ed. (Munich, 1897; repr. New York [1958], New York [1970])
Krumbacher, Κτήτωρ   K. Krumbacher, "Κτήτωρ. Ein lexikographischer Versuch," *Indogermanische Forschungen*, 25 (1909), pp. 393–421
Κυπρ.Σπουδ.   Κυπριακαὶ Σπουδαί

Legrand, *Notice biographique sur Jean et Théodose Zygomalas*   E. Legrand, *Notice biographique sur Jean et Théodose Zygomalas*, in Publications de l'Ecole des langues orientales vivantes, 3rd ser., vol. VI (Paris, 1889), pp. 67–264 (offprint Paris, 1889)
Λεξικὸν τῶν δήμων   Λεξικὸν τῶν δήμων, κοινοτήτων καὶ οἰκισμῶν τῆς Ἑλλάδος (Athens, 1963)
LThK Lexikon für Theologie und Kirche, 2nd ed., ed. J. Höfer and K. Rahner (Freiburg i.B., 1957–68)

Μεγ.Ἑλλ.Ἐγκυκλ.   Μεγάλη Ἑλληνικὴ Ἐγκυκλοπαιδεία, 24 vols. (Athens [1926–34])
Metzger, *The Text of the New Testament*   B. M. Metzger, *The Text of the New Testament. Its Transmission, Corruption, and Restoration*, 2nd ed. (New York–Oxford, 1968)
Migne, Patr. Gr.   J.-P. Migne, ed., Patrologiae cursus completus, Series graeca (or Series graeca prior or Series graeca posterior), Patrologia Graeca, 161 vols. (Paris,

1857–66) (references to first editions of Migne or to their anastatic reprints dated not later than 1866; later editions of some volumes published by Garnier Frères from 1880 on disregarded)
Miklosich–Müller, *Acta et diplomata*   F. Miklosich and I. Müller, *Acta et diplomata graeca medii aevi sacra et profana*, 6 vols. (Vienna, 1860–90; repr. Athens [1960], Aalen, 1968)

NachrGött   Nachrichten von der Königl. Gesellschaft der Wissenschaften zu Göttingen, Philol.-hist.Kl.
Nares, *Catalogue of the Harleian Manuscripts*, III   R. Nares, *A Catalogue of the Harleian Manuscripts, in the British Museum*, III ([London], 1808; repr. Hildesheim–New York, 1973)
Νέος Ἑλλ.   Νέος Ἑλληνομνήμων
Nestle, *Novum Testamentum graece*   Eb. Nestle, Er. Nestle, and K. Aland, eds., *Novum Testamentum graece*, 25th ed. (London [1973])
New Pal. Soc., Ser. I   *The New Palaeographical Society. Facsimiles of Ancient Manuscripts, etc.*, Ser. I, ed. E. M. Thompson, G. F. Warner, F. G. Kenyon, and J. P. Gilson (London, 1903–12)
New Pal. Soc., Ser. II   *Ibid.*, Ser. II, ed. E. M. Thompson, G. F. Warner, F. G. Kenyon, J. P. Gilson, J. A. Herbert, and H. I. Bell (London, 1913–30)

OC   Orientalia Christiana
Omont, *Fac-similés ... du IXᵉ au XIVᵉ siècle*   H. Omont, *Fac-similés des manuscrits grecs datés de la Bibliothèque Nationale du IXᵉ au XIVᵉ siècle* (Paris, 1891)
Omont, "Notes"   H. Omont, "Notes sur les manuscrits grecs du British Museum," *BECh*, 45 (1884), pp. 314–50, 584
OrChr   Oriens Christianus

Paléographie grecque et byzantine   La paléographie grecque et byzantine, Colloques Internationaux du Centre National de la Recherche Scientifique, no. 559 (Paris, 1977)
Pal. Soc., Ser. I   *The Palaeographical Society. Facsimiles of Manuscripts and Inscriptions*, ed. E. A. Bond and E. M. Thompson (London, 1873–83)
Papadopulos, *Genealogie der Palaiologen*   A. Th. Papadopulos, *Versuch einer Genealogie der Palaiologen 1259–1453* (Diss. Munich, 1938; repr. Amsterdam, 1962)
PLP, I and II   *Prosopographisches Lexikon der Palaiologenzeit*, ed. E. Trapp, with R. Walther and H.-V. Beyer, I–II, Österreichische Akademie der Wissenschaften, Veröffentlichungen der Kommission für Byzantinistik, I,1 and I,2 (Vienna, 1976–77)
Polemis, *The Doukai*   D. I. Polemis, *The Doukai. A Contribution to Byzantine Prosopography*, University of London Historical Studies, XXII (London, 1968)

Rahlfs, *Verzeichnis der griechischen Handschriften des Alten Testaments*   A. Rahlfs, *Verzeichnis der griechischen Handschriften des Alten Testaments*, NachrGött, 1914, Beiheft = Mitteilungen des Septuaginta-Unternehmens der Königl. Gesellschaft der Wissenschaften zu Göttingen, 2 (Berlin, 1914)
RBibl   Revue Biblique
RE   Paulys Real-Encyclopädie der classischen Altertumswissenschaft, new rev. ed. by G. Wissowa and W. Kroll (Stuttgart, 1893 – Munich, 1978)
REB   Revue des Etudes Byzantines
REG   Revue des Etudes Grecques
RHSEE   Revue Historique du Sud-Est Européen
de Ricci, *English Collectors*   S. de Ricci, *English Collectors of Books and Manuscripts (1530–1930) and Their Marks of Ownership* (Cambridge, 1930; repr. Bloomington, Ind. [1960]; London, 1960; New York [1969])

Richard, *Inventaire*   M. Richard, *Inventaire des manuscrits grecs du British Museum*, Publications de l'Institut de Recherche et d'Histoire des Textes, III (Paris, 1952)
ROL   Revue de l'Orient Latin
RQ   Römische Quartalschrift für christliche Alterthumskunde und für Kirchengeschichte
RSBN   Rivista di Studi Bizantini e Neoellenici

Sandys, *History of Classical Scholarship*, II and III   J. E. Sandys, *A History of Classical Scholarship*, II–III (Cambridge, 1908; repr. New York, 1958)
SBBerl   Sitzungsberichte der Königl. Preussischen Akademie der Wissenschaften, Berlin
SBMünch   Sitzungsberichte der Bayerischen Akademie der Wissenschaften, München
SBN   Studi Bizantini e Neoellenici
SBWien   Sitzungsberichte der kaiserlichen Akademie der Wissenschaften, Wien; or Akademie der Wissenschaften in Wien, Sitzungsberichte
SC   Sources Chrétiennes. Collection dirigée par H. de Lubac et J. Daniélou (Paris)
S.C. (followed by a number)   prefix of the consecutive number of a MS of the Bodleian Library indicated in *Summary Catalogue* (see below)
Schreiner, *Die byzantinischen Kleinchroniken*, I and II   P. Schreiner, *Die byzantinischen Kleinchroniken*, I–II, CFHB, XII,1 and XII,2 (Vienna, 1975–77)
Scrivener, I   F. H. A. Scrivener, *A Plain Introduction to the Criticism of the New Testament*, 4th ed. by E. Miller, I (London, 1894)
Scrivener, *Codex Augiensis*   F. H. Scrivener, *An Exact Transcript of the Codex Augiensis* (Cambridge, 1859)
Scrivener, *Full and Exact Collation*   F. H. Scrivener, *A Full and Exact Collation of about Twenty Greek Manuscripts of the Holy Gospels* (Cambridge–London, 1853)
von Soden, I,1 and I,2   Hermann von Soden, *Die Schriften des Neuen Testaments in ihrer ältesten erreichbaren Textgestalt hergestellt auf Grund ihrer Textgeschichte*, I,1 and I,2 (Berlin, 1902–6; repr. as 2nd ed., Göttingen, 1911)
ST   Studi e Testi
StPB   Studia Patristica et Byzantina
Studia Codicologica   Studia Codicologica, ed. K. Treu, TU, 124 (Berlin, 1977)
SubsHag   Subsidia Hagiographica
Summary Catalogue   F. Madan, H. H. E. Craster, N. Denholm-Young, R. W. Hunt, and P. D. Record, *A Summary Catalogue of Western Manuscripts in the Bodleian Library at Oxford*, 7 vols. (Oxford, 1895–1953)
Synaxarium CP   Synaxarium Ecclesiae Constantinopolitanae, Propylaeum ad Acta Sanctorum Novembris, ed. H. Delehaye (Brussels, 1902)

Teubner   Bibliotheca Scriptorum Graecorum et Romanorum Teubneriana (Leipzig; or Stuttgart when so indicated in reference)
TFByzNgPhil   Texte und Forschungen zur byzantinisch-neugriechischen Philologie
ThLL   Thesaurus Linguae Latinae (Leipzig, 1900–   )
Thompson, *Introduction*   E. M. Thompson, *An Introduction to Greek and Latin Palaeography* (Oxford, 1912; repr. New York [1964])
Θρησκ.'Ηθ.'Εγκυκλ.   Θρησκευτικὴ καὶ 'Ηθικὴ 'Εγκυκλοπαιδεία, 12 vols. (Athens, 1962–68)
Trevisan, I and II   P. Trevisan, ed., *S. Giovanni Climaco, Scala Paradisi*, I–II, Corona Patrum Salesiana, Serie Greca, VIII–IX (Turin, 1941)
TU   Texte und Untersuchungen zur Geschichte der altchristlichen Literatur (Leipzig–Berlin, 1882–   )
Turyn, *Codices*   A. Turyn, *Codices graeci Vaticani saeculis XIII et XIV scripti annorumque notis instructi*, Codices e Vaticanis selecti quam simillime expressi, XXVIII (Vatican City, 1964)
Turyn, *DGMItaly*, I and II   A. Turyn, *Dated Greek Manuscripts of the Thirteenth and Fourteenth Centuries in the Libraries of Italy*. I, Text, II, Plates (Urbana–Chicago–London, 1972)

Van de Vorst–Delehaye, *Catalogus*   C. Van de Vorst and H. Delehaye, *Catalogus codicum hagiographicorum graecorum Germaniae, Belgii, Angliae*, SubsHag, 13 (Brussels, 1913)
VizVrem   Vizantijskij Vremennik
Vogel–Gardthausen   M. Vogel and V. Gardthausen, *Die griechischen Schreiber des Mittelalters und der Renaissance*, Beiheft zum Zentralblatt für Bibliothekswesen, 33 (Leipzig, 1909; repr. Hildesheim, 1966)

Wilson, *Mediaeval Greek Bookhands*   N. Wilson, *Mediaeval Greek Bookhands. Examples Selected from Greek Manuscripts in Oxford Libraries*, 2 vols., Text and Plates (Cambridge, Mass. [1973, 1972])
Wright, *Fontes Harleiani*   C. E. Wright, *Fontes Harleiani. A Study of the Sources of the Harleian Collection of Manuscripts Preserved in the Department of Manuscripts in the British Museum* (London, 1972)

Zepos, *Jus*   J. Zepos and P. Zepos, *Jus Graecoromanum*, 8 vols. (Athens, 1931; repr. Aalen, 1962)
Zeugoles, Λεξιχόν   G. Zeugoles, Λεξιχὸν τῆς ἑλληνικῆς γλώσσης (Athens, 1933)
ZNW   Zeitschrift für die neutestamentliche Wissenschaft und die Kunde der älteren Kirche

GENERAL ABBREVIATIONS AND SYMBOLS

a (after a figure) = left column of a page
b (after a figure) = right column of a page
A.D. = anno Domini
A.M. = anno mundi
b. = born
bombycine = Oriental paper, of Oriental paper
CP. = Constantinople
d. = died
des. = *desinit*
ed. = editor, edited by, edition, published by, published in the edition (of)
gr., Gr. = Greek, graecus, grec, greco (codex, manuscript), grečeskaja (rukopis')
graec. = graecus (codex)
greč. = grečeskaja (rukopis')

inc. = *incipit*
χτλ. = χαὶ τὰ λοιπά
n.d. = no date
n.p. = no place
paper = Western paper
Plate(s), Pl(s). (capitalized) = Plate(s) in this book
Progr. = program, *Programm* (Ger.), paper published in a report or announcement of a school or university

* after an author's name indicates doubtful or false authorship; before the title of a work marks a work of doubtful authenticity or a spurious work

CRITICAL NOTATION

Greek quotations from MSS, especially the subscriptions, are in general printed as they were written, with all the errors of the originals; corrections are made rarely and in such cases proper critical notation is applied. Letters marked in the MS by tachygraphic signs are printed fully without any mark added. The letter ς (except when it is a numeral) is printed as two characters στ. Letters ἴ and ϋ are printed as ι and υ, unless there is a diaeresis which is not indicated by the position of the breathing or the accent. In proper names, the initial letter is capitalized, even when it is written as a small letter in the MS.

....	illegible letters are marked by a corresponding number of dots
---	illegible letters of an uncertain number are marked by three dashes
α̣β̣γ̣δ̣	dotted characters mark letters mutilated or faded or doubtful
( )	parentheses enclosing a blank space mark the omission by contraction or suspension of letters that cannot be supplemented with reasonable certainty
(αβγδ)	letters αβγδ omitted in the MS by contraction or suspension or conventional omission are supplemented in parentheses
(ἥλιος)	words marked by special symbols are printed in parentheses
[ ]	square brackets indicate a lacuna caused by damage to parchment or paper of the MS
[....]	a lacuna of four letter spaces
[---]	a lacuna of an uncertain number of letter spaces
[αβγδ]	a lacuna in the MS is supplemented by letters αβγδ which presumably were lost in it
⟦ ⟧	double square brackets mark a deletion made in the MS
⟦....⟧	illegible letters deleted in the MS are marked by a corresponding number of dots inside double square brackets
⟦---⟧	illegible letters of an uncertain number deleted in the MS are marked by three dashes inside double square brackets
⟦αβγδ⟧	letters αβγδ were deleted in the MS
⟦α̣β̣γ̣δ̣⟧	letters deleted in the MS are mutilated or faded or doubtful, but probably they were αβγδ
⟨αβγδ⟩	angular brackets enclose letters αβγδ not extant in the MS, but added by an editor
{αβγδ}	braces enclose letters αβγδ extant in the MS, but expelled as superfluous by an editor
(?)	question mark in parentheses implies that the reading or form or meaning of the preceding word is doubtful
|	a vertical stroke marks the end of a line in the MS and the beginning of the next line
‖	a double vertical stroke marks the end of a page (or column) in the MS and the beginning of the next page (or column)

NOTE ON GREEK PROPER NAMES

Christian or given names of scribes, sponsors, and owners of MSS are rendered in the English text in their Latin forms (e.g., Andreas, Basilius, Ioannes, Theodorus), while given names of any other persons are used, on the whole, in their accepted English forms (e.g., Andrew, Basil, Clement, John, Theodore), or else in their generally accepted Latin forms (e.g., Andronicus). The surnames or family names of all persons are presented in the English text in their conventionally latinized or anglicized forms (e.g., Climacus, Palaeologus, Papadopulus, Ducas, Sinaita, Choniates, Hagiopetrites, Chrysostom). Unusual names are simply transliterated (e.g., Pastil).

DESCRIPTIONS AND ANALYSES
OF MANUSCRIPTS

Plate 1: A.D. 1214.

Edinburgh, University Library, ms 224. Parchment, 168 × 128 mm., III + 87 fols. The flyleaves, fols. I–III and 86–87, are parchment fragments from two older MSS with theological contents. Fols. I, II, 87 (passages on heresies) are from a 12th-century MS; fols. III and 86 (comments on John 1:1, Ἐν ἀρχῇ ἦν ὁ λόγος) are from a 10th-century MS. The main body of this MS (fols. 1–85) contains, on fols. 1ʳ–83ʳ, St. Neophytus the Recluse, Typicon (Τυπικὴ Διαθήκη) of the monastery Ἐγκλείστρα in Cyprus (near Ktima, in the Paphos district), which he founded. After the conclusion of the Typicon, there originally remained 5 blank pages. On fols. 84ʳ–85ᵛ passages from Psalms 137:2–8, 138:1–5, 139:3–8 were added subsequently (in a handwriting similar to that of the main scribe); on fol. 83ᵛ a partly illegible two-line note was written by Neophytus, and various notes were added later.

The MS originally comprised 13 quires marked with consecutive Greek numeral letters, of 8 leaves each, i.e., a total of 104 leaves. However, it suffered some losses prior to its *editio princeps* by Kyprianos in 1779. It lost, between the present fols. 16 and 17, leaves 5 and 6 of the quire γ′; 2 leaves between fols. 43 and 44 (in the quire ζ′, now comprising fols. 41–46); 1 leaf between fols. 52 and 53 (in the quire η′, now comprising fols. 47–53); 6 leaves between fols. 55 and 56 (in the quire ϑ′, now comprising fols. 54–55); 1 leaf between fols. 67 and 68 (in the quire ια′, now comprising fols. 64–70); 1 leaf between fols. 77 and 78 (in the quire ιβ′, now comprising fols. 71–77). Thus the MS lost 13 leaves prior to the edition by Kyprianos. At a later date, before the edition by Warren was prepared in 1878 (and published in 1882), 6 more leaves (leaves 1–4 and 7–8 of the quire γ′) were lost; so that the whole quire γ′, i.e., 8 leaves between fols. 16 and 17, was lost and is missing in the present state of the MS. This means that the total loss in the MS amounts now to 19 leaves. Fortunately, the text of the 6 leaves which were extant at the time of Kyprianos was printed by him and has been reprinted from his edition in the later editions of the Typicon (except for the one by Warren). The present foliation of the MS, referred to above, was made after all the losses took place.

This MS was transcribed from an exemplar revised by Neophytus himself, so that the text of this Typicon represents the second version of the Typicon. This Edinburgh MS was written by the priest Basilius, teacher and tabularius, i.e., notary, of the diocese of Paphos, son of a catechist, and was subscribed by him on 9 May A.M. 6722 = A.D. 1214 on fol. 83ʳ (Pl. **97**): Ἡ παροῦσα σὺν ϑ(ε)ῶ τυπικὴ | μου διαθήκη διὰ τεσσά|ρων κ(αὶ) εἴκοσι κεφαλαίων, | Ἐγράφη διὰ χειρὸς εὐτε|λοῦς Βασιλείου ἱερέως | διδασκάλου καὶ ταβου|λλαρίου τῶν ταβουλ-λα|ρίων τῆς ἁγιωτάτης ἐπι|σκοπῆς Πάφου τοῦ υἱοῦ τοῦ | κατηχητ(οῦ)· μη(νὶ) μαΐω ϑ ἰν(δικτιῶνος) β | τῶ ͵ϛψκβ ἔτει ++++[1]

---

[1] In the year date of this subscription, the rough breathing and the circumflex above the numeral letter ϛ refer to the initial rough breathing and the final circumflex of the ordinal numeral ἑξακισχιλιοστῷ. The smooth breathing above κ refers to the smooth breathing in εἰκοστῷ. On breathings

The authenticity of this MS of the Typicon was validated by some autographic notes of Neophytus himself. On this fol. 83ʳ, in the four lines at the beginning of the page, the conclusion of the Typicon (on fol. 82ᵛ) is followed, and the subscription of Basilius is preceded, by the following note in the handwriting of Neophytus, which is arranged below metrically in dodecasyllables[2] (Pl. 97):

† Νεοφύτου ἐγκλείστου τίσδε τῆς | βίβλου
προτάξασα χεὶρ, ἐπε|σφράγισεν ἤδη·
τεθηκὼς | ὡς ερκίον, σφέτερον γράμμα. +

Neophytus refers in lines 1–2 to his note at the beginning of the Typicon (on fol. 4ᵛ), with which I deal below. A different hand prefixed to the note on fol. 83ʳ the following headline at the top of the page (in red): Νεοφυτου πρε(σβυτ)έρ(ου) μ(ονα)χ(οῦ) κ(αὶ) ἐγκλείστου.

A late note written by a reader in the right margin of fol. 83ʳ on 6 June 1619 states that this MS was written in the time of St. Neophytus, as shown by his autographic notes at the beginning of the MS and here at its end. The text of the note on fol. 83ʳ was printed twice by I. P. Tsiknopoullos, Νεοφύτου πρεσβυτέρου μοναχοῦ καὶ ἐγκλείστου Τυπικὴ σὺν Θεῷ Διαθήκη. *Laing MS III 811* τῆς Πανεπιστημιακῆς Βιβλιοθήκης τοῦ ᾽Εδιμβούργου (Larnaca, 1952), p. IΑ; *idem*, Κυπριακὰ Τυπικά, in Κέντρον ᾽Επιστημονικῶν ᾽Ερευνῶν. Πηγαὶ καὶ μελέται τῆς Κυπριακῆς ἱστορίας, II (Nicosia, 1969), p. 5* (the two transcripts published by Tsiknopoullos differ from each other in some details).[3] In the lower margin of fol. 83ʳ, an invocation (partly trimmed in the bottom line) was written at a late date by the priest Theodore of Leucara (in Cyprus); its text was printed by Tsiknopoullos, Νεοφύτου ... Τυπικὴ σὺν Θεῷ Διαθήκη, p. I. Apart from my Plate 97, reproductions of fol. 83ʳ can be found also in these publications: F. E. Warren, "The 'Ritual Ordinance' of Neophytus," *Archaeologia*, 47, pt. 1 (1882), pl. ı (fols. 4ʳ and 83ʳ; in the reproduction of fol. 83ʳ, the later notes in the right and the lower margins were touched out so that they do not appear on the plate); Tsiknopoullos, Κυπριακὰ Τυπικά, pl. ıv (fols. 82ᵛ–83ʳ).

---

and accents marked above ordinal numeral letters, cf. Turyn, *Codices*, pp. 40, 112, 137; *idem*, *DGMItaly*, I, pp. 81, 113, 117, 124, 125, 130, 205, 257; cf. below, pp. 71, 137f., 143, 146, 148.

[2] The metrical character of the note of Neophytus was recognized by H. Delehaye, "Saints de Chypre," *AnalBoll*, 26 (1907), p. 279.

[3] The note in the right margin of fol. 83ʳ actually reads as follows: τὸ παρὸν βιβλίου | εἶναι γραμμέν[ον] | ἀπὸ τὸν κερὸν του ἁ[γίου] | Νεοφύτου καθ[ὼς] | ἀποδίχνη κ(αὶ) τὸ [ἰδι]|οχειρόν του γρά|μμαν εἰς τὴν | ἀρχὴν· κ(αὶ) ὥδε | εἰς τὸ τέλος [κ(αὶ)] | ἔχει ἀπὲ τόνδ[ε τὸν] | κερὸν ὅπου δ[είχνει?] | ὁ ἅγιος ὥδε μέσα | τετρακοσίους | ἐξίντα χρόνους· κ(αὶ) | ἀφὸν ἐγράφη | ἡ αὐτη βιβλος | εἶναι χρόνοι | τετρακόσιοι πεν|τε· εγραψα | τῆ ϛ ιουνίου | ͵αχιθ ετους | ταπεινὸς | Χριστοφορος (? a monogram) ταχα και γραμμ[ατι]κος | The first reference to the time of Neophytus obviously points to the statement of Neophytus made in his Typicon (ὥδε μέσα, i.e., here within this MS: cf. Tsiknopoullos, Κυπριακὰ Τυπικά, p. 77, 3–4) that he found the spot for his hermitage on 24 June A.M. 6667 = A.D. 1159. According to this note, 460 years passed since the point in Neophytus' life indicated in the Typicon. If we add A.M. 6667 + 460, the result is A.M. 7127 or (considering that this note was written in June) A.D. 1619. The next statement means that 405 years elapsed since the date of the writing of this MS. The MS was subscribed on this same folio 83ʳ on 9 May A.M. 6722 = A.D. 1214. The addition A.M. 6722 + 405 results in A.M 7127 or (in view of the June date of this note) A.D. 1619. This computation makes it certain that the date at the end of this note was indeed A.D. 1619, and that the last numeral letter in the date was written ϑ.

Another autographic authentication of the Typicon by Neophytus appears in this MS after the headline of the Typicon, before its chapter one, on fol. 4ᵛ: Νεόφυτο(ς) εὐτ(ε)λ(ὴς) (μον)αχ(ὸς) πρεσβύτ(ε)ρ(ος) κ(αὶ) | ἔγκλειστο(ς) ὁ Τιμιοστ(αυ)ρίτης | τῆς τυπηκῆς μου διαθήκης | οἰκεία χειρὶ πρωέταξα + This fol. 4ᵛ was reproduced several times: Tsiknopoullos, Νεοφύτου ... Τυπικὴ σὺν Θεῷ Διαθήκη, plate facing p. 2; *idem*, Κίνητρα καὶ πηγαὶ τοῦ συγγραφικοῦ ἔργου τοῦ Ἐγκλείστου ἁγίου Νεοφύτου. Ἡ ἁγία Βιβλιοθήκη, in Κυπρ.Σπουδ., 18 (1954), pl. 26 (cf. p. πζ'); *idem*, Ὁ ἅγιος Νεόφυτος πρεσβύτερος μοναχὸς καὶ ἔγκλειστος καὶ ἡ ἱερὰ αὐτοῦ μονή (Ktima, 1955), p. 199; *idem*, Κυπριακὰ Τυπικά, pl. III (fols. 4ᵛ–5ʳ).

For reproductions of notes by Neophytus found in other MSS which once belonged to the Encleistra library, cf. *idem*, Ὁ ἅγιος Νεόφυτος ... καὶ ἡ ἱερὰ αὐτοῦ μονή, p. 176 (from MS Paris Grec 1189, fol. 24ᵛ: three lines in the lower margin were written by Neophytus; cf. Delehaye, in *AnalBoll*, 26 [1907], pp. 279f.), p. 214 (from MS Paris Coislin 71, fols. 135ᵛ and 136ʳ; from MS Paris Coislin 245, fol. 56ᵛ; only the fourth line in the cut from this MS was written by Neophytus); I. P. Tsiknopoulos, Τὸ συγγραφικὸν ἔργον τοῦ ἁγίου Νεοφύτου, in Κυπρ.Σπουδ., 22 (1958), pp. 81, 193 (the same facsimiles).[4] On some textual interventions of Neophytus in the Edinburgh MS, cf. *idem*, Κυπριακὰ Τυπικά, p. 15*.

On Plate **1**, as a specimen of Basilius' handwriting, we reproduce folios 59ᵛ–60ʳ from the Edinburgh MS. These pages contain a passage from ST. NEO-PHYTUS THE RECLUSE, TYPICON OF THE ENCLEISTRA (ed. Tsiknopoullos, Κυπριακὰ Τυπικά, pp. 94, 26–95, 4). I listed above facsimiles of a few pages of this MS (fols. 4ʳ, 4ᵛ, 5ʳ, 82ᵛ, 83ʳ) already published elsewhere. This MS, being a foundation typicon (κτητορικὸν τυπικόν), is written calligraphically, without the abundant use of abbreviations which is a characteristic feature of liturgical typica.[5] Basilius' handwriting is calligraphic and in general accords with the well-known calligraphy of Cypriot MSS (cf. Turyn, *Codices*, pp. 122f., pl. 96; Follieri, *Codices*, pp. 76f., pl. 53; Omont, *Fac-similés ... du IXᵉ au XIVᵉ siècle*, pl. LXXIX/II; Turyn, *DGMItaly*, I, p. 119; II, pl. 93; below, pp. 82f., Pl. **56**; pp. 83ff., Pls. **57, 58**). However, Basilius' script is not yet as strikingly Cypriot as that of the MSS just referred to. Perhaps the more pronounced specifically Cypriot style of the regional calligraphy of that island developed a century later.[5a]

The same scribe Basilius wrote also some other MSS containing works of Neophytus, as we can judge from their scripts. The MS Paris, Supplément

[4] On corrections and additions made by Neophytus in several MSS which once belonged to the Encleistra library, cf. I. P. Tsiknopoulos, Ἡ ὀρθογραφικὴ ἰδιομορφία τῶν συγγραφῶν τοῦ Ἐγκλείστου Ἁγίου Νεοφύτου, in Κυπρ.Σπουδ., 19 (1955), pp. 47–51.

[5] On this feature of liturgical typica, cf. Turyn, *Codices*, p. 166, pl. 144; *idem*, *DGMItaly*, I, pp. 3, 96, 187, 238; II, pls. 1, 75, 150, 195, 196. On the difference between the two kinds of typica, κτητορικὰ τυπικά and λειτουργικὰ τυπικά, cf. Krumbacher, pp. 314–19; H. Delehaye, *Deux Typica byzantins de l'époque des Paléologues* (Brussels, 1921), pp. 3ff., 7 (under no. 21, on the Typicon of Neophytus).

[5a] On characteristically Cypriot MSS, cf. now the fundamental study by P. Canart, "Un style d'écriture livresque dans les manuscrits chypriotes du XIVᵉ siècle: la chypriote 'bouclée'," in *Paléographie grecque et byzantine*, pp. 303–21 (p. 310, on the script of Basilius; p. 321 fig. 7, a segment of MS Edinburgh Univ. 224, fol. 13ᵛ, is reproduced).

grec 1317 contains Catecheses of Neophytus, written in the handwriting of Basilius and showing corrections and additions by Neophytus himself.[6] A facsimile specimen of this MS (fol. 56ᵛ) was published by Tsiknopoullos, Ὁ ἅγιος Νεόφυτος ... καὶ ἡ ἱερὰ αὐτοῦ μονή, p. 196. The MS Paris Coislin 287, containing mainly Neophytus' Homilies on Divine Commandments, was written by the same Basilius and corrected by Neophytus.[7] A facsimile specimen of this MS (fol. 104ᵛ) was published by Tsiknopoullos, *op. cit.*, p. 165. Basilius also shared in the writing of MS Paris Grec 1189 which was written by several scribes. This MS contains Neophytus' Panegyricon for the months September–December and shows several autographic notes by Neophytus.[8]

According to Neophytus' wish stipulated in his Typicon,[9] the Edinburgh MS of the Typicon was to be kept in the Encleistra; indeed, it was kept there at least until 1779, when a transcript was made and published, within a collection of Neophytus' writings, by Archimandrite Kyprianos of the archdiocese of Cyprus. The book appeared in Venice in 1779: Τυπικὴ σὺν Θεῷ Διάταξις, καὶ λόγοι εἰς τὴν Ἐξαήμερον, τοῦ ὁσίου πατρὸς ἡμῶν Νεοφύτου τοῦ Ἐγκλείστου ... Ἐπιμελείᾳ δὲ καὶ διορθώσει τοῦ πανοσιωλογιωτάτου Κυπριανοῦ, ἀρχιμανδρίτου τῆς ἁγιωτάτης ἀρχιεπισκοπῆς Κύπρου, τοῦ ἐκ πολιτείας Κοιλανίου (Venice, 1779); the Typicon of Neophytus was printed on pages ε′–η′, 1–33. This *editio princeps* of the Typicon shows gaps in the text caused by the loss of 13 folios which occurred prior to Kyprianos' time, but it includes the text of the 6 folios which were extant at that time (see above). At a later date, probably after 1821, this MS left the monastery and subsequently came into the possession of David Laing (1793–1878) of Edinburgh.

The Laing collection of MSS was bequeathed by him to the University of Edinburgh, to the Library of which it came after Laing's death in 1878.[10]

---

[6] MS Paris, Supplément grec 1317 is identical with the MS which was once at Constantinople, Μετόχιον τοῦ Παναγίου Τάφου 370. On this MS, cf. A. Papadopoulos-Kerameus, Ἱεροσολυμιτικὴ Βιβλιοθήκη, IV (St. Petersburg, 1899), pp. 338–45 (under no. 370); Ehrhard, *Überlieferung und Bestand*, III,1, pp. 684–86; J. Darrouzès, "Manuscrits originaires de Chypre à la Bibliothèque Nationale de Paris," *REB*, 8 (1950), pp. 185f.; Ch. Astruc, in Ch. Astruc and M.-L. Concasty, *Bibliothèque Nationale, Département des manuscrits. Catalogue des manuscrits grecs*, pt. 3, *Le Supplément grec*, vol. III (Paris, 1960), pp. 602–8. Astruc (p. 607) identified the scribe of Paris Suppl. gr. 1317 with Basilius, scribe of Edinburgh Univ. 224, and recognized the autographic character of Neophytus' corrections and additions in this Paris MS (cf. Darrouzès, *loc. cit.*). Tsiknopoulos, in Κυπρ.Σπουδ., 19, p. 48 (under Κατηχήσεις), printed a complete list of Neophytus' interventions in Paris Suppl. gr. 1317.

[7] On MS Paris Coislin 287, cf. R. Devreesse, *Bibliothèque Nationale, Département des manuscrits. Catalogue des manuscrits grecs*, II, *Le fonds Coislin* (Paris, 1945), pp. 271f.; Darrouzès, *op. cit.*, p. 172; Astruc, *op. cit.*, p. 607; Tsiknopoulos, in Κυπρ.Σπουδ., 22, pp. 110–17. Neophytus' corrections and additions in this MS were listed by *idem, ibid.*, 19, p. 47 (under Εὐσύνοπτοι ἑρμηνεῖαι Δεσποτικῶν Ἐντολῶν).

[8] Cf. above, p. 5, on this MS Paris Grec 1189 and its facsimile specimen published twice by Tsiknopoullos, Ὁ ἅγιος Νεόφυτος ... καὶ ἡ ἱερὰ αὐτοῦ μονή, p. 176, and in Κυπρ.Σπουδ., 22, p. 81 (it should be pointed out that the text page reproduced from Paris Grec 1189 was not written by Basilius; the three lines in the lower margin were added by Neophytus). On this MS, cf. Delehaye, in *AnalBoll*, 26, pp. 161ff., 279ff.; Ehrhard, *Überlieferung und Bestand*, III,1, pp. 681–84; F. Halkin, *Manuscrits grecs de Paris. Inventaire hagiographique*, SubsHag, 44 (Brussels, 1968), pp. 136f.; Tsiknopoulos, in Κυπρ.Σπουδ., 22, pp. 80–99; *idem, ibid.*, 19, p. 48 (under Μειζοτέρα Πανηγυρική, Neophytus' corrections and notes in this MS are listed). Astruc, *op. cit.*, p. 607, discovered the participation of Basilius in the writing of this MS.

[9] Cf. Tsiknopoullos, Κυπριακὰ Τυπικά, p. 83, lines 10–13 and 30.

[10] On David Laing, cf. *DNB*, XI, pp. 401f.; Fletcher, *English Book Collectors*, pp. 377–81; G. Goudie, *David Laing, LL.D. A Memoir of His Life and Literary Work* (Edinburgh, 1913), especially pp. 126–28 on the bequest of Laing's collection of MSS.

When the MS was still in Laing's possession, Frederick Edward Warren (of Oxford) prepared a short study of this Typicon and an edition of the Greek text of the Edinburgh MS with short notes. Warren presented it to the Society of Antiquaries in London in April 1878 (a few months before Laing's death) and published his study and the Greek edition of the Typicon (*op. cit.*, pp. 1–36, pl. ɪ). As I said above, the Edinburgh MS at some time after Kyprianos' edition lost 6 more folios (in addition to the 13 folios lost before Kyprianos' edition). The edition of Warren represents the Edinburgh MS in its present state, with all its losses. Since Warren was unaware of the existence of the Kyprianos edition, he did not include in his text the passages extant in that edition but lost in the MS thereafter. A later edition of this Typicon was published by I. Ch. Chatzeïoannou, Ἱστορία καὶ ἔργα Νεοφύτου πρεσβυτέρου μοναχοῦ καὶ ἐγκλείστου (Alexandria, 1914), pp. 81–126; this is a reprint of the Kyprianos edition, with variants added from the Warren edition. The two most recent editions of the Typicon by Tsiknopoullos are based on a direct study of the Edinburgh MS, but they do include the passages published by Kyprianos from the 6 folios that were lost later and are missing now in this MS. I repeat references to these editions: Tsiknopoullos, Νεοφύτου ... Τυπικὴ σὺν Θεῷ Διαθήκη (1952), pp. 1–38 (with a critical apparatus in reference to the Edinburgh MS and to the Kyprianos edition); *idem*, Κυπριακὰ Τυπικά (1969), pp. 69–104 (the best critical edition, with ample prolegomena and with explanatory notes on pp. 117–22).

After the death in 1878 of the former owner of this MS, David Laing, his manuscript books at first formed, in accordance with the Laing bequest, Division III of the Laing Collection in the Edinburgh University Library. This MS of Neophytus' Typicon was marked within that collection with the number 811. This number was in the past occasionally combined with the Division mark into the call number Laing III 811, which was sometimes quoted by scholars. At any rate, the present call number of this volume within the Edinburgh University Library is MS 224. The older binding of the MS (described by Warren, *op. cit.*, p. 3) has been replaced by a new binding; its front and back covers have the imprint *Laing Bequest* and, in the middle of this imprint, the initials of the testator: *DL*.

On this MS, cf. *ibid.*, pp. 1–4; H. J. W. Tillyard, in C. R. Borland, *A Descriptive Catalogue of the Western Mediaeval Manuscripts in Edinburgh University Library* (Edinburgh, 1916), p. 321 (under no. 224); Vogel–Gardthausen, p. 55; Tsiknopoullos, Νεοφύτου ... Τυπικὴ σὺν Θεῷ Διαθήκη, pp. Θ–ΙΕ; J. Darrouzès, "Autres manuscrits originaires de Chypre," *REB*, 15 (1957), p. 143; Tsiknopoulos, in Κυπρ.Σπουδ., 22 (1958), pp. 172–81; *idem*, Κυπριακὰ Τυπικά, pp. 2*ff. and *passim*. On Neophytus, his Typicon, the Encleistra, and its MSS, cf. *BHG³* no. 1325m; Beck, *Kirche und theologische Literatur*, pp. 633f.; C. Mango and E. J. W. Hawkins, "The Hermitage of St. Neophytus and Its Wall Paintings," *DOP*, 20 (1966), pp. 119–206, especially pp. 122–29; K. A. Manaphes, Μοναστηριακὰ Τυπικὰ – Διαθῆκαι, in Ἀθηνᾶ. Σειρὰ διατριβῶν καὶ μελετημάτων, 7 (Athens, 1970), pp. 151–53 and *passim*.

Plate 2: A.D. 1225.

Oxford, Bodleian Library, ms Cromwell 11. Parchment, 215 × 155 mm., 2 pages (numbered fol. 1ᵃ, belonging to the main body of the MS) + 416 pages. At the beginning, fol. 1aʳ–1aᵛ line 3 contains a prayer written by the scribe of the MS; the rest of left-hand page fol. 1aᵛ contains a miniature (of almost full-page size) of the B.V.M. with the Infant Jesus. The text of the MS begins on right-hand page 1ᵇ. The MS contains liturgical texts: Office of the Lucernarium (Λυχνικόν) and Lauds; Liturgy of St. John Chrysostom, Liturgy of St. Basil, Liturgy of the Presanctified; New Testament lessons for the great feasts and for the feasts of some saints; offices for feasts of some saints; some prayers. It was written by the lector Michael Papadopulus, son of the priest Georgius from the theme of Ioannina, residing in the mountainous district (δρόγγος) of Τζερμέρνικος (rather Τζεμέρνικος, now τὰ Τζουμέρκα), and was subscribed by him on 13 February A.M. 6733 = A.D. 1225, on page 416. The subscription faded in several spots and can best be read under ultraviolet light. This is its text (page 416 – Pl. **98a**):

   † ὥς πὲρ ξένοι χαίρωντες ιδεῖν π(ατ)ρίδας, οὗτος | καὶ οἱ γράφωντες βιβλίου τέλος. ὦ Χ(ριστ)ε σ(ωτ)ηρ τοῦ κοσ|μου φρούρισον καὶ φύλαξον· τοὺς πόθω σὲ δοξάζωντας· | καὶ ὑμνοῦντας σου. τὴν ἐκ παρθ(ε)νοῦ σάρκωσιν· ἀμήν |

   † καὶ Ἐγρά(φ)η ιερὰ βίβλο(ς)· αὕτη· δια χειρὸ(ς) ἐμου· του ἐλαχιστοῦ· καὶ ἀμαρτ(ω)λ(οῦ) | παρὰ παντας· καὶ χωρικοῦ καλογράφοῦ, καὶ οι ἀναγινοσκωντες | ἐν αυτη τη βίβλω. εὔχεσθαι πρὸ(ς) κ(ύριο)ν ὑπὲρ εμου του ἀμαρτολοῦ ὅπως | καὶ ἡμᾶς ἐλεήσῃ. καὶ ἐν τω νὶν αἰῶνι καὶ εν τω μέλωντη: |

   Ἐγρα(φ)ῆ· παρεμου ἡ δέλτος αὕτη· Μιχ(αὴλ) ἀναγνώστ(ου), του Παπαδο-πούλ(ου) | ἠὸς· Γεωργ(ίου) ιερέως. του απὸ του θέμ(α)το(ς)· Ιωαννίνων. κ(α)τικῶν ἐστὶν ἐν | τῶ δρόγγω του Τζερμερνικου .... (perhaps ἐτελειώθ(η)?) δὲ επληρωθ(η) καὶ ὑπεγρά(φ)η δὲ· | ἐπὶ ἔτο(ς) ͵ϛψλγ´ ἰν(δικτιῶνος) ιγ̅ μη(νὶ) δε φευρουαρ(ίω) ιγ̅· ἡμέρ(α) ε̅· | ωρ(α) ε´ αὐθεντεύοντο(ς) δὲ· κ(υρο)ῦ Θεοδ(ώ)ρ(ου) του Δοῦκα ✝ ἐπικούρου | δὲ ὥντος εν τη Αρτη τοῦ Κλήμη· (μον)αχ(οῦ). του Μονομάχου:– |

   † Μιχ(αὴλ) ἐλάχιστο(ς) Παπαδόπουλος ψάλλω δόξα σοι (except for the last two words, this line is written in monocondylia, and the reading of its initial four words is probable, but tentative).

Over the text of this subscription, there is yellow wash; it appears elsewhere in this MS over headlines, rubrics, and some noteworthy elements. The use of yellow wash over noteworthy elements is known from MSS, especially from MSS of South Italian origin, although this practice was not limited to South Italian MSS, as we can see in the case of this MS.[11] Paleographically, the sampi-like shape of the letter ξ in line 3 of the subscription is interesting.[12] The subscription begins with two dodecasyllables which were a commonplace of many subscriptions.[13] The scribe characterizes himself as χωρικός, i.e., "inexperienced."[14]

The MS was written in Epirus. The father of the scribe was a native of the theme of Ioannina; the scribe himself resided in the δρόγγος τοῦ Τζερμερ-

   [11] Cf. Turyn, *Codices*, p. 20; *idem, DGMItaly*, I, pp. 170, 189, 202; below, pp. 14, 16, 70.
   [12] Cf. Turyn, *DGMItaly*, I, pp. 11, 19f., xvf., 59; II, pls. 9, 229a; Komines, Πίνακες, pp. 16f., pl. 28 left-hand page, line 4 from the bottom; or Komines–Naoumides, *Facsimiles*, pp. 32f., pl. 28 left-hand page, line 4 from the bottom.
   [13] Cf. Gardthausen, *Griechische Palaeographie*, II, p. 433; Turyn, *Codices*, pp. 114, 48, 73, 85; *idem, DGMItaly*, I, pp. 20, 101f., 127, 186, 260; K. Treu, "Der Schreiber am Ziel. Zu den Versen Ὥσπερ ξένοι χαίρουσιν ... und ähnlichen," in *Studia Codicologica*, pp. 473–92 (pp. 476f., on the above verses and their variant in this MS); below, pp. 38, 117, 127.
   [14] Cf. Turyn, *DGMItaly*, I, pp. 101f., 116, 127, 146; below, pp. 101f.

νίκου (the paroxytone acute is not visible now and is, therefore, uncertain; perhaps a circumflex was intended to be marked above the final -ου). The meaning of δρόγγος in this case is clear: it must be "mountain range" or "mountainous district or area." This accords with the well-known medieval usage of the word in the Chronicle of Morea and in some other sources.[15] The name of the mountainous area where the scribe resided was, according to the subscription, Τζερμέρνικος. I suspect that the scribe made a slight slip and that the toponym was actually Τζεμέρνικος. We know this place-name from a chrysobull of Andronicus II Palaeologus addressed to the Metropolitan of Ioannina in June 1321.[16] In this chrysobull, the Emperor confirmed various possessions and privileges of the Metropolitan Church of

[15] For the occurrence of δρόγγος in the Chronicle of Morea, cf. J. Schmitt, *The Chronicle of Morea* (London, 1904; repr. Groningen, 1967), Index, p. 605, *s.v.*; P. P. Kalonaros, Τὸ Χρονικὸν τοῦ Μωρέως [Athens, 1940], Index, p. 377, *s.v.* The translation of δρόγγος by Schmitt, *loc. cit.*, as "a defile," is wrong. Δρόγγος meant a mountainous area or district in which there were certain populated places. In the Chronicle of Morea, δρόγγος and ζυγός are synonyms. Δρόγγος is a topographical term. If it is followed by a proper name in the genitive, it becomes a geographical definition or possibly a term of administrative geography. For an extensive discussion of the meaning of the word in question, as used in the Chronicle of Morea, cf. S. Kougeas, Περὶ τῶν Μελιγκῶν τοῦ Ταϋγέτου ἐξ ἀφορμῆς ἀνεκδότου Βυζαντινῆς ἐπιγραφῆς ἐκ Λακωνίας, in Πραγματεῖαι τῆς 'Ακαδημίας 'Αθηνῶν, XV,3 (Athens, 1950), especially pp. 6 ff. (p. 4, δρόγγου Μελιγῶν in an inscription of A.D. 1337/1338). Cf. also V. Laurent, "Charisticariat et commende à Byzance," *REB*, 12 (1954), p. 101, ἐν τῷ χωρίῳ Σελτζιάνῳ δρούγγου 'Αχελώου. The upper Achelous or Aspropotamos flows through mountains (cf. N. G. L. Hammond, *Epirus* [Oxford, 1967], pp. 248 ff.). Thus the δρόγγος 'Αχελώου obviously refers to that mountainous district. There was a monastery of the B.V.M. in the diocese of Naupactus, situated ἐν τῷ δρούγγῳ Τρεβενίων (cf. S. Pétridès, "Jean Apokaukos, lettres et autres documents inédits," *IRAIK*, 14 [1909], p. 75 line 4), but this location is unknown and we cannot say anything about its topographical character. Apart from Kougeas, for a discussion of the meaning of δρόγγος, cf. D. A. Zakythinos, *Le Despotat grec de Morée*, II (Athens, 1953), pp. 26–29; H. Glykatzi-Ahrweiler, "Recherches sur l'administration de l'empire byzantin aux IXe–XIe siècles," *BCH*, 84 (1960), p. 81; *eadem*, "Une inscription méconnue sur les Mélingues de Taygète," *BCH*, 86 (1962), p. 7 note 5; *eadem*, *Byzance et la mer* (Paris, 1966), p. 278 note 3; *eadem*, "La région de Smyrne," p. 136 note 83 (the best formulation to the effect that ζυγός often denotes a mountain system of a region and that δρούγγος is often used as a counterpart of ζυγός in references to the Greek mainland).

For a discussion of δρούγγος (so spelled) in a different meaning in connection with the evolution of Byzantine military terminology, cf. Jul. Kulakovskij, "Drung i drungarij," *VizVrem*, 9 (1902), pp. 1–30, especially pp. 1–15; G. Stadtmüller, "Michael Choniates, Metropolit von Athen (ca. 1138–ca. 1222)," *OC*, 33,2, no. 91 (1934), pp. 301–5; pp. 304 f., on the meaning of δρόγγος (δρούγγος) in the Chronicle of Morea.

It seems that a phonetic confusion of *o* and *u* sounds caused the occasional interchange of δρόγγος and δρούγγος, two words with basically different roots. The word δρούγγος, originally "a troop," is certainly of Germanic origin; cf. A. Thumb, "Die germanischen Elemente des Neugriechischen," in *Germanistische Abhandlungen Hermann Paul zum 17. März 1902 dargebracht* (Strasbourg, 1902), pp. 235 f.; F. Kluge, *Etymologisches Wörterbuch der deutschen Sprache*, 19th ed., ed. W. Mitzka (Berlin, 1963), p. 141, *s.v.* Drang; *ThLL*, V,1, col. 2071, *s.v.* drungus; G. W. H. Lampe, *A Patristic Greek Lexicon* (Oxford, 1961), p. 388, *s.v.* δρούγγος; Du Cange, *Glossarium graecitatis*, I, cols. 332 f. On the other hand, δρόγγος, "mountain," derives most probably from the Slavic *drǫgъ*, "pole," "log" (cf. E. Berneker, *Slavisches etymologisches Wörterbuch*, 2nd ed., I [Heidelberg, 1924], p. 229; M. Vasmer, *Die Slaven in Griechenland*, AbhBerl, Philos.-hist.Kl., 1941, 12 [Berlin, 1941], p. 109). Δρόγγος is known from medieval Greek also as a proper name of a mountain, seat of the monastery of the B.V.M. Μακρινίτισσα near Demetrias (cf. Miklosich–Müller, *Acta et diplomata*, IV, pp. 330 ff.; N. I. Giannopoulos, Αἱ παρὰ τὴν Δημητριάδα Βυζαντιναὶ μοναί, in 'Επ.'Ετ.Βυζ.Σπ., 1 [1924], pp. 210, 216, 222).

[16] The original of the chrysobull is preserved in MS London Additional 24382 (cf. Richard, *Inventaire*, p. 45; *New Pal. Soc.*, Ser. II, pl. 80). Its text was published four times; cf. A. Moustoxydes, 'Ελληνομνήμων ἢ σύμμικτα ἑλληνικά (Athens, 1843–1853; repr. 1965), pp. 489ά–496ή; P. Arabantinos (= P.A.P.), Χρονογραφία τῆς 'Ηπείρου, II (Athens, 1857), pp. 307–11; Miklosich–Müller, *Acta et diplomata*, V, pp. 84–87; S. P. Lampros, Χρυσόβουλλον 'Ανδρονίκου Α' Παλαιολόγου ὑπὲρ τῆς 'Εκκλησίας 'Ιωαννίνων, in Νέος 'Ελλ., 12 (1915), pp. 38–40; the document was summarized by Dölger, *Regesten*, IV, pp. 87 f. (under no. 2460).

Ioannina and stated, among other things, that this Metropolis had, as one of its jurisdictions (ἐνορίαι),[17] also the district of Τζεμέρνικος (MS London Addit. 24382; Miklosich–Müller, *Acta et diplomata*, V, p. 85 lines 24–26; Lampros, in Νέος Ἑλλ., 12, p. 39 lines 38–39, with an inadvertent omission of several words): ἔτι δὲ καὶ εἰς τὴν ἐκτὸς χώραν ἐν τῷ θέματι τῶν Ἰωαννίνων ἔχει ἐνορίας πέντε· ἤγουν τὴν ἐνορίαν τῶν ἔξω Ἰωαννίνων· τοῦ Ζαγορίου· τοῦ Τζεμερνίκου. τοῦ Σμοκόβου· καὶ τοῦ Σεστρουνίου κτλ. This shows that the Metropolis of Ioannina had in the outside territory (i.e., outside the city of Ioannina) in the theme of Ioannina five jurisdictional districts and, among them, had under its jurisdiction the district of Τζεμέρνικος (I assume that it was a masculine name, though there is no cogent indication that it was not a neuter ending in -ον). The Τζερμέρνικος of our subscription (considering the reference to the Ioannina theme in the mention of the scribe's father) must be identical with the Τζεμέρνικος of the chrysobull just quoted. The identity of the Τζεμέρνικος of this chrysobull with the modern (τὰ) Τζουμέρκα was stated as something evident by Arabantinos.[18] Tzumerka (or Tsumerka) is a *mountain* area southeast of Ioannina (not too far from the city of Ioannina).[19] The use of the term δρόγγος was then perfectly appropriate in reference to Tzemernikos. This identification of the territory in which the scribe of our MS resided corroborates that this MS was indeed written in Epirus.[20]

[17] On the meaning of the term ἐνορία, cf. Ahrweiler, "La région de Smyrne," pp. 55f. and *passim*.

[18] Arabantinos, *op. cit.*, II, p. 309 note 8, notes in reference to the toponym τοῦ Τσεμερνίκου (so printed by him in the text of the chrysobull): Τσουμέρνικον, τὸ Τσουμέρκον, and remarks (in a glossary of geographic names): Τσουμέρκα ἤ Τσουμέρνικον κατὰ τοὺς Βυζαντινούς (*ibid.*, II, p. 170). In this connection, I refer to W. M. Leake, *Travels in Northern Greece*, IV (London, 1835), pp. 228f., who described the district of Arta as consisting of eight subdivisions, one of which was "Tzumérka, or Tzumérniko." On p. 229 note 1, Leake quoted in Greek the names of those subdivisions, and for the area in question he printed in Greek: "Τζουμέρκα, or Τζουμέρνικος." This is the same evidence as that given later by Arabantinos, with the slight difference between Τζ- in Leake and Τσ- in Arabantinos. There is also a difference in the gender of the older place-name between Τζουμέρνικος in Leake and Τσουμέρνικον in Arabantinos. It is difficult to determine whether the original name Τζεμέρνικος (-ον) and its later form Τζουμέρνικος (-ον) were masculine or neuter. I am inclined to believe that Leake had some learned informants in Ioannina with whom he discussed his records, and therefore I prefer to consider that the name in question was masculine.

The toponym Τζεμέρνικος seems to be of Slavic origin. It probably derives from Old Slavic čemerъ, "hellebore," and from *Čemerъnikъ, "hellebore-place" (cf. F. Miklosich, *Die Bildung der slavischen Personen- und Ortsnamen* [Heidelberg, 1927], p. 235 no. 62; Berneker, *op. cit.*, I, pp. 142f.; Vasmer, *op. cit.*, p. 55 no. 323, p. 53 no. 313).

[19] On the mountain region of Tzumerka, cf. Eleutheroudakes, Ἐγκυκλ.Λεξ., XII, p. 364; Μεγ.Ἑλλ. Ἐγκυκλ., XXIII, p. 473; Leake, *Travels in Northern Greece*, I (1835), pp. 271, 288f.; Hammond, *Epirus*, map 1 (on p. 5), pp. 11f., 167, and *passim*. The official name of the region at present is τὰ Τζουμέρκα. In a document dated 1696, the form τὸ Τζιουμέρκα is attested (cf. Miklosich–Müller, *Acta et diplomata*, III, p. 278 line 12).

[20] Incidentally, it should be pointed out that our place Τζεμέρνικος near Ioannina was probably not the only place with this name in Epirus. At least one other place in Epirus with an almost identical name Τζερμενικός (or -όν) appears in a letter of Bishop Demetrius of Butrinto (Buthrotum) which is quoted in the response of Demetrius Chomatenus, archbishop of Bulgaria (ed. J. B. Pitra, *Analecta sacra et classica Spicilegio Solesmensi parata*, VII, *Juris ecclesiastici Graecorum selecta paralipomena* [Paris–Rome, 1891; repr. as vol. VI, Farnborough, 1967], cols. 339–50). We find in col. 343, line 38 Τζερμενικῷ; in col. 350, line 24, in the response of Chomatenus himself, Τωρμενικὸν in a distorted form. The place in question (col. 343, lines 37–38, ὑπὸ τὴν ἀρχοντείαν ὄντι τοῦ Χοτεαχόβου) was ruled by the chieftain of Χοτεάχοβον, and it was situated in the diocese of Butrinto (cf. col. 343, lines 5–8 and 37–41). The place Χοταχόβα (Χόντα Χόβα, Χοντόβα) was in North Epirus, northeast of Butrinto, near the town Πρεμετή (or Πρεμέτι, now Përmet in Albania); cf. S. P. Lampros, Ἠπειρωτικά, in Νέος Ἑλλ., 10 (1913), p. 389; Μεγ.Ἑλλ.Ἐγκυκλ., XX, p. 662 (*s.v.* Πρεμετή). The place Τζερμενικός (or

The reference to Theodore Ducas, ruler of Epirus, in the subscription dated 13 February 1225, is very interesting. This reference was made after Theodore Angelus Ducas conquered Thessalonica at the end of 1224 and before his coronation in Thessalonica as βασιλεὺς καὶ αὐτοκράτωρ which took place in 1227–1228.[21] The subscription shows that, while Theodore (Angelus) Ducas was in Thessalonica, a lieutenant (ἐπίκουρος) of his, the monk Clement Monomachus,[22] administered the affairs of Epirus in Arta.

On Plate **2** we reproduce page 230, containing a part of a LESSON FROM THE GOSPELS, viz., a passage from the Gospel of St. Matthew 26:42–50 (ed. Nestle, *Novum Testamentum graece*, pp. 74f.). This is a part of the Gospel lesson for the evening Mass (λειτουργία) on Maundy Thursday (ed. Εὐαγγέλιον [1880], p. 133ᵃ, 22–41; or Εὐαγγέλιον [1968], p. 154ᵃ, 36 – 154ᵇ, 7). On the time and the contents of the whole lesson for this office, cf. Gregory, I, p. 362. The page reproduced begins with the words ἀπεμοῦ which do not appear in the present-day printed vulgate of the New Testament; they are, however, recorded as a variant in the critical apparatus to Matthew 26:42 (cf. Nestle, *op. cit.*, p. 74). It is noteworthy that these words are included in the lectionary text of this MS and in the printed lectionary vulgate (cf. Εὐαγγέλιον [1880], p. 133ᵃ, 22; Εὐαγγέλιον [1968], p. 154ᵃ, 36).[23] On this page, it can be seen that the sentences end, according to the practice of lectionaries, with the τελεία sign (+), a full-stop mark.[24]

The MS is one of the Cromwell MSS, which were presented to the Bodleian Library by Oliver Cromwell in 1654, when he was chancellor of the Oxford University (cf. *Summary Catalogue*, II,1, p. 11).

On this MS, cf. Coxe, I, cols. 433f.; *Summary Catalogue*, II,1, p. 12 (under S.C. 296); Vogel–Gardthausen, p. 317;[25] Scrivener, I, p. 330 (under Evst. 30); Gregory, I, p. 390 (under Evangelia 30); Aland, I, p. 206 (under the Gregory–Aland symbol *l* 30).

Plate 3: A.D. 1228.

Oxford, Bodleian Library, ms Holkham Greek 64. Parchment, 290 × 215 mm., III + 300 fols., 42 lines to a page. Fols. I–II are modern fly-

---

-ον) must have been within the diocese of Butrinto, if the bishop of Butrinto presented to Chomatenus his grievance that a regional chieftain Taronas infringed on his jurisdiction by establishing under patriarchal σταυροπήγιον a church of St. Nicholas even though there already was a church dedicated to the same saint under the authority of a former bishop of the same diocese (cf. Pitra, cols. 343, 42 – 344, 7; 350, 19–35). Accordingly, we must consider the Tzermenikos (-on) of the Butrinto diocese to be a place different from our Tzemernikos near Ioannina. It is possible that Taronas (col. 343, bottom line) is identical with a Vlach chieftain Taronas known from other historical sources (cf. D. M. Nicol, *The Despotate of Epiros* [Oxford, 1957], pp. 73 note 27, 155, 156 note 17; Polemis, *The Doukai*, p. 97 under no. 52).

[21] Cf. Nicol, *op. cit.*, pp. 62–66; G. Ostrogorsky, *Geschichte des byzantinischen Staates*, 3rd ed. (Munich, 1963), pp. 357f.; Polemis, *The Doukai*, pp. 89f. (under no. 42).

[22] On the Monomachus family, cf. Ahrweiler, "La région de Smyrne," p. 156.

[23] On the preservation of older readings in New Testament lectionaries, cf. Metzger, *The Text of the New Testament*, p. 31.

[24] On the τελεία sign used in lectionaries, cf. below, p. 18 note 45, and Pls. **6, 7, 11, 56.**

[25] Vogel–Gardthausen, p. 317, wrongly attributed MS Paris Grec 1571 to Michael Papadopulus, scribe of Oxford Cromwell 11. The Paris MS was written in an entirely different handwriting (cf. Omont, *Fac-similés ... du IXᵉ au XIVᵉ siècle*, pl. LIV). Moreover, the family name of the Paris scribe is illegible in the subscription and completely uncertain.

leaves; parchment folio III belongs to the main body of the MS. Contents: Theophylact ⟨Hephaestus⟩, archbishop of Bulgaria, Commentary on the Four Gospels. There are decorated headpieces in crimson ink. The MS was written by the monk Gregorius and subscribed by him in red in October A.M. 6737 = A.D. 1228 (fol. 300ᵛ – Pl. **98b**): † ἐγράφη ἡ παροῦσα θεόπνευστο(ς) βίβλο(ς) χειρὶ τοῦ ταπεινοῦ (μον)αχ(οῦ) Γρηγ(ο)ρ(ίου) | μη(νὶ) ὀκτωβρίω ἰν(δικτιῶνος) β τοῦ ͵ϛψλζ ἔτους· In this MS, Gospel passages, marked by double quotation marks to the left of the lines, and commentary sections alternate. On Plate **3** we reproduce folio 291ᵛ, containing a passage from THEOPHYLACT OF BULGARIA, COMMENTARY ON THE FOUR GOSPELS (ed. Migne, Patr. Gr., **124**, cols. 273 B 1 – 276 B 12; this is a comment on John 19:17–22).

This MS once was in the collection of Greek MSS owned by Ἰωάννης Μορεζῆνος (b. *ca.*1550, d. 1613) and his son, Μᾶρκος Μορεζῆνος (b. *ca.* 1570, d. 1634–1636), priests in Crete.[26] The MS was numbered λβ in their library (the number is marked on fol. 1ʳ). One of these owners annotated this MS.[27] Subsequently the MS was, along with other MSS of the Morezenus collection, owned by Giulio Giustiniani (1624–1699), a procurator of San Marco in Venice.[28] Montfaucon examined the Greek MSS of the Giustiniani library in 1698, supplied most of them with numbers, and made a summary and incomplete catalogue of these MSS without referring to their consecutive numbers.[29] This MS was no. 11 in the collection of Greek Giustiniani MSS (the number 11 and the date 1698 are written on fol. 1ʳ).

The next owner of almost the entire Giustiniani collection of Greek MSS was Thomas Coke of Holkham (1697–1759), Earl of Leicester, who acquired most of the Greek MSS of the Giustiniani library in 1721.[30] This MS carried in the Holkham library the mark 104. On the inside of the

[26] On Ioannes Morezenus and Marcus Morezenus, cf. H. D. Kakoulide, Ὁ Ἰωάννης Μορεζῆνος καὶ τὸ ἔργο του, in Κρ.Χρον., 22 (1970), pp. 7–78, 389–506 (pp. 48–57, on their library; p. 51, on this MS). Cf. also S. de Ricci, *A Handlist of Manuscripts in the Library of the Earl of Leicester at Holkham Hall*, Supplement to the Bibliographical Society's Transactions, 7 (Oxford, 1932), p. x; R. Barbour, "Greek Manuscripts from Holkham," *The Bodleian Library Record*, 5 (1954–1956), p. 62; *eadem*, "Summary Description of the Greek Manuscripts from the Library at Holkham Hall," *The Bodleian Library Record*, 6 (1957–1961), p. 591; Ch. G. Patrineles, Κρῆτες συλλέκται χειρογράφων κατὰ τοὺς χρόνους τῆς Ἀναγεννήσεως, in Πεπραγμένα τοῦ Β' Διεθνοῦς Κρητολογικοῦ Συνεδρίου, III (Athens, 1968), pp. 202, 205f.; Turyn, *DGMItaly*, I, pp. 202f.

[27] On the difficulty of distinguishing whether notes in some MSS of the Morezenus collection were written by Ioannes Morezenus or Marcus Morezenus, cf. Kakoulide, *op. cit.*, pp. 52–54. Cf. also P. Canart, "Scribes grecs de la Renaissance," *Scriptorium*, 17 (1963), p. 65 note 17.

[28] On Giulio Giustiniani, cf. P. Litta, *Famiglie Celebri Italiane*, VII (n.p., n.d.), under Giustiniani di Venezia, table VII; Kakoulide, *op. cit.*, p. 49 note 3. On the Morezenus MSS in the Giustiniani library, cf. de Ricci, *A Handlist*, p. x; Barbour, "Greek Manuscripts from Holkham," p. 62; *eadem*, "Summary Description," p. 591; Kakoulide, *op. cit.*, pp. 49–51; Turyn, *loc. cit.*

[29] This catalogue of Greek MSS in the Giustiniani library was published by B. de Montfaucon, *Diarium Italicum* (Paris, 1702), pp. 433–36 (cf. p. 69 on Montfaucon's visit to the Giustiniani library in August 1698); the same catalogue was reprinted: *idem*, *Bibliotheca bibliothecarum manuscriptorum nova*, I (Paris, 1739), pp. 483f. On Montfaucon's notes written on flyleaves of the Giustiniani MSS and on the numbers inscribed by him, cf. de Ricci, *A Handlist*, p. x; Barbour, *Summary Description*, p. 591. For a concordance of the present numbers of Oxford Holkham Greek MSS with Morezenus numbers and Giustiniani numbers (inscribed by Montfaucon), cf. Kakoulide, *op. cit.*, p. 51. Incidentally, the present MS Oxford Holkham Greek 72 cannot be Giustiniani MS 50 as marked with a question mark by Barbour, *Summary Description*, p. 605, and by Kakoulide, *loc. cit.* The Giustiniani MS 50 is the present MS Venice Greco 579 (colloc. 416), which carries on fol. 6ʳ a note by Montfaucon: *1698 Codex num. 50* (cf. C. E. Zachariä von Lingenthal, in *Neue kritische Jahrbücher für Deutsche Rechtswissenschaft*, VI,12 [1847], pp. 622f.; repr. in new ed. of J.-A.-B. Mortreuil, *Histoire du droit byzantin ou du droit romain dans l'empire d'Orient*, III [Osnabrück, 1966], at end, with the original pagination, pp. 622f.; Turyn, *op. cit.*, I, p. 203).

[30] On Thomas Coke, Baron Lovel, Earl of Leicester, cf. *Encyclopaedia Britannica*, XIII (Chicago [1973]), p. 917. On his activities as a collector of MSS, cf. de Ricci, *English Collectors*, pp. 42f.; *idem*, *A Handlist*, pp. VIII–XI (p. x, on the Giustiniani purchase); Barbour, "Greek Manuscripts from

front cover, there is the bookplate of Thomas William Coke, Earl of Leicester (1754–1842). In 1954, nearly all Greek MSS of the Earl of Leicester collection at Holkham (Norfolk), including this MS, were purchased by the Bodleian Library from Thomas William Edward Coke, fifth Earl of Leicester (born 1908).[31]

On this MS, cf. Barbour, "Summary Description," p. 604 (under no. 64); *eadem*, in *Greek Manuscripts in the Bodleian Library*, p. 21 (under no. 22); Vogel–Gardthausen, p. 96 (with a wrong date); Montfaucon, *Diarium Italicum*, p. 435 lines 9–10; *idem*, *Bibliotheca bibliothecarum manuscriptorum nova*, I, p. 483ᵇ C 4–6; *idem*, *Palaeographia graeca, sive de ortu et progressu literarum graecarum* (Paris, 1708; repr. [Farnborough, 1970]), p. 63 lines 4–3 from the bottom; de Ricci, *A Handlist*, p. 9 (under the former Holkham number 104): Gregory, I, p. 212 (under Vier Evangelien 684); Aland, I, p. 97 (under the Gregory–Aland number 684); von Soden, I,1, p. 264 (under Θᵉ³⁴), with an incorrect date.

Plate 4: A.D. 1252.

London, British Museum, ms Additional 27359. Paper (without watermarks), 289 × 207 mm., 267 fols. This MS, inasmuch as we know, is one of the earliest dated Greek MSS written on Western paper.[32] Contents: John Zonaras, Commentary on the Resurrectional Canons (ἀναστάσιμοι κανόνες) of the Octoechus (in the longer version), incomplete at the beginning and at the end. The ᾠδαί, εἱρμοί, and τροπάρια commented upon are marked as such by proper prefixes written in red. The comments have a prefix ἑρμηνεία (in full or in an abbreviated form). This MS carries Zonaras' Commentary in its longer version.[33] It agrees only in a general way in many longer stretches of text with the shorter version, which was published for the first time by Spyridon Lauriotes (see below). However, the longer version differs considerably from the shorter version by its very size and by the length and wording of countless longer passages. It may be assumed that the longer version is the original one, while the shorter version is an epitome of the original. It should be noted that Zonaras' Commentary in this London MS includes references to the commentary of Zonaras' predecessor in this field, the "late" (μακάριος ἐκεῖνος, ἐκεῖνος, μακαρίτης ἐκεῖνος) archbishop of Thessalonica, identified as Nicetas of Maroneia (archbishop of Thessalonica *circa* 1132–1145), who earlier

---

Holkham," pp. 61f.; Kakoulide, *op. cit.*, p. 48. As was rightly observed by de Ricci, *A Handlist*, p. x note 4, some Giustiniani MSS were not among those purchased by Thomas Coke and consequently were not found at Holkham Hall. For instance, I pointed out (*DGMItaly*, I, pp. 202f.) that two MSS which formerly belonged to the Morezeni and then to Giustiniani were acquired by Giovan Battista Recanati (1687–1734) and were willed by him to the Biblioteca Marciana in Venice; these are now MSS Venice Greco 578 (colloc. 866) and Venice Greco 579 (colloc. 416). They were obviously removed from the Greek collection of Giustiniani after his death and before Coke purchased it.

[31] On the acquisition of Greek Holkham MSS by the Bodleian Library, cf. Barbour, "Greek Manuscripts from Holkham," pp. 61–63; *eadem*, "Summary Description," p. 591; R. W. Hunt, in *Greek Manuscripts in the Bodleian Library. An Exhibition Held in Connection with the XIIIth International Congress of Byzantine Studies* (Oxford, 1966), p. 10.

[32] Cf. J. Irigoin, "Les premiers manuscrits grecs écrits sur papier et le problème du bombycin," *Scriptorium*, 4 (1950), p. 201 and note 1; cf. also *idem*, "Les conditions matérielles de la production du livre à Byzance de 1071 à 1261," *XVᵉ Congrès International d'Etudes Byzantines. Rapports et co-rapports*, II,3 (Athens, 1976), p. 9 and especially p. 10. In the paper of MS London Addit. 27359, the thickness of 20 laid marks varies from 51 to 60 mm. Chain marks are hardly visible; when discernible, they are 80 mm. apart.

[33] The existence in the manuscript tradition of two versions of Zonaras' Commentary was established by A. D. Komines, Γρηγόριος Πάρδος μητροπολίτης Κορίνθου καὶ τὸ ἔργον αὐτοῦ, Testi e Studi Bizantino-Neoellenici, II (Rome–Athens, 1960), p. 110.

wrote an incomplete commentary only on an initial part of the Resurrectional Canons of the Octoechus.[34] These references are a characteristic feature of the longer version of Zonaras' Commentary.

This MS Additional 27359 was subscribed in two scribal notes. The first note, dated 5 June A.M. 6760 = A.D. 1252, was written in red on fol. 191ᵛ (Pl. **99a**): + μηνὶ ἰουν(ίῳ) ε̄ ἡμέ(ρᾳ) δ′ ἰν(δικτιῶνος) ῑ τοῦ ͵ϛψξ ἔτους:– (The whole page, fol. 191ᵛ, which includes this note, was reproduced in *Pal. Soc.*, Ser. I, pl. 203.) The second note, dated 6 July A.M. 6760 = A.D. 1252, was likewise written in red, on fol. 239ᵛ (Pl. **99b**): μη(νὶ) ἰουλ(ίῳ) ϛ ἡμέ(ρᾳ) ϛ′ ἰν(δικτιῶνος) ῑ τοῦ ͵ϛψξ ἔτους:– The 6th of July in 1252 fell on a Saturday, not on a Friday (sixth day of the week), as marked in the note; the scribe must have made a slip in one of the two elements, either the number of the day of the month or the day of the week (5 July 1252 was a Friday).

On Plate **4** we reproduce the lower part of fol. 126ᵛ, containing a passage from JOHN ZONARAS, COMMENTARY ON THE RESURRECTIONAL CANONS OF THE OCTOECHUS (cf. Spyridon Lauriotes, ed., Ἀναστασίμων κανόνων ἑρμηνεία ὑπὸ Ἰωάννου Ζωναρᾶ, in Ὁ Ἄθως, ἁγιορειτικὸν περιοδικόν, ἔτος Α′. τρίτη τριμηνία [Athens, 1920], pp. 102, 13–103, 2). The page part reproduced contains comments on the Resurrectional Canon of the Octoechus for the ὄρθρος service on Sunday of the third mode (ἦχος γ′), ᾠδὴ η′, εἱρμός.[35] The text reproduced can be compared in general with the corresponding passage in the edition of Spyridon Lauriotes; however, it does not agree strictly with the published text. Another specimen from this MS was published in *Pal. Soc.*, Ser. I, pl. 203 (fol. 191ᵛ). A part of the same plate was reproduced by Thompson, *Introduction*, p. 252 (facsim. no. 71), with a transcript on p. 253, and a comment on the MS on pp. 250, 254.

In this MS, a yellow wash appears over some capital initials and sometimes covers larger letters at the beginning of a line, especially round or oval letters or parts thereof, or even triangular parts of letters (e.g., of a capital-like Δ). Yellow wash was used in this MS over some headpieces also.[36] Occasionally, red blobs cover round letters (such as ο) in the text of this MS.[37]

[34] Cf. *ibid.*, pp. 106–8, 111. On the references to the Archbishop of Thessalonica in the Commentary of Zonaras, i.e., to Nicetas of Maroneia, cf. *ibid.*, p. 106 notes 4, 6, 7. The same references as those quoted by Komines in notes 4 and 6 appear in London Addit. 27359, on fols. 78ʳ, 80ʳ, 72ʳ; the reference quoted in note 7 was lost in the London MS, which is incomplete at the end.

On Nicetas of Maroneia, archbishop of Thessalonica, cf. Krumbacher, pp. 89f.; M. Jugie, "Notes de littérature byzantine," *EO*, 26 (1927), pp. 408–16; *idem*, "Nicétas de Maronée," *DTC*, XI,1, cols. 473–77; Beck, *Kirche und theologische Literatur*, pp. 621f.

[35] For the text of the Canon in the version used in the above Commentary, cf. Ὀκτώηχος τοῦ ἐν ἁγίοις πατρὸς ἡμῶν Ἰωάννου τοῦ Δαμασκηνοῦ, ed. N. P. Papadopoulos (Athens [1947]), pp. 73–83 (for the text of the εἱρμός commented upon on Plate **4**, cf. p. 80, 24–28); or cf. Παρακλητική, in Ἐκδόσεις Φῶς (Athens, 1959), pp. 126–30 (for the text of the same εἱρμός, cf. p. 129ᵇ, 23–28). The text of this εἱρμός is printed in full also in Ὀκτώηχος ... (Rome, 1886), p. 49, 22–26; or in Παρακλητικὴ ἤτοι Ὀκτώηχος ἡ μεγάλη (Rome, 1885), p. 198, 22–26; or in Εἱρμολόγιον, ed. I. Nikolaïdes (Athens, 1906), p. 56, lines 9–6 from the bottom.

[36] Cf. also p. 8 and note 11, pp. 16, 70, 96.

[37] Red blobs were used over round or oval letters, or parts thereof, especially in South Italian MSS (cf. Turyn, *Codices*, pp. 36, 84; *idem*, *DGMItaly*, I, pp. 5f.), but this practice was not limited to South Italian MSS (cf. *ibid.*, pp. 169f., 192). This MS London Addit. 27359 was certainly not of South Italian origin.

This MS was acquired by the British Museum in 1866. On this MS, cf. Richard, *Inventaire*, p. 48; *Catalogue of Additions to the Manuscripts in the British Museum in the Years MDCCCLIV–MDCCCLXXV*, II [London, 1877], p. 306; *Pal. Soc.*, Ser. I, pl. 203, description.

Plate 5: A.D. 1253.

Oxford, Bodleian Library, ms E. D. Clarke 8. Parchment, 205 × 170 mm., 198 fols. (and one more fol. 166ᵇ), 2 columns, 23 lines to a column. The MS is incomplete at the beginning (two initial quires were lost) and at the end. Contents: Lectionary of the Gospels (daily in John, Saturdays and Sundays in Matthew and Luke; lessons for some feasts of the calendar year and for some occasions). The MS was written by the lector Demetrius Brizopulus (most probably in Epirus) and subscribed by him on 1 August A.M. 6761 = A.D. 1253, according to a partially mutilated subscription on the damaged folio 196ʳ right column – 196ᵛ left column (Pl. **99c**):

Πόθω τέτευχα· ἱερὰν | ταύτην βίβλον·
εὔ|ριθμον ἐσίνοπτον· | ὡς ψάλλει θέμης· |
ὑπο χειρὸς μὲν αν|δράνοῦς· Δημητρίου |
ἀναγνώστου, καὶ ἐλ|λαχίστου·
5 ἡ χεὶρ μὲν | ἡ γράψασα· σίπεται | τάφω·
γραφὴ μέ|νη δὲ εἰς μακροῦς | φεύ μοι χρόνους:· |

Πέρας ἤλειφεν ἡ | θεία ταύτη βίβλο(ς) | τοῦ ἱεροῦ Εὐα(γγελίου), | διὰ χειρὸς ἐμοῦ Δη|μητρίου ἀναγνώ|στου τοῦ Βριζωπούλου, ‖ [– – –] | [– – – Βαγε]|νετίας. το[. . . .] | ἄρχοντ( ) Μηκρὰν Βαγε|νετίαν, +++ | Καὶ ὅσοι ἐπὶ χείρας | ταύτην δέξασθ(ε), ἤτοι | ἴσως σφάλμα εὕρειται, | εὔξασθ(ε) καμοὶ τῶ ἁ|μαρτωλῶ καὶ μὴ κα|τηράσθ(ε), ἰδότες ὅτι | τὸ μὴ σφάλλειν παρὰ | ἀν(θρώπ)οις ἀδύνατον ἐ|στὶν, ἵνα καὶ ὁ θ(εὸ)ς | σώσει καὶ συγχωρή|σει καὶ ὑμᾶς πάν|τας, ἐγρά(φη) δὲ καὶ | ἐτελειώθ(η), ἐπὶ ἔτ(ους) | ͵ϛψξᾱ ἰν(δικτιῶνος) ιᾱ + | Μηνὶ αὐγούστω | εἰς τ(ὴν) πρώτ(ην), ἡμέρα | παρα(σκευῆ), ὥρα ΄θ, | δό(ξα) τὸ δόντ(ι) τὸ τέ(λος) τοῖς | πᾶ(σ)ην ἀμήν +++

In the above subscription, I have arranged the poem at the beginning metrically in dodecasyllables, as it was composed by the scribe. Verse 4 is metrically defective; three syllables are missing because of the scribe's inadvertence. In verse 2, on ἐσίνοπτον instead of εὐσύνοπτον, on ἐ- instead of εὐ-, cf. Dieterich, *Untersuchungen*, pp. 79f. In the word ψάλλει, the final -ν was dropped (cf. *ibid.*, pp. 88–91). In verse 3, ἀδρανοῦς would be the correct form.[38] Verses 5–6, ἡ χεὶρ μὲν ἡ γράψασα κτλ., were frequently used as a commonplace of subscriptions.[39] After the dodecasyllabic colophon there is

---

[38] The word ἀδρανεῖ was used by a scribe about himself in MS Vatic. graec. 2138, fol. 91ʳ (cf. Follieri, *Codices*, p. 50 under no. 32).

[39] Cf. P. Garitte, "Sur une formule des colophons de manuscrits grecs (ἡ μὲν χεὶρ ἡ γράψασα)," *Collectanea Vaticana in honorem Anselmi M. Card. Albareda a Bibliotheca Apostolica edita*, I, ST, 219 (Vatican City, 1962), pp. 359–90; S. Y. Rudberg, "Note sur une formule des colophons de manuscrits grecs," *Scriptorium*, 20 (1966), pp. 66f.; K. Treu, "Weitere Handschriften mit der Schreiberformel Ἡ μὲν χεὶρ ἡ γράψασα . . .," *Scriptorium*, 24 (1970), pp. 56–64; Turyn, *Codices*, pp. 53, 55, 83, 139, 157; idem, *DGMItaly*, I, p. 258; Follieri, *Codices*, pp. 56, 58; B. Atsalos, "La terminologie médiévale du livre dans ses rapports avec la description codicologique," in *Paléographie grecque et byzantine*, pp. 87–89.

a tailpiece, below which the subscription proper begins. The initial words of this subscription, Πέρας – βίβλο(ς), were probably conceived by the scribe as a dodecasyllable. In the left margin of fol. 196ᵛ, opposite the lines in which sections of the subscription begin, there are asterisks (opposite Καὶ ὅσοι, opposite τας, ἐγρά(φη), opposite Μηνὶ αὐγούστω). The upper part of fol. 196 was torn off so that an important part of the subscription is missing. I assume that two lines are entirely missing at the top of fol. 196ᵛ; in this less formal part of the MS, page fol. 196ᵛ contained probably 24 lines to a column, as was the case on the facing page fol. 197ʳ. The missing part of fol. 196ᵛ, left column, contained, as it seems, a mention of the man who commissioned this MS. It is obvious that there are in the subscription references to the well-known region of southwestern Epirus, Βαγενετία, or, strictly speaking, to Μικρὰ Βαγενετία. It may be that the first mention Βαγε]|νετίας had the same attribute in the preceding lost line. If so, we should supplement the line immediately preceding (cf. fol. 196ᵛ, left column, top: Pl. **99c**) Μικρᾶς Βαγε]| νετίας. The second mention of that region in the subscription is explicit: Μηκρὰν Βαγε|νετίαν. Most probably the MS was commissioned or paid for by somebody who was ἄρχων of Little Bagenetia. The participle ἀρχοντ( ) here governs the accusative; it was not substantivized (as was usual) to be used with the genitive.

On Bagenetia (or Vagenetia), a region (θέμα) of Epirus, cf. M. Lascaris, "Vagenitia," *RHSEE*, 19 (1942), pp. 423–37. On Bagenetia and its particular administrative feature of being governed by an ἄρχων, cf. D. A. Zakythenos, Μελέται περὶ τῆς διοικητικῆς διαιρέσεως καὶ τῆς ἐπαρχιακῆς διοικήσεως ἐν τῷ Βυζαντινῷ κράτει, in Ἐπ.Ἐτ.Βυζ.Σπ., 21 (1951), pp. 196–205. It is somewhat striking that the region mentioned in the subscription is referred to as Μικρὰ Βαγενετία. Such a term is known from a mention in a decree by John Apocaucus, metropolitan of Naupactus (cf. S. Pétridès, "Jean Apokaukos, lettres et autres documents inédits," *IRAIK*, 14 [1909], p. 75 line 30): Ὁ ἀπὸ Μικρᾶς Βαγενετίας, χωρίον Βρεστίανες, Θεόδωρος ὁ Βοδινόπουλος. κτλ. (cf. Lascaris, *op. cit.*, pp. 430 f.). Perhaps this "Little Bagenetia" was a lower administrative subdivision of Bagenetia proper. It is interesting that Μεγάλη Βαγενιτεία is mentioned in the subscription of MS Athos, Σκήτη Προδρόμου (Μονῆς Ἰβήρων) 11, dated A.D. 1624/1625 (cf. L. Polites with the collaboration of M. I. Manousakas, Συμπληρωματικοὶ κατάλογοι χειρογράφων Ἁγίου Ὄρους, in Ἑλληνικά, Suppl. 24 [Thessalonica, 1973], p. 246 no. 566).

In MS E. D. Clarke 8, the whole subscription, both the dodecasyllabic colophon and the subscription proper, is covered with yellow wash. Such wash was often used in this MS over headlines or rubrics and other noteworthy elements. It should be especially noted that in this case yellow wash was applied in a MS written in Epirus.[40]

On Plate **5** we reproduce folio 141ᵛ. This page of the LECTIONARY OF THE GOSPELS contains passages from the Gospel of St. John 19:26–28 and 19:30–35. This is a part of the lesson for the Mass on September 14, the feast of the

---

[40] On yellow wash, cf. above, p. 8 and note 11, pp. 14, 70.

Exaltation of the Holy Cross (ed. Εὐαγγέλιον [1880], p. 161ᵇ, 5–23; in the edition of the Εὐαγγέλιον [1968], p. 184, this lesson is shorter). The lesson for the Mass on September 14 partly coincides with the lesson for the Mass on May 8, the feast of St. John the Evangelist (a pertinent marginal note was made in this MS on fol. 141ʳ). For the time and extent of the lessons in question, cf. Gregory, I, pp. 366, 379. On the page reproduced, a larger omicron at the beginning of a text section (in the left column's line 17) shows yellow wash. Round or oval letters, or parts thereof, were traditionally prone to receive colored wash.[41] The MS is written in two-column pages; such an arrangement prevailed in lectionaries, since it made the reading more convenient (cf. Gregory, I, p. 328). For two-column lectionaries, cf. below, Plates **6, 7, 11, 56.**

This MS once belonged to Edward Daniel Clarke (1769–1822). The Clarke MSS were purchased by the Bodleian Library in 1809. On Clarke and his MSS, cf. *DNB*, IV, pp. 421–24 (p. 423, on his MSS); *Summary Catalogue*, IV, p. 297.

On this MS, cf. Th. Gaisford, *Catalogus sive notitia manuscriptorum qui a cel. E. D. Clarke comparati in Bibliotheca Bodleiana adservantur*, I (Oxford, 1812), p. 13; *Summary Catalogue*, IV, p. 300 (under S.C. 18370); Vogel–Gardthausen, p. 101; Scrivener, I, p. 337 (under Evst. 157); Gregory, I, p. 400 (under Evangelia 157); Aland, I, p. 213 (under the Gregory–Aland symbol *l* 157).

Plate 6: A.D. 1255/1256.

London, British Museum, ms Additional 40754. Parchment, 257 × 203 mm., 151 fols., 2 columns, 28 lines to a column. Fols. 119–121, 126–134, 136–140, 144–148 are later replacements on paper. The MS has been bound anew,[42] and the former dark brown leather binding (with identical gilt-stamped floral designs in the center of the upper front cover and in the lower back cover), containing on the verso of the upper cover important ownership entries, has been separated from the MS and is kept in a box which has on the spine an imprint "Binding of Brit. Mus. Additional Ms. 40,754." Contents: Lectionary of the Gospels (daily in John, Saturdays and Sundays in Matthew and Luke, παννυχίδες, νηστεῖαι, Holy Week, πάθη, ὧραι, daily for saints' days and immovable feasts, ἑωθινά). The MS was written by the lector Georgius S(?)udarias in A.M. 6764 = A.D. 1255/1256, according to the subscription on fol. 151ʳ (Pl. **100a**): δόξα σοι ὁ θ(εὸ)ς | ἀμήν:– | † Γεωργ(ίου) ἀναγνώστου | Σοῦδαρία: | † ἔτους ͵ϛψξδ ἰνδ(ικτιῶνος) ιδ | εὔχεσθαι καὶ μὴ κατηρά-σθαι. Lines 3–4 of this subscription, containing the name of the scribe, are written in red. In the scribe's family name, the initial letter σ- is somewhat uncertain.

On Plate **6** we reproduce folio 25ᵛ. This page of the LECTIONARY OF THE GOSPELS contains passages from the Gospel of St. John 14:9–11 and 14:10–19. The passages represent the end of the lesson for Friday of the sixth week after Easter (the whole lesson is John 14:1–11) and the beginning of the lesson

---

[41] Cf. above, p. 14 and note 37; Turyn, *DGMItaly*, I, pp. 5f., 202 lines 9–12.

[42] The new binding was probably made after 1950, when the description of the MS still with its old binding was published in the *Catalogue of Additions 1921–1925* (see below).

for Saturday of the same week (the whole lesson is John 14:10–21). The text of the page reproduced can be found in printed lectionaries of the Gospels (ed. Εὐαγγέλιον [1880], pp. 18ᵇ, 35 – 19ᵃ, 23; or ed. Εὐαγγέλιον [1968], p. 32ᵃ, 32 – 32ᵇ, 18). The beginning of the latter lesson is preceded in the MS by a liturgical note (in red) which indicates the time of the lesson and the Gospel from which the lesson is taken: τῷ σα(ββάτῳ) τῆς ϛ | εὐδ(ο)μάδ(ος) | ἐκ τ(οῦ) κατ(ὰ) Ἰω(άννην). Liturgical notes in New Testament MSS adapted for liturgical use and in New Testament lectionaries are usually written in red.⁴³ The text of the latter lesson begins (John 14:10) with a lesson formula prefixed to the standard text: Εἶπεν ὁ κ(ύριο)ς τοῖς ἑαυτοῦ μαθηταῖς.⁴⁴ On the time and extent of the lessons just mentioned, cf. Gregory, I, p. 346. The lesson which begins on the page reproduced has the initial letter E in a large-size decorated shape, traced in black and red, projected to the left into the margin. Within the text, there appears the τελεία sign (+), i.e., the full-stop mark, at the end of sentences.⁴⁵ The MS is written in two-column pages, as befits a lectionary (cf. above, p. 17; cf. Pls. **5, 7, 11, 56**).

In the *old* binding of this MS (kept separately), there are ownership entries of two former owners; they appear on the pastedown on the inside of the upper cover. This is the earlier entry written, probably in the 18th century, on the upper part of the pastedown: Τὸ παρῶν καὶ θήων καὶ ἱερόν ἐβανγγέλιων ὑπάρχῆ | ἐμοῦ τοῦ εὐτελοῦς Διαμαντάκη ἐκ της | χῶρας του Μεγάλου Ρεύματος τῶν | Ἀσωμάτων καὶ ὅστης βουληθῆ | ἀποξενόσι χορῆς θέλιμα | ἐδικῶν μου ἔστω | τοῦ ἀναθέματος | ἐν παντῆ | κερῶ: | Since Ῥεῦμα (or Ἀνάπλους) meant the Bosporus, it is clear that the owner Diamantakes indicated as the place of his origin or residence the area near Constantinople, on the European shore of the Bosporus, called Ἀσώματος, or Michaelion, from the church or monastery of St. Michael ἐν τῷ Ἀνάπλῳ. This was most probably the area on the Bosporus coast near the present cape Akıntıburnu.⁴⁶

The second ownership entry was written on a pink piece of paper pasted on the lower part of the same inside of the upper cover of the old binding:⁴⁷ Χειρόγραφον εἰς Μεμβράναν .[. . . . .] | Εὐαγγέλιον εἰς Περικοπὴν τεκμέρεται της | δεκάτης [[πέμπτης]] προχωρούσης (this word was written by a different hand above the preceding canceled word which was covered by ink) Ἑκατονταετηρίδος, καταγό|μενον ὡς ἐν τῇ ἄνω ἐπιγραφῇ. ἔλαβον | τοῦτο παρὰ Διονυσίου Φαραντάτου ἐκ τοῦ | δῆμου Θηνιᾶς, κατὰ τό ἔτος 1853.– | νῦν δὲ ὑπάρχει ἐμοῦ τοῦ ὑποσημειουμένου. | –Χαραλάμπους Τσημ. Γεννατᾶ. This note shows that up to 1853 the MS was owned by Dionysius Pharantatus from Cephalonia's district Θηναία.⁴⁸ From him it was obtained by

---

⁴³ Cf. Turyn, *DGMItaly*, I, p. 18. Cf. below, p. 43 note 101 (on red color of liturgical notes in New Testament MSS adapted for liturgical use).

⁴⁴ On formulaic additions to the standard text of the New Testament at the beginnings of pericopes in lectionaries, cf. Gregory, I, p. 341; von Dobschütz, *Eberhard Nestle's Einführung*, p. 37.

⁴⁵ On the τελεία sign, used in both Old Testament lectionaries (Prophetologia) and New Testament lectionaries, cf. G. Zuntz, "Das byzantinische Septuaginta-Lektionar (»Prophetologion«)," *ClMed*, 17 (1956), p. 193; Turyn, *DGMItaly*, I, p. 46; *idem, Codices*, pl. 70; cf. below, Pls. **2, 7, 11, 56**.

⁴⁶ Cf. R. Janin, *Constantinople byzantine. Développement urbain et répertoire topographique*, 2nd ed., AOC, 4A (Paris, 1964), p. 1, on Ῥεῦμα; p. 469, *s.v.* Asomatos; map XI; *idem, La géographie ecclésiastique de l'empire byzantin*, pt. 1, *Le siège de Constantinople et le Patriarcat oecuménique*, vol. III, *Les églises et les monastères*, 2nd ed. (Paris, 1969), pp. 338–40; E. Follieri, "Un Theotocarion Marciano del sec. XIV," *Archivio Italiano per la Storia della Pietà*, 3 (1962), pp. 40–42.

⁴⁷ Cf. below, p. 19 note 52 (on the color and placement of ownership labels in MSS which once belonged to Charalampos Tsemaratos Gennatas). On the typical contents of an ownership entry of Gennatas in his MSS, cf. P. G. Nikolopoulos, Κώδικες τῆς Βατικανῆς Βιβλιοθήκης ἐκ τῆς συλλογῆς Χαραλάμπους Τσιμαράτου Γεννατᾶ, in Πρακτικὰ Τρίτου Πανιονίου Συνεδρίου, II (Athens, 1969), p. 134.

⁴⁸ Cf. O. Riemann, *Recherches archéologiques sur les îles ioniennes*, II, *Céphalonie*, BEFAR, 12 (Paris, 1879), p. 7 (on the division of Cephalonia, as of 1873, into 19 districts, i.e., δῆμοι, according to p. 7 note 2), p. 8 (on the district Θηναία), map at the end (district 18).

Χαράλαμπος Τσημαρᾶτος Γεννατᾶς (1816–1884), of Hagia Thekla (then in the district of ᾿Ανωγή, therefore called also ῾Αγία Θέκλα ᾿Ανωγῆς) in Cephalonia (in the eparchy of Πάλη), collector of manuscripts as well as coins and other objects.[49] This MS was seen in the house of Gennatas by the French scholar Othon Riemann about 1879 and was listed by him as MS 2 of the Gennatas collection.[50]

Even after Gennatas' death, the MS was seen still in the Gennatas house by E. A. Tsitseles in 1887.[51] Later, the manuscript collection of Gennatas was obviously dispersed.[52] In July 1909, S. P. Lampros[53] saw it in Argostolion (in Cephalonia) in the possession of Νικόλαος Βλαχούλης, manager of the Hôtel des Etrangers.[54] Lampros described the MS[55] and quoted verbatim the ownership entries[56] that are identical with those reported from this London MS in the *Catalogue of Additions 1921–1925* (see below) and quoted by me from the pastedown on the inside of the upper cover of the old binding of the MS.

The identity of these ownership entries provides the identification of this London MS with the former Gennatas–Blachoules MS. It should be pointed out that Lampros[57] reported from the back flyleaf of this MS the following entry: ᾿Αριθ. 89 τοῦ Καταλόγου Π. Καπλανίδου. This must be a reference to a consecutive number in a catalogue made by Panagiotes Kaplanides (probably in the 19th century; the catalogue was not published).[58] It may be that the catalogue of Kaplanides comprised some other objects, apart from the Gennatas collection of MSS.[59] At any rate, the back flyleaf with the Kaplanides reference must have been lost before this MS reached London, because the description of the MS published in the *Catalogue of Additions* does not indicate any back flyleaves. After Blachoules, the next known owner of the MS was H. Bagge from whom the British Museum bought it on 9 June 1923 (according to a note written on the second new front flyleaf of the present new binding).

On this MS, cf. Richard, *Inventaire*, p. 83; *British Museum. Catalogue of Additions to the Manuscripts 1921–1925* (London, 1950), pp. 168f.; K. Aland, "Zur Liste der Neutestamentlichen Handschriften. V.," *ZNW*, 45 (1954), p. 216 (under *l* 1743); Aland, I, p. 302 (numbered according to the Gregory–Aland system as *l* 1743).

---

[49] On Charalampos Tsemaratos Gennatas (sometimes referred to as Tsimaratos with one family name only), cf. *ibid.*, pp. 26, 30, 32, 43, 44, 45, 52; on his collection, pp. 67–70; E. A. Tsitseles, Κεφαλ-ληνιακὰ Σύμμικτα, I (Athens, 1904), p. 72; on his MSS, cf. pp. 17, 24, 59, 272 note 1, 348 note 1.

[50] On the collection of MSS of Gennatas at Hagia Thekla, cf. Riemann, *op. cit.*, pp. 68–70; on this London MS, cf. *ibid.*, p. 68, under b) Manuscrits, 2. Riemann listed it as a lectionary of the Gospels on parchment; his dating was vague: "Les quatre Evangiles arrangés selon le rite grec; parchemin; antérieur au quinzième siècle, à ce qu'il me semble."

[51] Cf. E. A. Tsitseles, ᾿Αρχαῖα εὐαγγέλια ἐν Κεφαλληνίᾳ, in ῾Εστία, 24 (1887), p. 766. Tsitseles mentioned here two Gennatas MSS of the Gospels (Riemann, *op. cit.*, p. 68 under nos. 1 and 2). The Gennatas MS 2 is identical with London Additional 40754. Tsitseles, *loc. cit.*, added some details about the purported provenance of the Gennatas MS 2, but these details conflict with the autographic statement of Gennatas concerning the former owner of the MS from whom he obtained it.

[52] On the dispersion of the Gennatas collection and the present whereabouts of several MSS from that collection, cf. the fundamental study by Nikolopoulos, *op. cit.*, pp. 133–42; and the important contributions by L. Polites, Παλαιογραφικά, in ῾Ελληνικά, 21 (1968), pp. 172–76 (with an essential observation on p. 172 regarding Gennatas' ownership labels, often of pink paper, pasted customarily to the inside of the front cover of a MS, as is the case in London Additional 40754: cf. above, p. 18); *idem*, Παλαιογραφικά, *ibid.*, 24 (1971), pp. 140–43.

[53] Cf. S. P. Lampros, Τρεῖς κώδικες ἐν Κεφαλληνίᾳ, in Νέος ῾Ελλ., 6 (1909), pp. 322, 323f.

[54] This hotel and its manager (perhaps owner?), Blachoules, are mentioned in K. Baedeker, *Griechenland*, 5th ed. (Leipzig, 1908), p. 268 (under Argostóli): "H.[ôtel] des Etrangers, bei Wlachulēs."

[55] Lampros, *op. cit.*, pp. 323f. (on p. 323 he misprinted the Arabic figure of the date of the subscription converted to the Christian era).

[56] On the basis of the Gennatas entry quoted from the Blachoules MS by Lampros (*ibid.*, p. 324), Nikolopoulos (*op. cit.*, pp. 136 and 141) recognized that the lectionary MS of Blachoules was identical with the Gennatas MS 2 as numbered by Riemann.

[57] Cf. Lampros, *op. cit.*, p. 324.

[58] On Panagiotes Kaplanides, cf. E. A. Tsitseles, Κεφαλληνιακὰ Σύμμικτα, II (Athens, 1960), p. 618.

[59] The highest figure, 91, so far known from the Kaplanides catalogue (cf. Nikolopoulos, *op. cit.*, pp. 136, 139) is unlikely to indicate a consecutive manuscript number in the Gennatas collection. On the possibility that Kaplanides may also have included in his catalogue some other objects of the Gennatas collection, perhaps printed books, cf. *ibid.*, p. 139; Polites, in ῾Ελληνικά, 24, p. 143.

Plate 7: A.D. 1258/1259.

Glasgow, University Library, ms Hunter 440. This MS was formerly in the Hunterian Museum of the University of Glasgow (under the pressmark V.5.10); however, the Hunter MSS are now housed in the University Library. Parchment, 254 × 196 mm., 111 fols. numbered as pages 1–224 (page numbers 172 and 173 were skipped inadvertently), 2 columns, 27–36 lines to a column. Between pages 64 and 65 about 20 folios were lost. Contents: Lectionary of the Gospels (daily in John, Saturdays and Sundays in Matthew and Luke; lessons for some feasts and saints' days). The MS was subscribed in A.M. 6767 = A.D. 1258/1259 (page 224 – Pl. **100b**): ἔτ(ους or -ει) ͵ϛψ$\overline{ξζ}$|ἰν(δικτιῶνος)β ++++ On Plate **7** we reproduce page 131. This page of the LECTIONARY OF THE GOSPELS contains a passage from the Gospel of St. Matthew 27:16—27. This is a part of the fifth Gospel of the Passions read on Good Friday (the whole fifth Gospel lesson comprises Matthew 27:3–32). On the time and extent of this lesson, cf. Gregory, I, p. 363. The ends of sentences on the page reproduced are marked with the τελεία sign (+), a full-stop mark (cf. above, p. 18 note 45). In the text, the letters projected to the left of the column indicate the beginning of a sentence (or of an important part of a sentence) in the preceding line (cf. below, p. 22 and note 63).

This MS was once owned by Caesar de Missy, according to his ownership entry on page 224: *Ex libris Caesaris De Missy, Berolinensis*: — | *Londini*: *Anno Dⁿⁱ 1748*:~ On Caesar de Missy (b. Berlin, 1703 – d. London, 1775), priest, critic, and New Testament scholar, cf. *Nouvelle Biographie Générale*, XXXV (Paris, 1861), col. 675; Gregory, I, p. 139; III, p. 1403 (Index, *s.v.* Missy, Caesar de); J. Young and P. H. Aitken, *A Catalogue of the Manuscripts in the Library of the Hunterian Museum in the University of Glasgow* (Glasgow, 1908), p. 325. Subsequently, the MS was acquired in 1776 (along with several other MSS of de Missy) by Dr. William Hunter (1718–1783), renowned anatomist and physician, who bequeathed his museum to the University of Glasgow; the bequest was to take effect 30 years after his death. Actually, the Hunterian Museum came into the possession of the University of Glasgow in 1807. On William Hunter, his museum, and his MSS, cf. Young and Aitken, *op. cit.*, p. ix; *DNB*, X, pp. 302–5; de Ricci, *English Collectors*, p. 53.

On this MS, cf. Young and Aitken, *op. cit.*, p. 363 (under no. 440); Scrivener, I, p. 343 (under Evst. 230); Gregory, I, p. 407 (under Evangelia 239); Aland, I, p. 218 (under the Gregory–Aland symbol *l* 239).

Plates 8, 9, 10: A.D. 1271/1272.

London, British Museum, ms Additional 39597. Parchment, 143 × 110 mm., IV + 230 + I fols., 20–22 lines to a page. The inside of the upper cover is numbered I; the next flyleaves are II, III, an unnumbered flyleaf with the stamped call number of the MS, and IV; the first back flyleaf is numbered V. Between fols. 103 and 104, one leaf was lost, containing Luke 1:34–56; this text was supplemented by a later hand in the margins of fols. 103ᵛ–104ᵛ. Contents: Four Gospels, with occasional liturgical notes for lesson use. The MS seems to have been written by at least six alternating scribes—or certainly in at least six different scripts, which I shall denote by letters A, B, C, D, E, and F. Some of the scribes wrote within the MS with a varying size of lettering and a varying degree of calligraphic effort, so that pages written by the same scribe occasionally might assume a somewhat different appearance. All these scribes were linked by some common features like the similar or identical shapes of some characteristic letters, e.g., the ζ or the open ϑ. It seems that these scribes were trained in the same scriptorium of which this MS is a product. The MS was concluded in A.M. 6780 = A.D. 1271/ 1272, according to the subscription (in red) on fol. 230ᵛ (Pl. **100c**): † ἔτους ͵ϛψπ̄ + ἰν(δικτιῶνος) ιε̄ × The whole page fol. 230ᵛ was reproduced by R. Curzon, *Catalogue of Materials* (see below), opposite p. 40, and in *New Pal. Soc.*, Ser. II, pl. 119*c*; a facsimile of the same page (with its blank parts cut off) was published by A. Ehrhard, "Das griechische Kloster Mar-Saba in Palaestina, seine Geschichte und seine litterarischen Denkmäler," *RQ*, 7 (1893), pl. xiv, 6 (cf. *ibid.*, p. 64 under no. 17, on this MS).

As a specimen of script A, on Plate **8a** we reproduce folio 19ᵛ, containing a passage from the GOSPEL OF ST. MATTHEW 10:16–24. For another published sample of the same handwriting from this MS, cf. *New Pal. Soc.*, Ser. II, pl. 119*a* (= fols. 17ᵛ–18ʳ). The same handwriting, but in a more compact and calligraphic form, seems to be represented *ibid.*, pl. 119*b* (= fol. 102ʳ).

As a specimen of script B, on Plate **8b** we reproduce folio 109ʳ, containing a passage from the GOSPEL OF ST. LUKE 3:16–23.

As a specimen of script C, on Plate **9a** we reproduce folio 146ʳ, containing a passage from the GOSPEL OF ST. LUKE 15:13–20. It should be noted that several breathings, both smooth and rough, appear on this page in an angular form (such rough breathings are here in a rectangular form, while smooth breathings are angular). This is an archaistic mannerism,[60] which may be observed also in pages written by other scribes of this MS. The occasional (not consistent) use of angular breathings should be considered a common feature of most of the scribes of this MS.

As a specimen of script D, on Plate **9b** we reproduce folio 157ʳ, containing a passage from the GOSPEL OF ST. LUKE 19:47 – 20:9. In the right margin, there is a red figure ξ̄ϑ̄ (with a reference mark prefixed) which indicates the number of the κεφάλαιον, i.e., chapter 69 of Luke, which begins in the line to the left. The τίτλος (title or summary) of this chapter, preceded by the reference mark, is written in red in the upper margin: πε(ρὶ) τῶν ἐπερωτησάν-των τὸν κ(ύριο)ν ἀρχιερέων. κ(αὶ) γραμματαίων (cf. von Soden, I,1, p. 410). The usual place for the τίτλος is the top or the bottom of the page (some-times the τίτλος is written at the side of the text).[61] The whole chapter 69 of Luke comprises Luke 20:1–8. The chapter figure and the τίτλος of the chapter are written in red, since these and other elements of the usual equip-ment of New Testament MSS were normally written in red.[62]

---

[60] On angular breathings, cf. Gardthausen, *Griechische Palaeographie*, II, pp. 383–88; Turyn, *DGMItaly*, I, pp. 5, 11, 50, 124–26; II, pls. 2, 4, 36, 98, 99.

[61] Cf. Scrivener, I, p. 58; Hatch, *Facsimiles and Descriptions*, p. 26.

[62] On red color often used in the writing of τίτλοι of κεφάλαια, cf. Hatch, *loc. cit.* On red color used in liturgical and other notes in New Testament MSS, cf. above, p. 18 note 43; below, p. 43 note 101.

As a specimen of script E, on Plate **10a** we reproduce folio 183^r, containing a passage from the GOSPEL OF ST. JOHN 4:31–39. In the first line, the large letter projected to the left marks emphatically that in the preceding line (i.e., in the bottom line of the preceding page) a text section begins.[63]

As a specimen of script F, on Plate **10b** we reproduce folio 219^v, containing a passage from the GOSPEL OF ST. JOHN 17:4–12. The letter projected to the left in this case marks the beginning of an important text section.[64] For another published sample of the same handwriting from this MS, cf. *New Pal. Soc.*, Ser. II, pl. 119*c* (= fol. 230^v).

This MS once belonged to the monastery of St. Sabas, called Mâr Sâbâ, situated southeast of Jerusalem.[65] There are several ownership entries of this monastery in the MS (on fols. IV^v, 173^v, 230^v, v^r). In the early 19th century, J. M. A. Scholz saw this MS in the monastery.[66] According to an autographic note of Robert Curzon on fol. I (this is the inside of the front cover), he bought this MS for 10 dollars at the monastery of St. Sabas the first time he went there[67] in 1834. Subsequently, the MS belonged to the collection formed at Parham, Sussex, by Robert Curzon (1810–1873), afterward 14th Baron Zouche, as the result of his acquisitions during his travels in the Levant in 1833 and later.[68] On Robert Curzon, cf. *DNB*, V, pp. 354f.; de Ricci, *English Collectors*, p. 118. In the Curzon collection at Parham, this MS was numbered 78, 13 (i.e., MS 78 of the whole collection, MS 13 of the Greek series). Cf. *Catalogue of Materials for Writing, Early Writings on Tablets and Stones, Rolled and Other Manuscripts and Oriental Manuscript Books, in the Library of the Honourable Robert Curzon at Parham in the County of Sussex* (London, 1849), p. 22 (this MS is listed as Greek 13; in the copy of this book in the Department of MSS at the British Museum, a figure 78, i.e., the consecutive number of this MS within the entire collection of MSS at Parham, was added in pencil). Later, this MS was marked Parham XV (on the binding of the MS, there are imprints *Parham MS. XV*, and *Bequeathed by Darea, Lady Zouche*). After the death of Robert Curzon, the Parham MSS were deposited on loan in the British Museum on 19 April 1876. This was done by his son, Robert Nathaniel Cecil George Curzon, 15th Baron Zouche (1851–1914). These MSS became the property of the British Museum through the bequest of Darea Curzon, Baroness Zouche (1860–1917), daughter of Robert Curzon and heiress of R. N. C. G. Curzon, after she died on 7 April 1917. There is a note (concerning the deposit of the Curzon MSS in 1876 and their acquisition by the British Museum in 1917) written on the flyleaf of the copy of Curzon, *Catalogue of Materials*, in the British Museum's Department of MSS. Also cf. *British Museum. Catalogue of Additions to the Manuscripts 1916–1920* (London, 1933), pp. III, 54f.

On this MS, cf. Richard, *Inventaire*, p. 75; *Catalogue of Additions ... 1916–1920*, p. 76; Curzon, *Catalogue of Materials*, p. 22 (under Greek 13), pl. opposite p. 40 (= fol. 230^v); *New Pal. Soc.*, Ser. II, pl. 119 (description of the MS, facsimiles of fols. 17^v–18^r, 102^r, 230^v, with transcripts); Scrivener, I, p. 253 (under Evan. 541); Gregory, I, p. 202 (under Vier Evangelien 554); Aland, I, p. 90 (under the Gregory–Aland number 554); von Soden, I,1, p. 176 (under ε332). It should be noted that Vogel–Gardthausen, p. 301 note 3, mistakenly tried to identify the MS Curzon Greek 13 (i.e., this MS London Additional 39597) with the MS London Additional 28818 (cf. below, p. 23).

---

[63] Large (often capital) letters (often in red) projected to the left mark the beginning of a sentence or of a text section either in the preceding line or in the same line. On this habit, cf. Turyn, *DGMItaly*, I, p. 14 and *passim*; Index, p. 287 (under "projection (ἔκθεσις) to the left," etc.).

[64] Cf. note 63.

[65] Cf. Ehrhard, in *RQ*, 7 (1893), pp. 32–79; Beck, *Kirche und theologische Literatur*, p. 204; R. Curzon, *Visits to Monasteries in the Levant*, intro. by D. G. Hogarth (London, 1916), pp. 214ff.

[66] Cf. J. M. A. Scholz, *Biblisch-kritische Reise in Frankreich, der Schweitz, Italien, Palästina und im Archipel, in den Jahren 1818, 1819, 1820, 1821, nebst einer Geschichte des Textes des N. T.* (Leipzig-Sorau, 1823), p. 146, lines 4–6 (with an explicit reference to the subscription of this MS).

[67] Cf. Curzon, *Visits to Monasteries in the Levant*, p. 225, line 3 from the bottom (on the first purchase of three MSS which he made in the monastery of St. Sabas).

[68] Cf. D. G. Hogarth, *ibid.*, pp. XIVf.

Plate 11: A.D. 1272.

London, British Museum, ms Additional 28818. Parchment, 245 ×
180 mm., 118 fols., 2 columns, about 25–28 lines to a column. Contents:
Lectionary of the Gospels (daily in John, Saturdays and Sundays in Matthew
and Luke). At the beginning of the MS, three quires were lost. The MS was
written by the priest Metaxares and concluded by him in July A.M. 6780 =
A.D. 1272 (fol. 118ʳ – Pl. **100d**): Τω συντελεστῇ τῶν κα|λῶν, ϑ(ε)ῷ χάρις· – |
Επληρωϑ(η) τὸ παρὸν εὐα(γγέλιον) δι|ὰ χειρὸς ἐμοῦ τοῦ ἁμαρ|τωλοῦ τολμῶ εἰπεῖν
καὶ | ἱερέως τοῦ Μεταξάρη· | μηνὶ ἰουλ(ίῳ) ἰν(δικτιών)ης ιε: Ἔτους | ͵ϛψπ· ἀμήν· –
(the end of the penult line -τους and the last line are written in red). Metaxares
is obviously the family name of the scribe. The etymology of the name is
clear: it probably meant "silk merchant." The indication by the scribe of
his family name without his given name is rare, but not unique (cf. below,
p. 27, on Syropulus, scribe of Oxford Barocci 122).

On Plate **11** we reproduce folio 33ᵛ. This page from the LECTIONARY OF THE
GOSPELS contains a passage from the Gospel of St. Mark 2:2–12. This is the
major part of the lesson for the second Sunday of Lent, i.e., κυριακὴ β̄ τῶν
νηστειῶν (ed. Εὐαγγέλιον [1880], p. 118ᵃ, 39–118ᵇ, 22; or ed. Εὐαγγέλιον
[1968], p. 138ᵇ, 15–44). The whole lesson for this day is Mark 2:1–12 (cf.
Gregory, I, p. 361). On the page reproduced, there appears at the end of a
few sentences the τελεία sign (+), a full-stop mark used in lectionaries.[69]
Another specimen of Metaxares' handwriting from this MS was published in
Pal. Soc., Ser. I, pl. 204 (with a description of the MS and a transcript of the
page reproduced). The MS is written in two-column pages; this arrangement
prevails in lectionaries (cf. above, p. 17; cf. Pls. **5, 6, 7, 56**).

This MS was bought by the British Museum from Ivor B. Guest on 11 November 1871 (there
is a note to this effect on the recto of the flyleaf which precedes fol. 1). The British Museum
acquired from the same source the MSS Additional 28815–28830 in 1871 (cf. Richard, *Inventaire*,
pp. 49–52). On Ivor Bertie Guest (1835–1914), later first Baron Wimborne, of Canford Manor,
Dorset, cf. *The Times* (London), no. 40,454 (February 23, 1914), p. 11.

On this MS, cf. Richard, *Inventaire*, p. 50; Vogel–Gardthausen, p. 301 (Vogel–Gardthausen,
p. 301 note 3, erroneously identified the former Curzon MS Greek 13 with this MS London Additional 28818; on MS Curzon Greek 13, which is now MS London Additional 39597, cf. above,
p. 22); Omont, "Notes," p. 345; Scrivener, I, p. 347 (under Evst. 280); Gregory, I, p. 416
(under Evangelia 331); Aland, I, p. 224 (under the Gregory–Aland symbol *l* 331). This MS is
occasionally cited as *l* 331 in Aland et al., *The Greek New Testament*, cf. p. XXIV.

Plate 12: A.D. 1278/1279.

Oxford, Bodleian Library, ms Roe 7. Parchment, 225 × 160 mm.,
III + 333 fols. Contents: Euthymius Zigabenus, Commentary on the Psalms
and Odes. The MS was subscribed in red by the monk Galaction in A.M. 6787 =
A.D. 1278/1279 (fol. 331ᵛ – Pl. **101a**): † δόξα τῷ ἁγίῳ ϑ(ε)ῷ, ἀμήν + | † χεὶρ
Γαλακτίωνος μοναχοῦ· | καὶ ἐν μοναχοῖς ἀναξίου: | † Ἔτους ͵ϛψπζ ἰν(δικτιῶνος)

[69] On the τελεία sign, used in both Old Testament and New Testament lectionaries, cf. above,
p. 18 note 45; below, Pls. **2, 6, 7, 56**.

ζ· + On Plate **12** we reproduce folio 26ʳ, containing a passage from EUTHY-MIUS ZIGABENUS, COMMENTARY ON THE PSALMS (ed. Migne, Patr. Gr., 128, cols. 136 B 8 – 137 A 12; these are comments on Ps. 8:7–9). In the MS, the passages commented upon are written in red; they are followed by comments written in black.[70] For other facsimile specimens of MS Roe 7 published before, cf. *New Pal. Soc.*, Ser. II, pl. 161 (fol. 125ᵛ and part of fol. 314ᵛ, with transcripts of the texts reproduced and a description of the MS); Ruth Barbour, in *Encyclopaedia Britannica*, XVII (Chicago [1973]), *s.v.* "Pale-ography," p. 127, fig. 21 (segment of fol. 60ᵛ, with a comment on the MS on pp. 126f.).

Vogel–Gardthausen, p. 63 note 5, assumed the possibility that the monk Galaction, scribe of MS Roe 7, may be identical with the hieromonk Galaction the Blind of Mount Galesion (near Ephesus) who commissioned MS Roe 13 in A.D. 1284/1285 (cf. below, pp. 34f.). The same guess was formulated in *New Pal. Soc.*, Ser. II, pl. 161 (in the description of MS Roe 7). If this assumption is correct, it would mean that MS Roe 7 was written on Mount Galesion. There seems to be a certain affinity of the script style of Roe 7 and script C of Roe 13 (cf. below, Pls. **12** and **24**).

MS Roe 7 was owned in A.M. 7022 = A.D. 1513/1514 by Paulus Colybas of Modon in the Peloponnesus (fol. 332ʳ): τὸ παρὸν ψαλτήριον | ἐστὶν ἐμοῦ Παύλου | ἐκ τῆς οἰκτρωτάτης πόλεως | Μεθώνης:· | ζκβω ἰν(δικτιῶν)ος β'ης | Above and below this Greek note, there is a Latin note: *1514 Indictione secunda | hic liber est mei Pauli Coliuani: de Ciuitate | Methona:· +++*[71] Later, the MS was owned by Metrophanes III, patriarch of Constantinople (1565–1572 and 1579–1580), and the monastery of the Holy Trinity τοῦ 'Εσόπτρου in Chalce (one of the Princes' Islands in the Sea of Marmara). The pertinent entries were written on fol. IIIᵛ. In the lower part of the page, there is a dodecasyllable: οἱ π(ατέ)ρες μέμνησθε του Μ(ητ)ροφανους, written prob-ably by Metrophanes himself. In the upper part of fol. IIIᵛ, there is an ownership entry of the monastery τοῦ 'Εσόπτρου, in five political verses, used customarily in MSS of this monastery:

† ἡ βίβλος αὕτη πέφυκε τῆς παντουργου τριᾶδος, |
τῆς ἐν τη νήσῶ[72] Χάλκῆς τε μονῆς της του ἐσόπτουρ[72a] |
καὶ εἴ τὶς βοὐληθῆ ποτὲ{ται} ταύτην ἀποστερῆ|σαι
κεχῶρισμένος ἔσεται τριᾶδος της ἀγί|ας
ἐν τῶ αἰῶνι τούτῶ γε καὶ τῶ ἐλευσωμενω:– |

Such entries appear in the Chalce MSS with occasional slight variations.[73] This MS can be easily identified in the catalogue of Metrophanes' MSS subsequently owned by the Chalce monastery. The catalogue compiled in January 1572 was published by Legrand, *Notice biographique sur Jean et Théodose Zygomalas*, pp. 207–16; MS Roe 7 is evidently the item listed by Legrand on p. 210, line 6: Ψαλτήριον μετ' ἐξηγήσεως, ἐν μεμβράναις, μῆκος δεύτερον.

---

[70] On such a practice in MSS, cf. Turyn, *Codices*, pp. 26, 41, 102; *idem, DGM Italy*, I, pp. 50, 148, 219.

[71] On Paulus Colybas of Modon, cf. Vogel–Gardthausen, p. 377; H. Omont, "Les manuscrits grecs datés des XVᵉ et XVIᵉ siècles de la Bibliothèque Nationale et des autres bibliothèques de France," *Revue des bibliothèques*, 2 (1892), p. 147; *idem, Fac-similés de manuscrits grecs des XVᵉ et XVIᵉ siècles* (Paris, 1887; repr. Hildesheim–New York, 1974), p. 14 (under no. 43), pl. 43; S. Lampros, Σύμμικτα, in Νέος 'Ελλ., 17 (1923), p. 95; Ch. G. Patrineles, ''Ελληνες κωδικογράφοι τῶν χρόνων τῆς 'Αναγεννήσεως, in 'Επ.Μεσ.'Αρχ., 8–9 (1958–1959), p. 92.

[72] νή- *post correctionem.*

[72a] *sic codex*: ἐσόπτρου *legendum.*

[73] On the monastery of the Holy Trinity τοῦ 'Εσόπτρου in Chalce, cf. R. Janin, *Les églises et les monastères des grands centres byzantins* (Paris, 1975), pp. 74f. On its MSS, cf. Legrand, *Notice bio-graphique sur Jean et Théodose Zygomalas*, p. 206; Turyn, *Codices*, p. 68; W. Weinberger, *Beiträge zur Handschriftenkunde*, II, SBWien, Philos.-hist.Kl., 161,4 (1909), p. 18.

The MS was among the MSS brought from the Levant by Sir Thomas Roe (1580 or 1581–1644) and presented by him to the Bodleian Library in 1628 (they arrived in 1629). There is this entry on fol. 1ʳ: *Thomas Roe Eques auratus, et Ser(enissi)mi magnae Bri|tanniae etc, regis apud Turcarum Imperatorem | Orator, in gratitudinis suae erga matrem Acad: | perpetuum testimonium, hunc Librum quem ex | Oriente secum aduexit publicae Biblioth. D. D. | 1628.* On the Roe MSS in the Bodleian Library, cf. *Summary Catalogue*, II,1, p. 10; Legrand, *op. cit.*, pp. 205f. (p. 206, on this MS). On Thomas Roe, cf. *DNB*, XVII, pp. 89–93 (p. 91, on MSS presented by him to the Bodleian Library).

On this MS, cf. Coxe, I, col. 463; *Summary Catalogue*, II,1, p. 10 (under S.C. 253); Vogel–Gardthausen, p. 63; Rahlfs, *Verzeichnis der griechischen Handschriften des Alten Testaments*, pp. 174, 407; *New Pal. Soc.*, Ser. II, pl. 161 (description); Barbour, in *Greek Manuscripts in the Bodleian Library*, p. 21 (under no. 23).

Plate 13: A.D. 1279.

Cambridge, University Library, ms Ii.5.44. Parchment, 291 × 223 mm., 143 fols. (plus 4 extra fols. 85a, 85b, 85c, 85d, which are a 15th-century replacement of a lost text portion), 26–27 lines to a page. The MS contains works of Aristotle (or ascribed to Aristotle): (fols. 1ʳ–30ᵛ) *Magna Moralia; (fols. 30ᵛ–102ᵛ) Nicomachean Ethics; (fols. 102ᵛ–134ᵛ) Eudemian Ethics; (fols. 134ᵛ–143ᵛ) *Oeconomics. The MS was written by Nicolaus ⟨Damenus⟩, lector at the Hours (evidently in the abbey below), at the behest of the monk Iacobus, sceuophylax of the abbey of St. Savior at the Cape of the Lighthouse, de Lingua Phari, in Messina, and subscribed by him (in red) on 16 June A.M. 6787 = A.D. 1279 (fol. 143ᵛ – Pl. **101b**): Ἐγρά(φ)η τὸ παρὸν βιβλίον τῆς ἠθικῆς τοῦ Ἀριστοτέλους, διὰ χειρὸς | Νικολάου εὐτελοῦς ἀναγνώστ(ου) τῶν ὡρῶν, αἰτήσει τοῦ θεοτι|μήτ(ου) μοναχ(οῦ) κυρ(οῦ) Ἰακώβ(ου), σκευοφύλακ(ος) μάνδρας | ἀκρωτηρίου, μη(ν)ὶ Ἰουν(ίῳ) ιϛ, ἰνδ(ικτιῶνος) ζ, ἔτ(ους) ͵ϛψπζ. | οἱ ἀναγινώσκοντ(ες) εὔχεσθε ὑπὲρ αὐτῶν: + The scribe Nicolaus, lector at the Hours, to judge also from his handwriting, is identical with Nicolaus Damenus who wrote MS Venice Greco 362 (collocazione 817) in A.D. 1278/1279, and who referred to himself (in line 10 of the Venice subscription): τῷ τῶν ὡρῶν ὑπάρχοντι Δαμηνῷ Νικολάῳ. He wrote the Venice MS likewise at the behest of Iacobus, sceuophylax of the abbey of St. Savior de Lingua Phari in Messina. For the identity of Nicolaus, scribe of Cambridge Ii.5.44, with Nicolaus Damenus, scribe of Venice Greco 362, we should compare the Cambridge subscription on Plate **101b** with the informal script of the Venice subscription in Turyn, *DGMItaly*, II, pl. 224. The identity of the leaf ornaments on both sides of the two subscriptions (at their ends) is noteworthy. For the same leaf as a favorite ornament of Nicolaus Damenus, cf. D. Harlfinger, "Die Überlieferungsgeschichte der Eudemischen Ethik," in *Untersuchungen zur Eudemischen Ethik, Akten des 5. Symposium Aristotelicum*, Peripatoi, 1 (Berlin, 1971), pls. I and II; Turyn, *op. cit.*, I, p. XVI. On Nicolaus Damenus, on MS Venice Greco 362, on Iacobus, sceuophylax of the abbey of St. Savior de Lingua Phari in Messina from at least 1277 and later abbot from 1282 to about 1290, cf. *ibid.*, I, pp. 25–27, XVI (in reference to the Cambridge MS); II, pls. 14, 15; on Iacobus the sceuophylax, cf. also *ibid.*, I, p. 40. On the abbey of St. Savior de Lingua Phari, cf. M. Scaduto, *Il monachismo basiliano nella Sicilia medievale* (Rome, 1947), pp. 165ff., *passim*. Nicolaus Damenus probably was a novice in that monastery, and was appointed to be a lector at the Hours.

To present the handwriting of Nicolaus Damenus in this Cambridge MS, on Plate **13** we reproduce folio 120ʳ, which contains a passage from ARISTOTLE, EUDEMIAN ETHICS, Book III, chaps. 5, 14 – 6, 3, p. 1233ᵃ, 2 – 1233ᵇ, 6 Bekker (ed. F. Susemihl, [*Aristotelis Ethica Eudemia*], *Eudemi Rhodii Ethica. Adiecto de virtutibus et vitiis libello*, Teubner [1884; repr. Amsterdam, 1967], p. 62 penult line – p. 64 antepenult line). The script, with its abundance of abbreviations, should be considered as written in "student-book cursive" used especially in philosophical MSS.[74] Round letters in the page reproduced and elsewhere in this MS, as well as round or oval parts of letters in other pages, are filled with red blobs, in accordance with the South Italian practice.[75] For another facsimile specimen from this Cambridge MS, cf. Harlfinger, *op. cit.*, pl. II, pp. 6ff. It seems that cod. Vaticanus graec. 1342 was written by the same scribe, i.e., by Nicolaus Damenus (cf. *ibid.*, pl. I), and that the Aristotelian texts transmitted in both MSS are *gemelli*.[76] For specimens of the *formal* script of Nicolaus Damenus from Venice Greco 362, cf. Turyn, *DGM Italy*, II, pls. 14 and 15.

I have noticed another MS very similar in script style to the Cambridge MS. The part of MS Paris Grec 106 (New Testament, Gregory–Aland 5), exemplified by Hatch, *Facsimiles and Descriptions*, pl. XCI (described on facing page 254), strongly resembles MS Cambridge Ii.5.44. Except for the fact that Paris Grec 106, as a scriptural MS, is written in a more formal manner without abbreviations, the stylistic resemblance of both MSS is striking. MS Paris Grec 106 came from Calabria.[77] The part in question of this MS (fols. A–D and 1ʳ–192ʳ) was probably written in South Italy about the same time and possibly in the same scriptorium as MS Cambridge Ii.5.44.

This MS was once owned by John Moore (1646–1714), bishop successively of Norwich and Ely. It was MS 981 in Moore's collection. On his death in 1714, his library was bought by King George I and presented by him in 1715 to the University of Cambridge. There is in the MS a bookplate referring to this royal donation. On John Moore and his library in the Cambridge

---

[74] On student-book cursive, cf. Omont, *Fac-similés ... du IXᵉ au XIVᵉ siècle*, pl. LII/1; Thompson, *Introduction*, p. 251, facsim. no. 70, with a comment on p. 250; Turyn, *DGM Italy*, I, pp. XVI, 72f., 78, 205, 208; II, pls. 53, 56, 166, 169. Cf. also Wilson, *Mediaeval Greek Bookhands*, pl. 54 (cf. pp. 27f. under no. 54). In this connection, on the script style of Nicolaus Damenus, cf. now *idem*, "Nicaean and Palaeologan Hands: Introduction to a Discussion," in *Paléographie grecque et byzantine*, pp. 263f.

[75] Cf. Turyn, *Codices*, pp. 36, 84; *idem*, *DGM Italy*, I, pp. 5f.; and above, p. 14 note 37.

[76] Cf. H. Jackson, "On a MS. of the Nicomachean Ethics," *JPh*, 6 (1876), pp. 210f.; F. Susemihl, *Aristotelis quae feruntur Magna Moralia*, Teubner (1883), p. VI note 1; H. Jackson, "Eudemian Ethics ...," *JPh*, 32 (1913), p. 171 note 1; Harlfinger, *op. cit.*, pp. 2, 6ff.; H. Goldbrunner, in *Gnomon*, 42 (1970), pp. 336f.

[77] Cf. Gregory, I, p. 129 (under Vier Evangelien 5). MS Paris Grec 106 belonged (cf. fol. 342ʳ) to the monk Romanus of the monastery Θ(εοτό)κου τῆς ἐπόψης κράτος Βεβαληνου Καλαβρίας επαρχίας. On the monastery Sanctae Mariae de Popsi, or de Ypopsi, in Greek also Θεοτόκου του εποψιου, in the district of Bovalino, in the province of Calabria, cf. P. Batiffol, *L'Abbaye de Rossano* (Paris, 1891; repr. London, 1971), pp. XXXIII, 107; M.-H. Laurent and A. Guillou, *Le 'Liber Visitationis' d'Athanase Chalkéopoulos*, ST, 206 (Vatican City, 1960), p. 274, map at end (under no. 23). On MS Paris Grec 106, cf. A. Vaccari, "La Grecìa nell'Italia meridionale," *OC*, 3,3, no. 13 (1925), p. 308; G. Garitte, "Deux manuscrits italo-grecs," *Miscellanea Giovanni Mercati*, III, ST, 123 (Vatican City, 1946), p. 35; R. Devreesse, *Les manuscrits grecs de l'Italie méridionale*, ST, 183 (Vatican City, 1955), p. 38 note 1.

University Library, cf. *DNB*, XIII, pp. 806–8 (on his library, p. 808); Fletcher, *English Book Collectors*, pp. 125–29 (on the bookplate of George I, cf. p. 127, figure); de Ricci, *English Collectors*, pp. 34f.

On this MS, cf. C. Hardwick, *A Catalogue of the Manuscripts Preserved in the Library of the University of Cambridge*, III (Cambridge, 1858), pp. 495f. (under no. 1879); A. Wartelle, *Inventaire des manuscrits grecs d'Aristote et de ses commentateurs* (Paris, 1963), p. 26 (under no. 400); Jackson, in *JPh*, 6, pp. 208–11; *idem, ibid.*, 32, p. 171 note 1; Harlfinger, *op. cit., passim*; P. Schreiner, "Notizie sulla storia della Chiesa greca in Italia in manoscritti greci," in *La Chiesa greca in Italia dall'VIII al XVI secolo*, II, Italia Sacra, Studi e documenti di storia ecclesiastica, 21 (Padua, 1972), p. 904 (under no. 50a). Cf. now also J. Wiesner, in P. Moraux et al., *Aristoteles Graecus. Die griechischen Manuskripte des Aristoteles*, I, Peripatoi, 8 (Berlin–New York, 1976), pp. 104–7, 465.

Plates 14, 15, 16: A.D. 1279/1280.

Oxford, Bodleian Library, ms Barocci 122. Parchment, 240 × 163 mm., two parchment flyleaves II and III + 223 fols. Contents: Euthymius Zigabenus, Commentary on the Psalms and Odes. The MS was, as it seems, written by at least three scribes and it was subscribed by its main scribe, Syropulus, in A.M. 6788 = A.D. 1279/1280 (fol. 223^v – Pl. **101c**): τὸ τέρμ(α) γέγονεν, ἐν ἔτη ͵ϛψπη'· οὔσης ἰν(δικτιῶνος) τὲ η'+ τοῦ Συρροπούλου | οὗ τὸ πόνημα ἁμαρτ(ωλ)οῦ δέξου ὑπὲρ τῶν αὐτοῦ πολλῶν ἀμπλακιμάτων + ἀμήν + The family name Συρόπουλος is well known.[78] The scribe recorded only his family name, without his given name. This is rare in subscriptions, but by no means unique (cf. above, p. 23, on Metaxares, scribe of MS London Addit. 28818). This MS Barocci 122 is not listed by Vogel–Gardthausen, because Coxe, I, cols. 199f., failed to record its subscription. I owe to Mr. Nigel Wilson (Oxford) the knowledge of its existence.

As an example of the handwriting of Syropulus, on Plate **14** we reproduce folio 64^r, containing a passage from Euthymius Zigabenus, Commentary on the Psalms (ed. Migne, Patr. Gr., 128, cols. 380 D 11 – 384 B 3). These are comments on Psalm 33:1–6. The Psalm versicles quoted and commented upon are written in red; the comments are in black (the same distinction of colors appears on the other two pages reproduced from this MS on Pls. **15** and **16**). On this habit of writing in commentaries the original passages in red and the comments in black, cf. above, p. 24 and note 70. The marginal mark ἑρμ(η)νεία as a distinctive element is written in red.

For the handwriting of another scribe of this MS, on Plate **15** we reproduce folio 82^v, containing a passage from Euthymius Zigabenus, Commentary on the Psalms (ed. Migne, Patr. Gr., 128, cols. 489 C 6 – 492 D 1). These are comments on Psalm 44:2–5.

On Plate **16** we reproduce folio 140^r, containing a passage from Euthymius Zigabenus, Commentary on the Psalms (ed. Migne, Patr. Gr., 128, cols. 861 C 1 – 864 D 5). These are comments on Psalms 82:15–83:3. In the upper

---

[78] Cf. Vogel–Gardthausen, p. 411; Polemis, *The Doukai*, pp. 182f.; V. Laurent, *Les «Mémoires» du Grand Ecclésiarque de l'Eglise de Constantinople Sylvestre Syropoulos sur le concile de Florence (1438–1439)* (Paris, 1971), pp. 3f.

part of this page, lines 1–14 αἰσχύνονται seem to be written by Syropulus. However, the rest of the page, lines 14 εἴτουν– 41, is written by yet another, third scribe of the MS.

On fol. 5ᵛ (on the lower part of the page), there is an obituary note written by a later hand: † μηνὶ ἰουνίω κδ'· ἡμέρα παρασκευῇ· τὸ γεννέσ(ιον) τοῦ ἀγ(ί)ου ἐνδό|ξου πρ(οφήτου) (this word πρ' was added above the line) προδρόμ(ου) καὶ βαπτιστοῦ Ἰω(άνν)ου ὥρα θ' τῆς ἡμέρας, ἐκοιμή(θη) ἡ | δούλ(η) τοῦ θ(εο)ῦ Μαρία ἡ Μακρυδούκενα ἡ διὰ τοῦ θείου καὶ ἀγγελικοῦ σχή|μ(α)τος μετονομασθεῖσα Μάρθα μοναχή· ἔτους ϛοῦ· | ῶοῦ· ο' : ἰν(δικτιῶνος) ιε'⁻ⁿˢ:[79] The note reports that Maria, as nun Martha, Μακρύδουκαινα died on 24 June A.M. 6870 = A.D. 1362.[80]

The Barocci MSS were originally collected by Giacomo Barocci (or Barozzi) of Venice, who died before 1617. A complete catalogue of his collection of MSS was published in 1617; cf. *Indice Barocci*. This catalogue was repeated (in a Latin form) by I. Ph. Tomasini, *Bibliothecae Venetae manvscriptae pvblicae et privatae* (Udine, 1650), pp. 64–92. The Barocci MSS were brought to England in 1628 and purchased by William Herbert, third Earl of Pembroke, chancellor of the University of Oxford, who presented them to the University in May 1629. On Giacomo Barocci, cf. Frati, *Dizionario bio-bibliografico*, pp. 52f. On William Herbert, Earl of Pembroke (1580–1630), and the donation of Barocci MSS to the Bodleian Library, cf. *DNB*, IX, pp. 677–82 (on the donation, p. 681); *Summary Catalogue*, II,1, p. 3; Fletcher, *English Book Collectors*, pp. 137f.; de Ricci, *English Collectors*, pp. 22f. The present MS Barocci 122 was once in the Barocci collection MS Greco in Quarto 30 (cf. *Indice Barocci*, fol. 30ʳ).

On this MS, cf. Coxe, I, cols. 199f.; *Summary Catalogue*, II,1, p. 6 (under S.C. 122); Rahlfs, *Verzeichnis der griechischen Handschriften des Alten Testaments*, pp. 169, 408.

Plate 17: A.D. 1281.

London, British Museum, ms Harley 5575. Bombycine, 262 × 190 mm., 338 fols. Contents: (fols. 1ʳ–307ʳ) Euthymius Zigabenus, Commentary on the Psalms and Odes; (fols. 307ʳ–326ᵛ) Pseudo-Nonnus, Histories of St. Gregory of Nazianzus; (fols. 327ʳ–338ʳ) Nicholas of Andida, de Liturgiae symbolis (ed. Migne, Patr. Gr., 140, cols. 417–68); (fol. 338ʳ) prayer for a deceased priest (by a different hand). Fols. 339ʳ–346ᵛ are modern additions with some comments; among them, fols. 339ʳ–341ʳ contain notes written in the handwriting of Dr. John Covel on the contents of this MS. The MS was written and subscribed by the hieromonk Maximus on 8 July A.M. 6789 = A.D. 1281 (fol. 307ʳ – Pl. **102a**): Τέλους ἔτυχεν ὁ πα|ρὼν ψαλτὴρ, ὁ ἑρμηνευθεὶς παρὰ Ἰω-(άννου) (μον)αχ(οῦ) τ(ο)ῦ Ζιγαβην(οῦ). καὶ γρα|φεὶς παρὰ ἁμαρτωλοῦ καὶ ἀθλίου, Μαξίμου ἱερο(μον)άχ(ου), ἐν μη(ν)ὶ ἰ|ουλίω, ῆ, ἰν(δικτιῶνος) θ: Ἔτους ϛψπθ:– By inadvertence, Maximus recorded Zigabenus' given name as Ioannes, instead of Euthymius. The subscription is followed by a poem in 20 dodecasyllables, obviously composed by the scribe Maximus. In it he praises the monk (and

---

[79] This note was reprinted (from Coxe, I, col. 200) by S. P. Lampros, Ἐνθυμήσεων ἤτοι χρονικῶν σημειωμάτων συλλογὴ πρώτη, in Νέος Ἑλλ., 7 (1910), p. 144 no. 69; it was repeated from Lampros by Polemis, *The Doukai*, p. 210 note 3.

[80] The name Μακρυδούκας occurs in a document of A.D. 1325 (cf. Miklosich–Müller, *Acta et diplomata*, I, p. 140). On Maria-Martha Μακρυδούκαινα of the above note, cf. Papadopulos, *Genealogie der Palaiologen*, p. 80 no. 132; Polemis, *op. cit.*, p. 210.

physician, ἀκέστωρ) Ioannes who owned, or rather commissioned (κτησάμενος), this MS; he also mentions the monk Martinianus; and then refers to himself.

On Plate **17** we reproduce folio 185ʳ, containing a passage from EUTHYMIUS ZIGABENUS, COMMENTARY ON THE PSALMS (ed. Migne, Patr. Gr., 128, cols. 829 A 2–832 B 7; these are comments on Ps. 78:9–79:1). Initial letters of Psalm versicles commented upon and initial letters of comments are written in red. If they begin a line, they are projected to the left. Another facsimile specimen of this MS was published in *Pal. Soc.*, Ser. I, pl. 157 (= fol. 93ʳ), with a description of the MS and a transcript of the text reproduced.

The MS was once owned by Dr. John Covel (1638–1722), scholar and traveler, master of Christ's College in Cambridge (cf. *DNB*, IV, pp. 1280f.; Wright, *Fontes Harleiani*, pp. xvi, 113). In the Covel collection, this was MS Greek XVIII. Covel's MSS were acquired by Edward Harley, second Earl of Oxford, in 1716. On Edward Harley (1689–1741), cf. *DNB*, VIII, pp. 1278–80; Wright, *op. cit.*, pp. xvff. The MSS of the Harley library, accumulated by Robert Harley, first Earl of Oxford (1661–1724), and his son, Edward Harley, were sold to the nation by Lady Oxford, widow of Edward Harley, in 1753 and placed in the British Museum in 1757. On Robert Harley, cf. *DNB*, VIII, pp. 1283–90; on his library, cf. *ibid.*, p. 1289; Wright, *op. cit.*, pp. xvff. On the history of the Harley library, cf. Fletcher, *English Book Collectors*, pp. 150–55; de Ricci, *English Collectors*, pp. 33–38; Wright, *op. cit.*, pp. xv–xxxv.

On this MS, cf. Nares, *Catalogue of the Harleian Manuscripts*, III, p. 278; Vogel–Gardthausen, p. 287; *Pal. Soc.*, Ser. I, pl. 157; Omont, "Notes," p. 344; Rahlfs, *Verzeichnis der griechischen Handschriften des Alten Testaments*, pp. 110, 407; Wright, *Fontes Harleiani*, pp. 115, 459.

Plate 18: A.D. 1281.

Oxford, Bodleian Library, ms Auct.E.5.8. Parchment, 275 × 220 mm., 142 fols., 2 columns to a page (only the terminal fols. 137ʳ–142ᵛ are written as single-column pages). A modern flyleaf is numbered fol. I; moreover, there is a Latin fragment on paper, numbered at the beginning of the volume as fols. II–IV and at the end of the volume as fols. 143–144, plus an unnumbered pastedown on the inside of the back cover. Contents: Synaxarion (Lives of Saints) for the months from February through August. The MS was subscribed on 6 September A.M. 6790 = A.D. 1281 (fol. 142ᵛ – Pl. **102b**): Ἐτελειώθ(η) τὸ παρὸν συναξάριον μη(νὶ) σεπτ(εμβ)ρ(ίῳ) ϛ Ἔτο(ς) ͵ϛψϟ ἰν(δικτιῶνος) ι. On Plate **18** we reproduce folio 62ʳ, containing a passage from the SYNAXARION for the 4th of May (ed. *Synaxarium CP*, cols. 655, 13–656, 14; or Μηναῖον τοῦ Μαΐου, ἔκδοσις τῆς Ἀποστολικῆς Διακονίας τῆς Ἐκκλησίας τῆς Ἑλλάδος [Athens, 1972], pp. 20ᵇ, 60 – 21ᵃ, 16; Μηναῖον τοῦ Μαΐου [ἐκδόσεις Φῶς, Athens, 1961], p. 45ᵃ, 45 – 45ᵇ, 41). This is a passage from a synaxarion on St. Irene, martyr under Licinius; on this text, cf. *BHG Auct.* 953b.

This MS was formerly owned by Robert Huntington (1637–1701), orientalist, who visited Palestine, Cyprus, and Egypt. The MS was number 304 in the Huntington collection (there is an imprint *304* on the spine of its binding). The bulk of the Huntington collection of MSS was bought by the Bodleian Library in 1693. On Huntington and his MSS in the Bodleian Library, cf. *DNB*, X, pp. 308f.; *Summary Catalogue*, II,2, p. 742.

On this MS, cf. Coxe, I, col. 657 (under Misc. gr. 73; Coxe published the subscription with a wrong date which he indicated with a question mark added); *Summary Catalogue*, II,2, p. 1023 (under S.C. 5767).

Plates 19 and 20: A.D. 1282.

Manchester, The John Rylands University Library, ms Rylands Gaster 1574. Parchment, 92 × 65 mm., II + 377 fols. (+ 6 unnumbered fols. 270ᵃ, 274ᵃ, 285ᵃ, 285ᵇ, 299ᵃ, 359ᵃ), 20 lines to a page. Contents: (fols. 1ʳ–345ʳ) St. John Climacus, Ladder of Paradise (with the usual additions at the beginning); (fols. 346ʳ–376ᵛ) Liber ad pastorem. The text is concluded on fol. 376ᵛ (which is damaged) by a colophon (in red), which appears, e.g., in MS Oxford, Christ Church 63, fol. 362ʳ (on this MS, cf. below, pp. 118 ff.). I quote here the Manchester colophon supplemented on the basis of the Oxford MS: [τέλος το]ῦ ὑστάτου καὶ ἰδικω|[τάτου λόγο]υ καὶ ἰδιογράφου· | [καὶ κεχωρι]σμένου τῶν τριάκοντα | [κεφαλ]ῖδων· ἢ βαθμίδων· | [ἢ ἀναβ]άσεων τῆς ἐναρέτου κλι|[μακος]: | The subscription that follows immediately on fols. 376ᵛ–377ʳ shows that the MS was probably owned or commissioned by Father Iacobus, that the subscription's writer (and one of the scribes of the MS) was presumably Ioasaph and that the MS was concluded and subscribed on 11 November A.M. 6791 = A.D. 1282 (fols. 376ᵛ–377ʳ – Pl. **102c**): [ὁ κεκ]τημέ-νο(ς) π(άτ)ερ κῦρ 'Ιάκωβε | [τ(ὴν) βίβλ(ον) or τ(ὴν) δέλτ(ον)] ταύτην, 'Ιωάσαφ τὸν | [γραφέα?], εὔχου προθύμως | [ἵν' ἀμ]φοῖν ὁ κ(ύριο)ς, συγχώ|[ρησιν π]αρά-σχει:+ : | [ἀμ]ήν, ἀμήν + ‖ † ἔτους ‚ςψϟα ἰν(δικτιῶνος) ια | μη(νὶ) νοεμβρίω ια ἡμέρ(α) δ [ ] | δόξα σοι κ(ύρι)ε πάντων ἕνεκα [ ] | δόξα σοι:+ + [ ] In the last three lines I have marked the damaged margin with square brackets; however, nothing seems to have been lost because of the damage. One of the scribes of the MS, the one who wrote the above subscription, inscribed at the conclusion of the Ladder, on fol. 345ᵛ, a dodecasyllabic poem in 14 verses, headlined Στίχοι τοῦ γράψαντο(ς) τὴν παροῦσαν | βίβλον· περὶ τῶν ἀναβαινόντων | τὴν τῶν ἀρετῶν κλίμακα, addressed to John Climacus. The scribe begs him to grant that the monk Iacobus (obviously the above-mentioned owner or sponsor of the MS) may ascend the Ladder (verses 11–14):

11   ἥνπερ (i.e., τὴν κλίμακα) δίδου σαῖς λιταῖς 'Ιωάννη· |
      ὁ τήνδ' ἐγείρας ὡς λίθοις στερροῖς λόγοις: |
      ὁ τήνδε πήξας ἄγαν εὐτεχνετάστως |
      μοναχὸν 'Ιάκωβον ἀναβαίνειν ὡς γρά(φ)εις·

Verses 11 and 14 are metrically faulty.

The whole MS was written mainly by two alternating scribes, A and B. Scribe A wrote the subscription, and is presumably the Ioasaph referred to therein. Moreover, scribe C wrote a few pages and scribe D wrote one page, fol. 87ʳ.

On Plate **19a** we reproduce folios 344ᵛ–345ʳ, written by scribe A (presumably Ioasaph), containing a passage from St. John Climacus, Ladder of Paradise, chap. 30 (ed. Migne, Patr. Gr., 88, cols. 1160 C 11 – 1161 A 15; ed. Trevisan, II, pp. 317, 5 – 319, 10). Red capitals projected to the left mark the beginnings of text sections or emphasize a sentence.

On Plate **19b** we reproduce folios 181ᵛ–182ʳ, written by scribe B, containing a passage from St. John Climacus, Ladder of Paradise, chap. 15 (ed.

Migne, Patr. Gr., 88, cols. 892 B 3 – C 10; ed. Trevisan, I, pp. 379, 14 – 381, 9).
A large red letter projected to the left, if it begins a sentence, indicates the
beginning of a text section (as on the right-hand page, line 3). A larger red
letter projected to the left, if it is either an initial of a word inside a sentence
or even a middle letter of a word, means that a text section begins in the
preceding line (cf. right-hand page, last line, and left-hand page, line 7,
respectively).[81]

On Plate **20a** we reproduce folios 343ᵛ–344ʳ, written by scribe C, containing a passage from St. John Climacus, Ladder of Paradise, chap. 30
(ed. Migne, Patr. Gr., 88, col. 1160 B 4 – C 11; ed. Trevisan, II, pp. 315, 8 –
317, 5). On the meaning of the red capital letters projected to the left, cf.
above.

On Plate **20b** we reproduce folio 87ʳ, written by scribe D, a fortuitous
collaborator who wrote only this page in the MS. The page contains a passage
from St. John Climacus, Ladder of Paradise, chap. 4 (ed. Migne, Patr. Gr.,
88, cols. 720 C 15 – 721 A 12; ed. Trevisan, I, pp. 187, 21 – 189, 4). On this
page it happens that all four large red letters projected to the left indicate
that a text section begins in the preceding line.

This MS once belonged to Moses Gaster (1856–1939) of Bucharest, later resident of London.
On him, cf. *The Dictionary of National Biography, 1931–1940*, ed. L. G. Wickham Legg (London,
1949), pp. 309f.; *Encyclopaedia Judaica*, VII (Jerusalem [1971]), cols. 332–34. On the acquisition
of the Gaster collection of MSS by the John Rylands Library (in or shortly before 1954), cf.
"Notes and News," *Bulletin of the John Rylands Library Manchester*, 37 (1954–1955), pp. 2–6.
The Gaster MSS were partly sold and partly donated by the Gaster family. Among the MSS
donated, there were 28 Greek MSS (cf. *ibid.*, p. 5). In July 1972 the John Rylands Library and
the Library of Manchester University merged to form the John Rylands University Library of
Manchester.

I am grateful to Mr. Nigel Wilson (Oxford) who called my attention to the existence of
this MS and communicated to me essential information on it.

Plate 21: A.D. 1284.

London, British Museum, ms Harley 5535. Parchment, 113 × 80 mm.,
277 fols. Contents: Psalms and Odes (of the Old and New Testaments), with
some prayers added at the end. The MS was written and subscribed by Andreas
of Brindisi twice, on 8 May and 14 May, A.M. 6792 = A.D. 1284. This is the
first subscription (in red) on fol. 221ᵛ (Pl. **102d**): Ετελειώθ(η) τὸ παρὸν βι-
βλίον | τοῦ ψαλτ(η)ρ(ίου), δ(ιὰ) χειρὸ(ς) Ἀνδρέου | ἁμαρτ(ω)λ(οῦ) τῆς πό(λε)ως
Βρενδησίου, ἐν μη(νὶ) | μαΐω, εἰς τ(ὰς) η″, ἡμέρ(ᾳ) ε″, ὥρα | δὲ ὡσεὶ ϑ″· ἐν ἔτει
͵ϛψϟβ″· | τῆς ἰνδικτ(ιῶνος) ιβ̄:+ The second subscription (likewise in red)
appears on fol. 260ᵛ (Pl. **102e**): Ετελ(ειώ)θ(η) ὁ κα(νὼν) οὗτο(ς) δ(ιὰ) χειρὸ(ς)
Ἀνδρ(έου) ἁμαρτ(ω)λ(οῦ) τοῦ Βρενδ(η)σίου· | μη(νὶ) μαΐω ιδ̄, ἡμέρ(ᾳ) δ″· ἐν
ἔτει ͵ϛψϟβ″· | τῆς ιβ″ ἰν(δικτιῶνος): οἱ δὲ ἀναγινώσκοντες, | εὔχεσθαι ὑπ(ὲ)ρ
ἐμοῦ τοῦ ἁμαρτ(ω)λ(οῦ) πρὸ(ς) τὸν κ(ύριο)ν:+ The year A.M. 6792 was indeed the
12th indiction. The dates 8 May and 14 May A.M. 6792 fell on Monday
and Sunday, not Thursday and Wednesday, respectively, as reported in

[81] Cf. above, p. 22 note 63.

the subscriptions. The scribe may have made a mistake in indicating in both cases May instead of June, because 8 June A.M. 6792 = A.D. 1284 fell on a Thursday, and 14 June of the same year fell on a Wednesday. The same Andreas of Brindisi wrote MS Milan, Biblioteca Ambrosiana G 8 sup., in A.D. 1286 (cf. Turyn, *DGM Italy*, I, pp. 51f.; II, pls. 37 and 227*a*). The identity of the scripts in both MSS is obvious. The scribe Andreas was a native of Brindisi, a town of the Terra d'Otranto (or Salento) in South Italy. This MS is, therefore, to be considered a South Italian product, since Andreas was likely to have written his MSS in his region. It should be pointed out that the indication of the hour in the first subscription quoted above is a habit that prevailed in South Italian MSS.[82] In this MS, in most psalms, the initial letter is illuminated with the use of several colors, such as red, blue, green, gold, white; this practice accords with the habit of South Italian MSS.[83] Within the text, round or oval letters (or even triangular letters like Δ), or parts thereof, are occasionally covered with red blobs. This habit was a prevailing (but not exclusive) feature of South Italian MSS.[84]

On Plate **21** we reproduce folios 165ᵛ–166ʳ, which contain a part of Psalm 117:8–22 (ed. A. Rahlfs, *Septuaginta id est Vetus Testamentum graece iuxta LXX interpretes*, 6th ed., II [Stuttgart (1962)], pp. 129f.; or ed. Rahlfs, *Psalmi cum Odis*, 2nd ed. = *Septuaginta. Vetus Testamentum Graecum Auctoritate Academiae Litterarum Gottingensis editum*, X [Göttingen, 1967], pp. 285f.). The Psalm is written στιχηρῶς; the versicles are written with the initial capital (in red) projected to the left, i.e., they are written μετ' ἐκθέσεως; this arrangement was frequent in manuscript Psalters from olden times on.[85] On red blobs inside round or oval letters (or their parts), cf. above. On other published specimens of the handwriting of Andreas of Brindisi, cf. above. The handwriting of Andreas of Brindisi is the typical script of the Terra d'Otranto of that time. On this script style at the end of the 13th century, cf. Omont, *Fac-similés ... du IXᵉ au XIVᵉ siècle*, pl. LXXI/I; A. Turyn, *Studies in the Manuscript Tradition of the Tragedies of Sophocles*, Illinois Studies in Language and Literature, XXXVI, 1–2 (Urbana, 1952; repr. Studia Philologica, 15 [Rome, 1970]), pp. 110–14, pls. IV–V; Devreesse, *Les manuscrits grecs de l'Italie méridionale*, pp. 48ff., pls. VII *a–b*; Turyn, *Codices*, pp. 71f., pl. 40; Follieri, *Codices*, pp. 86f., pls. 61, 62; Turyn, *DGM Italy*, I, pp. 42–44, 109f.;

---

[82] This observation was made by J. Irigoin, "Les manuscrits grecs. II. Nouveaux recueils de fac-similés," *REG*, 85 (1972), p. 561. In order to observe the habit of indicating the hour in dated subscriptions of South Italian MSS, one may look through dated subscriptions and various notes printed, along with undated subscriptions, in P. Batiffol, *L'Abbaye de Rossano* (Paris, 1891; repr. London, 1971), pp. 151–67.

[83] On the use of such various colors in South Italian MSS, cf. Batiffol, *op. cit.*, pp. 89–91 and *passim*; A. Vaccari, "La Grecía nell'Italia meridionale," *OC*, 3,3, no. 13 (1925), p. 284; M.-L. Concasty, "Manuscrits grecs originaires de l'Italie méridionale conservés à Paris," *Atti dello VIII Congresso Internazionale di Studi Bizantini*, I = *SBN*, 7 (1953), pp. 22–34; R. Devreesse, *Introduction à l'étude des manuscrits grecs* (Paris, 1954), pp. 55f.; idem, *Les manuscrits grecs de l'Italie méridionale*, ST, 183 (Vatican City, 1955), pp. 29f.; Turyn, *Codices*, pp. 20, 33; idem, *DGM Italy*, I, p. 18.

[84] Cf. *idem, Codices*, pp. 36, 84; *idem, DGM Italy*, I, pp. 5f., 270 (Index, *s.v.* colors: —use of color blobs).

[85] Cf. *idem, Codices*, pp. 55f.; *idem, DGM Italy*, I, pp. 65f.

II, pls. 26, 27, 84; M. Petta, "Codici greci della Puglia trasferiti in biblioteche italiane ed estere," *BGrottaf*, N.S. 26 (1972), pls. 1, 2 (the script of a later MS reproduced on pls. 3 and 4 is similar to the script of MSS from the Terra d'Otranto written at the end of the 13th and early in the 14th centuries). In general, on MSS from the Terra d'Otranto, cf. now A. Jacob, "Les écritures de Terre d'Otranto," in *Paléographie grecque et byzantine*, pp. 269–81 (pp. 273–76, on MSS of the 13th and 14th centuries; p. 278, on this MS).

This MS once belonged to John Gibson (*fl.* 1720–1726), from whom it was acquired by Robert Harley (1661–1724), first Earl of Oxford, on 13 September 1722 (cf. Wright, *Fontes Harleiani*, pp. 162, 458). On John Gibson and his MSS in the Harleian collection, cf. *ibid.*, pp. XXIV, 162–64. The Harleian MSS were sold to the nation in 1753 and placed in the British Museum in 1757. On Robert Harley, Edward Harley, and the history of the Harley library, cf. above, p. 29.

On this MS, cf. Nares, *Catalogue of the Harleian Manuscripts*, III, p. 274; Vogel–Gardthausen, p. 16; Omont, "Notes," p. 334; Turyn, *DGMItaly*, I, pp. 51f.; R. Holmes and J. Parsons, *Vetus Testamentum Graecum cum variis lectionibus*, V (Oxford, 1827), at end, fol. 4v (under no. 166); Rahlfs, *Verzeichnis der griechischen Handschriften des Alten Testaments*, p. 109 (symbol 166); Batiffol, *L'Abbaye de Rossano*, p. 95; Vaccari, *op. cit.*, p. 308; Devreesse, *Les manuscrits grecs de l'Italie méridionale*, p. 50; Petta, *op. cit.*, p. 106.[86]

Plates 22, 23, 24: A.D. 1284/1285.

Oxford, Bodleian Library, ms Roe 13. Bombycine, 265 × 185 mm., 224 fols., about 32–38 lines to a page. Contents: (fols. 1r–87r) ⟨Hesychius of Jerusalem⟩, Expositiones in Psalmos 77–107 (only the comments on Psalms 77–99 are printed in Migne, Patr. Gr., 55, cols. 711–84);[87] (fols. 87r–132r) St. John Chrysostom, Expositiones in Psalmos 108–17 (ed. Migne, Patr. Gr., 55, cols. 258–338); (fols. 132r–146r) ⟨Hesychius of Jerusalem⟩, Expositio in Psalmum 118;[88] (fols. 146r–224r) St. John Chrysostom, Expositiones in Psalmos 119–50 (ed. Migne, Patr. Gr., 55, cols. 338–498). The expositions of the Psalms in this MS that are attributed by scholars to Hesychius of Jerusalem stem from Hesychius' third or great Commentary on the Psalms.[89] The MS was written in the monastery on Mount Galesion (or Galesios), near Ephesus,

---

[86] The assertion of Petta, *op. cit.*, p. 112 note 142, to the effect that Andreas of Brindisi, scribe of two MSS dated A.D. 1284 and 1286, is identical with the notary Andreas of Brindisi to whom Nicholas-Nectarius of Otranto, later abbot of Casole (b. *ca.* 1155–1160, d. 1235), addressed a poem, seems to be improbable for chronological reasons. On the poem, cf. J. M. Hoeck and R. J. Loenertz, *Nikolaos-Nektarios von Otranto, Abt von Casole*, StPB, 11 (Ettal, 1965), pp. 26, 141f.; on the chronology of Nicholas-Nectarius, cf. *ibid.*, p. 25.

[87] On fragments of Hesychius' Commentary on Psalms 77–99 that are found elsewhere and on published fragments of Hesychius' Commentary on Psalms 100–7, cf. R. Devreesse, *Les anciens commentateurs grecs des Psaumes*, ST, 264 (Vatican City, 1970), pp. 257–60.

[88] On Hesychius' Commentary on Psalm 118, cf. *ibid.*, pp. 260f.

[89] On the three commentaries on the Psalms by Hesychius of Jerusalem, cf. *idem*, "La chaîne sur les Psaumes de Daniele Barbaro," *RBibl*, 33 (1924), pp. 498–521 (on MS Roe 13, p. 510); *idem*, "Chaînes exégétiques grecques," *DB*, Suppl. I (Paris, 1928), cols. 1134f. (on MS Roe 13, col. 1135); *idem*, *Les anciens commentateurs grecs des Psaumes*, pp. 243–301; on Hesychius' third or long Commentary on the Psalms, *ibid.*, pp. 250–61; on MS Roe 13, *ibid.*, pp. 257–61.

For the text of Hesychius' *first* Commentary on the Psalms, the so-called *De titulis Psalmorum*, cf. Migne, Patr. Gr., 27, cols. 649–1344. For the text of Hesychius' *second* Commentary on the Psalms, cf. V. Jagić, *Supplementum Psalterii Bononiensis. Incerti auctoris explanatio Psalmorum graeca* (Vienna, 1917); cf. Turyn, *DGMItaly*, I, pp. 202–4.

most probably the monastery of the Theotocos,[90] at the behest of the hieromonk Galaction the Blind (probably the abbot of the monastery, to judge
from the adjective πανοσιωτάτου), in A.M. 6793 = A.D. 1284/1285, according
to the subscription on fol. 224ʳ (Pl. **103a**): + ἐγράφη ἡ παροῦ(σ)α βίβλο(ς)
τῶν ψαλμῶν ἐν τῇ π[ε]ριβοήτω μο(ν)ῇ | τοῦ Γαλησίου προτροπὴ τοῦ πανοσιω-
τ(ά)τ(ου) π(ατ)ρ(ὸ)ς ἡμῶν ἱερο(μον)άχ(ου) | κυρ(οῦ) Γαλακτίωνο(ς), τοῦ τυφλοῦ,
ἐν ἔτει ͵ςψϟγ ἰν(δικτιῶνος) ιγ | ἔστι δὲ ἡ ἑρμη(νεία) τοῦ ἡμίσους βίβλου τῶν
ψαλμῶν, τοῦ ἐν ἁγίοις | π(ατ)ρ(ὸ)ς ἡμῶν, Ἰω(άννου) ἀρχ(ι)επισκ(ό)π(ου) Κω(ν-
σταντινου)πόλ(ε)ως τοῦ Χρ(υσοστό)μου·– (The right margin of this subscription was torn off and repaired with a strip of paper, but nothing seems
to have been lost from the text of the subscription.) Galaction the Blind of
Mount Galesion was blinded by order of Michael VIII Palaeologus because of
his opposition to the Emperor's religious policies.[90a]

In general, on MSS which are known to have been written on Mt. Galesion
or to have been in the possession of the Galesion monasteries, cf. F. Halkin,
"Manuscrits galésiotes," *Scriptorium*, 15 (1961), pp. 221–27 (p. 223, on this
MS), pls. 17, 18 (repr. in F. Halkin, *Recherches et documents d'hagiographie
byzantine*, SubsHag, 51 [Brussels, 1971], pp. 157–63, with plates on pp. 164–65;
p. 159, on this MS); N. G. Wilson, "Notes on Greek Manuscripts," *Scriptorium*,
15 (1961), pp. 318f., pl. 18; Turyn, *Codices*, pp. 44–46, pls. 19, 20, 165*b*;
Follieri, *Codices*, pp. 73f., pl. 50.

MS Oxford Roe 13 was written by three scribes whom I denote with
letters A, B, C. Scribe A wrote fols. 1ʳ and 9ʳ–43ᵛ, scribe B fols. 1ᵛ–8ᵛ and
44ʳ–111ᵛ, and scribe C fols. 112ʳ–224ʳ.

To show handwriting A, on Plate **22** we reproduce folio 30ʳ, containing a
passage from ⟨Hᴇsʏᴄʜɪᴜs ᴏғ Jᴇʀᴜsᴀʟᴇᴍ⟩, (third or great) Cᴏᴍᴍᴇɴᴛᴀʀʏ ᴏɴ
ᴛʜᴇ Psᴀʟᴍs, Expositio in Psalmum 88 (ed. Migne, Patr. Gr., 55, col. 752,
20–72).

For handwriting B, on Plate **23** we reproduce folio 103ᵛ, containing a passage from Sᴛ. Jᴏʜɴ Cʜʀʏsᴏsᴛᴏᴍ, Exᴘᴏsɪᴛɪᴏ ɪɴ Psᴀʟᴍᴜᴍ 110 (ed. Migne,
Patr. Gr., 55, cols. 283, 44 – 284, 34). Double quotation marks in the left
margin were placed opposite lines that contain quotations from the Scrip-
tures.

[90] On the monasteries on Mount Galesion (or Galesios), cf. Beck, *Kirche und theologische Literatur*,
pp. 210, 676, 692; V. Laurent, in *LThK*, IV, cols. 491f.; S. G. Papadopoulos, in Θρησκ.ʼΗθ.ʼΕγκυκλ.,
IV, cols. 171f.; R. Janin, *Les églises et les monastères des grands centres byzantins* (Paris, 1975), pp. 241–50
(on MS Roe 13, p. 248 and note 6, p. 249). At the time MS Roe 13 was being written (A.D. 1284/1285),
the monastery of Galesion referred to in the subscription was most probably the monastery of the
Theotocos, since this was the most important monastery and apparently the only one that still existed
there after 1283: cf. W. Nissen, in *BZ*, 9 (1900), pp. 542f. Cf. also Dölger, *Regesten*, IV, pp. 2f. (no.
2085).

[90a] Cf. George Pachymeres, History (de Andronico Palaeologo, I.3), Bonn ed., II (1835), p. 17,
7–13; Macarius Chrysocephalus, Life of Meletius Galesiotes (*BHG*³ 1246a), ed. Spyridon Lauriotes,
in Γρηγόριος ὁ Παλαμᾶς, 5 (1921), pp. 582–84, 609–24, and esp. p. 621, 27–29 (on the blinding of
Galaction); and in ʽΟ ῎Αθως, ἁγιορειτικὸν περιοδικόν, 2,8–9 (1928), pp. 9–11 (*passim*); or (in a
Modern Greek version by Nicodemus Hagiorites) in K. Chr. Doukakes, ʽΟ Μέγας Συναξαριστής,
2nd ed., V (Athens, 1956), under January 19, pp. 324–37 (*passim*), esp. p. 334, penult line – p. 335,
2 (on the blinding of Galaction); Janin, *op. cit.*, p. 248; V. Laurent and J. Darrouzès, *Dossier grec de
l'Union de Lyon (1273–1277)*, AOC, 16 (Paris, 1976), pp. 85, 100, 102 (esp. note 1), 105; *PLP*, II
(1977), pp. 141f., no. 3473.

For handwriting C, on Plate **24** we reproduce folio 126^r, containing a passage from St. John Chrysostom, Expositio in Psalmum 115 (ed. Migne, Patr. Gr., 55, cols. 326, 31 – 327, 29). This script C resembles in its style the handwriting of Manuel Spheneas (but is not identical with it). So far as we know, Manuel Spheneas wrote MS Florence Laur. 31, 3 + Laur. 86, 3 (fols. 210^r–231^v), of A.D. 1287, and MS Moscow, Gosud. Istorič. Muzej, from Mosk. Sinod. Bibl., greč. 348 Savva (349 Vladimir), of A.D. 1297. For samples of these two MSS, cf. Turyn, *DGMItaly*, II, pl. 42 (from Laur. 31, 3); Cereteli–Sobolevski, *Exempla*, I, pl. xxx, lower part (from Moscow 348); for other published specimens of these two MSS, cf. Turyn, *op. cit.*, I, p. 56.

Vogel–Gardthausen, p. 63 note 5, suggested the possibility that the monk Galaction who wrote MS Oxford Roe 7 in A.D. 1278/1279 (cf. above, pp. 23f., and below, Pl. **12**) might be identical with the hieromonk Galaction the Blind who commissioned this MS Roe 13. There appears indeed a certain resemblance of script styles between MS Roe 7 represented on Plate **12** and the handwriting C of this MS Roe 13 shown on Plate **24**. As I stated above (cf. p. 24), there is therefore a probability that MS Roe 7 was written on Mount Galesion. Moreover, the script of Manuel Spheneas shows the same style. It seems that this particular variety of script style was cultivated on Mount Galesion toward the end of the 13th century.

On fol. 224^r, an Arabic note, purported to be not later than the 14th century, records the donation of this MS by Athanasius to a religious foundation in (?) Ephesus; the name of Athanasius was written in Greek at the beginning of the second line of the note.

This MS Roe 13 at some time before A.D. 1514 was in the library of the Patriarchate in Alexandria. It was held transiently around A.D. 1514 by the hieromonk Manuel, ex-abbot from Mount Sinai, a native of Cyprus. It is possible (but by no means certain) that after June 1514 the MS was returned to Alexandria. Such is the evidence.

The bottom part of the original fol. 224^r was cut off below the subscription at some later time (probably early in the 16th century). Later, a new sheet of Western paper, in the normal page size of this MS, was pasted under the verso of the remaining part of fol. 224^r. Below the subscription on fol. 224^r, a Greek note (quoted below) was mounted on the lower front side of that repair sheet. A colophon of the writer of the note was pasted at the top of fol. 224^v (which is the verso of the repair sheet). This is the text of the Greek note on fol. 224^r:

^{1} κατα την παρουσα· ειμερα· ωρ(α) της αυτις εχρον(ίας)· ͵αφιδ Χ(ριστ)ου· ειμερα δευτερα· κ̅ε̅· |^2 ιουν(ίου)· εθελισεν· ο θ(εο)ς να πιηση την εσπλαχνιαν του· ης εμενα· κε ακομι εβρησκο|^{3}με ιστον κοσμον· να με κατ(α)θεσι ιστον· θανατον· οπο χροστουμε· κε εβρεθικα ιστην Αλεξαν|^{4}δρια κε ειβρα διο βιβλια ηστο πατριαρχιο το μεν προτ(ον)· αυτο· κε ενα νομοκανονο· |^5 ει ψαλτιρα ιχεν δεσμον ιεραρχικον· κε η τολμι μου κε ι αμαρτια μου· ετζακισα το εχον ττα |^6 κε δεν εβρισκουν ττα Σουριανι. κε δια τουτο δεομε κε παρακαλο να μου σιχορισε|^{7}τε κε να πισετε μια ευχι δια τον· θ(εο)ν· κε στελο τα τις αρχιεροσινι σου κε μετα|^{8}νια ιστην αρχυιεροσινι σου κε δια ονομαν θ(εο)υ να εχο μιαν ευχι σιχοριτικι κε υ |^9 ευχι σου μεθ ιμον αμην· Μανουλ· ταχα κε ιε[ρ]ομοναχος κε προϊγουμενος γρα|^{10}φ[ω or ει] ||

At the top of fol. 224^v, there is a colophon written by the same Manuel and pasted to the verso of that repair sheet. The colophon in its left part is written in a contorted manner, with words and word parts extending upward and downward, with a monogram of Manuel's name at the outset. Following is the left part of the colophon:

† Μανουηλ τάχα δὲ προηγούμενος ἀπού τοῦ ὥρους Συνὰ ὁ ἁμαρτολὸς ουτω γράφη

Following is the conclusion of the colophon written normally in the right-hand part of the page:

δια ονομα θ(εο)υ να εχο μιαν ευχιν | σιχοριτικῆν δια να μιδε χαθ(ῶ).

The writer of the note was a Cypriot by birth, as evidenced by the use (in line 1) of εχρον(ίας) instead of ἔτους (cf. below, p. 82 and note 219) and some Cypriot dialectal features of the text.

The note was written by Manuel, hieromonk and προηγούμενος (probably ex-abbot) from **Mount Sinai**,[90b] on 25 June 1514, on Monday (that day was actually a Sunday). The opening sentence means: "God had mercy on me, because I am still alive" (in spite of the sin which is recounted below). Manuel states that he previously found in Alexandria, in the patriarchate, two MSS: the present one, a "Psalter" (so called because it contained expositions of the Psalms), and another one, a Nomocanon. The "Psalter" (this MS Roe 13) carried (line 5) δεσμον ιεραρχικον, obviously an ecclesiastical censure to be imposed on those who would purloin the MS, a censure in the customary form of curses inflicted by the 318 Fathers of the First Council of Nicaea (cf. below, p. 80 and note 212), or in the form of excommunication (cf. above, p. 24), or both (cf. Clark, *Greek New Testament Manuscripts in America*, p. 64). Evidently, the censure colophon was inscribed in the original bottom part of fol. 224r which was cut off (obviously by Manuel himself). Manuel explicitly confesses that he committed a foolhardy sin and stole these MSS from the Patriarchate of Alexandria.

Manuel begged the church dignitary whom he addressed to grant him absolution and at the same time sent him these MSS (line 7, στελο τα). It would be logical to assume that Manuel was returning the MSS to their rightful owner, the Patriarch of Alexandria, and that he was writing this note to the same Patriarch. If so, the addressee would be Patriarch Joachim ὁ Πάνυ, who headed the Patriarchate of Alexandria from 1487 to 1567 and was himself a scribe and collector of MSS for his patriarchate.[91] However, it is strange that Manuel styled the addressee as ἀρχιερωσύνη, which would befit a bishop or archbishop; the patriarch of Alexandria should have been addressed as παναγιότης or μακαριότης. We can surmise that perhaps Manuel addressed his note to the then Abbot of Sinai, Clement, who was at the same time (arch)bishop of Sinai (cf. above, note 90b). Or, if Manuel (after the conclusion of his tenure as abbot of Sinai) was transferred to another monastery and resided elsewhere, he may have addressed the (arch)bishop of the proper jurisdiction. In any case, he certainly assumed that both MSS returned by him would be duly transmitted to Alexandria. It is likely that Manuel's note and his colophon were written originally on a single piece of paper, and that the repair of fol. 224 and the pasting of the note and the colophon on the repaired fol. 224r–224v were made subsequently. The text of the note by Manuel is easily understood, in spite of its illiterate misspellings. Still, a few points call for a comment.

In line 3, in οπο the final -ς was dropped before two consonants following; the word is to be understood οπο⟨ς⟩, i.e., ὅπως. Line 5, δεσμον ιεραρχικον: the δεσμός, ecclesiastical censure (or rather, warning of a censure), is called ιεραρχικός either because it contained a reference to the 318 Fathers of Nicaea who were hierarchs, or because it was signed in this MS by a bishop or archbishop or possibly, in this particular case, by a patriarch of Alexandria. It is noteworthy that many MSS that are now extant in the Patriarchal Library at Alexandria show censure colophons signed by a patriarch of Alexandria (cf. Moschonas, *op. cit.*, *passim*).

With reference to line 5, the verb τζακίζω used in medieval Greek has several meanings: "to break" (literally, e.g., a tree, or metaphorically, e.g., an oath), "to defeat," "to devastate," "to destroy" (a building), "to steal," "to take away." Cf. Io. Mevrsius, *Glossarivm Graeco-barbarvm*, 2nd ed. (Leiden, 1614), p. 558b lines 3–1 from the bottom, *s.v.* τζακκίζειν: "Hinc τζάκκισμα. Glossae Graecobarbarae. κάταγμα, τζάκκισμα, κλέμμα, κλεψιά." It was observed by M. Beaudouin, *Etude du dialecte chypriote moderne et médiéval*, BEFAR, 36 (Paris, 1884), pp. 109f., that the "Glossae Graecobarbarae" in Meursius referred to specifically Cypriot idioms and derived from a Cypriot glossary. Thus it is warranted to assume that the noun explanations κλέμμα, κλεψιά in Meursius

90b On the meaning of προηγούμενος, cf. P. de Meester, *De monachico statu iuxta disciplinam byzantinam*, Sacra Congregazione per la Chiesa Orientale, Codificazione canonica orientale, Fonti, Ser. II, fasc. X (Vatican City, 1942), pp. 203f. No record of a Manuel, abbot of Mount Sinai before A.D. 1514, is known (cf. K. Amantos, Σιναϊτικὰ μνημεῖα ἀνέκδοτα, in Ἑλληνικά, Suppl. 1 [Athens (1928)], pp. 9f., 22; *idem*, Σύντομος ἱστορία τῆς ἱερᾶς μονῆς τοῦ Σινᾶ, in Ἑλληνικά, Suppl. 3 [Thessalonica, 1953], p. 83). For 1513/1514 there is a record of Clement, abbot of Mount Sinai, whose ownership entries dated A.M. 7022 = A.D. 1513/1514 appear in MSS Sinai Greek 648, 649, and 659 (cf. V. Gardthausen, *Catalogus codicum graecorum Sinaiticorum* [Oxford, 1886], pp. 149, 151; Amantos, Σιναϊτικὰ μνημεῖα, p. 10; *idem*, Σύντομος ἱστορία, p. 83).

91 On Patriarch Joachim ὁ Πάνυ of Alexandria, cf. T. A. Gritsopoulos, in Θρησκ.ʼΗθ.ʼΕγκυκλ., VI, cols. 1092–94. On his activities as scribe and collector of MSS, cf. Vogel–Gardthausen, p. 164 (with old MS numbers); Th. D. Moschonas, Πατριαρχεῖον ʼΑλεξανδρείας. Κατάλογοι τῆς Πατριαρχικῆς Βιβλιοθήκης, I, Χειρόγραφα, 2nd ed., Studies and Documents, XXVI (Salt Lake City, 1965), *passim*.

point to the Cypriot meaning of the verb τζακίζω as "to steal." J. Darrouzès, "Notes pour servir à l'histoire de Chypre. Troisième article," Κυπρ.Σπουδ., 22 (1958), pp. 227–40, published several Cypriot notes which record commemorative donations to a church (ψυχικόν). The verb τζακίζω is used there in a context which warns of an ecclesiastical censure to be inflicted on him who would try to steal (νὰ τζακίση) the donation or to take it away from the church in question. Cf. *ibid.*, *passim*, especially p. 234 line 3 from the bottom (νὰ τζακίσι τὸ αὐτὸν ψυσικὼν καὶ δόσην απ' των αὐτω(ν) ναὼν); p. 239 line 6 from the bottom (νὰ τζακίσι τὸ αὐτὸ ψιχικὸ απ τὸν ναγ(ὸ) κτλ.). The construction of the verb τζακίζω with ἀπ(ὸ) or ἀπ(ὲ) proves clearly its meaning as "to steal, to take away unlawfully from." The sense "to take away, to remove *illicitly*" fits the situation described in line 5. In the note (line 5) the meaning of the context is ἐτζάκισά το ἔχον ττα (i.e., ἔχων τα): "I removed it (or 'cut it out') illicitly ('it' = το, i.e., the lower part of the original page fol. 224ʳ, containing the threat of ecclesiastical censure, δεσμὸς ἱεραρχικός), while keeping them (τα)," i.e., the διο βιβλια (line 4), the two MSS. It is noteworthy that Manuel used the literary participle form ἔχων (he misspelled it εχον), instead of the vulgar Cypriot form ἔχοντα.

Line 6, κε δεν εβρισκουν ττα Σουριανι, i.e., καὶ δὲν εὑρίσκουν τα Σουριάνοι: "and (or 'there-fore') the Surians do not (i.e., cannot) find them," i.e., the two MSS. The form εβρισκουν is either a Modern Greek present (in the third person plural) or a historical present (on the use of the latter, cf. A. Thumb, *Handbuch der neugriechischen Volkssprache*, 2nd ed. [Strasbourg, 1910], p. 114, § 186). There is also some possibility that in this instance εβρισκουν may be not a Modern Greek present, but a literary imperfect εὕρισκον (the vulgar imperfect would be εὕρισκαν) with a phonetic change of -ο- to -ου-, known to occur in Cypriot Greek especially after a preceding κ (cf. Chr. G. Pantelides, Φωνητικὴ τῶν νεοελληνικῶν ἰδιωμάτων Κύπρου, Δωδεκανήσου καὶ Ἰκαρίας [Γλωσσικὴ Ἑταιρεία Ἀθηνῶν, 1] [Athens, 1929], p. 13 penult line – p. 14 line 3; cf. p. 12 under V). The orthographic gemination of τ in the sequence ν-ττα (in lines 5 and 6), in a close syntactic juncture (of a verbal form followed by an enclitic pronominal object), seems to imply that, according to the phonetic habit of the note's writer, the sequence ντ was here pronounced *nt*, not *nd* (in general, on the vicissitudes of ντ in various Greek dialects, cf. S. C. Caratzas, *L'origine des dialectes néo-grecs de l'Italie méridionale* [Paris, 1958], pp. 135–41).

The context suggests that, after Manuel stole the two MSS in the patriarchate in Alexandria, the Surians were unable to find them there. The Surians probably acted in the patriarchate as guards or custodians. Σουριανι is to be understood Σουριάνοι, Surians, i.e., Christians of Syrian background, the well-known lower class of the population of the Holy Land.[91a] During the Crusades, they were reported to speak Arabic in daily life and to be in touch with the Greek language only in church. As Arabic-speaking Christians they were likely to be employed by the Greek Patriarchate in Alexandria in the 16th century.

Line 8 ευχι σιχοριτικι, and on fol. 224ᵛ (at the end of the colophon) ευχιν σιχοριτικῆν, i.e., εὐχὴν συγχωρητικήν: "an absolution prayer," a formula of absolution pronounced by the absolver. For various absolution formulas (εὐχαὶ συγχωρητικαί), cf. J. Goar, Εὐχολόγιον *sive Rituale Graecorum*, 2nd ed. (Venice, 1730; repr. Graz, 1960), pp. 531 ff.

In the colophon on fol. 224ᵛ, the penult word μιδε is to be understood μιδε⟨ν⟩, i.e., μηδὲν in which the final -ν was dropped before the initial consonant of the next word. In Cypriot Greek, μηδέν is just a negation which corresponds to the classical μή (cf. Beaudouin, *op. cit.*, p. 96), or to the medieval μήν (μή), or to the Cypriot μέν (μέ); on this particle, cf. Beaudouin,

---

[91a] On the phonetic change of -υ- to -ου-, Συρία to Σουρία, and consequently Συριάνος to Σουριάνος, cf. Dieterich, *Untersuchungen*, pp. 23 ff., 28, 275, 289; M. D. Chabiaras, Περὶ τοῦ κάστρου τῆς Σουριᾶς, in Λαογραφία, 2 (1910), p. 567 (on Σουριά). On the Surians during the Crusades, cf. H. Prutz, *Kultur-geschichte der Kreuzzüge* (Berlin, 1883), pp. 146–50, with excellent documentation from medieval sources on pp. 531 f. Cf. especially C. Du Fresne Du Cange, *Glossarium ad Scriptores mediae et infimae latinitatis*, III (Paris, 1678), col. 1028 (also ed. L. Favre, VII [Niort, 1886], p. 678), *s.v.* Suriani; William of Tyre, *Historia*, XVIII.5 (ed. Migne, Patr. Lat., 201 [Paris, 1855], col. 713 D 5–9); Jacques de Vitry, *Historia Hierosolimitana*, chap. 74, in J. Bongars, *Gesta Dei per Francos*, II (Hanau, 1611), pp. 1089–91. In Latin historians of the Crusades and in Latin documents of that period, the ethnic name of the Surians is *Surianus* (singular), *Suriani* (plural). Cf. E. de Rozière, *Cartulaire de l'Eglise du Saint Sépulcre de Jérusalem* (Paris, 1849), pp. 87 f., 96, 105, 107 f., 123, 159 f., 179, 265. In the French text of the Assizes of Jerusalem, the Surians were called *Surien* (singular), *Suriens* (plural): cf. Comte Beugnot, ed., *Assises de Jérusalem*, I–II, Recueil des historiens des croisades, Lois, I–II (Paris, 1841–1845), *passim*.

p. 32; on the particles μηδέ(ν) and μέ(ν) in Cypriot Greek, cf. S. Menardos, Φωνητικὴ τῆς διαλέ-
κτου τῶν σημερινῶν Κυπρίων, in Ἀθηνᾶ, 6 (1894), p. 150. The meaning of the colophon's last
four words is: διὰ νὰ μηδὲν χαθῶ, "lest I perish."

     This MS was among the MSS brought from the Levant by Sir Thomas Roe (1580 or 1581–1644)
and presented by him to the Bodleian Library in 1628. On flyleaf VIᵛ (facing fol. 1ʳ), there is
the characteristic entry of Thomas Roe (cf. above, p. 25). On the Roe MSS in the Bodleian
Library and on Roe himself, cf. *ibid.*

     The MS is the unique direct source of Hesychius of Jerusalem, (third)
Commentary on the Psalms, for the expositions indicated above. At the
request of Bernard de Montfaucon, John Potter (1674?–1747), classical scholar,
later archbishop of Canterbury,[92] made from this MS a transcript of Hesychius' comments, which Montfaucon used for his *editio princeps* of the Expositions on Psalms 77–99 printed in his edition of St. John Chrysostom (cf.
B. de Montfaucon, *Sancti Patris Nostri Joannis Chrysostomi opera omnia quae
exstant*, V [Paris, 1724], Praefatio § XIV, unnumbered pages; repr. in Migne,
Patr. Gr., 55, cols. 29–30, Praefatio § XIV). Also cf. Montfaucon, *op. cit.*, V,
p. 722 (repr. in Migne, Patr. Gr., 55, both Greek and Latin cols. 709–10, at
the bottom, Monitum).

     On this MS, cf. Coxe, I, cols. 465f.; *Summary Catalogue*, II,1, p. 11 (under S.C. 259);
Barbour, in *Greek Manuscripts in the Bodleian Library*, pp. 21f. (under no. 24); Aubineau,
Codices Chrysostomici graeci, I, pp. 244–46; Devreesse, *Les anciens commentateurs grecs des
Psaumes*, pp. 257–61; Vogel–Gardthausen, p. 63 note 5.
     On this MS, especially on Manuel's note on fol. 224ʳ–224ᵛ, I had the privilege of consulting
the Rev. Fr. Jean Darrouzès, A.A. (Paris), and Dr. Renée Kahane (Urbana, Illinois).

Plate 25: A.D. 1285.

Oxford, Bodleian Library, ms Auct.T.3.6. Parchment, 280 × 205 mm.,
202 fols. Contents: (fols. 1ʳ–130ᵛ) Triodion; (fols. 130ᵛ–201ᵛ) Prophetologion.
The MS was written by the priest Nilus Cucubistianus and concluded by him
on 7 April A.M. 6793 = A.D. 1285. The scribe wrote two subscriptions, one in
a more formal script (on fols. 201ᵛ line 29 – 202ʳ line 3), and another one
in a more cursive script (fol. 202ʳ lines 4–14). On Plate **104** we reproduce both
subscriptions. This is the text of the first subscription, many elements of
which have faded, but can be read to a certain degree in ultraviolet light:

     †   Ὥσπερ ξένοι χέρουσιν ἰδεῖν π(ατ)ρίδ(α)·
        κ(αὶ) οἱ κινδυνεύοντ(ες) εὑρεῖν λιμένα |
        οὕτως κ(αὶ) οἱ γράφοντ(ες) ἰδεῖν βιβλίου τέλος + + + + + |

† Επληρώθ(η) τὸ παρὸν τριώδ(ιον) σὺν τῆς πρόφητ(είας) ἀποστόλων κ(αὶ) εὐάγ-
γελίων ἐκ | προστάξεως τοῦ κ(υρίο)υ ἡμῶν Ἰ(ησο)ῦ Χ(ριστο)ῦ ἐξ επιδρομ(ῆς)
κ(αὶ) κόπ(ου) κ(αὶ) μόχθου πολλοῦ | καμοῦ τλήμονο(ς) καὶ ἀβελτέρου· κ(αὶ)
αλλοτρίου απο (? this word was added above the line) χώρας τῆς λεγομένης Κρῖ·|
Θεσσαλοῦ δὲ τοῦ Κουκουβιστιανοῦ ἡμέρ(α) σαββάτω· ὥρα θ̅ | οἱ μέλλοντ(ες) διέρ-
χεσθαι αὐτῶ εὔχεσθαι μοι διὰ τὸν θ(εὸ)ν· περὶ τῶν | σφαλμάτων ἵνα εὕρω σ(ωτη)ρίαν

[92] On John Potter, cf. *DNB*, XVI, pp. 216f.

ἐν τῇ φρικώδη ἡμέρ(ᾳ) | δευτέρα παρουσία μικρὰν ἀνάπαυσιν ὁ πάνυ τάλας ++ |
++++++++++++ | ἀμὴν ἀμὴν ἀμὴν ++ ‖

Ἔτους ͵ϛψϟγ′ ἰν(δικτιῶνος) γ̄ κ(ύρι)ε Ἰ(ησο)ῦ Χ(ριστ)έ ὁ θ(εό)ς ἡμῶν ἐλέησὸν
ἡμᾶς ἀμήν:+ | † ἐπληρῶθη ἐν μη(νὶ) ἀπρηλλ(ίῳ) εἰς τ(ὰς) ἑπτά. |

    † ἡ γὰρ χεῖρ ἡ γράψασα σήπετε τάφω. |

(What follows is the second subscription in a more cursive script:)

    † ἐπληρώθ(η) τὸ παρὸν τριῶδ(ιον) συν της προφιτ(είας) διὰ χειρός.
καμοῦ τλήμονος· καὶ τάχα | ευτελέστάτου· ἱερεως Διαδωρίτ(ου) Νείλ(ου) τοῦ
Κουκουβιστιᾶνοῦ· τοῦ ὁρμενοῦ· τοίνυν· ἐκ θεόσό|στου πόλ(ε)ως· χῶρ(ας) τὲ τῆς
καλομ(έ)ν(ης) (?)· ἐκ προστάξεως τοῦ φιλαν(θρώπ)ου θ(εο)ῦ· καμοῦ τοῦ ταποινοῦ
συνδρομῆς | καὶ οἱ μέλλοντες διέρχεσθ(αι) τούτω, εὔχεσθαι διὰ τὸν θ(εό)ν· τὸν
και κτισάμενον τούτω τὸ οἰ|κτρότ(α)τον· βιβλίον· πρὸ⟨ς⟩ δοξολογίαν δόμου θ(εο)ῦ
τοῦ φιλαν(θρώπ)ου· και τῶν του αυτ(οῦ) θεραπ(ώ)των (the penult ών is marked
by an abbreviation) | συνᾶμα τῶ γράψαντ(ι) τουτω ευτελῆ γραφαίω. και
ἔκτρομα πάντ(α) γηγενῶν καὶ ο θ(εὸ)ς | καὶ π(ατ)ήρ τοῦ κ(υρίο)υ ἡμῶν, Ι(ησο)ῦ
Χ(ριστο)ῦ δώει ὑμῖν τὴν ἀντιμισθίαν εν τη φρικώδ(ει) αυτοῦ δευτέρα | παρου-
σία·:· ἀμήν ἀμήν γενον γένοι εἰς τοὺς ἀπεράντους ἀμήν:– |

    † τὸ δὲ ἔτο(ς) ͵ϛψϟγ̄ ἰν(δικτιῶνος) γ̄ ἡμέρ(ᾳ) σα(ββάτῳ) ὥρα θ̄ ἀπριλ-
λ(ίῳ) εἰς τ(ὰς) ἑπτά:– |

    † ἡ γὰρ χεὶρ η γράψασα τῆν βίβλον ταύτην σίπ(ε)ται τάφῳ:– |

    † ἡ γὰρ χεὶρ η γράψασα τῆν βίβλον τάυτην σίπεται τάφω

The second subscription in substance resembles the first one, although
there are some other elements added. Though it is written in a cursive writing
which differs from the script of the first subscription, it should be attributed
to the hand of the same scribe for several reasons. The numeral letters in
the year date of both subscriptions ϛψϟγ have identical shapes which point
to the identity of their scribe in both cases. The second subscription is written
in the name of the scribe (καμοῦ) as was the first subscription. The second
subscription carries personal references (lacking in the first subscription) to
the priestly status of the scribe and to his name Διαδωρίτ(ου) Νείλ(ου) which
the scribe himself would know and would be eager to include. The use of the
humility term ευτελέστάτου with regard to the scribe can be conceived only
as coming from the scribe himself.

The date of the conclusion of the MS was marked in both subscriptions as
Saturday, 7 April A.M. 6793 = A.D. 1285, indiction 3. The 7th of April in
A.D. 1285 fell indeed on a Saturday. However, the indiction number was
incorrectly marked as 3, since the year A.M. 6793 was the 13th indiction.
Obviously the scribe made a slip in the first subscription and repeated it in
the second; in both places he should have marked the indiction number as ιγ (and
not γ). The scribe wrote his name Κουκουβιστιᾶνοῦ in the first subscription.
In the second he referred to himself as διαδωρίτ(ου) Νείλ(ου) τοῦ Κουκουβιστιᾶνοῦ. What διαδωρίτης or Διαδωρίτης means, I do not venture to explain.
Is it a proper name? Does this word refer to some particular place where the
scribe then resided? The etymology of the family name Κουκουβιστιανός is an

interesting problem.[93] The scribe stated in the first subscription that he was a stranger (scil., in the place where he wrote the MS), a native (?) of a place called Κρίτ( ), which I was unable to identify. Perhaps he was at the time of writing this MS a resident of Thessaly, if my tentative reading Θεσσαλοῦ is correct. The reference in the second subscription τοῦ ὁρμενοῦ (i.e., ὁρμένου)· τοίνυν· ἐκ θεοσόστου πόλ(ε)ως may mean that the scribe came from[93a] Thessalonica, since the epithet θεόσωστος was applied to important cities (only Constantinople was called θεοφύλακτος).[94] Then the scribe continued χώρ(ας) τὲ τῆς καλομ(έ)ν(ης) (?), but by inadvertence he failed to name explicitly that χώρα. He bade the readers to pray for the sponsor of the MS, τὸν καὶ κτισάμενον (i.e., κτησάμενον), etc.[95] The scribe referred in the first subscription to his own ἐπιδρομή; he should have used the word συνδρομή, which meant the contribution to the cost of producing a MS.[96] In the second subscription, he referred to his own συνδρομή. If he used this term in the usual meaning practiced in subscriptions, we may assume that, apart from being the scribe of this MS, he himself defrayed the expense of buying the parchment for this volume. Thus he was probably both the scribe of this MS and the κτησάμενος.

The first subscription is preceded by conventional dodecasyllables (Ὥσπερ ξένοι κτλ.) often used by scribes in subscriptions.[97] The dodecasyllabic line which concludes the first subscription (ἡ γὰρ χεῖρ κτλ.), and is twice repeated at the end of the second subscription, is the beginning line of a few dodecasyllables frequently used in subscriptions.[98] On σύν used with the genitive (σὺν τῆς προφητείας), cf. Jannaris, *Historical Greek Grammar*, p. 396, § 1670. On προφητεία, meaning what is now called προφητολόγιον, cf. Rahlfs, *Verzeichnis der griechischen Handschriften des Alten Testaments*, p. xx; G. Zuntz, "Das byzantinische Septuaginta-Lektionar («Prophetologion»)," *ClMed*, 17 (1956), p. 184.

---

[93] The name Κουκουβιστιανός looks like an ethnic name ending in -ιανός (cf. Jannaris, *Historical Greek Grammar*, p. 291, § 1031.2; p. 300, §§ 1078 and 1079), derived from a place-name. Perhaps the primary root was κουκουβ-, the root of the verb κουκουβίζω ("to squat," "to crouch," "to perch," "to roost"); there is also a verbal adjective κουκουβιστός (cf. Zeugoles, Λεξικόν, p. 1410; Demetrakos, Μέγα Λεξικόν, V, p. 4079).

There may be an entirely different connection of this family name with the word κουκοῦβαι, "grapes" (cf. Eustathii Thessalonicensis *Opuscula*, ed. Th. L. F. Tafel [Frankfurt am Main, 1832], p. 309, 5; Ph. I. Koukoules, Βυζαντινῶν τροφαὶ καὶ ποτά, in Ἐπ.Ἑτ.Βυζ.Σπ., 17 [1941], pp. 79f.; idem, Ἡ ἀμπελουργία παρὰ Βυζαντινοῖς, ibid., 20 [1950], p. 25; or idem, Βυζαντινῶν βίος καὶ πολιτισμός, V, Collection de l'Institut Français d'Athènes, 76 [Athens, 1952], pp. 105, 288). Perhaps the place-name Κουκουβίτσα (with a Slavic suffix) in the Peloponnesus (cf. Λεξικὸν τῶν δήμων, p. 232) stems from this root κουκουβ-. It has been pointed out that sometimes the Slavic suffix -ιστα was substituted for -ιτσα in toponyms (cf. M. Vasmer, *Die Slaven in Griechenland*, AbhBerl, Philos.-hist.Kl., 1941, 12 [Berlin, 1941], p. 305). Thus we can presume also the existence of a place-name *Κουκουβίστα (cf. Vasmer, op. cit., p. 116, no. 30, where a similar place-name Κουκοβίστα from the eparchy of Parnassis is quoted). From Κουκουβίστα an ethnic name, Κουκουβιστιανός, could conceivably be derived.

[93a] "Came from" or rather "was a native of." It is somewhat strange that this medieval scribe should have used the form ὅρμενος, the Homeric participle aorist middle of the verb ὅρνυμι (cf., e.g., Iliad Λ 326). Perhaps the scribe made a slip and actually intended to write τοῦ ὁρμωμένου. On the meaning of ὁρμώμενος ἀπό (or ἐκ), "a native of," cf. L. Robert, *Opera minora selecta*, II (Amsterdam, 1969), pp. 925f.; idem, "Des Carpathes à la Propontide," *Studii Clasice*, 16 (1974), p. 85 note 43.

[94] Cf. F. Dölger, *Aus den Schatzkammern des Heiligen Berges* (Munich [1948]), p. 123.

[95] On the special meaning of κτισάμενος, or rather κτησάμενος, "sponsor of the MS, he who commissioned or paid for the MS," cf. Krumbacher, Κτήτωρ, pp. 396f.

[96] Cf. ibid., p. 410.   [97] Cf. above, p. 8 and note 13; below, pp. 117, 127.

[98] Cf. above, p. 15 and note 39.

On Plate **25** we reproduce folio 12ʳ, containing a passage from the Tʀɪᴏᴅɪᴏɴ which carries the conclusion of Lauds for Tuesday in the τυρινή week, then the troparia for the evening service of the same day, and troparia and a part of the canon for Matins on Wednesday of the same week (ed. Τριῴδιον κατανυκτικόν [Rome, 1879], pp. 52 last line – 53, 5; p. 53, 15–25; p. 54, 7–12; p. 55, 26–34; p. 55, 38–40; p. 56, 8–11; p. 58, 28–38; or Τριῴδιον κατανυκτικόν, ἔκδοσις τῆς Ἀποστολικῆς Διακονίας τῆς Ἐκκλησίας τῆς Ἑλλάδος [Athens, 1960], p. 39ᵇ, 37–44; p. 40ᵃ, 11–26; p. 40ᵇ, 8–13; p. 41ᵃ, 34–44; p. 41ᵇ, 5–8; p. 41ᵇ, 18–22; p. 43ᵃ, 2–13). A part of the page at its end, from the end of line 6 from the bottom through the end of the page (τας χείρας – τῆς ψυχῆς) was written by a hand different from that of the main scribe of the MS. Thus we gain from this MS another (albeit small) specimen of a Greek script belonging to the same time (A.D. 1285), since these lines were written obviously by some friend of the main scribe, who allowed a casual collaborator to write this small portion while the MS was being produced. On the page reproduced, headings and εἱρμοί are marked by red initials. Significant words in the headings are likewise distinguished by red initials. The troparia have capital initials in red, projected to the left; this projection follows the established arrangement practiced in liturgical books.[99]

On fol. 24ᵛ, a later owner of the MS recorded the birth dates of his children in A.M. 6815 = A.D. 1306/1307; on 4 December A.M. 6821 = A.D. 1312; on 24 January A.M. 6827 = A.D. 1319; on 14 July A.M. 6829 = A.D. 1321.

This MS was owned early in the 18th century by Giovanni Saibante of Verona; it was Greek MS 21 in the Saibante collection. On the Saibante collection of Greek MSS, cf. S. Maffei, *Verona illustrata*, pt. 3 (Verona, 1732), cols. 241–44; on this MS Greek 21, col. 243. A major part of the Saibante collection of Greek MSS was purchased by the Bodleian Library in 1820 (cf. *Summary Catalogue*, IV, p. 422). On the collection of Giovanni Saibante, cf. Frati, *Dizionario bio-bibliografico*, pp. 508f.

The library of Giovanni Saibante, who seems to have died sometime before 1732, was inherited by Giulio Saibante. A catalogue of the whole Saibante library (including both books and MSS) was published in 1734: *Indice delli libri, che si ritrovano nella raccolta Del Nobile Signor Giulio Saibanti* (sic) *Patrizio Veronese* (Verona, 1734); a list of Greek MSS is printed therein on pp. 217–19. It was reported that during the French revolution, or, rather, the Napoleonic wars (in Verona, probably after 1797), the Saibante library was dispersed (cf. F. Blume, *Iter italicvm*, I [Berlin–Szczecin, 1824], p. 270). A note written in the copy of *Indice Giulio Saibanti* in the Biblioteca Nazionale Marciana in Venice (shelfmark 226.D.198), on the verso of a flyleaf facing the title page, states that the painter Bossi acquired Greek and Latin MSS of the Saibante library; that the Greek MSS were listed in the catalogue of the Bossi library published in Milan in 1817; that Celotti bought them (i.e., the Greek MSS) and was shipping them to Oxford in March 1818. This note seems to have been written about that time (1818) and appears to be very trustworthy. Bossi was the famous painter and collector Giuseppe Bossi (1777–1815) in Milan. On him and his library, cf. U. Thieme and F. Becker, *Allgemeines Lexikon der bildenden Künstler*, IV (Leipzig, 1910), pp. 406f.; S. Samek Ludovici, in *Dizionario Biografico degli Italiani*, XIII (Rome [1971]), pp. 314–19; M. Parenti, *Aggiunte al Dizionario bio-bibliografico dei bibliotecari e bibliofili italiani di Carlo Frati*, I (Florence, 1952), p. 178.

The catalogue of the Bossi library is purported to have been compiled by a bookseller, C. Salvi, and was published after Bossi's death: C. Salvi, *Catalogo della libreria del fu Cavaliere Giuseppe Bossi* (Milan, 1817). There is on the title page a printed *Avviso*, in Italian and French, dated Milan, 20 February 1818, to the effect that the entire Bossi library was sold to the book-

---

[99] Cf. Turyn, *Codices*, pp. 25, 56, pls. 4, 19, 20, 93, 148; *idem, DGMItaly*, I, p. 5; II, pls. 2, 7, 10, 24, 25, 77, 145, 157; Follieri, *Codices*, pls. 38, 50, 56, 58.

seller G. P. Giegler of Milan, to whom interested persons were to apply for the purchase of books of their choice. On pp. 225–29, 25 Greek MSS are listed (they were included both in the Maffei list of Saibante Greek MSS and in the *Indice Saibanti*). All 25 (formerly Saibante–Bossi–Giegler MSS) are among the 51 Saibante MSS now extant in the Bodleian Library.

The priest Luigi Celotti (*ca.*1768–*ca.*1846) was a very active dealer in books, MSS, and art objects; he did a considerable amount of business in England (on him, cf. E. Jacobs, in *Zentralblatt für Bibliothekswesen*, 27 [1910], pp. 367 f.; Frati, *Dizionario bio-bibliografico*, pp. 154 f.; de Ricci, *English Collectors*, pp. 121 and note 3, 136). If the Venice note is accurate, it would mean that the sale of the Greek MSS of the Saibante library to the Bodleian Library in 1820 was negotiated by Luigi Celotti. The total number of Saibante Greek MSS bought by the Bodleian in the main purchase of 1820 was 50 (cf. *Summary Catalogue*, IV, p. 422). For this transaction Celotti probably acquired 25 Saibante Greek MSS from the Bossi–Giegler collection and the other 25 MSS from other sources.[99a]

On another Saibante MS in the Bodleian Library which is treated in this book, viz., MS Oxford Auct.T.3.16, cf. below, p. 71. It should be pointed out that the present MS Oxford Auct.T.3.6 (once Saibante Greek 21) and the other Oxford Saibante MS, Auct.T.3.16 (once Saibante Greek 26) never belonged to the Bossi library and were not listed in the Bossi *Catalogo*. On a Saibante MS in the British Museum (viz., MS Burney 21), cf. below, p. 62 and note 150.

On this MS Oxford Auct.T.3.6, cf. Coxe, I, col. 778 (under Misc. gr. 223); *Summary Catalogue*, IV, p. 422 (under S.C. 20502); Vogel–Gardthausen, p. 108.

Plate 26: A.D. 1285.

London, British Museum, ms Burney 20. Parchment, 190 × 153 mm., 317 fols., 22–23 lines to a page. Contents: Four Gospels, adapted for liturgical use. Full-page representations of the four Evangelists (on fols. 6^v, 90^v, 142^v, 226^v) precede the Gospels, and there are illuminated headpieces at the begin-

---

[99a] It is noteworthy that the Maffei list of Greek MSS in the Saibante library, compiled several years before its publication in 1732, indicated 80 MSS. The *Indice Giulio Saibanti* (1734) included 100 Greek MSS. Evidently Giovanni Saibante acquired the extra 20 Greek MSS between the time when Maffei made his earlier list and his own death. On the vicissitudes of Saibante Greek MSS, especially those which were subsequently owned by Paolino Gianfilippi of Verona, Guglielmo Libri of Paris, and the Ashburnham Library, and those which returned from Ashburnham Place to Italy to the Laurentian Library in Florence, cf. R. Foerster, *Mittheilungen über Handschriften des Libanios*, SBBerl (1885), pp. 901 f.; L. Delisle, *Notice sur des manuscrits du fonds Libri conservés à la Laurentienne*, Notices et Extraits des manuscrits de la Bibliothèque Nationale, XXXII,1 (Paris, 1886), pp. 1 ff.; de Ricci, *English Collectors*, pp. 131–35; Frati, *Dizionario bio-bibliografico*, pp. 258 f.; E. Rostagno and N. Festa, "Indice dei codici greci Laurenziani non compresi nel Catalogo del Bandini," *Studi Italiani di filologia classica*, 1 (1893), pp. 203 ff. (repr. in A. M. Bandini, *Catalogvs codicvm graecorvm Bibliothecae Lavrentianae*, III [repr. Leipzig, 1961], pp. 45*ff.); H. Rostagno, "Indicis codicvm graecorvm Bybliothecae Lavrentianae svpplementvm," *Studi Italiani di filologia classica*, 6 (1898), p. 144 (repr. in Bandini, *op. cit.*, p. 74*); G. Mercati, *Il frammento Maffeiano di Nestorio e la catena dei Salmi d'onde fu tratto*, ST, 154 (Vatican City, 1950), pp. 25 f. (this is a very important discussion).

It may be pertinent to note that the former Saibante Greek MS 2 (St. John Chrysostom, Homilies on St. Paul's First Epistle to the Corinthians) is now codex Vaticanus graecus 2155, which entered the Vatican Library not before 1813 (cf. Mercati, *op. cit.*, p. 25; Follieri, *Codices*, pp. 35 f., pl. 21). The former Saibante Greek MS 18 (Photius, Bibliotheca) is now in Paris, Bibliothèque Nationale, MS Supplément grec 471 (cf. Delisle, *op. cit.*, p. 118 under Gianfilippi 424; E. Martini, *Textgeschichte der Bibliotheke des Patriarchen Photios von Konstantinopel*, I, AbhLeipz, Philol.-hist.Kl., XXVIII,6 [Leipzig, 1911], pp. 35 f., 115–18). The former Saibante Greek MS 78 (St. Augustine, De Trinitate, translated into Greek by Maximus Planudes) is now MS 569 in the Biblioteca Civica at Verona (cf. H. Omont, "Les manuscrits grecs de la bibliothèque capitulaire et de la bibliothèque communale de Vérone," *Centralblatt für Bibliothekswesen*, 8 [1891], pp. 495, 489 note 4; G. Biadego, *Catalogo descrittivo dei manoscritti della Biblioteca Comunale di Verona* [Verona, 1892], p. 344).

On Saibante Greek MSS, cf. now E. M. Jeffreys, "The Greek Manuscripts of the Saibante Collection," in *Studia Codicologica*, pp. 249–62 (p. 254, under no. 21, on this MS Oxford Auct.T.3.6).

ning of each Gospel. The MS was subscribed by the hieromonk Theophilus on 30 May A.M. 6793 = A.D. 1285 on fol. 288ᵛ (Pl. **103b**): + ἐτελειώθ(η) κατ(ὰ) τὸν μάϊον μῆνα | εἰς τὰς τριάκοντα: ἡμέρα | τετάρτη: τῆς ἐνισταμένης: | ἔτους: ͵ξψϙγ (the letter ψ was written by the first hand; later the middle stem of ψ was erased by somebody to make the letter look like υ) ἰν(δικτιῶνος) ιγ̄: | διὰ συνεργ(ίας) τοῦ π(ατ)ρ(ὸ)ς καὶ τοῦ υἱ|οῦ καὶ τοῦ ἁγ(ίου) πν(εύματο)ς· εὔχεσθ(ε) | τὸν γράφοντ(α) διὰ τὸν κ(ύριο)ν: | (This beginning of the subscription was written in red; it is followed by a colophon written in black in full lines across the page and couched almost entirely in dodecasyllables, except for verse 3, which is two syllables too short, and for the invocation at the very end:)

'Ιδὼν τὸ τέρμα τοῦ παρόν|τος βιβλίου·
ἄν(θρωπ)ε κἀμοῦ | μνημόνευσον τοῦ τάλα· |
Θεοφίλου ἱερομονάχου· |
πανευτελοῦς τε καὶ ἀχρεί|ου τοῖς πᾶσι·
ὅπως θ(εο)ῦ | τύχοιμι προς τέλει βίου· |
νέμοντός μοι λύτρωσιν | ἀμπλακημάτων·

δ εἰς | τοὺς αἰῶνας ἀμήν· + | + ἀμήν· + ἀμήν: + | +

On Plate **26** we reproduce folio 17ʳ, containing a passage from the GOSPEL OF ST. MATTHEW 5:29–36. It comprises the end of the reading for Wednesday of the first week after Pentecost (the whole lesson is Matthew 5:20–30) and the beginning of the lesson for Thursday of the same week (the whole lesson is Matthew 5:31–41). The mark τέλ(ος) above line 5 at the end of the former lesson and the explanatory mark τῆς δ′ in the margin mean "end of the lesson for Wednesday" (of the first week). There is a mark αρχ(ή) in the margin opposite the same line 5 which is the initial line of the new pericope. In the upper margin a liturgical note indicates the time of the latter lesson, the customary prefix of the lesson, and the modification of the beginning of the pericope for lesson use:[100] τῇ ε̄ τῆς ᾱ ευδ(ο)μ(άδος) εἶπεν ὁ κ(ύριο)ς· ἠκούσατε ὅτι ἐρέθ(η) | ὅτι ὃς ἂν ἀπολύσ(η). The figure ιγ′ in the same margin indicates the consecutive number 13 of this pericope from Matthew (counting from the Sunday before Christmas: cf. Εὐαγγέλιον [1880], p. 23 under Περικοπαί ΙΓ′, p. 28ᵇ; or Εὐαγγέλιον [1968], p. [39] under Περικοπαί ΙΓ′, p. 42ᵇ). The red mark μα in the upper right-hand corner of the page means Μα(τθαίου); it shows that the page carries the Gospel of Matthew. All these marks and the liturgical note are in red, in accordance with the customary practice of New Testament MSS adapted for liturgical use.[101] For the time and extent of the lessons mentioned above, cf. Gregory, I, p. 347.

---

[100] On such features of the liturgical notes as the time of the lesson, a customary prefix to a Gospel lesson (like εἶπεν ὁ Κύριος or τῷ καιρῷ ἐκείνῳ), and the adaptation of the initial words of the pericope for lesson use, marked in New Testament MSS adapted for liturgical use (or completed in the text of New Testament lectionaries), cf. Gregory, I, pp. 16f., 341; von Dobschütz, *Eberhard Nestle's Einführung*, pp. 37f.

[101] On the liturgical notes and marks in New Testament MSS adapted for liturgical use and on their red color, cf. Scrivener, I, p. 76; Gregory, I, p. 17; Hatch, *Facsimiles and Descriptions*, p. 27; Metzger, *The Text of the New Testament*, pp. 30f.; Turyn, *DGM Italy*, I, pp. 62f. On red notes in New Testament lectionaries, cf. above, p. 18 note 43.

This MS was collated by Scrivener, *Full and Exact Collation*, with the symbol p (cf. pp. xlix–li: a description of this MS). The MS was occasionally quoted (with the Gregory–Aland number 482) by Aland et al., *The Greek New Testament*, cf. p. XIX.

The MS was once owned by Charles Burney (1757–1817), classical scholar and collector of books and MSS. After his death, his library was bought by Parliament and deposited in the British Museum in 1818 (cf. Forshall, *Catalogue*, I,2, pp. IIIf.). On Charles Burney, cf. *DNB*, III, pp. 418f.; Forshall, *loc. cit.*; Fletcher, *English Book Collectors*, pp. 306–8; de Ricci, *English Collectors*, p. 89.

On this MS, cf. Forshall, *op. cit.*, p. 4; Vogel–Gardthausen, p. 146; Omont, "Notes," p. 350; Scrivener, I, p. 257 (under Evan. 570); Gregory, I, p. 194 (under Vier Evangelien 482); Aland, I, p. 86 (under the Gregory–Aland number 482); von Soden, I,1, p. 175 (under ε329); N. Kondakov, *Istorija vizantijskago iskusstva i ikonografii po miniatjuram grečeskih rukopisej* (Odessa, 1876), p. 254; O. M. Dalton, *Byzantine Art and Archaeology* (Oxford, 1911; repr. New York [1961]), p. 476 note 2; J. J. Tikkanen, *Studien über die Farbengebung in der mittelalterlichen Buchmalerei*, Societas Scientiarum Fennica. Commentationes Humanarum Litterarum, V,1 (Helsinki, 1933), pp. 196f.; V. N. Lazarev, *Istorija vizantijskoj živopisi*, I (Moscow, 1947), pp. 166f., 340 note 29; II (1948), pls. 256a (fol. 6^v) and 256b (fol. 226^v); *idem*, in *VizVrem*, N.S. 2 = 27 (1949), pp. 369f.; K. Weitzmann, "A Fourteenth-Century Greek Gospel Book with Washdrawings," *GBA*, 6e Période, 62 (July–Dec. 1963), p. 97; D. Mouriki, in *Byzantine Art an European Art*, pp. 324 (no. 326), 546 (no. 326), pl 326 (fol. 6^v).

Plate 27: A.D. 1285/1286.

Oxford, Bodleian Library, ms Laud Greek 3. Parchment, 165 × 125 mm., 158 fols., 27–30 lines to a page. Contents: Four Gospels, adapted by a later hand for liturgical use. There are pictures of the Evangelists on fols. 41^r, 70^v, 121^v; the first picture of St. Matthew which should have faced the present fol. 1^r was lost. There are also ornamental headpieces of the Gospels. The MS was written by Nicetas Maurones, at the expense of Ioannes Pulumistrinus, in A.M. 6794 = A.D. 1285/1286 (fol. 158^r – Pl. **105a**):

Σὺν ϑ(ε)ῷ ἁγίω ἐπληρώϑη τὸ παρὸν τετραβάγγελ(ον). | διὰ χειρὸς ἐμοῦ Νικήτα τοῦ Μαυρώνη· διεξόδου | καὶ ἐνεργείας, Ἰωάννου τοῦ Πουλουμιστρινοῦ· | καὶ οἱ ἀναγὺνόσκοντες αὐτῷ εὔχεσϑε ἡμῖν· ἔτους | ͵ϛψϟδ ἔτη·

On Nicetas Maurones (later a lector), cf. Vogel–Gardthausen, p. 336; Cereteli–Sobolevski, *Exempla*, I, p. 12 (under no. XXVIII, on MS Moscow, Gosud. Istorič. Muzej, from Mosk. Sinod. Bibl., greč. 405 Savva = 416 Vladimir),[102] pl. XXVIII; Turyn, *DGMItaly*, I, p. XIV; Clark, *Greek New Testament Manuscripts in America*, pp. 179f., pl. LXV (from MS Princeton University, The Art Museum, now numbered 35–70; Gregory–Aland number 2420).[103] The wording of the Princeton subscription is similar to that of the Oxford subscription.

---

[102] Cf. Arhimandrit Vladimir, *Sistematičeskoe opisanie rukopisej Moskovskoj Sinodal'noj (Patriaršej) Biblioteki*, I (Moscow, 1894), pp. 621–24 (on p. 624, the subscription was quoted without its end). According to the subscription quoted in full by Cereteli–Sobolevski, *loc. cit.*, the Moscow MS was completed on Friday of the fourth week in Lent, A.M. 6797, indiction 2; this day was 18 March A.D. 1289.

[103] Clark, *op. cit.*, pl. XXXIV reproduced (on an enlarged scale) fol. 1^r of the Princeton MS. Even though the enlargement changed the appearance of the page, I do not think that fol. 1^r was written by Nicetas Maurones. There must have been more than one scribe of this MS. Therefore, I shall not refer to this plate as a published sample of Nicetas Maurones' handwriting. On this MS, cf. also S. de Ricci and W. J. Wilson, *Census of Medieval and Renaissance Manuscripts in the United States and*

On Plate **27** we reproduce folios 132ᵛ–133ʳ, containing a passage from the GOSPEL OF ST. JOHN 6:51 – 7:7. The red capitals projected to the left indicate that text sections begin in the preceding lines.[104] The later hand that adapted this MS of the Four Gospels for liturgical use added (in red) the marks αρχ(ή) and τέ(λος) in the margins while inserting red cross signs in the proper places in the text, added in the upper margins liturgical notes indicating the time of the lessons, and wrote in the outer vertical margins some numbers of Eusebian sections. The passage of the Gospel of John reproduced on the plate comprises: the end of the lesson for Friday of the third week after Easter (the whole lesson is John 6:48–54); the lesson for Monday of the fourth week after Easter (the whole lesson is John 6:56–69); the beginning of the lesson for Tuesday of the same week (the whole lesson is John 7:1–13). On the time and extent of these lessons, cf. Gregory, I, p. 345. The later annotator of the lesson equipment marked, as can be seen, the beginnings and ends of the lessons with crosses inside the text and then wrote in the margins αρχ(ή) or τέ(λος), as applicable. On both pages, he wrote in the top margins Ιω(άννου) to indicate that the Gospel of John is carried on these pages. On the right-hand page, in the upper margin, he wrote a note τη γ της δ εβδ(ο-μάδος), which indicates the time of the lesson that begins on this page. The red figures in the margins of the two pages, ξζ, ξη, οε, mark the numbers of the Eusebian sections included in the passage reproduced (on these Eusebian sections of John, cf. von Soden, I,1, p. 401). For other published specimens of the writing of Nicetas Maurones, cf. Savva, episkop Možajskij, *Paleografičeskie snimki s grečeskih i slavjanskih rukopisej Moskovskoj Sinodal'noj Biblioteki, VI–XVII věka* (Moscow, 1863), pl. ГІ (= XIII), fig. c (cf. p. 14); Arhimandrit Amfilohij, *Paleografičeskoe opisanie grečeskih rukopisej XIII i XIV v. opredělennyh lět*, III (Moscow, 1880), pl. VIII (cf. pp. 14–17); the facsimile is poor; Cereteli–Sobolevski, *op. cit.*, I, pl. XXVIII; Clark, *op. cit.*, pl. LXV (hardly pl. XXXIV: cf. above, p. 44 note 103).

On fol. 158ᵛ, a 14th-century hand wrote a poem[105] in political verses celebrating the arrival in Trebizond of the Emperor of Trebizond Basil Comnenus and the Empress Irene. Obviously Basil I Comnenus (who ruled from 22 September 1332 to 6 April 1340) and his wife Irene Palaeologina are

---

Canada, II (New York, 1937), p. 1175 (under no. 7); C. U. Faye and W. H. Bond, *Supplement to the Census of Medieval and Renaissance Manuscripts in the United States and Canada* (New York, 1962), p. 304 (under no. 7); *The Walters Art Gallery. Early Christian and Byzantine Art. An Exhibition Held at The Baltimore Museum of Art* (Baltimore, 1947), p. 144 (under no. 729); Aland, I, p. 188 (under the Gregory–Aland number 2420). The present number 35–70 of this MS is indicated in the Baltimore exhibition catalogue and in Aland.

[104] Cf. above, p. 22 note 63.

[105] Kirsopp Lake in the period 1902–1914 described several Laud Greek MSS. His handwritten descriptions were bound and are kept in the Old Bodleian Library in three volumes with the imprint *Catalogue of Mss. Laud. Gr. 1902–*, with the shelfmarks R 6.96/1, R 6.96/2, L[ibrary] R[ecords] 501/147. The first two parts are kept in Old Bodleian, in Duke Humfrey's Reading Room. The description of Laud Gr. 3 can be found in Lake, *Catalogue of Mss. Laud. Gr.* (in the first part, with the shelfmark R 6.96/1; the pages of the notebook are unnumbered).

Lake discovered the above poem in this MS, transcribed it, and made some comments on its contents.

meant.[106] The poem was composed after their wedding, which took place on 17 September 1335, when both of them arrived in Trebizond. I cannot say whether the person who wrote the poem was its author. Paleographically, this would be possible, since the script fits the period around A.D. 1335. However, some slips in the last line of the poem suggest that it was copied here by somebody else. This is the text of the poem (here it is arranged metrically):

$$καινὸν^{107} ὡράθη σήμερον ἐν Τραπε|ζοῦντι κλέος$$
$$καὶ καλλωπίζει \mid τὰς ψυχὰς φαιδρύνει τὰς ὁράσεις:- \mid$$
$$ἐκ γὰρ ἑώας ἥλιος· ἐκ δὲ δυσμῶν σελήνη:-^{108} \mid$$
$$Βασίλειος ὁ βασιλεύς ὁ Κομνηνός ὁ μέγας:- \mid$$
$$5 \quad καὶ βασιλὶς ἡ λαμπραυγής Εἰρήνη καὶ κοσμία:- \mid$$
$$συνεισδραμόντες ἐν ταυτῶ φωτίζουσι ἐν \mid κύκλω:$$
$$τοῦ κόσμου τὸ τετραμερές ἀρι|σταις δαδουχίαις:$$
$$ὡς ἐξ ἀντύγων οὐ(ρα)νοῦ τοῦ \mid φαινομένου δίφρου:$$
$$λοιπὸν ἀγάλλου Τραπεζοῦς \mid καὶ χόρεβε καὶ σκήρτα:$$
$$10 \quad καὶ δοξασμούς ἀνά|πεῦπε: σὺν κρότας εφημήα·^{108a}$$

The presence of the poem in this MS seems to indicate that in the 14th century the MS was in the area of Trebizond. It probably remained in Pontus until at least A.D. 1620/1621 (cf. below, note 108b).

On fol. 158ʳ, beneath the subscription by the original scribe, there are two notes written by different hands in the 17th century. The first note reads: αφου ἐγρεφη εινε τρακοσιοῦς | τριαντα πεντε χρονῶν:-· This note then was written in A.M. 6794 + 335 = A.M. 7129 = A.D. 1620/1621.[108b] The next note states that the nun Bartholomia died on Thursday, 24 March A.D. 1636 (according to the Julian calendar), and was buried in the quarter Yeni Mahalle (or Yenimahalle) of Scutari (now Üsküdar), a section of Constantinople on the Asian side of the Bosporus (fol. 158ʳ): :+: εμαρι η καλογρεα Βαρθολομια | μαρτηο εἰς τας· κ̄δ̄ ιμερα ε^{τη} | ‚αχλ̄ς̄:-· | ἰν-(δικτιῶν)ος δ | κ(αι) εταφι εἰς τω Γενη | Μαχαλα εις τω Σκοταρη. The word εμαρι obviously means "died."[109]

[106] On Basil I Comnenus of Trebizond and his wife Irene Palaeologina, cf. O. Lampsides, ed., Μιχαὴλ τοῦ Παναρέτου Περὶ τῶν Μεγάλων Κομνηνῶν, in Ποντικαὶ Ἔρευναι, II (Athens, 1958), pp. 64f.; Papadopulos, *Genealogie der Palaiologen*, pp. 50f. (under no. 80); Grumel, *Chronologie*, p. 372; J. Ph. Fallmerayer, *Geschichte des Kaiserthums von Trapezunt* (Munich, 1827; repr. Hildesheim, 1964), pp. 173–76; W. Miller, *Trebizond, the Last Greek Empire* (London, 1926), pp. 44–46.

[107] [κοι?]νὸν Lake (in his transcript of the poem, *loc. cit.*). No traces of letters to the left of -νὸν can be discerned even under ultraviolet light.

[108] The sun from the east points to Emperor Basil I of Trebizond, while the moon from the west refers to Irene Palaeologina from Constantinople.

[108a] The conclusion of the poem calls for a slight correction of the penult word; the last word is to be corrected orthographically and its final syllable is to be adjusted to the literary Greek of the poem. The text should be read and understood thus: σὺν κρότοις (-ας *codex*) ε⟨ὐ⟩φημία⟨ν⟩, (O Trebizond, send forth praises and) "acclamation with plaudits." On acclamations for an emperor accompanied by plaudits, cf. Du Cange, *Glossarium graecitatis*, I, col. 450, *s.v.* εὐφημεῖν; George Pachymeres, History, Bonn ed., I (1835), p. 97, 5–6; II (1835), p. 197, 10 κρότος καὶ ... εὐφημία.

[108b] The language of this note shows two phonetic peculiarities that are known from Pontic Greek. On the ε instead of α in ἐγρεφη, cf. D. E. Oeconomides, *Lautlehre des Pontischen* (Leipzig, 1908), p. 10, § 6.2; on the accent in χρονῶν, cf. *ibid.*, p. 129, § 79.II.6; p. 224 lines 1–3. It is likely that the note was written in Pontus. This MS, which I assume to have been in the area of Trebizond in the 14th century, presumably remained in Pontus until at least A.D. 1620/1621.

[109] It is probably a dialectal form of passive or intransitive aorist (possibly syncopated and perhaps also modified phonetically), closely related to the verb μαραίνω. It should be pointed out that there is in Modern Greek the form μαραμένος, meaning "dead person," considered to be the past participle

The Turkish term Yeni Mahalle means "new quarter of a town."[110] This note proves that in 1636 this MS was in the area of Constantinople. An ownership entry on fol. 1ʳ (in the upper margin) shows that the MS once belonged to the hieromonk Ioasaph: Ἰωάσαφ ἱερομονάχου.

In 1640, this MS was acquired by William Laud (cf. fol. 1ʳ), who donated it to the Bodleian Library in the same year. On William Laud (1573–1645), archbishop of Canterbury and chancellor of Oxford University, and on MSS donated by him to the Bodleian Library in the period 1635–1641, cf. *DNB*, XI, pp. 626–35; *Summary Catalogue*, II,1, pp. 12ff.; *ibid.*, I, pp. 128–35; Fletcher, *English Book Collectors*, pp. 66–72; de Ricci, *English Collectors*, p. 23.

On this MS, cf. Coxe, I, cols. 493f.; *Summary Catalogue*, II,1, p. 30 (under S.C. 680); *ibid.*, I, pp. 134f.; Lake, *Catalogue of Mss. Laud. Gr.*, *1902–*; Vogel–Gardthausen, p. 336; Scrivener, I, p. 198 (under Evan. 52); Gregory, I, p. 140 (under Vier Evangelien 52); Aland, I, p. 63 (under the Gregory–Aland number 52); von Soden, I,1, p. 177 (under ε345).

Plates 28–39: A.D. 1286.

Oxford, Bodleian Library, ms Roe 22. Parchment, 307 × 230 mm., IV + 560 fols., 33 (occasionally 34) lines to a page. Fol. I is a modern flyleaf; fols. II–IV are parchment leaves with Greek additions on fols. IIᵛ–IIIʳ and IVʳ; the original body of the MS consists of fols. 1–560. On fols. 1ʳ–288ᵛ (quires 1–36), the written page area is about 23 × 17 cm.; on fols. 289ʳ–559ᵛ (quires 37–70; I do not take into account the written area of the terminal leaf with the subscription), the written page area is about 22 × 17 cm.; however, the number of lines to a page in both parts of the MS is the same. In the first part, the ink is mostly black; in the second part, it is often brownish. At the beginning of the second part, the quality of parchment is poorer in a few quires. The MS is noteworthy, because its major part contains works of Nicetas Choniates. The MS contains: (fols. IIᵛ–IIIʳ) Index of Nicetas Choniates' Panoplia dogmatica (sive Thesaurus orthodoxiae), added by a hand of the 14th century (ed. Migne, Patr. Gr., 139, cols. 1093 A 1 – 1101 B 8);[111] (fol. IVʳ) a legal fragment, added by still another hand of the 14th century; (fols. 1ʳ–423ʳ line 27) Nicetas Choniates, Panoplia dogmatica, in 27 books;[112] (fols. 423ʳ line 28 – 447ʳ line 12) Nicetas Choniates,

---

passive of μαραίνω: cf. P. Blastos, Συνώνυμα καὶ συγγενικά. Τέχνες καὶ σύνεργα (Athens, 1931), p. 141 (*s.v.* νεκρός). Cf. also Zeugoles, Λεξικόν, p. 1539 (*s.v.* μαραίνω).

[110] On the meanings of the Turkish words *yeni* and *mahalle*, cf. H. C. Hony and Fahir İz, *A Turkish-English Dictionary*, 2nd ed. (Oxford [1957]), pp. 400 and 225. The Yeni Mahalle section of Scutari was shown on the plan in K. Baedeker, *Konstantinopel, Balkanstaaten, Kleinasien, Archipel, Cypern*, 2nd ed. (Leipzig, 1914), between pp. 220 and 221. There are several such place-names transliterated in Modern Greek as Γενῆ-μαχαλέ or Γενῆ Μαχαλέ (cf. Μεγ.Ἑλλ.Ἐγκυκλ., VIII, p. 190). The Turkish word *mahalle* appears in Modern Greek as a loan-word in the form μαχαλᾶς (or-άς): cf. Zeugoles, Λεξικόν, p. 1552; Demetrakos, Μέγα Λεξικόν, V, p. 4501; the Greek meaning offered in both dictionaries is συνοικία, ἐνορία, γειτονιά.

[111] For a critical edition of this Index, cf. J. L. van Dieten, *Zur Überlieferung und Veröffentlichung der Panoplia Dogmatike des Niketas Choniates*, Zetemata Byzantina, 3 (Amsterdam, 1970), pp. 50–56 line 8 (symbol R for this MS Roe 22).

[112] Nicetas Choniates' Panoplia dogmatica or Thesaurus orthodoxiae has not yet been published in a complete edition. Books I–V in a Latin translation are given in Migne, Patr. Gr., 139, cols. 1101–1444; parts of Books VI–XXV are printed in Greek, *ibid.*, 140, cols. 9–284; Book XXVII was published completely by S. Eustratiades, Μιχαὴλ τοῦ Γλυκᾶ εἰς τὰς ἀπορίας τῆς Θείας Γραφῆς κεφάλαια, I, in Βιβλιοθήκη Μαρασλῆ (Athens, 1906), pp. κ'–μ'. A very useful list of parts of the Panoplia dogmatica published in modern times was compiled by van Dieten, *Zur Überlieferung und Veröffentlichung*, pp. 28–42.

part of History, in its earliest version[113] (ed. I. A. van Dieten, *Nicetae Choniatae Historia*, CFHB, XI,1, Series Berolinensis [Berlin–New York, 1975], pp. 535, 3 – 611, 30/35; cf. Bonn ed. [1835], pp. 710–807; Migne, Patr. Gr., 139, cols. 917–97 C 14), containing, moreover, from Nicetas Choniates' History, (on fols. 447ʳ line 12 – 450ʳ line 24) the famous fragment De statuis Constantinopolitanis, for which this MS is one of the best sources (ed. van Dieten, *Nicetae Choniatae Historia*, pp. 647, 1 – 655, 65; cf. Bonn ed., pp. 854–68; Migne, Patr. Gr., 139, cols. 1041–57; E. Miller, in *Recueil des historiens des croisades. Historiens grecs*, I [Paris, 1875], pp. 503 C 5 – 514 A 3);[114] (fol. 450ʳ) Explanation of the Lord's Prayer; (fol. 451ʳ) Michael Attaleiates, Law Treatise, titles α′–λα′ (ed. Zepos, *Jus*, VII, pp. 418–56 line 10), with excerpts from legal texts added in the margins (on fols. 454ᵛ–461ᵛ);[115] (fol. 464ᵛ) St. Sophronius, patriarch of Jerusalem, Epitome of his Synodal Epistle (ed. Archiman-

---

[113] On the fact that MS Roe 22 contains the earliest version of a part of Nicetas Choniates' History, cf. van Dieten, *Nicetae Choniatae Historia*, pp. xcv–c. Cf. also *idem*, "Noch einmal über Niketas Choniates," *BZ*, 57 (1964), pp. 302–28, on various versions of Nicetas Choniates' History; cf. especially pp. 304, 314–21, on the character of MS Roe 22 (symbol O) in this connection.

[114] Variant readings and divergent text passages of Nicetas Choniates' History (including the fragment De statuis Constantinopolitanis) are reported from MS Roe 22 in van Dieten's critical apparatus, with the symbol O for this MS. On gaps and transpositions in the History in this MS, cf. van Dieten, *Nicetae Choniatae Historia*, p. xxvi.

[115] I owe the identification of the marginalia in Roe 22, fols. 454ᵛ–461ᵛ, to the great kindness and learning of Professor H. J. Scheltema of Groningen. Below, I record the identification of these marginalia by indicating the folio number of Roe 22 and the line numbers of the marginal writing on which a given marginal note is written and by referring its text to a printed edition. These are the editions: P. Krueger, *Corpus Iuris Civilis*, II, *Codex Iustinianus*, 12th ed. (Berlin, 1959); R. Schoell and G. Kroll, *Corpus Iuris Civilis*, III, *Novellae*, 6th ed. (Berlin, 1959); G. E. Heimbach, Ἀνέκδοτα, II (Leipzig, 1840; repr. Aalen, 1969), pp. 145–201: *Collectio XXV capitulorum*; pp. 202–34: *Collectio LXXXVII capitulorum*; for the *Collectio constitutionum ecclesiasticarum Tripartita*, I shall use below the symbol *Tripartita* and refer to pages and lines of its publication in G. Voellus and H. Ivstellus, *Bibliotheca ivris canonici veteris*, II (Paris, 1661), pp. 1217–1361 (from this edition the *Tripartita* was reprinted in Migne, Patr. Gr., 138, cols. 1077–1336). The references of the marginalia in Roe 22 to printed editions are:

   fols. 454ᵛ, *marginal* line 1 – 455ʳ, line 46 = *Collectio LXXXVII capitulorum*, chaps. 14–15 (ed. Heimbach, pp. 214ᵃ, 25 – 215ᵃ, 40).

   fols. 455ʳ, line 47 – 455ᵛ = *Codex Iustinianus* I.3,55 (ed. Krueger, pp. 38ᵃ, 44 – 39ᵃ, 33, without headline). This text was drawn from the *Collectio XXV capitulorum*, const. 12 (ed. Heimbach, pp. 165ᵃ, 24 – 167ᵃ, 29).

   fols. 456ʳ–459ʳ (in the margins) = Justinian, *Novella* 120 (ed. Schoell–Kroll, pp. 578ᵃ, 8 – 591ᵃ, 5). This text version was drawn from the *Collectio XXV capitulorum* (ed. Heimbach, pp. 192ᵃ, 7 – 200ᵃ, 32).

   fol. 459ᵛ, line 1 (headline) = *Tripartita*, p. 1243, 8–9.

   fol. 459ᵛ, lines 1–2 = *Tripartita*, p. 1244, 9–14.

   fol. 459ᵛ, lines 2–34 = *Tripartita*, pp. 1244, 22 – 1245, 2.

   fols. 459ᵛ, line 34 – 460ʳ, line 35 = *Tripartita*, pp. 1245, 23 – 1246, 41.

   fols. 460ʳ, line 35 – 460ᵛ, line 1 = *Tripartita*, pp. 1247, 35 – 1248, 16.

   fol. 460ᵛ, lines 1–24 = *Tripartita*, p. 1266, 3–27.

   fol. 460ᵛ, lines 25–26 (headline) = *Tripartita*, p. 1339, 6–8.

   fol. 460ᵛ, lines 26–52 = *Tripartita*, pp. 1339, 35 – 1340, 16.

   fol. 460ᵛ, lines 52–53 = *Tripartita*, p. 1340, 34–39.

   fol. 460ᵛ, lines 53–54 = *Tripartita*, p. 1341, 8–9.

   fols. 460ᵛ, line 54 – 461ʳ, line 1 = *Tripartita*, pp. 1340, 40 – 1341, 5.

   fol. 461ʳ, lines 1–3 = *Tripartita*, p. 1341, 11–17.

   fol. 461ʳ, lines 3–15 = *Tripartita*, p. 1341, 22–35.

   fol. 461ʳ, lines 16–41 = *Tripartita*, pp. 1341, 42 – 1342, 12.

   fol. 461ʳ, lines 41–53 = *Tripartita*, pp. 1342, 29 – 1343, 14.

   fol. 461ᵛ, lines 1–3 = *Tripartita*, p. 1344, 3–11.

   fol. 461ᵛ, line 3 = *Tripartita*, p. 1345, 9–11.

drites Hippolytos, in Νέα Σιών, 17 [1922], pp. 178–86); (fol. 466ᵛ) Abbot Cyril, Enigmas – αἰνίγματα θαυμαστὰ διὰ στοίχων· δηλοῦντα ἱστορίας παλαιάς· καὶ θαύματα οὐκ ὀλίγα· ποίημα Κυρίλλ(ου) μοναχοῦ καθηγουμένου τῆς μονῆς τοῦ Κώνσταντο(ς), τοῦ Καλλινίκου (inc. ἐρώ(τησις)· ἀπιστηθεὶς καὶ πιστευθεὶς – des. ἡ μαρτυρία δὲ πιστη· κἂν εἷς ὁ μαρτυρήσας); (fol. 470ʳ) Sermon on St. Paul, 1 Cor. 15:28, τότε ὁ υἱὸς ὑποταγήσεται τῷ ὑποτάξαντι κτλ. (inc. οὐ δοκεῖ μοι πρὸς τὸν ἴδιον θ(εὸ)ν καὶ λόγον – des. τὴν πολλὴν ὁμόνοιαν τοῦ υἱοῦ, πρὸς τὸν π(ατέ)ρα δεικνύς); (fol. 470ᵛ) κε(φά)λ(αια) περὶ τοῦ κινηθέντο(ς) ⟦δόγμ(α)το(ς)⟧ ζητήματο(ς)· τοῦ, ὁ π(ατ)ήρ μου μείζων μου ἐστίν (inc. Τοὺς σοφοὺς ὁ ἰδιώτης ἐρήσομαι – des. τῆς θεότητο(ς) φυσικῶν ἰδιωμ(ά)των); (fol. 475ʳ) Patriarch Dominic of Grado, Epistle to Patriarch Peter of Antioch (ed. Migne, Patr. Gr., 120, cols. 752 A 2 – 756 A 6); (fol. 475ᵛ) Response of Peter of Antioch to Dominic of Grado (ed. Migne, Patr. Gr., 120, cols. 756 A 8 – 781 B 2); (fol. 480ʳ) Leo of Achrida, archbishop of Bulgaria, Epistula 1 de azymis et sabbatis (ed. Migne, Patr. Gr., 120, cols. 836–44);[116] (fol. 482ʳ) Leo of Achrida, Epistula 3 de azymis (ed. in Ἐκκλησιαστικὴ Ἀλήθεια, περίοδος δευτέρα, 4 [1887], pp. 150–62);[117] (fol. 486ʳ) ⟨Nicon of Μαῦρον Ὄρος⟩*, Adversus Armenios (ed. A. Gallandi, Bibliotheca Veterum Patrum antiquorumque scriptorum ecclesiasticorum, III [Venice, 1767], pp. 249–251 B 4); (fol. 487ᵛ) Ἀναθεματισμός, abjuration against Jacobites; (fol. 488ᵛ) Tarasius, patriarch of Constantinople, Prayer at the opening of a church profaned by heretics; (fol. 489ʳ) St. Anastasius Sinaita, Viae dux – Ὁδηγός (ed. Migne, Patr. Gr., 89, cols. 40 A 5 – 309); (fol. 549ᵛ) Probus orthodoxus, Quaestiones ad Iacobitam; (fol. 550ʳ) St. Sophronius, patriarch of Jerusalem, Synodal Epistle to Sergius, patriarch of Constantinople (ed. Migne, Patr. Gr., 87, part 3, cols. 3148–3200 C 2); (fol. 560ʳ–560ᵛ) subscription of the MS.

The monk Ionas (= scribe A), who subscribed this MS, was its chief scribe, and was responsible for all but several smaller portions written sporadically by ten other scribes (marked below with capital letters B–L). Ionas produced this MS at the expense of Constantinus Maurozumes and subscribed it (on fol. 560ʳ–560ᵛ) on 15 May A.M. 6794 = A.D. 1286. The subscription consists of a dodecasyllabic poem in 9 verses, a colophon with the scribe's name and a reference to his monastic status, a commonplace dodecasyllable used in subscriptions, the dated subscription proper, and an invocation of the scribe. This is the text of the entire subscription (fol. 560ʳ–560ᵛ – Pl. 106):

Εὕρηκε τέρμα τὸ παρόν μοι πυκτίον: |
Καὶ παύλαν οὐχ᾽ εὕρηκε χεὶρ ἡ γραφέως: |
Μοχθεῖ γὰρ ἀπέραντα φεῦ ἕως πότε: |
Ἄρα μέχρις οὗ τάφος αὐτὴν δαμάσει: |
Εἰ τοῦτό σοι δέδοκτω Χ(ριστ)έ μου λόγε: |

[116] Also ed. C. Will, *Acta et scripta quae de controversiis Ecclesiae Graecae et Latinae saeculo undecimo composita extant* (Leipzig–Marburg, 1861), pp. 56–60; J. B. Pitra, *Analecta sacra et classica Spicilegio Solesmensi parata*, VII, *Juris ecclesiastici Graecorum selecta paralipomena* (Paris–Rome, 1891; repr. as vol. VI, Farnborough, 1967), cols. 745–52 (Auctarium VII).

[117] Partly printed in Greek, partly summarized in Latin, by Pitra, *ibid.*, cols. 759–62 (Auctarium IX).

Καί με προσεκλήρωσας ἐργῶδι βίω: |
Τοῦ ζῆν ἀφορμᾶς ἐκ τῶν χειρῶν μου ἔχειν,: |
Στέργων φέρω πλὴν καρδιακῶ τῶ πόνω: |
Ἰσχὺν μόνον μοι τὸ κράτος σου διδότω:– |
Χεὶρ Ἰωνᾶ ταπεινοῦ ῥακενδύτου, | Καὶ τάχα μονοτρόπου + |
ἔληξεν αὐχὴν δάκτυλοι τρεῖς καὶ γόνυ:– (this dodecasyllable is
written in red) ||

† ἐγράφει ἡ παροῦσα βίβλος διὰ συνδρομῆς καὶ | ἐξόδου τοῦ πανευ-
γενεστάτου κυρ(οῦ) Κων(σταντίνου) τοῦ | Μαυροζούμη:– † ἐγράφει δὲ ἐν ἔτει
τῶ | ͵ϛψϙδ: μηνὶ μαΐω ιε ἡμέρ(α) ε̄:– | ἰν(δικτιῶνος) ιδ:– |

† οἱ ἀναγινώσκοντες εὔχεσθαί μοι τῶ τολμητεία· | τῶ τολμήσαντι
βαλλεῖν χεῖρα ἐπὶ τοσοῦτον | ἔργον +

The 8 lines of the subscription proper and of the terminal invocation were
written originally in red and then retraced in black. The initial capitals of
the 9 dodecasyllables at the beginning and the initial capital of Ionas' colophon
are in red. It should be pointed out that the 15th of May 1286 fell on Wednesday (not on Thursday, as stated erroneously in the subscription).[118]

The sponsor of the MS, Constantinus Maurozumes, must belong to the
well-known family Μαυροζούμης or Μαυροζώμης of Peloponnesian origin which
appears in the later Middle Ages in various parts of the Byzantine Empire.[119]
This Constantinus Maurozumes may be identical with Constantinus Maurozomes mentioned by George Pachymeres (Bonn ed. [1835], II, p. 156, 5) in
a narrative of an incident (*ibid.*, p. 154, 10 ff.) which took place in Nymphaeum (during the stay there of Emperor Andronicus II Palaeologus) on
29 June 1292.[120] The incident involved the widow of Constantine Strate-

---

[118] The subscription of MS Roe 22 was reprinted (from Coxe, I, col. 482) and commented upon
by S. P. Lampros, Λακεδαιμόνιοι βιβλιογράφοι καὶ κτήτορες κωδίκων κατὰ τοὺς μέσους αἰῶνας καὶ ἐπὶ Τουρκοκρατίας, in Νέος Ἑλλ., 4 (1907), pp. 157–60. Lampros wrongly identified Ionas, scribe of Roe 22,
with the monk Ionas of Mistra who wrote, in Cyprus, MS Jerusalem, Patriarchal Library, Σάβα 67
(cf. A. Papadopoulos-Kerameus, Ἱεροσολυμιτικὴ Βιβλιοθήκη, II [St. Petersburg, 1894], pp. 115f.).
MS Σάβα 67 is written in an entirely different script (I checked its microfilm reproduction in the
collection of the Library of Congress). Lampros was so misled by his erroneous identification of Ionas
of Mistra, scribe of Σάβα 67, with Ionas of Roe 22 that he wrongly posited that MS Roe 22 was
probably written in Mistra. Moreover, he tried to corroborate this assumption by pointing to the
fact that Roe 22 was sponsored by Constantinus Maurozumes and that the Maurozumes or Maurozomes
family was of Peloponnesian origin (cf. note 119). The mistaken view of Lampros to the effect that
MS Roe 22 was written in the Peloponnesus was followed by D. A. Zakythinos, *Le Despotat grec de
Morée*, II (Athens, 1953), p. 316.

[119] On the Maurozumes (or Maurozomes) family in the Middle Ages, its Peloponnesian origins,
and its spread in the Byzantine Empire, cf. Lampros, *op. cit.*, pp. 158–60; N. A. Bees, Χριστιανικαὶ
ἐπιγραφαὶ Μεσσηνίας μετὰ σχετικῶν ἀρχαιολογημάτων, in Δελτ.Ἱστ.Ἐθν.Ἑτ., 6 (1901), p. 382 and pp.
382–83 (on the sponsor of MS Roe 22); idem, Ἀναγνώσεις καὶ κατατάξεις Βυζαντινῶν μολυβδοβούλλων
(Ἀνακοίνωσις δευτέρα), in *JIAN*, 13 (1911), pp. 19–21 (*ibid.*, on MS Roe 22); idem, *Die Inschriften-
aufzeichnung des Kodex Sinaiticus Graecus 508 (976) und die Maria-Spiläotissa-Klosterkirche bei
Sille (Lykaonien)*, TFByzNgPhil, 1 (Berlin-Wilmersdorf, 1922), pp. 71–73 (on MS Roe 22, p. 71
note 1), 76 note 3; V. Laurent, *Les bulles métriques dans la Sigillographie byzantine*, AOC, 2 (Athens,
1932), pp. 69f. (no. 194), 105 (no. 302); Ahrweiler, "La région de Smyrne," p. 172; N. Oikonomidès,
Actes de Dionysiou, Archives de l'Athos, IV (Paris, 1968), p. 148, doc. 25 line 9.

[120] On the chronology of this incident, cf. J. Verpeaux, "Notes chronologiques sur les livres II
et III du *De Andronico Palaeologo* de Georges Pachymère," *REB*, 17 (1959), pp. 169f. (especially
p. 169 note 4); Turyn, *DGMItaly*, I, p. xix (addendum to p. 80, lines 15–24).

gopulus (a grandaunt of the Emperor)[121] and Irene Palaeologina, wife of Constantine Palaeologus Porphyrogenitus (the Emperor's brother).[122] Constantinus Maurozomes was a friend of the Strategopulina and was rumored to be her lover.[123] In the aftermath of that incident he was outrageously mistreated by Constantine Palaeologus Porphyrogenitus (cf. Pachymeres, II, p. 156, 5–12). It is obvious that Constantinus Maurozomes moved in court circles. It can easily be assumed that in normal circumstances, when the Emperor and his family and retinue were in Constantinople, Constantinus Maurozomes was there as well. We can dismiss the variant spelling of the family name (Maurozumes, Maurozomes) and adopt the possibility that the sponsor of the Oxford MS and the man mentioned by Pachymeres are identical. If this identification is correct, it is likely that in A.D. 1286, six years before the incident in Nymphaeum and its sequel, Constantinus Maurozomes was in Constantinople and that this MS was commissioned by him and produced likewise in Constantinople. The characteristic Planudean script B of one of the collaborators of Ionas, which was cultivated especially in Constantinople in the Planudean scriptorium, supports the assumption that the MS was written in Constantinople. Of course, this is only a hypothesis.

As I stated above, the chief scribe of the MS was the monk Ionas (= scribe A). However, small text portions of varying length were written by ten other scribes marked by me with capital letters B–L. Since these sporadic copyists were writing their portions in the continuous production of the MS, they enrich our repertory of dated scripts and are duly represented by samples of their writings. Below I list the text portions written by each scribe within this MS.

Scribe A, i.e., the monk Ionas (cf. Plates **28–31**), wrote fols. 1^r–5^v; 6^r line 25 καταστρεψαμένου – 12^v line 12; 13^r–13^v; 14^v line 15 τοῦ αὐτοῦ – 19^r line 5 ἀρχῆς; 19^r line 15 Ἔτι – 33^r; 34^v–47^r line 15 τοῦτον; 47^v–50^r; 51^r–52^v line 10; 53^r–54^v line 5 εἰσφέρηται; 54^v line 16 ἢ κατά – 56^v line 22 (middle); 57^r–61^r line 10

---

[121] The widow of Constantine Strategopulus was a daughter of Isaac Ducas and a niece of John III Batatzes. Her niece, Theodora Ducaena Palaeologina, married the future Emperor Michael VIII Palaeologus. Thus the elder Strategopulina was a grandaunt of Emperor Andronicus II Palaeologus. On her and these relationships, cf. Polemis, *The Doukai*, p. 109 (nos. 73 and 74). I refer to the elder Strategopulina as a widow, since it can be inferred from Pachymeres (Bonn ed., II, p. 154, 20: συνοικήσασα in the aorist on Strategopulina; p. 155, 16: ζῶντα μηδενὸς ἐπιβῆναι ἀξιώματος on Constantine Strategopulus) that at the time of the incident Constantine Strategopulus was no more among the living. On Constantine Strategopulus, cf. Pachymeres, Bonn ed., I, p. 24, 6–10; pp. 64, 17 – 65, 4.

[122] On Irene Palaeologina and Constantine Palaeologus Porphyrogenitus (son of Michael VIII Palaeologus), cf. Papadopulos, *Genealogie der Palaiologen*, p. 23 (under no. 37).

[123] George Pachymeres (Bonn ed., II, p. 156, 3–6) clearly stated that Constantine Maurozomes was a friend of the elder Strategopulina and that he was said to be her lover. Lampros, in Νέος Ἑλλ., 4, p. 159, misinterpreted the statement of Pachymeres and wrongly related Constantine Maurozomes to Irene Palaeologina (wife of Constantine Palaeologus Porphyrogenitus) as her lover. Bees, in *JIAN*, 13, p. 20, followed Lampros' error and compounded it by mistakenly considering Constantine Palaeologus to have been a son of the co-Emperor Michael IX (1294 or 1295–1320), instead of a son of Emperor Michael VIII Palaeologus and brother of Emperor Andronicus II Palaeologus. As a result of this mistake and its chronological implications, Bees, *loc. cit.*, wrongly denied the possibility of identifying the Constantine Maurozomes mentioned by Pachymeres with Constantinus Maurozumes, the sponsor of MS Roe 22.

λόγω; 61ᵛ lines 1–21; 62ʳ–67ᵛ line 11; 68ʳ–69ʳ line 21 καλοῦνται; 70ʳ–70ᵛ; 72ʳ–78ᵛ line 5; 78ᵛ line 10 εἰρήκαμεν – 79ᵛ line 4 ἄβελ; 80ʳ–81ᵛ; 82ᵛ–90ʳ line 14 ἐπήγαγεν; 90ᵛ line 16 αἱ παιδαγωγὸν – 94ʳ line 3; 94ᵛ–97ᵛ line 3 νικήσαντες; 98ᵛ–108ʳ; 109ᵛ–112ʳ line 26; 113ʳ–114ᵛ line 26 ἀπεσχοινισμένος; 115ʳ–115ᵛ line 15 θεοδώριτο(ς); 116ᵛ–118ᵛ line 1; 119ʳ–132ʳ; 133ʳ–173ᵛ; 174ᵛ; 175ᵛ–176ʳ line 16 ἐγκατέλιπες; 177ʳ–178ᵛ line 9 δώσομεν; 179ᵛ–186ᵛ line 7; 186ᵛ line 18 – 187ᵛ line 27 ἐκρίθη; 188ʳ–190ᵛ line 7 ἐπιστολὴν; 191ʳ–194ᵛ; 195ᵛ–201ᵛ line 13; 202ʳ– 210ᵛ line 8; 211ʳ–214ᵛ; 215ᵛ–227ᵛ line 30; 228ʳ line 6 κατὰ τὸ ἐνδεχόμενον – 257ᵛ line 21 γνωμικὸν; 258ʳ–259ᵛ line 19; 260ʳ–266ᵛ line 4 ἄν(θρωπ)ος; 267ʳ–268ʳ line 18 σωζόμενον; 268ᵛ–275ᵛ line 8; 276ʳ–287ᵛ line 8 μὲν; 288ᵛ–389ᵛ; 391ʳ–399ʳ line 17; 399ᵛ–454ʳ; 454ᵛ–460ᵛ text line 16 ὕποπτοι (on these pages, only the text was written by scribe A); 461ʳ–501ʳ; 502ʳ–534ᵛ line 10 γῆς; 535ʳ–550ʳ line 23; 550ᵛ–553ʳ; 554ʳ–560ᵛ line 8.

The appearance of script A (of Ionas) varies in the MS, depending on the mood of the scribe, the part of the volume in which the script appears, the quality of parchment, and the color of the ink (black or brownish). However, the shapes of characteristic letters are so similar throughout as to vouch for the identity of the scribe, even though sometimes, especially as a result of poorer quality parchment and brownish ink, the immediate optical impression of the writing in some portions of the volume is somewhat different. The most calligraphic script of A appears within the first part of the volume, i.e., within quires 1–36; I give a sample of this script on Plate **28**. The writing of Ionas in this part of the MS is very careful and pleasing. The lettering is slightly taller than in the rest of the volume, owing to the fact that the area of the written page is somewhat greater in height. At the very beginning the writing has a certain vertical buoyancy not encountered in the rest of the volume. The basic slant of Ionas' script is to the right. On Plate **29** we see a similarly calligraphic script of Ionas which is more compact vertically. On Plate **30** Ionas' script, as a result of poorer parchment, is less calligraphic; moreover, it does not have the usual slant to the right, but is rather upright; the lettering is somewhat roundish and more cursive. On Plate **31** a relaxed and more cursive variety of Ionas' script is represented. The writing still slants to the right, but the lettering tends to be roundish, without the angular discipline which may be observed in Ionas' calligraphic pages, especially on Plate **29**. It is interesting that on Plate **31** the three top lines of the page are in rather angular calligraphy similar to Plate **29**, but the remainder switches to the relaxed cursive script style. It is not surprising to find such a variety of Ionas' writing in this large volume, the production of which taxed the strength and endurance of this scribe.

Scribe B (cf. Plate **32**, and marginal additions on Plate **36**) wrote fols. 6ʳ lines 1–25 ταύτην; 12ᵛ lines 13–33; 14ʳ–14ᵛ line 15 ἀγνωσίαν; 19ʳ lines 5 μίαν – 15 ἔσχατον; 33ᵛ–34ʳ; 47ʳ lines 15 πρὸς – 33; 50ᵛ; 52ᵛ lines 11–34; 54ᵛ lines 5 πάλιν – 16 ἀξίωμα; 56ᵛ lines 22 μέγα – 33; 61ʳ lines 10 Διάκρινον – 33; 61ᵛ lines 22–33; 67ᵛ lines 12–33; 69ʳ line 21 διὰ τὸν – 69ᵛ; 71ᵛ; 79ᵛ lines 4 καὶ σεμνύνονται – 33; 82ʳ; 90ʳ line 14 ὅτι τῶ – 90ᵛ line 16 Ἀντίρρησις; 97ᵛ line 3 ζηνοβία – 98^r; 108^v–109^r; 112^r line 27 – 112^v; 114^v lines 26 τῆς τοῦ θεοῦ – 33; 115^v line 15 πρῶτος – 116^r; 118^v lines 2–33; 132^v; 174^r; 175^r; 176^r line 16 ὅτι – 176^v; 178^v line 9 καὶ τὴν ὁμοίαν – 179^r; 186^v lines 8–17; 187^v lines 27 ἀμφοτέρους – 34; 190^v lines 7 τοῦ – 33; 195^r; 201^v lines 14–33; 210^v lines 9–33; 215^r; 257^v lines 21 αὐθαίρετος – 33; 259^v lines 20–33; 266^v lines 4 τὸ συναμφότερον – 33; 268^r lines 18 Εἰ τοίνυν – 33; 275^v lines 9–33; 287^v line 8 ἡμᾶς – 288^r; only marginal additions on fols. 454^v–461^v.

Scribe C (cf. Plate **33**) wrote fols. 71^r; 78^v lines 6–10 πρὸς δ' οἷς; 94^r lines 4–33.

Scribe D (cf. Plate **38a**) wrote fols. 227^v line 31 – 228^r line 6 νοεῖται.

Scribe E (cf. Plate **34**) wrote fol. 390^r–390^v.

Scribe F (cf. Plate **35**) wrote fol. 399^r lines 18–33 and the marginal note opposite lines 26–28 which concerns the authorship of a scholium included in the text.

Scribe G (cf. text lines on Plate **36**) wrote fol. 460^v text lines 16 ἤγουν – 33.

Scribe H (cf. Plate **37**, lines 1–6) wrote fol. 501^v lines 1–6 περιεργάζεσθαι τὰ.

Scribe J (cf. Plate **37**, lines 6–33) wrote fol. 501^v line 6 σεσιωπημένα – 33.

Scribe K (cf. Plate **38b**) wrote fol. 534^v lines 10 ἀπαύγασμα – 33.

Scribe L (cf. Plate **39**) wrote fols. 550^r lines 24–33; 553^v.

For scribe A, the monk Ionas, the chief copyist of this MS, we give four samples, in order to represent the whole variety of his handwriting (cf. my remarks above). On Plate **28** we reproduce folio 146^v, containing a passage from Nicetas Choniates, Panoplia dogmatica (Thesaurus orthodoxiae), Book VI, chaps. 5–8 (ed. Migne, Patr. Gr., 140, col. 13 A 1 – D 14). This is a specimen of Ionas' very calligraphic and somewhat exuberant script. On Plate **29** we reproduce folio 440^v, containing a passage from Nicetas Choniates, History (Post urbem captam: ed. van Dieten, *Nicetae Choniatae Historia*, pp. 614, 3–7; 615, 11–15; 615, 16 – 616, 52; the variants of MS Roe 22 and its divergent text passages are reported in van Dieten's critical apparatus with the symbol O for this MS; for earlier editions, cf. *Nicetae Choniatae Historia*, Bonn ed. [1835], pp. 811, 6–11; 14–19; 811, 21 – 813, 18; or Migne, Patr. Gr., 139, cols. 1001 A 13 – B 3; B 7–13; 1001 C 1 – 1004 B 10). This fol. 440^v is the final page of the quire νε'; the quire mark νε which is written in the lower right-hand corner of this page was cut off in the reproduction. Plate **29** is a sample of Ionas' calligraphic, but more compact, writing. On Plate **30** we reproduce folio 290^v, containing a passage from Nicetas Choniates, Panoplia dogmatica (Thesaurus orthodoxiae), Book XX, chaps. 5–7 (ed. Migne, Patr. Gr., 140, cols. 109 B 6 – 112 B 4). This is a sample of Ionas' less calligraphic, upright (not slanted), roundish lettering. On Plate **31** we reproduce folio 507^r, containing a passage from St. Anastasius Sinaita, Viae dux, chap. 7 (ed. Migne, Patr. Gr., 89, cols. 117 C 12 – 120 A 15; 120 B 4 – D 9). This specimen shows Ionas' roundish and more cursive writing.

For scribe B, on Plate **32** we reproduce folio 195^r, containing a passage from Nicetas Choniates, Panoplia dogmatica (Thesaurus orthodoxiae), Book IX, chaps. 28–31 (ed. Migne, Patr. Gr., 140, cols. 64 B 3 – 65 B 10).

I consider script B to show the "Planudean" style and to be influenced by the kind of writing which was cultivated in the last quarter of the 14th century in the Planudean scriptorium in Constantinople.[123a] One may confer some scripts represented in the famous Planudean MS Laurentianus 32, 16: cf. Turyn, *DGMItaly*, II, pls. 16, 18–23; also cf. below, Plate **41**. I have invoked the Planudean style of script B as a basis for the assumption that this MS was produced in Constantinople (see above). A very small lettering of script B can be seen in the marginal scholia reproduced on Plate **36**.

For scribe C, on Plate **33** we reproduce folio 71^r, containing a passage from NICETAS CHONIATES, PANOPLIA DOGMATICA (THESAURUS ORTHODOXIAE), Book IV, chap. 4 (unpublished in Greek; in Latin translation, ed. Migne, Patr. Gr., 139, cols. 1250 C 15 – 1252 A 6).

For scribe D, on Plate **38a** we reproduce fols. 227^v lines 31–33 and 228^r lines 1–6 νοεῖται, containing a passage from NICETAS CHONIATES, PANOPLIA DOGMATICA (THESAURUS ORTHODOXIAE), Book XIII (unpublished). Scribe D obviously was a friend or amanuensis of Ionas and was permitted to write just a few lines.

For scribe E, on Plate **34** we reproduce folio 390^v, containing a passage from NICETAS CHONIATES, PANOPLIA DOGMATICA (THESAURUS ORTHODOXIAE), Book XXIV (ed. Migne, Patr. Gr., 140, cols. 181 A 4 – D 5).[124]

For scribe F, on Plate **35** we reproduce the lower part of folio 399^r (lines 18–33), containing a passage from NICETAS CHONIATES, PANOPLIA DOGMATICA (THESAURUS ORTHODOXIAE), Book XXV (ed. Migne, Patr. Gr., 140, cols. 217 B 13–14; C 10 – D 7; 220 A 4–10; on lines 19–26, the excerpt quoted is from St. Gregory of Nazianzus, Oratio 29: ed. Migne, Patr. Gr., 36, col. 97 A 8–10, B 10 – C 2), with a scholium on lines 26–30 of Elias of Crete on the preceding passage of Gregory of Nazianzus (the pertinent passage of the scholium of Elias of Crete, which must have been somewhat more explicit in its original form than it appears here, can be found in Latin translation in I. Levvenklaivs, *Opervm Gregorii Nazianzeni tomi tres*, I [Basel, 1571], p. 131 B 24–26). The authorship of the scholium is explicitly marked here in the marginal note. The lines reproduced on this plate are the only ones written by this scribe in the MS.

For scribe G, on Plate **36** we reproduce the lower part of folio 460^v, with text lines 16–33, written from text line 16 ἤγουν through the end of the page text by scribe G, with marginal additions written by scribe B. The text portion reproduced contains a passage from MICHAEL ATTALEIATES, LAW TREATISE (Πόνημα), titles ΚΕ΄, δ΄ – ΚΖ΄, β΄ (ed. Zepos, *Jus*, VII, pp. 446, 34 – 447, 28).

[123a] This is the kind of writing which Herbert Hunger characterized with his terms "Fettaugenstil" or "Fettaugen-Mode": cf. H. Hunger, "Antikes und mittelalterliches Buch- und Schriftwesen," in *Geschichte der Textüberlieferung der antiken und mittelalterlichen Literatur*, I (Zurich [1961]), pp. 101 f., 103 fig. 22; *idem*, "Die sogenannte Fettaugen-Mode in griechischen Handschriften des 13. und 14. Jahrhunderts," *ByzF*, 4 (1972), pp. 105–13. Now cf. also *idem*, "Archaisierende Minuskel und Gebrauchsschrift zur Blütezeit der Fettaugenmode," in *Paléographie grecque et byzantine*, pp. 283–85.

[124] Also ed. Th. L. F. Tafel, *Annae Comnenae supplementa historiam ecclesiasticam Graecorum seculi XI et XII spectantia. Accedunt Acta synodi Constantinopolitanae in Soterichi Panteugoni dogmata de Christi crucifixi sacrificio habitae* (Progr. Tübingen [1832]), pp. 21, 1 – 22, 12.

The marginal additions written by scribe B are excerpts from the Collectio Constitutionum Ecclesiasticarum Tripartita (ed. G. Voellus and H. Ivstellus, *Bibliotheca ivris canonici veteris*, II [Paris, 1661], p. 1339, 6–8; pp. 1339, 35 – 1340, 16; p. 1340, 34–39; p. 1341, 8–9; pp. 1340, 40 – 1341, 2; or ed. Migne, Patr. Gr., 138, col. 1304 A 1–2; B 11 – D 2; col. 1305 A 6–11; B 11–12; A 12 – B 4).

For scribes H and J, on Plate **37** we reproduce folio 501ᵛ, written jointly by these scribes. On this page, lines 1–6 περιεργάζεσθαι τὰ were written by scribe H; lines 6 σεσιωπημένα – 33 (through the end of the page) were written by scribe J. The page reproduced contains a passage from St. Anastasius Sinaita, Viae dux, chap. 4 (ed. Migne, Patr. Gr., 89, cols. 93 C 4 – 96 D 13). The script of these two scribes appears in the MS on this page only.

For scribe K, on Plate **38b** we reproduce from folio 534ᵛ lines 15–33, which contain a passage from St. Anastasius Sinaita, Viae dux, chap. 13 (ed. Migne, Patr. Gr., 89, cols. 240 C 12 – 241 B 9). The upper part of the page from line 1 through the middle of line 10 γῆς was written by Ionas. However, the rest of the page from the middle of line 10 ἀπαύγασμα through the end of the page was written by scribe K, who is represented in the MS only in the major part of folio 534ᵛ. In view of the space available on this plate, I can accommodate on Plate **38b** the part of the page beginning with line 15.

For scribe L, on Plate **39** we reproduce folio 553ᵛ, containing a passage from St. Sophronius, patriarch of Jerusalem, Synodal Epistle (ed. Migne, Patr. Gr., 87, 3, cols. 3160 D 6 – 3161 C 15).

This MS once belonged to Metrophanes III, patriarch of Constantinople (1565–1572 and 1579–1580), and then to the monastery of the Holy Trinity τοῦ ᾽Εσόπτρου in Chalce near Constantinople; the typical ownership entry of the monastery (in political verses) and the dodecasyllabic invocation of Metrophanes[125] appear on fol. 560ᵛ. In the catalogue of Metrophanes' MSS subsequently owned by the Chalce monastery, compiled in 1572, two MSS of Panoplia dogmatica were listed (cf. Legrand, *Notice biographique sur Jean et Théodose Zygomalas*, p. 210 lines 3–4): Δογματικαὶ πανοπλίαι δύο· ἡ μὲν ἐν μεμβράναις, μῆκος πρῶτον, ἡ δὲ βαμβίκινος. The first MS, a parchment MS of large size, should be identified with the present MS Roe 22 (the second MS mentioned was listed as a bombycine MS, presumably of smaller or intermediate size, and is obviously a different MS).[126]

MS Roe 22 was among the MSS brought from the Levant by Sir Thomas Roe and presented by him to the Bodleian Library in 1628. His characteristic entry is written on fol. IVᵛ.[127]

On this MS, cf. Coxe, I, cols. 480–82; *Summary Catalogue*, II,1, p. 11 (under S.C. 268); Barbour, in *Greek Manuscripts in the Bodleian Library*, p. 22 (under no. 25); Vogel–Gardt-

---

[125] Cf. above, p. 24.

[126] Some difficulty underlies this identification. First of all, we do not know whether the famous Panoplia dogmatica of Euthymius Zigabenus is not meant in the catalogue of Metrophanes' MSS. There is a possibility that the first MS listed there is identical with Roe 22, and that the second one may be a MS of Euthymius Zigabenus' Panoplia. A more serious difficulty appears in the fact that MS Roe 22 itself does not carry a title of Δογματικὴ πανοπλία. (Only cod. Vatic. graec. 680 does have the title Δογματικὴ πανοπλία τοῦ Χωνιάτου: cf. van Dieten, *Zur Überlieferung und Veröffentlichung*, p. 1.) The cataloger of the Metrophanes MSS may have been an intelligent scholar who read attentively the prologue of Nicetas Choniates' religious work at the beginning of our MS and whose eyes were caught by the reference in the prologue to the δογματικὴ πανοπλία (of Euthymius Zigabenus): cf. MS Roe 22, fol. 1ᵛ, lines 29/30 (ed. van Dieten, *op. cit.*, p. 58 line 25). The cataloger may have perceptively applied these words to the present MS as a convenient title or reference.

[127] On Roe's typical donation entry in this MS and on the Roe MSS in the Bodleian Library. cf. above, p. 25.

hausen, p. 219; Migne, Patr. Gr., 139, cols. 1037–40 (preface to Nicetas Choniates, fragment De statuis Constantinopolitanis, repr. from F. Wilken, *Nicetae Acominati Choniatae Narratio de statuis antiquis, quas Franci post captam anno 1204 Constantinopolin destruxerunt. Ex codice Bodlejano emendatius edita* [Leipzig, 1830], pp. III–VI); A. Heisenberg, *Zu den armenisch-byzantinischen Beziehungen am Anfang des 13. Jahrhunderts*, SBMünch, Philos.-philol. und hist.Kl., 1929, Heft 6 (Munich, 1929), pp. 10ff. (symbol B for this MS); G. Moravcsik, *Byzantinoturcica*, 2nd ed., I, Berliner byzantinistische Arbeiten, 10 (Berlin, 1958), p. 448; M. E. Colonna, *Gli storici bizantini dal IV al XV secolo*, I. *Storici profani* (Naples [1956]), p. 90; J. A. J. van Dieten, "Noch einmal über Niketas Choniates," *BZ*, 57 (1964), pp. 304, 314–21 (symbol O for this MS); J. van Dieten, "Zur Überlieferung der Panoplia Dogmatike des Niketas Choniates. Codex Parisiensis Graecus 1234," in *Polychronion. Festschrift Franz Dölger zum 75. Geburtstag* (Heidelberg, 1966), pp. 166–80, especially pp. 166 note 1, 167 note 4, 169f. (symbol R for this MS); van Dieten, *Zur Überlieferung und Veröffentlichung*, pp. 8–13, *passim* (symbol R for this MS); *idem, Niketas Choniates. Erläuterungen zu den Reden und Briefen nebst einer Biographie*, Supplementa Byzantina, 2 (Berlin–New York, 1971), pp. 43 note 53, 44f., 110ff., 114, 181–83 (symbol O for this MS); I. A. van Dieten, *Nicetae Choniatae orationes et epistulae*, CFHB, III, Series Berolinensis (Berlin–New York, 1972), p. XVI (symbol O for this MS); *idem, Nicetae Choniatae Historia*, pp. XXV–XXVII, LVII, LXXXIV–LXXXVI, XCV–CIII (symbol O for this MS).

Plate 40: A.D. 1289/1290.

Oxford, Bodleian Library, ms Laud Greek 40. Bombycine, 26 × 17 cm., VII (modern flyleaves) + 308 fols., 29 lines to a page. Contents: (fols. 1r–207v) Antiochus, monk of the Laura of St. Sabas, Pandectes Sacrae Scripturae (incomplete at the beginning), and Exomologesis; (fols. 208r–308r) Michael Glycas, Capitula in Sacrae Scripturae dubia (only 14 epistles). The MS was written by Macarius and completed in A.M. 6798 = A.D. 1289/1290, according to the subscription (partially cryptographic) on fol. 308r (Pl. **105b**):

† τῶ συντελεστῇ τῶν καλῶν ϑ(ε)ῶ χάρις:– +++ |

† τὸν δακτύλοις γράψαντα τὸν κεκτημένον·
τὸν ἀναγινώσκοντα | μετ εὐλαβείας,
φύλαττε τοὺς τρεῖς ἢ τριᾶς τρι|σολβίως:– |

† ἐτελειώϑ(η) ἡ παροῦσα βίβλος ἐν ἔτει ͵ϛψϙη ἰν(δικτιῶνος) γ· καὶ οἱ | ἐντυγχάνοντες ταύτῃ, εὔχεσϑέ μοι διὰ τὸν κ(ύριο)ν ὅπως λάβω | λύσην ἀπλέτων ἀμπλακημάτων:–|

† βϧꝉ.]ωλχηλβαβψϛ꙼ᴈϑτϑνψꝩωχνψϛῦλνψꝩϑξꝩν: | υꝩᴧἐξᴧχκϑνψοꝩ-ξλνλωψᴧχꝫϑπϑᴈꝩᴧχ +++

The cryptographic part of the subscription is to be understood[128] as follows: Ἡἱꝅ.]σοῦ[129] βοήϑη τῶ γράψαντι σὺν τῶ ἔχοντι ἀμίν: χὶρ ἐμοῦ παντλίμονος τοῦ Μακαρίου. On the first iambic line often used by scribes in the conclusion of a manuscript, cf. below, p. 122. On the dodecasyllables τὸν δακτύλοις – τρισολβίως, used frequently as a commonplace of subscriptions, cf. Turyn,

---

[128] On this well-known cryptographic alphabet, cf. E. Thompson and S. P. Lampros, trans., Ἐγχειρίδιον ἑλληνικῆς καὶ λατινικῆς παλαιογραφίας, in Βιβλιοϑήκη Μαρασλῆ (Athens, 1903), p. 157; Gardthausen, *Griechische Palaeographie*, II, p. 311; R. Devreesse, *Introduction à l'étude des manuscrits grecs* (Paris, 1954), p. 44; L. Polites, Ὁδηγὸς καταλόγου χειρογράφων, in Γενικὸν Συμβούλιον Βιβλιοϑηκῶν τῆς Ἑλλάδος, 17 (Athens, 1961), pp. 40f.; A. Sigalas, Ἱστορία τῆς ἑλληνικῆς γραφῆς, 2nd ed., in Βυζαντινὰ κείμενα καὶ μελέται, 12 (Thessalonica, 1974), pp. 332f.

[129] It means Ἰησοῦ.

Codices, p. 100; *idem, DGMItaly*, I, pp. 215, 58/59, 102, 127, 260. The colophon χὶρ – Μακαρίου is a dodecasyllable.

As a sample of the handwriting of Macarius, on Plate **40** we reproduce folio 113ʳ, containing a passage from ANTIOCHUS, MONK OF THE LAURA OF ST. SABAS, PANDECTES SACRAE SCRIPTURAE, chap. 81 (ed. Migne, Patr. Gr., 89, col. 1677 B 10 – D 8).

This MS once belonged to Archbishop William Laud (1573–1645), who acquired it in 1635 (cf. the note on fol. VIIᵛ facing fol. 1ʳ); it was in the group of MSS donated by him to the Bodleian Library in 1636. On William Laud and his MSS in the Bodleian Library, cf. above, p. 47.

On this MS, cf. Coxe, I, cols. 525f.; *Summary Catalogue*, II,1, p. 32 (under S.C. 733); I, p. 131; Vogel–Gardthausen, p. 273.

Plates 41 and 42: *circa* A.D. 1290.

Edinburgh, National Library of Scotland, ms Advocates' 18.7.15.
Bombycine, 168 × 125 mm., 126 fols. Contents: (fols. 1ʳ–54ʳ) Cleomedes, Circular Theory of the Stars; (fol. 54ᵛ) a note on the calendar reform of Julius Caesar; (fols. 55ʳ–72ʳ, 73ʳ–126ʳ) Aratus, Phaenomena, with the Planudean collection of subsidiary texts and scholia;[130] (fol. 72ᵛ) various lists of the months. The MS carries the following note on a lunar eclipse which took place on the night of 21/22 August A.M. 6798 = A.D. 1290 (fol. 54ᵛ – Pl. **105c**):

+ τῷ ͵ϛψϟη ἔτει τῇ κα αὐγούστου νυκτὸ(ς) εἰς κβ, γέγονεν ἔκλειψις σελήνης | μ(ε)τ(ὰ) τὸ μεσονύκτιον μέχρι πρωΐας. This eclipse of 22 August 1290 is indeed confirmed to have occurred.[131] The MS was written mainly by scribe A, who was identical with Maximus Planudes, and to a lesser extent by scribe B, who was obviously an amanuensis of Maximus Planudes. Scribe A, i.e., Maximus Planudes, wrote fols. 1ʳ–1ᵛ, 8ʳ–8ᵛ, 17ʳ–126ʳ. Scribe B wrote fols. 2ʳ–7ᵛ and 9ʳ–16ᵛ.

The original quire composition of this MS cannot be checked, because in the process of binding many leaves, especially in the initial two quires, were repaired along the inner edge. However, the original existence of the leaves written by scribe B within this volume at the time when it was written is vouched by the fact that on some B-written folios there are notes written by scribe A, i.e., by Planudes himself, e.g., on fols. 4ᵛ (right margin), 14ᵛ (left margin), 15ᵛ (upper margin).

The identification of scribe A with Maximus Planudes is easily confirmed by a comparison of the A script exemplified on Plate **41** with published samples of MS Venice Greco 481 (colloc. 863), subscribed by Maximus Planu-

---

[130] On the Planudean collection of scholia on Aratus, cf. J. Martin, *Histoire du texte des Phénomènes d'Aratos*, Etudes et Commentaires, XXII (Paris, 1956), pp. 289–91 and *passim*. The peculiar scholium of Planudes on *Arat. Phaen.* 96ff. (*ibid.*, p. 290) appears in the Edinburgh MS on fol. 80ʳ.

[131] Cf. Th. v. Oppolzer, *Canon der Finsternisse*, DenkWien, Math.-naturwiss.Cl., LII (Vienna, 1887), p. 363 (under no. 3867); Grumel, *Chronologie*, p. 467. According to v. Oppolzer, *loc. cit.*, the lunar eclipse in question began at 2ʰ8ᵐ Greenwich time and lasted (2 × 74ᵐ =) 148ᵐ. If Planudes was observing the eclipse in Constantinople (which is most likely), then this eclipse lasted there (since Constantinople lies 29° east of Greenwich, which accounts for a time difference of 29 × 4ᵐ = 116ᵐ) from 2ʰ8ᵐ + 116ᵐ = 4ʰ4ᵐ local time until 4ʰ4ᵐ + 148ᵐ = 6ʰ32ᵐ local time. This accords with Planudes' statement that the lunar eclipse began (scil., in Constantinople) during the night after midnight and lasted until the morning.

des in A.D. 1299 (before this date was corrected by him): cf. Turyn, *DGMItaly*, I, pp. 90–96; II, pls. 71 (from the Planudean Anthology), 72 (from Nonnus, Paraphrase of the Gospel of John); cf. also K. Preisendanz, *Zur Griechischen Anthologie*, Beilage zum Jahresbericht des Grossherzoglichen Gymnasiums zu Heidelberg 1910 (Progr. Leipzig, 1910), pl. II; E. Mioni, in T. Gasparrini Leporace and E. Mioni, *Cento codici bessarionei. Catalogo di mostra*, Biblioteca Nazionale Marciana – Venezia, V Centenario della fondazione 1468–1968 (Venice, 1968), pl. 40.[132] We can also compare specimens from other MSS written (partially or entirely) in the handwriting of Planudes: cf. Turyn, *DGMItaly*, II, pls. 16 (Laur. 32, 16: A.D. 1280), 57 (Ambros. & 157 sup.: about A.D. 1292–1293), 60 (Ambros. C 126 inf.: about A.D. 1294–1295); A. Cameron, *Porphyrius the Charioteer* (Oxford, 1973), fig. 11 (Laur. 32, 16: from a section written after A.D. 1283, part of fol. 383^r, on a reduced scale). The calligraphic script of Planudes in MS Edinburgh Adv.18.7.15 points to the mature period of Planudes and allows us to surmise that this MS (or at least its Cleomedes part) was written by Planudes shortly before (or shortly after) the lunar eclipse recorded by him on fol. 54^v occurred. This is why I date this MS to about A.D. 1290. The script of Planudes in the Edinburgh MS especially resembles his handwriting in Ambrosianus & 157 sup. and in his parts of Ambrosianus C 126 inf.

Scribe B, as I pointed out above, played a modest role in the writing of this MS. We may presume that he belonged to the entourage of Maximus Planudes. I am inclined to identify his handwriting (cf. Pl. **42**) with that of scribe A of the famous Planudean MS Laurentianus 32, 16 of A.D. 1280, represented in Turyn, *DGMItaly*, II, pl. 17 (cf. I, p. 34, with the data on other published specimens of that scribe). If this identification is correct, it means that scribe B of the Edinburgh MS belonged to the Planudean scriptorium already in A.D. 1280, some ten years before the Edinburgh MS was produced.

As I observed before,[133] the Aratus part of this MS represents Planudes' own autographic edition of Aratus. Its most striking features are Planudes' famous interpolations of the poetic text of Aratus which he wrote on fols. 98^r–99^v as substitutions for the original text passages of Aratus (vv. 481–96, 501–6, 515–24). Planudes either erased the original lines (on fol. 98^r) or crossed them out (on fols. 98^v–99^v).[134] Cf. the description of this MS by I. C. Cunningham, "Greek Manuscripts in the National Library of Scotland," *Scriptorium*, 24 (1970), pp. 367f., and pl. 24 (= fols. 98^v–99^r) which shows most of the interpolations just mentioned. On the Planudean recension of

---

[132] The specimen from Venice Greco 481, fol. 20^r, reproduced by E. Mioni, *Introduzione alla paleografia greca*, Università di Padova, Studi Bizantini e Neogreci, 5 (Padua, 1973), pl. XXI (cf. p. 140), represents not the handwriting of Planudes but that of scribe B of the Planudean Anthology (cf. Turyn, *DGMItaly*, I, p. 92; II, pl. 73).

[133] Cf. Turyn, *DGMItaly*, I, pp. XVI/XVII. The handwriting of Maximus Planudes in the Edinburgh MS of Aratus was recognized also by J. Martin, *Scholia in Aratvm vetera*, Teubner (Stuttgart, 1974), p. VII.

[134] The genuine passages of Aratus and the interpolated passages of Planudes intended as substitutions are conveniently printed in Martin, *Histoire du texte*, pp. 295–99.

Aratus and the Planudean interpolations in Aratus, there exists ample scholarly literature.[135] After Planudes, within the framework of Palaeologan philology, Demetrius Triclinius is known to have dealt with the Planudean edition of Aratus.[136] It is then of considerable interest that in this Edinburgh MS, on fol. 105^r (top), above the line Arat. Phaen. 669, there is a short scholium ὅτι ἐξόπισθεν ἀνατέλλ(ει). It was added later in a handwriting which looks like that of Demetrius Triclinius.[137] If this is so, it means that later the MS probably came into the possession of Demetrius Triclinius and was used by him as a basis for his own work on Aratus.

The importance of the Aratus part of this MS as the authentic exemplar of the Planudean edition of Aratus (both of the text and of the scholia) is obvious. The whole volume was evidently written in Constantinople where Planudes resided at that time. The Cleomedes part of this MS should be examined for the purpose of finding out whether there are any peculiar Planudean interpolations.

In order to show a sample of handwriting A, i.e., of Maximus Planudes, from this MS, on Plate **41** we reproduce folio 52^v, containing a passage from CLEOMEDES, CIRCULAR THEORY OF THE STARS, Book II, chap. 6, pp. 121–23 Balforeus (ed. H. Ziegler, *Cleomedis de motu circulari corporum caelestium libri duo*, Teubner [1891], pp. 218, 26 – 220, 26). For another published specimen of Planudes' handwriting from this MS, cf. Cunningham, *op. cit.*, pl. 24.

In order to show a sample of script B in this MS, on Plate **42** we reproduce folio 12^v, containing a passage from CLEOMEDES, CIRCULAR THEORY OF THE STARS, Book I, chap. 7, pp. 35–36 Balforeus (ed. Ziegler, pp. 64, 16 – 66, 21). For a sample of the same handwriting from MS Florence Laur. 32, 16 (of A.D. 1280), cf. Turyn, *DGMItaly*, II, pl. 17 (cf. my remark above on the presumable identity of the two scripts).

In the 15th century this Edinburgh MS was in Florence, since it was transcribed there in Laurentianus 28, 37 by Ioannes Thettalus Scutariotes in 1465.[138]

The MS was formerly owned by the Faculty of Advocates in Edinburgh and, along with a considerable part of the Advocates' library, became the property of the National Library of Scotland in 1925. Cf. H. Schenkl, *Bibliotheca patrum latinorum Britannica. VII.*, SBWien, Philos.-hist.Cl., 133,7 (1896), p. 8 (under no. 3038).

On this MS, cf. Cunningham, *op. cit.*, pp. 367f., pl. 24; Turyn, *DGMItaly*, I, p. XVII; Martin, *Scholia in Aratvm vetera*, pp. VIIf. (symbol E).

[135] Cf. E. Maass, *Arati Phaenomena* (Berlin, 1893; repr. as 2nd ed., 1955), pp. XVIIf.; C. Wendel, "Planudes, Maximos," in *RE*, XX, col. 2221, § 27; Martin, *Histoire du texte*, pp. 247–55, 295–99; L. D. Reynolds and N. G. Wilson, *Scribes and Scholars. A Guide to the Transmission of Greek and Latin Literature*, 2nd ed. (Oxford [1974]), pp. 66, 224; Martin, *Scholia in Aratvm vetera*, pp. VIIf.

[136] Cf. Martin, *Histoire du texte*, pp. 250–53 and *passim; idem, Scholia in Aratvm vetera*, pp. XXIX–XXXIII. On Demetrius Triclinius' interest in astronomy, cf. A. Wasserstein, "An Unpublished Treatise by Demetrius Triclinius on Lunar Theory," *JÖBG*, 16 (1967), pp. 153–74.

[137] For facsimiles of Demetrius Triclinius' handwriting which can be compared for the identification of the script, cf. below, Pls. **49, 110a**; Turyn, *DGMItaly*, II, pls. 96–99, 237*d*, 237*e*; for a list of other published facsimiles of Triclinius, cf. *ibid.*, I, p. 126. Now cf. also D. Harlfinger, "Zu griechischen Kopisten und Schriftstilen des 15. und 16. Jahrhunderts," in *Paléographie grecque et byzantine*, pp. 333, 347 fig. 8.

[138] Cf. Martin, *Histoire du texte*, pp. 247f.; *idem, Scholia in Aratvm vetera*, p. VIII; Vogel–Gardthausen, p. 198. On Ioannes Scutariotes, now cf. also D. Harlfinger, *Specimina griechischer Kopisten der Renaissance*, I (Berlin, 1974), pp. 34f. (no. 76), pl. 76; *idem*, "Zu griechischen Kopisten und Schriftstilen," pp. 339, 358 figs. 30 and 31.

Plate 43: A.D. 1291/1292.

London, British Museum, ms Burney 21. Bombycine, 34 × 25 cm., 258 fols., 24 lines to a page. Contents: Four Gospels, adapted for liturgical use. Elaborately ornamented headpieces in several colors precede each Gospel (on fols. 9ʳ, 76ʳ, 121ʳ, 197ʳ). The MS has suffered considerably from humidity. It was written by the well-known scribe of New Testament MSS, Theodorus Hagiopetrites,[139] at the expense of the monk Gerasimus, grand sceuophylax of the monastery τοῦ Φιλοκάλου (situated in Thessalonica), and concluded in A.M. 6800 = A.D. 1291/1292, according to the subscription on fol. 258ʳ (Pl. **107a**):

† ἐτελειώϑ(η) σὺν ϑ(ε)ῶ ἀγ(ίῳ) τὸ παρὸν ϑεῖον καὶ ἱερὸν τετραευά(γγελον or -γγέλιον) μετὰ τοῦ πρα|ξαπο(στόλου), μετὰ πά(σ)ης αὐτῶν ἀκολουϑ(ίας), διὰ χειρὸ(ς) κἀμοῦ τοῦ ταπεινοῦ | Θεοδ(ώ)ρ(ου) τοῦ Ἁγιωπετρίτ(ου) τάχα καὶ καλλιγρά(φ)ου· διὰ συνδρομῆς δὲ καὶ ἐξόδ(ου) | καὶ πόϑ(ου) πολλοῦ, τοῦ τιμιωτ(ά)τ(ου) ἐν μοναχοῖς, καὶ μ(ε)γ(ά)λ(ου) σκευοφύλακο(ς) μο(νῆς) τοῦ | Φιλοκάλ(ου)[140] κ(υρο)ῦ Γερασίμου· καὶ οἱ ἀναγινώσκοντες ταῦτα τὰ ἱερὰ | βιβλία, εὔχεσϑε ὑπ(ὲ)ρ τοῦ πόϑ(ῳ) πολλῶ κτησαμένου· κἀμοῦ δὲ τοῦ γρά|ψαντο(ς), λύσιν πολλῶν ἁμαρτημάτων:–:–:– |

    † Θ(εὸ)ν ἱλεούμενος τίμιε π(άτ)ερ,
       Θεοδώρου μέμνησο τοῦ | καλλιγρά(φ)ου +++ |[141]

† Ἔτους ͵ϛῶ· (σελήνης) κύ(κλος) ιζ (ἡλίου) κύ(κλος) κδ νομικ(ὸν) φάσκ(α) ἀπ(ριλλίου) ε ἡμ(έ)ρ(ᾳ) ζ· χρ(ιστιανῶν) πάσχ(α) ἀπ(ριλλίου) ϛ | ἡ ἀπ(όκρεως) φε(β)ρ(ουαρίου) ι +[142]

All the calendar data indicated above in the dated part of the subscription agree. The year A.M. 6800 = A.D. 1291/1292 was lunar year 17 and solar year 24.[143] The liturgical dates listed for the early part of A.D. 1292, which

---

[139] On MSS written by Theodorus Hagiopetrites, cf. Gregory, I, p. 146; von Soden, I,2, pp. 781–93; Vogel–Gardthausen, pp. 135 f.; Clark, *Greek New Testament Manuscripts in America*, p. 18; Turyn, *Codices*, pp. 57 f.; L. Politis, "Die Handschriftensammlung des Klosters Zavorda und die neuaufgefundene Photios-Handschrift," *Philologus*, 105 (1961), p. 139 (on Zaborda MS written by Theodorus Hagiopetrites in A.D. 1307); N. A. Bees, Τὰ χειρόγραφα τῶν Μετεώρων, I (Athens, 1967), pp. 544–46 (on MS Meteora, Μονὴ Μεταμορφώσεως 545, written by him in A.D. 1296/1297); Belting, *Das illuminierte Buch*, pp. 8 f. Now cf. also L. Politis, "Quelques centres de copie monastiques du XIVᵉ siècle," in *Paléographie grecque et byzantine*, pp. 291 f.

[140] The words τοῦ | φιλοκά᷎ are written more heavily, in larger letters and darker ink than the rest. In the spot where φιλοκά᷎ is written there appears a slight horizontal rift in the paper, or rather a certain strain in the paper surface. However, there is no trace of an erasure, and the words τοῦ Φιλοκάλ(ου) must be considered absolutely authentic and written in the original process of writing. Perhaps they were written in the above-mentioned manner for a more emphatic appearance. I record this matter in view of the fact that the reference to the monastery of Philocales in this subscription provides us with a decisive clue for an approximate localization of Theodorus Hagiopetrites' activities as a scribe.

[141] I have arranged these two lines metrically as dodecasyllables. A similar wording of dodecasyllables in colophons of two other MSS written by Theodorus Hagiopetrites is noteworthy: cf. Bees, *op. cit.*, I, p. 545, pl. LXI (from MS Meteora, Μονὴ Μεταμορφώσεως 545); Turyn, *DGMItaly*, I, p. 100; II, pl. 233c (from MS Venice Greco I, 19).

[142] The dated part of this subscription was printed by Gardthausen, *Griechische Palaeographie*, II, p. 470.

[143] On solar and lunar cycles, their years indicated in subscriptions, and the method of computing them, cf. *ibid.*, pp. 468–72. The solar and lunar years corresponding to the years of the Byzantine era are conveniently tabulated *ibid.*, pp. 488 ff.; for A.M. 6800, cf. *ibid.*, p. 494. For finding solar and lunar years, one can also use the table in Grumel, *Chronologie*, pp. 266–77, which ends in an

was a leap year, are indicated correctly. The "legal Easter," i.e., the Easter limit, was on Saturday, 5 April 1292; Easter was on Sunday, 6 April 1292; the Sexagesima Sunday (κυριακὴ τῆς ἀπόκρεω) fell on Sunday, 10 February 1292.[144]

The monastery of Philocales is known to have existed in Thessalonica.[145] The fact that Theodorus Hagiopetrites was commissioned by a dignitary of that monastery to write this MS suggests that Theodorus was active as a copyist in an important cultural center of the Byzantine Empire, either in Thessalonica itself or in Constantinople.[146] In the invocation regarding Gerasimus, the idiom τοῦ κτησαμένου means not so much the owner of the MS as the person who commissioned and paid for the MS.[147] It is most peculiar that the subscription mentions that the MS contains the Four Gospels with the Praxapostolus (i.e., the Acts of the Apostles and the Epistles), for there is no trace of the Praxapostolus in the MS in its present state. Either Theodorus Hagiopetrites mentioned the Praxapostolus by some inadvertence or, if he did write it while producing this MS, the Praxapostolus somehow was detached, and we do not know what became of it.

On Plate **43** we reproduce folio 249^v, containing a passage from the GOSPEL OF ST. JOHN 20:22–29. This is a part of the εὐαγγέλιον ἑωθινὸν θ′, which comprises John 20:19–31 (cf. Gregory, I, p. 364). According to the liturgical note on fol. 249^r (in the upper margin), this Gospel lesson was used on four occasions: ἑωθ(ι)νὸν θ̄: καὶ τῇ μεγ(ά)λ(η) κυ(ριακῇ) ἑσπ(έ)ρ(ας): καὶ κυ(ριακῇ) τοῦ ἀντ(ι)πάσχα: καὶ κυ(ριακῇ) τῆς ῡστ(ῆς) (i.e., πεντηκοστῆς) εἰς τὸν ὄρθρον: καὶ εἰς τὸν ἅγ(ιον) ἀπο(στολον) Θωμᾶν (i.e., on 6 October). On the page reproduced, a liturgical note written in line 4, τέ(λος) ὄρθρ(ου) ῡστ(ῆς) (i.e., πεντηκοστῆς), means that this Gospel lesson when used at Matins of Pentecost ends at this point, because it comprises for this service only John 20:19–23 (cf. Gregory, I, p. 347). In line 13 there is a liturgical note, τέ(λος) μεγ(ά)λ(ης) κυρ(ιακῆς) ἑσπ(έ)ρ(ας), which means that this Gospel lesson when used at Vespers on Easter Sunday ends at this point, because the lesson appointed for this service comprises only John 20:19–25. On the extent of the lesson in question, cf. Εὐαγγέλιον (1880), pp. 1f.; Εὐαγγέλιον (1968), p. 14.

---

explicit form with A.M. 6400 on p. 277, although it can be used for the later years in accordance with the instruction on p. 277.

[144] For verification of all these data, cf. Grumel, *Chronologie*, p. 260 (in A.D. 1292, the Easter limit, i.e., the νομικὸν φάσκα, falls on 5 April and Easter on 6 April), p. 311, table XII (for lunar year 17 and solar year 24, the Easter limit falls on Saturday, 5 April, and Easter on 6 April), p. 312 table XIII (when Easter is on 6 April, the Sexagesima, ἡ κυριακὴ τῆς ἀπόκρεω, is in this leap year A.M. 6800 on 10 February).

[145] On the monastery τοῦ Φιλοκάλου and its location in Thessalonica, cf. Turyn, *Codices*, pp. 58–60; R. Janin, *Les églises et les monastères des grands centres byzantins* (Paris, 1975), pp. 418f. To the evidence adduced by me (*loc. cit.*), this reference should have been added: cf. L. Petit, *Actes de Xénophon*, Actes de l'Athos, I, *VizVrem*, 10, Suppl. 1 (1903; repr. Amsterdam, 1964), p. 64, no. VIII, line 104. Now cf. also P. Magdalino, "Some Additions and Corrections to the List of Byzantine Churches and Monasteries in Thessalonica," *REB*, 35 (1977), p. 282.

[146] Follieri, *Codices*, p. 62 and note 143, agrees that cod. Vaticanus graec. 644, written by Theodorus Hagiopetrites, was produced either in Thessalonica or, more likely, in Constantinople. Politis, "Quelques centres de copie monastiques," p. 291 note 2, decidedly places Theodorus Hagiopetrites in Constantinople.

[147] Cf. Krumbacher, Κτήτωρ, pp. 396f.

On the use of this Gospel lesson to its full extent (John 20:19–31) at Ἀντι-
πάσχα (Octave of Easter) and on the feast of St. Thomas the Apostle (6 October), cf. Gregory, I, pp. 345, 368.

For specimens of MS Burney 21 published before, cf. Forshall, *Catalogue*,
I,2, pl. [II] at the bottom; Scrivener, I, pl. VI (15) facing p. 145. For data
on other published samples of Theodorus Hagiopetrites' handwriting from
various MSS, cf. Turyn, *Codices*, pp. 60f. For specimens of Theodorus Hagiopetrites' handwriting published in recent years, cf. Turyn, *Codices*, pls. 34,
169; Follieri, *Codices*, pl. 41; Bees, *op. cit.*, I, pls. LX, LXI; Turyn, *DGM Italy*, II,
pls. 79, 233c. Now cf. also Politis, "Quelques centres de copie monastiques du
XIVᵉ siècle," pp. 291, 296 fig. 2. On Theodorus Hagiopetrites in general, now
cf. *PLP*, I (1976), p. 23, no. 249.

This MS was collated by Scrivener, *Full and Exact Collation*, with the
symbol r (cf. pp. li–liv: a description of MS Burney 21).

This MS must have originally belonged to the monastery of Philocales in Thessalonica. At
some later date, the monk Dositheus, son of the γραμματικός Demetrius of Thessalonica,
presented it to the archon Alexius, according to a very illiterate note written possibly in the
middle of the 14th century on fol. 8ᵛ: † Δήμητριοῦ τοῦ γραμματικοῦ, | τοῦ απε τι Θεσαλωνηκι
καλωγερὸς | μὰιγαλὼσκιμὸς Δοσῆθαίος | προς τὸν πρὸτὸν καλῶν αρ|κων Αλὰιξηὸν να μαι εμνη-|
μωναιεῆς. Forshall,[148] in his description of the MS, suggested an identification of the archon
Alexius, mentioned in the note, with Alexius Metochites who was cogovernor of Thessalonica
in 1349–1350.[149]

Early in the 18th century the MS was in the collection of Giovanni Saibante in Verona,[150]
whose library was inherited by Giulio Saibante.[151] Toward the end of the 18th century the
Saibante collection was dispersed.[152] This particular MS came into the possession of Charles
Burney (1757–1817).[153] After Burney's death, his whole library, including his MSS, was bought
by Parliament and deposited in the British Museum in 1818.[154]

On this MS, cf. Forshall, *Catalogue*, I,2, pp. 4f., pl. [II] at the bottom; Omont, "Notes,"
p. 349; Vogel–Gardthausen, p. 135 and note 6, p. 470 (addendum to p. 135 note 6); Scrivener,
I, p. 257 (under Evan. 571), pl. VI (15) facing p. 145; Gregory, I, p. 194 (under Vier Evangelien
484); Aland, I, p. 87 (under the Gregory–Aland number 484); von Soden, I,1, p. 175 (under
ε322).

Plate 44: A.D. 1294.

Oxford, Bodleian Library, ms Barocci 16. Parchment, 162 × 110 mm.,
v + 285 fols., 22 lines to a page. Fols. I–III are modern paper flyleaves; IV–V

---

[148] Cf. Forshall, *Catalogue*, I,2, p. 4.

[149] On the πρωτοσέβαστος Alexius Metochites, one of the two ἄρχοντες of Thessalonica in 1349–1350,
cf. John Cantacuzenus, History, IV.15–16, Bonn ed., III (1832), pp. 104, 9–11; 108, 11; 108, 22–23;
O. Tafrali, *Thessalonique au quatorzième siècle* (Paris, 1913), pp. 76, 159 note 3 (on p. 160), 249–52;
Papadopulos, *Genealogie der Palaiologen*, p. 76, no. 120; F. Dölger, *Byzantinische Diplomatik* (Ettal
[1956]), pp. 325–32; G. Ostrogorsky, *Geschichte des byzantinischen Staates*, 3rd ed. (Munich, 1963),
p. 430; Dölger, *Regesten*, V, p. 21, no. 2951.

[150] This MS was listed as Saibante Greek MS 1 in the list of Saibante Greek MSS published by
S. Maffei, *Verona illustrata*, pt. 3 (Verona, 1732), col. 242. (B. De Montfaucon, *Bibliotheca bibli-
othecarum manuscriptorum nova*, I [Paris, 1739], p. 490, used Maffei's list.) On the collection of
Giovanni Saibante and on numerous Saibante Greek MSS now in the Bodleian Library at Oxford,
cf. above, pp. 41f. Now cf. also E. M. Jeffreys, "The Greek Manuscripts of the Saibante Collection," in
Studia Codicologica, pp. 249–62 (pp. 251 f., under no. 1, on this MS).

[151] Cf. above, p. 41.   [152] Cf. above, p. 41.

[153] On Charles Burney, cf. above, p. 44.

[154] Cf. Forshall, *Catalogue*, I,2, pp. IIIf.

are preliminary parchment leaves of the main body of the MS; 284 is parchment back flyleaf of the main body; 285 is modern paper back flyleaf. Contents: (fols. 1ʳ–241ᵛ) St. John Climacus, Ladder of Paradise, and (fols. 241ᵛ–263ʳ) Liber ad pastorem; (fols. 263ʳ–279ᵛ) St. Basil the Great, Sermo asceticus et exhortatio de renuntiatione saeculi et de perfectione spirituali (ed. Migne, Patr. Gr., 31, cols. 625–48), and (fols. 280ʳ–282ᵛ) Sermo de ascetica disciplina, quomodo monachum ornari oporteat (ed. Migne, Patr. Gr., 31, cols. 648–52). The MS was concluded on 18 December A.M. 6803 = A.D. 1294, according to the subscription on fol. 283ʳ. The subscription was first so written that the scribe made a mistake in the year date in the second numeral letter. He, therefore, canceled the two numeral letters of the year date already written and, beginning in the next line, wrote anew the subscription with the correct year date and additional chronological data (fol. 283ʳ – Plate **107b**):

τελειώθη τὸ παρὸν βιβλίον εἰς | τὴν ῑη ἡμέραν τοῦ δικεμβρί|ου μηνὸ(ς)· ἔτους ⟦͵ϛψ⟧ |

ἐτελειώθη τὸ παρὸν βιβλίον εἰς | τὴν ῑη ἡμέραν τοῦ δικεμβρίου | μηνὸ(ς)· ἔτους ͵ϛῶγ ἰν(δικτιῶνος) η κύ(κλος) (σελήνης) ᾱ | κύ(κλος) (ἡλίου) κζ··¹⁵⁵

The subscription is followed by an obituary in the same handwriting, commemorating the scribe's mother who died on Friday, the 10th of the same month and year, i.e., 10 December A.M. 6803 = A.D. 1294 (it was eight days before this MS was concluded). Above the first subscription's first line, there is a repetition of almost the whole first line, scribbled by somebody else.

On Plate **44** we reproduce folios 168ᵛ–169ʳ, containing a passage from St. John Climacus, Ladder of Paradise, chap. 25 (ed. Migne, Patr. Gr., 88, cols. 996 C 1 – 997 A 14; ed. Trevisan, II, pp. 109, 16 – 113, 3). On the left-hand page, the red capitals projected to the left indicate that a text section begins in the preceding line. On the right-hand page, the projected red capital marks the beginning of a section.¹⁵⁶

The MS once belonged to Giacomo Barocci (d. before 1617) of Venice; in his collection it was MS Greco in Ottauo 11 (cf. *Indice Barocci*, fol. 39ʳ⁻ᵛ). On the Barocci collection of Greek MSS now in the Bodleian Library, cf. above, p. 28.

On this MS, cf. Coxe, I, col. 25; *Summary Catalogue*, II,1, p. 4 (under S.C. 16).

Plate 45: A.D. 1297.

Cambridge, University Library, ms Dd.9.69. Parchment, 205 × 145 mm., 324 fols. (there is a new foliation in pencil throughout the volume). A fragment of an older leaf pasted to the inside of the front cover is numbered

---

¹⁵⁵ On years of the lunar and solar cycles in subscriptions, cf. above, p. 60 note 143. According to Gardthausen, *Griechische Palaeographie*, II, p. 494, the Byzantine year ͵ϛωγ (Gardthausen misprinted it as ͵ϛφγ) was solar year 27 and lunar year 1, as is marked in the subscription of Barocci 16. The computation of such years can be made very easily. To obtain the solar year in the case of A.M. 6803, we divide 6803 by 28 (the number of years in the solar cycle); the quotient is 242, and the remainder 27 indicates the year of the solar cycle. To obtain the lunar year in the same case of A.M. 6803, we divide 6803 by 19 (the number of years in the lunar cycle); the quotient is 358, and the remainder 1 indicates the year of the lunar cycle.

¹⁵⁶ On the meaning of letters projected to the left, cf. above, p. 22 note 63.

fol. 1ᵇ; the recto of the front flyleaf is numbered fol. 2; a parchment leaf with Greek prayers, written perhaps in the 15th century, is numbered fol. 3. The volume (fols. 4–324) consists of three independent parts written at different times and now bound together. The first part, numbered fols. 4–294 (fol. 294 is blank), 24–26 lines to a page, contains the Four Gospels, adapted for liturgical use. There are full-page miniatures on fols. 13ᵛ (St. Matthew), 88ᵛ (St. Mark), 139ʳ (Christ with the Evangelists), 139ᵛ (St. Luke), 230ᵛ (St. John). The owner of this part of the volume was Georgius Mugduphes, who commissioned it; the scribe of this part was Michael Mantylides, who completed it in June A.M. 6805 = A.D. 1297. I deal below especially with this part of the volume.

The second part of the volume, numbered fols. 295–316 (fol. 316ᵛ is blank), 27 lines to a page, contains the Apocalypse, written in the latter part of the 14th century in the script style of the monastery τῶν Ὁδηγῶν in Constantinople.[157] The third part, fols. 317–324 (the text ends on fol. 324ʳ), written by another scribe perhaps about the same time as the second part, i.e., in the latter part of the 14th century, in a script likewise similar to that of the monastery τῶν Ὁδηγῶν, contains prayers from the Office of Genuflection recited on Pentecost at Vespers (ed. Πεντηκοστάριον χαρμόσυνον [Rome, 1883], pp. 409, 17 – 411, 6; 411, 21 – 413, 13; 413, 26 – 415, 19; or Πεντηκοστάριον χαρμόσυνον, ἔκδοσις τῆς Ἀποστολικῆς Διακονίας τῆς Ἐκκλησίας τῆς Ἑλλάδος [Athens, 1959], pp. 210ᵃ, 28 – 211ᵃ, 11; 211ᵃ, 27 – 212ᵃ, 13; 212ᵃ, 28 – 213ᵃ, 16). A title added on fol. 316ᵛ attributes the authorship of these prayers to St. Basil the Great (εὐχαὶ τοῦ Μεγάλου Βασιλῆου).[158]

I am concerned here especially with the first part of this MS (fols. 4–294), since it is dated. For its subscription written on fols. 293ʳ–293ᵛ we reproduce the text of both pages entirely on Plate **108**. Before the subscription begins, at the top of fol. 293ʳ (the left-hand page) there is the end of the Gospel of St. John 21:25, χωρῆσαι τὰ γραφόμενα, with the conclusion, βιβλία ἀμήν,[159] written beneath the center of the first line vertically and followed below by a double dot (··) and a vertical downward flourish. These vertical words are flanked on both sides by the following dodecasyllables written on four lines:

τέλος εἴληφε τὸ ποθού|μενον ἔργον· |
ἔλθης βοηθὸς Χ(ριστ)ὲ τῷ | γεγραφότι·

and an explanation of the nature of these verses: στίχ(οι) εἰς τ(ὸ) τέλος. | written at the end of the fourth line.

The subscription of the MS was begun by the scribe, immediately below the colophon just quoted, so that the first two lines of the subscription were written across the ornamental flourish with the double dot, which falls above the final -ς of the word τοῖς. One must be careful not to consider these dots

---

[157] On the scriptorium of the monastery τῶν Ὁδηγῶν in Constantinople and its script style, cf. below, pp. 131 ff., Pls. **89**, **90**; pp. 142 ff., Pl. **96**; pp. 146 ff., Pl. **96A**.

[158] On the attribution of the prayers in the Office of Genuflection to St. Basil the Great, cf. J. Goar, Εὐχολόγιον *sive Rituale Graecorum*, 2nd ed. (Venice, 1730; repr. Graz, 1960), pp. 605 f.

[159] ἀμήν is carried by many New Testament MSS as the final word of the Gospel of John: cf. Nestle, *Novum Testamentum graece*, p. 296, note in the critical apparatus.

an expunction or cancellation mark. The subscription on fol. 293ʳ–293ᵛ consists of three components. The first one, couched in 23 dodecasyllables, indicates the sponsor and owner of this part, Γεώργιος ὁ Μουγδουφῆς. The second component is worded in 4 political verses and indicates that the writing was concluded in June A.M. 6805 = A.D. 1297, lunar cycle year 3, solar cycle year 1,[160] indiction 10. The last component of the subscription, presented in the conventional cryptographic code,[161] obviously offers the name of the scribe, which is Μιχαὴλ ὁ Μαντυλίδης (some later hand wrote this name below the line in plain writing). The complete text of the subscription follows (fol. 293ʳ–293ᵛ – Plate **108**):

    †   πᾶσι μὲν τοῖς βλέπουσι πρὸ(ς) φθαρτὰ φύλλα· |
         χρυσὸς λίθοι μάργαρος ἀργύρου φύ(σις)· |
         τῷ δεσπότῃ δὲ τοῦ παρόντος βιβλίου· |
         τῷ τε Μουγδουφῇ κυρ(ῷ) τῷ Γεωργίῳ. |
    5   οὐ χρυσὸς οὐκ ἄργυρο(ς) οὐκ ἄλλο τούτων· |
         εἰ μὴ μελωδῶν εὐλογεῖν τὸν δεσπότην· |
         κατὰ τὸν Δα(υὶ)δ ἑπτάκις τῆς ἡμέρας· |
         οἵῳ πόθῳ τέτυχε τὴν βίβλον ταύτην |
         ἐκ καρδίας ὅλης τε αὐτοῦ ἰσχύος· |
   10   ἐξόδου πολλοῦ καὶ τύρβου καὶ μεμίμνων·[162] |
         ἀνθ᾽ ὧν βροτουργὲ παντάναξ κοσμ᾽ἐργάτα |
         εὐθυμίαν πάρεσχε καὶ σ(ωτη)ρίαν· |
         τοὺς υἱοὺς εὐλόγησον σ(ωτ)ὴρ τοὺς τούτου· |
         καὶ τὰ διαβήματα εὔθυνον αὖθις ||
   15   τῶν παίδων τούτου καὶ τῆς μ(ητ)ρ(ὸ)ς ὡσαύτως· |
         ὅπως παραμένουσι τῷδε τῷ βίῳ· |
         ἐκ πάσης νόσου καὶ λύπης ἄτερ· |
         καὶ πληροῖν προστάγματα τῶν ἐντολῶν σου, |
         τύχωσιν αὖθις τὴν Ἐδὲμ κατοικίαν. |

   20   Πάντων τῶν καλῶν τὸ πλήρω|μα τεκοῦσα·
         πλήρωσον ἡμῶν | παρθένε τὴν καρδίαν.
         ἁμαρ|τιῶν γὰρ λύτρωσιν αἰτουμέ|νη·
         καὶ ἱλασμὸν καὶ μέγα ἔλεος:— |

         ἐτελειώθ(η) τοῦτο γε τῷ μη(νὶ) ἰουννίῳ. |
   25   σελήνης κύ(κλος) τρίτος τε (ἡλίου) κύ(κλος) πρῶτος.[163] |

---

[160] On years of the lunar and solar cycles, cf. above, pp. 60 note 143, 63 note 155.

[161] On this cryptographic alphabet, cf. above, p. 56 note 128.

[162] The paroxytone accent μερίμνων (instead of μεριμνῶν) is noteworthy; it is absolutely necessary here for metrical reasons in the sixth foot of a dodecasyllable. This accent follows the practice of Byzantine and Modern Greek. Cf. G. N. Hatzidakis, *Einleitung in die neugriechische Grammatik*, Bibliothek indogermanischer Grammatiken, V (Leipzig, 1892), p. 420; S. B. Psaltes, *Grammatik der Byzantinischen Chroniken*, Forschungen zur griechischen und lateinischen Grammatik, 2 (Göttingen, 1913; repr. 1974), p. 145, § 262.

[163] The nominative forms τρίτος τε and πρῶτος show that in references to the years of the lunar and solar cycles the word κύ(κλος) or κύκλος was often used in the nominative, and not necessarily

ἐν ἔτει ͵ϛ ὀκτακοσιωστῷ δε· |
πρὸ(ς) τούτοις δὲ καὶ πέμπτῳ τε, | ἰνδικτιὼν δεκάτης + |

ξ͵υθβολξθνψχο͡ϛ͵ϛβω +

Verses 17 and 23 are short by two syllables each.[164] In the political verses of the dated subscription proper, the redundant use of the particles γε, τε, δέ signals the metrical nature of the text and the scribe's effort to meet its requirements. In verse 26 the numeral ͵ϛ evidently was intended to be spelled out as ἐξ χιλιοστῷ (instead of ἑξακισχιλιοστῷ) in oral delivery or in explicit reading in order to fill out the verse properly.[164a]

On Plate **45** we exhibit a specimen of the handwriting of Michael Mantylides by reproducing from his part of the MS folio 240ᵛ, containing a passage from the GOSPEL OF ST. JOHN 4:26–35. This is part of the lesson for the κυριακή τῆς Σαμαρείτιδος, i.e., the fourth Sunday after Easter. The whole lesson for this day is John 4:5–42 (cf. Gregory, I, p. 346).

This MS was once owned by John Moore (1646–1714), bishop successively of Norwich and Ely. It was MS 14 in Moore's collection (cf. E. Bernard, *Catalogi librorum manuscriptorum Angliae et Hiberniae in unum collecti* [Oxford, 1697], II,1, p. 362 under no. 9200). On Moore's death in 1714, his library was bought by King George I and presented by him in 1715 to the University of Cambridge. A bookplate in the MS refers to this royal donation. On John Moore and his MSS in the Cambridge University Library, cf. above, pp. 26f.

On this MS, cf. C. Hardwick, *A Catalogue of the Manuscripts Preserved in the Library of the University of Cambridge*, I (Cambridge, 1856), pp. 411f. (under no. 556); Vogel–Gardthausen, p. 316; Scrivener, I, p. 199 (under Evan. 60); Gregory, I, pp. 142 (under Vier Evangelien 60), 316 (under Apokalypse 10); Aland, I, p. 64 (under the Gregory–Aland number 60); von Soden, I,1, pp. 182 (under ε1321), 248 (under α1594).

Plate **46**: A.D. 1304/1305.

London, British Museum, ms Additional 22506. Parchment, 243 × 182 mm., 279 fols., 22 lines to a page. The MS actually consists of fols. 3–279; fols. 1–2 are an inserted paper sheet with a note by H. O. Coxe written on

---

in the genitive κύκλου or in the dative κύκλῳ. Moreover, scribes often applied a simplified usage. Instead of saying "in the year of the lunar, or solar, cycle," they said "lunar, or solar, cycle," meaning "in the indicated year of the respective cycle." Cf. Turyn, *DGMItaly*, I, pp. 64, 144; II, pls. 228c, 240d. It appears that the strict remark on this subject by G. Mercati, *Nuove note di letteratura biblica e cristiana antica*, ST, 95 (Vatican City, 1941), p. 76, note on subscription 4, in favor of reading in general κύ. with the suspended ending as κύ(κλου), goes too far. Cf. also Follieri, *Codices*, p. 52 note 123, who seems to follow Mercati's view in this respect.

[164] In verse 17, for instance, a supplement ἐκ⟨τός γε⟩ would heal the defect. In verse 23 a paroxytone and disyllabic verbal form in the imperative (with the meaning παράσχου) is missing at the end. Perhaps ⟨δίδου⟩ would do as a conclusion of the verse.

[164a] The regular form ἑξακισχιλιοστῷ would infringe the middle caesura and would result in exceeding the length of the political verse by two syllables. With the form ἐξ χιλιοστῷ suggested by me the whole verse would agree with the proper length, the middle caesura, and the usual accentuation requirements. This form is conceivably possible, since morphological irregularities and peculiar circumlocutions in numerals of metrical (or metrically inclined) subscriptions are a well-known phenomenon (cf. L. Polites, Παλαιογραφικά, in Ἑλληνικά, 26 [1973], pp. 315–21; Krumbacher, p. 743, § 3; Turyn, *Codices*, p. 26). A striking analogy to the form proposed by me is the cardinal numeral ἐξ χιλίοις in the dodecasyllabic colophon of MS Sinai Greek 2110 (cf. V. N. Beneševič, *Opisanie grečeskih rukopisej monastyrja Svjatoj Ekateriny na Sinaě*, III,1 [Petrograd, 1917], p. 329).

fol. 1ʳ (the rest, fols. 1ᵛ–2ᵛ, is blank, except for the date of acquisition by the British Museum recorded on fol. 2ʳ). Contents: Four Gospels, adapted (by a different hand) for liturgical use. There are four full-page miniatures of the Evangelists, damaged by the peeling of the colors: (fol. 5ᵛ) St. Matthew, (fol. 87ᵛ) St. Mark, (fol. 138ᵛ) St. Luke, (fol. 219ᵛ) St. John.[165] The MS was written by the monk and deacon (ἱεροδιάκονος) Neophytus of Cyprus and subscribed by him in red in A.M. 6813 = A.D. 1304/1305 (fol. 219ʳ – Plate 109a): + ἐγράφη ἐν ἔτη ͵ϛ·ω·ιγ′:+ | ἰν(δικτιῶνος) γ̄:+ | Δι᾽ ἐμοῦ τοῦ ἐν ἱεροδιακόνοις ἐλαχίστου | ὀικτροῦ Νεοφύτου· καὶ τάχα μοναχοῦ:+ | τοῦ Κυπρίου:– | καὶ ὀι ἐντυγχάνοντες ἀυτὸ, ἔυχεσϑ(ε) ὑπὲρ ἐμοῦ διατὸν κ(ύριο)ν:+

On Plate 46 we reproduce fol. 47ʳ, containing a passage from the GOSPEL OF ST. MATTHEW 15:37 – 16:4. This passage comprises the end of the lesson for Saturday of the ninth week after Pentecost (the whole lesson is Matthew 15:32–39) and the beginning of the lesson for Monday of the eighth week after Pentecost (the whole lesson is Matthew 16:1–6). The end of the former lesson is marked in red above line 7: τέλος τοῦ σα(ββά)τ(ου). The beginning of the latter lesson is likewise marked in red above the same line: ἀρχή. In the upper margin there is a liturgical note in red: τῇ β̄′ τῆς η̄′ ευδ(ο)μ(άδος) | τῶ καιρ(ῷ ἐκείνῳ)· προσελθόντες. τῶ ᾽Ι(ησο)ῦ οἱ Φαρισαῖοι καὶ Σαδδουκ(αῖοι): This note indicates the time of the lesson which begins on this page, the customary opening formula of the lesson, and a slight modification of the initial words of the pericope for lesson use.[166] On the time and extent of these lessons, cf. Gregory, I, p. 350. The τέλος note, the ἀρχή mark, and the liturgical note in the upper margin are written in red, in accordance with the accepted custom of New Testament MSS adapted for liturgical use.[167] The figure ξϛ′ in red in the right margin indicates the consecutive number 66 of the pericope from Matthew (counting from the Sunday before Christmas) which begins in the line to the left.[168] The black figures in the right margin, ρ̄ξ̄β′ and ρ̄ξ̄γ′, mark the Eusebian sections 162 and 163 of the Gospel of Matthew as they begin here. These sections comprise Matthew 16:2–3 and 16:4 (cf. von Soden, I,1, p. 397). Actually, the figure ρ̄ξ̄β′ is marked here opposite the beginning of Matthew 16:1 (the figure should have been marked 4 lines lower, to the right of the line containing the words ὁ δὲ ἀποκριϑεὶς). The liturgical note quoted above and all the marks discussed here were written not by the scribe of the MS, but by some different later hand which adapted the MS for liturgical use. In the main text of the page, the red capitals projected to the left indicate either that in the preceding line an important text part begins (this appies to the first and the second projected initials), or that in the same line such a text part begins (this applies to the third projected initial).[169] Another

---

[165] For published reproductions of some miniatures from MS London Additional 22506, cf. the publications by A. M. Friend, Jr., and K. Weitzmann (see below, pp. 68f.).

[166] Cf. above, p. 43 note 100.

[167] Cf. above, p. 43 note 101.

[168] In the printed vulgate of Gospel lectionaries, this lesson is marked as pericope ξε′ or 65 from Matthew: cf. Εὐαγγέλιον (1880), pp. 24 (under Περικοπαί ΞΕ′), 41ᵃ; Εὐαγγέλιον (1968), pp. [40] (under Περικοπαί ΞΕ′), 56ᵇ.

[169] Cf. above, p. 22 note 63.

facsimile specimen of this MS was published in *Pal. Soc.*, Ser. I, pl. 205. There is nothing specifically Cypriot[170] in the script style of the scribe Neophytus of Cyprus. This MS shows, rather, the conventional calligraphy of New Testament MSS which sometimes overwhelms the expected regional features of the scribe's native habits. A similar case can be found in another Cypriot MS with scriptural contents (a lectionary of the Gospels), viz., MS London Burney 22 (cf. below, pp. 82f., Plate **56**), which likewise does not show in its text any characteristic features of Cypriot calligraphy. Nonetheless, it is possible that, although Neophytus was a native of Cyprus, he may have grown up elsewhere and may have shaped his writing habits in some other area of the Byzantine world. In such a case this MS Additional 22506 may have been written outside Cyprus.[171]

On fol. 279^v there is a note: $\overline{α\,χ}$′μη μινι ... | (then in different ink) *1645.* καὶ νυν | N. Σ. Apparently, whoever wrote lines 2–3 of this note mistakenly converted A.D. 1648 written in Greek letters into 1645; the same person wrote the letters N. Σ., which must be the initials of the person who was then the owner of the MS. In the upper margin of fol. 142^r there is the following note: σχεδὸν κοντιύει (this word in its standard form is κοντεύει)[171a] χρόνος. | *1849* (ἔτος) (this word is written between parentheses and underscored with a wavy line) | Slightly to the right of the first and second lines of the note, there is this notation: A (which seems to be a monogram, possibly involving elements of some more letters) | A. Συρμαλένιος. We know from a note written by Henry Octavius Coxe of Oxford, inserted in this MS (fol. 1^r), dated 31 March 1857,[172] and from Coxe's published *Report*,[173] that he found the MS at Melos (Milo) in the hands of a dealer in antiquities and curiosities, Μιχαηλ Συρμαλενεα, who told him that he got it from a relative who had been the abbot of the monastery of Preveli (Πρέβελη) in Crete.[174] Coxe, in his note on fol. 1^r, stated that he bought this MS from Michael Syrmalenea, obviously on 31 March 1857. I am inclined to believe that the note on fol. 142^r, signed in 1849 by A. Syrmalenios, is due perhaps to that abbot of the Preveli monastery, who signed his name with a formal ending, slightly different from the ending of the name of Michael Syrmalenea at Melos as reported by Coxe. On Coxe's return from his travels to the Levant, this MS was acquired by the British Museum on 29 July 1858 (according to a note on fol. 2^r).

On this MS, cf. *Catalogue of Additions, MDCCCLIV.–MDCCCLX.*, pp. 654f.; Richard, *Inventaire*, p. 39; Omont, "Notes," p. 347; Vogel–Gardthausen, pp. 331, 237; *Pal. Soc.*, Ser. I, pl. 205 (description of the MS); Scrivener, I, p. 259 (under Evan. 591); Gregory, I, p. 208 (under Vier Evangelien 645); Aland, I, p. 95 (under the Gregory–Aland number 645); von Soden, I,1, p. 194 (under ε434); A. M. Friend, Jr., "The Portraits of the Evangelists in Greek and Latin Manuscripts, Part II," *Art Studies, Medieval, Renaissance, and Modern* (1929), p. 13; pl. VII, fig. 14

---

[170] For the characteristic calligraphy of Cypriot MSS, cf. Omont, *Fac-similés ... du IXe au XIVe siècle*, pl. LXXIX/II (cf. Notice des planches, p. 16); Turyn, *Codices*, pl. 96 (cf. pp. 117–24); Follieri, *Codices*, pl. 53 (cf. pp. 76–78). Also cf. Turyn, *DGMItaly*, II, pl. 93 (cf. I, p. 119); below, Pls. **57, 58** (cf. pp. 83ff.); Thompson, *Introduction*, p. 262, facsimile no. 76; Wilson, *Mediaeval Greek Bookhands*, pl. 66 (cf. p. 31 under no. 66).

[171] J. Darrouzès, "Autres manuscrits originaires de Chypre," *REB*, 15 (1957), p. 149 (under no. 81), assumed that MS London Additional 22506 was probably written outside Cyprus.

[171a] For the accented -ε- changed to -ι- in κοντιύει ("is near"), cf. A. Thumb, *Handbuch der neugriechischen Volkssprache*, 2nd ed. (Strasbourg, 1910), p. 6, § 7.1 (on changes of unaccented vowels in northern dialects of Modern Greek), esp. line 10 from the bottom.

[172] The note by Coxe which appears on fol. 1^r has a date, "Melos. 31 March 1857," added in the handwriting of Frederic Madden. The whole note was printed in *Catalogue of Additions to the Manuscripts in the British Museum, in the Years MDCCCLIV.–MDCCCLX.* [London, 1875; repr. 1965], pp. 654f.

[173] Cf. H. O. Coxe, *Report to Her Majesty's Government, on the Greek Manuscripts Yet Remaining in Libraries of the Levant* (London, 1858), pp. 24, 73 (under no. 18).

[174] On the monastery of the B.V.M. at Πρέβελη, on the south coast of Crete, in the community Λευκόγεια, in the eparchy of Ἅγιος Βασίλειος (due south of Ῥέθυμνον, in the province Ῥέθυμνα, very close to the south shore of Crete), cf. Μεγ.Ἑλλ.Ἐγκυκλ., XX, pp. 660f.; cf. also Coxe, *op. cit.*, p. 22.

(= fol. 87ᵛ); pl. VIII, fig. 19 (= fol. 5ᵛ); K. Weitzmann, *Geistige Grundlagen und Wesen der Makedonischen Renaissance*, Arbeitsgemeinschaft für Forschung des Landes Nordrhein-Westfalen. Geisteswissenschaften, 107 (Cologne–Opladen [1963]), p. 45, fig. 45 (= fol. 5ᵛ).

Plate 47: A.D. 1305/1306.

London, British Museum, ms Additional 29714. Parchment, 283 × 215 mm., 178 fols., 28–29 lines to a page. Contents: Lectionary of the Acts and Epistles (i.e., the so-called Ἀπόστολος). The MS was written by Ignatius in A.M. 6814 = A.D. 1305/1306, according to the subscription written in red on fol. 178ᵛ (Plate **109b**): † ἐγρ(άφη) διὰ χειρὸς ἐμοῦ ἁμαρτωλοῦ Ἰγνατ(ίου). | ἐν ετ(ει): ͵ϛω ιδ. ἰν(δικτιῶνος) δ | εὔχεσθαί μοι διὰ τὸν κ(ύριο)ν οἱ ἀναγινώσ|κοντες αὐτόν:–

On Plate **47** we reproduce fol. 114ʳ. This is a page of the LECTIONARY OF THE ACTS AND EPISTLES, containing passages from St. Paul*, Epistle to the Hebrews 7:1–6 and 7:18–19 (ed. Ἀπόστολος ἤτοι Πράξεις καὶ Ἐπιστολαὶ τῶν ἁγίων Ἀποστόλων καθ' ὅλον τὸ ἔτος ἐπ' Ἐκκλησίας ἀναγινωσκόμεναι [Rome, 1881], pp. 180, last line – 181, 17; or ed. Ἀπόστολος ..., Ἀποστολικὴ Διακο-νία τῆς Ἐκκλησίας τῆς Ἑλλάδος [Athens, 1954], pp. 229, 27 – 230, 16). This is the major part of the lesson appointed for Thursday of the 29th week after Pentecost (the whole lesson is Hebrews 7:1–6), and the beginning of the lesson for Friday of the same week (the whole lesson is Hebrews 7:18–25). On the time and the extent of these lessons, cf. Gregory, I, p. 357. The beginning of the latter lesson is preceded by a liturgical note in red and a heading (likewise in red): τῇ ϛ τῆς κθ (i.e., ἑβδομάδος):· | : πρὸς Ἑβραίους:· The note indicates the time for which the lesson is appointed; it is followed by the indication of the Epistle from which the lesson is drawn. According to the accepted custom of New Testament MSS, the entire note (including the title of the Epistle) is written in red.[175] Since this is a lectionary, the customary prefix of the lesson (in this case, Ἀδελφοί) is written in the text itself; ἀδελφοί is the most frequent prefix of an Epistle lesson. Another modification of the text opening here is the omission of the words μὲν γὰρ which follow after the word ἀθέτησις in the standard text of this Epistle (in the printed vulgate of the Apostolus, μὲν is retained and only γὰρ is omitted).[176] This lectionary is written in single-column pages, while in general a two-column arrangement prevails in lectionaries (cf. above, p. 17; cf. Plates **5, 6, 7, 11, 56**). However, the lectionary reproduced on Plate **67** is written in single-column pages.

The MS was bought by the British Museum from Nicolas Parassoh on 27 June 1874 (according to a note recorded on the recto of the first front flyleaf).

On this MS, cf. Richard, *Inventaire*, p. 52; Omont, "Notes," p. 339; Vogel–Gardthausen, p. 159; Scrivener, I, p. 371 (under Apost. 69); Gregory, I, p. 469 (under Apostel 81), and III,

---

[175] Cf. above, p. 18 and note 43.

[176] On customary prefixes in New Testament lessons and modifications of the beginnings of the standard text which appear in New Testament lectionaries, cf. the remarks on the analogous situation in the Gospel lectionaries made by Gregory, I, p. 341, and by von Dobschütz, *Eberhard Nestle's Ein-führung*, p. 37.

pp. 1255, 1437 (Gregory replaced his former symbol apl 81 by a new symbol *l*ᵃ 257); C. R. Gregory, *Die griechischen Handschriften des Neuen Testaments* (Leipzig, 1908; repr. 1973), pp. 130 (under *l*⁺ᵃ 257), 272 (symbol *l* 257); Aland, I, p. 219 (under the Gregory–Aland symbol *l* 257).

Plate 48: A.D. 1306/1307.

Oxford, Bodleian Library, ms Auct.T.3.16. Parchment, 27 × 20 cm., II + 125 fols., 2 columns, 49–57 lines to a column. Fols. ɪ, ɪɪ, and 1 are modern flyleaves; fol. 125 is the back flyleaf. Contents (fols. 2ʳ–124ᵛ): Synaxarion (Lives of Saints) of Constantinople for the whole year (from September through August). The MS was written by the lector Georgius Saracinopulus and subscribed by him in A.M. 6815 = A.D. 1306/1307 (fol. 124ᵛ – Plate **109c**): Ἐτελειώθ(η) τὸ παρὸν συναξάρ(ιον), διὰ | χειρὸς ἁμαρτωλοῦ πάνυ | Γεωργ(ίου) ἀναγνώστου, τοῦ ἐκ γένους | μὲν τυγχάνοντ(ος), τῶν Σαρακι|νοπούλων: | Ἔτους τρέχοντος, ͵ϛωιε: | (then in monocondylia) Γεώργιος ἔγρα(ψεν) | ἀρετῶν θείων | ξένος +++ On the family name Σαρακηνόπουλος, its meaning and its use in Byzantium, cf. G. Moravcsik, *Byzantinoturcica*, 2nd ed., II, Berliner Byzantinistische Arbeiten, 11 (Berlin, 1958), p. 268.

On Plate **48** we reproduce folio 45ᵛ, containing passages from the Sʏɴᴀxᴀʀɪᴏɴ ᴏғ Cᴏɴsᴛᴀɴᴛɪɴᴏᴩʟᴇ for 26 and 27 January (ed. *Synaxarium CP*, cols. 425, 17 – 426, 19; col. 425, 20–22; cols. [in the lower sections] 425–26 line 41 – 427–28 line 41; cols. 425, 31 – 427, 3).[177] These passages contain: the very end of the commemoration of an earthquake at Constantinople (in A.D. 447);[178] Life of Symeon the Old; Translation of the Relics of St. John Chrysostom (cf. *BHG*³ 877e); Passion of Ananias the Priest, Peter the Jailer, and Seven Soldiers in Phoenicia (almost entirely).

In this MS, yellow wash covers some headlines.[179]

[177] For the text of Plate **48**, cf. also Μηναῖον τοῦ Ἰανουαρίου, ἔκδοσις τῆς Ἀποστολικῆς Διακονίας τῆς Ἐκκλησίας τῆς Ἑλλάδος (Athens, 1961), pp. 216ᵇ, 38–40; 216ᵇ, 44–54; 226ᵃ, 9–12; 226ᵃ, 18 – 226ᵇ, 1 (with considerable differences); 216ᵇ, 55–57; 217ᵃ, 4–11; or Μηναῖον τοῦ Ἰανουαρίου [ed. Φῶς, Athens, 1960], pp. 387ᵇ, 4–7; 387ᵇ, 13–31; 404ᵃ, 34–38; 404ᵇ, 7 – 405ᵃ, 47 (with considerable differences); 387ᵇ, 32–36; 388ᵃ, 1–14.

[178] The earthquake in Constantinople mentioned in the commemoration notice under 26 January in the *Synaxarium CP*, col. 425, 1–17 (cf. also Μηναῖον for January [ed. 1961], p. 216ᵇ, 30–38), is commonly referred to 26 January 450 (cf. G. Downey, "Earthquakes at Constantinople and Vicinity, A.D. 342–1454," *Speculum*, 30 [1955], p. 597; Grumel, *Chronologie*, p. 477). However, the commemoration notice (both in the *Synaxarium CP*, col. 425, 6, and in the Μηναῖον for January, p. 216ᵇ, 31) explicitly states that the earthquake occurred on a Sunday. January 26, 450, was a Thursday (not a Sunday). But 26 January 447 fell indeed on a Sunday. An earthquake occurred in A.D. 447 (cf. Downey, *op. cit.*, p. 597; Grumel, *Chronologie*, p. 477). The earthquake of A.D. 447 is most probably the one commemorated in the *Synaxarium CP* and in the Μηναῖον under 26 January. There is a certain difficulty in this matter. According to the Chronicon Paschale, Bonn ed. (1832), p. 586, 6–14, the earthquake of A.D. 447 was commemorated on 6 November (*ibid.*, p. 586, 13; cf. Grumel, *op. cit.*, p. 477 under A.D. 447). But this statement of the Chronicon Paschale must have resulted from some confusion. The liturgical commemoration on 6 November pertains to the burning clouds which appeared over Constantinople toward the end of the reign of Leo I the Great, probably on 6 November 472 (cf. *Synaxarium CP*, cols. 198, 7 – 199, 12; Μηναῖον τοῦ Νοεμβρίου, ἔκδοσις τῆς Ἀποστολικῆς Διακονίας τῆς Ἐκκλησίας τῆς Ἑλλάδος [Athens, 1960], pp. 40ᵇ, 52 – 41ᵃ, 23; N. Nilles, *Kalendarium manuale utriusque Ecclesiae orientalis et occidentalis*, 2nd ed., II [Innsbruck, 1897], pp. 530–32; Grumel, *Chronologie*, p. 478 under 472, 6 Nov.). It appears that the author of the Chronicon Paschale confused the date elements of the events of A.D. 447 and 472.

[179] On yellow wash applied in some MSS to noteworthy elements, a frequent (but not exclusive) feature of South Italian MSS which appears also in MSS produced in other areas of the Byzantine world, cf. Turyn, *DGMItaly*, I, pp. 6, 170, 189, 202.

Early in the 18th century the MS was owned by Giovanni Saibante in Verona; it was Greek MS 26 in the Saibante library.[180] A major part of the Saibante collection of Greek MSS was purchased by the Bodleian Library in 1820 (cf. *Summary Catalogue*, IV, p. 422).

On this MS, cf. Coxe, I, col. 786 (under Misc. gr. 233); *Summary Catalogue*, IV, p. 422 (under S.C. 20512); Vogel–Gardthausen, p. 83; H. Delehaye, in *Synaxarium CP*, cols. xvif. (symbol **Da**); Barbour, in *Greek Manuscripts in the Bodleian Library*, p. 22 (under no. 26).

Plate 49: A.D. 1308.

Oxford, New College, ms 258. (The MSS of New College are now on deposit in the Bodleian Library.) Parchment, 248 × 172 mm., 252 fols., 22 lines to a page. Fols. 1–2 are front flyleaves; fols. 251–252 are back fly-leaves. Contents: (fols. 3ʳ–27ʳ) Aphthonius, Progymnasmata; (fols. 27ᵛ–250ᵛ) Hermogenes, Rhetorical Writings (Περὶ στάσεων, Περὶ εὑρέσεως, Περὶ ἰδεῶν, Περὶ μεθόδου δεινότητος). The MS was written by the famous scholar and scribe of the Palaeologan period, Demetrius Triclines (or Triclinius) of Thessalonica, and subscribed by him in red on fol. 250ᵛ in August A.M. 6816 = A.D. 1308 (Plate **110a**): + ἐτελειώθη ἡ παροῦσα βίβλος. διὰ χειρὸ(ς) Δημητρίου | τοῦ Τρικλίνη, ἐν μηνὶ αὐγούστω ἰν(δικτιῶν)ος ϛ́, τοῦ ζω̅ιϛ̅ου′ ἔτους ++ [181] The change of the name form Τρικλίνης to Τρικλίνιος was made later (around A.D. 1316–1319) by Demetrius Triclinius himself.[182] The accents and breathings above the numeral letters in the subscription are easily understood: ϛ́ corresponds to ἕκτης; in ζ and ω̅ the initial breathings and the final accents of the ordinal numerals in question were marked in correspondence with ἑξακισχιλιοστοῦ and ὀκτακοσιοστοῦ, respectively.[183]

On Plate **49** we reproduce folio 93ʳ, containing a passage from HERMOGENES, RHETORICAL WRITINGS (from Περὶ εὑρέσεως, Book Γ, chap. 10: ed. H. Rabe, *Hermogenis opera*, Rhetores Graeci, VI, Teubner [1913; repr. Stuttgart, 1969], pp. 155, 16 – 156, 14). This is the earliest dated MS written by Demetrius Triclinius, as far as we know, and probably the earliest known in the handwriting of Demetrius Triclinius. It is written in his round-breathing style, as opposed to his angular-breathing style, which he began using after A.D. 1316 and before A.D. 1319.[184] For other facsimile specimens of this MS, cf. Turyn,

---

[180] Cf. S. Maffei, *Verona illustrata*, pt. 3 (Verona, 1732), col. 243; E. M. Jeffreys, "The Greek Manuscripts of the Saibante Collection," in *Studia Codicologica*, p. 255 (under no. 26). On the Saibante collection, cf. above, pp. 41f. On a Saibante MS in the Bodleian Library, MS Auct.T.3.6, treated in this book, cf. above, p. 42; on another Saibante MS in the British Museum, MS Burney 21, cf. above, p. 62.

[181] For other facsimiles of this subscription, cf. A. Turyn, *The Byzantine Manuscript Tradition of the Tragedies of Euripides*, Illinois Studies in Language and Literature, 43 (Urbana, 1957; repr. Studia philologica, 16 [Rome, 1970]), pl. vi, lower part; W. J. W. Koster, *Autour d'un manuscrit d'Aristophane écrit par Démétrius Triclinius*, Scripta Academica Groningana (Groningen–Djakarta, 1957), pl. i.

[182] On this question, cf. A. Turyn, *The Manuscript Tradition of the Tragedies of Aeschylus*, Polish Institute Series, 2 (New York, 1943; repr. Hildesheim, 1967), pp. 103–4 note 89; idem, *The Byzantine Manuscript Tradition of the Tragedies of Euripides*, pp. 26–27 note 43; idem, *DGMItaly*, I, pp. 124f. In general, on such variations in Greek names, cf. idem, *Codices*, p. 125.

[183] On the habit of scribes of putting breathings and accents above numeral letters, cf. idem, *Codices*, pp. 40, 112, 125, 137; idem, *DGMItaly*, I, pp. 81, 113, 117, 124f. (here, on the practice of Demetrius Triclinius), 130, 132, 205, 257.

[184] Cf. Turyn, *DGMItaly*, I, pp. 124–26.

The Byzantine Manuscript Tradition of the Tragedies of Euripides, pl. VI, lower part (part of fol. 250^v); Koster, *op. cit.*, pl. I (= fol. 250^v); Barbour, in *Greek Manuscripts in the Bodleian Library*, pl. XI (= fol. 100^v); *eadem*, in *Encyclopaedia Britannica*, XVII (Chicago [1973]), *s.v.* "Paleography," p. 127 fig. 22 (segment of fol. 205^r).

For other published facsimiles of Demetrius Triclinius' handwriting, cf. G. Wattenbach and A. von Velsen, *Exempla codicum graecorum litteris minusculis scriptorum* (Heidelberg, 1878), pl. XXI; U. de Wilamowitz-Moellendorff, *Aeschyli tragoediae* (Berlin, 1914), pls. II, III; E. Fraenkel, *Aeschylus Agamemnon*, I (Oxford, 1950), pl. I; Turyn, *The Byzantine Manuscript Tradition of the Tragedies of Euripides*, pls. VIII–XI, XVI, XVII; Koster, *op. cit.*, pls. II, III; Turyn, *DGMItaly*, II, pls. 96–99. Now cf. also D. Harlfinger, "Zu griechischen Kopisten und Schriftstilen des 15. und 16. Jahrhunderts," in *Paléographie grecque et byzantine*, pp. 333, 347 fig. 8. For references to other published facsimiles of Demetrius Triclinius' handwriting, cf. Turyn, *DGMItaly*, I, pp. 124, 126.

On MS Oxford, New College 258, cf. H. O. Coxe, *Catalogus codicum mss. qui in collegiis aulisque Oxoniensibus hodie adservantur*, I (Oxford, 1852; repr. *idem, Catalogue of the Manuscripts in the Oxford Colleges*, I [East Ardsley, 1972]), in the part "Catalogus codicum mss. Collegii Novi," p. 92 (with a misprint in the A.M. date quoted in Greek in the subscription and a corresponding error in the A.D. year indicated in the description of the MS); Barbour, in *Greek Manuscripts in the Bodleian Library*, pp. 23 f. (under no. 29), pl. XI; *eadem*, in *Encyclopaedia Britannica*, XVII, p. 127 (comment on the script style of this MS) and fig. 22; Vogel–Gardthausen, p. 106 (with the erroneous date repeated from Coxe); Rabe, *op. cit.*, p. XVII (symbol Og).

Plate 50: A.D. 1311/1312.

London, British Museum, ms Additional 38538. Parchment, 208 × 145 mm., 1 + 269 fols., 25–26 lines to a page. Contents: (fols. 1^r–234^r) Acts of the Apostles, Catholic Epistles, Pauline Epistles (i.e., the so-called Πραξαπόστολος), adapted for liturgical use; (fols. 234^r–238^v) Dorotheus of Tyre*, Index of the Apostles and the Disciples (ed. Migne, Patr. Gr., 92, cols. 1060 C 2 – 1065 D 8; 1071 + 1072 B 11 Ὑποκατιὼν – 12; 1072 B 13 – 1073 A 16; or ed. Th. Schermann, *Prophetarum vitae fabulosae, indices apostolorum discipulorumque Domini Dorotheo, Epiphanio, Hippolyto aliisque vindicata*, Teubner [1907], pp. 132, 3 – 144, 4; 152, 8 – 157, 4; cf. *BHG*³ 151, and *BHG Auct.* 152b, pars posterior); (fols. 239^r–269^v) Tables of lessons. The MS was written by Ioannes in A.M. 6820 = A.D. 1311/1312, according to the subscription written in red and an invocation following in black which includes the scribe's name (fol. 238^v – Plate **110b**): † ἐγρά(φ)η τὸ παρὸν βιβλίον ὁ πραξαποστ(ο)λο(ς), ἐν ἔτει ͵ϛωκ, | ἰν(δικτιῶνος) δεκάτης ++ | Μνήσθητι κ(ύρι)ε τοῦ δούλου σου Ἰωάννου ἁμαρτωλοῦ καὶ τῶν | κατασάρκα συγγενῶν αὐτοῦ καὶ ἐλέησον αὐτοὺς διὰ τὸ μέ|γα σου ἔλεος:

> καὶ βασάνων λύτρωσαι τῶν πικρο|τάτων,
> ἀμὴν τῶν ἀιτήσαιων γένοιτο πέρας ++

The end of the invocation is couched in two dodecasyllables, which I have arranged correspondingly.

On Plate **50** we reproduce folio 114ᵛ, which contains a passage from St. Paul, Epistle to the Romans 14:8–17. This passage includes the end of the lesson for Saturday of the 9th week after Pentecost (the whole lesson is Romans 14:6–9) and the beginning of the lesson for Tuesday of the 5th week after Pentecost (in the MS, the time of this lesson was marked by inadvertence as Tuesday of the 4th week; the whole lesson is Romans 14:9–18). For the time and the extent of these lessons, cf. Gregory, I, pp. 350, 349. The end of the former lesson is marked in red τέ(λος) τοῦ σα(ββάτου):– For the beginning of the latter lesson, the proper liturgical note, likewise in red, is written within the text (instead of in a margin, as is usual).[185] The note runs thus: τῇ γ̄ τῆς δ̄ ἑβδ(ομάδος): πρ(ὸς) ῾Ρωμ(αίους): ἀδε(λφοί), | εἰς τοῦτο Χ(ριστὸ)ς κὰι ἀ(πέθανε):· In addition to the time of the lesson (with the week marked mistakenly) and the title of the Epistle, the usual prefix of an Epistle lesson (ἀδελφοί) and the beginning of the text as modified for lesson use are indicated.[186] The projected capital X in red indicates that an important text part begins in the preceding line;[187] in this case, it is the beginning of the lesson that takes place in the preceding line. The marginal mark κε(φάλαιον) ρκ: in red is the consecutive section number from the Praxapostolus to which the Tables of lessons at the end refer (the Praxapostolus is divided in this MS into 360 sections). The liturgical notes and this marginal mark are in red, in accordance with the custom of New Testament MSS adapted for liturgical use.[188] The placement of the liturgical note which precedes the beginning of the latter lesson suggests that the MS was copied from one which had the liturgical equipment and that the scribe of the present MS, in the course of transcribing his immediate source, was anxious to place those notes and marks within the text, while using the proper red color for them.[189] This explains the situation in lines 2 and 3 of the page reproduced.

The MS was purchased by the British Museum from N. Giannacopulo on 8 June 1912 (according to a note written on the inside of the front cover).

On this MS, cf. Richard, *Inventaire*, p. 71; *Catalogue of Additions to the Manuscripts in the British Museum in the Years MDCCCXI–MDCCCXV* (London, 1925; repr. 1969, pt. 1), pp. 147f.; K. Aland, "Zur Liste der Neutestamentlichen Handschriften. V.," *ZNW*, 45 (1954), p. 201 (under no. 2484); Aland, I, p. 192 (numbered according to the Gregory–Aland system as 2484).

Plate 51: A.D. 1312.

Oxford, Bodleian Library, ms Lyell 94. Parchment, 133 × 95 mm., 223 fols., 19 lines to a page. Contents: (fols. 1ʳ–189ʳ) Theotocarion, comprising

[185] On the occurrence of liturgical notes within the text of New Testament MSS adapted for liturgical use, cf. Gregory, I, p. 17 lines 5–6.

[186] On such features of the liturgical notes as the time of the lesson, a customary prefix to a lesson (in an Epistle lesson it is mostly ἀδελφοί), and the adaptation of the initial words of the pericope for lesson use, marked in New Testament MSS adapted for liturgical use (or completed in the text of New Testament lectionaries), cf. Gregory, I, pp. 16f., 341; von Dobschütz, *Eberhard Nestle's Einführung*, pp. 37f. Cf. also above, p. 43 note 100.

[187] Cf. above, p. 22 note 63.   [188] Cf. above, p. 43 note 101.

[189] For a similar appearance of a liturgical note within the text of a New Testament MS, cf. Hatch, *Facsimiles and Descriptions*, pl. xliv.

48 canons, one for Vespers on each day of the week from Sunday to Friday for each of the eight ἦχοι (each ode has 3 troparia, and each canon is followed by its proper stichera);[190] (fols. 189ᵛ–223ʳ) Metrophanes of Smyrna, Triadic Canons; (fol. 223ʳ–223ᵛ) κονδά(κιον) to the Theotocos.[191] The MS was completed on 15 August A.M. 6820 = A.D. 1312, according to the subscription written in red on fol. 189ʳ (Plate **110c**): Ἔτους ͵ϛῶκ μη(νὶ) αὐγ(ούστῳ) ιε̄: ἰν(δικτιώ-ν)ης ι:+

On Plate **51** we reproduce folios 102ᵛ–103ʳ, containing a passage from this THEOTOCARION, viz., a part of a Canon to the Theotocos, in the ἦχος πλάγιος α', for Vespers on Monday, from the continuation of ᾠδὴ ε' through the beginning of ᾠδὴ η' (ed. Παρακλητικὴ ἤτοι Ὀκτώηχος ἡ Μεγάλη [Rome, 1885], pp. 373, 18–26; 374, 11–19; 375, 15–24; 376, 14–16; or ed. Παρακλητική, ἐκδόσεις Φῶς [Athens, 1959], pp. 244ᵃ, 2–13; 244ᵇ, 9–18; 245ᵃ, 27–37; 246ᵃ, 1–4). In each ᾠδή, its heading with the initial words of the εἱρμός and the first troparion are written in red; the second and third troparia are written in black.

The MS was once owned by James P. R. Lyell (1871–1949), a lawyer in London, who acquired it from A. Rosenthal of Oxford on 2 April 1943. Lyell willed a sizable part of his collection of MSS, including this one, to the Bodleian Library (cf. R. W. Hunt, "The Lyell Bequest," *The Bodleian Library Record*, 3 [1950–1951], pp. 68–82; on this MS, p. 81; N. R. Ker, in A. de la Mare, *Catalogue of the Collection of Medieval Manuscripts Bequeathed to the Bodleian Library, Oxford, by James P. R. Lyell* [Oxford, 1971], pp. xv–xviii).

On this MS, cf. R. Barbour, in de la Mare, *op. cit.*, pp. 271–73; *ibid.*, p. xxvi, on the time of the acquisition of this MS by Lyell; Winkley, *op. cit.*, pp. 267–73 (a detailed study of this MS).

Plate 52: A.D. 1312/1313.

London, British Museum, ms Arundel 523. Bombycine, 197 × 130 mm., ɪɪ + 149 fols. Contents: (fols. 3ʳ–144ᵛ) Constantine Manasses, Chronicle; (fol. 144ᵛ) subscription by the priest Michael Lulludes; (fols. 145ʳ–146ʳ) a poem in political verses composed and written by Michael Lulludes, addressed to Manuel Hyalinas who commissioned this MS, headlined as follows on fol. 145ʳ: τοῦ αὐτοῦ ἱερέως στίχοι πρὸ(ς) τὸν προστάξαντα τούτῳ | τὴν βίβλον γράψαι εὐγενέστατον ἄρχοντα κῦρ | Μα(νουὴλ) τὸν Ὑαλινᾶν + (this poem was published, from a 16th-century MS Munich graec. 153, fols. 116ᵛ–117ᵛ, by I. Hardt, *Catalogus codicum manuscriptorum graecorum Bibliothecae Regiae Bavaricae*, II [Munich, 1806], pp. 172–74); (fol. 147ʳ–147ᵛ) a later insert, πε(ρὶ) τῆς ἀλφαβήτ(ου). The MS was written and completed by the priest Michael Lulludes of Ephesus in Crete in A.M. 6821 = A.D. 1312/1313, according to the subscription in red on fol. 144ᵛ (Plate **110d**): ✳ ἡ παροῦσα βίβλος ἐτε-λειώθη διὰ χειρὸ(ς) | τοῦ ἐλαχίστου καὶ εὐτελοῦς ἱερέως Μιχ(αὴλ) τοῦ | Λουλλούδη

---

[190] S. Winkley, "A Bodleian Theotokarion," *REB*, 31 (1973), pp. 270f., listed the incipits of the canons in this MS with references to their publications, if any.

[191] The text of this κοντάκιον can be found in the following publications: P. G. Nikolopoulos, Ὕμνοι (κοντάκια) σῳζόμενοι εἰς χειρόγραφα τῆς Βαλλικελλιανῆς Βιβλιοθήκης τῆς Ῥώμης, in Ἐπ.Ἑτ.Βυζ.Σπ., 28 (1958), p. 309 (under no. 43); S. Eustratiades, Ῥωμανὸς ὁ Μελῳδὸς καὶ τὰ ποιητικὰ αὐτοῦ ἔργα. Β', *ibid.*, 25 (1955), pp. 274, line 6 from the bottom – 275, line 13.

τοῦ ἀπὸ τῆς 'Εφέ(σ)ου· μετοι|κισμένου ὄντο(ς) ἐν τῇ τρισμεγίστω νήσω | Κρήτῃ, διὰ τὸ τὴν αὐτοῦ π(ατ)ρίδα κρατηθῆναι | ὑπὸ Περσῶν· ἔτους ͵ϛωκα ἰν(δικτιῶνος) ια:–

Michael Lulludes (or Luludes) of Ephesus was a learned copyist who fled from Ephesus after its capture by the Turks on 24 October 1304 and settled down as a refugee in Crete, where he continued writing manuscripts. The above subscription recalls a similar historical allusion in another subscription by Lulludes in MS Venice Greco 292 (colloc. 914), fol. 327ᵛ, of A.D. 1306, when he was only a lector (cf. Turyn, *DGMItaly*, I, p. 106). At some later time (after A.D. 1312/1313, the date of MS Arundel 523), Lulludes, who in the meantime changed the spelling of his name to Luludes, became πρωτο- ψάλτης of the Greek Church of Crete.

On Michael Lulludes (Luludes), his life and activities, his MSS, and the capture of Ephesus by the Turks, cf. S. P. Lampros, Μιχαὴλ Λουλλούδης ὁ 'Εφέσιος καὶ ἡ ὑπὸ τῶν Τούρκων ἅλωσις τῆς 'Εφέσου, in Νέος 'Ελλ., 1 (1904), pp. 209–12 (p. 209, on MS Arundel 523); Vogel–Gardthausen, pp. 314f.; P. Lemerle, *L'Emirat d'Aydin, Byzance et l'Occident. Recherches sur «La Geste d'Umur Pacha»*, Bibliothèque Byzantine, Etudes, 2 (Paris, 1957), p. 20 note 4 (*ibid.*, on this MS); Turyn, *DGMItaly*, I, pp. 105–8 (p. 107, on this MS); *idem*, "Michael Lulludes (or Luludes), a Scribe of the Palaeologan Era," *RSBN*, N.S. 10–11 (XX–XXI) (1973–1974), pp. 3–15 (on this MS, pp. 4f., 15).[191a]

In reference to Manuel Hyalinas, who commissioned this MS, it should be pointed out that the Hyalinas (Ialinas) family belonged to the local Cretan nobility and is well attested there from the Middle Ages on through the 17th century.[192] The title of εὐγενέστατος ἄρχων, attributed to Manuel Hyalinas in the headline of the dedicatory poem on fol. 145ʳ, simply means that he was a nobleman.[193] Conceivably, this sponsor of the MS may be identical with Hemanuel Jalina of Candia recorded in a Venetian document of 28 February 1334.[194]

On Plate **52** we reproduce folio 22ʳ, containing CONSTANTINE MANASSES, CHRONICLE, verses 863–87 (ed. I. Bekker, *Constantini Manassis Breviarium historiae metricum*, Bonn ed. [1837], pp. 40f.; or ed. Migne, Patr. Gr., 127,

---

[191a] A. Markopoulos presented a paper, Συμπληρωματικὰ γιὰ τὸν Μιχαὴλ Λουλούδη, to the 4th International Congress of Cretan Studies in Herakleion in August 1976. The paper (which was delivered too late to be taken into account in this book) is expected to be published in Πεπραγμένα τοῦ Δ' Διεθνοῦς Κρητολογικοῦ Συνεδρίου.

[192] On the Ὑαλινᾶς family in Crete, cf. P. Canart, "Les épigrammes de Thomas Trivizanos," Θησαυρίσματα, 8 (1971), p. 241; *idem*, "L'unique exemplaire connu de l'œuvre grecque de Thomas Trivizanos," in *Studi offerti a Roberto Ridolfi, direttore de «La Bibliofilia»*, Biblioteca di bibliografia italiana, LXXI (Florence, 1973), p. 181 note 35; Turyn, "Michael Lulludes (or Luludes)," p. 5; N. B. Tomadakes, Βυζαντινὰ καὶ Μεταβυζαντινά, II (Athens, 1978), pp. 328f.

[193] On the indigenous ἄρχοντες, the local Greek aristocracy, in Venetian-dominated Crete, cf. E. Gerland, "Histoire de la noblesse crétoise au moyen âge," *ROL*, 10 (1903–1904), pp. 211ff. (on the meaning of εὐγενέστατος ἄρχων, p. 213 note 1); F. Thiriet, *La Romanie vénitienne au Moyen Age*, BEFAR, 193 (Paris, 1959), pp. 128–33 and *passim*.

[194] Cf. S. M. Theotokes, Θεσπίσματα τῆς Βενετικῆς Γερουσίας *1281–1385*, in 'Ακαδημία 'Αθηνῶν. Μνημεῖα τῆς ἑλληνικῆς ἱστορίας, II,1 (Athens, 1936), p. 143, document xvi 35; the same document was summarized by F. Thiriet, *Régestes des délibérations du Sénat de Venise concernant la Romanie*, I (Paris – The Hague, 1958), p. 32, no. 44; also cf. *idem*, La Romanie vénitienne au Moyen Age, p. 299.

cols. 252 B 6 – 253 B 2). For other specimens of Michael Lulludes' handwriting, cf. G. Wattenbach and A. von Velsen, *Exempla codicum graecorum
litteris minusculis scriptorum* (Heidelberg, 1878), pl. xx (from MS Venice
Greco 292); Turyn, *DGMItaly*, II, pls. 83, 235*b* (from the same MS); Omont,
Fac-similés ... du IXe au XIVe siècle, pl. lxxii (from MS Paris Grec 2207).
It should be comprehensively recorded here that Michael Lulludes (Luludes)
is known to have written these MSS subscribed by him: Paris Grec 2207
(of A.D. 1299), Venice Greco 292 (of A.D. 1306), London Arundel 523 (of
A.D. 1312/1313), Vienna theolog. graec. 311, Sinai Greek 1342. Apart from
these MSS, I attributed to the hand of Lul(l)udes the following MSS: Paris
Grec 1251; Paris Grec 205 (of A.D. 1326/1327); Paris, Bibliothèque Sainte-
Geneviève 3400 (major part); Vatic. graec. 329. On all these MSS, cf. Turyn,
DGMItaly, I, pp. 105–8; *idem*, "Michael Lulludes (or Luludes)."

MS London Arundel 523 once belonged to Metrophanes III, patriarch of Constantinople
(1565–1572 and 1579–1580), who donated his MSS to the monastery of the Holy Trinity τοῦ
'Εσόπτρου on the island of Χάλκη (southeast of Constantinople, in the Sea of Marmara).[195]
On fol. 2^v there is the characteristic ownership entry of the monastery in five political verses
and, below it, the dodecasyllabic invocation in behalf of Metrophanes.[196] In the catalogue of
the Metrophanes MSS at Chalce, compiled in A.D. 1572 and published by Legrand, *Notice biographique sur Jean et Théodose Zygomalas*, pp. 207–16, there are two MSS of Manasses' Chronicle
listed (p. 210, lines 3–1 from the bottom). One of these MSS is evidently identical with the
present MS Arundel 523.[197] Possibly this is the MS which was borrowed from Metrophanes by

[195] Cf. above, p. 24 and note 73.
[196] Cf. above, pp. 24, 55; below, pp. 77, 116.
[197] This is the listing of the two MSS of Manasses' Chronicle in the catalogue of the Metrophanes
MSS at Chalce (Legrand, *Notice biographique*, p. 210, lines 3–1 from the bottom): Κωνσταντίνου τοῦ
Μανασσῆ ἱστορικὰ βιβλία δύο, μήκος δεύτερον, βαμβίκινα· περιέχει τὸ ἓν καὶ τὰ πάτρια τῆς πόλεως καὶ τὰ ὀφφίκια
τὰ βασιλικά. Thus there were, among the Metrophanes MSS in the monastery at Chalce, one with
Manasses' Chronicle only, and another containing, in addition to Manasses, Pseudo-Codinus' Πάτρια
Κωνσταντινουπόλεως and Pseudo-Codinus' De officiis. It is then obvious that one of these MSS, containing
Manasses without the other two texts, is identical with Arundel 523. The other MS, which also contained Pseudo-Codinus' Πάτρια and Pseudo-Codinus' De officiis in addition to Manasses, is most
probably identical with the main bulk of the present MS Vienna Supplem. graec. 174 (as was pointed
out by J. Verpeaux, *Pseudo-Kodinos, Traité des Offices*, Le Monde Byzantin, 1 [Paris, 1966], pp. 89f.;
cf. also Th. Preger, *Scriptores originvm Constantinopolitanarvm*, II, Teubner [1907], p. viii, on the
same MS when it was MS Nikolsburg I.132). On this MS, cf. H. Hunger, *Katalog der griechischen
Handschriften der Österreichischen Nationalbibliothek. Supplementum Graecum*, Biblos-Schriften, **15**
(Vienna, 1957), pp. 108–10. Actually, some other part at the beginning, also supplied with the
ownership entry of the Chalce monastery, was added to the main MS, and both parts were bound
together. The Vienna MS was once owned by Ferdinand Hoffmann, Baron von Grünpichel (Grünbüchel, Grünpühel)-Strechau (1540–1607), then was from 1679 on (along with the other MSS of the
Hoffmann collection) the property of Prince Ferdinand von Dietrichstein in Nikolsburg, i.e., Mikulov
(in Czechoslovakia). Around 1935, the Dietrichstein library in Mikulov was dissolved, and this MS was
bought by the Österreichische Nationalbibliothek in Vienna. On the Hoffmann and the Dietrichstein
libraries, cf. B. Dudík, "Handschriften der fürstlich Dietrichstein'schen Bibliothek zu Nikolsburg
in Mähren," *Archiv für österreichische Geschichte*, 39 (1868), pp. 420–23; E. Gollob, *Verzeichnis der
griechischen Handschriften in Österreich ausserhalb Wiens*, SBWien, Philos.-hist.Cl., 146,7 (1903),
pp. 57–90 (pp. 70–74, on the former MS Nikolsburg I.132, i.e., the present MS Vienna Supplem.
graec. 174); W. Weinberger, *Beiträge zur Handschriftenkunde*, II, SBWien, Philos.-hist.Kl., **161**,4
(1909), p. 46 note 2.
    With regard to the above listing in the catalogue of the Metrophanes MSS, it should be pointed
out that the listing recorded both MSS of Manasses as bombycine MSS. While Arundel 523 is bombycine, the other MS, Vienna Supplem. graec. 174, both on account of its age (*ca.* 1500) and its size,
is obviously of Western paper. The Chalce cataloger evidently distinguished only parchment MSS,
ἐν μεμβράναις, and paper MSS which were called βαμβίκινα, without any distinction whether they were
of Oriental or Western paper.

German Ambassador Albert von Wise (Wyss), who did not return it. Metrophanes complained about it to Stephan Gerlach, preacher of the German embassy, on 28 December 1577.[198]

If this MS was not returned to Metrophanes by Albert von Wyss, who died in Constantinople in 1569, then it is likely that, after his death, the MS was carried by some of his associates from Constantinople to the territory of the German empire or to the Netherlands. It is noteworthy that there are in the Arundel collection a few more MSS from this Chalce monastery with the characteristic ownership entries and the Metrophanes invocations.[199] Some of the Chalce MSS were obviously sold by the monastery to scholars, diplomats, and travelers from Western Europe. It is conceivable that the Chalce MSS that found their way to the Arundel collection were bought together in one lot by the founder of the collection, Thomas Howard, second Earl of Arundel, perhaps when he was on a diplomatic mission on the Continent in 1636 and visited Holland and such centers as Nuremberg and Vienna, or on some other of his travels to the Continent, or through some agent.[200]

At any rate, MS Arundel 523 belonged to the collection gathered by Thomas Howard, second Earl of Arundel (1586–1646). His grandson, Henry Howard, sixth Duke of Norfolk (1628–1684),[201] presented the bulk of the Arundel collection in 1667 to the Royal Society of London (cf. the

---

[198] Cf. Stephan Gerlach der Aeltere, *Tage-Buch Der ... An die Ottomannische Pforte zu Constantinopel Abgefertigten ... Gesandtschafft* (Frankfurt am Main, 1674), p. 425ᵇ, lines 22 ff.: "Er [i.e., Metrophanes] redet auch mit mir von allerhand Griechischen Büchern *de argumento* τῆς μεγάλης βιβλιοθήκης τοῦ φωτίου πατριάρχου: *de Manasse Chronographo*, welchen er dem Hn. Gesandten Albert von Wise / ihn abzuschreiben / gelehnet / aber ihn nit wieder bekommen habe / auch nit die παραλλήλα *Damasceni*, ein herrliches Buch" (cf. Legrand, *op. cit.*, p. 209 note 1). The same complaint of Metrophanes was reported by Gerlach in a letter addressed to Martin Crusius on 29 December 1577; cf. Martinvs Crvsivs, *Tvrcograeciae libri octo* (Basel [1584]; repr. Modena, 1972), p. 512, lines 36 f.: [Metrophanes] *conquestus, sibi aliquot libros furto ablatos esse*: παράλληλα *Damasceni, & Chronicon Manassis*. I assume that of the two Manasses MSS at Chalce Ambassador von Wyss borrowed the older MS, i.e., the present Arundel 523, rather than the newer one, the present Vienna Supplem. graec. 174.

Albert von Wyss, a Dutchman, was at first a diplomatic agent of the German empire in Constantinople, and then German ambassador to Turkey from 1563 until his death on 21 October 1569 (cf. J. von Hammer, *Geschichte des Osmanischen Reiches*, III [Pest, 1828], pp. 400, 529, 776; A. J. van der Aa, *Biographisch Woordenboek der Nederlanden*, XX [Haarlem, 1877], pp. 497 f.). Von Wyss died and was buried in Constantinople in 1569. This means that the MS of Manasses was borrowed by him from Metrophanes in 1569 at the latest. It is noteworthy that, although the borrowed MS was not at its place in Chalce in 1572, it was nonetheless listed in the catalogue of 1572, obviously on the basis of Metrophanes' or the monastery's records.

On Stephan Gerlach (1546–1612), preacher to the German embassy to Turkey in the period 1573–1578, cf. *ADB*, IX, p. 23.

[199] MSS Arundel 519 and Arundel 541 carry the well-known ownership entries of the Chalce monastery and the Metrophanes invocations (cf. Forshall, *Catalogue*, I,1, pp. 153, 165). According to Omont, "Notes," p. 325, MS Arundel 535 also shows the same characteristic features.

[200] On Thomas Howard, second Earl of Arundel (1585–1646), cf. *DNB*, X, pp. 73–76; on his visits to Holland, Nuremberg, and Vienna in 1636, p. 74. It is a well-known fact that in 1636 he purchased in Nuremberg a considerable part of the library of the prominent humanist, statesman, and military leader, Bilibald Pirkheimer (1470–1530), obviously from his heirs, and that most MSS in the Arundel collection came from the Pirkheimer library (cf. Forshall, *Catalogue*, I,1, p. v; *DNB*, X, p. 76). On Bilibald Pirkheimer, cf. J. Ch. Adelung and H. W. Rotermund, *Fortsetzung und Ergänzungen zu Christian Gottlieb Jöchers allgemeinem Gelehrten-Lexiko*, VI (Bremen, 1819), cols. 253–59 (col. 255, on the purchase of a part of Pirkheimer's library by the Earl of Arundel in 1636); *ADB*, XXVI, pp. 810–17; Sandys, *History of Classical Scholarship*, II, pp. 259 f. In 1636 the Pirkheimer library was in the possession of the successor to the preceding heir, Johann III Im Hof (1563–1629) of Nuremberg (cf. G. A. Will, *Nürnbergisches Gelehrten-Lexicon*, II [Nuremberg–Altdorf, 1756], p. 231). However, Pirkheimer himself died in 1530, and MS Arundel 523 was in Chalce around 1563 (when von Wyss became German ambassador) and was removed from the Chalce library by von Wyss in 1569 at the latest. Thus this MS could not conceivably have been in the Pirkheimer library during Pirkheimer's life or in 1636 at the time of the purchase by the Earl of Arundel, unless we assume that the heirs of Pirkheimer continued to add some acquisitions to the Pirkheimer library during the century following his death. We have no information to this effect.

[201] On Henry Howard, sixth Duke of Norfolk (1628–1684), and his disposal of the Arundel library, cf. *DNB*, X, pp. 32 f.

stamp on fol. 3ʳ of this MS). The Royal Society sold the Arundel MSS to the British Museum in 1831.[202]

On this MS, cf. Forshall, *Catalogue,* I,1, p. 155; Vogel–Gardthausen, pp. 314f.; Omont, "Notes," p. 346.

Plate 53: A.D. 1314/1315.

Oxford, Bodleian Library, ms Cromwell 22. Parchment, 325 × 240 mm., 464 pages (pages 463–64 are a back flyleaf), 2 columns to a page, 30 lines to a column. Contents: (pages 1–20) two tables of contents, in red; (pages 21–22) St. John Chrysostom*, Sermo catecheticus in Sanctum Pascha (ed. Migne, Patr. Gr., 59, cols. 721–24); (pages 22–450) St. Theodore the Studite, Short Catecheses;[203] (pages 451–61) St. Theodore the Studite, Testament (ed. Migne, Patr. Gr., 99, cols. 1813–24). The MS was completed by the hieromonk Marcus, who recorded his name cryptographically and wrote openly the rest of the subscription in A.M. 6823 = A.D. 1314/1315 (page 450 – Plate **111a**): ξϑ'ᾱπλχ ʹϞεᾱλξλνϑʹ|υλχ | ∙:∙ τέλος πληρῶ, καὶ ϑ(εὸ)ς χά|ριν νέμει:– | ∙:∙ ἔτους ͵ϛῶκγ̅· ἰν(δικτιῶνος) ιγ̅: The cryptographic part of the subscription is to be read as follows: Μάρκου ἱερομονά|χου.[204]

On Plate **53** we reproduce page 37, containing a passage from Sᴛ. Tʜᴇᴏᴅᴏʀᴇ ᴛʜᴇ Sᴛᴜᴅɪᴛᴇ, Sʜᴏʀᴛ Cᴀᴛᴇᴄʜᴇsᴇs (from Catechesis 7, On the Ascension of Our Savior, Jesus Christ: ed. I. Cozza-Luzi, in A. Mai, *Nova Patrvm Bibliotheca,* IX [Rome, 1888], 1, pp. 16, 14 – 17, 10; or ed. E. Auvray, *Sancti patris nostri et confessoris Theodori Studitis praepositi Parva catechesis* [Paris, 1891], pp. 23, 25 – 24, 51). The red capitals projected to the left indicate the beginning of a section in the preceding line.[205]

On the Cromwell MSS in the Bodleian Library, cf. above, p. 11.

On this MS, cf. Coxe, I, cols. 450f.; *Summary Catalogue,* II,1, p. 12 (under S.C. 282); Vogel–Gardthausen, p. 292; Aubineau, *Codices Chrysostomici graeci,* I, p. 217.

Plate 54: A.D. 1315.

Oxford, Christ Church, ms 71. Parchment, 265 × 205 mm., 342 fols., 18 lines to a page. Contents: St. John Climacus, Ladder of Paradise. The MS was subscribed in May A.M. 6823 = A.D. 1315 (fol. 342ᵛ – Plate **111b**): ἐτελειώϑη τὸ παρὸν βιβλίον, μηνὶ | μαΐῳ ἰν(δικτιῶνος) ιγ̅· ἔτους ͵ϛῶκʹγ· δέομαι δὲ |

---

[202] On the history of the Arundel collections, cf. Forshall, *Catalogue,* I,1, pp. ɪ–ᴠ; Fletcher, *English Book Collectors,* pp. 91f.; de Ricci, *English Collectors,* pp. 25f.

[203] The correct title of this collection of sermons by St. Theodore the Studite is "Short Catecheses" in the plural (not "Short Catechesis" in the singular); this was demonstrated by J. Leroy, "Les Petites Catéchèses de S. Théodore Studite," *Le Muséon,* 71 (1958), pp. 329–58. On the Short Catecheses of St. Theodore the Studite, cf. Ch. Van de Vorst, "La Petite Catéchèse de S. Théodore Studite," *AnalBoll,* 33 (1911), pp. 43f. For a characterization of the collection of homilies carried, among other similar MSS, by MS Cromwell 22, cf. J. Leroy, "Un nouveau témoin de la Grande Catéchèse de saint Théodore Studite," *REB,* 15 (1957), pp. 75f. (symbol C for Cromwell 22). On the manuscript tradition of the Short Catecheses of St. Theodore the Studite, now cf. I. Ševčenko, "Kosinitza 27, a Temporarily Lost Studite Manuscript Found Again," in *Studia Codicologica,* pp. 433–42.

[204] On the conventional cryptographic code, cf. above, p. 56 note 128.

[205] On the meaning of the projection of a letter to the left, cf. above, p. 22 note 63.

ὑμῶν, ὅσοις τῶ παρόντι ἐντυχεῖν | ἐξέσται, ὑπερεύχεσθαι ⟦τῆς ἐμῆς⟧ | ψυχῆς +
On Plate **54** we reproduce folio 158ʳ, containing a passage from Sт. John
Climacus, Ladder of Paradise, chap. 14 (ed. Migne, Patr. Gr., 88, col. 865
A 13 – B 11; ed. Trevisan, I, p. 343, 5–16).

This MS once belonged to the monastery of Ὀμπλός, according to the ownership entry
written in the handwriting of the latter part of the 17th century on fol. 342ᵛ: † αὕτη ἡ βηλως
ὑπαρχη τῆς πανα|αγίας μοῦ τῆς ἐν τῶ Ωμπλώ | καὶ ἢ τῆς τὴν ἐξιλεῶσί²⁰⁵ᵃ απαυτου | να ἐνε ἀφόρη-
σμένος απ(ὸ) τῶ π(ατ)ρ(ὸ)ς | υἱοῦ καὶ ἁγίου πνέματός²⁰⁶ ἐν τω | νην ἀιωνὶ καὶ εν τω μελωτι:–²⁰⁷
The monastery of the Presentation (τῶν Εἰσοδίων) of the B.V.M. in Ὀμπλός, μονὴ τῆς Θεοτόκου
Ὀμπλοῦ, in the Peloponnesus, southeast of Patras, near the community of Κρήνη (in the
eparchy of Patras), is sufficiently attested and is still in existence.²⁰⁸ To the left of the above
ownership entry, the name of the hieromonk Ioasaph is recorded (the name of Ioasaph was
written in a monocondylion): † Ἰωάσαφ ἱερο(μον)αχὸ(ς). This entry was repeated twice on the
same page, to the lower left and in the lower margin.

The MS presumably belonged to William Wake (1657–1737), archbishop of Canterbury, who
willed his library to Christ Church, Oxford. On Wake, cf. *DNB*, XX, pp. 445f. On his MSS at
Christ Church, cf. C. H. Hoole, *An Account of Some Greek Manuscripts Contained in the Library
of Christ Church, Oxford* (London, 1895), pp. 4–19 and 23–31, mainly on Greek MSS.

On this MS, cf. G. W. Kitchin, *Catalogus codicum mss. qui in bibliotheca Aedis Christi apud
Oxonienses adservantur* (Oxford, 1867), p. 29 (under no. LXXI); Van de Vorst–Delehaye, *Catalogus*, p. 384.

Plate 55: A.D. 1315/1316.

Cambridge, Trinity College, ms B.10.16. Bombycine, 185 × 127 mm.,
363 fols., 28 lines to a page. Contents: New Testament, without the Apocalypse (Four Gospels, Acts of the Apostles, Catholic Epistles, Pauline Epistles),
adapted for liturgical use. Included are also two hagiographic texts: (fols.
333ᵛ–335ᵛ) Dorotheus of Tyre*, Index of the 72 Disciples (*BHG*³ 152n);
(fol. 350ʳ–350ᵛ) Hippolytus of Thebes, Chronicle on the Genealogy of the
B.V.M., fragment on St. James, the Lord's brother (Ἰάκωβος γενόμενος ἐπί-

---

[205a] On the meaning of this verb ("to take away," "to remove") in such ownership entries, cf.
L. Polites, Παλαιογραφικά, in Ἑλληνικά, 24 (1971), p. 137.

[206] On πνέματος instead of πνεύματος, cf. Jannaris, *Historical Greek Grammar*, p. 93, § 179.

[207] On μελωτι, i.e., μέλλοτι, instead of μέλλοντι, cf. Dieterich, *Untersuchungen*, pp. 114, 284 (on ντ
changed to τ). On the malediction against a thief of the MS contained in this subscription, cf. below,
p. 80 note 212.

[208] The monastery of Omplos is listed in Λεξικὸν τῶν δήμων, p. 259 (Μονὴ Ὀμπλοῦ). On the history
and documents of this monastery, and on its place-name, cf. Eleutheroudakes, Ἐγκυκλ.Λεξ., X,
p. 81; Μεγ.Ἑλλ.Ἐγκυκλ., XVIII, p. 892; Θρησκ.Ἠθ.Ἐγκυκλ., IX, cols. 921f.; S. N. Thomopoulos, Ἡ
ἱερὰ μονὴ Ὀμπλοῦ (Patras, 1903), especially pp. 13ff.; *idem*, Ἱστορία τῆς πόλεως Πατρῶν ἀπὸ ἀρχαιοτάτων
χρόνων μέχρι τοῦ *1821*, 2nd ed. by K. N. Triantaphyllou (Patras, 1950), pp. 595–98; D. A. Zakythinos, *Le Despotat grec de Morée*, II (Athens, 1953), pp. 307f.; L. Polites, Ἡ μονὴ τοῦ Ὀμπλοῦ κοντὰ
στὴν Πάτρα, in Πελοποννησιακά, 1 (1956), pp. 238–52; K. N. Triantaphyllou, Ἱστορικὸν Λεξικὸν
τῶν Πατρῶν (Patras, 1959), pp. 444–49; A. Bon, *Le Peloponnèse byzantin jusqu'en 1204*, Bibliothèque Byzantine, Etudes, 1 (Paris, 1951), p. 144 and note 3; *idem*, *La Morée franque*, BEFAR, 213
(Paris, 1969), Text, p. 353 and note 1; M. Richard, *Répertoire des bibliothèques et des catalogues
de manuscrits grecs*, Suppl. 1, Documents, Etudes et Répertoires publiés par l'Institut de Recherche
et d'Histoire des Textes, IX (Paris, 1964), p. 47 (no. 692d); N. A. Bees, in *BZ*, 15 (1906), p. 479;
S. P. Lampros, Ὀγδοήκοντα πατριαρχικὰ σιγίλλια καὶ τεσσαράκοντα τέσσαρα μοναστηριακὰ ἔγγραφα τῆς ἐν
Παρισίοις Ἐθνικῆς Βιβλιοθήκης, in Νέος Ἑλλ., 3 (1906), pp. 386f. (no. 31); D. A. Zakythenos, Ἀνέκδοτα
πατριαρχικὰ ἔγγραφα τῶν χρόνων τῆς Τουρκοκρατίας, in Ἑλληνικά, 3 (1930), pp. 115–18; Ph. D. Apostolo-
poulos, "44 documents ecclésiastiques inédits du XVIIIᵉ siècle," Ἑλληνικά, 27 (1974), pp. 327f. (no.
33); D. I. Georgakas, Συμβολὴ εἰς τὴν τοπωνυμικὴν ἔρευναν, in Ἀθηνᾶ, 48 (1938), pp. 49–53 (on the place-
name Ὀμπλός).

σκοπος πρῶτος Ἱεροσολύμων – ἀνεψιοῖ λέγοντες εἶναι· τουτέστιν ἐξάδελφοι· υἱὸς δὲ τοῦ Ἰωσὴφ ὁ κ(ύριο)ς ἐνομίζετο: *BHG Auct.* 766f).[209] The MS was written by the hieromonk Iacobus on Mount Sinai in A.M. 6824 = A.D. 1315/1316, according to the subscription on fol. 160ᵛ, which was partially canceled and partially erased (Plate **111c**): † αὔτη ἡ βίβλο(ς), ἤγουν τὸ ἅγιον εὐαγγ(έλιον), ὁμοίως καὶ ὁ ἀπόστολο(ς) | ἐγράφησαν ἐν τῷ ὄρει τῷ ἁγίῳ Συνᾶ· ἔνθα Μωυσῆς | οἶδεν τὴν ἁγίαν βάτον· καὶ ἐδέξατο τὸν νόμον· | ἐγράφησαν δὲ ἐνέτη ͵ϛωκδ. διαχειρὸς ἐμοῦ ἀμαρ|⁵τωλοῦ Ἰακώβου ἱερο(μον)αχ(ου)· ⟦καὶ ἐ––– ἄτην⟧ | ⟦πρὸ(ς) τὴν μονὴν τῆς ὑπεραγίας Θ(εοτό)κου τῆς Σπηλαιωτήσης, τοῦ ἐν⟧ | ⟦τῇ νῆσσω Χίω χάριν δια τὰς πολλάς μου ἀμαρτίας⟧ | ⟦καὶ τῶν γονέων ἡμῶν· καὶ εἴ τις ταύτην ἀποστερή⟧⟦ση ἀπὸ τῆς τοιαύτης μονῆς, –––⟧ | ¹⁰⟦δόλω ––– κατάραν –––⟧ | ⟦τ––– ἀνάλωσις καὶ –––⟧ +

The erased part of line 5 presumably contained words to the effect that this MS was being sent[210] (to the monastery of the Θεοτόκος Σπηλαιώτισσα, as indicated in line 6). It is impossible to determine with certainty the location of the monastery in question.[211] The same erasure makes it difficult to explain the reference to the island of Chios. Perhaps Iacobus was sending the MS to that monastery located on Chios because of some past event in his life which took place on the island. Or perhaps by inadvertence he omitted a word after Χίω which would have made the sentence clearer. At any rate, he was sending the MS as an expiation for his own and his parents' sins. It is likely that Iacobus was a native of Chios and that the monastery mentioned in the above subscription was situated there. There is no mention in the subscription that Iacobus was a hieromonk in the monastery of St. Catherine on Sinai. He may have been simply a pilgrim to Sinai at the time of writing this MS. The end of the subscription, erased on lines 8–11, seems to have contained a malediction (cf. line 10 κατάραν) against those who would purloin the MS.[212]

---

[209] Cf. F. Diekamp, *Hippolytos von Theben. Texte und Untersuchungen* (Münster, 1898), pp. 7, 4 – 10, 3; Migne, Patr. Gr., 72, cols. 457 D 10 – 458 D 17; A. Xerouchakes, Τὰ σύσσημα τῆς Ὑπεραγίας Θεοτόκου καὶ τοῦ Κυρίου ἡμῶν Ἰησοῦ Χριστοῦ, in Θεολογία, 11 (1933), p. 349, lines 5–28 (in a version identical with that of the Cambridge MS, but the manuscript text as reprinted by Xerouchakes is marred by a few slips); cf. also Migne, Patr. Gr., 117, cols. 1040 B 5 – 1041 B 12.

The two texts from Pseudo-Dorotheus and Hippolytus of Thebes appear often in New Testament MSS: cf. von Soden, I,1, pp. 363–65, 361f.

[210] I assume that the obliterated part of line 5 referred to the sending of this MS, because the preposition πρὸς (in πρὸ(ς) τὴν μονὴν) seems to imply it. The 'donating' or 'dedicating' or 'depositing' would call for the prepositions εἰς or ἐν (cf. Krumbacher, Κτήτωρ, pp. 411–14).

[211] There were several monasteries known under this name in the Middle Ages. One is especially tempted to think of the monastery of the Assumption of the B.V.M. Σπηλαιώτισσα in Crete (in the place Ἅγιος Βασίλειος, in the eparchy of Πεδιάς), because this monastery was a μετόχιον of the Sinai monastery (cf. Μεγ.Ἑλλ.Ἐγκυκλ., XXII, p. 233). It would be natural for a Sinai monk to donate a MS to the μετόχιον of his monastery. However, as I point out below, there is no basis for assuming that our hieromonk Iacobus was a monk of the Sinai monastery.

[212] On such maledictions (which usually threatened the thief of a MS with the curses of the 318 Fathers of the First Council of Nicaea) in colophons and ownership entries of Greek MSS, cf. B. de Montfaucon, *Palaeographia graeca, sive de ortu et progressu literarum graecarum* (Paris, 1708; repr. [Farnborough, 1970]), pp. 57f., 63, 69, 75f., 89, 385; Gardthausen, *Griechische Palaeographie*, II, pp. 433f.; Clark, *Greek New Testament Manuscripts in America*, pp. 15, 64, 66f., 96 (with the word κατάραν), 188, 196 (κατάρας), 236, 303, 363, 364 ([κ]ατάρας); R. Devreesse, *Introduction à l'étude des manuscrits grecs* (Paris, 1954), p. 55; L. Polites, Ὁδηγὸς καταλόγου χειρογράφων, in Γενικὸν Συμβούλιον

On Plate **55** we reproduce folio 141ᵛ, containing a passage from the GOSPEL OF ST. JOHN 8:58 – 9:12. This passage contains the end of the lesson for Tuesday of the 5th week after Easter (the whole lesson is John 8:51–59) and the beginning of the lesson for the 5th Sunday after Easter, or the 6th Sunday from Easter, counting Easter Sunday as the 1st one (the whole lesson is John 9:1–38). For the time and extent of these lessons, cf. Scrivener, I, p. 80; Gregory, I, p. 346. In line 4, there is to the right of the line the mark τέλ(ος) γ̄, indicating the end of the lesson for Tuesday (viz., of the 5th week after Easter). To the left of line 5, there is the mark ἀρχ(ὴ), which points to the beginning of the next lesson. In the upper margin, there is the liturgical note which indicates the time of this lesson, the customary lesson prefix, and the modification of the beginning of the standard text for lesson use:[213] κυ(ριακῇ) ϛ τ(ο)ῦ τυφλοῦ· τῶ και(ρῷ) ἐκεί(νῳ)· παράγων ὁ ’Ι(ησοῦ)ς ἴδεν. The capital letter Π in red projected to the left points out that an important text section begins in the preceding line.[214] The figure πθ in the left margin indicates that this pericope belongs to the Eusebian section 89 of John (the whole section 89 comprises John 8:21 – 10:14); the figure ῑ marked a little lower to the left shows that section 89 of John belongs to the Eusebian canon 10.[215] The liturgical note and the marks discussed are in red, in accordance with the accepted practice for the New Testament MSS.[216] Only the figure ῑ of the Eusebian canon is in black, while the Eusebian section number πθ is in red; this is irregular, because normally (at the beginning of a Eusebian section) the section number is marked in the margin in black, and the pertinent canon number is marked in red below the section number.[217] On the page reproduced, the Eusebian section number πθ was repeated there in order to mark that the pericope still belonged to the Eusebian section 89 which began before and continued here. The Eusebian canon number ῑ may have been added in black in the margin separately, perhaps by some other hand.

The MS was collated by F. H. Scrivener, according to his autographic note on the recto of the flyleaf that precedes fol. 1: "Collated Feb 9 1854 | F. H. Scrivener." Cf. Scrivener, *Codex Augiensis*, pp. xxxviii–xl (a description

Βιβλιοθηκῶν τῆς Ἑλλάδος, 17 (Athens, 1961), p. 31; Metzger, *The Text of the New Testament*, p. 20. On such maledictions in general, cf. W. Wattenbach, *Das Schriftwesen im Mittelalter*, 3rd ed. (Leipzig, 1896), pp. 527–34 (p. 529, on a Greek MS); L. S. Thompson, "A Cursory Survey of Maledictions," *Bulletin of The New York Public Library*, 56 (1952), pp. 55–75 (on Greek MSS especially, pp. 57, 59).

[213] On the usual features of the liturgical notes in New Testament MSS adapted for liturgical use, cf. above, p. 43 note 100.

[214] On the meaning of a letter (usually a capital) projected to the left, cf. above, p. 22 note 63.

[215] On the extent of the Eusebian section 89 in John and its listing in the Eusebian canon, cf. von Soden, I,1, p. 401. In general, on Eusebian sections and canons, cf. Gregory, II, pp. 861–68; von Soden, I,1, pp. 388–402; von Dobschütz, *Eberhard Nestle's Einführung*, pp. 35f.; Metzger, *The Text of the New Testament*, pp. 24f.; Nestle, *Novum Testamentum graece*, pp. 30*, 32*–37*.

[216] On the red color of liturgical notes and marks in New Testament MSS adapted for liturgical use, cf. above, p. 43 note 101.

[217] On the traditional manner of marking the Eusebian section numbers in black and the Eusebian canon numbers in red, cf. von Dobschütz, *Eberhard Nestle's Einführung*, p. 35; Turyn, *Codices*, p. 79, pl. 47. The letter of Eusebius of Caesarea to Carpianus, in which he expounded his system of sections and canons, can be found conveniently in Nestle, *Novum Testamentum graece*, pp. 32*f.; on the red color of canon numbers, cf. *ibid.*, p. 32*, lines 27–29.

of MS Trinity B.10.16), 287ff. (a collation of the same MS with the symbols w for the Gospels, k for the Acts and the Catholic and Pauline Epistles). The evidence from MS Trinity College B.10.16 was occasionally used (with the Gregory–Aland number 489) in the edition of Aland et al., *The Greek New Testament*, cf. p. xix.

This MS is presumed to have been in the Pantocrator monastery on Mount Athos. It was acquired by the famous classical scholar, Richard Bentley (1662–1742), along with a few other Greek MSS which came to him from the same Pantocrator monastery. Bentley, master of Trinity College in Cambridge in the period 1700–1742, willed Greek MSS in his possession to Trinity College, to which they passed on his death.[218]

On this MS, cf. M. R. James, *The Western Manuscripts in the Library of Trinity College, Cambridge*, I (Cambridge, 1900), pp. 315f. (under no. 227); Vogel–Gardthausen, p. 156; Scrivener, I, p. 248 (under Evan. 507); Gregory, I, p. 195 (under Vier Evangelien 489); Aland, I, p. 87 (under the Gregory–Aland number 489); von Soden, I,1, p. 114 (under δ459); Van de Vorst–Delehaye, *Catalogus*, p. 291.

Plate 56: A.D. 1319.

London, British Museum, ms Burney 22. Parchment, 30 × 22 cm., 248 fols., 2 columns, 27–29 lines to a column. Contents: Lectionary of the Gospels (for the liturgical year beginning at Easter and for saints' days). The MS was subscribed on 27 January A.M. ⟨6⟩827 = A.D. 1319 (fol. 248ᵛ – Plate **112a**): ἐτελειώθ(η) τὸ παρὸν | ἅγιον εὐα(γγέλιον) κ(α)τ(ὰ) τὴν κ̅ζ̅ | τοῦ ἰαν-νουαρ(ίου) μηνὸς | τῆς ὠκ̅ζ̅ ἐγχρον(ίας) + | + This subscription was previously reproduced by Scrivener, I, pl. xiii (37) facing p. 343; on the text of this subscription, cf. Scrivener, I, p. 43 note 3. The MS was obviously written in Cyprus, as is suggested by the use of ἐγχρονίας instead of ἔτους and the omission of the millenary letter in the year date.[219] In the year date of the subscription, we must understand ⟨ς⟩ωκζ, since this is the only possible A.M. date for a medieval manuscript. The script style of the subscription fits the Cypriot calligraphy of the 14th century.[220]

On Plate **56** we reproduce folio 133ᵛ, containing a passage from the Lec-tionary of the Gospels, viz., a passage from the Gospel of St Luke 20:9–16 (ed. Εὐαγγέλιον [1880], p. 88ᵃ, 37 – 88ᵇ, 14; or ed. Εὐαγγέλιον [1968], p. 106ᵇ,

---

[218] On Richard Bentley, cf. *DNB*, II, pp. 306–14; R. C. Jebb, *Bentley* (London, 1882); Sandys, *History of Classical Scholarship*, II, pp. 401–10. On the bequest of his Greek MSS to Trinity College, cf. J. H. Monk, *The Life of Richard Bentley*, 2nd ed., II (London, 1833), p. 415. On the provenience of some of these MSS from Mount Athos, cf. J. Duplacy, "La provenance athonite des manuscrits grecs légués par R. Bentley à Trinity College, Cambridge et en particulier de l'oncial 0131 du Nouveau Testament," in B. L. Daniels and M. J. Suggs, eds., *Studies in the History and Text of the New Testament in honor of Kenneth Willis Clark*, Studies and Documents, XXIX (Salt Lake City, 1967), pp. 113–26 (pp. 117 and 124 note 24, on MS Trinity College B.10.16).

[219] On the use of ἐγχρονίας instead of ἔτους, and the omission of the millenary letter in year dates in subscriptions of Cypriot MSS and in dated notes written in Cyprus, cf. J. Darrouzès, "Autres manuscrits originaires de Chypre," *REB*, 15 (1957), p. 132; Turyn, *Codices*, pp. 117, 119, 122 (also on MS Burney 22), pls. 190*a–c*.

[220] For facsimile samples of Cypriot calligraphy of the 14th century, cf. *ibid.*, pls. 96, 190*a–c* (cf. *ibid.*, pp. 117ff.); Follieri, *Codices*, pl. 53 (cf. *ibid.*, pp. 76–78). Also cf. Turyn, *DGMItaly*, II, pl. 93 (cf. I, p. 119). Now cf. also P. Canart, "Un style d'écriture livresque dans les manuscrits chy-priotes du XIVᵉ siècle: la chypriote 'bouclée'," in *Paléographie grecque et byzantine*, pp. 319f., figs. 2–5.

16–39). This is a part of the lesson for Thursday of the 11th week in Luke (or of the 28th week after Pentecost); the whole lesson for this day is Luke 20:9–18 (cf. Gregory, I, p. 357). On the page reproduced, sentences have a red τελεία mark (+) at the end.[221] The red capital 'I projected to the left indicates the beginning of a larger text section.[222] The conservative writing of this liturgical book somehow lacks a characteristic Cypriot appearance; but the subscription vouches for the Cypriot origin of the MS.[223] For other facsimile specimens of the MS, cf. Forshall, *Catalogue*, I,2, pl. [I] in the upper right-hand corner; B. F. Westcott, "New Testament," in W. Smith, *A Dictionary of the Bible Comprising Its Antiquities, Biography, Geography, and Natural History*, II (London, 1863), pl. II fig. 4. This MS is written in two-column pages, in accordance with the usage which prevailed in lectionaries (cf. above, p. 17; cf. Plates **5, 6, 7, 11**).

The MS was collated by Scrivener, *Full and Exact Collation*, with the symbol y (cf. pp. lxi–lxiii for a description of the MS).

The MS was once owned by the so-called Chevalière d'Eon (fol. 1ʳ, lower margin): *De la Bibliotheque de la Chevaliere D'Eon*. This owner was Charles G. L. A. A. T. d'Eon de Beaumont, French political adventurer (1728–1810), who resided for long periods in London and died there. His valuable library, which also contained MSS, was auctioned in London in 1791.[224] Later this MS belonged to Charles Burney (1757–1817), whose library was acquired by the British Museum in 1818. On Burney and his library, cf. above, p. 44.

On this MS, cf. Forshall, *Catalogue*, I,2, p. 5; pl. [I] in the upper right-hand corner; Scrivener, I, pp. 345f. (under Evst. 259), p. 43 note 3, pl. XIII (37) facing p. 343; Gregory, I, p. 402 (under Evangelia 184); Aland, I, p. 214 (under the Gregory–Aland symbol *l* 184).

Plates 57 and 58: A.D. 1320/1321.

London, British Museum, ms Harley 5579. Bombycine, 247 × 175 mm., 221 fols. The original body of this MS consists of fols. 11 and 13–210 (between fols. 11 and 13, there is a modern insert fol. 12); the quires are quinions.[225] Contents: (fols. 1ʳ–2ᵛ) parchment leaves, containing Latin liturgical matter written in the 11th century; (fols. 3–10) modern paper flyleaves; (fol. 11ʳ) a fragment from Eusebius of Caesarea, Ecclesiastical History, III.31, 2–3 (ed. E. Schwartz, *Eusebius Werke*, II,1, GCS, IX,1 [Leipzig, 1903], p. 264, 7–19),

---

[221] On the τελεία sign, used as full-stop mark both in Old Testament and New Testament lectionaries, cf. above, p. 18 note 45; cf. Pls. **2, 6, 7, 11.**

[222] On the meaning of a letter (usually a capital) projected to the left, cf. above, p. 22 note 63.

[223] We have encountered a similar situation in MS London Additional 22506, containing the Four Gospels and written by Neophytus of Cyprus in A.D. 1304/1305 (cf. above, pp. 66 ff.), of which a specimen appears on Plate **46**. As I have observed (p. 68), there is nothing specifically Cypriot in the conventional writing of this scriptural MS, in spite of the scribe's Cypriot origin.

[224] On the Chevalier d'Eon de Beaumont, cf. L. G. Michaud, *Biographie universelle ancienne et moderne*, XII (Paris, n.d.), pp. 500–3 (p. 503, on his library and its auction); *Encyclopaedia Britannica*, VIII (Chicago [1973]), p. 628, *s.v.* Eon, The Chevalier d'.

[225] On the quinions in Harley 5579, cf. F. Wallis, "On Some MSS of the Writings of St. Athanasius: Part I," *JThS*, 3 (1902), p. 103; Wilson, *Mediaeval Greek Bookhands*, p. 31 (under no. 66). Wilson observed this feature also in another MS Oxford, Bodleian Library, Barocci 27, which he identified as written by the same scribe as Harley 5579. The quinion composition is now reported also from MS Athos Lavra E 43 written by the lector Romanus, most probably the same scribe (cf. below, p. 87 and note 245).

added by a later hand; (fol. 11ᵛ) table of contents, written by the scribe of this MS; (fol. 12ʳ, a modern insert) Latin list of contents by a modern hand, with references to the *editio Commeliniana* of St. Athanasius of Alexandria; (fol. 12ᵛ) blank; (fols. 13ʳ–210ʳ) St. Athanasius of Alexandria, Writings; (fols. 211–219) modern paper flyleaves, blank; (fols. 220ʳ–221ᵛ) parchment leaves with Latin liturgical matter, being a continuation of fols. 1ʳ–2ᵛ. The original MS (fols. 11ᵛ, 13ʳ–210ʳ) was written by the lector Romanus ⟨Chartophylax⟩ in A.M. 6829 = A.D. 1320/1321, according to the subscription on fol. 210ʳ (Plate **112b**): χειρὶ ἁμαρτωλῷ· ῾Ρωμανῶ ἀναγνώστη· ἔτους ͵ϛῶκθ· In this subscription, the words ἁμαρτωλῷ ῾Ρωμανῶ ἀναγνώστη were certainly meant to be genitives; their peculiar forms were due partly to Cypriot phonetics (see below on the Cypriot origin of the scribe), partly to the influence of the common declension pattern of spoken medieval Greek.[226]

Some other MSS written by the same scribe are known to exist.[227] The handwriting of Harley 5579 can conveniently serve as a basis for confirming the identity of the same scribe in other MSS. As specimens of Romanus' handwriting we can use Plates **112b, 57, 58,** from this MS; also *Pal. Soc.*, Ser. I, pl. 133 (= Harley 5579, fol. 111ʳ). A part of this plate was reproduced by Thompson, *Introduction*, p. 262 facsim. no. 76 (cf. *ibid.*, p. 255).

The same scribe wrote MS Paris Grec 234 (fols. 30ʳ–444ʳ) and subscribed it in May A.D. 1318 (on fol. 444ʳ): χειρὶ ἁμαρτωλῷ. ῾Ρωμανῶ ἀναγνωστ'· τõυ Χαρτοφύλακο(ς)· | τοῦ ἀπὸ Χ(ριστο)ῦ καταβάσεως ἔτους· ͵ατιῆ. μαίω μηνί· | βίβλο(ς) πέφυκα, ζῶντο(ς) ὕδατος κρίνη· (these 5 words form a dodecasyllable).[228] There appear in this subscription (after χειρὶ) the same peculiar forms of genitives as in the subscription of Harley 5579; ἀναγνωστ' was doubtlessly intended to be read ἀναγνώστ(η). These words were followed by the genitive of the family name τοῦ Χαρτοφύλακο(ς). The use of the Christian era in the subscription is noteworthy. Since we assume that the scribe was a Cypriot, this manner of dating the MS seems to have been influenced by the regional habit.[229] MS Paris Grec 234 (once Colbertinus 4185) was one of a shipment of MSS sent to Colbert from Cyprus in 1676 by Balthasar Sauvan, French consul

---

[226] On the occasional change of ου to ω in medieval Cypriot Greek, cf. A. A. Sakellarios, Τὰ Κυπριακά, II (Athens, 1891), p. μά, lines 8–9. On similar changes attested in medieval Greek elsewhere, cf. Turyn, *Codices*, pp. XIII, 23, 61f., 160. On ἀναγνώστη instead of ἀναγνώστου, cf. Sakellarios, *op. cit.*, II, p. ξά, penult line; ἀναγνώστη in the genitive is the common form in medieval and modern Greek (cf. A. Thumb, *Handbuch der neugriechischen Volkssprache*, 2nd ed. [Strasbourg, 1910], p. 45, § 68).

[227] Cf. Vogel–Gardthausen, p. 394; also p. 395, lines 2–4 and note 1; M. Naoumides, Σύμμεικτα παλαιογραφικά, in ᾿Επ.῾Ετ.Βυζ.Σπ., 39–40 (1972–1973), Λειμὼν τιμητικὴ προσφορὰ Ν. Β. Τωμαδάκη, pp. 380–83.

[228] On MS Paris Grec 234, cf. H. Omont, *Inventaire sommaire des manuscrits grecs de la Bibliothèque Nationale*, I (Paris, 1886), p. 26; Ehrhard, *Überlieferung und Bestand*, III,1, pp. 534f. and 534 note 2; Scrivener, I, p. 270 (under Evan. 761); Gregory, I, p. 217 (under Vier Evangelien 740); Aland, I, p. 101 (under the Gregory–Aland number 740); von Soden, I,1, p. 267 (symbol Θε⁴¹⁰); the original MS (fols. 30–444) is bombycine, 25 × 18 cm. On the text of the subscription of this MS, cf. Omont, *Fac-similés ... du IXᵉ au XIVᵉ siècle*, Appendix, p. 20. On Paris Grec 234 in connection with Cyprus, cf. J. Darrouzès, "Manuscrits originaires de Chypre à la Bibliothèque Nationale de Paris," *REB*, 8 (1950), p. 170. Now cf. also P. Canart, "Un style d'écriture livresque dans les manuscrits chypriotes du XIVᵉ siècle: la chypriote 'bouclée'," in *Paléographie grecque et byzantine*, pp. 308, 309 note 28, 313, 320 fig. 4 (a facsimile specimen).

[229] Cf. Darrouzès, "Autres manuscrits originaires de Chypre," *REB*, 15 (1957), p. 132.

in Larnaca.[230] The provenience of this MS strongly supports the assumption that the lector Romanus Chartophylax was a Cypriot. His handwriting, which appears in Harley 5579 (cf. Plates **57** and **58**) and in Paris Grec 234[230a] as well as in other MSS written by him, shows unmistakably a Cypriot script style of the kind that has been called "notarial" Cypriot script.[231] This script style (used, for instance, in the obituary notes in the famous Cypriot codex Vat. Palatinus graec. 367) is well exemplified in Turyn, *Codices*, pl. 190*a*, 190*c*;[232] these specimens from a MS written in Cyprus in the same period as the MSS of Romanus Chartophylax decidedly resemble the script style of our scribe.

Another factor which may support the assumption of the Cypriot origin of this scribe is MS Paris Grec 2617 (once Colbertinus 4124).[233] This MS is written in the hand of Romanus Chartophylax.[234] It came to Colbert in 1674,[235] and it is very probable that it also was sent to Colbert from Cyprus by Consul Sauvan.[236]

Some doubts regarding the Cypriot origin of our scribe could be raised by the wrong reading of the subscription of MS Lesbos, Μονὴ Λειμῶνος 70, published in the past.[237] This MS (to judge from a microfilm of some pages at the end, which I examined)[238] was indeed written by our Romanus Chartophylax and subscribed by him on fol. 401^v in A.M. 6824 = A.D. 1315/1316. Except for the first three words in black ink, the rest of the subscription seems to have been written in red. The final portion of its first line, faded out in part, was repaired at the very end and covered by a strip of paper. At the beginning of the second line there may have been a few words which have faded out. This is how I read the subscription of Lesbos 70 (fol. 401^v), with the explicit reservation that the dotted characters at the end of the first line are very doubtful:[239] Ἐτελειώθη ἡ παρδῦσα βίβλο(ς) χειρὶ ἁμαρτωλῶ

[230] MS Paris Grec 234 (once Colbertinus 4185) was one of a shipment of 49 Greek and 2 Syriac MSS sent from Cyprus by Consul Sauvan to Jean-Baptiste Colbert, the French statesman (1619–1683). These MSS entered Colbert's library on 12 June 1676: cf. H. Omont, *Missions archéologiques françaises en Orient aux XVIIe et XVIIIe siècles*, Collection de documents inédits sur l'histoire de France (Paris, 1902), I, p. 237; II, p. 968 (under no. 37). On Colbert's quest for MSS in the Levant, cf. Omont, *Missions*, I, pp. 222–50; II, pp. 963–94; on the vicissitudes of Colbert's library, until his collection of MSS entered the Royal Library in Paris in 1732, cf. Omont, *Inventaire sommaire*, I, p. xiv.

[230a] Cf. Canart, *op. cit.*, p. 320 fig. 4.

[231] Cf. Darrouzès, in *REB*, 8, pp. 164–65; *idem, ibid.*, 15, p. 131.

[232] On cod. Vat. Palatinus gr. 367 (of A.D. 1317–1320), cf. Darrouzès, *op. cit.*, 15, p. 161; Turyn, *Codices*, pp. 117–24; Follieri, *Codices*, pp. 76f.; Canart, *op. cit.*, pp. 303–11.

[233] On Paris Grec 2617, cf. Omont, *Inventaire sommaire*, III (1888), p. 14.

[234] The identification of Romanus Chartophylax as the scribe of MS Paris Grec 2617 was made by M. Naoumides, in ᾽Επ.῾Ετ.Βυζ.Σπ., 39–40 (1972–1973), pp. 380f. I owe to the kindness of Professor Mark Naoumides † (Urbana, Illinois) a photographic sample of Paris Grec 2617 (fol. 153^r). Now cf. also Canart, *op. cit.*, p. 315 (under no. 23).

[235] MS Paris Grec 2617 (once Colbertinus 4124) entered Colbert's library on 12 October 1674: cf. Omont, *Missions archéologiques*, II, p. 964 (under no. 3).

[236] On shipments of MSS sent by Sauvan from Cyprus in 1673 and 1674, cf. *ibid.*, I, pp. 236f.

[237] Cf. A. Papadopoulos-Kerameus, Μαυρογορδάτειος βιβλιοθήκη ἤτοι γενικὸς περιγραφικὸς κατάλογος τῶν ἐν ταῖς ἀνὰ τὴν ᾽Ανατολὴν βιβλιοθήκαις εὑρισκομένων ἑλληνικῶν χειρογράφων, in ῾Ελλ.Φιλολ.Σύλλ., 16, Suppl. (1885), p. 68.

[238] I am grateful to Professor A. D. Komines of Athens for providing me with a microfilm of several pages of MS Lesbos Λειμῶνος 70.

[239] The subscription of MS Lesbos Λειμῶνος 70 deserves an examination under ultraviolet light. On this MS, now cf. also Canart, *op. cit.*, pp. 305 note 9, 309 note 28, 312 (under no. 3).

'Ρωμανοῦ Χαρτοφύλακο(ς) τοῦ λ.μ.[---] | --- (?) ἐν ἔτει· ςωκδ. Papadopoulos-Kerameus (*loc. cit.* [note 237 above]) too rashly published the end of the first line: χαρτοφύλακος τῆς Λαμείας.²⁴⁰ The reading τῆς Λαμείας would imply that our Romanus was chartophylax of the diocese of Lamia (in Thessaly), which was called at that time Ζητούνιον.²⁴¹ However, it has been pointed out already,²⁴² in reference to Papadopoulos' publication of the Lesbos subscription, that the use of Λαμία instead of Ζητούνιον was impossible for the time recorded in the subscription.²⁴³ Thus, it is obvious that the Papadopoulos-Kerameus reading of the end of the first line is untenable and unwarranted.

Moreover, it is obvious that Χαρτοφύλαξ must be considered the family name of 'Ρωμανός. If Romanus had been a chartophylax, he would have mentioned his affiliation with some administration in his subscription in MS Paris Grec 234. In view of his Cypriot origin, which we assume to be certain, it should be pointed out that in the 14th century the family name Χαρτοφύλαξ is attested in Cyprus, in Crete, and in the Peloponnesus, and that it was used even later.²⁴⁴

²⁴⁰ It seems probable that τοῦ was followed in the subscription by an ethnic adjective derived from a place-name in Cyprus and used in the genitive. There are several places in Cyprus with a similar beginning that would fit the traces of the beginning of that faded adjective (although I wish to emphasize that those traces are doubtful). We have to visualize some adjectives derived from place-names like Λάνια, Λεμεσός, Λεμίθου, and some others. It is possible that after μ there are traces of what could be the beginning of the conventional sign for ει. It is possible that Romanus, if he wrote this sign, may have made a misspelling instead of ι. For place-names in Cyprus, cf. L. de Mas Latrie, "Notice sur la construction d'une carte de l'île de Chypre," *BECh*, 24 (1863), pp. 29–50; *Cyprus. Index Gazetteer. Compiled by Survey Directorate, General Headquarters Middle East* (Cairo, 1946); *Cyprus. Census of Population and Agriculture 1946.* Tables (London [1949]), pp. 6ff.; N. G. Kyriazes, Τὰ χωρία τῆς Κύπρου (Larnaca, 1952). For an ample presentation and extensive discussion of Cypriot place-names, cf. S. Menardos, Τοπωνυμικὸν τῆς Κύπρου, in 'Αθηνᾶ, 18 (1905), pp. 315–421.
²⁴¹ Cf. Darrouzès, in *REB*, 8, p. 170 (under Paris. 234); O. Markl, *Ortsnamen Griechenlands in "fränkischer" Zeit,* Byzantina Vindobonensia, I (Graz–Cologne, 1966), p. 41, *s.v.* Lamia.
²⁴² Cf. N. A. Bees, "Beiträge zur kirchlichen Geographie Griechenlands im Mittelalter und in der neueren Zeit," *OrChr*, N.S. 4 (1915), p. 245.
²⁴³ It is also impossible to assume that Romanus of the Lesbos MS was χαρτοφύλαξ τῆς λαμίας. This was suggested by Bees, *loc. cit.*, who referred to E. A. Sophocles, *Greek Lexicon of the Roman and Byzantine Periods* (New York, 1888), p. 704 (*s.v.* λαμία, a reference to Constantine Porphyrogenitus, De caerim. 717, 18), and pointed to a seal of the 9/10th century published by K. M. Konstantopoulos, Βυζαντιακὰ μολυβδόβουλλα ἐν τῷ 'Εθνικῷ Νομισματικῷ Μουσείῳ 'Αθηνῶν, in *JIAN*, 6 (1903), p. 53 (under no. 206). This was a seal of a κόμης τῆς λαμίας. On this office, cf. Constantine Porphyrogenitus, De caerimoniis, II.52, Bonn ed., I (1829), p. 717, 18 (with a comment by Reiske, Bonn ed., II [1830], p. 845); R. Guilland, "Les logothètes. Etudes sur l'histoire administrative de l'Empire byzantin," *REB*, 29 (1971), p. 16 (under no. 8). There is no trace of the office of κόμης τῆς λαμίας in the later Middle Ages, and by the same token any speculation on the existence of the office of χαρτοφύλαξ τῆς λαμίας in the 14th century would be groundless. Thus we can safely dismiss the possibility that our Romanus was such an official.
²⁴⁴ The family name Χαρτοφύλαξ, Χαρτοφύλακας, is attested in Cypriot historical literature and documents (cf. Naoumides, in 'Επ.'Ετ.Βυζ.Σπ., 39–40, pp. 382f.). In a document of A.D. 1367 concerning the territory of the diocese of Limassol, there appears *Nicolle Hartofilaca*: cf. J. Richard, *Chypre sous les Lusignans. Documents chypriotes des Archives du Vatican (XIVᵉ et XVᵉ siècles),* Institut Français d'archéologie de Beyrouth, Bibliothèque archéologique et historique, LXXIII (Paris, 1962), p. 83 and note 7. Leontius Machaeras mentions τὸν σὶρ Τουμᾶς τὸν Χαρτοφύλακαν (in reference to the events of 1377–1380), most probably a relative of the person just mentioned: cf. Leontios Makhairas, *Recital Concerning the Sweet Land of Cyprus Entitled "Chronicle,"* ed. R. M. Dawkins (Oxford, 1932), I, p. 578, line 20, § 581 (cf. *ibid.,* II, p. 196, note on § 581.1). On the same person and name in Italian, cf. *Thomaso Cartofillaca* in the Chronicle of Amadi, *Tomas Cartofilaco* in the Chronicle of Strambaldi, and *Thomaso Cartophilaca* in the Chronicle of Florio Bustron. Cf. R. de Mas Latrie, *Chroniques d'Amadi et de Strambaldi,* I, *Chronique d'Amadi,* Collection de documents

To conclude the list of our scribe's known MSS, I have to mention MS Oxford, Bodleian Library, Barocci 27: it was written in the handwriting of the lector Romanus Chartophylax, although he did not subscribe it. The identification of the scribe of this MS was made by Wilson, *Mediaeval Greek Bookhands*, p. 31 (under no. 66), with a specimen published on pl. 66 (= Barocci 27, fols. 39ᵛ–40ʳ).[244a]

MS Athos Lavra E 43 was listed by Vogel–Gardthausen, p. 395, who suggested that the scribe of this MS might be identical with our Romanus. The subscription of this MS is reported[245] to run as follows (fol. 89ʳ): Χειρὶ ἁμαρτωλῷ Ῥωμανῷ ἀναγνώστῃ· | ἐν ἔτει ϛωλβ. The wording of the subscription (which resembles the wording of the Harley subscription), combined with the date of the subscription, A.M. 6832 = A.D. 1323/1324, which is near the period of our scribe's activities, makes the identification of the Athos scribe with our Romanus Chartophylax very likely. (I was unable to obtain photographic samples of the Athos MS and am not, therefore, in a position to make a more definite judgment on its scribe.)[245a]

To show the handwriting of Romanus Chartophylax in MS Harley 5579, on Plate **57** we reproduce folio 131ʳ, containing a passage from St. Athanasius of Alexandria, Oratio II contra Arianos (in the MS numbered γ′; ed. Migne, Patr. Gr., 26, cols. 153 A 6 – 156 D 1). This lettering of Romanus Chartophylax is rather small and perhaps approximates what was called Cypriot "notarial" script (used in legal acts, in obituary notes in MSS, etc.). In the page reproduced one can see a tendency to put an accent, or a breathing, or a combination of breathing and accent, above the first vowel of a diphthong: cf. line 6 ἀκόυοντες, line 7 ὄυτως, line 8 ἐαυτοῦ, line 15 ἐυθὺς; some-

---

inédits sur l'histoire de France, 1st ser.: Histoire politique (Paris, 1891), p. 487; II, *Chronique de Strambaldi, ibid.* (1893), p. 246; *idem*, "Chronique de l'île de Chypre, par Florio Bustron," in *Mélanges historiques. Choix de documents*, V, Collection de documents inédits sur l'histoire de France (Paris, 1886), p. 347.

The family name Χαρτοφύλαξ was used in Crete, probably in a likewise vulgarized form Χαρτοφύλακα(ς), in the Middle Ages, and in modern times. The family name *Carcofilaca* appears in a Venetian document of A.D. 1359 pertaining to this Cretan family: cf. F. Thiriet, *Régestes des délibérations du Sénat de Venise concernant la Romanie*, I (Paris–The Hague, 1958) p. 93 (under no. 350); S. M. Theotokes, Θεσπίσματα τῆς Βενετικῆς Γερουσίας *1281–1385*, in Ἀκαδημία Ἀθηνῶν. Μνημεῖα τῆς ἑλληνικῆς ἱστορίας, II,2 (Athens, 1937), p. 70; cf. also F. Thiriet, *La Romanie vénitienne au Moyen Age*, BEFAR, 193 (Paris, 1959), pp. 293f. (on p. 293, the family name in question is quoted as *Cartofilaca*). For the same family name in Crete of the 17th century, cf. M. I. Manousakas, Ἡ παρὰ *Trivan* ἀπογραφὴ τῆς Κρήτης *(1644)* καὶ ὁ δῆθεν Κατάλογος τῶν κρητικῶν οἴκων Κερκύρας, in Κρ.Χρον., 3 (1949), p. 49, lower part, no. 24 (*Cartoffilaca*); p. 52, no. 13 (*Cartofilaca*); p. 53, lower part, no. 15 (*Cartofilaca*). The family name *Cartofila* is attested in the Peloponnesus in A.D. 1354: cf. J. Longnon and P. Topping, *Documents sur le régime des terres dans la principauté de Morée au XIVᵉ siècle* (Paris–The Hague, 1969), p. 81, line 32.

In general, on the occurrence of family names Χαρτοφύλαξ, Χαρτοφύλακος, Χαρτοφύλακας, cf. D. B. Bagiakakos, Ἡ ἐκκλησιαστικὴ γλῶσσα καὶ ἡ μεσαιωνικὴ καὶ ἡ νεοελληνικὴ ὀνοματολογία, in Ἀθηνᾶ, 63 (1959), pp. 228f.

[244a] Now cf. also Canart, *op. cit.*, p. 313 (under no. 10) and note 47.

[245] Cf. Spyridon of the Laura and S. Eustratiades, *Catalogue of the Greek Manuscripts in the Library of the Laura on Mount Athos*, Harvard Theological Studies, XII (Cambridge, Mass., 1925), p. 79 (under no. 505). Now cf. also D. Reinsch, in P. Moraux et al., *Aristoteles Graecus. Die griechischen Manuskripte des Aristoteles*, I, Peripatoi, 8 (Berlin–New York, 1976), pp. 23–25 (p. 24, on the quinion composition of the MS; cf. above, p. 83 and note 225).

[245a] Now cf. also Canart, *op. cit.*, pp. 309 note 28, 312 (under no. 1).

times only the breathing is put above the first vowel, and the accent above the second vowel of a diphthong: e.g., line 27 ὁὶ, line 28 εἴρηκε. The most striking feature of this practice is the placing of the circumflex above the first vowel of a diphthong, as in line 30 τοῦ. Since the same practice appears also in another Cypriot MS of the same period,[246] we can safely assume that the practice in question is a peculiarity of the Cypriot script of that time. Romanus Chartophylax used a rather unusual abbreviation for the ending -αν, e.g., line 12 in διάνοιαν, line 13 in σοφίαν. It is a very characteristic feature of the handwriting of Romanus Chartophylax.[247] This abbreviation can be seen also in Plate **58** from this MS.

As a sample of a larger lettering by the same scribe in the same MS, on Plate **58** we reproduce folio 209ᵛ, containing a passage from St. Athanasius of Alexandria, Epistula IV ad Serapionem (ed. Migne, Patr. Gr., 26, cols. 673 A 8 – 676 B 8). This larger lettering of the scribe resembles the size of his lettering in MS Oxford Barocci 27 (cf. Wilson, *Mediaeval Greek Bookhands*, pl. 66; cf. *ibid.*, p. 31).

For other published facsimiles of the handwriting of Romanus Chartophylax from this MS, cf. above, p. 84.

This MS Harley 5579 is affirmed to be a copy of MS Paris Coislin 45.[248]

MS Harley 5579 was once owned by Justinus Goblerus (= Göbler), 1503 or 1504–1567, jurist and humanist, active mainly in Frankfort on the Main; from him this MS was called by scholars "codex Goblerianus."[249] A prominent classicist, Pieter Nanninck (Nannius), 1500–1557, professor in Louvain, used the codex Goblerianus for his Latin translation of Athanasius,

---

[246] For the occurrence of the same writing mannerism in Vatic. Palat. graec. 367, cf. Turyn, *Codices*, pl. 96, left column, line 8 ὁύτω, line 18 τοῦτο; right column, line 13 ὁπὸιον, line 15 τᾱῦτά σοι; pl. 190c, line 1 τοῦ; Follieri, *Codices*, pl. 53, line 1 τοῦ Δαμασκηνοῦ. Cf. also, in the subscription of MS Lesbos Λειμῶνος 70 (quoted above), παρὸῦσα and Ῥωμανοῦ.

[247] This abbreviation for -αν was recorded from Harley 5579 by G. Cereteli, *Sokraščenija v grečeskih rukopisjah preimuščestvenno po datirovannym rukopisjam S.-Peterburga i Moskvy*, 2nd ed. (St. Petersburg, 1904; repr. Hildesheim–New York, 1969), p. 12 note 2; pl. ii, top line, at right; cf. Gardthausen, *Griechische Palaeographie*, II, p. 335, lines 25–27 (on the basis of Cereteli). Actually, this peculiar abbreviation represents the normal abbreviation for -αν turned upside down. The use of this peculiar sign by Romanus in both Harley 5579 and Barocci 27 was pointed out emphatically by Wilson, *Mediaeval Greek Bookhands*, p. 31 (under no. 66); cf. *ibid.*, pl. 66. Now cf. also Canart, *op. cit.*, pp. 313 note 47, 307 (right column, penult line: facsimile of the abbreviation from Romanus).

[248] Cf. Wallis, *op. cit.* (note 225 above), pp. 102–4; H.-G. Opitz, *Untersuchungen zur Überlieferung der Schriften des Athanasius*, Arbeiten zur Kirchengeschichte, 23 (Berlin–Leipzig, 1935), pp. 60f.; G. J. Ryan, *The* De incarnatione *of Athanasius, Part 1*, Studies and Documents, XIV,1 (London–Philadelphia [1945]), pp. 45, 48f. Some doubts concerning the direct derivation of Harley 5579 from Coislin 45 were voiced by A. Robertson, "Additional Note," *JThS*, 3 (1902), pp. 109f.; and by L. Leone, *Sancti Athanasii archiepiscopi Alexandriae Contra gentes*, Collana di Studi Greci, 43 (Naples [1965]), pp. xxiif.

[249] On the name of Harley 5579 as codex Goblerianus, cf. Wallis, *op. cit.*, p. 102; Robertson, *op. cit.*, p. 109. Goblerus' ownership entries appear in this MS on fols. 2ʳ and 219ᵛ. The ownership entry on fol. 2ʳ written down the right-hand margin has been heavily obliterated: ⟦ *Sum Iustini Gobleri L L Doctoris – – –*⟧. The other entry on fol. 219ᵛ has been deleted: ⟦ *Iustini Gobleri Goarini L L doctoris codex*⟧ *sum* (this word was added by a different hand). This entry was apparently repeated by somebody else in the next line and then strongly obliterated (except for the final word *sum* due to the same hand which added *sum* in the preceding line). The attribute *Goarinus* refers to Goblerus' birthplace Sankt Goar (in the region of Hessen, Germany). On Goblerus' ownership, cf. Opitz, *op. cit.*, p. 60. On Justinus Goblerus (Göbler), cf. Ch. G. Jöcher, *Allgemeines Gelehrten-Lexicon*, II (Leipzig, 1750), col. 1029; *ADB*, IX, p. 301.

published for the first time in Basel in 1556.[250] In the 16th century, the Harley MS was transcribed in MS Geneva Grec 29 tomus III, fols. 1–238; this Geneva MS was used by Peter Felckmann as a part of the printer's copy for the *editio Commeliniana* of St. Athanasius of Alexandria (Heidelberg, 1600).[251] In the latter part of the 16th century, the present Harley MS was held by Jérôme (Hieronymus) Commelin (1560–1597 or 1598), a Frenchman, printer, and publisher in Heidelberg; the MS was found among his effects, but the identity of its actual owner was not known at that time.[252] At any rate, at the end of the 16th century Felckmann also used this codex Goblerianus, i.e., the present Harley MS, while preparing the *editio Commeliniana*.[253] Later the MS was owned by Dr. John Covel (1638–1722), master of Christ's College in Cambridge, scholar, and traveler. Covel's ownership entry is written in Greek on fol. 11ʳ. The MS was Greek XIX in his collection (cf. Wright, *Fontes Harleiani*, pp. 115, 459). He must have acquired it from a West European owner.[254] On the acquisition, in 1716, of the Covel library by Edward Harley, second Earl of Oxford, and the subsequent fate of the Harley library, cf. above, p. 29. The Harley MSS were placed in the British Museum in 1757.

On this MS, cf. Nares, *Catalogue of the Harleian Manuscripts*, III, p. 278; Wallis, *op. cit.*, pp. 102–4; Vogel–Gardthausen, p. 394; Omont, "Notes," p. 348; *Pal. Soc.*, I, pl. 133 (description of the MS); Opitz, *Untersuchungen*, pp. 60f.; R. P. Casey, "Greek Manuscripts of Athanasian Corpora," *ZNW*, 30 (1931), p. 53 (symbol H for this MS); Canart, *op. cit.*, pp. 309 note 28, 312 (under no. 4).

Plate 59: A.D. 1321/1322.

Oxford, Bodleian Library, ms Gr.bibl.d.1. Parchment, 244 × 175 mm., 277 fols. (the text of the MS is on fols. 2ʳ–271ʳ), 20 lines to a page. Contents: Four Gospels, adapted for liturgical use. The MS was subscribed (in brownish ink) in A.M. 6830, indiction 5 = A.D. 1321/1322 (fol. 271ʳ – Plate **112c**): ·:· ἔτους ͵ϛωλ⟦.⟧:· ἰν(δικτιών)ης ε̅. The erased letter was obviously due to an error by the scribe himself. The indiction figure 5 shows that A.M. 6830 was the only possibility (within the decade A.M. 6830–6839) for the date of the MS.

On Plate **59** we reproduce folio 167ʳ, containing a passage from the GOSPEL OF ST. LUKE 14:19–26. This is the end of the lesson for Sunday of the 11th week in Luke (i.e., of the 28th week after Pentecost) and the beginning of the lesson for Tuesday of the 9th week in Luke (i.e., of the 26th week after Pentecost). The extents of these entire lessons are Luke 14:16–24 and Luke 14:25–35 (cf. Gregory, I, pp. 357, 356). The end of the former lesson is marked with the usual τέ(λος); the beginning of the latter lesson is marked ἀρχ(ή). In the upper margin, there is a liturgical note indicating the time of the latter

[250] Cf. an excerpt from Nannius' preface reprinted in Migne, Patr. Gr., 25, p. xliiᵃ D 8ff. (with an explicit reference to the MS of Justinus Goblerus); Opitz, *op. cit.*, p. 60. On Pieter Nanninck (Nannius) of Alkmaar, cf. Sandys, *History of Classical Scholarship*, II, pp. 215f.; A. J. van der Aa, *Biographisch Woordenboek der Nederlanden*, XIII (Haarlem, 1868), pp. 60–65; *Biographie Nationale ... de Belgique*, XV (Brussels, 1899), cols. 415–25.

[251] On MS Geneva Grec 29 tomus III, cf. Wallis, *op. cit.*, pp. 108, 104; Opitz, *op. cit.*, pp. 61, 93, 95. On Peter Felckmann and the *editio Commeliniana* of St. Athanasius, cf. *ibid.*, p. 2.

[252] Cf. *ibid.*, p. 60 (or Migne, Patr. Gr., 25, p. xliiiᵇ A 8–11). On Jérôme (Hieronymus) Commelin, cf. L. G. Michaud, *Biographie universelle ancienne et moderne*, VIII (Paris, n.d.), p. 685; *ADB*, IV, p. 436.

[253] Cf. Migne, Patr. Gr., 25, p. xliiiᵃ D 12ff. (from the preface of the *editio Commeliniana*); Opitz, *op. cit.*, p. 2. In referring to the codex Gobleri (or Goblerianus), Felckmann quoted in the preface of the *editio Commeliniana* even the subscription of the Harley MS (cf. Migne, Patr. Gr., 25, p. xliiiᵇ A 7–8).

[254] On John Covel, cf. above, p. 29. The MS was in Western Europe since the 16th century, if it was owned by Goblerus and held by Commelin. The assumption of Wallis, *op. cit.*, p. 103, that Covel acquired it in Constantinople in 1664 is therefore untenable (cf. Robertson, *op. cit.*, p. 109).

lesson which begins on this page and the adaptation of the beginning of the standard text of the pericope for lesson use:[255] τῇ γ̄ τῆς θ̄ ἐβδ(ομάδος)· τῷ και(ρῷ ἐκείνῳ)· συνεπορεύοντο τῶ Ἰ(ησο)ῦ ὄχλοι πολλοί: The marginal mark ο̄ζ opposite the initial line of the latter lesson means that this is the 77th consecutive pericope from Luke.[256] All these marks and the liturgical note are in red, in accordance with the traditional practice of New Testament MSS adapted for liturgical use.[257] The red capital letter Π projected to the left indicates the beginning of the new lesson in the preceding line.[258]

This MS was purported to have been bought at the sale of the Meerman Library in The Hague in 1824 by the London bookseller, John Bohn.[259] Bohn sold the MS to the Rev. Theodore Williams, vicar of Hendon. At the Williams sale in 1827,[260] the MS was bought by the bookseller Thomas Thorpe, who sold it to the Rev. Joseph Mendham in 1827. Joseph Mendham (d. 1856) willed it to the Rev. John Mendham (d. 1869). The widow of John Mendham presented it to John W. Burgon (1813–1888), dean of Chichester, in 1871, on the condition that after Burgon's death it would become the property of the Bodleian Library. Burgon's nephew, W. F. Rose, conveyed the MS to the Bodleian Library on 31 August 1888 (cf. notes on fol. 1r).

On this MS Greek bibles d.1, cf. *Summary Catalogue*, V, pp. 697f. (under S.C. 29802); Scrivener, I, pp. 255f. (under Evan. 562); Gregory, I, p. 198 (under Vier Evangelien 521); Aland, I, p. 88 (under the Gregory–Aland number 521); von Soden, I,1, p. 195 (under ε443).

---

[255] Cf. above, p. 43 note 100.

[256] Cf. Εὐαγγέλιον (1880), p. 63 (under Περικοπαί OZ′), p. 84a; Εὐαγγέλιον (1968), p. 82 (under Περικοπαί OZ′), p. 101b.

[257] Cf. above, p. 43 note 101.

[258] On the meaning of a letter projected to the left, cf. above, p. 22 note 63.

[259] It is a meaningless coincidence that Meerman MS 117 had 277 folios, the same number that appears now in MS Oxford Gr.bibl.d.1 (in the past, this MS was reported to have 270 or 271 fols.). Since the latter MS was purported to have been bought at the Meerman sale, there was a tendency at one time to identify it with Meerman 117 (cf. Gregory, I, p. 198, under Vier Evangelien 521). However, Meerman 117 was an 11th-century *lectionary* of the Gospels, on parchment, 277 folios (cf. *Bibliotheca Meermanniana; sive Catalogus librorum impressorum et codicum manuscriptorum, quos maximam partem collegerunt viri nobilissimi Gerardus et Joannes Meerman; morte dereliquit Joannes Meerman* [The Hague, 1824], IV, p. 16 [under no. 117]). Earlier, Meerman 117 was MS 54 in the Jesuit Collège de Clermont at Paris (cf. G. Studemund and L. Cohn, *Codices ex Bibliotheca Meermanniana Phillippici graeci nunc Berolinenses*, Die Handschriften-Verzeichnisse der Königlichen Bibliothek zu Berlin, XI,1 [Berlin, 1890], p. xxxv, lines 1–4).

Gregory, *loc. cit.*, suspected that our Oxford MS might be identical with Meerman 117. He also dubiously suggested that the Oxford MS was perhaps identical with Meerman 76 (according to Studemund and Cohn, *op. cit.*, pp. XVII and XXX, MS Meerman 76 = Claromontanus 116 is now MS Oxford Misc. gr. 182, i.e., Auct.T.1.4 [S.C. 20582], which has different contents). Moreover, Gregory, I, p. 190 (under Vier Evangelien 436), listed MS Meerman 117 as lost. Also cf. Gregory, III, p. 1106, lines 9–13 (on [e 436]); J. G. Schomerus, "Erfahrungen bei der Bearbeitung früherer Handschriftenlisten," in K. Aland, *Materialien zur neutestamentlichen Handschriftenkunde*, I, Arbeiten zur neutestamentlichen Textforschung, 3 (Berlin, 1969), p. 286 (under e 436).

Studemund and Cohn, *op. cit.*, pp. XV (under Clarom. 54 – Meerm. 117) and XXX (under Meerm. 117 = Clarom. 54), by putting a question mark after the listings, implied that the present location of Meerman 117 is unknown; one may add that the very existence of this MS at present is uncertain. Scrivener, I, p. 238 (under Evan. 436), dealt with Meerman 117 as with a MS whose location was unknown, but in a puzzling manner he attributed to Meerman 117 the date A.D. 1322, which he probably drew from Oxford Gr.bibl.d.1. For some reason Scrivener, *loc. cit.*, made at this point a reference to the latter MS, i.e., to his Evan. 562 (cf. *ibid.*, pp. 255f.).

It should be stated that John W. Burgon (who owned the present MS Oxford Gr.bibl.d.1 from 1871 until his death in 1888), in a letter addressed to Scrivener and published as "Sacred Greek Codices at Home and Abroad, I.," *The Guardian*, vol. XXXVII, pt. 1, no. 1907 (June 21, 1882), p. 869, explained why his MS could *not* be identified with Meerman 117.

[260] On the sale of the library of Theodore Williams in April–May 1827, cf. Fletcher, *English Book Collectors*, p. 447.

Plate 60: A.D. 1325/1326.

London, British Museum, ms Additional 11838. Parchment, 240 ×
165 mm., 269 fols., 24 lines to a page. Contents: Four Gospels, adapted for
liturgical use. There are full-page miniatures of the four Evangelists prefixed
to the Gospels (fol. 12ᵛ, St. Matthew; 86ᵛ, St. Mark; 135ᵛ, St. Luke;²⁶⁰ᵃ 213ᵛ,
St. John), and ornamental headpieces at the beginning of each Gospel. The
MS was written by the priest and notary Constantinus Pastil, at the behest
of Callinicus, hieromonk and archimandrite of a monastery of St. Demetrius
ὁ Μυροβλύτης, and subscribed in red in A.M. 6834 = A.D. 1325/1326 (fol. 269ᵛ –
Plate **112d**): † ἐπληρώθ(η) τὸ κ(α)τ(ὰ) θ(εο)ῦ ἅγ(ιον) εὐα(γγέλιον)· διαχ(ει)-
ρ(ὸς) Κωνστ(α)ν(τίνου) ἱερ(έως) καὶ νομικ(οῦ) | ἀμαρτ(ω)λ(οῦ) δὲ καὶ ταπεινοῦ
ὁ τοῦ Παστὶλ· πρὸ(ς) Καλινίκ(ου) ἱερο|(μον)άχ(ου)· καὶ ἀρχιμανδρίτ(ου) τῆς ἀγ(ί)ας
μονῆς· τοῦ | ἁγ(ίου) καὶ ἐνδόξου μεγ(α)λ(ο)μ(ά)ρ(τυρος) καὶ ἰαματικοῦ, Δημη-
τρ(ίου) | τοῦ Μυροβρύτ(ου)· καὶ οἱ ἀναγινώσκοντες, εὔχεσθ(ε) δι|ὰ τὸν κ(ύριο)ν· –
ἔτους ͵ϛωλδ. ἰν(δικτιῶνος) θ. The family name of the scribe, Παστὶλ, is not
Greek.²⁶¹ The phonetic change of μυροβλύτης to μυροβρύτης is noteworthy.²⁶²
It is impossible to identify the location of the monastery of St. Demetrius mentioned in the subscription.

To represent the handwriting of Constantinus Pastil, on Plate **60** we reproduce
folio 69ʳ, containing a passage from the GOSPEL OF ST. MATTHEW 24:3–11.
This passage begins the Gospel lesson for the Mass on Monday in Holy Week
(the whole lesson for this service is Matthew 24:3–35). There is a liturgical
note in red in the margin, opposite the beginning of the lesson: μ(ε)γ(άλη) β̄
(i.e., δευτέρᾳ) (εἰς τὴν) λ(ει)τ(ου)ρ(γίαν):· Above the beginning of the lesson in
the first line, there is a mark in red, ἀρχ(ή). The initial capital Κ is likewise
in red and is projected to the left. Red is customarily used for liturgical notes
and marks in New Testament MSS adapted for liturgical use.²⁶³ On the time

---

²⁶⁰ᵃ This miniature was reproduced in *New Pal. Soc.*, Ser. I, pl. 130.

²⁶¹ The name Παστὶλ ends in -ὶλ, and it has a grave accent above the iota. The ending of the name
with a consonant like -λ shows that the name was not a genuine Greek name, and the grave accent
above the penult letter indicates that no suspension of some ending beyond the written end was
implied. It seems that the name Παστὶλ was related to the Romance loan-word παστῖλος, πάστιλλος
("cake") attested in Byzantine Greek. Cf. Du Cange, *Glossarium graecitatis*, I, cols. 1125 f., *s.v.*
παστῖλος, πάστιλλος; col. 1126, *s.v.* παστελοπούλης, and παστιλλᾶς; Demetrakos, Μέγα Λεξικόν, VII, p. 5581,
s.v. πάστιλλος. A surname Παστιλλᾶς is known from Byzantine times; cf. J. D. Mansi, *Sacrorum
Conciliorum nova, et amplissima collectio*, XIII (Florence, 1767; repr. Paris–Leipzig, 1902), cols.
400 A 4/5 and 416 C 2/3: Σισιννίῳ τῷ ἐπίκλην Παστιλλᾷ. We should expect a name like Παστὶλ to
assume in the nominative a grecized form like Παστῖλος, Παστίλας, or Παστίλης (cf. F. Dölger, *Aus
den Schatzkammern des Heiligen Berges* [Munich (1948)], text vol., p. 301, comment on grecized forms
of foreign names in document 110), and to be formed correspondingly in the genitive.

²⁶² The change μυροβλύτου to μυροβρύτου is linguistically peculiar. A change of λ to ρ is well known,
if λ is followed (not preceded) by a consonant (cf. Jannaris, *Historical Greek Grammar*, pp. 94 f., § 187;
Dieterich, *Untersuchungen*, pp. 107–9). On the rare change of λ to ρ after a consonant in South Italian
Greek, cf. G. Rohlfs, *Historische Grammatik der unteritalienischen Gräzität*, SBMünch, Philos.-hist.Kl.,
1949, IV (Munich, 1950), p. 59, § 49 (end). Moreover, a dissimilation of the same liquid in a word
is a known occurrence, but in this case there appears to be an assimilation. One may suspect that
the scribe was influenced by the verb βρύω in the meaning "to gush with," as it occurs in the New
Testament, James 3:11, and that he simply substituted -βρυ- for -βλυ-.

²⁶³ On the red color used in liturgical notes and marks in New Testament MSS adapted for
liturgical use, cf. above, p. 43 note 101.

and extent of this Gospel lesson, cf. Gregory, I, p. 362. Another facsimile specimen of this MS was published in *New Pal. Soc.*, Ser. I, pl. 130 (= fol. 41**r**).

The MS was once owned by the monastery of Mount Sinai, according to the note of Samuel Butler on the inside of the upper cover, up to the time when it was procured, at a price of above 100 guineas, by Butler (1774–1839), bishop of Lichfield and classical scholar. On the same verso of the upper cover, there is an imprint of Butler's seal. Butler's MSS were acquired by the British Museum in 1841. On Samuel Butler and his MSS, cf. *DNB*, III, pp. 528 f.; Sandys, *History of Classical Scholarship*, III, pp. 398 f.; *Catalogue of Additions to the Manuscripts in the British Museum in the Years MDCCCXLI–MDCCCXLV* (London, 1850; repr. 1964), pp. VI, 9 (on this MS, p. 10); de Ricci, *English Collectors*, pp. 114 f.

On this MS, cf. Richard, *Inventaire*, p. 19; Omont, "Notes," pp. 332, 337; *New Pal. Soc.*, Ser. I, pl. 130 (description of the MS); Vogel–Gardthausen, pp. 250, 253, 474 (additions and corrections to p. 250 and to p. 253); V. N. Benešević, *Opisanie grečeskih rukopisej monastyrja Svjatoj Ekateriny na Sinaě*, I (St. Petersburg, 1911), p. 649; Scrivener, I, p. 258 (under Evan. 577); Gregory, I, p. 195 (under Vier Evangelien 492); Aland, I, p. 87 (under the Gregory–Aland number 492); von Soden, I,1, p. 194 (under ε433); J. W. Bradley, *A Dictionary of Miniaturists, Illuminators, Calligraphers, and Copyists*, I (London, 1887; repr. New York [1958]), pp. 248 f.; O. M. Dalton, *Byzantine Art and Archaeology* (Oxford, 1911; repr. New York [1961]), p. 476 note 2; D. Mouriki, in *Byzantine Art an European Art*, pp. 325 (no. 328), 546 (no. 328).

Plates 61–65: A.D. 1326.

London, British Museum, ms Additional 5117. Parchment, 192 × 145 mm., 225 fols. Contents: (fols. 1**r**–25**v**) Tables of Gospel lessons, including the letter of Eusebius to Carpianus and Eusebian canon tables, and some minor texts;[264] (fols. 26**r**–224**r**) Four Gospels, adapted for liturgical use by a different hand. This main body of the MS (fols. 26**r**–224**r**) was written by two main scribes, A and B, with small portions written by four other scribes: C, D, E, and F.

A different scribe (different from those who shared in the writing of the main body of the MS) decided to include the *Pericope de Adultera* (Gospel of John 7:53 – 8:11). For this purpose, he erased the writing on fol. 198**r** which previously contained John 7:40–52 and 8:12 πάλιν – λέγων, and inserted a new leaf, fol. 197. He wrote on fols. 197**r–v** and 198**r**, lines 1–11 (he left the rest of page 198**r** blank), the text of John 7:40–52; 7:53 – 8:11; 8:12 πάλιν – λέγων. Since this portion written subsequently did not belong to the original production of the MS, we shall disregard it in representing the scripts of this MS.

The MS was subscribed on 24 February A.M. 6834 = A.D. 1326 (fol. 224**r** – Plate **113a**): πληρώθ(η) τὸ παρὸν τετραυάγγελον, μη(νὶ) φευρουαρίω εἰς τ(ὰς) | x̄δ̄ ἔτους ⟦ϛ̄⟧ω̄λ̄δ̄: ἰν(δικτιῶνος) ϑ + The subscription must have been written by scribe B, because it was written below the conclusion of this scribe's portion; however, it was written in a less formal and more cursive lettering than the usual script of B. It seems that ϛ̓ was erased in the year date;

---

[264] There are two sets of tables of Gospel lessons, and this resulted in a duplication of some tables. Among the minor texts there is (on fols. 9**v**–10**v**) a fragment of Hippolytus of Thebes, Syntagma chronologicum de Christi prosapia, on St. James, the Lord's brother (cf. F. Diekamp, *Hippolytos von Theben. Texte und Untersuchungen* [Münster, 1898], pp. 31–32; *BHG Auct.* 766h). On fols. 10**v**–11**r** we find Theodore Prodromus, some Tetrastichs (iambic and hexametric) on the New Testament (I refer only their first lines to the printed texts): ed. Migne, Patr. Gr., 133, cols. 1175 D 2, 1177 A 2, 1177 A 7, 1178 A 4, 1197 C 2, 1197 C 7, 1177 C 8, 1178 B 6, 1197 C 12, 1198 C 3, 1179 B 1.

actually, the trace of the presumably erased letter with its rough breathing is quite weak. At the very beginning of the subscription, either the scribe expected the initial 'E to be added in red in a position projected to the left and this was not done, or the unaccented augment was simply omitted (as happens in medieval and modern Greek). The term τετραυάγγελον used in the subscription is not unusual.[265]

Some older quire marks written on the last verso of a quire (in the lower margin, to the right of the center) reveal that at first this MS began with the text of the Gospels on the present fol. 26ʳ (cf. such quire marks on fols. 33ᵛ α, 41ᵛ β̄', 57ᵛ δ̄, 65ᵛ ε̄', 137ᵛ ῑδ, 153ᵛ ῑϛ) and that it included the Four Gospels within the present fols. 26–225, which formed 25 quires. After the Gospels were written, the preliminary matter (tables of lessons) comprising 3 quires (the present fols. 1–25) was prefixed to the main, primary body of the MS. The person who added the lesson equipment (liturgical notes, titles of chapters, numbers of Eusebian sections, marks ἀρχή and τέλος) introduced new quire marks beginning with a new ᾱ on fol. 8ᵛ, and inscribed them throughout the MS (on the last verso of each quire, in the center of the lower margin) up to the end of the final quire 28 as counted from the new beginning (there is a mark κη on fol. 225ᵛ). These new quire marks were obviously intended to be observed by the binder who was to make the first binding of the volume.

In the primary body of the MS (fols. 26ʳ–224ʳ), with regard to the handwriting of these folios, we can distinguish two large parts: fols. 26ʳ–137ᵛ (the present quires 4–17) written almost entirely by scribe A (except for small portions indicated below), and fols. 138ʳ–224ʳ (the present quires 18–28, except for the terminal 3 pages) written entirely by scribe B (except for fols. 197ʳ–198ʳ: see above). I should add that the initial quire of A (fols. 26ʳ–33ᵛ), as a result of its somewhat different quality of parchment and ink, makes a slightly different impression than the rest of the A portion. The scripts of A and B are very similar in their conventional letterings which fit this scriptural MS. However, script A is evenly calligraphic, while script B is much less consistent in its carefulness and occasionally assumes a somewhat slack appearance. Still, it is obvious that both writings are kindred and belong to the same style.

In the part of the MS which I attributed to A, there are some small portions written by different scribes. They are valuable for our paleographical knowledge, because they depart from the conventional style of this New Testament MS and reveal interesting varieties of minuscule script of the date stated. On fol. 39ᵛ, lines 1–8 αὐτοῦ were written by A, the main scribe of this part of the MS; but lines 8 διὰ τί με – 10 σας εἴ were written by C; and lines 10 πεν αὐτοῖς – 24 were written by D (cf. Plate **63**). Scribe E wrote fols. 58ᵛ–59ʳ, 60ʳ, 61ᵛ, lines 1–17 εἰμι (cf. Plate **64**). Scribe F wrote fols. 82ᵛ–83ʳ (cf. Plate **65**).

As for the preliminary matter on fols. 1ʳ–25ᵛ, it agrees in its script style and some details with the script of B, although we must take into account

---

[265] On the term τετραυάγγελον, cf. Gregory, I, p. 334; Clark, *Greek New Testament Manuscripts in America*, pp. 179 (pl. LXV, top cut, τετραβάγγελον), 234, 301.

the difference between the minute and more cursive lettering of the preliminary matter (containing mainly tables of lessons) and the conventional and more formal style of B in the text of the Gospels. It seems to me that fols. 1ʳ–15ᵛ especially should be attributed to scribe B. The older quire marks of the MS show that the preliminary matter originally did not begin the production of this MS. We have no cogent basis to assume that the preliminary matter was written immediately after the text of the Gospels was completed. Of course, there is some likelihood that the preliminary matter was produced at about the same time as the main body of the MS. Yet, there is no absolute certainty that the dated subscription of this MS covers also the preliminary matter. I shall not, therefore, include a sample of this preliminary matter in the set of specimens of the MS which I offer in this publication.

To represent script A, on Plate **61** we reproduce folio 40ᵛ, containing a passage from the GOSPEL OF ST. MATTHEW 9:25–35 (ed. Nestle, *Novum Testamentum graece*, p. 22; cf. critical note on Matthew 9:35, *ibid.*). This passage comprises the end of the lesson for Saturday of the 6th week after Pentecost (the whole lesson was Matthew 9:18–26) and the beginning of the lesson for Sunday of the 7th week after Pentecost (the whole lesson was Matthew 9:27–35). On the time and extent of these lessons, cf. Gregory, I, pp. 349, 350. The end of the former lesson is marked in the second line by a red note τε(λος) σα(ββάτῳ). The beginning of the latter lesson has in the same second line a red initial K and two red notes in the margin, οε and αρχ(ῆ) κυ(ριακ)ῆ. In line 3 also, above τῷ Ἰ(ησο)ῦ· ἠκολούθησαν, there is a red note ἀρ(χὴ) κυ-(ριακῇ). The beginning of this lesson coincides with the beginning of the Eusebian section 75 of Matthew, marked by the red numeral οε in the margin (the whole section 75 comprises Matthew 9:27–34). The red initial K signals the beginning of the section. The next Eusebian section 76 is marked in the left margin, farther down, by a red numeral ο𝟈 written to the left of the line which carries the beginning of this section; its initial word καὶ is written in the form of a tachygraphic sign which has a red blob for emphatic appearance. This section 76 comprises Matthew 9:35. On sections 75 and 76 in Matthew, cf. von Soden, I,1, p. 397. In the upper and lower margins, written in red, are the τίτλοι of the κεφάλαια which begin on this page. The title of chapter ιζ (the number is not marked here) is πε(ρὶ) τῶν δύο τυφλῶν (the chapter begins in Matthew 9:27), written in the upper margin. The title of chapter ιη (no number written here) is πε(ρὶ) τοῦ δαιμονιζομένου κωφοῦ, written in the lower margin (the chapter begins in Matthew 9:32). On the τίτλοι of κεφάλαια, cf. von Soden, I,1, pp. 402ff. (specifically on the titles quoted above, cf. p. 406); Metzger, *The Text of the New Testament*, p. 23. The liturgical note pertaining to the lesson which begins on this page is written in red in the upper margin: κυ(ριακῇ) ζ Τῷ καιρ(ῷ ἐκείνῳ) παράγοντ(ι) τῷ Ἰ(ησο)ῦ. This note indicates the time for which this lesson is appointed, the customary prefix of the Gospel lesson, and the modification of the initial words of the pericope for lesson use.[266] The liturgical note and all the other titles, numbers, and marks are

---

[266] Cf. above, p. 43 note 100.

written in red, in accordance with the accepted practice of New Testament MSS adapted for liturgical use.[267]

To represent script B, on Plate **62** we reproduce folio 158ᵛ, containing a passage from the GOSPEL OF ST. LUKE 15:12–21.

To exemplify some other scripts that appear in this MS, I shall reproduce three more pages. On Plate **63** we reproduce folio 39ᵛ. This page (as observed above) was written by three scribes. The page contains a passage of the GOSPEL OF ST. MATTHEW 9:9–16. This passage includes the lesson for Saturday of the 5th week after Pentecost, which comprises Matthew 9:9–13 (ed. Nestle, *Novum Testamentum graece*, pp. 20f.; cf. critical note on Matthew 9:13, *ibid.*, p. 21), and the beginning of the lesson for Friday of the 2nd week after Pentecost, which usually comprises Matthew 9:14–17, but here its beginning is indicated by a liturgical note (in the upper margin) as taking place at Matthew 9:12 (on the time and extent of these lessons, cf. Gregory, I, pp. 349, 348). For the former lesson, there are red marks: ἀρχ(ὴ) σα(ββάτῳ), to the left of line 1; τέ(λος) σα(ββά)τ(ῳ), inside line 14. A liturgical note (in red) in the upper margin indicates the time of the lesson, a customary prefix of a Gospel lesson, and the modification of the beginning of the pericope for lesson use: σα(ββά)τ(ῳ) ε̄ Τῷ καιρ(ῷ ἐκείνῳ) παράγων ὁ Ἰ(ησοῦ)ς εἶδεν. For the latter lesson, the rubricator failed to mark the beginning of the lesson in the text with a mark ἀρχ(ή); yet he wrote a liturgical note (in red) in the upper margin. The note indicates the time of the lesson and the modification of the beginning of the standard text for lesson use: τῇ ς τῆς β Εἶπεν ὁ κ(ύριο)ς οὐ χρείαν. Also in the upper margin, the first line exhibits (in red) the τίτλος of the 14th κεφάλαιον of Matthew: ῑδ πε(ρὶ) τοῦ Ματθ(αίου). This chapter comprises Matthew 9:9–17 (on the title of this chapter and its extent, cf. von Soden, I,1, p. 406). In the left margin of the page, there appear red figures which are numbers of Eusebian sections: ο̄ᾱ (Matthew 9:9), ο̄β̄ (9:10–11), ο̄γ̄ (9:12–17). On these Eusebian sections in Matthew, cf. *ibid.*, p. 397.

To show the handwriting of scribe E, on Plate **64** we reproduce folio 60ʳ, containing a passage of the GOSPEL OF ST. MATTHEW 19:8–19. This passage comprises the end (Matt. 19:8–12) of the lesson for Saturday of the 11th week after Pentecost (the whole lesson was Matthew 19:3–12); also the end (Matt. 19:13–15) of the lesson for Tuesday of the 9th week after Pentecost (the whole lesson was Matt. 18:18–22; 19:1–2; 19:13–15); and the beginning (Matt. 19:16–19) of the lesson for Sunday of the 12th week after Pentecost (the whole lesson was Matt. 19:16–26). On the time and extent of these lessons, cf. Gregory, I, pp. 351, 350, 351. There are appropriate marks (in red) for the ends and the beginnings of the lessons: above line 13, τ(έ)λ(ος) (this is exceptionally in black) σα(ββάτῳ); to the left of line 13, ἄρξ(ου) γ; above line 13, ἀρχ(ὴ) τῆς γ; to the right of line 18, τελ(ος) γ; to the right of line 19, αρχ(ῆ) κυ(ριακ)ῆ. In the lower margin, there is (in red) the τίτλος of the 41st κεφάλαιον of Matthew: μᾱ περ(ὶ) τοῦ επερωτήσαντ(ος) πλουσίου τὸν Ι(ησοῦ)ν (on the title of this chapter which comprises Matthew 19:16–30, cf. von Soden,

---

[267] Cf. above, p. 43 note 101.

I,1, p. 406). Thereafter, there is in the lower margin the liturgical note (in red) which indicates the time of the lesson that begins on this page, the customary prefix of a Gospel lesson, and the modification of the initial words of the pericope for lesson use: κυ(ριακ)ῇ ιβ̄ τῶ κερ(ῶ ἐκείνῳ) | νεἀνίσκος τίς προσῆλθ(ε) τῶ Ἰ(ησο)ῦ καὶ εἶπεν. In the right margin there are red figures which are numbers of the Eusebian sections in Matthew: ρ̄ϟ (Matthew 19:9), ρ̄ϟα (19:10–12), ρ̄ϟβ (19:13–15), ρ̄ϟγ (19:16–20). On these Eusebian sections in Matthew, cf. von Soden, I,1, p. 397.[268]

To show the handwriting of scribe F, on Plate **65** we reproduce folio 83ʳ, containing the end of the HYPOTHESIS and the beginning of the LIST OF CHAPTERS TO THE GOSPEL OF ST. MARK. The end of the hypothesis which appears in this page is published in von Soden, I,1, pp. 323, 34 – 324, 8 and p. 311, 9–12. Since this hypothesis is based on the προοίμιον to Mark in Theophylact of Bulgaria, Commentary on the Four Gospels, lines 1–14 of this page can be found also in Migne, Patr. Gr., 123, col. 493 A 13 – C 2. The beginning of the list of chapters, the τίτλοι of κεφάλαια α′–ζ′ (the scribe by inadvertence skipped the number ζ′ and numbered the chapters α′–η′) can be found in von Soden, I,1, p. 407, 31–38. This scribe obviously sensed that the hypothesis was a scholarly additament that did not call for a formal and conventional script of the kind practiced in the text of the Gospels. He, therefore, wrote the hypothesis (on fols. 82ᵛ–83ʳ, line 19) in a more cursive style which abounds in abbreviations. This particular feature gives a special paleographical value to the script style exhibited on Plate **65**, in view of the fact that this specimen comes from a New Testament MS.

It is noteworthy that in this MS yellow blobs occasionally cover round or oval letters or round or oval parts of letters.[269]

On fol. 224ᵛ, a later hand wrote an act by which Constantine Στρηλίτζα(ς) and his wife Constantina donated a vineyard to a church of Ἁγία Κυριακή in June A.M. 6965 = A.D. 1457.

This MS belonged in the past to Richard Mead (1673–1754) of London, physician and collector, and subsequently to Anthony Askew (1722–1774), physician, classical scholar, and collector. Askew's MSS went on sale in 1785. Some of them (including the present MS) were acquired at that time by the British Museum. This MS Additional 5117 must be[270] the former Askew MS 620. On Mead and Askew, and on their MSS, cf. Fletcher, *English Book Collectors*, pp. 160–64, 219–21; de Ricci, *English Collectors*, pp. 47 (and note 2), 52f., 55; Richard, *Inventaire*, p. x.

On this MS, cf. Richard, *Inventaire*, p. 4; Scrivener, I, p. 209 (under Evan. 109); Gregory, I, pp. 152f. (under Vier Evangelien 109); Aland, I, p. 67 (under the Gregory–Aland number 109); von Soden, I,1, p. 194 (under ε431).

[268] Von Soden, *loc. cit.*, misprinted the Greek figures of these sections (placed in correct location, after ρπθ) as ρζ, ρζα, ρζβ, and ρζγ.

[269] On the yellow wash used predominantly (but *not* exclusively!) in South Italian MSS, cf. Turyn, *Codices*, p. 20; *idem*, *DGMItaly*, I, pp. 6, 170, 189, 202. On colored blobs applied to round or oval letters or to parts of such letters, cf. *idem*, *Codices*, pp. 36, 84; *idem*, *DGMItaly*, I, pp. 5, 192 (on MS Laur. Conv. Soppr. 20), especially p. 202, and *passim*.

[270] The present MS Additional 5117 is listed in the sale catalogue of Askew MSS: *Bibliotheca Askeviana manu scripta. Sive Catalogus Librorum Manuscriptorum Antonii Askew, M.D. ... Horum omnium publicè fiet Auctio, Apud G. Leigh & J. Sotheby, ... Londini ... M.DCC.LXXXV* [London, 1785], p. 40 (under no. 620, as I demonstrate below). I have examined a microfilm of the British Museum copy of this catalogue (shelfmark 679.e.26), in which purchasers' names and prices were marked. The Greek parchment MSS of the New Testament are listed on pp. 40–41. It should be

Plate 66: A.D. 1333.

Oxford, Bodleian Library, ms Auct.T.5.28. Bombycine, 244 × 172 mm., 263 fols., 23 lines to a page. Contents: St. Gregory of Nazianzus, Sixteen Orations (or. 1, 45, 44, 41, 15, 24, 19, 38, 43, 39, 40, 11, 21, 42, 14, 16, as numbered in Migne; I indicate their beginnings in Migne, Patr. Gr., 35, col. 396; 36, 624; 36, 608; 36, 428; 35, 911; 35, 1169; 35, 1044; 36, 312; 36, 493; 36, 336; 36, 360; 35, 832; 35, 1081; 36, 457; 35, 857; 35, 933).[271] The MS was completed in January A.M. 6841 = A.D. 1333, according to the subscription on fol. 263^r (Plate 113b): + τῷ ϑ(ε)ῷ χάρις, ἀμήν: | † ἔτους ͵ϛ°ᵘ ω°ᵘ. μα̅°ᵘ′: μηνὶ ἰαννουαρίω· ἰν(δικτιῶν)ος α̅ⁿˢ′:

On Plate 66 we reproduce folio 194^r, containing a passage from St. Gregory of Nazianzus, Oration 21, In laudem magni Athanasii episcopi Alexandrini, chap. 8 (ed. Migne, Patr. Gr., 35, cols. 1089 B 6 – 1092 A 1). The capital O (in red) projected to the left indicates that a text section begins in the preceding line.[272]

Another facsimile specimen of this MS was published in *Catalogue of the Extraordinary Collection of Splendid Manuscripts, Chiefly upon Vellum, in Various Languages of Europe and the East, Formed by M. Guglielmo Libri, ... Which Will Be Sold by Auction, by Messrs. S. Leigh Sotheby & John Wilkinson. ... On Monday, 28th of March, 1859, and Seven following Days* [London, 1859], pl. II (under no. 1130: part of fol. 3^v).

This MS was formerly owned by Guglielmo Libri-Carrucci (1803–1869).[273] It was listed and described in the auction *Catalogue* of Libri MSS (see above), pp. 248f. (under no. 1130). The Libri MSS that are now in the Bodleian Library were purchased at the Libri auction at Sotheby and Wilkinson in 1859 (cf. *Summary Catalogue*, V, p. 47).

In the Bodleian Library, this MS was for a while marked Graec. misc. 296. It is listed, with the present shelfmark Auct.T.5.28, and described in *Summary Catalogue*, V, p. 71 (under S.C. 24777).

---

pointed out that Gregory, in the descriptions of former Askew MSS that are now in the British Museum, in some cases wrongly indicated their Askew numbers and in others simply did not indicate them. I list here the Askew MSS of the New Testament on parchment sold to the British Museum according to the entries recorded in the Museum's copy of the Askew catalogue, and I indicate their present shelfmarks wherever the identification is obvious (cf. Richard, *Inventaire*, pp. 2–4): Askew 609 = Brit. Mus. Additional 5115; Askew 621 = Additional 5153 A, 5153 B (this MS in 2 volumes was successively first bought by Lowes, then again sold by Leigh to the British Museum on 15 May 1786); Askew 622 = Additional 5111, 5112; Askew 623 = Additional 5107; Askew 630 = Additional 5116. The only New Testament MS on parchment bought by the British Museum in the Askew sale that remains to be identified is Askew 620, which must be identical with the present MS Additional 5117.

[271] On the selection of Gregory Nazianzenus' sixteen orations which were used as homilies on certain feasts and were carried in many MSS, cf. I. Sajdak, *Historia critica scholiastarum et commentatorum Gregorii Nazianzeni*, I, Meletemata Patristica, I (Cracow, 1914), pp. 96f., 120ff.; Ehrhard, *Überlieferung und Bestand*, II, pp. 210–14; T. Sinko, *Literatura grecka*, III,2 (Wroclaw, 1954), p. 188; F. Halkin, "Le Marcianus gr. 494 et l'hagiographie byzantine," in *Miscellanea Marciana di studi bessarionei*, Medioevo e Umanesimo, 24 (Padua, 1976), p. 158.

[272] On the meaning of a letter projected to the left, cf. above, p. 22 note 63.

[273] On Guglielmo Libri-Carrucci, cf. Frati, *Dizionario bio-bibliografico*, pp. 296–303; *Summary Catalogue*, V, p. 47; de Ricci, *English Collectors*, pp. 131ff., 135f.

Plate 67: A.D. 1334/1335.

London, British Museum, ms Additional 19993. Bombycine, 250 ×
175 mm., 281 fols., 23–25 lines to a page. Contents: Lectionary of the Gospels.
The MS was subscribed in A.M. 6843 = A.D. 1334/1335 (fol. 281ᵛ – Plate **113c**):
Ἔτ[ει] ͵ϛωμγ [   ] | † [᾽Ε]τελειώθ(η)· τὸ παρὸν [ἅ]γιον εὐαγγέλιον· | καὶ ἐτέθη
ἐν τῇ ἁγίᾳ [[μονῇ]] ἐκκλησίᾳ (this word was probably written by the same scribe
above the deleted word), τοῦ ἁγ(ίου) μ(ε)γ(α)λ(ο)|μάρτ(υ)ρ(ος) Γεωργίου· τοῦ
βαϑῦ: δι ἐξόδ(ου) | κυρ(οῦ) π(α)π(ᾶ) Γε(ω)ρ(γίου) τοῦ ῾Αγιασοματ(ί)τ(ου) (?):
καὶ οἱ ἐντυ|χάν[ο]ντες, εὔχεσϑ[ε], αὐτόν + The term εὐαγγέλιον means a
lectionary of the Gospels (cf. Gregory, I, pp. 334f.). This MS was deposited
in, i.e., donated to, a church of St. George. On this meaning of the word
τιϑέναι, "to donate" (a MS), cf. Krumbacher, Κτήτωρ, pp. 413–14. For τοῦ
βαϑῦ, Gregory (I, p. 403) read τοῦ βαϑῦ (? καϑῦ); Richard (*Inventaire*, p. 36)
read τοῦ βαϑύ. This obviously was (in the genitive) the name of the locality
in which the church in question was situated. It should be pointed out that
the place-name τὸ Βαϑύ is frequent in modern Greece.[274] I was unable to
identify in Cyprus the location of the place mentioned in the above subscription (on the presumable Cypriot origin of this MS, see below). The subscription states that the MS was written at the expense of the priest Georgius
Hagiasomatites (?) and was donated to the church of St. George τοῦ βαϑῦ.
The priest Georgius was a native or resident of a place, or pastor of a church,
from whose name the apposition τοῦ ῾Αγιασοματ(ί)τ(ου) was derived. My reading ασο is uncertain. The misspelling ασο (instead of ασω) is a necessary
assumption, because the space between ι and μ is too narrow for ασω and
the traces before μ could be those of σο; the letter α (after ἀγι) is my con-
jectural reading not supported by any trace of the letter (there is, in fact,
a complete blank).[274a] I assume that the place-name, or the name of a church,
from which the noun as read by me was derived was ῞Αγιος ᾽Ασώματος or
῞Αγιοι ᾽Ασώματοι. Places with the name ᾽Ασώματος (in a more formal manner
certainly supplied with the prefix ῞Αγιος) existed in Cyprus in the Middle
Ages; two still exist there; one monastery with such a name is known to
have existed in Cyprus.[275] Since this MS was bought in Cyprus, there is a strong

---

[274] On the frequency of τὸ Βαϑύ in Greece as name of towns, villages, harbors, bays, and rivers,
cf. Μεγ.῾Ελλ.᾽Εγκυκλ., VI, p. 471; for a list of such names in the Greek world, cf. *ibid.*, pp. 471–75.
Also cf. Λεξικὸν τῶν δήμων, pp. 26, 183f.; only one village with the masculine name ὁ Βαϑύς is listed,
ibid., p. 184. From Cyprus, three rivers or streams with the name Vathys, i.e., ὁ Βαϑύς, are listed
in *Cyprus. Index Gazetteer. Compiled by Survey Directorate, General Headquarters Middle East* (Cairo,
1946), p. 32. However, a more specific appellation of a church usually refers, after the name of the
patron saint, to the name of a place in the genitive (not to the name of a river); therefore, we can
dismiss these Cypriot river (or stream) names in reference to the church of St. George, if it was in
Cyprus.

[274a] There is some other difficulty in that the byname of the sponsor suggested above should
have been ῾Αγιοασωματίτης in the nominative, in accordance with the usual pattern of such names
like ῾Αγιοαϑανασίτης, ῾Αγιοαναστασίτης (cf. *PLP*, I [1976], p. 21, nos. 232, 233, 234). But there is no
room in the subscription to assume that there were two letters οα in that blank, something that
would allow a reading ῾Αγιοασωματ(ί)τ(ου).

[275] On two villages named ᾽Ασώματος in Cyprus, cf. S. Menardos, Τοπωνυμικὸν τῆς Κύπρου, in ᾽Αϑηνᾶ,
18 (1905), p. 380.

basis for an assumption that it was written there, all the more so since the writing of the subscription is consistent with the characteristic script style practiced in Cyprus in the first half of the 14th century.²⁷⁶ This is why I support my reading τοῦ Ἁγιασραματ(ί)τ(ου) by a reference to Cypriot place-names.

On Plate **67** we reproduce folio 131ᵛ. This is a page of the LECTIONARY OF THE GOSPELS which contains a passage from the Gospel of St. Matthew 25:18–24. It is a part of the lesson for the Mass on Tuesday in Holy Week (ed. Εὐαγγέλιον [1880], pp. 127ᵇ, 36 – 128ᵃ, 12; or ed. Εὐαγγέλιον [1968], pp. 148ᵇ, 38 – 149ᵃ, 8). The entire lesson for this office is Matthew 24:36 – 26:2 (on the time and extent of this lesson, cf. Gregory, I, p. 362). It is noteworthy that this lectionary is written in single-column pages (cf. also Plate **47**), while in general a two-column arrangement prevailed in lectionaries (cf. above, p. 17; cf. Plates **5, 6, 7, 11, 56**). Even if this MS was presumably written in Cyprus, its script style does not show any characteristic features of Cypriot calligraphy. It is only the subscription (Plate **113c**) which manifests an appearance related to the Cypriot calligraphy of the period in question. The uncharacteristic style of the main body of the MS, if it was (as I believe) written in Cyprus, may be explained by the fact that this is a scriptural MS and that in scriptural MSS particular regional features were avoided. We have already encountered the phenomenon of an uncharacteristic script style in two scriptural MSS written presumably in Cyprus (cf. above, pp. 68, 83; cf. Pls. **46, 56**). Another facsimile specimen of this MS was published in *Pal.*

There is a village named Asomatos in the Kyrenia (Kerynia) district of Cyprus. Cf. *Cyprus. Census of Population and Agriculture 1946.* Tables (London [1949]), p. 8; L. de Mas Latrie, "Notice sur la construction d'une carte de l'île de Chypre," *BECh,* 24 (1863), p. 45 (under XIII, 15); N. G. Kyriazes, Τὰ χωρία τῆς Κύπρου (Larnaca, 1952), pp. 57 (no. 366), 163 (under no. 1453); L. de Mas Latrie, *Histoire de l'île de Chypre sous le règne des princes de la maison de Lusignan,* II (Paris, 1852; repr. Famagusta, 1970), p. 110 and note 2.

Another village named Asomatos is situated in the Limassol district. Cf. *Cyprus. Census,* p. 11; de Mas Latrie, "Notice," p. 32 (under III, 20); Kyriazes, *op. cit.,* p. 57 (no. 367); J. Richard, *Chypre sous les Lusignans. Documents chypriotes des Archives du Vatican (XIVᵉ et XVᵉ siècles),* Institut Français d'archéologie de Beyrouth, Bibliothèque archéologique et historique, LXXIII (Paris, 1962), p. 68 and note 5.

On villages named Asomatos or San Asomatos in Cyprus, cf. also de Mas Latrie, *Histoire de l'île de Chypre,* III (1855, repr. 1970), pp. 503, 507, 509; Kyriazes, *op. cit.,* p. 10 (under nos. 20 and 21). Ruins of churches called Asomatos in Cyprus are listed in *Cyprus. Index Gazetteer,* p. 5, lines 1 and 2. Cf. also A. Stylianou, Αἱ περιηγήσεις τοῦ Βάρσκυ ἐν Κύπρῳ, in Κυπρ.Σπουδ., 21 (1957), p. 89 and note 149.

On a monastery called Asomatos, μονὴ τοῦ Ἀσωμάτου, in Lefkara in Cyprus, cf. Richard, *Chypre sous les Lusignans,* p. 69 note 5, p. 80 note 1; N. G. Kyriazes, Τὰ μοναστήρια ἐν Κύπρῳ (Larnaca, 1950), p. 28 (no. 13); S. P. Lampros, Κυπριακὰ καὶ ἄλλα ἔγγραφα ἐκ τοῦ Παλατίνου κώδικος 367 τῆς βιβλιοθήκης τοῦ Βατικανοῦ, in Νέος Ἑλλ., 15 (1921), p. 159; or K. Chatzepsaltes, Ἐκ τῆς ἱστορίας τῆς Ἐκκλησίας Κύπρου κατὰ τὴν Φραγκοκρατίαν, in Κυπρ. Σπουδ., 22 (1958), p. 15 (doc. 5, line 12); Turyn, *Codices,* p. 120.

It should be added that the place-names Ἀσώματος and Ἀσώματοι (even Ἀσώματα) are well known from the territory of Greece: cf. Λεξικὸν τῶν δήμων, pp. 24, 182.

²⁷⁶ For samples of Cypriot script of the first half of the 14th century, cf. Pls. **57, 58, 112b** (from London Harley 5579: cf. above, pp. 83 ff.); Omont, *Fac-similés ... du IXᵉ au XIVᵉ siècle,* pl. LXXIX/II (from Paris Grec 2133, certainly a Cypriot MS: cf. Turyn, *Codices,* p. 122); J. Schmitt, in *BZ,* 1 (1892), p. 329; S. P. Lampros, in Νέος Ἑλλ., 5 (1908), pl. Α'; 15 (1921), p. 346; 16 (1922), p. 83; Turyn, *Codices,* pls. 96, 190a–c; Follieri, *Codices,* pl. 53; Turyn, *DGMItaly,* II, pls. 93, 237a (cf. I, p. 119). Now cf. also P. Canart, "Un style d'écriture livresque dans les manuscrits chypriotes du XIVᵉ siècle: la chypriote 'bouclée'," in *Paléographie grecque et byzantine,* pp. 319–20, figs. 2–4.

Soc., Ser. I, pl. 206 (with a description of this MS and a transcript of the page reproduced).

This MS was bought in Cyprus by G. Alefson in 1851; then was owned by the bookseller Boone, who sold it to the British Museum in 1854.

On this MS, cf. Richard, *Inventaire*, pp. 35f.; J. Darrouzès, "Autres manuscrits originaires de Chypre," *REB*, 15 (1957), p. 149 (under no. 80, with a misprint in the number of the MS); Scrivener, I, p. 346 (under Evst. 266); Gregory, I, p. 403 (under Evangelia 193); Aland, I, p. 215 (under the Gregory–Aland symbol *l* 193).

Plate 68: A.D. 1335/1336.

Oxford, Bodleian Library, ms Laud Greek 2. Parchment, 220 × 155 mm., 290 fols., 24 lines to a page. Contents: (fols. 1ʳ–14ᵛ) religious texts; (fols. 15ʳ–189ᵛ) Psalms and (fols. 190ʳ–201ᵛ) Odes; (fols. 202ʳ–290ʳ) religious hymns. The MS was subscribed (in gold over red) in A.M. 6844 = A.D. 1335/ 1336 (fol. 201ᵛ – Plate **113d**): ·:· Ἔτους, ͵ϛ, ωμδ΄: ἰν(δικτιῶνος), δ΄ ·:· On Plate **68** we reproduce folio 157ʳ containing a passage of PSALM 118:101–14 (ed. A. Rahlfs, *Septuaginta id est Vetus Testamentum graece iuxta LXX inter- pretes*, 6th ed., II [Stuttgart (1962)], pp. 136f.; or ed. Rahlfs, *Psalmi cum Odis*, 2nd ed. = *Septuaginta. Vetus Testamentum Graecum Auctoritate Acade- miae Litterarum Gottingensis editum*, X [Göttingen, 1967], pp. 296–98). The initial capital letters of the versicles are projected to the left, in accordance with the traditional arrangement of the Psalms in MSS; it means that the Psalms are arranged στιχηρῶς and μετ' ἐκθέσεως.[277] These projected letters are written here in gold over red; this combination of colors is used throughout the MS wherever normally we should expect red.

The MS was once owned by Robert Pember (cf. fol. 1ʳ, upper margin). Then it was acquired by William Laud in 1633 (cf. fol. 1ʳ, lower margin) and donated by him to the Bodleian Library in 1635. On Robert Pember (d. 1560), reader in Greek in Cambridge and collector of coins, cf. *DNB*, XV, pp. 722f. On William Laud (1573–1645) and MSS donated by him to the Bod- leian Library in the period 1635–1641, cf. above. p. 47.

On this MS, cf. Coxe, I, cols. 491–93; *Summary Catalogue*, II,1, p. 30 (under S.C. 693); I, p. 129; R. Holmes and J. Parsons, *Vetus Testamentum graece cum variis lectionibus*, III (Oxford, 1823), Praefatio ad librum Psalmorum, under no. 203; Rahlfs, *Verzeichnis der griechischen Hand- schriften des Alten Testaments*, p. 172 (symbol 203).

Plates 69 and 70: A.D. 1336.

Cambridge, University Library, ms Additional 3049. Parchment and paper (in each quire, the outer bifolium and the inner bifolium are of parch- ment, the rest is of paper),[278] 275 × 190 mm., 67 fols. (numbered 49–128),

---

[277] On the traditional arrangement of Psalms and Odes in MSS so that the text is divided into versicles which have the initial letter projected to the left (i.e., the arrangement is made στιχηρῶς and μετ' ἐκθέσεως), cf. Turyn, *Codices*, pp. 55f.

[278] In this MS, in each quire the conjoint leaves 1 + 8 and 4 + 5 are of parchment; the con- joint leaves 2 + 7 and 3 + 6 are of Western paper. On the composition of MSS in which parchment and paper were combined, cf. J. Irigoin, "Quelques particularités des manuscrits copiés en Crète avant le milieu du XVᵉ siècle," in Πεπραγμένα τοῦ Β΄ Διεθνοῦς Κρητολογικοῦ Συνεδρίου, III (Athens, 1968), pp. 93f. This MS shows a combination of parchment and paper of the kind indicated *ibid.*, p. 94, lines 4–2 from the bottom (not of the kind indicated in the upper part of p. 94); cf. *ibid.*, p. 93, lines 6–2 from the bottom.

about 40 lines to a page. The MS is incomplete at the beginning and at the end. According to the present foliation, fols. 1–48, 50, 104–105, 112–120, 127 are lost; some folios at the end are also lost. To judge from the quire marks, at the beginning of the original MS 16 quires are missing, i.e., 128 fols., not 48 fols., as implied by the modern foliation (which possibly was done after the MS had suffered some loss at its beginning). Presumably there was some unknown text, or texts, at the beginning of the original MS; thereupon followed the theological treatise (indicated below) of which the beginning is lost here. As of 1974, the MS has no binding and is kept in a box. Contents: (fols. 49ʳ–78ʳ) George Moschampar, Κεφάλαια ἀντιρρητικὰ κατὰ τῶν τοῦ Βέκκου δογμάτων τε καὶ γραμμάτων (Capita antirrhetica contra Ioannis Becci dogmata et scripta), chaps. 11–33 (incomplete at the beginning);[279] (fol. 78ᵛ) subscription; (fols. 79ʳ–128ᵛ) St. Anastasius Sinaita, Ὁδηγός (Viae dux), incomplete at the end (ed. Migne, Patr. Gr., 89, cols. 48 B 12 – 273 B 4), with gaps resulting from the loss of some folios (see above).

The MS was written almost entirely (the exceptions being some small portions indicated below) by Nicolaus, son of the priest Gregorius, of Clarentza (in the Peloponnesus), who wrote a subscription (in red) on 26 April A.M. 6844 = A.D. 1336, on fol. 78ᵛ, after the conclusion of the above theological treatise (Plate **114a**): Δόξα Χ(ριστ)ῷ τῷ Θ(ε)ῷ ἡμῶν τῷ δόντι ἀρχὴν καὶ τέλος + | Ἐ-γρά(φ)η τὸ τοιοῦτον βιβλίον διὰ χειρὸς ἁμαρτωλοῦ καὶ χω|ρικοῦ τάχα γραφέως· Νικολάου υἱοῦ παπᾶ Γρηγ(ο)ρ(ίου) ἀπὸ τὴν Κλαρενθ(αν)· | καὶ εὔχεσθαι διὰ τὸν κ(ύριο)ν οἱ μέλλοντες ἀναπτεῖν καὶ θεορεῖν αὐτὸ δι(ὰ) | τὸν κ(ύριο)ν· καὶ μὴ κατα-ρᾶσθαι· ὅτι χωρικός· εἰμὶ πολλὰ πολὰ πολὰ· | σφόδρ(α) τοῦ νοῦ τὲ καὶ γραμμάτ-των· + | Ἐγρά(φ)η ἐν μη(ν)ῆ ἀπριλλ(ίῳ) κϛ'· ἰνδικτιώνος τετάρτης: ὥρα ἦν | ὡσεὶ ϑ τῆς ἡμέρας· ἡμέρ(α) παρα(σκευ)ῆ τῆς μεσοπεντηκοστῆς· | τοῦ Ἔτους ͵ϛωμδ· | σωθείημεν ἅπαντες ἀμήν· +++++

In the subscription, it is noteworthy, from the paleographical point of view, that the capital initial E (in line 2) is traced doubly (also cf. the capital initial E in line 7 of the subscription). The double tracing of letters is a feature of the South Italian script.[280] Double tracing of initials appears also elsewhere in the MS. We must consider this feature an influence of South Italian manuscripts, which can be easily understood here, since this MS was written by a native of Clarentza, a town under Frankish rule at that time. Clarentza or Chiarentza (Κλαρέντσα, -τζα, also Γλαρέντζα) in the Peloponnesus, now called Κυλλήνη (in the eparchy Ἠλεία), situated northwest of Pyrgos, was an important harbor during the Frankish rule.[281] In line 4, ἀναπτεῖν is puzzling (one would expect, e.g., ἀναπτύσσειν). The commonplace of the subscriptions

---

[279] I am grateful to the Rev. Fr. Jean Darrouzès, A.A., of Paris for supplying me with the identification of this incomplete text of George Moschampar.

[280] On the double tracing of initial capitals in South Italian MSS, cf. M.-L. Concasty, "Manuscrits grecs originaires de l'Italie méridionale conservés à Paris," *Atti dello VIII Congresso Internazionale di Studi Bizantini*, I = *SBN*, 7 (1953), pp. 24, 28.

[281] On Clarentza, cf. O. Markl, *Ortsnamen Griechenlands in "fränkischer" Zeit*, Byzantina Vindobonensia, I (Graz–Cologne, 1966), p. 27, s.v. Chiarentza, p. 33, s.v. Glarentsa; Μεγ.Ἑλλ.Ἐγκυκλ., VIII, pp. 451f., s.v. Γλαρέντζα; D. A. Zakythinos, *Le Despotat grec de Morée*, I (Paris, 1932), Index, p. 320, s.v. Clarentza; II (Athens, 1953), Index, p. 390, s.v. Clarentza.

μὴ καταρᾶσθαι κτλ. was a frequent feature of South Italian subscriptions;[282] their influence in this MS should be noted. The adjective χωρικός used in reference to the scribe (in the meaning "inexperienced") is a known commonplace of the subscriptions.[283] The day of the subscription, 26 April 1336, fell indeed on Friday which was the third day after the Wednesday of Mid-Pentecost (in the 4th week after Easter); this Friday was then within the festal Mid-Pentecost season[283a] (as recorded in the subscription).

The main scribe of this MS, Nicolaus of Clarentza, whom I denote as scribe A, wrote the preserved dated part of the MS (except for fols. 62^r line 27 – 63^r, written by scribe B) and continued writing the MS beyond the subscription page. In this latter part of the volume, I noticed a few small portions written by other scribes. Folio 109^r was written by two scribes, C and D, both of them different from A. Scribe C wrote fol. 109^r lines 1–14 σευῆρος; scribe D wrote the rest of this page, i.e., fol. 109^r lines 14 καὶ οἱ – 39. Scribe E wrote folio 121^r. Scribe F wrote fol. 128^r–128^v. Some pages in this part of the volume (which follows the subscription) seem to have been written by the main scribe A in a different vein, in somewhat smaller lettering. Strictly speaking, the subscription on fol. 78^v pertains to the part of the volume which precedes it, i.e., to fols. 49^r–78^r. Still, it is conceivable that, after the whole volume was written, the scribe Nicolaus wrote the subscription on a blank page fol. 78^v which was available for this purpose. But there is no cogent proof that the subscription was written after the completion of the entire volume. Since the subscription is written in a script that appears identical with the handwriting of Nicolaus which precedes and follows it, but is somewhat different from the script of the final part of the volume, I assume that the subscription was written in the course of the writing immediately after the conclusion of the preceding part of the volume. For this reason, I consider that the subscription pertains only to the preceding part of the volume and I offer specimens only from that part of the MS.

As a specimen of the handwriting of the main scribe A, Nicolaus of Clarentza, on Plate **69** we reproduce folio 78^r, containing a passage from GEORGE MOSCHAMPAR, CAPITA ANTIRRHETICA CONTRA IOANNIS BECCI DOGMATA ET SCRIPTA, from chap. 33, viz., the conclusion of the treatise (except for the end of the page on line 5 from the bottom ἡ χάρις – last line ἀμήν, ed. A. K. Demetrakopoulos, Ὀρθόδοξος Ἑλλὰς ἤτοι περὶ τῶν Ἑλλήνων τῶν γραψάντων κατὰ Λατίνων καὶ περὶ τῶν συγγραμμάτων αὐτῶν [Leipzig, 1872], pp. 61, 20 – 62, 25).[283b] This polemic treatise of George Moschampar, consisting

---

[282] Cf. Turyn, *Codices*, p. 54.

[283] Cf. *idem, DGM Italy*, I, p. 102; above, p. 8 and note 14.

[283a] The Mid-Pentecost festival (μεσοπεντηκοστή) ran from the Wednesday indicated through its octave, i.e., through the next Wednesday (cf. N. Nilles, "Mitte-Pfingsten," *Zeitschrift für katholische Theologie*, 19 [1895], pp. 169f.; *idem, Kalendarium manuale utriusque Ecclesiae orientalis et occidentalis*, 2nd ed., II [Innsbruck, 1897], p. 346).

[283b] The book of Demetrakopoulos was reprinted in Athens in 1968 as volume 26 of Βιβλιοθήκη ἱστορικῶν μελετῶν.

in its complete form of 33 chapters, is not yet published, except for its conclusion (*ibid.*, pp. 61–62).[284]

In the dated part of this MS written and subscribed by Nicolaus, there is a small portion comprising fols. 62^r line 27 – 63^r, written by a different scribe B. He seems to be identical with the rubricator who wrote the headlines of the chapters in the dated part of the MS. This scribe B who participated to a slight degree in the production of the MS should, nevertheless, be represented here. To show the handwriting of scribe B, on Plate **70** we reproduce folio 63^r, containing a passage from GEORGE MOSCHAMPAR, CAPITA ANTIRRHETICA CONTRA IOANNIS BECCI DOGMATA ET SCRIPTA, from chap. 22 (unpublished).

This MS was acquired by the Cambridge University Library in 1891 from C. J. Cummings of Volo, through H. C. Rae of Liverpool. Several Additional MSS of this Library show the same provenience.[285]

On this MS, cf. Easterling, *op. cit.*, pp. 314f.; Irigoin, *op. cit.* (above, note 278), p. 94.

Plate 71: A.D. 1337.

London, British Museum, ms Additional 5468. Parchment, 220 × 158 mm., 226 fols. (the pencil foliation is valid), 29 lines to a page. Contents: Four Gospels, adapted for liturgical use. The MS was subscribed in red by Constantinus of Adrianople on 10 September A.M. 6846 = A.D. 1337 (fol. 225^v – Plate **114b**): † ἐτελιωθ(η) ἡ παρὸν δέλτο(ς) αὕτη τῶν τεσ|σάρων εὐαγγελιστῶν· διαχειρὸ(ς) Κωνστ(αν)|τίνου τοῦ Ανδρ(ια)νοπ(ο)λ(ίτου): ἦν δὲ κ(αὶ) τοῦ τρέχοντος | ἔτους ͵ϛωμϛ' μ(η)ν σεπ(τέμβ)ρ(ιος) εις τ(ὰς) ι ++ The confusion of genders in the participle παρὸν (i.e., παρὼν) used instead of παροῦσα is noteworthy.[286]

On Plate **71** we reproduce folio 129^r, which contains a passage from the GOSPEL OF ST. LUKE 5:25–35. This passage comprises the end of the lesson appointed for Saturday of the 19th week after Pentecost, the whole lesson for Saturday of the 20th week, and the beginning of the lesson for Wednesday of the 19th week. The entire lessons for these three days are: Luke 5:17–26; 5:27–32; 5:33–39 (on the time and the extent of these lessons, cf. Gregory, I, p. 354). There appear on this page liturgical and other notes in red. In

[284] On George Moschampar and this polemic treatise, cf. V. Laurent, "Un polémiste grec de la fin du XIIIe siècle. La vie et les œuvres de Georges Moschampar," *EO*, 28 (1929), pp. 129–58 (pp. 153–55, on the treatise); L. Allatius, *De Ecclesiae occidentalis Atque orientalis perpetua consensione, Libri Tres* (Cologne, 1648: repr. [Farnborough], 1970), cols. 778f. (under XIII); I. A. Fabricius and G. C. Harless, *Bibliotheca Graeca*, XII (Hamburg, 1809), pp. 46f.; Demetrakopoulos, *op. cit.*, pp. 60–63; V. Laurent, in *DTC*, X, cols. 2508f., *s.v.* Moschabar, Georges; Beck, *Kirche und theologische Literatur*, pp. 677f.; V. Laurent, in *LThK*, IV, cols. 704f., *s.v.* Georgios Moschambar. Now cf. also V. Laurent and J. Darrouzès, *Dossier grec de l'Union de Lyon (1273–1277)*, AOC, 16 (Paris, 1976), pp. 19–24 (esp. pp. 21f., on this treatise; p. 22, on this Cambridge MS), and *passim* (cf. Index, p. 601, *s.v.* Moschabar, Georges); G. Podskalsky, *Theologie und Philosophie in Byzanz*, ByzArch, 15 (Munich [1977]), p. 88 note 370.

[285] On the same provenience of the MSS Cambridge Univ. Libr. Additional 3046–3052 and 3076, cf. P. Easterling, "Hand-List of the Additional Greek Manuscripts in the University Library, Cambridge," *Scriptorium*, 16 (1962), pp. 305, 314, 309, 315, 319, 310, 322, 318.

[286] On the use of masculine participles with feminine nouns in late postclassical and Byzantine Greek, cf. Jannaris, *Historical Greek Grammar*, p. 315, § 1181^b; Dieterich, *Untersuchungen*, p. 208.

line 4, this note is written: τέλ(ος) τοῦ ιϑ̄' σα(ββά)τ(ου): σα(ββά)τ(ῳ) κ̄:· This note marks the end of the first lesson mentioned above and the beginning of the subsequent lesson. In line 5, αρχ(ή) marks the beginning of this lesson; the initial of this lesson is a red capital, projected to the left. In line 22, there is a note, τέλ(ος) τοῦ ιϑ̄ σα(ββά)τ(ου):,[286a] which marks the end of the lesson indicated. In line 23, the beginning of the next lesson is marked: τῇ δ' τῆς ιϑ̄' ευδ(ομά-δος): The red numerals in the right margin, λη̄', λϑ̄', and μ̄, are numbers of the Eusebian sections of Luke that begin here; these sections comprise Luke 5:27–28; 5:29–30; 5:31–39 (on the contents of these sections, cf. von Soden, I,1, p. 399). In the upper margin, there is in red a note indicating the number and the τίτλος of the κεφάλαιον in Luke which begins in line 5: ιδ̄'· πε(ρὶ) Λευὶ τοῦ τελώνου:· The chapter number ιδ̄ is marked in the left margin, to the left of line 4 (there was no room for it to the left of line 5). This chapter 14 of Luke comprises Luke 5:27 – 6:5 (cf. von Soden, I,1, p. 409). The red color is used in all these notes in accordance with the traditional practice of New Testament MSS adapted for liturgical use.[287]

On fol. 225ᵛ a note was recorded on 6 December 1718 by the priest Sophronius, at the end of which the protosyncellus of Alexandria, Iacobus, is mentioned: *1718* δεκεμβρίου ϛ τὸ παρὸν εγχειριζω εγώ | ο παπὰ Σωφρονιος· ἐμμοῦ τῆς αγίας μονῆς Ἀκακηου (?) | τοῦ αγιοῦ προτοσυγ-γέλλου ––– Ἰακοβου ϑρο|νου Αλεξανδρειας.

The MS was once owned by the London bookseller Conant of Fleet Street, from whom it was bought by John Jackson[288] in London in 1777 (according to the note on a front flyleaf).

On this MS, cf. Richard, *Inventaire*, p. 5; Scrivener, I, p. 257 (under Evan. 573); Gregory, I, p. 212 (under Vier Evangelien 686); Aland, I, p. 98 (under the Gregory–Aland number 686); von Soden, I,1, p. 194 (under ε432).

Plate 72: A.D. 1337/1338.

Oxford, Bodleian Library, ms Selden Supra 29. Parchment, 163 × 120 mm., 230 fols., 23–27 lines to a page. Contents: Four Gospels. The adaptation of the MS for liturgical use is indicated by the marks ἀρχή and τέλος in the text, and by the presence of lesson tables in the beginning of the MS. The MS was subscribed by the scribe Theodosius in A.M. 6846 = A.D. 1337/1338 (fol. 230ᵛ – Plate **114c**): ⟨Τ⟩ῶι τῆι πυξίδι ταύτῃ, τρισὶ δακτύλοις πεπλη-ρωκότι· | σὺ δ' ἀντιδοίηις ἄφε(σιν) ἁμαρτιῶν ὦ παντάναξ· υἱὲ καὶ λόγε | π(ατ)ρ(ὸ)ς τοῦ προανάρχου, ἵν' ὅπως τοῖς ἐξ αριστερῶν μὴ τύχαιεν, τοῖς | δ' ἐκ δεξιὼν, αὐτὸν συναριθμήσαις ἅμα· Θεοδοσίω λέγω, τῶ μετ(ὰ) | σοῦ, τῆς μ(ητ)ρ(ό)ς σου δούλωι:– ἔτους, ͵ϛ,ω̄,μϛ̄, ἰν(δικτιῶνος) ϛ':– At the beginning of the subscription, the initial capital T was to be added in red, in a position projected to the left, but inadvertently this was not done. The combination of final particles ἵν' ὅπως which appears here is known from late postclassical and Byzantine

---

[286a] The number ιϑ̄ was written mistakenly instead of κ'.
[287] Cf. above, p. 43 note 101.
[288] Perhaps this John Jackson was identical with John Jackson of London, amateur archeologist and traveler, who died in 1807 (cf. *DNB*, X, p. 533).

Greek.[289] The form τύχαιεν is a clumsy optative aorist in the third person singular coined by the scribe.[290]

On Plate **72** we reproduce folios 109v–110r, containing a passage from the GOSPEL OF ST. MARK 14:49–68. The red numerals in the outer margins (ρπε̄-ρϟε̄) are numbers of the Eusebian sections 185–195 of Mark carried on the pages reproduced (on their extents, cf. von Soden, I,1, p. 399). The capital letters in red projected to the left indicate, according to the custom of the scribes, either that a text section begins with such a capital (if the capital happens to begin a sentence), or that a text section begins in the preceding line.[291]

There are in the MS (in the lower margin of fol. 38v and in the right margin of fol. 193r) supplements of passages omitted, made in the handwriting of Ioannes Serbopulus (*fl. ca.* 1480–1500).[292]

This MS was once owned by the famous scholar John Selden (1584–1654). On him and MSS willed by him to the Bodleian Library, which came into possession of the Bodleian Library in 1659, cf. Sandys, *History of Classical Scholarship*, II, pp. 342–44; *Summary Catalogue*, II,1, pp. 594f.; Fletcher, *English Book Collectors*, pp. 85–91; de Ricci, *English Collectors*, p. 23.

On this MS, cf. Coxe, I, cols. 616–18 (under Seldenianus 54); *Summary Catalogue*, II,1, p. 626 (under S.C. 3417); Vogel–Gardthausen, p. 133; Scrivener, I, p. 198 (under Evan. 54); Gregory, I, p. 141 (under Vier Evangelien 54); Aland, I, p. 63 (under the Gregory–Aland number 54); von Soden, I,1, p. 195 (under ε445).

Plate 73: A.D. 1340.

Oxford, Bodleian Library, ms Selden Supra 9. Palimpsest parchment, about 225 × 150 mm. (within the first part, fols. 1–43, some leaves are smaller

[289] On ἵν' ὅπως, cf. Jannaris, *Historical Greek Grammar*, p. 418 note 1; S. G. Kapsomenos, "Zur Häufung synonymer Partikeln in der spätgriechischen Volkssprache," in *Polychordia. Festschrift Franz Dölger zum 75. Geburtstag*, III (Amsterdam, 1968) = *ByzF*, 3 (1968), pp. 134–40, esp. p. 135; also cf. below, pp. 125f.

[290] Cf. Jannaris, *op. cit.*, p. 204, § 805.   [291] Cf. above, p. 22 note 63.

[292] On Ioannes Serbopulus, cf. S. P. Lampros, Σύμμικτα, in Νέος Ἑλλ., 3 (1906), pp. 476f.; Vogel–Gardthausen, pp. 196f. Serbopulus wrote some MSS in the Reading Abbey in England between 1489 and 1497. I compared the writing of Serbopulus in MS Oxford Auct.D.5.2 (listed in Coxe, I, cols. 626f., under Misc. gr. 9; cf. *Summary Catalogue*, II,I, p. 89, under S.C. 1864; Gregory, I, pp. 139f., under Vier Evangelien 47); this MS of the Gospels carries on fol. 1v Serbopulus' inscription ΣΕΡΒΌΠΟΥΛΟC. Two other MSS of the Gospels were written by Ioannes Serbopulus, viz., Oxford, Lincoln College, Greek 18, and Oxford, New College 68. In both of them, the subscription of Oxford Selden Supra 29 was copied (without the date) in such a manner that Serbopulus substituted only his Christian name Ἰωάννη for the name Θεοδοσίω of the scribe of Selden Supra 29. These four Oxford MSS of the Gospels are closely linked by the affinity of their texts: Selden Supra 29, Auct.D.5.2, Lincoln College Greek 18, New College 68. On these MSS, cf. Gregory, I, pp. 139–42 (under Vier Evangelien 54, 47, 56, 58). It appears that MS Auct.D.5.2 was transcribed by Serbopulus directly from Selden Supra 29. MSS Lincoln College 18 and New College 68 either both derive directly from Selden Supra 29, or one of them was copied directly from Selden Supra 29 and was in turn copied in the other one.

On MSS Oxford, Lincoln College Greek 18 and New College 68, cf. also H. O. Coxe, *Catalogus codicum mss. qui in collegiis aulisque Oxoniensibus hodie adservantur*, I (Oxford, 1852; repr. *idem*, *Catalogue of the Manuscripts in the Oxford Colleges*, I [East Ardsley, 1972]), in "Catalogus codicum mss. Collegii Lincolniensis," p. 11, and in "Catalogus codicum mss. Collegii Novi," p. 20.

For Serbopulus' handwriting, cf. N. G. Wilson, in R. W. Hunt et al., *The Survival of Ancient Literature. Catalogue of an Exhibition of Greek and Latin Classical Manuscripts Mainly from Oxford Libraries Displayed on the Occasion of the Triennial Meeting of the Hellenic and Roman Societies 28 July – 2 August 1975* (Oxford, 1975), p. 42 (no. 87), pl. IX (facsimile specimen from MS Oxford, Corpus Christi College 106, written and subscribed by Ioannes Serbopulus in A.D. 1495).

and measure about 200 × 150 mm.), 120 fols. There are fols. 41ᵃ, 41ᵇ, 47ᵃ, 47ᵇ; folio numbers 46 and 69 were passed over; fol. 120 is badly mutilated; the foliation in the upper right-hand corners is valid. The palimpsest leaves consist of 3 different sets. Fols. 1–43 came from two MSS of the 10th century with liturgical contents (menology?). Fols. 44–113 belonged to an Old Testament lectionary of the 11/12th century. Fols. 114–120 came from a New Testament lectionary in majuscule script of the 9th century. The scriptura superior, with which we are concerned here, has the following contents: Panegyricon (hagiographic and homiletic texts). It was written by the priest and chartophylax Constantinus Magedon of Italy and subscribed by him on 21 March A.M. 6848 = A.D. 1340, according to the subscription written on fol. 110ᵛ, lines 6–5 from the bottom of the scriptura superior (Plate **114d**):
Κω(νσταν)τ(ῖ)ν(ος) ἱερεὺς καὶ χαρτωφύλαξ Μαγεδῶν ὁ ᾿Ιταλιώ|τις· μηνὶ μαρτ(ίῳ) κᾱ ἰν(δικτιῶνος) ῆ ἔτους ͵ςῶμῆ ·∴ [293]

On Plate **73** we reproduce folio 3ʳ, containing a passage from this Panegy-ricon. Specifically, this page includes a passage from Nectarius*, patriarch of Constantinople, Narratio de colybis sive Narratio in festum s. Theodori Tiro-nis (ed. Migne, Patr. Gr., 39, cols. 1832 C 15 – 1833 B 3). This text is listed in *BHG*³ 1768. In view of the fact that the ethnic name ᾿Ιταλιώτης is added as an apposition to the scribe's name in the subscription, it should be pointed out that the script of this copyist does not show a strikingly characteristic South Italian appearance.

There are in the MS, in the lower margins of fols. 111ᵛ and 112ʳ, two identical entries: † ὁ τιμιότατος ἱερεὺς παπ(άς) κυρ Μανοῆλ.

This MS once belonged to John Selden (1584–1654). On Selden and the Selden MSS in the Bodleian Library, cf. above, p. 105.

On this MS, cf. Coxe, I, cols. 588f. (under Seldenianus 8); Coxe², *loc. cit.*, reproduces some handwritten additions; *Summary Catalogue*, II,1, p. 621 (under S.C. 3397); p. xviii (under S.C. 3397), important corrections and additions; Van de Vorst–Delehaye, *Catalogus*, pp. 344f.; Ehrhard, *Überlieferung und Bestand*, III,2, pp. 760f., especially p. 760 note 1 (also II, p. 611); Leroy, *op. cit.*, p. 80; [R. Holmes], "*Index codicum rescriptorum Bodleianorum*," in H. Ph. C. Henke and P. I. Brvns, *Annales literarii*, I (Helmstedt, 1782), pp. 11f.; R. Holmes, *Vetus Testamentum Graecum cum variis lectionibus*, I (Oxford, 1798), Praefatio ad Pentateuchum, p. [*kii], caput III (under no. 132); Rahlfs, *Verzeichnis der griechischen Handschriften des Alten Testaments*, pp. 174f.; Scrivener, I, p. 371 (under Apost.74); Gregory, I, p. 469 (under Apostel 84); III, p. 1228, lines 3–1 from the bottom; C. R. Gregory, *Die griechischen Handschriften des Neuen Testaments* (Leipzig, 1908; repr. 1973), pp. 134 (under *l* 368), 277 (symbol *l*ᵃ 368); Aland, I, p. 226 (under the Gregory–Aland symbol *l* 368); Aubineau, *Codices Chrysostomici graeci*, I, p. 252.

Plate 74: A.D. 1340/1341.

Oxford, Bodleian Library, ms Auct.E.1.14. Parchment, 37 × 27 cm., 296 fols. (actually 297, since there are fols. 242a and 242b), 2 columns, 31 lines to a column. Contents: St. John Chrysostom, Homilies on Genesis. The MS was written in A.M. 6849 = A.D. 1340/1341, according to the sub-

---

[293] On this subscription, cf. F. J. Leroy, *L'homilétique de Proclus de Constantinople. Tradition manuscrite, inédits, études connexes*, ST, 247 (Vatican City, 1967), p. 80 and note 69.

scription on fol. 296ᵛ (Plate **115a**): † ἐγράφη τὸ παρὸν τοῦτο βιβλίον ἐν ἔτη ͵ς΄ωμ΄θ΄ + On Plate **74** we reproduce the upper part of folio 81ᵛ, containing a passage from St. John Chrysostom, Homily 11 on Genesis (ed. Migne, Patr. Gr., 53, col. 92, lines 40–50 and 53–63). The capital letter Π (in red) projected to the left indicates that a text section begins in the preceding line.[294]

This MS once belonged to the monastery of Chortaites (near Thessalonica, east of the city).[295] There is an ownership entry of this monastery in political verses on fol. 1ʳ; I arrange it here metrically:

> + αὕτη ἡ βήβλος πέφηκε | τῆς μονῆς Χορταΐτου·
> ⟨×⟩ ἀρχομένης πρω|τῆς τε, τῆς τεσαρακοστῆς γε |
> τοῦ Χρισωστώμου πανη γε, τοῦ φηλο|σωφοτάτου.

In the second verse one syllable was omitted by the person who wrote this entry; some monosyllabic word is missing (probably at the beginning of the verse); the wrong accent should be corrected to πρώτης. The note clearly implies that Chrysostom's Homilies on Genesis were here intended for homiletic use in Lent.[296] Another ownership entry of the same monastery in a political verse appears on fol. 296ᵛ: + αὕτη ἡ βήβλος πέφικεν τῆς μονὶς Χορταΐτου:– On fol.1ʳ, the hieromonk Arsenius entered his name twice: † ᾿Αρσενίου ἱερο(μον)άχ(ου) | † ᾿Αρσενίου ἱερο-(μον)άχ(ου).

This MS was presented to the Bodleian Library in 1608 by Sir Henry Lillo or Lille, late consul of the English merchants in Constantinople. Sir Henry Savile[297] used the MS for his edition of the works of John Chrysostom, published in Eton in 1610–1612.

On this MS, cf. Coxe, I, col. 634 (under Miscell. gr. 28); *Summary Catalogue*, II,1, p. 569 (under S.C. 3025); Aubineau, *Codices Chrysostomici graeci*, I, p. 110.

Plate 75: A.D. 1341/1342.

Oxford, Bodleian Library, ms Laud Greek 71. Bombycine, 24 × 17 cm., vi modern flyleaves (only fol. vi has some modern notes in Greek) + 270 fols. (rather 271, since there are fols. 256a and 256b), *ca.* 27–31 lines to a page. Contents: St. Augustine, De Trinitate, in the Greek translation by Maximus Planudes. The MS was subscribed in A.M. 6850 = A.D. 1341/1342 (fol. 270ᵛ – Plate **115b**): † ἐτελειώθη τὸ παρὸν βιβλίον, ἐν ἔτει ⟦.⟧ ͵ςω|ν̄ +

On Plate **75** we reproduce folio 256bᵛ, containing a passage from St. Augustine, De Trinitate, in the Greek translation by Maximus Planudes (ed. Migne, Patr. Gr., 147, cols. 1122 C 15 – 1123 D 3). This is a passage from De Trinitate, Book XV, chap. 19, §§ 33–34 (the original Latin text of St. Augustine can be found, above the Greek translation text, in Migne, Patr. Gr., 147, cols. 1122 A 10 – 1123 A 12; or it can be found in the edition of St. Augustine's works in Migne, Patr. Lat., 42 [Paris, 1865], cols. 1083 last line – 1084 line 29). The quotation marks in the left margin of the page reproduced pertain to the quotations from the Old and New Testaments in the text.

[294] On the meaning of a letter projected to the left, cf. above, p. 22 note 63.

[295] On the monastery Χορταΐτου, cf. Μεγ.῾Ελλ.᾿Εγκυκλ., XIV, p. 464, *s.v.* Κισσός (ancient name of the mountain ridge called in Byzantine times Χορταΐτης, now Χορτιάτης); A. Bakalopoulos, ῾Η παρὰ τὴν Θεσσαλονίκην Βυζαντινὴ μονὴ τοῦ Χορταΐτου, in ᾿Επ.῾Ετ.Βυζ.Σπ., 15 (1939), pp. 280–87; Vogel–Gardthausen, p. 15; O. Tafrali, *Thessalonique au quatorzième siècle* (Paris, 1913), pp. 213, 216. This monastery had in the city of Thessalonica a μετόχιον which should not be confused with the chief monastery: cf. R. Janin, *Les églises et les monastères des grands centres byzantins* (Paris, 1975), pp. 414f.

[296] Cf. Ehrhard, *Überlieferung und Bestand*, II, p. 304.

[297] On Henry Savile, cf. *DNB*, XVII, pp. 856–59; Sandys, *History of Classical Scholarship*, II, pp. 333–36.

On the translation of St. Augustine's De Trinitate by Maximus Planudes, cf. M. Rackl, "Die griechischen Augustinusuebersetzungen," in *Miscellanea Francesco Ehrle*, I, ST, 37 (Rome, 1924), pp. 9–17; C. Wendel, *RE*, XX, *s.v.* "Planudes, Maximos," col. 2241, § 43; G. Podskalsky, *Theologie und Philosophie in Byzanz*, ByzArch, 15 (Munich [1977]), pp. 123, 176f. MS Laud Greek 71 seems to be the oldest preserved MS of the Planudean Augustine. On another MS, Venice II, 2 (colloc. 1012), containing, among other things, St. Augustine's De Trinitate, in the Greek translation by Maximus Planudes, cf. Turyn, *DGM Italy*, I, pp. 232f.; II, pls. 188, 258c.

The MS was once owned by Gabriel ⟨Severus⟩, metropolitan of Philadelphia, according to the ownership entry on fol. 1ʳ (in the lower margin): ἐκ τῶν Γαβριήλου, τοῦ μητροπολίτ(ου) Φιλαδελφείας Γαβριήλ, τοῦ ἐκ Μονεμβασίας: Gabriel Severus (born *ca.* 1541) lived for most of his life (1572–1616) in Venice. In 1577, he was consecrated metropolitan of Philadelphia, but continued to reside in Venice. From about 1591 he was patriarchal exarch of Venice and Dalmatia, until he died in 1616 on a trip to Dalmatia; he was buried in Venice. Gabriel Severus owned several MSS.[298] This MS later was acquired by Archbishop William Laud in 1637 and was presented by him to the Bodleian Library in 1639. On William Laud (1573–1645) and MSS donated by him to the Bodleian Library, cf. above, p. 47.

On this MS, cf. Coxe, I, col. 556; *Summary Catalogue*, II,1, p. 30 (under S.C. 703); I, pp. 132f.; Barbour, in *Greek Manuscripts in the Bodleian Library*, p. 24 (under no. 31).

Plate 76: A.D. 1343.

Oxford, Bodleian Library, ms Barocci 197. Paper, 315 × 205 mm., 673 fols., 32 lines to a page. Contents: theological, patristic, hagiographic, homiletic texts. The MS was written in Constantinople, since several notes written by the scribe of the MS refer in a precise manner to earthquakes that took place in Constantinople during the writing of the MS between 14 October and 20 November A.M. 6852 = A.D. 1343. The notes of the scribe, including notes which refer to the ecclesiastic calendar, cover the period from 14 October to 5 December A.M. 6852 = A.D. 1343. This means that the MS was concluded after 5 December 1343; the conclusion of the writing may well have taken place in an early part of A.D. 1344. However, since the dated notes pertaining to the progress in the writing of the MS refer to A.D. 1343, I date the MS to A.D. 1343. The scribe's name is indicated cryptographically at the end of one of the dated notes (Pl. **115d**) as Γαλακτίων. His full name appears in several other notes (see below) as the hieromonk Γαλακτίων ὁ Μαδαράκης.

These are the dated notes written in the handwriting of the scribe of the MS. The earliest note is found on fol. 374ʳ (Plate **115c**): † γραφομένου μου τὸ παρὸν βιβλίον καὶ φθάσαντος ὧδε³ γέγονεν συσμὸς ἐν Κωνσταντινουπόλ(ει)· | κατὰ τὸ ͵ϛωνβ ἔτει· μη(νὶ) ὀκτωβρίω ιδ· ἰν(δικτιῶνος) ιβ:– + This earthquake occurred in Constantinople on 14 October A.M. 6852 = A.D. 1343.

---

[298] On Gabriel Severus, cf. E. Legrand, *Bibliographie hellénique ou description raisonnée des ouvrages publiés en grec par des Grecs aux XVᵉ et XVIᵉ siècles*, II (Paris, 1885; repr. 1962), pp. 144–51; Ch. G. Patrineles, in Θρησκ.'Ηθ.'Εγκυκλ., IV, cols. 117–19. On MSS once owned by Severus, cf. Legrand, *op. cit.*, p. 151; Ae. Martini and D. Bassi, *Catalogus codicum graecorum Bibliothecae Ambrosianae*, II (Milan, 1906), Index, p. 1276, *s.v.* Severus Gabriel (on his MSS in Milan); W. Weinberger, *Beiträge zur Handschriftenkunde*, II, SBWien, Philos.-hist.Kl., 161,4 (1909), p. 137; *idem, Wegweiser durch die Sammlungen altphilologischer Handschriften*, SBWien, Philos.-hist.Kl., 209,4 (1931), p. 117.

The next note was written on fol. 380ᵛ (Plate **115d**): † γραφομένου μου τὸ παρὸν βιβλίον καὶ φθάσαντος ὧδε, ἐγένετο σισμὸς | μέγας ἐν Κωνσταντινουπόλ(ει), κατὰ τὸ ͵ϛωνβ ἔτει, ἰν(δικτιῶνος) ιβ· μη(νὶ) ὀκτω|βρίω, ιη· ἐπεκράτησε δὲ ὁ σισμὸς, ἄχρι ἡμερῶν ιβ· ζϑοϑπψϟλν:· This earthquake began in Constantinople on 18 October A.M. 6852 = A.D. 1343 and extended over 12 days, i.e., through 29 October 1343. The name marked cryptographically is to be understood Γαλακτίον (the cryptogram should have been written at the end -σν for -ων).

There follows this note on fol. 425ᵛ (Plate **115e**): † γραφομένου μου τὸν παρόντα λόγον καὶ φθάσαντος ἐνταῦθα, | ἔτυχεν καὶ ἡ παραμονὴ τῆς Θ(εοτό)κου τῆς εἰσόδου· ἤγουν, τὰ ἅγια τῶν ἀγ(ί)ων:- This is a reference to the vigil of the Entry of the B.V.M. into the Temple. This feast fell on the 21st of November. The note was recorded during the vigil or on the eve of the feast, i.e., on the evening of 20 November (1343). There is also this note on fol. 426ᵛ (Plate **115f**): † τῇ παραμονῇ τῆς εἰσόδ(ου) γράφοντός μου καὶ φθάσαντος ἐνταῦθα, γέγονεν συσμὸς μέγας:· This means that on that eve of the feast of the Entry of the B.V.M. into the Temple, i.e., on 20 November (1343), there was an earthquake.[299]

This is the final dated note written by the scribe of the MS on fol. 434ʳ (Plate **116a**): † γραφομένου μου τὸν παρόντ(α) λόγ(ον) τοῦ ὁσ(ίου) π(ατ)ρ(ὸ)ς καὶ φθάσαντος ἐνθάδε· ἔλαχε γενέσθ(αι) καὶ ἡ παρα|μονὴ τῆς θείας μνήμης αὐτοῦ· καὶ μὴ θαυμάσῃς. μὴ ἔχον γὰρ ἀνθιβόλιον, ἀργὸς παρῆλθον | τὰς ἡμέρας, ἀπὸ τῆς εἰσόδου τῆς Θ(εοτό)κου, ἄχρι δεκεμβρίου τὰς τέσσαρης:-+ At the beginning of the note, the scribe refers to his transcribing the life of a saint. Indeed, on fol. 427ᵛ he began copying the Life of St. Nicholas of Myra from the Menology of Symeon Metaphrastes (ed. Migne, Patr. Gr., 116, cols. 317–356; *BHG*³ 1349). St. Nicholas of Myra was commemorated on 6 December. The eve of this commemoration mentioned by the scribe fell on the evening of 5 December (1343). The scribe explains that, since for a while he did not have at his disposal the exemplar which he was copying,[300] he did not work on this MS from the feast of the Entry, i.e., from 21 November, to 4 December.

---

[299] These notes on earthquakes, written on fols. 374ʳ, 380ᵛ, 426ᵛ, were reprinted (from Coxe, I, col. 351) by S. P. Lampros, Ἐνθυμήσεων ἤτοι χρονικῶν σημειωμάτων συλλογὴ πρώτη, in Νέος Ἑλλ., 7 (1910), p. 141 (under no. 58). On the earthquakes in Constantinople in October and November A.D. 1343, cf. Nicephorus Gregoras, Hist. XIV.2, Bonn ed., II (1830), pp. 694, 13 – 696, 11; E. de Muralt, *Essai de chronographie byzantine 1057–1453* (St. Petersburg, 1871; repr. Paris–Amsterdam, 1965), p. 592 (under October 1343); Metropolitan Athenagoras, Κατάλογος τῶν χειρογράφων τῆς ἐν Χάλκῃ μονῆς τῆς Παναγίας, in Ἐπ.Ἑτ.Βυζ.Σπ., 11 (1935), p. 178; V. Laurent, "Notes de chronographie et d'histoire byzantine," *EO*, 36 (1937), pp. 169f. (*ibid.*, on the notes in Barocci 197); Sp. Lampros and Κ. I. Amantos, Βραχέα Χρονικά, in Ἀκαδημία Ἀθηνῶν. Μνημεῖα τῆς ἑλληνικῆς ἱστορίας, I,1 (Athens, 1932), p. 80, no. 47 line 13; B. T. Gorjanov, "Neizdannyj anonimnyj vizantijskij hronograf XIV veka," *VizVrem*, N.S. 2 (XXVII) (1949), p. 285, lines 160–64 (under 18 October 1342); I. Ševčenko, "Nicolas Cabasilas' 'Anti-Zealot' Discourse: A Reinterpretation," *DOP*, 11 (1957), p. 167 note 164; Grumel, *Chronologie*, p. 481. (These earthquakes were not listed by G. Downey, "Earthquakes in Constantinople and Vicinity, A.D. 342–1454," *Speculum*, 30 [1955], p. 600.). Now cf. also Schreiner, *Die byzantinischen Kleinchroniken*, I, pp. 83 (Chronik no. 8/39), 93 (no. 9/10), 612 (no. 87/1), 681 (no. 113/1); II, pp. 258, 610 (Chron. Not. 35).

[300] In the note on fol. 434ʳ, the word ἀνθιβόλιον was used instead of ἀντιβόλαιον. On the meaning of ἀντιβόλαιον ("exemplar," "source"), cf. Du Cange, *Glossarium graecitatis*, I, col. 83, s.v. ἀντίβολιν; Demetrakos, Μέγα Λεξικόν, I, p. 625; E. Kriaras, Λεξικὸ τῆς μεσαιωνικῆς ἑλληνικῆς δημώδους γραμματείας 1100–1669, I (Thessalonica, 1969), pp. 115f., s.v. ἀθιβόλι(ν). On the interaspiration in ἀνθιβόλιον, cf. Dieterich, *Untersuchungen*, pp. 85f., § 3.

The name of the hieromonk Galaction Madaraces, who presumably was the scribe of the MS, appears in a few notes written in the MS in the same handwriting as is the text of the MS. Above, I called attention to the cryptogram with the name of Galaction in one note (cf. Pl. **115d**). For the other notes, I consider it fit to adduce the complete evidence.

A note on fol. 277ᵛ (Plate **116b**): † βιβλίον τοῦ ταπεινοῦ καὶ ἁμαρτωλοῦ τάχα καὶ ἱερο|μονάχου, Γαλακτίωνος τοῦ Μαδαράκη· Ἰ(ησο)ῦ σῶσον με:· +

A note on fol. 344ʳ (Plate **116c**): † βιβλίον Γαλακτίωνος ἱερομονάχου, τοῦ Μαδαράκη:· +

A note on fol. 460ʳ (Plate **116d**): † ζϑοϑπψ⁄λν, λ̒ ξϑςϑλϑπβω:· | † βιβλίον τοῦ ταπεινοῦ καὶ ἁμαρτωλοῦ τάχα | καὶ ἱερομονάχου, Γαλακτίωνος τοῦ Μαδα|ρά-κη:· The cryptographic part of this note means Γαλακτίον, ὁ Μαδαράκης.

A note on fol. 630ᵛ (Plate **116e**): † βιβλίον τοῦ ταπεινοῦ καὶ ἁμαρτωλοῦ τάχα καὶ ἱερο|μονάχου, Γαλακτίωνος τοῦ Μαδαράκη:· +[301]

The formula of the above notes, "book of Galaction Madaraces," does not explicitly point to his role as scribe of the manuscript, although it is obvious that he was indeed the scribe (and not the owner) of the MS.[302] If the scribe had wanted to indicate a Galaction Madaraces as the owner of this MS, he would have added some specific apposition to the name. At any rate, we find in this volume an explicit reference to Galaction Madaraces as the compiler and scribe of the MS. This is the evidence.

Toward the end of the volume there are three leaves, fols. 664ʳ⁻ᵛ and 668ʳ⁻669ᵛ, written in a handwriting slightly different from that of the whole volume. The script style is the same, but the writing of these folios is thinner, somewhat less calligraphic, and perhaps less orthographic. However, the copyist of these pages must have belonged to the same scriptorium or the same

---

[301] It should be recorded that on fol. 308ᵛ a *different* later hand (obviously under the influence of the above notes which mentioned Galaction Madaraces) added the following note: + βίβλίων Γα-λάκτίωνος· ἱερώμονάχου, τοῦ Μαδα (it should have been written Μαδαράκη). This note can be completely disregarded.

[302] V. Gardthausen, *Griechische Palaeographie*, 1st ed. (Leipzig, 1879), p. 236, referred to the cryptographic names of Galaction Madaraces in the above notes; on p. 321, he had doubts whether Galaction Madaraces was the owner or the scribe of Barocci 197; on p. 354, he expressed doubts whether Galaction was the scribe. Vogel–Gardthausen, p. 63 and note 4, referred to Gardthausen, *op. cit.*, p. 236, and expressed doubts whether Galaction Madaraces was the scribe of the MS. Incidentally, Gardthausen, *ibid.*, p. 236, and 2nd ed., II (1913), p. 313, by inadvertence dated MS Barocci 197 to A.D. 1279 (however, Gardthausen, *ibid.*, 1st ed., p. 354, dated Barocci 197 to A.D. 1344).

The cryptographic notes of Galaction Madaraces influenced a later scribe, the priest Hierotheus, who copied MS Laud Greek 29 in A.D. 1592/1593 and wrote there some cryptographic notes which clearly were intended to refer to Galaction Madaraces. In Laud Greek 29, fol. 23ᵛ, upper margin, there is a note, + ψλχ̒ψϑψϑζλϑξξϑψϑοέ̒ζλχωⅰν, ζϑοϑπψⅰσνλωξϑλςϑπβ, which means: ταῦτα (τούτα *codex*) τὰ γράμματα λέγουσιν, Γαλακτίωνος Μαρδάκη (cf. Coxe, I, col. 511 C). The note on fol. 21ᵛ, line 7, was reported by Coxe, I, col. 511B, with a mistake, because it means βίβλος Μακαρίου (this is perhaps a reference to the sponsor or owner of Laud Greek 29). Gardthausen, *op. cit.*, 1st ed., p. 236, and 2nd ed., II, p. 313, stated incorrectly that Galaction Madaraces put a cryptographic signature in MS Laud Greek 29, since this MS was copied by Hierotheus in 1592/1593. This statement was misleading, because the cryptographic note on fol. 23ᵛ was written in the handwriting of the scribe of MS Laud Greek 29, i.e., of Hierotheus. The same can be said of the note on fol. 21ᵛ. Gardthausen's statement (*ibid.*, 1st ed.) was so confusing that Vogel–Gardthausen, p. 161, prefixed (at the bottom of the text page) a question mark to two MSS listed under the priest Hierotheus, one of them being MS Laud Greek 29.

monastery as the scribe of the whole volume. There are some minute differences between the writing of the above three folios and of the whole volume—differences which preclude the identification of the scribe of the three folios with the scribe of the volume. I assume that, when the volume was already concluded, this particular scribe recopied the original three folios, because they were damaged, and in doing so retained the layout of the volume with regard to the number of lines to the page (32 lines). On fol. 664ᵛ the new scribe wrote a commemorative invocation for the hieromonk Galaction: † μνήσθ(η)τ(ι) κ(ύρι)ε τὴν ψυχὴν | τοῦ δούλου σου, Γαλακτίωνος ἱερομονάχου, ἀμήν:· + The reference to the soul of Galaction implies that the note was written after his death, and this would explain why some other scribe did the writing of the three folios indicated above.

This scribe copied on fol. 669ʳ (Plate **117a**) a lengthy colophon which states that Galaction Madaraces compiled and wrote this volume. It also includes information concerning the name of Galaction's father and Galaction's place of origin as Tiberiupolis or Strumica (in Southern Serbia);[303] I assume that this indication of the origin pertains to Galaction himself, not to his father. Strumica is mentioned as situated in the West; this is logical from the standpoint of Constantinople where Galaction resided. The precise information on Galaction's origins was most probably contained in the colophon on the original page, which was being transcribed after Galaction's death by this scribe who was conceivably one of his brethren in the same monastery. The colophon is written so that it flanks on both sides a longer dedication consisting of 15 seven-syllable lines and is surrounded on four sides by 4 dodecasyllables. The left vertical part of the colophon is written cryptographically.

Of the part of fol. 669ʳ reproduced here (Plate **117a**), this is the essential text which is of interest to us:

(On the left side) † ζϑοϑ|πψ4λν | ϑξϑ⅄|ψλολω, | ψϑυϑ | πϑ4 4ἐ|⅄λξλ|νϑυλω | λ ξϑςϑ|⅄ϑπβω· | ψλ κϑ⅄λν | η4ηο4λν | ἔζ⅄ϑ|τεν:· | This cryptographic text is to be understood thus: Γαλακτίον ἁμαρτολὸς, τάχα καὶ ἱερομόναχος ὁ Μαδαράκης· τὸ παρὸν βιβλίον ἔγραψεν.

(On the right side) † βιβλίον Γα|λακτίωνος | ἁμαρτωλοῦ τά|χα καὶ ἱερο|μονάχου, τοῦ | Μαδαράκη· | υἱοῦ Δημητρί|ου τοῦ Κημη|νίτζη, τοῦ | ἐκ τῆς Τιβερι|ουπόλεως | Στρουμμίτζης, | τῆς πρὸς τὴν δύ|σιν διακειμένης:· |

From the dedicatory text in the middle, the beginning is interesting, since it states that the compiler of the volume was also its scribe: σός εἰμὶ τίμιε σός· | ὁ βιβλίον σοι τόυτο· | συνϑῆς ἅμα καὶ γράψας· | κτλ.

The left side of the colophon is a most welcome statement to the effect that the hieromonk Galaction Madaraces was the scribe of this MS. The right

[303] On Τιβεριούπολις, now Strumica in Yugoslavia, a town situated north of Thessalonica, cf. Eleutheroudakes, ᾿Εγκυκλ.Λεξ., XI, p. 836; F. Dölger, *Aus den Schatzkammern des Heiligen Berges* (Munich [1948]), text vol., pp. 46 (note on doc. 9, line 21), 301 (note on doc. 110, line 51); A. Solovjev and V. Mošin, *Grčke povelje srpskih vladara* (Belgrade, 1936), pp. 38 (doc. VI, 35), 44 (doc. VII, 28/29).

side of the colophon restates that this is a MS of the hieromonk Galaction Madaraces, son of Demetrius Κημηνίτζης,[304] of Tiberiupolis or Strumica. I assume (as I stated above) that the apposition τοῦ ἐκ τῆς Τιβεριουπόλεως, etc., pertains to Galaction Madaraces rather than to his father, since Galaction Madaraces was the central figure of the statement. (Of course, it may be that both father and son were natives of Tiberiupolis.) This colophon, which contains such personal details on the scribe, his origin, and the name of the scribe's father, should be accorded full credence, even though the page is written in a handwriting different from that of Galaction Madaraces. Either an original colophon of Galaction Madaraces was recopied (as I believe to have happened) by someone from the same monastery shortly after Galaction's death, or the three leaves in this handwriting were inserted by someone from Galaction's fraternity who was so well informed about Galaction that he was able to report his father's name and Galaction's place of origin. At any rate, this colophon only confirms what was from the very beginning of my analysis the most likely assumption, namely, that Galaction Madaraces was indeed the scribe of this MS.

As a specimen of the handwriting of Galaction Madaraces from this MS, on Plate **76** we reproduce folio 374ᵛ, containing a passage from St. Gregory of Nazianzus, Oration 44 (In novam Dominicam: ed. Migne, Patr. Gr., 36, cols. 609 D 6 – 612 C 6). As I stated above, the MS was produced in Constantinople.

This MS once belonged to the collection of Giacomo Barocci of Venice (d. before 1617). The present Barocci collection of MSS was presented to the Bodleian Library in 1629 (on Barocci MSS in the Bodleian Library, cf. above, p. 28). In the Barocci Library this MS was Greco in foglio 7 (cf. *Indice Barocci*, fols. 3ʳ–6ʳ).

On this MS, cf. Coxe, I, cols. 341–51; *Summary Catalogue*, II,1, p. 8 (under S.C. 197); Vogel–Gardthausen, p. 63; Van de Vorst–Delehaye, *Catalogus*, pp. 311–13; Krumbacher, pp. 154, 744; Aubineau, *Codices Chrysostomici graeci*, I, pp. 187f.; Lampros, in Νέος Έλλ., 7 (1910), p. 141 (under no. 58).

In the past, five palimpsest parchment leaves were bound in MS Barocci 197 as its front flyleaves I–IV and its back flyleaf numbered fol. 674. On 6 December 1912, they were taken out of MS Barocci 197 and then bound separately as the present MS Barocci 197*, fols. 1–5 (followed by the Library's notes on this transfer and on the contents of these leaves, written on inserts numbered fols. 6–8). The scriptura inferior of these leaves, in a majuscule of the 10th century, contains fragments of a New Testament lectionary; the scriptura superior, of the 12th century, shows fragments of an Old Testament lectionary (i.e., of a Prophetologion). On the parchment leaves of the present Barocci 197* (formerly bound in Barocci 197), cf. Coxe, I, col. 351 (at the end of the description of Barocci 197); Coxe², I, col. 351 (note added in the margin); *Summary Catalogue*, II,1, p. 8 (under S.C. 197*); Scrivener, I, p. 341 (under Evst. 201); Gregory, I, p. 404 (under Evangelia 205); Aland, I, p. 216 (under the Gregory–Aland number *l* 205); notes on the contents of these leaves written by a librarian of the Bodleian Library, bound in Barocci 197*, fols. 6–8.

---

[304] The name Κημηνίτζης (in the nominative) seems to be of Slavic origin. I suspect that it was written in the above colophon with an error in the first vowel; the name probably was Καμηνίτζης, which would be an ethnic name derived from a place-name Kaminitza, or rather Καμινίτσα (the normal form would be Καμενίτσα). The place-name Καμινίτσα is attested: cf. M. Vasmer, *Die Slaven in Griechenland*, AbhBerl, Philos.-hist.Kl., 1941, 12 (Berlin, 1941), pp. 36 (no. 154), 154 (no. 37); cf. also pp. 134 (no. 48), 135 (no. 49).

Plate 77: A.D. 1344.

Oxford, Bodleian Library, ms Barocci 156. Paper (except for parchment fols. 1–2), 282 × 200 mm., 362 fols. Parchment fols. 1–2, in a majuscule script of the 10th century, 28 lines to a page, contain a fragment of a homily. Contents (fols. 3ʳ–362ʳ): Macarius Chrysocephalus, metropolitan of Philadelphia, Catena on the Gospel of St. Matthew, Book I. The MS was written by the compiler of the Catena, Macarius Chrysocephalus, and concluded by him on 22 December A.M. 6853 = A.D. 1344, according to the subscription on fol. 360ᵛ (Plate **117b**): Ἐτελειώθη ἡ παροῦσα πρώτη βίβλος τῆς ἐξηγήσεως τοῦ κατὰ Ματθαῖον | ἁγίου εὐαγγελίου, τῆς ἐκ διαφόρων συντεθείσης ἐξηγητικῶν λόγων τῶν θείων | π(ατέ)ρων, κατὰ τὴν παροῦσαν ἡμέραν· ἥτις ἐστίν, εἰκοστὴ δευτέρα, τοῦ δεκεμβρίου | μηνός· τῆς νῦν τρεχούσης τρι⟨σ⟩καιδεκάτης ἰνδικτιῶνος. τοῦ ἑξακισχιλιοστοῦ, ὀκτα|κοσιοστοῦ πεντηκοστοῦ, τρίτου{ς} ἔτους· ἡμέρα, τετράδι + |

> Τὸν συντεθέντα Φιλαδελφείας πόθῳ·
> + Μακάριον ταπεινὸν ἐν τοῖς σοῖς θύταις, |
> φύλαττε τριὰς ἁγία τρισολβίως + |

The subscription proper is concluded by an invocation in these three dodecasyllables. Since we know (from a note written by Chrysocephalus himself in MS Venice Greco 83, fol. 227ᵛ: cf. Turyn, *DGM Italy*, I, p. 163) that Macarius left Philadelphia for Constantinople in January 1345, it is likely that this MS Barocci 156, concluded a little earlier on 22 December 1344, was subscribed in Philadelphia.

Macarius Chrysocephalus indicated his authorship of this Catena also in dodecasyllabic headlines, which I consider relevant to quote here. On fol. 3ʳ, this headline is prefixed to a prologue and a table of contents:

> Μακαρίου ταῦτ' ἐστι Φιλαδελφείας·
> τοῦ οἰκέτου τῆς μακαρίας τριάδος + |
> Πίναξ ἀκριβὴς τῆς παρούσης πυκτίδος·
> ἔργον Φιλαδελφείας Χρυσοκεφάλου. |

On fol. 12ᵛ, after the table of contents of Book I, there are these four dodecasyllables:

> Πολλῶν πόνων ἔρανος ἠκριβωμένος·
> Οὐδὲν περιττὸν οὐδὲ λεῖπον ἐνθάδε· |
> Τὰ πάντα δ' ὡς χρὴ καὶ καλῶς ἐσκεμμένα,
> Μακάριος συνῆψε Φιλαδελφείας + |

This is followed by the elaborate title of Book I, concluded by six dodecasyllables (fols. 12ᵛ–13ʳ): Ἡ ἐπιγραφὴ τοῦ ὅλου βιβλίου:+ | Ἐξήγησις εἰς τὸ κατὰ Ματθαῖον ἅγιον εὐαγγέλιον· συλλεγεῖσα καὶ | συντεθεῖσα κεφαλαιωδῶς, παρὰ Μακαρίου μ(ητ)ροπολίτου Φιλα|δελφείας. τοῦ Χρυσοκεφάλου· ἥτις καὶ χρυσᾶ κεφάλαια ὠνόμασται, | διά τε τὴν τιμίαν καὶ διαλάμπουσαν τῶν ἐν τοῖς κεφαλαίοις θεω|ρουμένων ἔννοιαν, καὶ διὰ τὴν τοῦ συγγραψαμένου ἐπίκλησιν:+ |

> Χρυσῶν ἐπῶν ἐνθάδε σωρεία, ἔργον,
> Μακαρίου Φιλαδελφείας ποιμένος:+ ‖
> Σ(ωτῆ)ρ(ο)ς ἀρχιποίμενος θ(εο)ῦ λόγου,

ἀρνίον εἰμι καὶ πρὸς αὐτοῦ τοὺς λόγους. |
ὡς πρὸς πόαν ἢ γάλα τὸ γλυκὺ τρέχω·
φάσκει Μακάριος ὁ Φιλαδελφείας + |

Macarius Chrysocephalus originally planned to arrange his whole Catena on Matthew in five books, each of which was to contain 20 homilies (in this MS, fol. 3ᵛ, lines 1–4: ed. Migne, Patr. Gr., 150, col. 241 B 11 – C 1): καὶ γοῦν, πρώτην τὴν | τοῦ κατὰ Ματθαῖον εὐαγγελίου σεβασμίαν βίβλον, ἐν βιβλίοις ἐσπούδακα | πέντε συνθέσθαι· ἔχουσαν καθ᾽ ἕκαστον τούτων ἀνὰ τοὺς εἴκοσι λόγους· | ὡς ἅμα συμπληροῦσθαι ταύτην. εἰς ἑκατὸν λόγους ἅπασαν· κτλ.

The continuation of MS Barocci 156 is to be found in MS Patmos 381, written likewise by Macarius Chrysocephalus and subscribed by him in A.D. 1349. MS Patmos 381 contains Book II (likewise in 20 homilies) of the same Catena on the Gospel of St. Matthew.[305] However, it should be pointed out that in MS Patmos 381, at the end of the table of contents prefixed to Book II of that Catena, Macarius speaks of arranging the Catena on Matthew in *three* books,[306] contrary to the above statement on planning to arrange the entire Catena on Matthew in five books. The rest of this Catena (Book III) that would follow the Patmos MS (Book II) is lost or has not been located. The prologue of the Catena, contained in MS Barocci 156, fol. 3ʳ–3ᵛ line 9 ἁρμόζοντα, is published in Migne, Patr. Gr., 150, cols. 240 D 1 – 241 C 6.

On Michael-Macarius Chrysocephalus (b. before 1306, metropolitan of Philadelphia from 1336, d. 1382), cf. V. Laurent, in *LThK*, VI, col. 1311; I. Ch. Konstantinides, in Θρησκ.᾽Ηθ.᾽Εγκυκλ., VIII, cols. 480f.; Turyn, *DGMItaly*, I, pp. 157ff., 168ff. (on this Barocci MS, pp. 162, 164), and the bibliography quoted there; R. Walther, "Ein Brief an Makarios, den Metropoliten von Philadelphia," *JÖB*, 22 (1973), pp. 219ff.[306a] Now cf. also Schreiner, *Die byzantinischen Kleinchroniken*, I, pp. 614–17 (under Chronik 88 A and Chronik 88 B); II, pp. 234f., 260–67 (comments on Chr. 88 A and Chr. 88 B).

From this MS Barocci 156 written by Macarius Chrysocephalus, on Plate **77** we reproduce folio 177ʳ, containing a passage from MACARIUS CHRYSOCEPHALUS, CATENA ON THE GOSPEL OF ST. MATTHEW, Book I. The page reproduced includes a passage from St. Gregory of Nyssa, De beatitudinibus, Oratio 7 (ed. Migne, Patr. Gr., 44, cols. 1277 B 4 – 1280 A 8). For another published specimen of this same MS, cf. Wilson, *Mediaeval Greek Bookhands*, pl. 68 (cf. p. 32 under no. 68). For other published specimens of the handwriting of Michael-Macarius Chrysocephalus, cf. M. I. Manousakas, Μακαρίου Φιλαδελ-

---

[305] On MS Patmos, Μονὴ ᾽Ιωάννου τοῦ Θεολόγου 381, cf. I. Sakkelion, Πατμιακὴ Βιβλιοθήκη (Athens, 1890), pp. 174f. (under no. ΤΠΑ´); Komines, Πίνακες, pp. 18f. (under no. 31A); or Komines–Naoumides, *Facsimiles*, pp. 34f. (under no. 31A).

[306] Cf. the quotation from Macarius Chrysocephalus in Sakkelion, *op. cit.*, p. 175: ᾽Εν τρισὶ γὰρ ὅλοις Βιβλίοις τὴν τοῦ Εὐαγγελίου τούτου ποιούμεθα διατράνωσιν.

[306a] With regard to Walther, *op. cit.*, p. 223 note 24, I disagree with his interpretation of the words τοῦ οἰκέτου τῆς μακαρίας Τριάδος which Macarius used in apposition to his name in Barocci 156 (see above) and in Patmos 381 (cf. Komines, Πίνακες, p. 19, or Komines–Naoumides, *Facsimiles*, p. 35), or of the words ὁ οἰκέτης τῆς μακαρίας Τριάδος, likewise used by him and copied in Barocci 211 (cf. Coxe, I, cols. 368f.). These words do not mean "a *resident* of a monastery of the Holy Trinity" (in Constantinople), as Walther understood them, but simply "a *servant* of the Holy Trinity."

φείας τοῦ Χρυσοκεφάλου ἀνέκδοτα χρονικὰ σημειώματα *(1344-1346)* εἰς δύο αὐτογράφους Μαρκιανοὺς κώδικας, in Θησαυρίσματα, 4 (1967), pls. Α'-Ε'; Komines, Πίνακες (or Komines–Naoumides, *Facsimiles*), pl. 31A; Turyn, *DGMItaly*, II, pls. 135, 138, 245, 246*b*. Following are the other MSS written by Michael-Macarius Chrysocephalus, so far as we know at present: Patmos 381, cod. Vaticanus graec. 1597, Venice Greco 83 (colloc. 512), Venice Greco 452 (colloc. 796); cf. Turyn, *DGMItaly*, I, p. 164.

In this MS Barocci 156, on fol. 3ʳ, in the upper margin, a later hand wrote this obituary note: † ἐκοιμήθ(η) ὁ ἁγιώτ(α)τ(ος) μ(ητ)ροπολίτ[ης] Φιλαδε(λφείας) Μακάριος . . . . [. . . αὐ]γούστο[υ]. ἀρχιερατεύσας | χρόνους τεσσαρακοντα ἕξ. (blank space 5 letters wide) +++ On this note, which indicates the death of Macarius Chrysocephalus in August ⟨A.D. 1382⟩, cf. L. Petit, *DTC*, IX, cols. 1445f., *s.v.* Macaire Chrysoképhalos; Turyn, *DGMItaly*, I, pp. 162f.

This MS once belonged to Giacomo Barocci of Venice (d. before 1617); the collection of Barocci MSS was presented to the Bodleian Library in 1629 (cf. above, p. 28). In the Barocci library the MS was Greco in foglio 17 (cf. *Indice Barocci*, fol. 9ᵛ).

On this MS, cf. Coxe, I, cols. 266f.; *Summary Catalogue*, II,1, p. 7 (under S.C. 156); Barbour, in *Greek Manuscripts in the Bodleian Library*, p. 24 (under no. 30); Wilson, *Mediaeval Greek Bookhands*, p. 32 (under no. 68); J. A. Robinson, "Notes," *CR*, 1 (1887), p. 281; Krumbacher, p. 216; G. Karo and I. Lietzmann, *Catenarvm graecarvm catalogvs*, NachrGött, 1902, p. 568; E. A. De Stefani, "Ramenta," *Studi Italiani di filologia classica*, 8 (1900), p. 494 note 1.

Plate 78: A.D. 1348.

Oxford, Bodleian Library, ms Roe 18, now divided into two parts, MS Roe 18ᴬ and MS Roe 18ᴮ. Paper, 300 × 205 mm., altogether 476 fols. (Roe 18ᴬ comprises fols. 1–253; Roe 18ᴮ, fols. 254–476). Contents: various Byzantine legal and literary texts; legal texts (public law and church law) prevail in Roe 18ᴬ. The MS was written by Constantinus ὁ Σοφός and was subscribed by him in September A.M. 6857 = A.D. 1348 (MS Roe 18ᴮ, fol. 476ᵛ – Plate **117c**): † ἐτελειώθη ἡ βίβλος αὕτη, διὰ χειρὸς ἐμοῦ Κω(νσταντίνου) τοῦ Σοφοῦ· κ(α)τὰ μῆνα σεπτ(έμβ)ριον | τῆς β' ἰν(δικτιῶνος)· τοῦ ͵ϛωνζ ἔτους· ++ It seems that σοφός in this case was the family name of the scribe (not a nickname, "the wise"). This adjective was rarely used in Byzantium as a family name; still, it is attested as such (cf. Miklosich–Müller, *Acta et diplomata*, II, p. 488, document 641).[307]

As a sample of the handwriting of Constantinus Sophus, on Plate **78** we reproduce (from Roe 18ᴬ) folio 146ʳ, containing a passage from Theodore Balsamon, Responsa ad interrogationes Marci patriarchae Alexandrini (ed. Migne, Patr. Gr., 138, col. 1005 A 5 – D 1; or ed. Migne, Patr. Gr., 119, col. 1085 A 5 – D 1; or ed. G. A. Rhalles and M. Potles, Σύνταγμα τῶν θείων καὶ ἱερῶν κανόνων, IV [Athens, 1854], pp. 491, 4 – 492, 6).

---

[307] It is noteworthy that the signer of this document (of A.D. 1401) accented his family name as a paroxytone Σόφος. On such recessive accents in adjectives used as substantives in Byzantine and Modern Greek, cf. A. Thumb, *Handbuch der neugriechischen Volkssprache*, 2nd ed. (Strasbourg, 1910), p. 26, lines 7–11; cf. also Jannaris, *Historical Greek Grammar*, p. 296, § 1049. However, the scribe of MS Roe 18 accented his family name conservatively on the last syllable.

The whole MS was written by Constantinus Sophus, except for a few later
additions. Some later hand used blank spaces in Roe 18ᴮ, on fols. 435ʳ line 7 –
436ʳ line 4 and 436ʳ lines 6–1 from the bottom, to add in small script a letter
of St. Basil the Great to St. Gregory of Nazianzus (St. Basil, Epist. classis I,
epist. 2: ed. Migne, Patr. Gr., 32, cols. 224 A 1 – 233 B 8). Another later hand
added at the end of Roe 18ᴮ, on fol. 476ᵛ (in the lower part), a dodecasyllabic
poem on the death of some empress (*inc.* παστάς· τόκος· θάνατος· τῇ βασιλίδι).

In Roe 18ᴬ, on fol. 20ᵛ, a later hand added historical notes pertaining to events of A.D. 1422–
1425; they seem to have been copied in Constantinople. For the text of these notes, cf. Schreiner, *Die byzantinischen Kleinchroniken*, I, pp. 115–18 (under Chronik 13); for comments, cf.
II, pp. 414–30 (under Chr. 13).

The MS was once owned by Metrophanes III, patriarch of Constantinople (1565–1572 and
1579–1580), and subsequently by the monastery of the Holy Trinity τοῦ Ἐσόπτρου in Chalce
near Constantinople. In part Roe 18ᴮ, on fol. 476ᵛ, there is the usual ownership entry of the
monastery (in 5 political verses), and a dodecasyllabic invocation for Metrophanes. On the MSS
of Metrophanes in the Chalce monastery and their characteristic entries, cf. above, p. 24.
This MS seems to be listed in the catalogue of the Metrophanes MSS subsequently owned by
the Chalce monastery which was compiled in 1572: cf. Legrand, *Notice biographique sur Jean et
Théodose Zygomalas*, p. 213, lines 13–15. Later, Sir Thomas Roe (1580 or 1581–1644) acquired
this MS, brought it from the Levant, and presented it to the Bodleian Library in 1628. Roe's
entry is written in part Roe 18ᴬ, on fol. 1ʳ (in the lower margin). On the typical entry of Roe
in his MSS, on Roe and his MSS in the Bodleian Library, cf. above, p. 25. Legrand, *op. cit.*,
p. 206, listed this MS Roe 18 as one of the Chalce MSS brought by Roe from the Levant.

On this MS, cf. Coxe, I, cols. 471–79 (in Coxe², *loc. cit.*, there are some additional references);
Summary Catalogue, II,1, p. 11 (under S.C. 264ᵃ and S.C. 264ᵇ); Vogel–Gardthausen, p. 251;
Krumbacher, p. 780 (under 3); I. Sajdak, *Historia critica scholiastarum et commentatorum Gregorii Nazianzeni*, I, Meletemata Patristica, I (Cracow, 1914), p. 118; J. Bessières, "La tradition
manuscrite de la correspondance de Saint Basile," ed. C. H. Turner, *JThS*, 21 (1920), pp. 28f.
(= M. Bessières, *La tradition manuscrite de la correspondance de S. Basile. Réimpression* [Oxford,
1923], pp. 28f.); J. Darrouzès, *Recherches sur les ὀφφίκια de l'Eglise byzantine*, AOC, 11 (Paris,
1970), pp. 197, 269, 271, 547 note 33; Schreiner, *Die byzantinischen Kleinchroniken*, I, pp. 115–18.

Plate 79: A.D. 1348.

Glasgow, University Library, ms Hunter 424. This MS was formerly
in the Hunterian Museum of the University of Glasgow (under the pressmark
V.4.8); however, the Hunter MSS are now housed in the University Library.
Paper, 267 × 195 mm., 323 fols., 26–32 lines to a page. In the first gathering,
the original conjoint fols. 1 (a preliminary leaf) and 8 were lost and replaced
with two new fols. 1 and 8 in the late 15th century. Contents (fols. 2ʳ–323ʳ):
Plutarch, 18 Parallel Lives.³⁰⁷ᵃ On fols. 306ʳ–322ᵛ, there are Latin marginalia.
The MS was subscribed (in red) in September A.M. 6857 = A.D. 1348 (fol. 323ʳ–
Pl. **113e**): † ἐγράφη δι' ἡμερῶν τεσσαράκοντα. ἐτελειώθη δὲ | κ(α)τὰ μῆνα σε-
πτ(έμβ)ρ(ιον) τῆς β' ἰν(δικτιῶν)ος· τοῦ ͵ϛοῦ ωοῦ νζ' ἔτους + On Plate **79** we reproduce
folio 239ʳ, containing a passage from PLUTARCH, PARALLEL LIVES, from Life
of Crassus, chaps. 26–27, p. 560a–d (ed. K. Ziegler, *Plvtarchi Vitae Parallelae*,
Teubner, I,2, 2nd ed. [1959], pp. 164, 23 – 166, 2; or ed. R. Flacelière and E.

³⁰⁷ᵃ These eighteen Parallel Lives represent part one of the tripartite recension of Plutarch's Parallel
Lives: cf. K. Ziegler, *Die Überlieferungsgeschichte der vergleichenden Lebensbeschreibungen Plutarchs*
(Leipzig, 1907), pp. 5–12 (Ziegler did not examine the above Glasgow MS: cf. *ibid.*, p. 164 note 1);
idem, "Plutarchos von Chaironeia," *RE*, XXI, cols. 950f.

Chambry, *Plutarque, Vies*, VII, Collection Budé [Paris, 1972], pp. 242, 14 – 243, 22).

On fol. 1ʳ (which is a later insert), a late 15th-century hand wrote in Greek a table of contents (πίναξ), viz., a list of the 18 Lives contained in the MS, followed by this note: ·ῑῆ· + τῶν παραλλήλων τινὰ οὐκ ἐγράφθη, ὡς οἶμαι, διὰ τὸ· | θρυλλούμενον ἐκεῖνο ἰάμβιον:– | ὥσπερ ξένοι χαίρουσιν ἰδεῖν πατρίδα, | οὕτω καὶ οἱ γράφοντες βιβλίου τέλος: + | ζη⟨τη⟩τέον ἄρα τὸ, τε δεύτερον, καὶ τὸ τρίτον, ἅπερ οὐκ ἔστιν ἐνθάδε:– | The words ὥσπερ – τέλος are two dodecasyllables often used by scribes at the conclusion of a MS (cf. above, p. 8 and note 13, p. 38). The reference to the lack of the second and third books of Plutarch's Lives in this MS points to the other parts of the tripartite recension of the Lives (cf. above, note 307a). The same 15th-century hand supplied on fol. 8ʳ–8ᵛ the lost portion of the Plutarch text. A hand of the 14/15th century added on fol. 36ᵛ lists of months according to various calendars (Roman, Macedonian, Attic, Jewish, Egyptian), as well as a list of the signs of the zodiac.

At the bottom of fol. 1ʳ, there is an obliterated monogram ⟦*VF*⟧ of Victor Falchonius of Venice, who owned this MS early in the 16th century. On fol. 323ʳ, there are two ownership entries of Falchonius. The first one (in red) reads: ·:*1509: Die 10 Nouembris habui librum ego* ⟦+ *V.F.*⟧ The deleted initials indicate V⟨ictor⟩ F⟨alchonius⟩; on them, the letters *A. I. P.* were written, which are the initials of the next owner, Aulus Ianus Parrhasius (see below). The second ownership entry of Victor Falchonius was written in Greek (below the preceding entry) and has been partly obliterated (probably by Parrhasius): Ταῦτα τὰ παράλληλα· ἐστί (ἐισ- *incipiebat* Falchonius) · τοῦ ⟦Ὀυίκτωρος τοῦ Φαλχωνίου τῶν⟧ | ⟦μεγάλων Ὀυεννετίων⟧:·+++++++++:· This note explicitly points out the connection of Falchonius with Venice.

On fol. 323ᵛ, a different hand of the late 15th century inscribed (in the upper part of the page) a Greek epigram (Greek Anthology, Appendix 4.92, ed. Cougny). Below, in the middle part of the page, the hand which wrote on fol. 1ʳ the table of contents with the subsequent note copied Agathias' epigram on Plutarch (Greek Anthology, 16.331). Beneath, Victor Falchonius inscribed in red his ownership entry: *Iste liber est* ⟦*Victoris falchonij*⟧ *Nec mutuo ulli amicorum dandus, nisi fidei probatẹ:* (these three words were written additionally) | *nec precio quamuis magno alicuj vendendus:·++++* | Immediately below, Falchonius wrote his own metrical translation of Agathias' epigram into Latin elegiacs, preceded by this headline: *Victoris Falchonii metaphrasis In plutarchi statuam:–* (the text of the translation was published by J. Young and P. H. Aitken, *A Catalogue of the Manuscripts in the Library of the Hunterian Museum in the University of Glasgow* [Glasgow, 1908], p. 350). | Beneath the translation, Falchonius inscribed this note: *Anno ẹtatis uigesimo · 1510 · mense Iunij:·* This shows that Victor Falchonius (or Falconius) of Venice was born either in the later part of 1490 or in the earlier part of 1491.

Victor Falchonius must have been a humanist of some culture, if he was able to translate an epigram of Agathias into Latin elegiacs and if he valued the ownership of a MS of Plutarch's Parallel Lives. He also knew how to write Greek epigrams. He composed in Greek an epigram on the Venetian printer Ioannes ⟨Tacuinus de Tridino⟩ who printed an edition of Aulus Gellius, Noctes Atticae, under the title: *Accipite studiosi omnes Auli Gellii noctes micantissimas ...*, ed. Nicolavs Ferettvs Ravennas [Venice, 1509]. Falchonius' epigram appears on the verso of the title page and is headlined: οὐίκτωρ ὁ φαλχώνιος τοῖς σπουδαίοις.[307b] Thus, it can be assumed that Victor Falchonius (probably Falcone or Falconi in Italian), who was born in 1490 or 1491, already had some stature as a humanist *ca.* 1509, at a rather young age.

[307b] The epigram of Victor Falchonius was mentioned by M. E. Cosenza, *Biographical and Bibliographical Dictionary of the Italian Humanists and of the World of Classical Scholarship in Italy, 1300–1800*, 2nd ed., II (Boston, 1962), p. 1377, *s.v.* Feretrius, Johannes Petrus (Cosenza miswrote the name in question as Victor Falchorius). On the printer Ioannes Tacuinus de Tridino (i.e., of Trino), whose name appears in the colophon on the last page of Gellius' edition of 1509, cf. F. J. Norton, *Italian Printers 1501–1520*, Cambridge Bibliographical Society, Monograph no. 3 (London, 1958), p. 154.

The next owner of this MS was Aulus Ianus Parrhasius (Aulo Giano Parrasio, 1470–1522), whose initials *A. I. P.* are written on fol. 323ʳ over the initials ⟦*V. F.*⟧. From Parrhasius the MS was inherited by his friend, Antonio Seripando (d. 1531), according to the entry on fol. 323ʳ: *Antonij Seripandi ex Iani Parrhasij* | *testamento*. It is known that the library of Antonio Seripando was inherited by his brother, Cardinal Girolamo Seripando (1493–1563), who presumably was the next owner of this MS. In the 18th century, the MS was owned by Caesar de Missy (b. Berlin, 1703 – d. London, 1775), according to the entry on fol. 1ʳ: *Ex libris* | *Caesaris De Missy* | *Berolinensis*:∼ | *Londini*:∼ | *Anno Domini 1748*. The MS was acquired in 1776 (along with several other MSS of de Missy) by Dr. William Hunter (1718–1783), whose museum became the property of the University of Glasgow in 1807.

On Aulo Giano Parrasio, Italian humanist and son-in-law of Demetrius Chalcondyles, **cf.** Frati, *Dizionario bio-bibliografico*, pp. 438f.; F. Lo Parco, *Aulo Giano Parrasio. Studio biografico-critico* (Vasto, 1899); *Enciclopedia Italiana di scienze, lettere ed arti*, XXVI (Rome, 1935), pp. 402f. On Antonio Seripando, cf. Cosenza, *op. cit.*, IV (1962), p. 3252. On Cardinal Girolamo Seripando, cf. Frati, *op. cit.*, p. 516. On the successive ownership of MSS by Parrasio, Antonio Seripando, and Girolamo Seripando, cf. W. Weinberger, *Beiträge zur Handschriftenkunde*, II, SBWien, Philos.-hist.Kl., 161,4 (1909), p. 39 note 1. On Caesar de Missy, William Hunter, and the Hunterian Museum, cf. above, p. 20.

On this MS, cf. Young and Aitken, *op. cit.*, pp. 348–50 (under no. 424).

Plate 80: A.D. 1355/1356.

Oxford, Christ Church, ms 63. Paper, 29 × 22 cm., 366 fols., 19–21 lines to a page for the main body of the MS. Contents: (fols. 4ʳ–335ᵛ) St. John Climacus, Ladder of Paradise (including, on fols. 8ᵛ–16ʳ, Daniel of Rhaithu, Life of John Climacus); (fols. 336ʳ–362ʳ) John Climacus, Liber ad pastorem. On fols. 1ʳ–3ᵛ and 363ʳ–366ᵛ, there are fragments of an Old Testament Lectionary (or Prophetologion), written in the 14th century about the same time as the main MS. The original body of the MS was first written in part by the monk Germanus. After his death, the MS was continued by the hieromonk Gennadius and was concluded by him in A.M. 6864 = A.D. 1355/1356. This is stated in the subscription written by Gennadius on fol. 362ʳ–362ᵛ (Plate **118a** – this reproduction is made at three-fourths the original measurements): † ἐτελειώθη ἡ παροῦσα θεία καὶ ἱερὰ | κλίμαξ· ἐν ἔτει ͵ϛωξδ'· | ἰν(δικτιῶνος) θ'· συν{υν}εργὸς δὲ ταύτης, | θύτης μοναστὴς, Γεννάδιος τῇ κλήσει· ‖ ἐγράφησαν δὲ τέτραδα κ'γ· | παρὰ μοναχοῦ Γερμανοῦ· τελευτή|σαντος δὲ τούτου, ἔμεινεν ἀτελείωτος· | καὶ ἵνα μὴ (this particle was added in red color above the line) τῇ χρονία παραδρομῇ ἀ|φανεία παραδοθῶσιν, ἀνεδέξατο ταύτην | ὁ προειρημένος ἱερομόναχος κῦρ Γεν|νάδιος, καὶ ἀνεπλήρωσε· εἰς ἔ|παινον μὲν· καὶ δό(ξ)αν τοῦ φιλαν(θρώπ)ου θ(εο)ῦ· | καὶ εἰς ὠφέλειαν τῶν ἱερῶν καὶ ἁγίων | ἀνδρῶν· ὁμοῦ τὰ ὅλα, τέ|τραδα μϛ'· + | The subscription is followed by a colophon of the Ladder, one invocation, and another invocation in 2 dodecasyllables (written in red): Ἡ κλίμαξ ἥδε, τοῦ παμμάκαρος | καὶ χρυσοῦ Ἰω(άνν)ου ++ | ∴ μέμνησθε π(ατέ)ρες ὑπὲρ τοῦ ἐξαγοράσαντός με ∴ |

† γενοῦ βοηθὸς κἀμοὶ τῶ ξένω θύτα,
καὶ νεύσει θ(εὸ)ς ἐπὶ τῇ προ|σευχῇ σου·∙

Moreover, on fol. 333ᵛ (in the lower margin), there is this dodecasyllabic note (in red) by the scribe Gennadius (Plate **118b**):

+ θύτης μοναστὴς, Γεννάδιος τῇ κλήσει +

In the above subscription, the term τέτραδον is used (in the plural) for "quire," instead of the common form τετράδιον (or τετράς).[308]

As indicated in the subscription, there are indeed two different handwritings in two successive parts of the original MS. The former part is obviously to be attributed to the monk Germanus. The latter, written in a handwriting identical with that of the subscription, was evidently due to the hieromonk Gennadius. It appears that Germanus wrote fols. 4ʳ–178ᵛ; after him, Gennadius wrote fols. 179ʳ–362ᵛ. It can be assumed that the continuation of the unfinished MS was taken up by Gennadius almost immediately after the death of Germanus. Thus the date of the final subscription pertains also to the time of the writing of the Germanus portion of the MS.

As a specimen of the handwriting of the monk Germanus, on Plate **80a** we reproduce the upper part of folio 26ᵛ, containing a passage from St. JOHN CLIMACUS, LADDER OF PARADISE, chap. 1 (ed. Migne, Patr. Gr., 88, col. 637 C 15 – D 6; ed. Trevisan, I, pp. 57, 21 – 59, 4). The capital letters (in red) projected to the left indicate that a text section begins in the preceding line.[309]

As a specimen of the handwriting of the hieromonk Gennadius, on Plate **80b** we reproduce the upper part of folio 360ᵛ, containing a passage from ST. JOHN CLIMACUS, LIBER AD PASTOREM, chap. 15 (ed. Migne, Patr. Gr., 88, col. 1205 B 7 – C 1; ed. Trevisan, II, p. 373, 3–9). The capital letters (in red) projected to the left indicate either that they begin a text section (as is the case in line 4) or that a text section begins in the preceding line (as is the case in line 11).[310]

The handwritings of both Germanus and Gennadius are very calligraphic and show a strong stylistic resemblance. Both monks must have belonged to a scriptorium of the same monastery. Their scripts resemble the style cultivated in the monastery of the B.V.M. τῶν Ὁδηγῶν in Constantinople.[311]

This MS was once owned by the monastery of Philotheus, most probably the well-known monastery on Mount Athos. There is the following ownership entry on fol. 362ᵛ, in the left margin, written in a handwriting of the 15th century (Plate 118a): Φιλοθέου πέ|φυκεν ἡ θεία βί|βλος αὕτη μονῆς | πανάγνου τὲ καὶ θεο|μήτορος· καὶ τὸ | ἐπίκλην αὐτῆς | Πτέρρης, ἥτις λέ-|

---

[308] On the terms τετράδιον and τετράς, cf. Gardthausen, *Griechische Palaeographie*, I, pp. 157–60; E. Thompson and S. P. Lampros, trans., Ἐγχειρίδιον ἑλληνικῆς καὶ λατινικῆς παλαιογραφίας, in Βιβλιοθήκη Μαρασλῆ (Athens, 1903), pp. 119–22; Thompson, *Introduction*, pp. 53f.; R. Devreesse, *Introduction à l'étude des manuscrits grecs* (Paris, 1954), pp. 9, 20f.; L. Polites, Ὁδηγὸς καταλόγου χειρογράφων, in Γενικὸν Συμβούλιον βιβλιοθηκῶν τῆς Ἑλλάδος, 17 (Athens, 1961), pp. 11f.; idem, Παλαιογραφικά, in Ἑλληνικά, 21 (1968), pp. 168f.; B. Atsalos, *La terminologie du livre-manuscrit à l'époque byzantine*, I, in Ἑλληνικά, Suppl. 21 (Thessalonica, 1971), pp. 124, 183, 51, 131, 168 note 4; E. Mioni, *Introduzione alla paleografia greca*, Università di Padova, Studi Bizantini e Neogreci, 5 (Padua, 1973), p. 34; A. Sigalas, Ἱστορία τῆς ἑλληνικῆς γραφῆς, 2nd ed., in Βυζαντινὰ κείμενα καὶ μελέται, 12 (Thessalonica, 1974), p. 179.

[309] Cf. above, p. 22 note 63.

[310] Cf. above, p. 22 note 63.

[311] On MSS written in the monastery of the B.V.M. τῶν Ὁδηγῶν in Constantinople, or in the script style of that scriptorium, cf. below, pp. 120f., Pl. **81**; pp. 125f., Pl. **83**; pp. 131ff., Pls. **89, 90**; pp. 142ff., Pl. **96**; pp. 146ff., Pl. **96A**; Turyn, *Codices*, pp. 177–80, pl. 158; Komines, Πίνακες, pp. 20f. (no. 33), pl. 33; or Komines–Naoumides, *Facsimiles*, pp. 36f. (no. 33), pl. 33; Follieri, *Codices*, pp. 67f. (no. 45), pl. 45; Turyn, *DGMItaly*, I, pp. 164–67, 234; II, pls. 136, 189; Wilson, *Mediaeval Greek Bookhands*, p. 33 (no. 71), pl. 71.

γεται Φιλοθεῖ|τησα. The name Πτέρρη (or Πτέρη) seems to be an alternate form of Φτέρη. The place-name Φτέρη is known in reference to the monastery of Philotheus on Mount Athos.[312]

This MS presumably belonged to William Wake (1657–1737), archbishop of Canterbury, who willed his MSS to Christ Church, Oxford. On Wake and his bequest, cf. above p. 79.

On this MS, cf. G. W. Kitchin, *Catalogus codicum mss. qui in bibliotheca Aedis Christi apud Oxonienses adservantur* (Oxford, 1867), p. 27 (under no. LXIII); Vogel–Gardthausen, pp. 65, 69; Van de Vorst–Delehaye, *Catalogus*, p. 382; Rahlfs, *Verzeichnis der griechischen Handschriften des Alten Testaments*, p. 176.

Plate 81: A.D. 1357.

London, British Museum, ms Additional 11837. Parchment, 347 × 270 mm., 493 fols., 2 columns to a page, 22 lines to a column. Contents: the whole New Testament, adapted for liturgical use. Before each Gospel there is an illuminated headpiece in the form of a πύλη. For liturgical notes and projected capital letters, red on gold was used (instead of the customary red).[313] The MS was written by the hieromonk Methodius and subscribed by him on 7 October A.M. 6866 = A.D. 1357 (fol. 464ᵛ – Plate **119a**): Ἐτελειώθη μηνὶ | ὀκτωβρίω· ζ· | ἰνδικτιῶνος | ῑα | ἔτους ͵ϛ~ | ω̄ξ̄ϛ̄: | Μεθοδίου χεὶρ, τοῦ θυτο-| ρακενδύτου: | † The scribe's colophon Μεθοδίου – θυτορακενδύτου forms a dodecasyllabic verse. In the word θυτορακενδύτου, the first component indicates that Methodius was a priest (θύτης); the second that he was a ῥακενδύτης, i.e., a monk.[314] Consequently, he was a hieromonk.

On Plate **81** we reproduce the upper part of folio 12ʳ, containing in the two columns passages from the GOSPEL OF ST. MATTHEW 2: 4–6 and 2: 8–9. The quotation marks in the left margin denote a quotation from the Old Testament (Septuagint, Michaeas 5: 1), paraphrased in the text of the Gospel. The capital letters (in red on gold) projected to the left mark the beginnings of text sections.

The script style of this MS is that of the scriptorium of the monastery of the B.V.M. τῶν Ὁδηγῶν in Constantinople.[315] This style was cultivated in its characteristic appearance in that scriptorium for a long time, especially in the 14th and 15th centuries. For script specimens of the famous scribe of the scriptorium τῶν Ὁδηγῶν, Ioasaph, who was active in the period 1360–1406 (d. 1406), cf. below, pp. 131ff., Pls. **89** and **90**; pp. 142ff., Pl. **96**; pp. 146ff., Pl. **96A**; for specimens of other MSS that are attributable to the same scriptorium, cf. above, pp. 118ff., Pl. **80**; below, pp. 125f., Pl. **83**. There is a fundamental monograph on the scriptorium by L. Politis, "Eine Schreiberschule

---

[312] On Φτέρη in connection with the monastery of Philotheus on Mount Athos, cf. Μεγ.ʽΕλλ.ʼΕγκυκλ., II, p. 330 (third column, no. 27).

[313] It is noteworthy that in another MS written in the scriptorium τῶν Ὁδηγῶν in Constantinople, to which I attribute the above MS, a similar combination, gold over red, was used for liturgical notes and projected capitals: cf. below, p. 133, on MS London Burney 18. This coincidence seems to point to a special technique practiced in this respect in the scriptorium mentioned.

[314] On the meaning of θυτορακενδύτης, cf. V. Laurent, in *BZ*, 51 (1958), p. 429.

[315] On the monastery of the B.V.M. τῶν Ὁδηγῶν in Constantinople, cf. R. Janin, *La géographie ecclésiastique de l'empire byzantin*, pt. 1, *Le siège de Constantinople et le Patriarcat oecuménique*, vol. III, *Les églises et les monastères*, 2nd ed. (Paris, 1969), pp. 199–207.

im Kloster τῶν ʻΟδηγῶν,'' *BZ*, 51 (1958), pp. 17–36, 261–87, pls. I–III, XIII–XVIII. The above dodecasyllabic colophon with the name of the scribe accords with the tradition of dodecasyllabic colophons in MSS produced in the scriptorium.[316] For further bibliography on this scriptorium and its products, cf. below, pp. 133f.

A particular detail should be mentioned in reference to Plate **81**. In the script style of the monastery τῶν ʻΟδηγῶν there was a tendency to extend some letters upward in the top line and to extend some downward in the bottom line. Further, in the top line a vertical emphasis was sometimes effected by writing some letters above the line (in accordance with a general, otherwise accepted practice). This particular feature can be observed on Plate **81** in both top lines of the two columns. On the characteristics just mentioned of the ʻΟδηγῶν script, cf. below, p. 126, Pl. **83**; p. 133, Pls. **89, 90**; p. 143, Pl. **96**.

The MS was collated by Scrivener, *Full and Exact Collation*, with the symbol m (on the MS itself, cf. pp. xliv–xlvi).

It is possible (but not certain) that this MS once belonged to Niccolò Niccoli (1363–1437) of Florence, whose MSS after his death were donated by his trustees to the Dominican convent of San Marco in Florence in 1441 and placed in the San Marco library in 1444. This MS certainly was in that library *ca.* 1499–1500, when a catalogue of the San Marco MSS was compiled. Giovanni Lami (1697–1770) saw the MS there in 1738. In the 1768 catalogue of San Marco MSS it was listed as MS 701. On the spine of its binding (made around the time of the compilation of this catalogue) the number 701 is printed within a tooled frame. The vicissitudes of this MS, after the confiscation of the San Marco library in 1808 and the return of some of the MSS to the library in 1814, are uncertain. It is possible that John Thomas Payne of the firm of Payne and Foss, booksellers in London, acquired this MS along with several San Marco MSS which he purchased about 1830 and then shipped to England. These were offered for sale in London from 1832 on.[317] If this MS was among those obtained by Payne and Foss, then it was probably sold by this firm to its next owner, Samuel Butler. At any rate, the MS came subsequently into the possession of Butler (1774–1839), bishop of Lichfield and a classical scholar. On the inside of the back cover is the imprint *Bibliotheca Butleriana*. Butler's MSS were acquired after his death by the British Museum in 1841. On Samuel Butler and his MSS, cf. above, p. 92.

On this MS, cf. Richard, *Inventaire*, pp. 18f.; Omont, "Notes," p. 345; Vogel–Gardthausen, p. 299; Lami, *De eruditione apostolorvm*, pp. 218–21; Scrivener, I, pp. 218f. (under Evan. 201); Gregory, I, p. 166 (under Vier Evangelien 201); Aland, I, p. 71 (under the Gregory–Aland number 201); von Soden, I,1, p. 112 (under δ403).

---

[316] The colophon by Methodius differs from the prevalent pattern used in the scriptorium, as exemplified by the frequent colophons of Ioasaph: Θεοῦ τὸ δῶρον καὶ ᾽Ιωάσαφ πόνος (cf. Politis, *op. cit.*, p. 19).

[317] On the history of MS London Additional 11837 from the 15th century to the early 19th century, cf. B. L. Ullman and Ph. A. Stadter, *The Public Library of Renaissance Florence. Niccolò Niccoli, Cosimo de' Medici and the Library of San Marco*, Medioevo e Umanesimo, 10 (Padua, 1972), p. 65 and note 2, p. 72 and note 5 (on the presumable ownership of the MS by Niccolò Niccoli); p. 248 under no. 1054 (on the listing of this MS in the San Marco catalogue of MSS made *ca.* 1499–1500); p. 273 (under M 17, from an inventory of San Marco MSS made in the 16th century); p. 52 (on the catalogue of the San Marco MSS made in 1768 and the bindings of MSS made around that time); pp. 54f. and 55 note 4 (on the acquisition of some San Marco MSS, including possibly the present London Addit. 11837, by J. T. Payne of Payne and Foss).

On Giovanni Lami in connection with this MS, cf. Io. Lami, *De eruditione apostolorvm liber singvlaris* (Florence, 1738), p. 218.

On Payne and Foss, booksellers in London, cf. de Ricci, *English Collectors*, pp. 114f., who pointed out that Samuel Butler was a client of this firm and that the same firm, after Butler's death, bought the printed books of his library from his heirs.

Plate 82: A.D. 1357/1358.

Oxford, Bodleian Library, ms Laud Greek 18. Bombycine, 242 ×
173 mm., 288 fols., 30 lines to a page. Contents: Proclus Diadochus, On
Platonic Theology (Books I–VI), and Elements of Theology. The MS was
written by Stelianus (or rather Stylianus) Chumnus,[318] at the expense of
Ioannes Contostephanus of Constantinople, in A.M. 6866 = A.D. 1357/1358,
according to the subscription, partly couched in dodecasyllables, written on
fol. 288ᵛ (the essential parts of the subscription are reproduced on Plate **119b**):

     †   τῷ συντελεστῇ τῶν καλῶν ϑ(ε)ῷ, χάρις:— + |

     †   σὺ βίβλε μακάριζε τὸν γράψαντά σε, |
        πλὴν οὐ δι' αὐτῆς οὐδὲ γὰρ σϑένος ἔχεις· |
        ἀλλὰ δι' ἀνδρῶν εὐμαϑῶν φιλεμπόνων, |
        τῶν ἰδίαις σε κατεχόντων παλάμαις:— |

     †   Στηλιανὸς ἦν ὁ γράψας, ὁ καὶ τοῦ πίκλην (from ποίκλην corrected
by the scribe himself) Χοῦμνος:— |

     +   ϑ(εο)ῦ διδόντος, οὐδὲν ἰσχύει φϑόνος· |
        καὶ μὴ διδόντος, οὐδὲν ἰσχύει πόνος:— |

     +   ἐτελειώϑη δὲ Χ(ριστο)ῦ χάριτι, ἐν ἔτη ͵ϚωξϚ: ἐξόδῳ πολλῷ | τοῦ
κυρ(οῦ) Ἰω(άνν)ου τοῦ Κωντοστεφάνου τοῦ ἀπὸ τὴν Κωνσταντινούπ(ο)λ(ιν):—

On the iambic verse τῷ – χάρις, used as commonplace in subscriptions, cf.
Turyn, *Codices*, pp. 70, 172; *idem*, *DGMItaly*, I, pp. 148, 234, 245, 250;
Komines, Πίνακες, pp. 13, 55, 73 (or Komines–Naoumides, *Facsimiles*, pp. 28,
74, 94); Follieri, *Codices*, p. 59. The two iambic trimeters ϑ(εο)ῦ – πόνος, sometimes used by scribes, stem from St. Gregory of Nazianzus (Carmina I, 2,
32 vv. 127–28: ed. Migne, Patr. Gr., 37, col. 926): cf. Turyn, *Codices*, pp. 74,
135.

The sponsor of this MS, Ioannes Contostephanus of Constantinople, also
commissioned MS Florence, Laur. Conventi Soppressi 103, which was written
by four scribes and was completed on 3 November A.M. 6867 = A.D. 1358
and likewise contained philosophical texts, pertaining mainly to Plato and
Neoplatonism (cf. Turyn, *DGMItaly*, I, pp. 219–22). On Ioannes Contostephanus
and the Contostephanus family, cf. *ibid.*, pp. 220f. In the subscription of the
Laurentian MS, Ioannes Contostephanus was called a "professor" (τοῦ πανευγενεστάτου διδασκάλου). In view of the fact that the sponsor of the MS was a
Constantinopolitan, it is very likely that the MS was written in that city.

To represent the handwriting of Stelianus Chumnus in Laud Greek 18, on
Plate **82** we reproduce folio 19ʳ, containing a passage from PROCLUS DIA-
DOCHUS, ON PLATONIC THEOLOGY, Book I, chap. 11 (ed. H. D. Saffrey and L. G.
Westerink, *Proclus, Théologie platonicienne*, Book I, Collection Budé [Paris,
1968], pp. 52, 5 – 53, 18). Another specimen of this script was published from
this MS by Wilson, *Mediaeval Greek Bookhands*, pl. 69 (cf. p. 32). Apparently
the scribe of Laud Greek 18, Stelianus Chumnus, is identical with scribe B of

---

[318] On the Chumnus family in Byzantium, cf. J. Verpeaux, "Notes prosopographiques sur la
famille Choumnos," *Byzantinoslavica*, 20 (1959), pp. 252–66 (p. 264 under no. 34, on Stelianus Chumnus).

Laurentianus Conventi Soppressi 103, who wrote fols. 287^r–408^v of that MS and whose handwriting is represented in Turyn, *DGM Italy*, II, pl. 178 (cf. I, pp. 219, 221). The participation of Stelianus Chumnus in another MS commissioned by the same sponsor, Ioannes Contostephanus, is easily conceivable.

On fol. 288^v, there is an ownership entry (in brownish ink) of the famous philosopher Giovanni Pico della Mirandola (1463–1494):[319] *hic liber est Iohannis Pici de la Mirandula*. It seems that this MS was item no. 885 in the library of Pico della Mirandola.[320] The next owner was Cardinal Domenico Grimani (1461/63–1523), who bought the library of the deceased Pico in 1498.[321] The present MS Laud Greek 18 thus passed into the possession of Grimani.[322] On fol. 1^r (in the upper margin) of Laud Greek 18 is Grimani's ownership entry, which at a later time was erased to conceal the provenience of the MS, but which can be read under ultraviolet light:[323] *Liber Dominici Grimani Car(dina)^{lis} S. Marci*. In the Grimani collection, this MS became Greek MS 18.[324] In two wills, dated 1520 and 1523, Grimani donated the major part of his library, including, among others, all his Greek MSS, to the monastery of San Antonio di Castello in Venice with the proviso that his collection was to become a public library. Grimani's collection was sent from Rome to Venice in 1522 and presumably entered the newly constructed library building there in 1523 where it remained until it was destroyed by fire in 1687. In the course of time, between 1523 and 1687, many MSS disappeared from the monastery probably by illegal

---

[319] For comparison of this entry with other autographs of Pico della Mirandola, cf. G. Mercati, *Codici latini Pico Grimani Pio ... e i codici greci Pio di Modena*, ST, 75 (Vatican City, 1938), pl. I. On Giovanni Pico della Mirandola, cf. Sandys, *History of Classical Scholarship*, II, p. 82. On his library, cf. Frati, *Dizionario bio-bibliografico*, pp. 458 f.; F. Calori Cesis, *Giovanni Pico della Mirandola detto la Fenice degli Ingegni*, Memorie storiche della città e dell'antico ducato della Mirandola, XI (Mirandola, 1897), p. 31; pp. 32–76 for the inventory of Pico's library made in 1498 after his death; P. Kibre, *The Library of Pico della Mirandola* (Diss. New York, 1936), with an inventory of Pico's library from a 16th-century MS on pp. 119 ff.

[320] In the inventory of Pico's library made in 1498 this was the listing of no. 885 (cf. Calori Cesis, *op. cit.*, p. 45): *Proculi theologicha elementatio in greco manuscripta in papiro*. This inventory was not very precise in its listings, and therefore the omission of the Platonic theology in the indication of the contents of this MS is not at all surprising. This item no. 885 is entirely missing in the later copy of the inventory of Pico's library published by Kibre, *op. cit.*, but this has no significance, since the later copy of the inventory is less complete than the inventory of 1498 (cf. *ibid.*, p. 8).

[321] On Domenico Grimani and his library, cf. Frati, *Dizionario bio-bibliografico*, pp. 269–71; F. Paschini, *Domenico Grimani Cardinale di S. Marco († 1523)*, Storia e Letteratura, 4 (Rome, 1943). On Grimani's library, cf. esp. T. Freudenberger, "Die Bibliothek des Kardinals Domenico Grimani," *HJ*, 56 (1936), pp. 15–45; G. Mercati, *Opere minori*, IV, ST, 79 (Vatican City, 1937), pp. 159–61 (reprint of a paper published in 1920); *idem*, *Codici latini Pico Grimani Pio*, pp. 26–34; V. Capocci, *Codices Barberiniani graeci*, I (Vatican City, 1958), pp. 132–35 (description of Cod. Vatic. Barber. gr. 97); L. G. Westerink, "Nikephoros Gregoras, Dankrede an die Mutter Gottes," *Helikon*, 7 (1967), pp. 260 f.; M. Sicherl, "Der Codex Grimanianus graecus 11 und seine Nachkommenschaft," *BZ*, 67 (1974), pp. 313–36 (*passim*).

[322] Sicherl, in *BZ*, 67 (1974), pp. 334 f., did not take into consideration item no. 885 in the inventory of Pico's library of 1498. He believed that our Proclus MS is missing in both inventories of Pico's library and that this MS left Pico's library before his death and came into the possession of Grimani during Pico's lifetime, possibly as a gift.

[323] The note was first read (at some time between 1902 and 1914) by Kirsopp Lake in his description of Laud Greek 18, included in his *Catalogue of Mss. Laud. Gr., 1902–* (handwritten), at Oxford, Old Bodleian Library, Duke Humfrey's Reading Room, shelfmark R 6.96/1 (unnumbered pages).

[324] There are two indexes of Grimani Greek MSS and an index of Grimani's library in Venice, preserved in codex Vaticanus latinus 3960 (cf. Freudenberger, *op. cit.*, pp. 39 f.; Mercati, *Opere minori*, IV, p. 159; *idem*, *Codici latini Pico Grimani Pio*, p. 29 and note 2). The most authoritative document is the first index written probably around 1520, when Grimani was still alive; this is found in cod. Vatic. lat. 3960, at the very beginning of the volume, on fols. 1^r–13^r. (The other two indexes were made when Grimani's library was already in Venice in the monastery of San Antonio di Castello; see above.) Our present MS Laud Greek 18 is listed in the first index, in cod. Vatic. lat. 3960 (on fol. 2^r), as Grimani's Greek MS 18: *Procli commentariorum libri sex in Platonis theologiam. — Procli theologica elementatio* (cf. Saffrey and Westerink, *Proclus, Théologie platonicienne*, Book I, p. CXIV note 2).

sales, or by not being returned by borrowers, or by other despoliations; possibly some were purloined at the time of the fire.[325]

It is impossible to determine how long this Proclus MS remained at San Antonio di Castello. It was certainly there in 1539, when it was transcribed in Venice in the present MS Paris Grec 1830, and it was there between 1546 and 1555, when it was partially transcribed in the present MS Munich graec. 98.[326] Iacopo Filippo Tomasini examined the Grimani library at San Antonio di Castello around 1646 and published a list of its MSS in 1650. Among the Greek MSS listed by him there is no mention of this Proclus MS,[327] which would indicate that around 1646 the MS was no longer at San Antonio.

The binding of Laud Greek 18 is of the kind used for Greek MSS destined for, or owned by, Johann Jakob Fugger (1516–1575) of Augsburg, whose library was purchased by Albrecht V, duke of Bavaria, in 1571 and then entered the Ducal Library at Munich[328] (the present successor of which is the Bayerische Staatsbibliothek). This binding is also identical with the bindings of two other Laud Greek MSS,[329] 21 and 62. Presumably all three MSS, Laud Greek 18, 21, and 62, were at first in the Fugger collection at Augsburg.[330]

[325] Cf. esp. Freudenberger, *op. cit.*; Mercati, *opp. citt.*; cf. also W. Weinberger, *Beiträge zur Hand-schriftenkunde*, II, SBWien, Philos.-hist.Kl., 161,4 (1909), p. 69 note 1; *idem, Wegweiser durch die Sammlungen altphilologischer Handschriften*, SBWien, Philos.-hist.Kl., 209,4 (1931), p. 65.

[326] Cf. Saffrey and Westerink, *op. cit.*, pp. cxiv–cxviii (on the above-mentioned and other apographs of Laud Greek 18). Also cf. Sicherl, *op. cit.*, p. 318 and note 26.

[327] Cf. I. Ph. Tomasinus, *Bibliothecae Venetae manvscriptae publicae & privatae* (Udine, 1650), pp. 1–19 (list of MSS at San Antonio), especially pp. 15–18 (list of Greek MSS there).

[328] Cf. Saffrey and Westerink, *op. cit.*, p. cxv, on the identical bindings of the two MSS, Laud Greek 18 and Munich gr. 98 (which was produced for Johann Jakob Fugger). On the Fugger bindings, and bindings of Fugger Greek MSS in red leather, cf. O. Hartig, *Die Gründung der Münchener Hofbiblio-thek durch Albrecht V. und Johann Jakob Fugger*, AbhMünch, Philos.-philol. und hist.Kl., XXVIII,3 (Munich, 1917), pp. 235–40, pl. iii (reproduction of a red leather binding of a Fugger Greek MS).

[329] Cf. *Summary Catalogue*, II,1, pp. 15–16 (§ 4).

[330] The present MS Laud Greek 21 was transferred in due course from the Fugger library to the Ducal Library in Munich. It was listed in the *Catalogvs graecorvm manvscriptorvm codicvm Qvi asser-vantvr jn inclyta Serenissimi vtrivsqve Bauariae Ducis, &c. Bibliotheca* (Ingolstadt, 1602), pp. 40f. (under no. civ); it has two bookplates of the Ducal Library, one dated 1618 and the other not earlier than 1628 (cf. *Summary Catalogue*, II,1, p. 16). The Ducal Library in Munich was looted during the Thirty Years' War, when the Swedish troops of Gustavus Adolphus occupied Munich in 1632. The present Laud Greek 21 (once Fugger MS X, 22, then Ducal Library's MS VIII, 9) was one of three Greek MSS lost by the Ducal Library during that sack (cf. Hartig, *op. cit.*, pp. 123f. on the losses suffered then; p. 134 and note 1 and p. 136 on Laud Greek 21, with the indication of its former call numbers in the Fugger library and the Ducal Library). The other two lost Greek MSS, to judge from their contents (cf. *ibid.*, p. 134), cannot be identified with Laud Greek 18 or Laud Greek 62 (cf. Coxe, I, col. 542).

It appears that the latter MSS, if they were at first in the Fugger library, were not included in the transfer of the Fugger library to Albrecht V in 1571. Indeed, MSS Laud Greek 18 and Laud Greek 62 were not listed in the *Catalogvs* printed in Ingolstadt in 1602 (this was pointed out in the *Summary Catalogue*, II,1, p. 16). We should keep in mind that some MSS of Johann Jakob Fugger were most probably donated or bequeathed by him to some relatives or friends and thus did not go to Munich (on this question, cf. P. Lehmann, *Eine Geschichte der alten Fuggerbibliotheken*, I, Schwäbische Forschungsgemeinschaft bei der Kommission für Bayerische Landesgeschichte, Ser. 4, vol. 3, Studien zur Fuggergeschichte, 12 [Tübingen, 1956], pp. 72f.). MS Oxford Laud Greek 18 is not even listed in the catalogue of Fugger's Greek MSS (Munich, Bayerische Staatsbibliothek, Cod. bav. Cat. 48), which was made by Carolus Stephanus, Fugger's librarian, in 1565. Dr. Erwin Arnold of the Bayerische Staatsbibliothek kindly looked through this catalogue of Fugger's Greek MSS, and in a letter of 24 February 1976 advised me that he was unable to locate an item that could be identified with MS Laud Greek 18; I am grateful to Dr. Arnold for his assistance. If, then, this MS was not listed in the catalogue of Fugger's Greek MSS and was not transferred to the Ducal Library in Munich, it may have disappeared from the Fugger collection at an early date. It may have remained somewhere in the area of Augsburg or Munich, which was occupied by the Swedish army in 1632, and it may have been plundered at that time. It is conceivable that Laud Greek 18 fell into the hands of the same dealer who a few years later obtained the other two MSS, Laud Greek 62 and Laud Greek 21 (this one removed from the Ducal Library in Munich), and successively sold them to William Laud. At any rate, MS Laud Greek 18 must have left Germany before or in 1633, when it was acquired by Laud. MS Laud Greek 62 was acquired by Laud in 1638; MS Laud Greek 21, in 1639. (On the years in which Laud acquired these three MSS and which are recorded in his ownership entries, cf. *Summary Catalogue*, I, pp. 129, 133, 134, also p. 136.)

Laud Greek 18 was acquired by Archbishop William Laud (1573–1645) in 1633 (this is the date of the ownership entry on fol. 1ʳ, in the lower margin) and donated by him to the Bodleian Library in 1635. On Laud and the MSS donated by him to the Bodleian, cf. above, p. 47.

On this MS, cf. Coxe, I, cols. 501 f.; *Summary Catalogue*, II,1, pp. 30 (under S.C. 704), 15–16 (§ 4); I, p. 129; K. Lake, *Catalogue of MSS. Laud. Gr., 1902–* (handwritten), at Oxford, Old Bodleian Library, Duke Humfrey's Reading Room, shelfmark R 6.96/1 (with unnumbered pages); Vogel–Gardthausen, p. 407; H. D. Saffrey, "Sur la tradition manuscrite de la Théologie platonicienne de Proclus," in *Autour d'Aristote. Recueil d'études de philosophie ancienne et médiévale offert à Monseigneur A. Mansion*, Bibliothèque philosophique de Louvain, 16 (Louvain, 1955), pp. 399–402 (superseded by Saffrey and Westerink, *Proclus, Théologie platonicienne*, Book I, pp. cxi–cxvi); *ibid.*, Book I, pp. cxi–cxvi (symbol o), and pp. cxvi–cxix on apographs of this MS; Barbour, in *Greek Manuscripts in the Bodleian Library*, pp. 32f. (no. 54); Wilson, *Mediaeval Greek Bookhands*, p. 32 (no. 69), pl. 69; E. R. Dodds, *Proclus, The Elements of Theology*, 2nd ed. (Oxford, 1963), p. xxxvii (symbol O); *ibid.*, on apographs of this MS; Sicherl, in *BZ*, 67 (1974), pp. 318 and note 26, 330 note 82, 334f., on this MS and its apographs.

Plate 83: A.D. 1358.

London, Lambeth Palace, ms 1183. Paper, 255 × 175 mm., 236 fols. numbered as 472 pages (with valid page numbers marked in the upper right-hand corners of odd-numbered pages only), 27 lines to a page. The top margins of the MS were trimmed excessively in the binding process; the bottom margins were only slightly trimmed; the outer side margins were also trimmed too much. Many leaves were pasted to paper strips along the inner edge. Originally the MS had greater height and width. The present measurements of the excessively trimmed volume conflict, of course, with the normal size of MSS on Western paper.[331] Many leaves of this MS were misplaced in the process of binding.[332] Contents: Acts of the Apostles, Pauline Epistles, Catholic Epistles (i.e., the so-called Praxapostolus), adapted for liturgical use. This MS was written and subscribed by Theophanes on 23 May A.M. 6866 = A.D. 1358 (page 472 – only the essential parts of the subscription are reproduced on Plate **120a**): † Ἐγρ(άφη) ἐν ἔτει, ͵ϛωξϛ: ἰν(δικτιῶνος) ιαˉ· |

† 　Θ(εο)ῦ τὸ δῶρον καὶ πόνος | Θεοφάνους· |

† 　γόνυ μὲν ζεύξας καὶ ὑποκλίνας | κάραν,
　　χεῖρας ἐκτείνας | πρὸς τὰς θείας τετράδας, |
　　ἐκπεπλήρωκα τὴν θεόσ|δοτον δέλτον:+ [332a] |

† μὴν μάϊος. κγˉ· τοῦ ὁσ(ίου) Μιχαὴλ | Συνάδ(ων). τοῦ ὁμολογητοῦ· ἡμέ(ρᾳ) δˉ | καὶ οἱ τῆδε τῇ γραφῇ ἐντυχάνοντες, | τὸ, κ(ύρι)ε συγχώρησον καὶ ἐλέ(ησον) τὸν γρα|φέα τοῦ παρόντος βιβλίου. λέγετ(ε)· | ἶ ὅπως καὶ υμᾶς ἄλλοι πάλ(ιν)· μνησθῶσι[:]+

I have arranged the dodecasyllabic verses metrically. On the feminine κάραν (instead of the neuter κάρα), cf. Jannaris, *Historical Greek Grammar*,

---

[331] I suspect that MS Lambeth 1183 was bound twice and trimmed twice, and that the present binding is the second one. This MS is a quarto volume (the laid marks run vertically down the pages). It seems that the first trimmed size of a page was about 280 × 200 mm., which would be consistent with the page size of a Western-paper MS. On the average sizes of MSS on Western paper, cf. J. Irigoin, "Les premiers manuscrits grecs écrits sur papier et le problème du bombycin," *Scriptorium*, 4 (1950), pp. 197, 203f.; M. Wittek, "Manuscrits et codicologie," *Scriptorium*, 7 (1953), p. 277 note 6.

[332] Cf. Scrivener, *Codex Augiensis*, p. lvii note 2.

[332a] On the occurrence of the verses γόνυ – δέλτον in subscriptions, cf. B. Atsalos, *La terminologie du livre-manuscrit à l'époque byzantine*, in Ἑλληνικά, Suppl. 21 (Thessalonica, 1971), p. 131.

p. 103, § 249[b]. May 23, commemoration day of St. Michael of Synnada, in A.D. 1358 fell indeed on a Wednesday. On the combination of two final particles ἵν' ὅπως in the last line of the subscription, cf. above, pp. 104f. and note 289. The dodecasyllabic colophon, Θ(εο)ῦ - Θεοφάνους, by its typical form suggests that this MS was most probably produced in the monastery of the B.V.M. τῶν Ὁδηγῶν in Constantinople.[333]

On Plate **83** we reproduce page 332, containing a passage from ST. PAUL, 1 EPISTLE TO THE THESSALONIANS 4:1–11. In the bottom line, the middle stem of the letter φ extends down considerably. Incidentally, a tendency to extend some letters upward in the top line of a page (or to write some letters above the top line) and to extend some letters downward in the bottom line seems to be a characteristic feature of the Ὁδηγῶν style (cf. Turyn, *Codices*, pl. 158; Follieri, *Codices*, pl. 45; Turyn, *DGMItaly*, II, pl. 136; Omont, *Facsimilés ... du IXᵉ au XIVᵉ siècle*, pl. C; *New Pal. Soc.*, Ser. I, pl. 180; cf. below, Pls. **81, 89, 90, 96**). The script style of Theophanes shown on Plate **83** accords with the well-known style of MSS written in the Ὁδηγῶν scriptorium in Constantinople (cf. below, pp. 132f., 143; cf. especially Pls. **89, 90, 96**).

This MS was collated by Scrivener, *Codex Augiensis*, pp. 287ff. (a collation with symbol b for the Acts and the Catholic and Pauline Epistles); cf. p. lviif. (a description of the MS). Occasionally the MS was quoted with the Gregory–Aland number 216 in the apparatus of Aland et al., *The Greek New Testament*, cf. p. XIX.

The MS was once owned by Joseph Dacre Carlyle (1759–1804), orientalist and professor in Cambridge, who collected Greek and Syriac MSS on a tour through Asia Minor, Palestine, Greece, and Italy in 1799–1801. This MS was marked I. 9 in Carlyle's collection; the symbol I. stood for I(slands) and meant that this MS was brought from a Greek island of the Archipelago or in the Sea of Marmara. On J. D. Carlyle, cf. *DNB*, III, pp. 1018f.; on his MSS at Lambeth Palace, cf. H. J. Todd, *A Catalogue of the Archiepiscopal Manuscripts in the Library at Lambeth Palace* (London, 1812; repr. 1965), pp. IVf.

The next owner of this MS was Charles Manners-Sutton (1755–1828), archbishop of Canterbury (from 1805), who purchased the Carlyle MSS and gave them to the Lambeth Palace Library (cf. Todd, *loc. cit.*). On Charles Manners-Sutton, cf. *DNB*, XII, pp. 942f.

On this MS, cf. Todd, *op. cit.*, p. 261; Scrivener, *Codex Augiensis*, pp. lviif.; Vogel–Gardthausen, p. 146; Scrivener, I, p. 297 (under Act. 183); Gregory, I, p. 281 (under Apg und Kath 215); III, p. 1099 (under a changed number 216); C. R. Gregory, *Die griechischen Handschriften des Neuen Testaments* (Leipzig, 1908; repr. 1973), pp. 55 (under the new number 216), 270; Aland, I, p. 72 (under the Gregory–Aland number 216); von Soden, I,1, p. 234 (under α469).

Plate **84**: A.D. 1359/1360.

Oxford, Bodleian Library, ms Barocci 110. Paper, 212 × 140 mm., VIII + 386 fols. (fols. I–VIII are modern flyleaves, Vʳ–VIIʳ contain a Greek table of contents written in the 15th century; there are also fols. 99a and 99b, and 363a and 363b). Main contents: John Zonaras, Commentary on the Resurrectional Canons of the Octoechus; Theodore Prodromus, Commentary

---

[333] Cf. L. Politis, "Eine Schreiberschule im Kloster τῶν Ὁδηγῶν," *BZ*, 51 (1958), pp. 19, 17–36, and 261–84 *passim*; cf. below, pp. 132, 143, 148.

on the Canons for the Feasts of Our Lord by Cosmas of Maïuma and St. John of Damascus. There are also other Byzantine texts in the MS. Except for fols. 363aʳ–386ᵛ, written by different hands of the 14th century, the main body of the MS on fols. 1ʳ–362ᵛ was written by the priest Nicetas who subscribed the MS in A.M. 6868 = A.D. 1359/1360 (fol. 362ᵛ – Plate **121a**): Ἐτελειόθη τὸ παρὸν ἀναγνωστικὸν ἤγουν ὁ Δα|μασκηνὸς· δηὰ χειρὸς ἐμοῦ τοῦ τρισὰθλίου καὶ | τριπλοὲχμαλλώτ(ου)· τάχ(α) καὶ ἱερέως τῶ ἐπίκλην ὄ|νομα Νηκίτας·: + καὶ μη μεφθῶ διὰ τῶ πλεῖ|θος (an acute was replaced by a circumflex by the scribe himself) τοῦ σωλικησμοῦ καὶ βαρβαρυσ|μοῦ ὁ ταλέπορος:· ἔτος τρέ|χοντος: + + ϛ·ῶ·ξη· ἐν ἰν(δικτιῶνι) ιγ | This subscription proper is followed by five lines written in monocondylia³³³ᵃ which seem to contain a well-known dodecasyllabic commonplace used in subscriptions. I read these lines tentatively and arrange them below metrically:

> ὥσπερ ξένοι χέρουσιν ἠδὴν π(ατ)ρί|δα
> καὶ ἡ θαλαττεύοντες | εὑρὴν λιμένα
> οὗτος καὶ | ἡ γράφοντες βιβλίου τέλος, |
> ἀμὴν ἀμὴν + : + | + + + + + + | +

On this metrical composition used in subscriptions, cf. Turyn, *DGM Italy*, I, pp. 101 f., 127, 186, 260, 20; above, pp. 8 and note 13, 38, 117. The word τριπλοὲχμαλλώτ(ου) used by the scribe in reference to himself obviously means "thrice (i.e., utterly) unfortunate as αἰχμάλωτος," i.e., as a "refugee"; on this meaning of the word αἰχμάλωτος, cf. E. Kriaras, Λεξικὸ τῆς μεσαιωνικῆς ἑλληνικῆς δημώδους γραμματείας 1100–1669, I (Thessalonica, 1968), p. 140, *s.v.* αἰχμάλωτος 2); V. Laurent, *Les Regestes des Actes du Patriarcat de Constantinople*, I,4 (Paris, 1971), Index, p. 613, *s.v.* αἰχμάλωτοι, *passim*; Turyn, *DGM Italy*, I, pp. 106, 108.

On Plate **84** we reproduce from the main body of the MS (written by the priest Nicetas) folio 186ʳ, containing a passage from THEODORE PRODROMUS, COMMENTARY ON THE CANONS FOR THE FEASTS OF OUR LORD BY COSMAS OF MAÏUMA AND ST. JOHN OF DAMASCUS (ed. H. M. Stevenson, Sr., *Theodori Prodromi Commentarii in carmina sacra melodorvm Cosmae Hierosolymitani et Ioannis Damasceni* [Rome, 1888], pp. 10, 12 – 11, 4). The page reproduced includes comments of Theodore Prodromus on Cosmas of Maïuma's Canon on the Exaltation of the Cross (on ᾠδὴ γ′, τροπάριον β′; this text of Cosmas, here commented upon by Theodore Prodromus, can be found in Migne, Patr. Gr., 98, col. 504 C 3–6, or in W. Christ and M. Paranikas, *Anthologia graeca carminum christianorum* [Leipzig, 1871; repr. Hildesheim, 1963], p. 162 vv. 41–44).

The MS once belonged to Giacomo (Iacopo) Barocci of Venice (d. before 1617); in his collection it was MS Greco in Quarto 38 (cf. *Indice Barocci*, fol. 32ʳ). The Barocci collection of MSS was presented to the Bodleian Library in 1629 (cf. above, p. 28).

On this MS, cf. Coxe, I, cols. 179 f.; *Summary Catalogue*, II,1, p. 6 (under S.C. 110); Vogel–Gardthausen, p. 338.

---

³³³ᵃ On monocondylia, cf. above, p. 70, and Pl. **109c**; below, pp. 135 f. and note 349a, and Pl. **123b**, **123c**.

Plates 85 and 86: A.D. 1361/1362.

London, British Museum, ms Burney 50. Paper, 285 × 200 mm., in two parts foliated separately: part I has 165 fols., part II has 180 fols. Contents: (part I and part II, fols. 1ʳ–165ᵛ) Apophthegmata Patrum (referred to at the beginning, part I fol. 2ʳ, as Λειμονάρ(ι)ον); (part II, fols. 166ʳ–167ᵛ are blank); (part II, fols. 168ʳ–174ᵛ) Life of Mark the Athenian (*BHG³* 1040); (part II, fols. 176ʳ–179ʳ) Apophthegmata Patrum. The binding of part I is a little confused (folio 11 should have been set after folio 15). The MS (except for part I, fols. 161ʳ–163ʳ, written by a collaborating scribe) was written by Ioannes Philagrius at the expense of Georgius of Chandax and subscribed by the same Ioannes Philagrius in A.M. 6870 = A.D. 1361/1362 (part II, fol. 179ʳ – Plate **120b**): Ἐτελειώθ(η) το παρὸν βιβλιον. διὰ συνδρομῆς | καὶ ἐξόδ(ου) κυρ(οῦ) Γεωργ(ίου) του Χαντακήτ(ου)· καὶ διὰ | χειρὸς ἐμοῦ τοῦ εὐτελοὺς καὶ ἁμαρτωλ(οῦ) Ἰω(άνν)ου | τοῦ Φιλάγριού, καὶ οἱ ἀναγινώσκοντες, εὔ|χεσθε μοι διὰ τὸν κ(ύριο)ν:– Ἔτους ͵ϛωο ἰν(δικτιῶνος) ιε̅:— The same main scribe wrote an invocation in part I, on fol. 2ʳ, at the top of the page (Plate **120c**): + ὦ Χ(ριστ)ὲ βοήθει μ(οι) τῷ σῷ δούλ(ῳ) Ἰω(άνν)η τῷ Φιλαγρίω:– The fact that the person who commissioned this MS was from Chandax[333b] (Candia) suggests that the scribe was also a Cretan and that the MS was produced in Crete. Actually, the main scribe of Burney 50, Ioannes Philagrius, was (as shown by his handwriting) identical with the monk Ioseph Philagrius (or Philagres), a prominent Cretan churchman, writer, theologian, and philosopher, who wrote MS Rome, Biblioteca Angelica, Greco 30, around A.D. 1392–1395 (cf. Turyn, *DGM Italy*, I, pp. 253–56). To establish the identity of Ioannes Philagrius with the monk Ioseph Philagrius (Philagres), it is enough to compare Plates **85, 120b, 120c** below, from MS Burney 50, with specimens of MS Rome, Bibl. Angelica, Greco 30, reproduced in Turyn, *DGM Italy*, II, pls. 212, 264*a–g*. As was customary, on taking the monastic vows Ioannes Philagrius assumed a name with the same initial, Ioseph.

To exemplify the handwriting of Ioannes(-Ioseph) Philagrius in MS Burney 50, on Plate **85** we reproduce from part I of the MS folio 97ᵛ, containing a passage from the Apophthegmata Patrum (cf. Paul Euergetinus, Synagoge, I, 20, 4: ed. Biktor Matthaiou, Εὐεργετινός, ἤτοι Συναγωγὴ τῶν θεοφθόγγων ῥημάτων καὶ διδασκαλιῶν τῶν θεοφόρων καὶ ἁγίων πατέρων, 5th ed., I [Athens, 1957], p. 167, 17–40). Another facsimile specimen of the handwriting of Ioannes Philagrius in this MS was published in *Pal. Soc.*, Ser. I, pl. 207 (= Burney 50, part I, fol. 42ᵛ), with an accompanying description of the MS and a transcript of the page reproduced. This plate of *Pal. Soc.* was partially reproduced by Thompson, *Introduction*, p. 263 facs. no. 77 (with a transcript of the text); cf. *ibid.*, p. 255 (a comment on no. 77). For specimens of the handwriting by the same scribe, (Ioannes-)Ioseph Philagrius, from A.D. 1392–1395, cf. above.

[333b] Now Ἡράκλειον in Crete.

As I mentioned above, a different scribe wrote in part I of Burney 50 the folios 161ʳ–163ʳ. This scribe was a collaborator during the production of the MS, since he wrote leaves 4–6 within quire κᾱ; he was preceded and followed by Philagrius within this quire. Thus it is obvious that the pages written by this collaborator in the continuous course of the production of the MS pertain to the same date as that indicated in the subscription of Ioannes Philagrius. Evidently they were written in Crete, as was the rest of the MS.

To represent the handwriting of this collaborator, on Plate **86** we reproduce from part I of the MS folio 163ʳ, containing a passage from the APOPHTHEGMATA PATRUM (ed. Migne, Patr. Gr., 65, cols. 385 D 6 – 388 B 14).

This MS was once owned by Charles Burney (1757–1817) and was acquired by the British Museum in 1818. On Burney and his MSS, cf. above, p. 44.

On this MS, cf. Forshall, *Catalogue*, I,2, pp. 15–18; J.-C. Guy, *Recherches sur la tradition grecque des Apophthegmata Patrum*, SubsHag, 36 (Brussels, 1962), pp. 222, 223 ff., 229 f.; Omont, "Notes," p. 341; Vogel–Gardthausen, p. 202; Van de Vorst–Delehaye, *Catalogus*, pp. 260 f.; Ehrhard, *Überlieferung und Bestand*, III,2, p. 924.

I wish to acknowledge with gratitude additional information received from the Rev. Fr. Jean-Claude Guy, S.J. (Paris), with reference to the text of this MS.

Plate 87: A.D. 1362.

Oxford, Bodleian Library, ms Canonici Greek 93. Paper, 380 × 285 mm., 314 fols., 33 lines to a page. Contents: Plutarch, Parallel Lives (part). This is the first part of the original larger volume, of which the second is now in Milan, Biblioteca Ambrosiana, MS D 538 inf. (on this MS, cf. Ae. Martini and D. Bassi, *Catalogus codicum graecorum Bibliothecae Ambrosianae*, II [Milan, 1906], pp. 1072 f., under graec. 1000). This connection between the two parts was proved by K. Ziegler, *Die Überlieferungsgeschichte der vergleichenden Lebensbeschreibungen Plutarchs* (Leipzig, 1907), pp. 160 f.; cf. Turyn, *DGMItaly*, I, pp. 229–31. At the end of the Canonici MS, one leaf (the eighth leaf of quire μ) was lost (it contained the words of Plutarch, Philopoemen 10, 10 p. 362a προσθίοις – 14, 3 p. 363f λέγουσιν: Teubner, II,2 [1935], pp. 14, 25 – 19, 7/8). The whole MS (Canonici Greek 93 + Milan D 538 inf.) was written by the famous scribe Manuel Tzycandyles (of Constantinople) in Mistra (near Sparta, in the Peloponnesus), at the expense of Demetrius (-Daniel) Casandrenus of Thessalonica, and was concluded on 7 April A.M. 6870 = A.D. 1362, according to the subscription written at the end of the original entire volume, in the present MS Milan D 538 inf., on its fol. 305ᵛ (Plate **122a**): Ἐγράφη καὶ ἐτελειώθη ἡ βίβλος ἥδε, κατὰ τὴν Πελοπόννησον· ἐν | τῷ κάστρῳ Μυζιθρᾶ· ἐξόδω τὲ καὶ συνδρομῇ καὶ συνεργία, κυρ(οῦ) Δημητρί(ου) | τοῦ Κασανδρηνοῦ· κόπω δὲ καὶ γραφῇ Μανουὴλ τοῦ Τζυκανδύλη· ἐν | μηνὶ ἀπριλλίῳ ζⁿ· ἡμέρα πέμπτη· ἰνδικτιῶνος, πεντεκαιδεκάτης· | τοῦ ͵ϛ°ᵘω°ᵘ ἑβδομηκοστοῦ ἔτους + (This subscription was previously reproduced in Turyn, *DGMItaly*, II, pl. 243b.) On Manuel Tzycandyles, cf. the bibliography in Turyn, *Codices*, pp. 150 f., 162 f., 165 f.; Vogel–Gardthausen, pp. 281 f.; Belting, *Das illuminierte Buch*, pp. 16 f. On Demetrius (later monk Daniel)

Casandrenus, cf. D. Bassi, "Sette epigrammi greci inediti," *Rivista di filologia e d'istruzione classica*, 26 (1898), pp. 386 ff.; Turyn, *DGM Italy*, I, pp. 229 f.

On Plate **87** we reproduce from MS Canonici Greek 93 the middle part of folio 13ʳ, containing a passage from Plutarch, Parallel Lives, from Life of Romulus, chaps. 11–12, pp. 23e–24b (ed. K. Ziegler, *Plvtarchi Vitae Parallelae*, Teubner, I,1, 4th ed. [1969], pp. 47, 22 – 48, 23; or ed. R. Flacelière, E. Chambry, and M. Juneaux, *Plutarque, Vies*, I, Collection Budé [Paris, 1957], pp. 71, 21 – 72, 22). For another facsimile specimen of Manuel Tzycandyles' handwriting from this Canonici part of the original volume, cf. Wilson, *Mediaeval Greek Bookhands*, pl. 70 (cf. p. 32 under no. 70). For facsimiles from the Milan part of this MS, cf. F. Steffens, *Proben aus griechischen Handschriften und Urkunden* (Trier, 1912), pl. 19 (this plate was reprinted, on a reduced scale, by M. Imhof, "Zur Überlieferungsgeschichte der nichtchristlichen griechischen Literatur der römischen Kaiserzeit," in *Geschichte der Textüberlieferung der antiken und mittelalterlichen Literatur*, I [Zurich (1961)], p. 297, fig. 57); Turyn, *DGM Italy*, II, pls. 183, 184. For published facsimiles of Tzycandyles' handwriting from other MSS, cf., among others, Turyn, *Codices*, pls. 140, 142; *idem, DGM Italy*, II, pl. 186; Omont, *Fac-similés ... du IXᵉ au XIVᵉ siècle*, pls. LXXXVII–LXXXVIII, XCIII; Cereteli–Sobolevski, *Exempla*, I, pl. XLII; G. M. Prohorov, "Publicistika Ioanna Kantakuzina 1367–1371 gg.," *VizVrem*, 29 (1969), p. 321, fig. 2 (from MS Moscow, Gosud. Istorič. Muzej, once Mosk. Sinod. Bibl. greč. 143 Savva = 233 Vladimir, partly written by Tzycandyles); cf. *ibid.*, pp. 318 ff. on Manuel Tzycandyles and MSS written by him.

This MS once belonged to Matteo Luigi Canonici (1727–1805 or 1806), a great collector, who from 1773 resided in Venice. The major part of Canonici's collection of MSS was purchased by the Bodleian Library in 1817. On Canonici and the Canonici MSS in the Bodleian Library, cf. *Summary Catalogue*, IV, p. 313; de Ricci, *English Collectors*, pp. 136 f.; Frati, *Dizionario bio-bibliografico*, pp. 134–36.

On MS Canonici Greek 93, cf. Coxe, III, col. 87; *Summary Catalogue*, IV, p. 316 (under S.C. 18546).

Plate 88: A.D. 1362/1363.

London, British Museum, ms Harley 5782. Paper, 213 × 140 mm., 242 fols. (folio numbers in upper right-hand corners are valid), 24 lines to a page. Contents: Synaxarion (Lives of Saints) for September, October, November.[334] The MS was written by the hieromonk Iacobus in A.M. 6871 = A.D. 1362/1363 (fol. 241ʳ – Plate **121b**): † ἐτελειώθη τὸ παρὸν συναξάριον, διὰ

---

[334] This MS Harley 5782 was not listed in Van de Vorst–Delehaye, *Catalogus*. The Rev. Fr. François Halkin, S.J., of Brussels examined it and kindly communicated to me in a letter of 12 July 1962 the identifications of several hagiographic items contained in this MS, to which I have added a few more. I list below the items identified, each followed by its reference number marked in *BHG³*, with their locations in MS Harley 5782. The prefix *BHG³* is not repeated and is to be understood, unless reference is made to *BHG Auct.*:

(fols. 3ᵛ–6ʳ) Philippus diaconus et Hermione filia (*BHG Auct.* 2371d, des. a); (12ᵛ–15ᵛ) Narratio de diacono cum defuncto sacerdote reconciliato (*BHG³* 1322e); (19ʳ–20ᵛ) Euphrosynus coquus (628c);

χειρὸς κἀμοῦ | Ἰακώβου ἁμαρτωλοῦ· τάχα καὶ ἱερομονάχου· | ἐν ἔτει ͵ϛῶδᾱ: καὶ εὔχεσθαί μοι οἱ ἀναγινώσκοντες:· | ἰν(δικτιῶνος) ᾱ:·

     ἔχοντι κ(αὶ) γράψαντι, σῶτερ μου σῶσον + |

(then in red) τέλος Ἰάκωβος ἱερομόναχος + The words ἔχοντι – σῶσον form a dodecasyllable; on this formulaic element of subscriptions, cf. Krumbacher, Κτήτωρ, p. 416.

On Plate **88** we reproduce folio 147ʳ, containing a passage from this Synaxarion for October 29. More specifically, it is a passage from the Life of the nun Anna the Younger renamed Euphemianus (ed. *Synaxarium CP*, cols. 175–76, lines 19–30; or Μηναῖον τοῦ Ὀκτωβρίου, ἔκδοσις τῆς Ἀποστολικῆς Διακονίας τῆς Ἐκκλησίας τῆς Ἑλλάδος [Athens, 1960], p. 179ᵃ, 27–44; or Μηναῖον τοῦ Ὀκτωβρίου [ed. Φῶς, Athens, 1961], p. 300ᵇ, 11–38). This Life is listed in *BHG³* 2027.

This MS was once owned by the Jesuit College in Agen (in southwest France), according to the entry on fol. 1ʳ: *Collegij Agen(ensis) Socie(tatis) Jesu Catal(ogo) Ins(criptus)*. Several Greek MSS (and some books) in the library of this College presumably belonged earlier to the Spanish scholar Pedro Galés (*ca.* 1537–1595). Some Greek MSS, stemming probably from Pedro Galés and certainly from the Jesuits of Agen, were acquired in the 18th century by the Harley library.[335] On this MS, cf. Nares, *Catalogue of the Harleian Manuscripts*, III, p. 296; Omont, "Notes," p. 340; Vogel–Gardthausen, p. 156; Ehrhard, *Überlieferung und Bestand*, III,2, p. 724 note 1; I, p. 505 note 4; *BHG³* 498h, 1225m, 2276.

Plates 89 and 90: A.D. 1366.

London, British Museum, ms Burney 18. Parchment, 33 × 23 cm., 222 fols., 23 lines to a page. Contents: Four Gospels, part of St. Paul*, Epistle to the Hebrews (12:17–13:25); the MS was adapted for liturgical use. A part of the original body of this MS, comprising its quires κη′–νε′ and containing Acts of the Apostles, Catholic Epistles, Pauline Epistles, *Epistle to the Hebrews (without Hebrews 12:17–13:25 by the original hand, now bound in this Burney MS), was once in Metz, Bibliothèque Municipale, as its MS 4

(21ᵛ–22ᵛ) Iulianus m. in Galatia (*BHG Auct.* 2211g); (28ʳ–28ᵛ) Theodota m. Ancyrae, incomplete at end (*BHG Auct.* 2433); (38ʳ–39ʳ) Copres seu Copris mon. in Palaestina (2081); (41ʳ–51ᵛ) Ioannes theologus ap. (919e); (52ᵛ–53ᵛ) Ignatius abbas Bathyrrhyacis (*BHG Auct.* 2183g); (56ᵛ–62ᵛ) Dadas, Gobdelaas et Casdia seu Casdoa (480); (69ᵛ–72ᵛ) Ioannes Chozebita (2186); (81ʳ–86ʳ) Thomas apostolus (1836); (93ᵛ–96ʳ) Theophilus mon. confessor Nicaeae (2450); (117ʳ–119ᵛ) Artemius (174); (125ʳ–129ʳ) Macarius Romanus (1005m); (132ᵛ–138ᵛ) Demetrius m. Thessalonicae (498h); (140ʳ–141ᵛ) Hiberorum conversio (2175); (144ᵛ–148ᵛ) Anna-Euphemianus (2027); (162ᵛ–170ᵛ Ieremias propheta – Narratio de capta Ierusalem (778); (183ʳ–185ᵛ) Miles seu Milus (2276); (185ᵛ–189ᵛ) Menas m. in Aegypto (1269m); (195ᵛ–196ʳ) Philippus apostolus (1528e); (196ʳ–203ʳ) Philippus apostolus (1528f); (203ʳ–203ᵛ) Gurias, Samonas et Abibus (Epitome passionis: ed. O. von Gebhardt and E. von Dobschütz, *Die Akten der edessenischen Bekenner Gurjas, Samonas und Abibos*, TU, 37,2 [Leipzig, 1911], p. 228, 1–5; p. 225, 3–20: major part of *BHG³* 740f); (205ʳ–209ʳ) Matthaeus apost. evang. (1225m); (224ᵛ–227ʳ) Narratio – Visio Ioannis (1322i); (238ʳ–239ᵛ) Andreas apostolus (101b).

[335] Cf. H. Omont, "La bibliothèque de Pedro Galés chez les Jésuites d'Agen," *JSav*, N.S. 3 (1905), pp. 380–84 (p. 383, on this MS); *idem*, "Notes," pp. 323f. (p. 324, on this MS); Wright, *Fontes Harleiani*, pp. 159 (*s.v.* Galesius, on the fate of the library of Galés), XVI and XXIII (on the Agen MSS in the Harley collection), 47f. (*s.v.* Agen, on MSS from Agen in the Harley collection; p. 47, on Harley 5782), 462 (on the provenance of Harley 5782 from Agen).

and was destroyed during World War II.[336] The Burney MS was written by the famous calligrapher Ioasaph (of the monastery Θεοτόκου τῶν ῾Οδηγῶν in Constantinople)[337] and was subscribed by him on 4 June A.M. 6874 = A.D. 1366 (fol. 222ᵛ – Plate **122b**): Θ(εο)ῦ τὸ δῶρον· καὶ πόνος, ᾿Ιωάσαφ:— | ῎Ετους ͵ϛωōδ ἰν(δικτιῶνος) δ· μηνὶ ἰουνί(ῳ) δ. (A facsimile of this subscription was already published in *New Pal. Soc.*, Ser. I, pl. 180.) The first line of the subscription with the name of Ioasaph is couched in a dodecasyllabic form and has a characteristic wording, typical not only of Ioasaph's colophons, but also frequently used in colophons of other scribes of the same ῾Οδηγῶν scriptorium in Constantinople.[338] The identification of this Ioasaph, scribe of Burney 18, with the well-known Ioasaph of the monastery τῶν ῾Οδηγῶν in Constantinople is established beyond any doubt by the script style of Burney 18, the dodecasyllabic colophon of Ioasaph in this MS, and by a comparison of the handwriting in Burney 18 with the famous Ioasaph's handwriting in his explicitly certified autographs (referred to below).

In this MS, Ioasaph used two kinds of writing style. In one (cf. Plate **89**) he used a wide and rather large lettering, and in the other (cf. Plate **90**) a narrower and more compact lettering. Since the two differ somewhat in their optical effect, I provide specimens of both kinds from this MS.

For Ioasaph's wider style of lettering, on Plate **89** we reproduce the upper part of folio 10ʳ, containing a passage from the GOSPEL OF ST. MATTHEW 5:18–22. This passage comprises the end of the lesson read at Mass on the feast of the Three Holy Hierarchs on January 30 (the whole lesson is Matthew 5:14–19)[339] and the beginning of the lesson for Wednesday of the first week after Pentecost (the whole lesson is Matthew 5:20–30).[340] The note τέ(λος) is marked in the proper place in the text; the note αρχ(ή) appears in the left margin above the beginning of the pericope. The liturgical note in the upper margin indicates the time of the latter lesson and the beginning of the pericope modified for lesson use through the addition of a conventional prefix:[341] τῇ δ̄ τῆς ᾱ ἑβδ(ομάδος): εἶπεν ὁ κ(ύριο)ς τοῖς ἑαυτ(οῦ) μαθ(η)τ(αῖς), ἐὰν μὴ πε(ρισσεύσῃ). The initial letter of the pericope is written as a large capital projected to the left. The figure ιβ in the right margin is the consecutive

---

[336] On MS Metz 4, cf. *Catalogue général des manuscrits des bibliothèques publiques des départements*, V (Paris, 1879; repr. Farnborough, 1968), pp. 4f. (under no. 4). It was Gregory, I, p. 194 (under Vier Evangelien 480), who identified MS Metz 4 as a part of Burney 18. On the destruction of Metz 4 in World War II, cf. M. Richard, *Répertoire des bibliothèques et des catalogues de manuscrits grecs*, 2nd ed., Centre National de la Recherche Scientifique, Publications de l'Institut de Recherche et d'Histoire des Textes, I (Paris, 1958), p. 162.

[337] On the monastery of the B.V.M. τῶν ῾Οδηγῶν in Constantinople, cf. above, p. 120 note 315.

[338] Cf. L. Politis, "Eine Schreiberschule im Kloster τῶν ῾Οδηγῶν," *BZ*, 51 (1958), pp. 19, 27–33 (especially p. 27 under no. 4), 17–36 and 261–84 *passim*.

[339] This lesson is marked in Burney 18 for the feast of the Three Hierarchs which falls on January 30. For some reason, Gregory, I, p. 375, failed to indicate this lesson under January 30. However, the lesson is exhibited under this date in the printed vulgate of the Gospel lectionaries (cf. Εὐαγγέλιον [1880], p. 186; Εὐαγγέλιον [1968], p. 212). The same lesson is also read on January 18; it is recorded under this date by Gregory, I, p. 375, and it appears under this date in the printed Gospel lectionaries (cf. Εὐαγγέλιον [1880], p. 185; Εὐαγγέλιον [1968], p. 210).

[340] On the time and extent of this lesson, cf. Gregory, I, p. 347.

[341] On such features of the liturgical notes, cf. above, p. 43 note 100.

number of this pericope from Matthew as designated for lesson use.[342] All these notes and marks and the projected capital are written in gold over red, as is the liturgical note in the upper margin. All the liturgical notes and marks in this MS are written in this manner. Apparently, the use of this combination of colors for noteworthy elements was a special feature of the writing technique of the ʿΟδηγῶν scriptorium.[343] For another specimen of Ioasaph's handwriting from this MS, cf. *New Pal. Soc.*, Ser. I, pl. 180 (= fol. 101ʳ), with a description of the MS and a transcript of the page reproduced. This specimen represents Ioasaph's wider script, which resembles his script reproduced on Plate **89**. Still another facsimile specimen from this MS was published by Forshall, *Catalogue*, I,2, pl. [II], top part (= part of fol. 163ʳ).

To show Ioasaph's narrower lettering in this MS, on Plate **90** we reproduce folio 53ʳ, containing a passage from the GOSPEL OF ST. MATTHEW 25:32–43. It should be pointed out that in the bottom line some letters are extended downward. In the style of this scriptorium, there was a tendency to extend some letters upward in the top line and downward in the bottom line; also to write some letters above the top line (in accordance with the general practice accepted elsewhere).[344] We can observe these features on Plates **89** (top line of the text, last word), **90** (top line, last word; bottom line, three downward extensions), and **96** (top line, endings of four words on two upper levels).

On the scriptorium of the B.V.M. τῶν ʿΟδηγῶν in Constantinople and the consistent characteristic style of its manuscripts, and on its famous scribe Ioasaph (d. 1406), cf. the fundamental study by Politis, "Eine Schreiberschule im Kloster τῶν ʿΟδηγῶν," pp. 17–36, 261–87, pls. I–III, XIII–XVIII (pp. 26–36, especially on Ioasaph; p. 27, on this MS); also cf. H. Hunger, *Johannes Chortasmenos (ca. 1370–ca. 1436/37). Briefe, Gedichte und kleine Schriften*, Wiener Byzantinistische Studien, VII (Vienna, 1969), pp. 111, 193f., 55; Belting, *Das illuminierte Buch*, pp. 55f. For other specimens of Ioasaph's handwriting, cf. Omont, *Fac-similés ... du IXᵉ au XIVᵉ siècle*, pls. XCV (narrower lettering), C (wider lettering); Politis, *op. cit.*, pl. II, figs. 4, 5, 6; pl. III, figs. 7, 8, 9; Chrysostomos Lauriotes, Κατάλογος λειτουργικῶν εἰληταρίων τῆς ἱερᾶς Μεγίστης Λαύρας, ed. L. Polites, in Μακεδονικά, 4 (1955–1960), pl. 3, fig. 8 (cf. p. 394, no. 5); Turyn, *Codices*, pls. 158, 205e (cf. pp. 177–80); Komines, Πίνακες, pl. 33 (cf. pp. 20f.), or Komines–Naoumides, *Facsimiles*, pl. 33 (cf. pp. 36f.); Follieri, *Codices*, pl. 45 (cf. pp. 67f.); Wilson, *Mediaeval Greek Bookhands*, pl. 45

---

[342] In the printed Gospel lectionaries, in the repertory table (εὕρεσις) prefixed to each Gospel, the consecutive number of a lesson from a given Gospel is marked in the repertory's column headed Περικοπαί. The above lesson from Matthew 5:20–30 indeed carries in the printed Gospel lectionary the consecutive number ιβ′ as the 12th lesson from Matthew (cf. Εὐαγγέλιον [1880], p. 23, Περικοπαί ΙΒ′, p. 28ᵃ, line 7 from the bottom; Εὐαγγέλιον [1968], p. [39], Περικοπαί ΙΒ′, p. 42ᵇ, line 2).

[343] The combination of red on gold used in liturgical notes and in some noteworthy elements appears in MS London Additional 11837 which I attributed to the ʿΟδηγῶν scriptorium (cf. above, p. 120 and note 313, and Pl. **81**).

[344] Cf. above, pp. 121, 126, below, p. 143, and Pls. **81, 83, 96**; Omont, *Fac-similés ... du IXᵉ au XIVᵉ siècle*, pl. C (cf. *ibid.*, Notice des planches, p. 19), bottom line; *New Pal. Soc.*, Ser. I, pl. 180, bottom line.

(only the note in the lower margin; cf. pp. 24f.), pl. 71 (cf. p. 33); cf. below, Pls. **96, 125, 96A, 126a, 126b** (cf. below, pp. 142ff., 146ff.).[345]

On the velvet-covered binding of this MS there are, in the upper middle section of the front cover and in the lower middle section of the back cover, gold plaquettes in relief, representing the Adoration of the Shepherds and the Adoration of the Magi.[346]

For collations of the MS, cf. Scrivener, *Full and Exact Collation*, pp. xlvi–xlviii (description of the MS, with the symbol n), collation of the Gospels in the main body of the book; *idem, Codex Augiensis*, pp. lxiiif. (description of the fragment of the Epistle to the Hebrews), 287ff. (a collation of this fragment with the symbol j).

The MS was once owned by Charles Burney (1757–1817), whose library was acquired by the British Museum in 1818. On Burney and his MSS, cf. above, p. 44.

On this MS, cf. Forshall, *Catalogue*, I,2, pp. 3f.; Omont, "Notes," pp. 343, 584; Vogel–Gardthausen, p. 217; Scrivener, I, pp. 256f. (under Evan. 568); Gregory, I, p. 194 (under Vier Evangelien 480); Aland, I, p. 86 (under the Gregory–Aland number 480); von Soden, I,1, p. 114 (under δ462).

Plates 91 and 92: A.D. 1367.

Oxford, Christ Church, ms 69. Paper, 288 × 214 mm., 174 fols., 2 columns. Fols. 173–174 are an extraneous insert, on parchment. Contents: (fols. 1^r–14^v) various minor texts, selected mainly from religious literature; (fols. 15^r–155^r) Matthew Blastares, Syntagma with its Appendix; (fols. 155^r–156^r) Leo VI the Wise, Ὑποτύπωσις (so called here: usually Διατύπωσις); (fols. 156^v–172^r) minor texts of religious character; (fol. 172^v) scribbles by different hands; (fols. 173^r–174^r) religious stichera written by a different hand. The original body of the MS (fols. 1^r–172^r) was written mainly by scribe A and, to a small degree, by scribe B. Scribe A, who stated in two notes (see below) that he was Manuel Mauromates, hypomnematographus and ecclesiarch of the Metropolis of Zichnai, wrote fols. 1^r–150^v right column, line 1, and fols. 156^v–172^r. Scribe B wrote only a small portion of the MS, viz., fols. 150^v right column, line 2–156^r.

The first 14 folios, written by scribe A, were prefixed to the main body of the MS which contains Matthew Blastares' Syntagma with its Appendix.

---

[345] G. M. Proxorov, "A Codicological Analysis of the Illuminated *Akathistos* to the Virgin (Moscow, State Historical Museum, *Synodal Gr.* 429)," *DOP*, 26 (1972), pp. 237–52, with great probability attributed a few MSS to Ioasaph of the Ὁδηγῶν monastery: first of all, MS Moscow, Gosud. Istorič. Muzej, once Mosk. Sinod. Bibl., greč. 429 Savva (303 Vladimir); then, Mosk. Sinod. Bibl., greč. 279 Savva (261 Vladimir), and Leningrad, Akademija Nauk SSSR, Rukopisnyj Otdel, Collection of the former Russian Archaeological Institute in Constantinople, MS 2. Facsimile specimens of these MSS which include handwriting samples are given *ibid.*, figs. 2–7. Moreover, V. D. Lixačeva, "The Illumination of the Greek Manuscript of the *Akathistos* Hymn (Moscow, State Historical Museum, *Synodal Gr.* 429)," *DOP*, 26 (1972), pp. 253–62, published *ibid.*, figs. 1–3, reproductions that also include handwriting specimens from MS Moscow Synodal Greek 429 Savva (303 Vladimir), whose writing Proxorov, *loc. cit.*, attributed to our Ioasaph.

[346] On the binding of MS Burney 18, cf. G. F. Hill, "Notes on Italian Medals – XII," *Burlington Magazine*, 20 (Oct. 1911–March 1912), p. 201.

That scribe A began writing the text of Blastares as an independent MS is shown by the fact that quire-marks begin on fol. 15^r ($\overline{α}^{ου}$) and continue through fol. 150^r ($\overline{ιη}^{ου}$). For some unexplained reason scribe A, who wrote the preliminary gathering (fols. 1^r–14^v) and Blastares' Syntagma with the major part of its Appendix, ceased writing the Appendix on fol. 150^v right column, line 1. A different scribe, B, concluded the Appendix by writing fols. 150^v right column, line 2–155^r. After completing Blastares' Appendix, scribe B added (on fols. 155^r–156^r) the Διατύπωσις of Leo VI the Wise and marked the end of his work with a note written on 14 August A.M. 6875 = A.D. 1367 on fol. 156^r, at the bottom of the right column (Plate **123a**): † ἔτους ͵ϛῶδε'· | ἰν(δικτιῶν)ος ε'· ῑδ μηνὸς αὐγ(ού)στου: | ἡμέρα σαββάτω· | τοῦ ἁγίου ἐνδόξου | προφήτου, Μιχαίου +

It can be presumed that scribe B concluded the main body of the MS, containing Blastares' Syntagma with its Appendix, immediately after scribe A ceased writing on fol. 150^v right column, line 1. Thus the dated note of scribe B implicitly pertains to the whole main body of the MS, i.e., to fols. 15^r–156^r, written mainly by scribe A, Manuel Mauromates, and concluded by scribe B. The fact that scribe A resumed the writing of the MS on fol. 156^v, on the verso of the final page written by scribe B, proves that the intervention of scribe B was accepted and approved by scribe A, and that the portion of scribe B was an integral part of the MS written in the course of the production of the whole work. Therefore, I shall refer the preceding major part of Blastares' Syntagma with its Appendix written by scribe A (Manuel Mauromates) to A.D. 1367, since it was written just before the portion of scribe B was concluded on 14 August 1367. Regarding the final part of the main body of the MS, fols. 156^v–172^r, it cannot be related chronologically to the preceding part, since how soon scribe A resumed writing this part is not known. All that is certain is that it was after 14 August 1367. But, for my purposes, I shall disregard the final part of the volume since I shall give a specimen of the writing of scribe A from the part that precedes the portion written by scribe B.

Scribe A stated in two notes written at the end of the volume that he was Manuel Mauromates, ὑπομνηματογράφος[347] and ecclesiarch[348] of the Metropolis of Zichnai.[349] This is the text of the first of these notes (fol. 171^r – Plate **123b**): + ἁγία τριάς | βοήθει μοι τῶ σῶ δούλω | Μανουὴλ τῶ ὑπομνημα|τογράφω Ζιχνῶν καὶ | ἐκκλησιάρχη + This is the second note (fol. 172^r – Plate **123c**): † ὁ ὑπομνηματογράφος | τῆς ἁγιωτ(ά)της τῶν Ζιχνῶν | μ(ητ)ροπ(ό)λ(ε)ως, Μανουὴλ ὁ Μαυρομάτης, | καὶ γραφεὺς τῆς παρούσης | βίβλου +++ This note is actually an undated subscription. Its last four words show that Manuel Mauromates considered himself the scribe of the MS (which indeed he was, except for the

---

[347] On the ecclesiastic office of ὑπομνηματογράφος, cf. J. Darrouzès, *Recherches sur les ὀφφίκια de l'Eglise byzantine*, AOC, 11 (Paris, 1970), pp. 362–68.

[348] On the office of ἐκκλησιάρχης, cf. Darrouzès, *op. cit.*, pp. 179, 272f.; cf. *ibid.*, Index, p. 597, *s.v.*

[349] On the Metropolis of Zichnai (near Serrai) in Macedonia, established *ca.* 1328, cf. Beck, *Kirche und theologische Literatur*, p. 177.

small portion written by scribe B). Both notes by Manuel Mauromates are written in monocondylia.[349a]

The family name Mauromates (or Maurommates) is known from the Byzantine past.[350] Since Manuel Mauromates was an official of the Metropolis of Zichnai (at least when he was writing the final portion of the MS after 14 August 1367), we can safely assume that this MS is a product of Macedonia.

To represent the handwriting of scribe A, i.e., Manuel Mauromates, from the dated part of the MS, on Plate **91** we reproduce folio 44^r, containing a passage from MATTHEW BLASTARES, SYNTAGMA, letter A, chap. 13 (ed. Migne, Patr. Gr., 144, cols. 1085 A 8–1088 A 15; or G. A. Rhalles and M. Potles, Σύνταγμα τῶν θείων καὶ ἱερῶν κανόνων, VI [Athens, 1859], pp. 102, 7–103, 30).

To represent the handwriting of scribe B, on Plate **92** we reproduce folio 154^r, containing a passage from MATTHEW BLASTARES, SYNTAGMA, from its APPENDIX. The text is actually a passage from John of Kitros, Canonical Responses to Constantine Cabasilas of Dyrrhachium, as included in the Appendix to Blastares' Syntagma (ed. Migne, Patr. Gr., 119, col. 969 B 1–8; cols. 969 D 4–972 A 17; col. 972 C 1–4; col. 973 A 4–6; or Rhalles and Potles, *op. cit.*, V [1855], pp. 409, 29–410, 2; pp. 410, 23–411, 8; p. 411, 28–31; p. 412, 10–12). This text can be found also in Demetrius Chomatenus, Canonical Responses to Constantine Cabasilas of Dyrrhachium, Questions 18–19 (ed. J. B. Pitra, *Analecta sacra et classica Spicilegio Solesmensi parata*, VII: *Juris ecclesiastici Graecorum selecta paralipomena* [Paris–Rome, 1891; repr. as vol. VI, Farnborough, 1967], col. 654, 2–10; cols. 655, 13–656, 17; col. 657, 5–10; col. 658, 7–9).[351] The red mark in the upper margin of the page reproduced, + Κίτρους∶·, refers to the author of the text included on this page, i.e., Ἰωάννου τοῦ ἐπισκόπου Κίτρους.

This MS presumably belonged to William Wake (1657–1737), archbishop of Canterbury, who willed his MSS to Christ Church, Oxford. On Wake and his bequest, cf. above p. 79.

On this MS, cf. G. W. Kitchin, *Catalogus codicum mss. qui in bibliotheca Aedis Christi apud Oxonienses adservantur* (Oxford, 1867), p. 28 (under no. LXIX); C. H. Hoole, *An Account of Some Greek Manuscripts Contained in the Library of Christ Church, Oxford* (London, 1895), pp. 16, 29.

[349a] On monocondylia, cf. Gardthausen, *Griechische Palaeographie*, II, pp. 50–52; L. Polites, Ὁδηγὸς καταλόγου χειρογράφων, in Γενικὸν Συμβούλιον βιβλιοθηκῶν τῆς Ἑλλάδος, 17 (Athens, 1961), pp. 41, 91, pl. 1 figs. 1, 2; Follieri, *Codices*, p. 78 (no. 54), pl. 54; Turyn, *DGMItaly*, I, Index, p. 282, *s.v.* monocondylion; above, pp. 70, 127; below, Pls. **109c, 121a**.

[350] On the family name Μαυρομάτης (or Μαυρομμάτης), cf. Vogel–Gardthausen, pp. 177f., 246; P. Canart, *Codices Vaticani graeci. Codices 1745–1962*, I (Vatican City, 1970), pp. 163f. (on a different Manuel Mauromates of Philadelphia, of the 13th century, probably owner of cod. Vatic. gr. 1804); II (1973), Index, p. 132, *s.v.* Mauromates Iohannes; H. Moritz, *Die Zunamen bei den byzantinischen Historikern und Chronisten*, II (Progr. Landshut, 1897/98), p. 50. Moritz pointed out and explained the difference in spellings between the vulgar form -ομάτης and the classicistic one -ομμάτης in names with such endings (the vulgar form refers to μάτι; the classicistic form, to ὄμμα).

[351] On the relationship of canonical responses transmitted under the names of Demetrius Chomatenus and of John of Kitros, and the responses included under the name of John of Kitros in the Appendix to Matthew Blastares' Syntagma, cf. A. Pavlov, "Komu prinadležat kanoničeskie otvěty, avtorom kotoryh sčitalsja Ioann, episkop kitrskij (XIII věka)?," *VizVrem*, 1 (1894), pp. 493–502; J. Darrouzès, "Les réponses canoniques de Jean de Kitros," *REB*, 31 (1973), pp. 319–34.

Plates 93 and 94: A.D. 1378.

Oxford, Bodleian Library, ms Barocci 69. Paper (except for parchment fols. 280 and 281), 215 × 137 mm., 281 fols., 21 lines to a page. Contents: theological and ascetic texts. The MS was written alternately by two scribes, presumably in Crete (see below). One scribe, the hieromonk Niphon who subscribed the MS, wrote: fols. 1ʳ–16ᵛ, 65ʳ–96ᵛ, 156ʳ–157ʳ, 186ʳ–189ᵛ, 216ʳ–281ʳ. The other scribe wrote: fols. 17ʳ–64ᵛ, 97ʳ–155ᵛ, 158ʳ–185ᵛ, 190ʳ–215ᵛ. The MS was subscribed by the hieromonk (ῥακενδύτης, monk, and θύτης, priest) Niphon on 26 April A.M. 6886 = A.D. 1378 (fol. 280ʳ – Plate 124a): Εἴληφε τέλος ἡ παροῦσα βίβλος, | κατὰ τὸ ͵ϛὸν ᾽ὦὸν π̄ὸν ϛ ἔτος, ἰν(δικτιώ-ν)ου ᾱⁿˢ′ | ἐνισταμένης· ἐν μηνὶ ἀπριλλίω κϛ̄· | ἡμέρα δευτέρα ἐν (this preposition was added above the line) ὥρα γ̄ⁿ· [[ἐ̄τ̄ε̄λ?]] εγρά(φ)η | δὲ παρὰ ἀλιτροῦ Νίφωνος ῥα|κενδύτου καὶ θύτου:– | It is noteworthy that in this subscription (and in all the notes that follow on the same fol. 280ʳ) above the numeral letters there are breathings and accents which correspond to the breathings and accents of the ordinal numerals when they are spelled out.[352]

Beneath this subscription, there are seven notes quoted below (with consecutive figures added by me), referring to pestilences which occurred (1) in A.M. 6856 (= A.D. 1347/48), (2) in A.M. 6873 (= A.D. 1364/65), (3) in A.M. 6884 (= A.D. 1375/76), (4) in A.M. 6897 (= A.D. 1388/89), and (5) a pestilence that began in April A.M. ⟨6⟩906 (= A.D. 1398). Then a note (6) states that on Friday, 9 May A.M. ⟨6⟩907 (= A.D. 1399), the construction of a church in Βαϊονέα began. A final note (7) mentions a solar eclipse on 5 May A.M. 6868 (= A.D. 1360); this date was probably written by mistake and should have been A.M. 6869 (= A.D. 1361); see below. These notes have been published by Coxe, Lampros, G. Mercati, and recently by Schreiner.[353] Following is the text of the notes as it appears in the MS (on fol. 280ʳ):

(1) Ἰστέον ὅτι κατὰ τὸ ͵ϛὸν ᾽ὦὸν ν̄ὸν ϛ ἔτος, | ἐγεγόνει τὸ μέγα θανατικόν:– |

(2) Ἐγένετο δὲ πάλιν θανατικὸν ἕτε|ρον, κ(α)τ(ὰ) τὸ ͵ϛὸν ᾽ὦὸν ῾ō γ′ ἔτος, ὅτε καὶ μοῦρτον ἦν | ἐν τῇ | Κρή|τηι:– | (The words ὅτε – Κρήτηι were added later in the same script as that of note 7.)

(3) Εἶτα πάλιν ἐγένετο θανατικὸν | ἄλλο, κατὰ τὸ ͵ϛὸν ᾽ὦὸν ᾽π̄ὸν δ′ ἔτος:– |

(4) Ἐγένετο θανατικὸν ἄλλο, κ(α)τ(ὰ) τὸ ͵ϛὸν ᾽ὦὸν | ζ̄ⁿ ϛ ἔτος:– |

(5) + ἐγένετο καὶ ἄλλο | θανατικὸν μέγιστον, κ(α)τ(ὰ) τὸ ᾽λ̄ὸν ϛ ἔτος, ἐν | μηνὶ ἀπριλλίω ἀρξάμενον:– [[κ(α)τ(ὰ) δὲ]] |

---

[352] On accents and breathings marked above ordinal numeral letters, cf. Turyn, *Codices*, pp. 40, 112, 125, 137; *idem, DGMItaly*, I, pp. 81, 113, 117, 124f., 130, 132, 205, 257.

[353] Cf. Coxe, I, col. 111. The notes were reprinted from Coxe, with some mistakes, by S. P. Lampros, Ἐνθυμήσεων ἤτοι χρονικῶν σημειωμάτων συλλογὴ πρώτη, in Νέος Ἑλλ., 7 (1910), pp. 142 (no. 61), 147f. (no. 84). Most of these notes were also reprinted from Coxe by G. Mercati, "Per l'epistolario di Demetrio Cidone," *SBN*, 3 (1931), p. 226 (= *idem, Opere minori*, IV, ST, 79 [Vatican City, 1937], p. 416). The notes have been published recently by Schreiner, *Die byzantinischen Kleinchroniken*, I, pp. 618f. (under Chronik 89); for comments, cf. *ibid.*, II, pp. 271f., 292, 311, 337, 361, 363 (Schreiner, *op. cit.*, I, p. 619, and II, p. 323, referred the solar eclipse recorded in note 7 to A.M. 6888 = A.D. 1380).

(6) † τὸ ἀ᷎ον ζ, ἠρξάμεθ(α) κτίζειν τὴν ἐκκλησίαν | τῆς Βαϊονέας, μηνὶ μάϊω θ'· ἡμέρα | παρα(σκευ)ῆ·

(7) ἰστέον· ὅτι τῷ ͵ϛ᷉ ᾽ω᷉ ξ᷉ ᾽η' ἔτει, ἐγένετο | ἔκλειψις μεγ(ά)λ(η) τοῦ ἡλίου τῇ ε' τοῦ μαΐου | μηνὸ[ς] ὥρα γ᷎ʹ τῆς ἡμέρας ἐν ᾗ ἐφάνη | σαν πάντες οἱ ἀστέρες τοῦ οὐ(ρα)νοῦ:

It is obvious that notes 1–3 were written by the hieromonk Niphon, after he wrote the subscription. He recorded, in a script very similar to that of the subscription, the pestilences of two decades prior to the time of the subscription. Subsequently, the same Niphon, it seems, recorded in notes 4–5 two pestilences which occurred eleven and twenty years later; he wrote these notes as the events happened, in a script that changed in the course of time and grew thicker. Note 6, written a year later than note 5, is in a similar but somewhat coarser script. It should be borne in mind that note 6 is dated twenty-one years later than the subscription. Note 7, recording a solar eclipse which took place thirty-eight years earlier than note 6 (on the actual date of that eclipse, see below), seems to have been written on some later occasion just to record the eclipse for history. I suspect that it was the same Niphon who wrote note 7. At any rate, whoever wrote note 7 also added the words ὅτε καὶ μοῦρτον ἦν ἐν τῇ Κρήτηι at the end of note 2.

Giovanni Mercati, *loc. cit.*, in discussing references to pestilences in medieval sources, quoted the above notes 1–5.[354] The place Βαϊονέα mentioned in note 6 must be the present village Βαϊνιά in Crete (in the eparchy of Ἱεράπετρα, in the province of Λασίθιον).[355] This note is proof that the MS was in Crete in A.D. 1399; further, if we assume that note 6 was written by Niphon, then we can safely assert that the MS was written in Crete.

Moreover, the words added to note 2 in the coarser script contain an explicit reference to Cretan history, a reference which is interesting both historically and linguistically. The words ὅτε καὶ μοῦρτον ἦν ἐν τῇ Κρήτηι, added at a later date to the note 2 that recorded the pestilence of A.D. 1364/1365, explicitly refer to the well-known sedition against Venice which took place in Crete,

[354] Several references to the great pestilence of A.D. 1347/1348 as it affected Crete can be found in Venetian documents of that time. Cf. F. Thiriet, *Régestes des délibérations du Sénat de Venise concernant la Romanie*, I (Paris–The Hague, 1958), p. 64 (no. 214); *idem, Délibérations des assemblées vénitiennes concernant la Romanie*, I (Paris–The Hague, 1966), pp. 214 (nos. 545, 546), 215 (no. 550), 216 (no. 553), 218 (nos. 560, 562). Cf. also *idem, La Romanie vénitienne au Moyen Age*, BEFAR, 193 (Paris, 1959), esp. pp. 261f. (cf. Index, p. 458, s.v. Peste Noire); Th. E. Detorakes, Ἡ πανώλης ἐν Κρήτῃ. Συμβολὴ εἰς τὴν ἱστορίαν τῶν ἐπιδημιῶν τῆς νήσου, in Ἐπιστημονικὴ Ἐπετηρὶς τῆς Φιλοσοφικῆς Σχολῆς τοῦ Πανεπιστημίου Ἀθηνῶν, 2nd ser., 21 (1970–1971), pp. 120–22.

[355] Cf. Λεξικὸν τῶν δήμων, p. 26. Lampros, in Νέος Ἑλλ., 7, pp. 147–48, stated (obviously in view of note 2) that the above notes referred to Crete. The church mentioned in note 6 must be one in the convent Θεοτόκου τῆς Παντανάσσης in Βαιονία, founded by the hieromonk Νεῖλος Νταμιλᾶς (d. after April 1417) who wrote the Typicon for this convent. On this convent and on the hieromonk Nilus Damilas, cf. N. B. Tomadakes, in Θρησκ.᾽Ηθ.᾽Εγκυκλ., III, col. 561; *idem,* Ὁ Ἰωσὴφ Βρυέννιος καὶ ἡ Κρήτη κατὰ τὸ *1400* (Athens, 1947), pp. 89–92. The Typicon itself was published by S. Pétridès, "Le typicon de Nil Damilas pour le monastère de femmes de Baeonia en Crète (1400)," *IRAIK*, 15 (1911), pp. 92–111. Cf. K. A. Manaphes, Μοναστηριακὰ Τυπικὰ – Διαθῆκαι, in Ἀθηνᾶ. Σειρὰ διατριβῶν καὶ μελετημάτων, 7 (Athens, 1970), esp. pp. 168–71; S. P. Lambros, "Das Testament des Neilos Damilas," *BZ*, 4 (1895), p. 585.

There are now in Crete two places with similar names: Βαϊνιά (in the eparchy of Ἱεράπετρα) and Βαγιονιά (in the eparchy of Μονοφάτσιον). The former place is more probable as the seat of the convent founded by Nilus Damilas, since Damilas himself was a hieromonk of a monastery which was located in the same district of Ἱεράπετρα (cf. Pétridès, *op. cit.*, p. 93).

the so-called St. Titus revolt of A.D. 1363–1364, whose aftermath lasted for some time.[356] The word μοῦρτον used in this form in Crete was changed phonetically from μοῦλτον, which meant in Byzantine Greek "rebellion, sedition."[357] The phonetic change of λ to ρ before a consonant is a well-known feature of uncultivated Byzantine Greek.[358] The form μοῦρτον was, as it seems, prevalent in Crete.[359] The characteristic Cretan phonetic form μοῦρτον used in the addition to note 2 is an obvious indication that this addition, which pertained to Cretan history, was written in Crete. This addition and the reference in note 6 to the Cretan locality Vainiá support the assumption that the MS was written in Crete.

The last note, 7, contains an error in its date. The note was written on the basis of some records which its scribe had either made in his younger years or found elsewhere. The solar eclipse mentioned occurred (as I stated above) almost four decades earlier than the fact recorded in the preceding note 6. Note 7 states that there was a total (μεγάλη) solar eclipse on 5 May A.M. 6868 = A.D. 1360, in the third hour of the day (i.e., after sunrise). Obviously the scribe made a slight slip. He should have indicated the next year, A.M. 6869 = A.D. 1361. On 5 May 1361 there was indeed a total solar eclipse, at 8:48.9 a.m., Greenwich time.[360]

---

[356] Cf. J. Jegerlehner, "Der Aufstand der kandiotischen Ritterschaft gegen das Mutterland Venedig. 1363–65," *BZ*, 12 (1903), pp. 78–125; S. Xanthoudides, Ἡ Ἐνετοκρατία ἐν Κρήτῃ καὶ οἱ κατὰ τῶν Ἐνετῶν ἀγῶνες τῶν Κρητῶν, TFByzNgPhil, 34 (Athens, 1939), pp. 81 ff.; Thiriet, *La Romanie vénitienne au Moyen Age*, p. 174; idem, *Délibérations des assemblées vénitiennes concernant la Romanie*, I, pp. 261–66 (nos. 708–26); II (1971), pp. 17–25 (nos. 733–37, 739–41, 743–45, 749–51, 753); p. 272 (cf. nos. 736, 737); pp. 273–83 (cf. nos. 740, 743, 749, 753, 757, 758, 771, 773, 774); Schreiner, *Die byzantinischen Kleinchroniken*, II, p. 292 note 82.

[357] Cf. Du Cange, *Glossarium graecitatis*, I, col. 961: μοῦλτον, *Tumultus*; μουλτάριος, *Seditiosus*; μουλτεύειν, *Tumultum & seditionem excitare*. The entry *ibid.*, col. 963, μοῦρτος, *Murdrum, Homicidium*, is erroneous both in the gender of the noun listed and in its translation. The context quoted by Du Cange is: ἐπιβουλαῖς ... ἢ μούρτοις (cf. *ibid.*, col. 961, lines 14–17). It is most likely that a neuter μοῦρτον was used here in the dative plural and that the obvious meaning of this noun was here "sedition, rebellion"; the form μοῦρτον with ρ was transformed by the scribe from μοῦλτον, because it was more familiar to him (see above, and below, note 358).

[358] On the change of λ to ρ before a consonant, cf. Jannaris, *Historical Greek Grammar*, pp. 94f., § 187.

[359] The noun μοῦρτον, "rebellion," the verb μουρτεύω, "to make rebellion," and the participle μουρτεμένος, "a rebel," appear in the well-known treaty of Venice with Alexius Callierges of A.D. 1299. The recent edition of its Greek and Latin texts was published by K. D. Mertzios, Ἡ συνθήκη Ἐνετῶν–Καλλέργη καὶ οἱ συνοδεύοντες αὐτὴν κατάλογοι, in Κρ.Χρον., 3 (1949), pp. 264–75 (I refer in the following to the lines of this edition). The noun μοῦρτου appears in lines 59 and 128; with the metathesis of the consonants, μούτρου in line 48 (in the Latin text, the corresponding word is *guerre*, though clearly "rebellion" is meant). The verb μουρτεύω appears in μουρτεύσε (= μουρτεῦσαι) in lines 59/60, and in ἐμούρτευσες in line 185. The participle μουρτεμένος ("a rebel") is found in lines 29/30; in the plural, μουρτεμένοι in lines 94, 162, 245, 253; μουρτεμένων in lines 85, 229, 276; μουρτεμμένους in lines 193, 240.

For comments on these words, cf. E. Gerland, *Das Archiv des Herzogs von Kandia* (Strasbourg, 1899), p. 127 note 3; S. A. Xanthoudides, Συνθήκη μεταξὺ τῆς Ἐνετικῆς δημοκρατίας καὶ Ἀλεξίου Καλλιέργου, in Ἀθηνᾶ, 14 (1902), p. 302 note 4; A. Thumb, "Alt- und neugriechische Miszellen," *Indogermanische Forschungen*, 14 (1903), pp. 359–61; M. A. Triantaphyllidis, *Die Lehnwörter der mittelgriechischen Vulgärliteratur* (Strasbourg, 1909), pp. 57, 70, 123; Mertzios, *op. cit.*, p. 265 note 8.

[360] Cf. Th. v. Oppolzer, *Canon der Finsternisse*, DenkWien, Mathem.-naturwiss.Cl., LII (Vienna, 1887), pp. 246–47 (under no. 6122); J. Fr. Schroeter, *Spezieller Kanon der zentralen Sonnen- und Mondfinsternisse, welche innerhalb des Zeitraums von 600 bis 1800 n.Chr. in Europa sichtbar waren* (Kristiania, 1923), pp. 8–9 (no. 184), 50 (no. 184), 132 (no. 184), pl. xcii map 92b (the map shows that Crete was almost entirely, except for a tiny western tip, enveloped by the total solar eclipse in question). For a listing of this eclipse, cf. also Grumel, *Chronologie*, p. 468 (under A.D. 1361). Since the median meridian

As a specimen of the handwriting of the hieromonk Niphon (who subscribed this MS), on Plate **93** we reproduce folio 261ᵛ, containing passages from HESYCHIUS OF SINAI, abbot of the monastery Βάτου (of the Burning Bush) on Mount Sinai, DE TEMPERANTIA ET VIRTUTE (from Centuria II, 3, 4, 7–8: ed. Migne, Patr. Gr., 93, cols. 1512 D 1–5, 1512 D 10 – 1513 A 2, 1513 B 1–11).[361] The red letters in lines 5, 12, and 19 of the page reproduced mark the beginnings of text sections. The red crescents in line 19 and in the bottom line denote carry-overs which belong to the ends of the preceding lines.

To represent the handwriting of the other scribe of this MS, on Plate **94** we reproduce folio 102ʳ, containing a passage from NICETAS STETHATUS, PHYSICORUM CAPITUM CENTURIA II, from chaps. 14–16 (ed. Migne, Patr. Gr., 120, cols. 905 D 9 – 908 A 13). On the page reproduced, in the upper right-hand corner, the author's name appears in red, Στηθ(ά)τ(ου). The red numbers in the margin ιε΄ and ιϛ΄ indicate the numbers of the sections of the text. The red initials τ and ὁ in lines 1 and 18, respectively, mark the beginnings of these sections. In the margin, there appear the well-known marks: ὅρα ("look," "attention") and ση(μείωσαι), which means *nota bene*.[362]

On fol. 280ʳ, in the upper right-hand corner, is a later note: τοῦ αγιοῦ Μαρχου. This may be an ownership entry; the MS may have been owned by a monastery or church of St. Mark (probably in Crete).

---

of Crete is 25° east of Greenwich, we should assume that this solar eclipse became visible in Crete at 8ʰ48ᵐ9 a.m. + 1ʰ40ᵐ = 10ʰ28ᵐ9 a.m. local time. If the eclipse, as reported in the above note, occurred in the third hour of the day, it would mean that the first hour of the day was counted there in Crete at that time of the year as beginning *about* 8:00 a.m. local time (unless the hours at that time of the year were measured as having longer duration, in which case the day would be implied to begin at an earlier hour). On the hours of the Byzantines, cf. A. Mentz, "Zur byzantinischen Chronologie," *BZ*, 17 (1908), pp. 474–76 (especially p. 475); Gardthausen, *Griechische Palaeographie*, II, p. 477; in general, cf. Grumel, *Chronologie*, pp. 163–65.

In MS Vatic. Ottobon. gr. 210, written in the Terra d'Otranto in A.D. 1363, a different hand recorded (on fol. 64aʳ) the same solar eclipse of 5 May 1361 (cf. Turyn, *Codices*, p. 160). The person who wrote the note did it in or after A.D. 1363, the date of the MS, and therefore wrote the note from memory or on the basis of some records. The original MS was written by a native of Soleto in the Terra d'Otranto (cf. Turyn, *loc. cit.*), and we can presume that the MS was still in the same region when the note on the eclipse was written. The note indicates that the eclipse occurred ὥρα ϛ, i.e., in the sixth hour (presumably of the day). In order to compute approximately the local time of the eclipse in the region where the note was probably written, we take the longitude of the town of Lecce (near Soleto), which is 18°11′ east of Greenwich. The solar eclipse became visible in Lecce at 8ʰ48ᵐ9 a.m. + 1ʰ12ᵐ7 (this accounts for the difference in time because of the longitude of Lecce) = 10ʰ1ᵐ6 a.m. local time. If the writer of the note marked the time of the eclipse as the sixth hour (of the day), he somehow counted the hours of the day from the sunrise, or possibly the "sext" meant "forenoon" to him. On the intricate question of the computation of hours in the Middle Ages, cf. G. Bilfinger, *Die Mittelalterlichen Horen und die Modernen Stunden* (Stuttgart, 1892), pp. 8 ff.

The note on the solar eclipse in MS Vatic. Ottobon. gr. 210, fol. 64aʳ, was transcribed verbatim in MS Milan P 75 sup. (at the end) by a hand different from that of the scribe of the MS (cf. Ae. Martini and D. Bassi, *Catalogus codicum graecorum Bibliothecae Ambrosianae* [Milan, 1906], II, p. 714). It is interesting that the Milan MS was brought to Milan from San Pietro in Galatina (likewise in the Terra d'Otranto) in 1607.

[361] On the attribution of this text to Hesychius of Sinai, abbot of the monastery Βάτου on Mount Sinai, cf. Krumbacher, p. 147 (section 59, 3, with a misprinted reference to MS Oxford Cromwell 5 instead of Cromwell 6); Beck, *Kirche und theologische Literatur*, pp. 354, 453.

[362] On ση(μείωσαι), one of the marginal marks possibly introduced by Arethas of Caesarea, cf. Turyn, *DGM Italy*, I, p. 233. Cf. also R. Devreese, *Introduction à l'étude des manuscrits grecs* (Paris, 1954), p. 86 note 9 (end); Ch. Astruc, "Remarques sur les signes marginaux de certains manuscrits de S. Grégoire de Nazianze," *AnalBoll*, 92 (1974), p. 290.

The MS belonged to Giacomo (Iacopo) Barocci early in the 17th century. It was MS Greco in Quarto 79 in the Barocci collection (cf. *Indice Barocci*, fol. 37ᵛ). On the Barocci collection in the Bodleian Library, cf. above, p. 28.

On this MS, cf. Coxe, I, cols. 108–11; *Summary Catalogue*, II,1, p. 5 (under S.C. 69); Vogel–Gardthausen, p. 334; J. Darrouzès, *Syméon le Nouveau Théologien, Chapitres théologiques, gnostiques et pratiques*, SC, 51 (Paris, 1957), p. 16; Aubineau, *Codices Chrysostomici graeci*, I, p. 173.

Plate 95: A.D. 1383.

Oxford, Bodleian Library, ms Canonici Greek 102. Palimpsest parchment, 320 × 243 mm., 70 fols., 2 columns, 51–53 lines to a column. Contents of the scriptura superior: Pentecostarion. The scriptura inferior pertains to an Armenian lectionary of the Old Testament, written perhaps in the 9th century (cf. a note by F. C. Conybeare added at the end of the volume, on the recto of the back flyleaf numbered fol. 71). The Greek text of this MS was written by the priest Constantinus Charases, referendarius[363] of the Great Church, i.e., of the Patriarchate in Constantinople, and concluded by him on 14 October A.M. 6892 = A.D. 1383, according to the subscription written in red on fol. 70ʳ (Plate **124b**): Ἐτελειώθ(η) ἡ βίβλος αὕτη· διὰ χειρὸς | ἐμοῦ ἁμαρτωλοῦ· καὶ ραϊφερενδαρίου | εὐτελοῦς ἱερέως· καὶ κληρικοῦ, τῆς τοῦ θ(εο)ῦ μεγ(ά)λ(ης) | ἐκκλησίας. Κωνσταντίνου, τοῦ Χαράση· | ἐπὶ ἔτους ἐ(ξακισχι)λ(ιο-σ)τ(οῦ) ωϟβ. μη(νὶ) ὀκτωμβρίω, εἰς τὰς | ιδ· ἡμέρα δ΄:+ :+ :+ Since the scribe of this MS held office in Constantinople, we should consider the MS a product of Constantinople.

As a sample of Constantinus Charases' handwriting, on Plate 95 we reproduce the upper part of folio 30ᵛ, comprising, in the top sections of the two columns, passages from the PENTECOSTARION for Wednesday of the 4th week after Easter, i.e., for the Μεσοπεντηκοστή (Mid-Pentecost).[363a] More specifically, the page reproduced includes a part of the Office for Matins on the Μεσοπεντηκοστή. The canon chanted in this service is Andrew of Crete's Canon for Mid-Pentecost (ed. Migne, Patr. Gr., 97, cols. 1421–33). In the left column of the part of the page reproduced, the text begins within the canon for Matins, ᾠδὴ ς΄, with the θεοτοκίον; in the right column, the text begins with the synaxarion for this feast (for the upper part of the left column: ed. Πεντηκοστάριον χαρμόσυνον, ἔκδοσις τῆς Ἀποστολικῆς Διακονίας τῆς Ἐκκλησίας τῆς Ἑλλάδος [Athens, 1959], p. 91ᵇ, 44–47; p. 92ᵃ, lines 1, 29–32, 2–5, 10–17, 6–9, 19; for the upper part of the right column: *ibid.*, p. 92ᵇ, 8–21;[364]

[363] On the office of referendarius, cf. J. Darrouzès, *Recherches sur les ὀφφίκια de l'Eglise byzantine*, AOC, 11 (Paris, 1970), pp. 373f. and *passim*. It is noteworthy that Constantinus Charases, who was referendarius, was a priest, not a deacon (contrary to the tradition: cf. *ibid.*, p. 539).

[363a] On the feast of Mid-Pentecost, cf. above, p. 102 and note 283a.

[364] This text of the Office for Matins on Mid-Pentecost agrees (except for the sequence of troparia) with the Athens edition (1959) of the Pentecostarion. It agrees less exactly with the published text of Andrew of Crete, Canon for Mid-Pentecost (Plate 95, left column, lines 5–25: cf. Migne, Patr. Gr., 97, cols. 1425 C 12 – D 1, 1425 D 6 – 1428 A 2, 1425 D 2–5, 1428 A 4; right column, lines 1–16 and 18–24: *ibid.*, col. 1428 A 14 – B 15). This canon of Andrew of Crete was reprinted (on the basis of Migne [*ibid.*, cols. 1421–33], with slight modifications made on the basis of the Rome edition [1883] of the Pentecostarion [pp. 176–87]) by N. Nilles, *Kalendarium manuale utriusque Ecclesiae orientalis et occidentalis*, 2nd ed., II (Innsbruck, 1897), pp. 347–61 (cf. pp. 353–55, corresponding in general to the passages exhibited on Plate 95, though in a modified sequence).

or for the upper part of the left column: ed. Πεντηκοστάριον χαρμόσυνον
[Rome, 1883], p. 181, 31–34; p. 182, 19–21; p. 181, 35–37; p. 182, lines 4–9, 1–3, 11;
for the upper part of the right column, lines 1–2 only: *ibid.*, p. 183, 6–7; only the
iambic distich on the feast was printed in the Rome edition, without the synaxarion, which was omitted in this edition).[365] In the left column, the large capital initials (in red) of the troparia are projected to the left, in accordance
with the traditional practice of the liturgical books.[366] In line 4 of the left
column, the rubric εἱρμ(ὸς) ἄλλο(ς) is in red, as are the other rubrics in this
MS. The full text of the εἱρμός in lines 5–8 is also written in red, to emphasize it
as a noteworthy element in the text.[367] At the top of the right column, the
synaxarion on the feast of Mid-Pentecost begins with an iambic distich
stemming from the hagiographic iambic calendar commonly attributed to
Christopher of Mytilene.[368] This iambic distich likewise is written in red, as
a kind of poetic rubric prefixed to the synaxarion proper.

The MS once belonged to Matteo Luigi Canonici (b. 1727, d. 1805 or 1806) and was acquired
by the Bodleian Library in 1817. On Canonici and his MSS in the Bodleian Library, cf. above,
p. 130.
On this MS, cf. Coxe, III, col. 95; *Summary Catalogue*, IV, p. 316 (under S.C. 18555); Vogel–
Gardthausen, p. 252.

Plate 96: A.D. 1391.

Oxford, Christ Church, ms 61. Parchment, 28 × 17 cm., 222 fols.,
18–20 lines to a page. Contents: Psalms and Odes (of the Old and New Testaments), with some prayers. The MS has suffered some losses and is, therefore,
incomplete. Fols. 4, 5, 138, 140, 141, and 165 are later replacements on paper.
On fol. 1ʳ, there is a paschal table for A.M. 6912–6918 = A.D. 1404–1410,
added by a different hand. There are full-page miniatures on fols. 1ᵛ (David),
102ᵛ and 103ʳ (Virgin Mary presenting a monk to Christ). The MS was written
by the famous scribe Ioasaph (of the monastery τῶν Ὁδηγῶν in Constantinople)
and subscribed by him on fol. 222ᵛ on 21 January A.M. 6899 = A.D. 1391.

[365] In the Rome editions of the Greek liturgical books (especially in the Menaia), synaxaria on
saints or feasts were left out.
[366] On the projection (ἔκθεσις) of large initials of troparia in liturgical books, cf. Turyn, *Codices*,
pp. 25, 46, 56, 115, 170; *idem, DGMItaly*, I, pp. 5, 16–17, 21–22, 40, 41, 99, 181, 193.
[367] This εἱρμός is indicated in the printed editions of the Πεντηκοστάριον ([1959], p. 92ᵃ, 1;
[1883], p. 181, 34) by its three initial words Ὡς ὕδατα θαλάσσης, but its text is printed in full in the
Πεντηκοστάριον editions of this canon ([1959], p. 92ᵃ, 29–32; [1883], p. 182, 19–21) as καταβασία farther
down at the end of the same ᾠδή. The text of this εἱρμός can be found in editions of the Εἱρμολόγιον:
cf. I. Nikolaïdes, Εἱρμολόγιον (Athens, 1906), p. 136, 12–15; S. Eustratiades, Εἱρμολόγιον, in Ἁγιορει-
τικὴ Βιβλιοθήκη, 9 (Chennevières-sur-Marne, 1932), p. 228, no. 327, lines 35–39.
On the meaning of καταβασία and its relationship to εἱρμός, cf. W. Christ and M. Paranikas, *Anthologia graeca carminum christianorum* (Leipzig, 1871; repr. Hildesheim, 1963), p. LXVI; A. A. Papadopoulos, Λειτουργικοὶ ὅροι, in Ἀθηνᾶ, 40 (1928), p. 79; E. Mercenier and F. Paris, *La prière des Eglises
de rite byzantin*, I, 2nd ed. (Chevetogne [1947]), p. 120 notes, lines 7–3 from the bottom.
[368] On the iambic distichs on saints included in liturgical books and their probable attribution to
Christopher of Mytilene, cf. J. Darrouzès, "Les calendriers byzantins en vers," *REB*, 16 (1958),
pp. 59–84 (especially pp. 61–73); A. D. Komines, Τὸ βυζαντινὸν ἱερὸν ἐπίγραμμα καὶ οἱ ἐπιγραμματοποιοί,
in Ἀθηνᾶ. Σειρὰ διατριβῶν καὶ μελετημάτων, 3 (Athens, 1966), pp. 27, 151f.

Most of the subscription is faded, but can be read under ultraviolet light. This is its text (fol. 222ᵛ – Pl. **125**):

+ Θ(εο)ῦ τὸ δῶρον καὶ Ἰωάσαφ πόνος + |

Χ̣(ριστ)ὲ̣ δίδου μογήσαντι τεὴν πολύολβον ἀρωγήν + |

+ Ἔτους ͵ϛω|μθ ἰν(δικτιῶνος) ιδ | μηνὶ ἰαν|νουαρίῳ | + κᾱ· ἡμέρ(ᾳ) | σα(β-βάτῳ) | +³⁶⁸ᵃ

This subscription was detected in 1974 by P. L. Bokotopoulos and published for the first time by him, Ἕνα ἄγνωστο χειρόγραφο τοῦ κωδικογράφου Ἰωάσαφ καὶ οἱ μικρογραφίες του: τὸ ψαλτήριο *Christ Church Arch. W. Gr. 61*, in Δελτ. Χριστ.Ἀρχ.Ἑτ., 4th ser., 8 (1975–1976), p. 180, with a reproduction (on a reduced scale) of the whole page fol. 222ᵛ on pl. 103. Apart from the wording of the subscription, which is typical for Ioasaph of Constantinople, a comparison of its script and of the script of the whole MS with the known facsimiles of Ioasaph corroborates the identity of the scribe with Ioasaph of the monastery τῶν Ὁδηγῶν in Constantinople.

On this scribe and the monastery's scriptorium, cf. above, pp. 131 ff., below pp. 146 ff., and the bibliography quoted in both places; cf. especially the valuable study by L. Politis, "Eine Schreiberschule im Kloster τῶν Ὁδηγῶν," *BZ*, 51 (1958), pp. 17–36, 261–87, pls. I–III, XIII–XVIII. On the dodecasyllable at the beginning of the subscription, Θ(εο)ῦ – πόνος, which is a hallmark of MSS produced in the above scriptorium, cf. above, p. 132, below, p. 148, Pls. **122b**, **126b**; Politis, *op. cit.*, pp. 19, 27–33 (especially p. 27 under no. 4), and *passim*. The hexametric invocation which follows in line 2 of the subscription, Χ̣(ριστ)ὲ̣ – ἀρωγήν, is likewise a characteristic feature of MSS written by Ioasaph and other scribes of that scriptorium (cf. below, p. 148 and note 374, Pl. **126b**). On the monastery τῶν Ὁδηγῶν in Constantinople, cf. above, p. 120 note 315.

As a specimen of Ioasaph's handwriting in this MS, on Plate **96** we reproduce folio 106ʳ, containing a passage from Psalm 77, 28–36 (ed. A. Rahlfs, *Septuaginta id est Vetus Testamentum graece iuxta LXX interpretes*, 6th ed., II [Stuttgart (1962)], pp. 83 f.; or ed. Rahlfs, *Psalmi cum Odis*, 2nd ed. = *Septuaginta. Vetus Testamentum Graecum Auctoritate Academiae Litterarum Gottingensis editum*, X [Göttingen, 1967], pp. 214 f.). On the page reproduced, there appears in the top line the characteristic tendency of this scriptorium to place some endings of words above the line (cf. above, p. 133; and Pls. **89**, **90**); here they even appear on two upper levels above the line in a rather exaggerated manner. Sentences end with stop marks in the form of thick red dots. Initials of versicles (or of some of their parts), if they happen to begin a line, are larger red letters, projected to the left of the text area into the margin, in accordance with the traditional manner of writing psalm versicles μετ' ἐκθέσεως (cf. Turyn, *Codices*, pp. 55 f.; *idem, DGMItaly*, I, pp. 65 f.). However, the projection of versicles in this MS is rather limited, because the writing of versicles is not done στιχηρῶς, but is basically continuous. For other facsimiles from this MS, cf.

---

³⁶⁸ᵃ On the meaning of the breathings and accents above the numeral letters ϛω in the year date of the subscription, cf. above, p. 3 note 1.

Bokotopoulos, *op. cit.*, pl. 104 (fols. 17ᵛ–18ʳ and 40ᵛ–41ʳ, on a reduced scale). For facsimiles of Ioasaph's writing from other MSS, cf. Pls. **89, 90, 122b, 96A, 126a, 126b**. For facsimiles of Ioasaph's writing published elsewhere, cf. above, pp. 133f.

On the verso of the upper cover, there is the following note in a handwriting of the 17th century: † τὸν βηβλήον ἠνὲ του μονάστιρη ὁυ ηγε | † ἠερομόναχος κὰι πνἐυματηκός τοῦ σοτηρως Χ(ριστο)ῦ | ἐυχαστὲ ἤπερ ἐμο ἀγήή πατέραις κὰι σιχοράισετε μὲ | τον ἀμαρτολον ὡτι ἀμαθης ειμ(αι). In line 1, ἠνὲ means εῖναι, "is." The end of line 1 presents a considerable difficulty; this is a tentative interpretation of its text. μονάστιρη should probably be read μοναστηρί, the Pontic genitive of μοναστήρ' (on this form in Pontic Greek, cf. D. E. Oeconomides, *Lautlehre des Pontischen* [Leipzig 1908], pp. 89f., §68.ιι.2; on the declension, cf. A. A. Papadopoulos, Ἱστορικὴ γραμματικὴ τῆς Ποντικῆς διαλέκτου, in Ἀρχεῖον Πόντου, Suppl. 1 [Athens, 1955], p. 47). On the reasons for my referring to Pontic Greek, cf. below. ὁυ must be a relative pronoun taken (strangely enough) from literary Greek in a form changed phonetically: it is to be understood ὅ (on the change of a stressed *o* to *u*, cf. A. Thumb, *Handbuch der neugriechischen Volkssprache*, 2nd ed. [Strasbourg, 1910], p. 6, § 6.5; Oeconomides, *op. cit.*, p. 29, § 19.5.ιι). ηγε is a literary imperfect (with temporal augment), quite unusual in this style and in this late note. In line 2 of the note, the lack of its writer's name is contrary to the custom of such signatures. The meaning of lines 1–2 is: "The book belongs to the monastery which the hieromonk and confessor of St. Savior's (monastery) guided," i.e., of which he was the abbot.[368b] In line 3, εὔχεσθε is meant: on α instead of ε in Pontic Greek, cf. Oeconomides, *op. cit.*, p. 4, § 1.2; the change of σθ to στ is normal in Modern Greek (cf. Thumb, *op. cit.*, p. 15, § 18). In the same line, the words ἤπερ ἐμο are to be understood ὑπὲρ ἐμοῦ. On the phonetic change of *u* to *o* (from ἐμοῦ to ἐμο), cf. Turyn, *Codices*, pp. 23, xiii (examples from Palestine, Cilicia, and Cappadocia). This change may indicate that the note was indeed written in an eastern region of the Byzantine world. It seems that in the eastern part of that world the written expression of the normal sounds *o* and *u* in some cases oscillated between ο and ου. In Modern Greek, the word σιχοράισετε, i.e., συχωρέσετε, is the common form of the imperative aorist of the contract verb συχωρῶ (cf. Thumb, *op. cit.*, p. 132, line 7 from the bottom).

On fol. 202ʳ (in the upper margin), an ownership entry of a monastery of St. Savior, also containing the well-known malediction against those who would purloin the MS (cf. above, p. 80 note 212), was written by a hand of the 17th or early 18th century: ετουτο το ψαλτιρον γινε το αγηου σωταιρου και ὁπηος | το παροι ναχη την καταρ⟨αν⟩ του τρηακωσϊου τιη θεο|φορ⟨ων⟩ πατρε-ρον: In line 1, ψαλτιρον is written instead of ψαλτήριον. This contraction of *i* + *o*, resulting in *ŏ*, is a characteristic feature of Pontic Greek (cf. Oeconomides, *op. cit.*, p. 23, § 9.2; Thumb, *op. cit.*, p. 6, § 6.6; Papadopoulos, *op. cit.*, p. 11). In the same line, γινε means εῖναι. The next word το, instead of του, is phonetically interesting: I refer to my remark above on *o* instead of *u*. However, it is possible that the *-u* of the proclitic article του was changed to *o* under the influence of the next *a-* which followed in a close juncture (cf. Dieterich, *Untersuchungen*, pp. 72–74, under d.). In Pontic Greek, the article τῦ before a vowel could be pronounced simply τ' (cf. Oeconomides, *op. cit.*, p. 24, § 10; p. 76, § 62.xiii). The *-er-* in σωταιρ-, instead of *-ir-* in σωτηρ-, was due to the influence of ρ (cf. Oeconomides, *op. cit.*, p. 13, § 6.4.xi; cf. also Thumb, *op. cit.*, p. 5, § 6.2). The change of η to ε before ρ occurred in Pontic Greek regardless of whether the vowel was stressed or not. On the ending -ου in σωταιρου (instead of -ος), cf. Dieterich, *op. cit.*, p. 163 (under b.α.). In line 2, ναχη means νὰ ἔχῃ. In line 3, in reference to πατρερον instead of πατέρων, on parasitic ρ in Pontic Greek, cf. Oeconomides, *op. cit.*, p. 117, § 77.6. In lines 2–3, the whole reference to the curse of the 318 (τιη) Fathers of the First Council of Nicaea is spelled ungrammatically, although the text of the malediction had, on the whole, an established traditional form. Perhaps the writer of the note transcribed the malediction from some MS in which the final letters of κατάραν and θεοφόρων were marked by tachygraphic abbreviations which he was unable to understand; therefore, he dropped these letters. On the other hand, it is just possible that the writer spontaneously wrote καταρ and θεοφορ only, dropping the respective endings -αν and -ων in accordance with the characteristic habit of Pontic Greek of occasionally omitting word end-

---

[368b] Bokotopoulos, *op. cit.*, p. 183, read the words at the end of line 1 of the above note: μονάστι-ρηου ηνε. In such a text, ηνε would be a repetition of the foregoing predicate ἠνὲ. Moreover, the penult letter in line 1 looks more like γ than like ν.

ings (cf. Oeconomides, *op. cit.*, pp. 91–92, § 68.ɪɪɪ). Linguistically, the above note clearly points to Pontus as the territory where it originated.

On fol. 134ᵛ (in the lower margin), the monk Constantius, sexton (κανδηλάπτης, "lamplighter") of an unnamed metropolitan church, recorded his name and status in a note dated A.D. 1706: Κοστάτηος μοναχὸς της μητροπόλεος | καντηλαυτης | Ἔτος ͵αψϛ·³⁶⁸ᶜ To the left of the note, there are two letters Θϛ written by the same hand as the note. Although there is no contraction mark and no accent, this must be read Θ(εο)ϛ. It seems to be just a pious scribble of the note's writer. The spelling καντηλαυτης, i.e., κανδηλάφτης, represents the common spoken modern form (cf. Thumb, *op. cit.*, p. 12, § 14). The phonetic form κανδηλάφτης is reported from Cappadocia and Pontus, and κανδηλάφτ'ϛ from Pontus (cf. N. Andriotis, *Lexikon der Archaismen in neugriechischen Dialekten*, Österreichische Akademie der Wissenschaften, Philos.-hist.Kl., Schriften der Balkankommission, Linguistische Abteilung, XXII [Vienna, 1974], p. 294 no. 3021). This note shows that as late as A.D. 1706 this MS was in the Greek-speaking East.

On κανδηλάπτης, cf. Du Cange, *Glossarium graecitatis*, I, col. 571. On the office of κανδηλάπτης in a monastery, cf. P. de Meester, *De monachico statu iuxta disciplinam byzantinam*, Sacra Congregazione per la Chiesa Orientale, Codificazione canonica orientale, Fonti, Ser. II, fasc. X (Vatican City, 1942), pp. 24, 281. The responsibilities of a sexton in a diocesan church probably were similar. However, it is unusual that a monk should hold this office outside his monastery, as Constantius seems to state in his note, even if it were in the metropolitan church. A monk would be expected to be a sexton in his monastery. The language of at least one of the above notes implies that it was written in Pontus, and by the same token suggests that at the time when the note was inscribed, in the 17th or early 18th century, the MS was kept in Pontus. In view of this circumstance, a hypothesis may be formulated in connection with a metropolitan church located within a monastery in the territory of Pontus.

The church of St. Philip in Trebizond, which was the metropolitan church, was plundered by the Turks in A.D. 1665 and subsequently was confiscated and converted to a mosque. Thereupon, the seat of the Metropolis of Trebizond was transferred to the monastery of St. Gregory of Nyssa in Trebizond, the church of which was then used as *the* metropolitan church of the Metropolis of Trebizond.³⁶⁸ᵈ It seems possible that in A.D. 1706 Constantius was a monk of this monastery of St. Gregory of Nyssa and the sexton of its church, which was then the cathedral of the Metropolis of Trebizond. This situation would perfectly explain the wording of Constantius' note in the MS.

The monastery of St. Savior mentioned in the first note is likely to be identical with the monastery referred to in the second note. If this MS was kept in the 17th and the early 18th centuries in the area around Trebizond, then it is probable that this monastery of St. Savior was the monastery of St. Savior of Chaldes (so named for its founder), μονὴ τοῦ Σωτῆρος Χριστοῦ τοῦ Χάλδου, in τὰ Σύρμενα (or τὰ Σούρμενα), now Sürmene (by road *ca.* 40 km. east of Trebizond).³⁶⁸ᵉ Either Constantius saw this MS on a visit to the monastery in Sürmene and used the opportunity to inscribe his note therein, or it is likely that the MS was transferred by order of the metropolitan of Trebizond from the monastery of St. Savior of Chaldes in Sürmene to the monastery of St. Gregory of Nyssa in Trebizond, possibly for liturgical use in its church, which was then the cathedral church. The monk Constantius may then have written his note while the MS was in the church of his own monastery. The metropolitan of Trebizond conceivably could disregard the threat of ecclesiastical censure (contained in the note on fol. 202ʳ) for moving the MS from one monastery to another one within his province.

This MS presumably belonged to William Wake (1657–1737), archbishop of Canterbury, who willed his MSS to Christ Church, Oxford. On Wake and his bequest, cf. above, p. 79.

---

³⁶⁸ᶜ Bokotopoulos, *op. cit.*, p. 183, did not realize that the crosslike mark (written beneath the α) was a symbol for thousands and read it as χ; he also misread ψ as ϛ. As a result, he erroneously printed the date as ͵αχϛ' (i.e., A.D. 1696). For the crosslike mark for thousands used in dates, cf. Komines, Πίνακες (or Komines–Naoumides, *Facsimiles*), pls. 104 (A.D. 1690), 108 (A.D. 1701), 110 (top line, A.D. 1706).

³⁶⁸ᵈ On these events, cf. Chrysanthos [Philippides], Ἡ Ἐκκλησία Τραπεζοῦντος = Ἀρχεῖον Πόντου, 4–5 (1933), pp. 711–13, 412; on the monastery of St. Gregory of Nyssa and its church, pp. 454f., 531, 553–55, *passim*; R. Janin, *Les églises et les monastères des grands centres byzantins* (Paris, 1975), pp. 292f. on the church of St. Philip; pp. 264f. (under 2.) on the church and the monastery of St. Gregory of Nyssa.

³⁶⁸ᵉ Cf. Chrysanthos [Philippides], *op. cit.*, p. 506; N. Oikonomidès, *Actes de Dionysiou*, Archives de l'Athos, IV (Paris, 1968), pp. 99f., 155f.; Janin, *op. cit.*, pp. 295–97.

On this MS, cf. G. W. Kitchin, *Catalogus codicum mss. qui in bibliotheca Aedis Christi apud Oxonienses adservantur* (Oxford, 1867), pp. 26 f.; Rahlfs, *Verzeichnis der griechischen Handschriften des Alten Testaments*, pp. 175 f. (symbol 101); Bokotopoulos, *op. cit.*, pp. 179–95, pls. 100–4 (= fols. 1ᵛ, 102ᵛ, 103ʳ, 222ᵛ, 17ᵛ–18ʳ, and 40ᵛ–41ʳ, all on a reduced scale); R. Holmes and J. Parsons, *Vetus Testamentum Graecum cum variis lectionibus*, III (Oxford, 1823), Praefatio ad libros Psalmorum, page facing p. [b] (under no. 101); V (1827), at end, fol. 4ʏ (under no. 101); in both places the MS is listed with its old call number 20.

I wish to thank Dr. Renée Kahane (Urbana, Illinois), who contributed valuable suggestions to the interpretation of the later notes added in the MS.

Plate 96A: A.D. 1391.

Oxford, Bodleian Library, ms Auct.T.inf.1.10, addition on fols. 1ʳ–14ᵛ, containing Tables of New Testament lessons (the above date pertains to these folios *only*). The MS is written on parchment, 205 × 160 mm., 426 fols., 27 lines to a page in the original main body of the MS, 17–18 lines in the aforementioned addition. The original body of the MS, written in the 12th century, contains (on fols. 15*ʳ–424ʳ) the following parts of the New Testament: Four Gospels, Acts of the Apostles, Catholic Epistles, Pauline Epistles; (fol. 425ʳ) the Niceno-Constantinopolitan Creed concludes the MS. On fol. 426ʳ, a list of Epistles for the Hours on Good Friday was added by a later hand. The MS contains famous illustrations, which are unanimously attributed by art historians to an early part of the 12th century and are affirmed to have been produced in Constantinople. This MS is the Codex Ebnerianus of the New Testament (so called from the name of a former owner). Late in the 14th century, in A.D. 1391, the well-known scribe Ioasaph of the monastery τῶν Ὁδηγῶν in Constantinople, monk and later abbot of this monastery (d. A.D. 1406),[369] adapted the original body of the MS for liturgical use by writing the liturgical notes for lesson use, marking notes for ἀρχή and τέλος, and adding the consecutive numbers of the pericopes. In this undertaking Ioasaph enjoyed the cooperation of the hieromonk Gregorius (evidently from the same monastery). Ioasaph's work and the cooperation of Gregorius are attested in a note written (in red) by Ioasaph on 19 June A.M. 6899 = A.D. 1391, at the end of the main original body of the MS (fol. 424ʳ – Plate **126a**): + ἐπληρώθη τὸ καθ᾽ ἡμέρ(αν) εὐα(γγέλ)ι(ον) μετ(ὰ) τοῦ ἀποστ(ό)λ(ου) καὶ τῶν σα(ββατο)κυ(ριακ)ῶν καὶ ὅλων | τῶν ἑορτῶν τοῦ ἐνιαυτ(οῦ), κατ(ὰ) μῆνα ἰούνι(ον) τῆς ιδ ἰν(δικτιῶνος) τοῦ ͵ϛωϟθ ἔτους | ἡμέρ(ᾳ) β'· ιθ τοῦ εἰρημένου μηνός. καὶ οἱ ἐντυγχάνοντες ταύτῃ· εὔχεσθαι καὶ[370] τὸν | συνεργήσαντα ἐμοὶ εἰς τοῦτο ἱερομόναχον κύρ(ιον) Γρηγόριον. κἀμοὶ τῷ ἐλαχίστῳ | καὶ ἁμαρτωλῷ Ἰωάσαφ τὸ ἀπὸ τῆς μονῆς τῶν Ὁδηγῶν + (The whole fol. 424ʳ including this note by Ioasaph was reproduced by Wilson, *Mediaeval Greek Bookhands*, pl. 45; cf. p. 25.)

It is obvious that the word ἐπληρώθη, which in subscriptions and scribal

---

[369] Cf. above, pp. 132 ff., 142 ff. On the scriptorium τῶν Ὁδηγῶν in Constantinople, cf. L. Politis, "Eine Schreiberschule im Kloster τῶν Ὁδηγῶν," *BZ*, 51 (1958), pp. 17–36, 261–87, pls. ɪ–ɪɪɪ, xɪɪɪ–xvɪɪɪ; especially on this Ioasaph, cf. pp. 19, 26–36, pls. ɪɪ figs. 4, 5, 6, ɪɪɪ figs. 7, 8, 9; cf. also Turyn, *Codices*, pp. 177–80.

[370] Instead of καὶ, Wilson, *Mediaeval Greek Bookhands*, p. 25, read διὰ and followed it with a question mark.

notes usually means "was completed," i.e., written, here implies only the writing of liturgical notes and marks for lesson use. The note by Ioasaph is very explicit with regard to his own work done in the original body of the MS (with the "cooperation" of Gregorius). It should be pointed out emphatically that Ioasaph used in his note the term εὐαγγέλιον, which means "*lectionary* of the Gospels" (as opposed to the term τετραευαγγέλιον), and ἀπόστολος (not πραξαπόστολος), which in fact means "*lectionary* of the Acts and the Epistles."[371] These terms and the subsequent reference to the "feasts of the whole year" clearly indicate that what was accomplished (ἐπληρώθη) in this MS was an adaptation of the original MS for liturgical use as a lectionary of the Gospels, the Acts, and the Epistles for daily use from Easter Sunday on and for the immovable feasts of the whole calendar year (beginning September 1).

We know the handwriting of Ioasaph very well (cf. Pls. **89, 90, 96, 96A**; cf. above, pp. 133f.). Actually, all the liturgical notes and marks added in the original body of this MS look as though they were written by Ioasaph only. Ioasaph, however, stated in the above note that the hieromonk Gregorius "cooperated" with him on this lectionary or in this matter. If Gregorius was a hieromonk of the same monastery τῶν Ὁδηγῶν (as is most probable), then he had the same script style peculiar to that scriptorium, and it would, therefore, be very difficult to distinguish his share of the writing, if any, in the adaptation of this MS for lesson use.[372]

Regarding the role of Gregorius, we have to rely on the note of Ioasaph and to interpret it properly. It is probable that Ioasaph's reference to the cooperation or assistance of Gregorius (fol. 424^r τὸν συνεργήσαντα ἐμοὶ εἰς τοῦτο – Γρηγόριον) simply meant that Gregorius helped by defraying the cost of parchment for the initial folios 1–14 (which Ioasaph himself was to use in the following days in order to prefix them to the original body of the MS: see below) and by paying the cost of rebinding the whole volume. The verb συνεργεῖν is most likely to have in this context the meaning "to assist," "to defray the expenses." I can support this interpretation by referring to the subscription of MS Oxford Canonici Greek 93 + Milan D 538 inf., written by Manuel Tzycandyles in A.D. 1362. In this subscription (cf. above, p. 129), Tzycandyles mentioned the sponsorship of Demetrius(-Daniel) Casandrenus, who commissioned the MS, in these words: ἐξόδω τὲ καὶ συνδρομῆ καὶ συνεργία, κυρ(οῦ) Δημητρί(ου) τοῦ Κασανδρηνοῦ. It is obvious from the first two nouns that the third noun συνεργία also had a related meaning and in this context meant "(financial) assistance."[372a] This is decisive proof that the

---

[371] On the meaning of εὐαγγέλιον and ἀπόστολος, cf. Gregory, I, pp. 334, 335.

[372] Politis, *op. cit.*, p. 31 (under no. 22), surmised that this Gregorius was perhaps identical with the hieromonk Gregorius who wrote the Athos Vatopedi roll no. 19 of A.M. 6888 = A.D. 1379/ 1380 (cf. *ibid.*, p. 267, pl. xiv fig. 13; *idem*, Κατάλογος λειτουργικῶν εἰλητταρίων τῆς Ἱερᾶς Μονῆς Βατοπεδίου, in Μακεδονικά, 4 [1955–1960], pp. 406–7, under no. 19).

[372a] A similar wording was used in reference to the sponsor of a MS, e.g., in the subscription of MS Sinai Greek 877 (of A.D. 1466): ἐγεγόνει δὲ ἐκ συνεργείας καὶ ἐξόδου τοῦ κτλ. (cf. V. N. Beneševič, *Opisanie grečeskih rukopisej monastyrja Svjatoj Ekateriny na Sinaĕ*, I [St. Petersburg, 1911], pp. 127f.). Also cf. the subscription of cod. Vatic. gr. 1755 (of A.D. 1294): διὰ συνεργίας καὶ κελεύσεως, κυροῦ κτλ. (cf. Turyn, *Codices*, p. 85; P. Canart, *Codices Vaticani graeci. Codices 1745–1962*, I [Vatican City, 1970], p. 54).

words τὸν συνεργήσαντα ἐμοὶ εἰς τοῦτο in the above note of Ioasaph most
probably meant "the one who assisted me financially in this matter." If it
was so, then we should not expect to see in our MS any trace of Gregorius'
handwriting.

It should be added that on fols. 222ᵛ–223ʳ, after the end of the Gospel of
St. John, Ioasaph added the *Pericope de Adultera*[373] (John 8:3–11), which
was omitted by the original scribe. On fol. 302ʳ, Ioasaph duplicated the end
of the Second Epistle of St. Peter (2 Pet. 3:18 ἡμῶν – αἰῶνος, ἀμήν:), though
it was written by the original scribe on fol. 303ʳ.

Within the next ten days Ioasaph wrote, and prefixed to the original **MS**,
additional matter on fols. 1ʳ–14ᵛ intended to facilitate the liturgical use of
the MS. On fol. 1ʳ–1ᵛ he wrote an instruction on Gospel lessons; on fols.
2ʳ–7ʳ, a Table of lessons from the Gospels, the Acts, and the Epistles for the
liturgical year (beginning with Easter Sunday); on fols. 8ʳ–14ᵛ, a Table of
lessons from the Gospels, the Acts, and the Epistles for the fixed feasts of the
calendar year (beginning September 1), i.e., a Menologion (here called Συναξάριον). The writing of fols. 1ʳ–14ᵛ by Ioasaph is certified by the subscription
of Ioasaph written on fol. 14ᵛ on 29 June A.M. 6899 = A.D. 1391, in the form
of a well-known conventional dodecasyllabic colophon (in red), characteristic
of the Ὁδηγῶν scriptorium and of Ioasaph himself, followed by the date note
proper (written in the dark brown ink used for the liturgical notes and marks
in the original MS), and a hexametric invocation, also characteristic of the
same scriptorium and used elsewhere by Ioasaph[374] (fol. 14ᵛ – Plate **126b**):

+ θ(εο)ῦ τὸ δῶρον καὶ Ἰωάσαφ πόνος + |
ἔτους ͵ϛωϞθ ἰν(δικτιῶνος) ιδ' μηνὶ ἰουνί(ῳ) κθ· ἡμέρ(ᾳ) ε̄·· |

Χ(ριστ)έ· δίδου μογήσαντι, τεὴν πολύολβον | + ἀρωγήν + | + (The whole
fol. 14ᵛ written by Ioasaph and including this subscription was reproduced
by Wilson, *Mediaeval Greek Bookhands*, pl. 71; cf. p. 33.)

To represent the writing of Ioasaph from the part of this volume written
by him in A.D. 1391, on Plate **96A** we reproduce folio 10ʳ, containing a part of
the MENOLOGION (TABLE OF LESSONS) for the days November 25–December 20
(cf. Gregory, I, pp. 371–73, under the proper dates). For another facsimile
of Ioasaph's writing from this part of the MS, cf. Wilson, *loc. cit.* By its very
nature, the addition of Ioasaph prefixed to the main body of this New Testament MS, since it contains subsidiary texts like a Synaxarion and a Menologion,
is written in a somewhat cursive, less formal, and less calligraphic manner
than Ioasaph's formal MSS. The page reproduced abounds in abbreviations,
in accordance with the conventional script of such tables of lessons. For a

---

[373] On the *Pericope de Adultera*, cf. Metzger, *The Text of the New Testament*, pp. 223f.; Aland et al.,
The Greek New Testament, pp. 355, 413–15. This pericope is marked in this MS (fol. 222ᵛ, lower
margin) εἰς μετανοοῦντας (cf. Gregory, I, p. 340, lines 17–20); the time for which this lesson is
appointed is marked in the MS (fol. 223ʳ, lower margin) ἰουλί(ου) ιβ; for dates to which this lesson is
usually assigned in MSS, cf. Gregory, I, p. 340, lines 12–15.

[374] On the dodecasyllabic colophon of Ioasaph, cf. Politis, in *BZ*, 51, pp. 19, 27–33 (esp. p. 27
under no. 4), 17–36 and 261–84 *passim*. On the above hexametric invocation used in MSS of Ioasaph
and other scribes of the scriptorium τῶν Ὁδηγῶν, cf. *ibid.*, pp. 30–32 (under nos. 19, 20, 21, 24, 28),
262 (under nos. 2, 3), 265, 277 (under no. 1); above, pp. 132, 143.

formal and calligraphic style of Ioasaph, cf. Plates **89** and **90** from MS London Burney 18 (Four Gospels, of A.D. 1366), and Plate **96** from MS Oxford, Christ Church 61 (Psalter, of A.D. 1391). The reader may compare several other published specimens of Ioasaph's writing quoted above, pp. 133f.

At the end of the MS, on fol. 424ᵛ, a 16th-century owner of this MS recorded in five successive notes the births of his five children. He indicated in each case the date of the birth, the name of the child, and the name of the baptizing priest (only in the last note was the name of the baptizer not written in). I repeat here the essentials of the notes—the year of birth, the name of the child, and the name of the baptizer: 1532, child Smaragda, baptizer Μανουὴλ ὁ Κουνοῦπης; 1534, child Alexandra, baptizer Μανουὴλ ὁ Κουνουπης; 1535, child Constantine, baptizer 'Αντώνιος, ὁ φηλῶσοφος, καὶ μέγας ῥήτωρ; 1537, child George, baptizer Μανουὴλ, Σοφιάνός; 1539, child Manuel, the baptizer's name was not indicated. Of the baptizers mentioned, 'Αντώνιος, μέγας ῥήτωρ (viz., of the Patriarchate in Constantinople), is otherwise known.[375] The reference to him above is proof that in 1535 the owner of this MS resided in Constantinople and that, by the same token, the MS was in 1535 and possibly in 1539 still in Constantinople. If, as art historians assert, the illuminations of this MS were executed early in the 12th century in Constantinople and the MS, therefore, was written about the same time in Constantinople, this shows that the MS remained in Constantinople for at least four centuries, certainly until 1535. Manuel Sophianus, mentioned above in the note of 1537, belonged apparently to the Sophianus family which originated in Constantinople and settled later in Chios. We know of a few members of the Sophianus family in Chios, like the humanist Michael Sophianus, who died shortly before or in 1565; Manuel Sophianus, merchant, heir of Michael Sophianus; Theodorus Sophianus, who owned a few MSS which are now in the Ambrosian Library in Milan. MSS of Michael Sophianus and his heir, Manuel Sophianus, were brought from Chios in 1606 and acquired by the Ambrosian Library.[376]

On the upper cover of the binding (of the 16th or 17th century), there is an ivory plaque of the 10th century, probably from Constantinople, representing Christ Pantocrator. The original background of this plaque has been replaced by a more recent silver one which shows an incised inscription in capital letters. It is an invocation in Greek on behalf of Hieronymus Wilhelm (viz., Ebner von Eschenbach, the 18th-century owner of the MS) and his family: ΔΕΣΠΟΤΑ ΕΥΛΟΓΗΣΟΝ | ΤΟΝ ΔΟΥΛΟΝ ΣΟΥ ΕΛΑΧΙΣΤΟΝ | ΙΕΡΟΝΥΜΟΝ ΙΟΥ-ΛΙΕΛΜΟΝ ΚΑΙ ΤΗΝ ΟΙΚΙΑΝ ΑΥΤΟΥ. This inscription was engraved before 1738, when M. Conradus Schoenleben reproduced the upper cover of the MS which already showed the inscription (*Notitia egregii codicis graeci Novi Testamenti manuscripti qvem Noribergae servat vir illvstris Hieronymvs Gvilelmvs Ebner ab Eschenbach* [Nuremberg, 1738], pl. [i]). Specifically on the ivory fixed on the upper cover of this MS, cf. C. Diehl, *Manuel d'art byzantin*, 2nd ed., II (Paris, 1926), p. 666, fig. 328 (on p. 668); A. Goldschmidt and K. Weitzmann, *Die byzantinischen Elfenbeinskulpturen des X.–XIII. Jahrhunderts*, II (Berlin, 1934), pp. 43f. (under no. 62), pl. xxiv, 62; *Masterpieces of Byzantine Art*, Edinburgh International Festival 1958 (Edinburgh–London [1958]), p. 57 (no. 159); or *ibid.*, 2nd ed. (Edinburgh, 1958), p. 56 (no. 159); D. Talbot Rice, *The Art of Byzantium* (New York [1959]), pl. 107, p. 315 (under no. 107); D. Mouriki, in *Byzantine Art an European Art*, pp. 164 (no. 62), 524 (no. 62).

---

[375] On 'Αντώνιος (probably Καρμαλῆς or Καρμαλίκης), grand rhetor of the Patriarchate in Constantinople from 1532 until at least 1537, cf. Ch. G. Patrineles, Οἱ μεγάλοι ῥήτορες Μανουὴλ Κορίνθιος, 'Αντώνιος, Μανουὴλ Γαλησιώτης καὶ ὁ χρόνος τῆς ἀκμῆς των, in Δελτ.'Ιστ.'Εθν.'Ετ., 16 (1962), pp. 17–38; *idem*, in Θρησκ.'Ηθ.'Εγκυκλ., II, cols. 998f. (under no. 7).

On the office of μέγας ῥήτωρ of the Patriarchate, cf. F. Fuchs, *Die höheren Schulen von Konstantinopel im Mittelalter*, ByzArch, 8 (Leipzig–Berlin, 1926; repr. Amsterdam, 1964), pp. 40f., 57, 75; J. Darrouzès, *Recherches sur les ὀφφίκια de l'Eglise byzantine*, AOC, 11 (Paris, 1970), Index, p. 610, *s.v.* rhètôr.

[376] On Michael Sophianus, cf. E. Legrand, *Bibliographie hellénique ou description raisonnée des ouvrages publiés en grec par des Grecs aux XVᵉ et XVIᵉ siècles*, II (Paris, 1885; repr. 1962), pp. 168–76; Vogel–Gardthausen, pp. 320f.; on his heir, Manuel Sophianus, cf. Legrand, *op. cit.*, II, pp. 175f. On Michael, Manuel, and Theodorus Sophianus, and on MSS of the Sophianus family now in the Ambrosian Library at Milan, cf. Ae. Martini and D. Bassi, *Catalogus codicum graecorum Bibliothecae Ambrosianae* (Milan, 1906), I, pp. xvf.; II, Index, p. 1276, *s.v.* Sophianus.

This MS was once owned by Hieronymus Wilhelm Ebner von Eschenbach (1673–1752), scholar and statesman in Nuremberg.[377] From the name of this owner, the MS was called by New Testament scholars "codex Ebnerianus." While it was in the possession of Ebner, its detailed description was published by Schoenleben (*op. cit.*, 44 pp. and 12 pls.). This publication was reprinted by Chr. Th. de Mvrr, *Memorabilia bibliothecarvm publicarvm Norimbergensivm et Vniversitatis Altdorfinae*, II (Nuremberg, 1788), pp. 100–31 and plates (reproduced from Schoenleben). The MS was bought by the Bodleian Library from Payne and Foss[378] of London in 1819.

On this MS, cf. Coxe, I, cols. 703–5 (under Misc. Gr. 136; the former shelfmark was Auct.C. subtus); *Summary Catalogue*, V, p. 412 (under S.C. 28118); Vogel–Gardthausen, p. 215; Scrivener, I, p. 208 (under Evan. 105); Gregory, I, p. 152 (under Vier Evangelien 105); Aland, I, p. 66 (under the Gregory–Aland number 105); von Soden, I,1, p. 107 (under δ257); L. Politis, *BZ*, 51 (1958), pp. 30f. (under no. 22); Barbour, in *Greek Manuscripts in the Bodleian Library*, p. 43 (under no. 80); Belting, *Das illuminierte Buch*, p. 56; Wilson, *Mediaeval Greek Bookhands*, pp. 24f. (under nos. 44, 45), p. 33 (under no. 71), pls. 44, 45, 71. On the MS illuminations specifically, cf. O. Pächt, *Byzantine Illumination*, Bodleian Picture Book No. 8 (Oxford [1952]), pp. 7, 8, 9, pls. 3, 8, 9*b*, 11, 17; J. Beckwith, *The Art of Constantinople* (Greenwich, Conn. [1961]; repr. London–New York [1968]), pp. 125f., fig. 166; Mouriki, in *Byzantine Art an European Art*, pp. 307 (no. 296), 542 (no. 296), pl. 296; C. Meredith, "The Illustrations of Codex Ebnerianus. A Study in Liturgical Illustration of the Comnenian Period," *JWarb*, 29 (1966), pp. 419–24, pls. 69, 70.

---

[377] On Hieronymus Wilhelm Ebner von Eschenbach, cf. J. Ch. Adelung, *Fortsetzung und Ergänzungen zu Christian Gottlieb Jöchers allgemeinem Gelehrten-Lexico*, II (Leipzig, 1787), cols. 812f.; *ADB*, V, pp. 593f.

[378] On Payne and Foss, booksellers in London, cf. de Ricci, *English Collectors*, pp. 92f.; also cf. above, p. 121 and note 317.

GENERAL INDEX

by

ELIZABETH BRYSON BONGIE

Ordinary figures refer to text pages; **boldface** figures refer to plates.

abbreviations: of ending -αν in script of Romanus ⟨Chartophylax⟩, 88 and note 247, **57, 58**; – in foundation typica, lack of, 5, **1**; in liturgical typica, abundance of, 5; – in scriptural MSS, lack of, 26; in scholarly additament to a scriptural MS, abundance of, 96, **65**; – in students' cursive (in philosophical MSS), 26, **13**; – in tables of lessons (Menologia), 148, **96A**; – *see* prefixes

accents and breathings: marked above first vowel of diphthongs in Cypriot scripts, 87f. and note 246, **57, 58**; – marked in ordinal numeral letters, 3 note 1, **97**, 71, **110a**, 137f., **124a**, 143 and note 368a, **125**; – *see* breathings

ἀδρανής, adjective used by scribes, 15

Advocates, Faculty of, in Edinburgh: *see* Faculty of Advocates, Edinburgh

Agathias, epigram on Plutarch, translated into Latin elegiacs by Victor Falchonius, 117

Agen (in southwest France), Jesuit College, owner, 131

αἰχμάλωτος, meaning "refugee," 127

Albrecht V, duke of Bavaria, owner, 124

Alefson, G., owner, 100

Alexius Metochites: *see* Metochites, Alexius

alphabet, cryptographic: *see* cryptography; – πε(ρὶ) τῆς ἀλφαβήτ(ου), later insert, 74

Ambrosian Library in Milan, acquisition of MSS: *see* Sophianus, Manuel

ἀμήν, as final word of the Gospel of John, 64 note 159

Ananias the Priest, Peter the Jailer, and Seven Soldiers in Phoenicia, Passion of, 70, **48**

ἀναπτεῖν, possibly for ἀναπτύσσειν, 101

Anastasius Sinaita, St., Ὁδηγός (Viae dux), 49, 53, **31**, 55, **37, 38b**, (incomplete) 101

ἀναθεματισμός, abjuration, against Jacobites, 49

Andreas of Brindisi, notary, addressed in a poem by Nicholas-Nectarius of Otranto, 33 note 86; – *see* next entry

Andreas of Brindisi, scribe (A.D. 1284), 31–33, **21, 102d, 102e**

Andrew of Crete, Canon for Mid-Pentecost, 141, **95**

Andronicus II Palaeologus, emperor, chrysobull to the Metropolitan of Ioannina, 9f.; – his stay in Nymphaeum, 50f.

Anna the Younger, nun, renamed Euphemianus, Life of (*BHG*[3] 2027), 131 and note 334, **88**

ἀνθιβόλιον, for ἀντιβόλαιον, meaning "exemplar," "source," 109 and note 300

Antiochus, monk of the Laura of St. Sabas, Exomologesis, 56; – Pandectes Sacrae Scripturae (with incomplete beginning), 56f., **40**

Antonius ⟨Καρμαλῆς or Καρμαλίκης⟩: *see* ⟨Καρμαλῆς or Καρμαλίκης⟩, Antonius

ἀπ' ἐμοῦ, variant reading in the Gospel lesson of Matthew 26:42, 11

Aphthonius, Progymnasmata, 71

Apocaucus, John, metropolitan of Naupactus, a decree of, 16

Apophthegmata Patrum (Λειμωνάριον), 128f., **85, 86**

Apostles and Disciples, Index of: *see* Dorotheus of Tyre*

ἀπόστολος: *see* Bible: New Testament, lectionary of the Acts and the Epistles; – term ἀπόστολος (i.e., lectionary of the Acts and the Epistles), used for πραξαπόστολος (i.e., text of the Acts and the Epistles) adapted for liturgical use, 146f.

Arabic note in MS, 35

Aratus, Phaenomena (with scholia, subsidiary texts, and Planudean interpolations), edited and written by Maximus Planudes, vii, 57–59 ἀρχιερωσύνη, term of address for a bishop or archbishop, 36

ἄρχων, term used for a governor of Bagenetia, 16; – ἄρχοντες, term used for local Greek aristocracy in Venetian-dominated Crete, 75

Arethas of Caesarea, marginal marks of, 140 note 362

Aristotle, Eudemian Ethics, 25 f., **13**; – Nicomachean Ethics, 25; – *Magna Moralia, 25; – *Oeconomics, 25; – MS-tradition of these texts, 26 and note 76

Armenian Prophetologion, fragments (in palimpsest, scriptura inferior), 141

Arsenius, hieromonk, name recorded in MS, 107

Arundel: *see* Howard, Henry; – Howard, Thomas

Ashburnham Library, 42 note 99a

Askew, Anthony, owner, 96; – identification of his MSS, 96 note 270

Ἀσώματος, place-name in Cyprus, 98; – *see* St. Michael ἐν τῷ Ἀνάπλῳ, church or monastery of

asterisks in a subscription, 16, **99c**

Athanasius, owner, 35

Athanasius of Alexandria, St., Writings, 84, 87 f., **57, 58**; – *editio Commeliniana*, 84, 89; – Latin translation by Pieter Nanninck (Nannius), 88 f.

Athos: *see* Pantocrator, monastery of; – Philotheus, monastery of

Attaleiates, Michael, Law Treatise, 48, 54, **36**

Augustine, St., De Trinitate (translated into Greek by Manuel-Maximus Planudes), 42 note 99a, 107 f., **75**

Βαγενετία, a region of Epirus, 16; – Μικρὰ Βαγενετία, perhaps a lower administrative subdivision of Bagenetia, 15 f.; – Μεγάλη Βαγενιτεία, 16

Bagge, H., owner, 19

Βαϊονέα (probably Vainiá in Crete), village mentioned in a note in MS, 138

Balsamon, Theodore, Responsa ad interrogationes Marci patriarchae Alexandrini, 115, **78**

Barocci (or Barozzi), Giacomo, owner, xxix, 28, 63, 112, 115, 127, 141

Bartholomia, nun, death of, recorded in a note (A.D. 1636 in Julian calendar), 46

Basil I Comnenus, emperor of Trebizond, arrival in Trebizond (A.D. 1335) commemorated in a poem, 45 f.

Basil the Great, St.: Liturgy of, 8; – Sermo asceticus et exhortatio de renuntiatione saeculi et de perfectione spirituali, 63; – Sermo de ascetica disciplina, quomodo monachum ornari oporteat, 63; – letter to St. Gregory of Nazianzus, 116; – prayers from the Office of Genuflection, attributed to, 64

Basilius of Paphos, priest, teacher, notary, scribe (A.D. 1214), 3, 5 f., **1, 97**

Βαθύ, τὸ, place-name, frequent in modern Greece, 98

Βάτου, monastery (of the Burning Bush) on Mt. Sinai, 140

Bentley, Richard, owner, 82 and note 218

Bible

1. Old Testament:

Psalms, passages from, 3; – Psalms and Odes (of the Old and New Testaments), 31 f., **21**, 100, **68**, 142 f., **96**

Prophetologion (lectionary of the Old Testament), 38; fragments, 118; fragments (in palimpsest, scriptura inferior), 106; fragments (in palimpsest, scriptura superior), 112; fragments of an Armenian Prophetologion (in palimpsest, scriptura inferior), 141

2. New Testament:

New Testament, adapted for liturgical use, 120, **81**; – without the Apocalypse, adapted for liturgical use, 79, 81, **55**, 131; 12th-century MS adapted for liturgical use (in A.D. 1391), Codex Ebnerianus, 146–50, **96A**

Four Gospels, adapted for liturgical use, 42 f., **26**, 44 f., **27**, 60 ff., **43**, 64–66, **45**, 67 f., **46**, 89 f., **59**, 91 f., **60**, 92, 94 ff., **61–65**, 103 f., **71**, 104 f., **72**, 131 ff., **89, 90**; Four Gospels, partially adapted for liturgical use, 20–22, **8a–10b**; – modifications of the beginnings of passages adapted for liturgical use, 43 and note 100, 67, 81, 90, 94–96, 132; – *Pericope de Adultera*, 92, 148 and note 373

Acts of the Apostles and the Epistles (Praxapostolus), adapted for liturgical use, 72 f., **50**, 125 f., **83**; a MS destroyed in World War II, 131 f.; a MS lost, or listed by error of scribe, 61

Epistle to the Hebrews, 131

Apocalypse, 64

Odes of the Old and New Testaments: *see above* Bible, Old Testament, *under* Psalms and Odes

lectionaries of the Gospels, 15, 16f., **5**, 17, **6**, 20, **7**, 23, **11**, 82, **56**, 98f., **67**, (scriptura inferior) 106, 112; – εὐαγγέλιον, meaning "lectionary of the Gospels," 98, 146f.; – lectionary of the Acts and the Epistles (ἀπόστολος), 69, **47**; – modification of the standard text for lesson use, 18, 69; – lectionaries in two columns, 16f., **5**, 17f., **6**, 20, **7**, 23, **11**, 82f., **56**; – in one column (irregular), 69, **47**, 99, **67**; – see prefixes: lesson prefixes in Gospel lectionaries and New Testament MSS adapted for liturgical use; – see also τελεία sign

Biblical Writings

1. on Old Testament:

Genesis: see Chrysostom, St. John, Homilies on Genesis

Psalms: see Hesychius of Jerusalem, Commentary on the Psalms; – Chrysostom, St. John, Expositiones in Psalmos; – Zigabenus, Euthymius, Commentary on the Psalms and Odes

2. on New Testament:

Tables of lessons from N.T. for the calendar year: see Menologion; – tables of lessons for the Four Gospels, 92; – see Theophylact, abp. of Bulgaria, Commentary on the Four Gospels; – see Chrysocephalus, Michael-Macarius, Catena on the Gospel of St. Matthew (Book I); – Gospel of St. Mark, Hypothesis and List of Chapters, 96, **65**; – Gospel of St. John, comments on, 3; – Sermon on St. Paul, 1 Corinthians 15:28, 49; – see Chrysostom, St. John, Homilies on St. Paul's First Epistle to the Corinthians; – see Eusebius of Caesarea; – see Prodromus, Theodore, Tetrastichs on the New Testament

Biblical MSS, script style in: see script styles under conservative style in scriptural and liturgical MSS

bindings: characteristic of books owned by Johann Jakob Fugger, 124 and note 328; characteristic of certain MSS of the Dominican library of San Marco in Florence, 121 and note 317; – decorated, velvet with gold plaquettes in relief, 134; with ivory plaque of the 10th century, 149; with gilt-stamped floral designs, 17f.; – with ownership entries, 18

Blachoules, Nikolaos, owner, 19

Blastares, Matthew, Syntagma with its appendix, 134–36, **91, 92**

Bodleian Library (Oxford), acquisition of MSS: see Barocci (or Barozzi), Giacomo; – Canonici, Matteo Luigi; – Clarke, Edward Daniel; – Coke, Thomas, of Holkham, Earl of Leicester; – Coke, Thomas William, Earl of Leicester; – Coke, Thomas William Edward, 5th Earl of Leicester; – Cromwell, Oliver; – Ebner von Eschenbach, Hieronymus Wilhelm; – Herbert, William; – Holkham MSS; – Huntington, Robert; – Laud, William, archbishop of Canterbury; – Libri-Carrucci, Guglielmo; – Lillo (Lille), Sir Henry; – Lyell, James P. R.; – Roe, Sir Thomas; – Rose, W. F.; – Saibante, Giovanni; – Saibante, Giulio; – Selden, John

Bohn, John, bookseller in London, 90

bombycine (Oriental paper): MSS written on, 28, 33, 55, 56, 57, 60, 74, 79, 83, 84 note 228, 97, 98, 107, 122; – βαμβίκινα, term used in a 16th-century catalogue for Oriental or Western paper MSS without distinction, 76 note 197

booksellers: see Bohn, John; – Boone; – Celotti, Luigi; – Conant of Fleet Street; – Giegler, G. P.; – Payne, John Thomas; – Payne and Foss; – Rosenthal, A.; – Salvi, C.; – Thorpe, Thomas

Boone, English bookseller, 100

Bossi, Giuseppe, painter in Milan, owner, 41f.

breathings, angular and rectangular (archaistic feature), 21, **9a**; – angular and round style of Demetrius Triclines (or Triclinius), 71, (round breathings) **49, 110a**; – see accents and breathings

Brindisi (Terra d'Otranto, South Italy), MS from the area of, 31f., **21, 102d, 102e**

British Museum (London), acquisition of MSS, 15; – see Alefson, G.; – Askew, Anthony; – Bagge, H.; – Boone; – Burney, Charles; – Butler, Samuel; – Coxe, Henry Octavius; – Curzon, Darea; – Giannacopulo, N.; – Guest, Ivor Bertie; – Harley, Edward; – Harley, Robert; – Howard, Henry; – Howard, Thomas; – Jackson, John; – Parassoh, Nicolas

Brizopulus, Demetrius, lector, scribe (A.D. 1253), 15, **5, 99c**

Burgon, John W., dean of Chichester, owner, 90 and note 259

Burney, Charles, owner, 44, 62, 83, 129, 134

Butler, Samuel, bp. of Lichfield, owner, 92, 121 and note 317

Calabria (South Italy), MS from, 26

calendar: various lists of the months, 57; – lists of the months according to various calendars, 117; – ecclesiastic calendar, notes referring to, 108; – hagiographic iambic calendar: *see* Christopher of Mytilene; – reform of calendar by Julius Caesar, a note on, 57

Callierges, Alexius, treaty of Venice with (A.D. 1299), 139 note 359

calligraphy: in foundation typica, 5, **1**; – conventional calligraphy in scriptural and liturgical MSS, viii, 26, 68, **46**, 83 and note 223, **56**, 93–95, **61, 62**, 99, **67**; – *see also* Cyprus *under* script style; Planudes, Manuel-Maximus, *under* "Planudean" script style; Θεοτόκου τῶν Ὁδηγῶν, monastery, in CP. *under* script style

Callinicus, hieromonk and archimandrite of a monastery of St. Demetrius ὁ Μυροβλύτης, sponsor, 91

Cambridge University Library, acquisition of MSS: *see* Cummings, J. C.; – George I, king of England; – Moore, John

Canonici, Matteo Luigi, owner, 130, 142

canons, liturgical: *see* Andrew of Crete, Canon for Mid-Pentecost; – Metrophanes of Smyrna, Triadic Canons; – Nicetas of Maroneia, incomplete commentary on the initial part of the Resurrectional Canons of the Octoechus; – Prodromus, Theodore, Commentary on the Canons of Cosmas of Maïuma and St. John of Damascus; – Theotocarion; – Zonaras, John, Commentary on the Resurrectional Canons of the Octoechus

Carlyle, Joseph Dacre, owner, 126

Casandrenus, Demetrius-Daniel, of Thessalonica, sponsor, 129f., 147

catenae: Michael-Macarius Chrysocephalus, Catena on the Gospel of St. Matthew, Book I, 113f., **77**

Celotti, Luigi, bookseller, 41f.

censure, ecclesiastical (δεσμός), to be imposed on those who would purloin a MS, 35f., 80, 144, 145; – in form of excommunication, 24, 79; *see* Holy Trinity, monastery of, τοῦ Ἐσόπτρου, in Chalce

Cephalonia, 18 and note 48, 19

chain marks in Western paper, 13 note 32

Chalce: *see* Holy Trinity, monastery of, τοῦ Ἐσόπτρου, in Chalce

Chalcondyles, Demetrius, 118

Chandax (Ἡράκλειον) in Crete, 128 and note 333b

Charases, Constantinus, priest, scribe (A.D. 1383), 141 and note 363, **95, 124b**

⟨Chartophylax⟩, Romanus, lector, scribe (A.D. 1320/1321), 83 note 225, 84, 85; 86 and notes 240, 243, 244; 87f., **57, 58, 112b**; – family name, 86 and note 244

Chios, island, reference in subscription, 80, **111c**

Chomatenus, Demetrius, abp. of Bulgaria, letter to Demetrius, bp. of Butrinto, 10 note 20; – Canonical Responses to Constantine Cabasilas of Dyrrhachium, 136 and note 351

Choniates, Nicetas, Works, viii; – History, a part in its earliest version containing the fragment De statuis Constantinopolitanis, 47f., 53, **29**; – Panoplia dogmatica (or Thesaurus orthodoxiae), 47, 53f., **28, 30, 32–35, 38a**, 55 and note 126; – Index to Panoplia dogmatica, a 14th-century addition in a MS, 47

χωρικός, meaning "inexperienced," referring to a scribe, 8, 101, 102

Chortaites, monastery at, near Thessalonica, owner, 107

Christ Church, Oxford, acquisition of MSS: *see* Wake, William

Christopher of Mytilene, iambic distich from hagiographic iambic calendar attributed to, 142, **95**

Χριστοφορος (? a monogram), γραμματικός, writer (A.D. 1619) of a note in a MS, 4 note 3

Chrysocephalus, Michael-Macarius, metropolitan of Philadelphia, scribe (A.D. 1344) and author, 113–15; – Catena on the Gospel of St. Matthew, Book I, compiler of, 113f., **77, 117b**; – Life of Meletius Galesiotes (*BHG*³ 1246a), 34 note 90a

Chrysostom, St. John, Expositiones in Psalmos 108–17, 33–35, **23, 24**; – Expositiones in Psalmos 119–50, 33; – Homilies on Genesis, 106f., **74**; – Homilies on St. Paul's First Epistle to the Corinthians, 42 note 99a; – *Sermo catecheticus in Sanctum Pascha, 78; – Liturgy of, 8; – Translation of the Relics of St. John Chrysostom (from the Synaxarion of Constantinople: cf. *BHG*³ 877e), 70, **48**

Chumnus, Stelianus, scribe (A.D. 1357/1358), 122f., **82, 119b**; – family, 122 note 318 churches: *see* Ἁγία Κυριακή; – St. George; – St. Gregory of Nyssa; – St. Mark; – St. Michael ἐν τῷ Ἀνάπλῳ; – St. Philip

Clarentza (Peloponnesus) or Chiarentza, now called Κυλλήνη, MS from, 101, **69, 70, 114a**

Clarke, Edward Daniel, owner, 17

Clement, abbot of Sinai, 36 note 90b

Clement Monomachus, monk: *see* Monomachus, Clement, monk

Cleomedes, Circular Theory of the Stars, 57–59, **41, 42**

codicology: *see* bombycine (Oriental paper); – chain marks; – laid marks; – palimpsests; – paper (i.e., Western paper); – parchment; – quire; – watermarks: *see* paper (i.e., Western paper) *under* without watermarks

Coke, Thomas, of Holkham, Earl of Leicester, owner, 12

Coke, Thomas William, Earl of Leicester, owner, 13

Coke, Thomas William Edward, 5th Earl of Leicester, owner, 13

Colbert, Jean-Baptiste, owner, 84f.

Collectio constitutionum ecclesiasticarum Tripartita, marginal excerpts in a MS of Law Treatise of Michael Attaleiates, 48 note 115, 54f., **36**

Collectio LXXXVII capitulorum, marginal excerpts in a MS of Law Treatise of Michael Attaleiates, 48 note 115

Collectio XXV capitulorum, marginal excerpts in a MS of Law Treatise of Michael Attaleiates, 48 note 115

colophons: written in a contorted manner, 35; – *see* monocondylia. – *See* subscription commonplaces (*especially under* metrical, characteristic of MSS from the scriptorium of the monastery Θεοτόκου τῶν Ὁδηγῶν); – subscriptions, cryptographic; – subscriptions, ownership entries, and scribal notes, metrical; – verses of scribes, owners, users. *See also* colors *under* use of red in subscriptions

colors, use of, in MSS: color combinations, in MSS of South Italian origin (red, blue, green, gold, and white), 32; in MSS from the monastery Θεοτόκου τῶν Ὁδηγῶν in Constantinople (red and gold), 120, 133; red and gold, 100; – use of color blobs in round, oval, or triangular letters or parts thereof, in MSS of South Italian origin, (red) 26, 32; in MSS of non-South Italian

origin, (red) 14 and note 37; in MSS of non-specified origin, (red) 94, (yellow) 14, 96 and note 269; – use of color wash over noteworthy elements, (yellow) 14, 70 and note 179; in MSS from Epirus, (yellow) 8, 16f.; – use of separate colors for text (red) of Psalms and commentary (black), 24, 27; – use of red for table of contents, 78; for author's name, 4, 136, 140; for headpieces, 12; for τίτλοι of κεφάλαια, 21, 94, 95 (twice), 104; for marginal notes like ἑρμ(η)νεία, 27; – use of red for liturgical notes in New Testament MSS adapted for liturgical use and in New Testament lectionaries, 18, 21, 43, 45, 67, 69, 73, 81, 90, 91, 94f., 103f.; use of brown, 148; use of red and gold, 120, 133; normal use of black for Eusebian section number when followed by Eusebian canon number in red, 81 and note 217; exceptional use of black for τ(έ)λ(ος), 95, for Eusebian canon number, 81 and note 217; use of red for Eusebian section numbers alone (when not followed by Eusebian canon numbers), 45, 93f., 95, 96, 104, 105; use of black for Eusebian section numbers (alone), 67; – use of red for prefixes, rubrics, or noteworthy elements in liturgical hymnbooks, 13, 74, 142; – use of red for signs, (crescents) 140, (crosses) 45, (thick dots as stop marks) 143, (τελεία marks) 83; – use of red in projected initials (mostly capitals), to mark the beginning of a new sentence or of a new section in the same line or in the preceding line or to emphasize a sentence, 22, 30f., 45, 63, 67, 73, 78, 81, 83, 97, 105, 107, 119, (red and gold) 120, (red and gold) 133; to mark the beginning of a Gospel lesson, 90, 91, 104, (red and black) 18; to mark the beginning of versicles in Psalms, 29, (red and several colors) 32, (red and gold) 100; to mark the beginning of comments on Psalms, 29; to mark the beginning of a troparion, 41, 142; – use of red for non-projected initials, to mark the beginning of sections, 140; to mark the beginning of a Gospel lesson, 94; to mark significant words in headings of a liturgical book, 41; to mark the beginnings of εἱρμοί, 41; to mark the beginning of a line of verse, 50; – use of red in subscriptions, 12, 14, 17, 21, 23, 25, 31, 43, (retraced in black) 50, 67, 69, 71, 72, 74 (twice), 85, 91, 101, 103, 116, 131, 141, 146,

148, (in scribal note) 118; use of brown ink in subscriptions, 89, 148; – use of red in Latin ownership entry, 117; use of brown in Latin ownership entry, 123; – use of red in an invocation, 118; – use of red in a colophon, 30; – correction (particle μή) added in red above the line, 118; – failure of rubricator to fill in space left for him, 93, **113a**, 104, **114c**; – see projection

Colybas, Paulus, of Modon, owner, 24

Commelin, Jérôme, 89; – see Athanasius of Alexandria, St., *under editio Commeliniana*

Comnenus, Basil I, emperor of Trebizond: *see* Basil I Comnenus

Conant of Fleet Street, bookseller in London, 104

Constantine Palaeologus Porphyrogenitus, brother of the emperor Andronicus II Palaeologus, 51 and notes 122, 123

Constantinople: MSS from, 50f., **28–39, 106,** 57–59, **41, 42, 105c,** 61, 64, 108, **76, 115c–f, 116a–e, 117a,** 120f., **81, 119a,** 122f., **82, 119b,** 126, **83, 120a,** 131–34, **89, 90, 122b,** 141, **95, 124b,** 142f., **96, 125,** 146–49, **96A, 126a, 126b;** – earthquake in CP. (A.D. 447), 70; notes on earthquakes in CP. (A.D. 1343), 108f. and note 299; – notes written in CP. on the events of A.D. 1422–1425, 116; – script styles: *see* Planudes, Manuel-Maximus, *under* "Planudean" script style; – Θεοτόκου τῶν Ὁδηγῶν, monastery in CP., script style

Constantinus of Adrianople, scribe (A.D. 1337), 103, **71, 114b**

Constantinus Charases, scribe: *see* Charases, Constantinus

Constantinus Magedon, scribe: *see* Magedon, Constantinus

Constantinus Pastil, scribe: *see* Pastil, Constantinus

Constantinus Sophus, scribe: *see* Sophus, Constantinus

Constantius, monk, κανδηλάπτης, note in MS, 145

Contostephanus, Ioannes, of Constantinople, sponsor, 122

Conybeare, F. C., note in MS, 141

Cosmas of Maïuma, Commentary on the Canons of, by Theodore Prodromus, 126f., **84**

Covel, John, owner, 29, 89; – notes in MS, 28

Coxe, Henry Octavius, owner, 68; – note in MS, 66f., 68

Creed, Niceno-Constantinopolitan, 146

crescent marks (in red), to indicate carry-over from preceding lines, 140, **93**

Crete: MSS from, 74, **52, 110d,** 128f., **85, 86, 120b, 120c,** 137–41, **93, 94, 124a;** – the St. Titus revolt against Venice (A.D. 1363–1364), 138f. and note 356; – dialect: *see* Greek language; – *see* Preveli, monastery of the B.V.M.; Θεοτόκου τῆς Παντανάσσης, church and convent, in Crete; Θεοτόκου τῆς Σπηλαιωτίσσης, monastery of the Assumption, in Crete

Cromwell, Oliver, owner, 11, 78

crosslike sign beneath a numeral letter, symbol for thousands, 145 note 368c

Crusius, Martin: *see* Gerlach, Stephan

cryptography, conventional, 56 and note 128, **105b,** 65f., **108,** 78, **111a,** 108f., **115d,** 110 and note 302, **116d,** 111, **117a**

Cucubistianus, Nilus, priest, scribe (A.D. 1285), 38–41, **25, 104;** – family name, 39f. and note 93

Cummings, C. J., owner, 103

curses against book thieves: *see* censure, ecclesiastical

Curzon, Darea, Baroness Zouche, owner, 22

Curzon, Robert, 14th Baron Zouche, owner, 22

Curzon, Robert Nathaniel Cecil George, 15th Baron Zouche, owner, 22

cycles, solar and lunar, 60f. and notes 143, 144; 63 and note 155, 65 and note 163

Cyprus: MSS from, 3–6, **1, 97,** 50 note 118, 66–68, **46, 109a,** 82f., **56, 112a,** 83–88, **57, 58, 112b,** 98–100, **67, 113c;** – script style, Cypriot calligraphy, 5 and note 5a, **1, 97,** 67f., 82f., **56, 112a,** 98–100, **67, 113c;** "notarial," 85, 87f., **57, 58, 112b;** accent, or breathing, or breathing and accent marks placed above the first vowel of a diphthong, or breathing placed above the first vowel of the diphthong and accent above the second vowel, 87f., **57, 58;** – dating practices: omission of the millenary letter in dates, 82, **112a;** use of the Christian era, 35, 84; use of ἐγχρονίας for ἔτους, 35, 82, **112a;** – dialect: *see* Greek language. – *See* Encleistra, monastery, in Cyprus

Cyril, abbot, Enigmas, 49

⟨Damenus⟩, Nicolaus, lector at the Hours, scribe (A.D. 1279), 25f., **13, 101b**

Damilas, Nilus, founder of the convent Θεοτόκου τῆς Παντανάσσης in Βαϊοναία in Crete, 138 note 355

Daniel of Rhaithu, Life of St. John Climacus (*BHG*³ 882), 118

Darias, Georgius, lector, scribe (A.D. 1255/1256), 17 and 173 (*Corrigendum*), **6, 100a**

dating: discrepancies, 14, 32, 39, 50, 63, 89, 92f., 137, 139; – indication of the hour in subscriptions of MSS from South Italy, 32; – omission of the millenary letter in dates written in Cyprus, 82; – use of the Christian era in dates written in Cyprus, 35, 84; – use of a crosslike mark beneath a numeral letter, symbol for thousands, 145 note 368c

decoration in MSS: headpieces, 12, 14, 42, 44, 60, 91, (in the form of a πύλη) 120; – initial capitals, 18, **6**, (doubly traced) 101, **114a**; – leaf ornament favored by scribe Nicolaus Damenus, 25, **101b**

Demetrius, bp. of Butrinto (Buthrotum), letter quoted by Demetrius Chomatenus, 10 note 20

Demetrius, γραμματικός, of Thessalonica, father of the monk Dositheus, 62

Demetrius Brizopulus, scribe: *see* Brizopulus, Demetrius

Demetrius Κημηνίτζης: *see* Κημηνίτζης, Demetrius

Demetrius Triclines (or Triclinius) of Thessalonica, scribe and scholar: *see* Triclines (or Triclinius), Demetrius

δεσμός, meaning "ecclesiastical censure," 36; – *see* censure, ecclesiastical, to be imposed on those who would purloin a MS

διαδωρίτης, of unknown meaning, 39

Diamantakes, of Ἀσώματοι on the Bosporus (near Constantinople), owner, 18

διδασκάλου, τοῦ πανευγενεστάτου, meaning "professor," 122

Dietrichstein, Prince Ferdinand von, owner, 76 note 197

Dominic of Grado, patriarch, Epistle to Patriarch Peter of Antioch, 49

Dorotheus of Tyre*, Index of the Apostles and the Disciples (cf. *BHG*³ 151 and *BHG Auct.* 152b, pars posterior), 72; Index of the 72 Disciples (*BHG*³ 152n), 79, 80 note 209

Dositheus, monk, son of the γραμματικός Demetrius of Thessalonica, owner, 62

double dots, a decorative element, not an expunction or cancellation mark, 64f., **108**

δρόγγος (δροῦγγος), meaning of, 8–10

Ducas, Theodore Angelus, ruler of Epirus, reference in a subscription, 11

earthquakes in Constantinople (A.D. 1343), notes on, 108f. and note 299; – commemoration of the earthquake of A.D. 447, 70

Easter, the date of (A.D. 1292), 60f.

Ebner von Eschenbach, Hieronymus Wilhelm, owner, 149f.

ecclesiastical censure to be imposed on those who would purloin a MS: *see* censure, ecclesiastical

eclipses: lunar (22 August 1290), vii, 57, 58; – solar (5 May 1361), 137, 139

Edinburgh, National Library of Scotland, acquisition of MSS, 59

Edinburgh University Library, acquisition of MSS, 6f.

ἐκκλησιάρχης, ecclesiastical office, 135

ἔκθεσις, μετ' ἐκθέσεως: *see* projection

Elias of Crete, scholium on Gregory of Nazianzus, 54, **35**

ἐγχρον(ίας), or εχρον(ίας), used for ἔτους, in dates written in Cyprus, 35, 82

Encleistra, monastery, in Cyprus, 3; – library, 5; – Typicon of, 3–7, **1**

ἐνορία, meaning "jurisdiction," 10

Eon, Chevalière d' (Charles G. L. A. A. T. d'Eon de Beaumont), owner, 83

Ephesus, note in MS on the capture of, by the Turks on 24 October 1304, 75; – *see* Mt. Galesion

ἐπιδρομή (for συνδρομή), meaning "contribution to the cost of producing a MS," 40

epigrams, Greek Anthology, 117; – Agathias' epigram on Plutarch, translated into Latin by Victor Falchonius, 117

Epirus: MSS from, 7–11, **2, 98a**, 15–17, **5, 99c**; – *see* Βαγενετία; Tzemernikos

ἐπληρώθη, meaning of, 146f.

εὐαγγέλιον, lectionary of the Gospels, 98, 147

εὐχὴ συγχωρητική, "an absolution prayer," 37

Euergetinus, Paul: *see* Paul Euergetinus

εὐγενέστατος ἄρχων, term of address, 75

Eusebian section and canon numbers in New Testament MSS, 81 and note 217, **55**; – section numbers (alone), 45, **27**, 67, **46**, 93f., **61**, 95, **63**, 96, **64**, 104, **71**, 105, **72**; – *see* colors

Eusebius of Caesarea, Ecclesiastical History (fragment), 83; – letter to Carpianus, 81 note 217, 92; – canon tables to the New Testament, 92 εὐτελεστάτου, term of humility used by scribe in reference to himself, 39

excerpts, legal, 48 note 115, 55, **36**

ἐξίλεῶσί, meaning "to take away," "to remove," 79 and note 205a

Faculty of Advocates, Edinburgh, owner, 59

Falchonius, Victor, humanist, owner, 117

Felckmann, Peter, use of MSS by, 89

Fettaugenstil (or Fettaugen-Mode), paleographical term used by Herbert Hunger, 54 note 123a

Fugger, Johann Jakob, of Augsburg, owner, 124

Galaction, monk, scribe (A.D. 1278/1279), 23f., **12, 101a**, 35

Galaction the Blind, of Mt. Galesion, hieromonk, sponsor, 34f.; – suggested identification with the Galaction of the preceding entry, 24, 35

Galaction Madaraces, hieromonk, scribe: see Madaraces, Galaction

Galés, Pedro, owner, 131

Galesios: see Mt. Galesion

Gaster, Moses, owner, 31

Gennadius, hieromonk, scribe (A.D. 1355/1356), 118f., **80b, 118a, 118b**

Gennatas, Charalampos Tsemaratos, owner, 18f.

George I, king of England, owner, 26, 66

Georgius, priest, father of the scribe Michael Papadopulus, 8

Georgius of Chandax, sponsor, 128

Georgius Darias, lector, scribe: see Darias, Georgius

Georgius ὁ Ἁγιασομάτ(ί)τ(ης), sponsor, 98

Georgius Saracinopulus, lector, scribe: see Saracinopulus, Georgius

Georgius Sudarias: see Darias, Georgius

Gerasimus, monk, grand sceuophylax of the monastery τοῦ Φιλοκάλου in Thessalonica, sponsor, 60f.

Gerlach, Stephan: statement of Metrophanes III, patriarch of CP., to Gerlach, 77; – Gerlach's letter to Martin Crusius, 77 note 198

Germanus, monk, scribe (A.D. 1355/1356), 118f., **80a**

Gianfilippi, Paolino, of Verona, owner, 42 note 99a

Giannacopulo, N., owner, 73

Gibson, John, owner, 33

Giegler, G. P., of Milan, bookseller, 42

Giustiniani, Giulio, owner, 12

Glasgow University Library, acquisition of the Hunter MSS, 20, 116, 118

Glycas, Michael, Capitula in Sacrae Scripturae dubia, 56

Göbler (Goblerus), Justinus, owner, 88, 89 note 254

Greek Anthology, epigrams from, 117

Greek language

1. Phonetics and Prosody: recessive accent in adjective used as substantive in Byzantine and Modern Greek (Σόφος), 115 note 307; accent of χρονῶν in Pontic Greek, 46; – interaspiration (ἀνθιβόλιον for ἀντιβόλαιον), 109 and note 300; – ανδράνοῦς for ἀδρανοῦς, 15; – α for ε (εὐχαστὲ for εὔχεσθε) in Pontic Greek, 144; – ε for α (ἔγρεφη) in Pontic Greek, 46; – ε for ευ (ἐσίνοπτον), 15, (πνέματος), 79; – η changed to ε before ρ regardless of whether or not vowel was stressed (σωταιρ- for σωτηρ-) in Pontic Greek, 144; – ι for accented ε (κοντιύει for κοντεύει), 68 and note 171a; – contraction of i + o to give ö (ψαλτιρον for ψαλτήριον) in Pontic Greek, 144; – change of o to ου, especially after a preceding κ in Cypriot Greek, 37; a stressed o to u (ὀυ for ὀ) in Pontic Greek, 144; confusion of o and u sounds (δροῦγγος for δρόγγος), 9 note 15; occasional change of ου to ω (e.g., ἁμαρτωλῷ Ῥωμανῶ for genitive singular) in Cypriot Greek, 84, 87 (cf. 85f.); – change of υ to ου (Σουρία for Συρία), 37 note 91a; oscillation in the written expression of the normal sounds o and u (ἐμο for ἐμοῦ) in the eastern part of the Byzantine world, 144; λ changed to ρ before a consonant (μοῦρτον for μοῦλτον) in uncultivated Byzantine Greek, 139; irregularly after a consonant (μυροβρύτης for μυροβλύτης) and rarely in South Italian Greek, 91 and note 262; – pronunciation of the sequence νττ as nt not nd in Cypriot Greek, 37; τ for ντ (μελωτι, i.e., μέλλοτι, instead of μέλλοντι), 79; – parasitic ρ (πατρερον) in Pontic Greek, 144; – στ for σθ in Modern Greek, 144; – vulgar form -ομάτης and classicistic form -ομμάτης as name component, 136 note 350; – Πτέρρη (Πτέρη), alternate form of Φτέρη, 119f.; – metrical influences: presumably ἐξ χιλιοστῷ for ἑξακισχιλιοστῷ, 66 and note 164a; – par-

oxytone accent (μερίμνων) in the sixth foot of a dodecasyllable, 65 and note 162

2. Morphology and Syntax: occasional omission of word endings in Pontic Greek, 144; – omission of unaccented augment, 93; – εμαρι with meaning of "died," closely related to the verb μαραίνω, 46; – τύχαιεν, an aorist optative form coined by scribe, 104f.; – εχον (for ἔχων), literary participle for vulgar Cypriot form ἔχοντα, 37; – ὅρμενος, Homeric form used (?) by scribe, 39f. and note 93a; – Pontic genitive μονάστιρη, i.e., μοναστηρί, 144; – feminine κάραν for neuter κάρα, 125; – ending -ου for -ος in σωταιρου, in a Pontic note, 144; – final -ν dropped from the infinitive, 15; – final -ς dropped from οπο (for ὅπως) before two consonants, in Cypriot Greek, 36; – μηδέν in Cypriot Greek for classical μή, medieval μήν, or Cypriot μέν or μέ, 37; – ἵν' ὅπως, combination of particles (postclassical and Byzantine), 104f., 125f.; – σύν governing the genitive, 40; – use of masculine participle with feminine noun, 103

3. Dialects: Cretan, 139; – Cypriot, 35–38, 84, 85, 87; – Pontic, 46 note 108b, 144f.

Gregorius, hieromonk, presumably of the monastery Θεοτόκου τῶν Ὁδηγῶν in Constantinople, sponsor, 146–48

Gregorius, monk, scribe (A.D. 1228), 12, **3, 98b**

Gregorius, priest, father of the scribe Nicolaus of Clarentza, 101

Gregory of Nazianzus, St.: Orations, 97, **66**; – excerpt from Oration 29, 54, **35**; – Oration 44, 112, **76**; – source of two iambic trimeters sometimes used by scribes, 122; – letter of St. Basil to, 116; – see Pseudo-Nonnus

Gregory of Nyssa, St., De beatitudinibus, Oration 7, 114, **77**

Grimani, Domenico Cardinal, owner, 123f.

Guest, Ivor Bertie, 1st Baron Wimborne, owner, 23

Gustavus Adolphus, the occupation of Munich in 1632 and the looting of the Ducal Library, 124 note 330

Ἁγία Κυριακή, church of, reference in a MS, 96

Ἁγία Θέκλα Ἀνωγῆς, place in Cephalonia, 19

Ἁγιασομματ(ι)τ(ης), Georgius: see Georgius ὁ Ἁγιασομματ(ι)τ(ης)

hagiographical texts, 106, 108, esp. 130 note 334; – see Ananias the Priest, Peter the Jailer, and Seven Soldiers in Phoenicia; Anna the Younger, nun, renamed Euphemianus; Apostles and Disciples, Index of; Chrysostom, John, Translation of the Relics of; Irene, martyr under Licinius; James, the Lord's brother; John Climacus; Mark the Athenian; Meletius Galesiotes; Nicholas of Myra; Symeon the Old; Theodore Tiro. – See also Chrysocephalus, Michael-Macarius; – Daniel of Rhaithu; – Dorotheus of Tyre*; – Hippolytus of Thebes; – Nectarius*, patriarch of Constantinople; – Symeon Metaphrastes. – See Apophthegmata Patrum; – Menology; – Panegyricon; – Synaxarion

Hagiopetrites, Theodorus, scribe (A.D. 1291/1292), 60f., **43, 107a**

Ἅγιος Ἀσώματος (or Ἅγιοι Ἀσώματοι), place-names in Cyprus, 98; – see Ἀσώματος

Harley, Edward, 2nd Earl of Oxford, owner, 29, 33, 89; – his widow, Lady Oxford, 29

Harley, Robert, 1st Earl of Oxford, owner, 29, 33; – the Harley Library, 29, 33, 89, 131

εἱρμοί, 41, **25**, 142; – see colors

Herbert, William, 3rd Earl of Pembroke, owner, 28

heresies, passages on, from a 12th-century MS, 3

Hermogenes, Rhetorical Writings, 71, **49**

⟨Hesychius of Jerusalem⟩, Commentary on the Psalms (the third or great), 33, 34, **22, 38**; – three commentaries on the Psalms, 33 note 89

Hesychius of Sinai, abbot of the monastery Βάτου, De temperantia et virtute, 140 and note 361, **93**

εὕρεσις, repertory table prefixed to each Gospel in printed lectionaries of the Gospels, 133 note 342

Hierotheus, priest, scribe (A.D. 1592/1593), 110 note 302

Hippolytus of Thebes, Chronicle on the Genealogy of the B.V.M., fragment on St. James, the Lord's brother (*BHG Auct.* 766f), 79f. and note 209, (*BHG Auct.* 766h) 92 note 264

Hoffmann, Ferdinand, Baron von Grünpichel (Grünbüchel, Grünpühel)-Strechau, owner, 76 note 197

Holkham MSS, 12f.

Holy Trinity, monastery of, τοῦ 'Εσόπτρου, in Chalce near Constantinople, owner, 24 and note 73, 55; 76f. and notes 197, 199; 116

homiletic texts, 106, 108, (fragment) 113

ὅρα, marginal mark, meaning "look," "attention," 140, **94**

Howard, Henry, 6th Duke of Norfolk, owner, 77; – dispersal of the Arundel library, 77f.

Howard, Thomas, 2nd Earl of Arundel, owner, 77

Hunter, William, anatomist and physician, owner, 20, 118

Hunterian Museum of the University of Glasgow, MSS of: see Glasgow University Library

Huntington, Robert, owner, 29

Hyalinas, Manuel, sponsor, 74f.; – Hyalinas (Ialinas) family in Crete, 75

hymns, liturgical, 100; – see canons, liturgical; – κονδάκιον to the Theotocos; – Octoechus; – Pentecostarion; – Theotocarion; – Triodion; – troparia

ὑπομνηματογράφος, ecclesiastical office, 135

Iacobus, hieromonk, scribe (A.D. 1362/1363), 130f., **88, 121b**

Iacobus, hieromonk, on Mt. Sinai, scribe (A.D. 1315/1316), 80, **55, 111c**

Iacobus, monk, sponsor or owner, 30

Iacobus, monk, sceuophylax of the monastery of St. Savior de Lingua Phari in Messina (later abbot), sponsor, 25

Iacobus, protosyncellus of Alexandria, reference in MS, 104

Ignatius, scribe (A.D. 1305/1306), 69, **47, 109b**

illustrated MSS, 7, 42, 44, 64, 67, 91, 142, 146

Im Hof, Johann III, of Nuremberg, owner, 77 note 200

initial capitals: decorated and of large size, 18, **6**; – double-traced, South Italian feature in MS from the Peloponnesus, 101, **114a**; – omitted by the rubricator, 93, **113a**, 104, **114c**; – see colors; – projection

invocations, non-metrical, of scribes, 43, 49f., 72, 111, 118, 128; – added by later hands, 4, 149; – metrical: see subscription commonplaces; – verses of scribes, owners, users

Ioannes, monk and physician, sponsor, 28f.

Ioannes, scribe (A.D. 1311/1312), 72, **50, 110b**

Ioannes Tacuinus de Tridino: see Tacuinus, Ioannes, de Tridino

Ioannes(-Ioseph) Philagrius, scribe: see Philagrius, Ioannes(-Ioseph)

Ioannina in Epirus, 8–10

Ioasaph, hieromonk, owner, 47

Ioasaph, hieromonk, reference in MS from the monastery of 'Ομπλός in the Peloponnesus, 79

Ioasaph, scribe (?) (A.D. 1282), 30, **19a, 102c**

Ioasaph, of the monastery τῶν 'Οδηγῶν in Constantinople, scribe (A.D. 1366; 1391), 120, 121 note 316, 132–34, 134 note 345, **89, 90, 122b**, 142–44, **96, 125**, 146–49, **96A, 126a, 126b**

Ionas, monk, scribe (A.D. 1286), 49–53, **28–31, 106**

Ionas of Mistra, scribe, 50 note 118

Irene, St., martyr under Licinius, synaxarion on (cf. BHG Auct. 953b), 29, **18**

Irene Palaeologina, wife of Emperor Basil I Comnenus of Trebizond, 45f.

Irene Palaeologina, wife of Constantine Palaeologus Porphyrogenitus, 51

Italy (South Italy): see Brindisi; – Calabria; – Messina; – Terra d'Otranto

Jackson, John, owner, 104; – see next entry

Jackson, John, of London, amateur archeologist and traveler, 104 note 288

Jalina, Hemanuel, of Candia, 75

James, St., the Lord's brother, fragment on, by Hippolytus of Thebes (BHG Auct. 766f), 79f. and note 209; (BHG Auct. 766h), 92 note 264

Joachim ὁ Πάνυ, patriarch of Alexandria, owner, 36

John Chrysostom, St.: see Chrysostom, St. John

John Climacus, St., Ladder of Paradise, 30f., **19, 20**, 63, **44**, 78f., **54**, 118f., **80a**; – Liber ad pastorem, 30, 63, 118f., **80b**; – Life of, by Daniel of Rhaithu (BHG³ 882), 118

John of Damascus, St., Commentary on the Canons of, by Theodore Prodromus, 126f.

John of Kitros, Canonical Responses to Constantine Cabasilas of Dyrrhachium, 136

κανδηλάπτης, ecclesiastical and monastic office, 145

Kaplanides, Panagiotes, compiler of an unpublished catalogue of the Gennatas collection, 19

⟨Καρμαλῆς or Καρμαλίκης⟩, Antonius, grand rhetor of the Patriarchate of Constantinople, mentioned in a note, 149 and note 375 καταβασία, its relationship to εἰρμός, 142 note 367

Κημηνίτζης, Demetrius, father of the scribe Galaction Madaraces, 111f.; – family name, 112 note 304

κεφάλαιον of a Gospel, number of, 21, **9b**; – see colors; – τίτλοι of κεφάλαια

κόμης τῆς λαμίας, Byzantine office, 86 note 243

κονδάκιον to the Theotocos, 74

κτησάμενος (κτισάμενος), meaning "sponsor" of a MS, 40 and note 95, 61 and note 147

Ktima, in Cyprus: see Encleistra, monastery, in Cyprus

Κουνοῦπης, Μανουὴλ ὁ, reference in a note, 149

Kyprianos, archimandrite of the archdiocese of Cyprus, editor of the Typicon of St. Neophytus the Recluse, 3, 6

labels, ownership: see ownership labels

laid marks in Western paper, 13 note 32, 125 note 331

Laing, David, owner, 6f.

Lake, Kirsopp, 45 note 105

Lambeth Palace Library, acquisition of MSS: see Manners-Sutton, Charles

Lami, Giovanni, reference to seeing a MS in the library of the Dominican convent of San Marco in Florence, 121 and note 317

Lamia (in Thessaly), later Ζητούνιον, 86

Lampros, S. P., witness to the past location of a MS, 19

Laud, William, abp. of Canterbury, owner, 47, 57, 100, 108, 124 and note 330, 125

lectionaries: see Bible, Old Testament under Prophetologion; – Bible, New Testament under lectionaries

legal texts and writings, public law and church law, 115; – excerpts from legal texts, 48, 54f., **36**; – fragment, 47; – see Attaleiates, Michael; – Balsamon, Theodore; – Blastares, Matthew; – Collectio constitutionum ecclesiasticarum Tripartita; – Collectio LXXXVII capitulorum; – Collectio XXV capitulorum

Leo of Achrida, abp. of Bulgaria, Epistula 1 de azymis et sabbatis, 49; – Epistula 3 de azymis, 49

Leo I the Great, emperor, appearance of the burning clouds over CP. during the reign of, 70 note 178

Leo VI the Wise, emperor, Ὑποτύπωσις (or Διατύπωσις), 134f.

lesson formulas in New Testament MSS, 18

and note 44. See prefixes: lesson prefixes in Gospel lectionaries and New Testament MSS adapted for liturgical use

letter forms: ζ and open ϑ, characteristic of scribes trained in the same scriptorium, 21, **8–10**; – sampi-like shape of ξ in a MS from Epirus, 8 and note 12, **98a**; – letters extended above the top line and below the bottom line, characteristic of the script style of the monastery τῶν Ὁδηγῶν in CP., 121, **81**, 126, **83**, 133, **89, 90**; – letters written above the top line to achieve a vertical emphasis, characteristic of the script style of the monastery τῶν Ὁδηγῶν in CP., 143, **96**

libraries in Great Britain, acquisition of MSS: see cross-references under Bodleian Library (Oxford); – British Museum (London); – Cambridge University Library; – Christ Church, Oxford; – Edinburgh, National Library of Scotland; – Edinburgh University Library; – Glasgow University Library; – Hunterian Museum of the University of Glasgow; – Lambeth Palace Library (London); – Manchester, The John Rylands University Library; – Trinity College, Cambridge

Libri-Carrucci, Guglielmo, owner, 42 note 99a, 97

Lillo (Lille), Sir Henry, owner, 107

literary texts, Byzantine, 115

liturgical books and texts: see Bible, Old Testament under Prophetologion; Bible, New Testament under lectionaries; – canons liturgical; – hymns; – liturgies; – Menologion; – Menology; – Octoechus; – offices, liturgical; – Panegyricon; – Pentecostarion; – Psalter; – Synaxarion; – Triodion; – typica, Typicon

liturgical hymnbooks: see projection in liturgical hymnbooks

liturgical matter, in Latin, written in the 11th century, 83

liturgical notes in New Testament MSS adapted for liturgical use and in New Testament lectionaries, 18, **6**, 43, **26**, 45, **27**, 61, **43**, 67, **46**, 69, **47**, 73, **50**, 81, **55**, 89f., **59**, 91, **60**, 94, **61**, 95f., **63, 64**, 132f., **89, 90**, 146f.; – features of liturgical notes, 43 note 100, 73 note 186; – liturgical notes written within the text instead of in the margins, 73, **50**; – see colors, use of red for liturgical notes; – marginal marks; – prefixes liturgies: of St. Basil, 8; – of St. John Chrysostom, 8; – of the Presanctified, 8

Lord's Prayer, an explanation of, 48

Lulludes (Luludes), Michael, of Ephesus, priest, scribe (A.D. 1312/1313), 74–76, **52, 110d**

Lyell, James P. R., owner, 74

Macarius, scribe (A.D. 1289/1290), 56f., **40, 105b**

Macedonia: *see* Thessalonica; – Zichnai

Madaraces, Galaction, hieromonk, scribe (A.D. 1343), 108–12, **76, 115c–f, 116a–e**

Madden, Frederic, date added to note in MS, 68 note 172

Maffei, S., list of Greek MSS of Saibante, 41f., 42 note 99a

Magedon, Constantinus, of Italy, priest, chartophylax, scribe (A.D. 1340), 106, **73, 114d**

Μακρυδούκαινα, Maria-Martha, reference in MS (A.D. 1362), 28

Μακρυδούκας, reference in a document (A.D. 1325), 28 note 80

maledictions against those who would purloin a MS, 80 and note 212; – *see* censure, ecclesiastical

Manasses, Constantine, Chronicle, 74–76, **52**; – 2 MSS recorded in the collection of Patriarch Metrophanes III at Chalce, 76f.

Manchester, The John Rylands University Library, acquisition of MSS: *see* Gaster, Moses

Manners-Sutton, Charles, abp. of Canterbury, owner, 126

Μανοήλ, ὁ τιμιότατος ἱερεὺς παπ(ᾶς) κυρ, reference in MS, 106

Mantylides, Michael, scribe (A.D. 1297), 64–66, **45, 108**

Manuel, hieromonk, ex-abbot from Mt. Sinai, owner, 35–38

Manuel Mauromates, scribe: *see* Mauromates, Manuel

Manuel Planudes, scribe: *see* Planudes, Manuel-Maximus

Manuel Spheneas, scribe: *see* Spheneas, Manuel

Manuel Tzycandyles, scribe: *see* Tzycandyles, Manuel

manuscripts (other than those represented in this book):

Athos, Lavra, MS *E 43*, 83 note 225, 87; – Σκήτη Προδρόμου (Μονῆς 'Ιβήρων), *11*, 16; – Vatopedi, *roll no. 19*, 147 note 372

Cambridge, University Library, *Additional 3046–3048, 3050–3052*, and *3076*, 103 note 285

Florence, Biblioteca Medicea Laurenziana, *plut. 28, 37*, 59; *plut. 31, 3*, 35; *plut. 32, 16*, 54, 58f.; *plut. 86, 3*, 35; *Conventi Soppressi 20*, 96 note 269; *Conventi Soppressi 103*, 122f.

Geneva, Bibliothèque Publique et Universitaire, *Grec 29, tomus III*, 89

Jerusalem, Patriarchal Library, *Saba 67*, 50 note 118

Leningrad, Akademija Nauk SSSR, Rukopisnyj Otdel, Collection of the former Russian Archaeological Institute in Constantinople, *2*, 134 note 345

Lesbos, Μονὴ Λειμῶνος, *70*, 85f.

London, British Museum, *Additional 5107, 5111, 5112, 5115, 5116, 5153 A, 5153 B*, 97 note 270; *Additional 24382*, 9f. and note 16; *Additional 28815–28817* and *28819–28830*, 23; *Additional 37002*, vii; *Arundel 519, 535*, and *541*, 77 note 199

Meteora, Μονὴ Μεταμορφώσεως, *545*, 60 notes 139, 141

Metz, Bibliothèque Municipale, once *4* (destroyed), 131f.

Milan, Biblioteca Ambrosiana, *C 126 inf.*, 58; *D 538 inf.*, 129f., **122a**, 147; *G 8 sup.*, 32; *P 75 sup.*, 140 note 360; *& 157 sup.*, 58

Moscow, Gosudarstvennyj Istoričeskij Muzej, Sinodal'noe sobranie, *greč. 143* Savva (233 Vladimir), 130; *greč. 279* Savva (261 Vladimir), 134 note 345; *greč. 348* Savva (349 Vladimir), 35; *greč. 405* Savva (416 Vladimir), 44; *greč. 429* Savva (303 Vladimir), 134 note 345

Munich, Bayerische Staatsbibliothek, cod. bav. Cat. 48, 124 note 330; *graec. 98*, 124; *graec. 153*, 74

Oxford, Bodleian Library, *Auct.D.5.2*, 105 note 292; *Auct.T.1.4*, 90 note 259; *Barocci 27*, 83 note 225, 87, 88 note 247; *Barocci 135*, vii; *Barocci 197**, 112; *Barocci 211*, 114 note 306a; *Laud Greek 21*, 124 and note 330; *Laud Greek 29*, 110 note 302; *Laud Greek 62*, 124 and note 330; – Corpus Christi College, *106*, 105 note 292; – Lincoln College, *Greek 18*, 105 note 292; – New College, *68*, 105 note 292

Paris, Bibliothèque Nationale, *Grec 106*, 26; *Grec 205*, 76; *Grec 234*, 84f., 86; *Grec 1189*, 5, 6; *Grec 1251*, 76; *Grec 1571*, 11 note

25; *Grec 1830*, 124; *Grec 2207*, 76; *Grec 2617*, 85; *Coislin 45*, 88; *Coislin 71*, 5; *Coislin 245*, 5; *Coislin 287*, 6; *Supplément grec 471*, 42 note 99a; *Supplément grec 1317*, 5f. and note 6; – Bibliothèque Sainte-Geneviève, *3400*, 76

Patmos, Μονὴ Ἰωάννου τοῦ Θεολόγου, *381*, 114f.

Princeton, New Jersey, Princeton University, The Art Museum, *35–70*, 44

Rome, Biblioteca Angelica, *Greco 30*, 128

Sinai, Monastery of St. Catherine, *Greek 648*, *649*, and *659*, 36 note 90b; *Greek 877*, 147 note 372a; *Greek 1342*, 76; *Greek 2110*, 66 note 164a

Vatican City, Biblioteca Apostolica Vaticana, *Ottoboni gr. 210*, 140 note 360; *Palatin. gr. 367*, 85; *Vatic. gr. 329*, 76; *Vatic. gr. 644*, 61 note 146; *Vatic. gr. 680*, 55 note 126; *Vatic. gr. 1342*, 26; *Vatic. gr. 1597*, 115; *Vatic. gr. 1755*, 147 note 372a; *Vatic. gr. 2138*, 15 note 38; *Vatic. gr. 2155*, 42 note 99a; *Vatic. lat. 3960*, 123 note 324

Venice, Biblioteca Nazionale Marciana, *Greco 83* (collocazione 512), 113, 115; *Greco 292* (colloc. 914), 75, 76; *Greco 362* (colloc. 817), 25, 26; *Greco 452* (colloc. 796), 115; *Greco 481* (colloc. 863), 57f. and note 132; *Greco 578* (colloc. 866), 13 note 30; *Greco 579* (colloc. 416), 12 note 29, 13 note 30; *Greco I, 19* (colloc. 1416), 60 note 141; *Greco II, 2* (colloc. 1012), 108

Verona, Biblioteca Civica, *569*, 42 note 99a

Vienna, Österreichische Nationalbibliothek, *theol. gr. 311*, 76; *Supplem. graec. 174*, 76 note 197, 77 note 198

Zaborda, Μονὴ τοῦ ὁσίου Νικάνορος, *3*, 60 note 139

manuscripts, provenance of: *see* Brindisi; – Clarentza; – Constantinople; – Crete; – Cyprus; – Epirus; – Messina; – Mistra; – Mt. Galesion; – Mt. Sinai; – Philadelphia; – South Italy; – Thessalonica; – Tzemernikos; – Zichnai

Mâr Sâbâ: *see* St. Sabas, monastery of

Marcus, hieromonk, scribe (A.D. 1314/1315), 78, **53, 111a**

marginal marks: Ιω(άννου), 45, **27**; – Μα(τθαίου), 43, **26**; – Κίτρους, 136, **92**; – ση(μείωσαι) and ὅρα, 140 and note 362, **94**; – asterisks, 16, **99c**; – quotation marks, double, to distinguish text from commentary, 12, **3**;

single, to mark passage from Old Testament paraphrased in New Testament, 120, **81**; double or single, to mark scriptural quotation, 34, **23**, 107, **75**; – *see* colors; – liturgical notes; – prefixes

Mark the Athenian, Life of (*BHG*³ 1040), 128

Martinianus, monk, reference in a scribal poem, 29

Mauromates, Manuel, of Zichnai, scribe (A.D. 1367), 134–36, **91, 123b, 123c**; – family name, 136

Maurones, Nicetas, scribe (A.D. 1285/1286), 44f., **27, 105a**

Maurozumes, Constantinus, sponsor, 49–51; – family name, 50

Maximus, hieromonk, scribe (A.D. 1281), 28, **17, 102a**

Maximus Planudes: *see* Planudes, Manuel-Maximus

Mead, Richard, owner, 96

Meerman Library, in The Hague, owner, 90

Μεγάλη Βαγενιτεία (in Epirus): *see* Βαγενετία

μέγας ῥήτωρ, office of the Patriarchate of Constantinople 149 and note 375

Meletius Galesiotes, Life of, by Macarius Chrysocephalus, (*BHG*³ 1246a), 34 note 90a

Mendham, John, owner, 90; – his widow, 90

Mendham, Joseph, owner, 90

Menologion (Table of New Testament lessons for the calendar year), here called Synaxarion, 148, **96A**

Menology (?), palimpsest, scriptura inferior of the 10th century, 106

Menology of Symeon Metaphrastes, 109

Messina (Sicily, South Italy), MSS written in, 25, **13, 101b**

Metaphrastes, Symeon: *see* Symeon Metaphrastes

Metaxares, priest, scribe (A.D. 1272), 23, **11, 100d**

Methodius, hieromonk, scribe (A.D. 1357), 120, **81, 119a**

Metochites, Alexius, cogovernor of Thessalonica, owner, 62

Metrophanes of Smyrna, Triadic Canons, 74

Metrophanes III, patriarch of Constantinople, owner of MSS at Chalce, 24, 55, 76f., 116; – characteristic invocation for, 77 and note 199, in addition to above references

Michael Lulludes, scribe: *see* Lulludes (Luludes), Michael

Michael Mantylides, scribe: *see* Mantylides, Michael

Michael VIII Palaeologus, emperor, 34, 51
notes 121, 122, 123

Michael IX Palaeologus, co-emperor, 51 note
123

Michael Papadopulus, scribe: *see* Papadopulus, Michael

Michaelion: *see* St. Michael ἐν τῷ Ἀνάπλῳ,
church or monastery of

Mid-Pentecost (Μεσοπεντηκοστή), feast of,
102; – Canon for, 141, **95**

Μικρὰ Βαγενετία (in Epirus): *see* Βαγενετία

miniatures: *see* illustrated MSS

Missy, Caesar de, owner, 20, 118

Mistra, Μυζιθρᾶς (near Sparta, in the Peloponnesus), MS from, 129, **87, 122a**; – MS
wrongly said to come from, 50 note 118; –
see Ionas of Mistra

monasteries: *see* Βάτου, monastery (of the
Burning Bush) on Mt. Sinai; – Chortaites,
monastery at, near Thessalonica; – Encleistra, monastery, in Cyprus; – Holy
Trinity, monastery of, τοῦ Ἐσόπτρου, in
Chalce, near Constantinople; – Pantocrator, monastery of, on Mt. Athos; – Philocales, monastery of, in Thessalonica; –
Philotheus, monastery of, on Mt. Athos; –
Preveli (Πρέβελη), monastery, in Crete; –
St. Acacius (?), monastery of; – St. Catherine, monastery of, on Mt. Sinai; – St. Demetrius ὁ Μυροβλύτης, monastery of, location unknown; – St. Gregory of Nyssa,
monastery and church of, in Trebizond; –
St. Sabas, monastery of (Mâr Sâbâ), southeast of Jerusalem; – St. Savior, monastery
of, of Chaldes, in Sürmene (near Trebizond); – St. Savior, monastery of, de Lingua Phari, τοῦ ἀκρωτηρίου, in Messina; –
San Antonio di Castello, monastery of, in
Venice; – San Marco, Dominican monastery
of, in Florence; – Sanctae Mariae de Popsi
or de Ypopsi (Θεοτόκου τῆς Ἐπόψης),
monastery, in Calabria; – Θεοτόκου, monastery, on Mt. Galesion, near Ephesus; –
Θεοτόκου τῶν Ὁδηγῶν or τῆς Ὁδηγητρίας,
monastery, in Constantinople; – Θεοτόκου
Ὀμπλοῦ, monastery of the Presentation,
southeast of Patras; – Θεοτόκου τῆς Παν-
ταννάσσης, church and convent, in Crete; –
Θεοτόκου τῆς Σπηλαιωτίσσης, monastery,
probably in Chios; – Θεοτόκου τῆς Σπηλαιωτίσσης, monastery of the Assumption, in
Crete

monocondylia, 8, **98a**, 70, **109c**, 79, 127,
121a, 136 and note 349a, **123b, 123c**

Monomachus, Clement, monk, ἐπίκουρος of
Theodore (Angelus) Ducas in Arta (Epirus),
8, 11; – family, 11 note 22

Montfaucon, Bernardus de, 12, 38

Moore, John, bp. of Norwich and Ely successively, owner, 26, 66

Morezenus, Ioannes, priest in Crete, owner, 12

Morezenus, Marcus, priest in Crete, son of
the above, owner, 12

Moschampar, George, Capita antirrhetica
contra Ioannis Becci dogmata et scripta,
101–3, **69, 70**

Mt. Athos: *see* Pantocrator, monastery of; –
Philotheus, monastery of

Mt. Galesion (or Galesios), near Ephesus in
Asia Minor: MS possibly from, 24, **12, 101a**;
MS from a monastery on Mt. Galesion, 33f.,
22–24, 103a; – script style, 24, 35

Mt. Sinai: MS written on, 80, **55, 111c**; –
monastery of, owner, 92; – *see* Βάτου,
monastery (of the Burning Bush); – St.
Catherine, monastery of

Mugduphes, Georgius, owner, 64f.

Munich, Ducal Library (now Bayerische
Staatsbibliothek), acquisition of the Fugger
MSS, 124 and note 330

μοῦρτον, i.e., μοῦλτον, meaning "rebellion,"
"sedition," in Byzantine Greek, 139

name, use of a family name by a scribe without a given name, 23, 27

Nanninck (Nannius), Pieter, Latin translation of St. Athanasius of Alexandria,
88f.

Nectarius*, patriarch of Constantinople, Narratio de colybis sive Narratio in festum s.
Theodori Tironis (*BHG*³ 1768), 106, **73**

Neophytus of Cyprus, monk, deacon, scribe
(A.D. 1304/1305), 67f., **46, 109a**, 83 note
223

Neophytus the Recluse, St., Typicon of the
Encleistra monastery, 3–7, **1**; – *editio
princeps* by Kyprianos in 1779, 3, 6; – edition by Warren in 1882, 3f., 7; – autographic
notes represented in this book, 4, **97** (top);
represented in other publications, 5f.; –
Catecheses, 6; – Homilies on Divine Commandments, 6; – Panegyricon for the
months September to December, 6

New Testament: *see* Bible; – Biblical Writings

Niccoli, Niccolò, owner (?), 121

Niceno-Constantinopolitan Creed: see Creed, Niceno-Constantinopolitan

Nicetas, priest, scribe (A.D. 1359/1360), 127, **84, 121a**

Nicetas of Maroneia, abp. of Thessalonica, incomplete commentary on the initial part of the Resurrectional Canons of the Octoechus, 13f.

Nicetas Maurones, scribe: see Maurones, Nicetas

Nicholas of Andida, de Liturgiae symbolis, 28

Nicholas of Myra, St., Life of, by Symeon Metaphrastes (*BHG*³ 1349), 109; – see Symeon Metaphrastes

Nicholas-Nectarius of Otranto, later abbot of Casole, a poem addressed to the notary Andreas of Brindisi, 33 note 86

Nicolaus of Clarentza, scribe (A.D. 1336), 101–3, **69, 114a**

Nicolaus ⟨Damenus⟩, scribe: see ⟨Damenus⟩, Nicolaus

⟨Nicon of Μαῦρον Ὄρος⟩*, Adversus Armenios, 49

Nilus Cucubistianus, scribe: see Cucubistianus, Nilus

Niphon, hieromonk, scribe (A.D. 1378), 137–40, **93, 124a**

N. Σ., owner's initials, 68

numerals: accents and breathings of ordinal numerals marked with numeral letters, 3 and note 1, **97, 71, 110a,** 137f., **124a,** 143, **125;** – irregular form of an ordinal numeral in a metrical subscription, 66 and note 164a, **108;** – omission of the millenary letter in Cypriot dates, 82, **112a;** – cross-like mark beneath a numeral letter used for thousands, 145 note 368c

Nymphaeum, stay of Emperor Andronicus II Palaeologus there, 50

Octoechus, Commentary on the Resurrectional Canons of the: see Nicetas of Maroneia; – Zonaras, John

offices, ecclesiastical and monastic: see ἐκκλησιάρχης; – ὑπομνηματογράφος; – κανδηλάπτης; – μέγας ῥήτωρ; – ῥαιφερενδάριος

offices, liturgical: of the Genuflection, 64 and note 158; – of the Lucernarium and Lauds, 8; – for the feasts of some saints, 8

Old Testament: see Bible; – Biblical Writings

Ὀμπλός: see Θεοτόκου Ὀμπλοῦ, monastery of the Presentation

Oriental paper: see bombycine

ὅρμενος (from ὄρνυμι), meaning "one who came from," "was a native of," 39f. and note 93a; – ὁρμώμενος ἀπὸ (or ἐκ), meaning "a native of," 40 note 93a

Österreichische Nationalbibliothek in Vienna, acquisition of MSS from the Dietrichstein library in Mikulov (Nikolsburg), 76 note 197

owners of MSS (represented in this work and others mentioned incidentally): see Agen (in southwest France), Jesuit College; – Albrecht V, duke of Bavaria; – Alefson, G.; – Askew, Anthony; – Athanasius; – Bagge, H.; – Barocci, Giacomo; – Bentley, Richard; – Blachoules, Nikolaos; – Bossi, Giuseppe; – Burgon, John W.; – Burney, Charles; – Butler, Samuel; – Canonici, Matteo Luigi; – Carlyle, Joseph Dacre; – Chortaites, monastery at; – Clarke, Edward Daniel; – Coke, Thomas, of Holkham; – Coke, Thomas William; – Coke, Thomas William Edward; – Colbert, Jean-Baptiste; – Colybas, Paulus; – Commelin, Jérôme; – Covel, John; – Coxe, Henry Octavius; – Cromwell, Oliver; – Cummings, C. J.; – Diamantakes; – Dietrichstein, Prince Ferdinand von; – Dositheus; – Ebner von Eschenbach, Hieronymus Wilhelm; – Eon, Chevalière d'; – Faculty of Advocates, Edinburgh; – Falchonius, Victor; – Fugger, Johann Jakob; – Galés, Pedro; – Gaster, Moses; – Gennatas, Charalampos Tsemaratos; – George I, king of England; – Gianfilippi, Paolino; – Giannacopulo, N.; – Gibson, John; – Giustiniani, Giulio; – Göbler (Goblerus), Justinus; – Grimani, Domenico Cardinal; – Guest, Ivor Bertie; – Harley, Edward; – Harley, Robert; – Herbert, William; – Hoffmann, Ferdinand; – Holy Trinity, monastery of, τοῦ Ἐσόπτρου, in Chalce; – Howard, Henry; – Howard, Thomas, 2nd Earl of Arundel; – Hunter, William; – Huntington, Robert; – Iacobus, monk; – Im Hof, Johann III, of Nuremberg; – Ioasaph, hieromonk; – Jackson, John; – Joachim ὁ Πάνυ; – Laing, David; – Laud, William; – Libri-Carrucci, Guglielmo; – Lillo (Lille), Sir Henry; – Lyell, James P. R.; – Manners-Sutton, Charles; – Manuel, hieromonk; – Mead, Richard; – Meerman Library, in The Hague; – Mendham, John; – Mendham, Joseph; – Metochites,

Alexius; – Metrophanes III, patriarch of Constantinople; – Missy, Caesar de; – Moore, John; – Mugduphes, Georgius; – Niccoli, Niccolò (?); – N. Σ.; – Pantocrator, monastery of, on Mt. Athos; – Parassoh, Nicolas; – Paris, Jesuit Collège de Clermont; – Parrhasius, Aulus Ianus; – Pember, Robert; – Pharantatus, Dionysius; – Philotheus, monastery of, on Mt. Athos; – Pico della Mirandola, Giovanni; – Pirkheimer, Bilibald; – Recanati, Giovan Battista; – Roe, Sir Thomas: – Romanus, monk; – Rose, W. F.; – Royal Society of London; – Saibante, Giovanni; – Saibante, Giulio; – St. Catherine, monastery of, on Mt. Sinai; – St. Mark, church or monastery of, probably in Crete; – San Antonio di Castello, monastery of, in Venice; – San Marco, Dominican monastery of, in Florence; – Selden, John; – Seripando, Antonio; – Seripando, Cardinal Girolamo; – ⟨Severus⟩, Gabriel; – Syrmalenea, Michael; – Syrmalenios, A.; – Θεοτόκου Ὀμπλοῦ, monastery of the Presentation, southeast of Patras; – Wake, William; – Williams, Theodore; – *see also* booksellers; – sponsors of MSS

ownership entries, metrical: *see* verses of scribes, owners, users

ownership labels: pink paper labels, characteristic of Gennatas, 18 and note 47, 19 note 52

Pachymeres, George, historian, 34 note 90a, 50f.

Palaeologina, Irene: *see* Irene Palaeologina, wife of Emperor Basil I Comnenus of Trebizond; – Irene Palaeologina, wife of Constantine Palaeologus Porphyrogenitus

Palaeologina, Theodora Ducaena: *see* Theodora Ducaena Palaeologina, wife of Michael VIII Palaeologus

Palaeologus, Andronicus II: *see* Andronicus II Palaeologus, emperor

Palaeologus, Constantine Porphyrogenitus: *see* Constantine Palaeologus Porphyrogenitus

Palaeologus, Michael VIII: *see* Michael VIII Palaeologus, emperor

Palaeologus, Michael IX: *see* Michael IX Palaeologus, co-emperor

paleography: *see* abbreviations; – accents and breathings; – bombycine (Oriental paper); – breathings; – calligraphy; – colors; – cryptography; – decoration in MSS; – double dots; – illustrated MSS; – initial capitals; – letter forms; – marginal marks; – monocondylia; – numerals; – palimpsests; – paper (i.e., Western paper); – parchment; – prefixes; – projection (ἔκθεσις); – scribes with two script styles; – script styles; – στιχηρῶς; – Bible, New Testament *under* lectionaries in two columns; in one column

palimpsests, 105f., **73, 114d**, 112, 141, **95**

Pancratius, Manuel, scribe, vii

Panegyricon, hagiographic and homiletic texts, 6, 106, **73**

πανοσιωτάτου, adjective appropriate for an abbot, 34

Pantocrator, monastery of, on Mt. Athos, owner, 82

Papadopulus, Michael, of Tzemernikos in Epirus, lector, scribe (A.D. 1225), 8–11, **2, 98a**

paper (i.e., Western paper): MSS written on, 13, 108, 113, 115, 118, 125 and note 331, 126, 128, 129, 130, 134, 137; – combined with parchment, 100 and note 278; – replacement leaves in a parchment MS, 17; – repair sheet of paper in a bombycine MS, 35; – usual size of paper MSS, 125 note 331; – unusual size, 125 and note 331; – without watermarks, 13; paper MSS listed in a 16th-century catalogue as βαμβίκινα, 76 note 197; *see* chain marks; – laid marks

paper, modern, 62f., 83, 84, 142

paper, Oriental: *see* bombycine

Paphos (Cyprus): *see* Cyprus; – Encleistra, monastery, in Cyprus

Parassoh, Nicolas, owner, 69

parchment: MSS written on, 3, 7, 11, 15, 17, 20, 23 (twice), 25, 27, 29, 30, 31, 38, 42, 44, 47, 62, 63, 66, 69, 70, 71, 72, 73, 78 (twice), 82, 89, 91, 92, 100, 103, 104, 106, 120, 131, 142, 146; – combined with Western paper in quires, 100 and note 278; – parchment fragments attached to parchment MSS, 3, 112; – parchment fragments attached to Western paper MSS, 113, 134; – parchment fragments attached to a bombycine MS, 83, 84; – parchment leaves attached to a Western paper MS, 137; – missing leaves of parchment, replaced by paper, 17, 142; – different qualities intermingled, 47, 93; –

different qualities of parchment affecting appearance of script, 52; – see palimpsests

Parham, library of Robert Curzon at, 22

Paris, Jesuit Collège de Clermont, MSS of (once Claromontani), 90 note 259

Parrhasius, Aulus Ianus (Parrasio, Aulo Giano), owner, 117, 118

Pastil, Constantinus, priest and notary, scribe (A.D. 1325/1326), 91, **60, 112d**; – family name, 91 note 261

Patriarch of Alexandria, owner: see Joachim ὁ Πάνυ

patristic texts, 108

Paul Euergetinus, Synagoge, 128, **85**

Payne, John Thomas, of London, bookseller, 121 and note 317

Payne and Foss, of London, booksellers, 121, 150

Peloponnesus: see Clarentza; – Mistra

Pember, Robert, owner, 100

Pentecostarion, 141, **95**; – see Andrew of Crete

pericopes, consecutive numbers of, 132f. and note 342, 146

pestilences, notes on, in Crete in the 14th century, 137f. and notes 353, 354

Peter of Antioch, patriarch, Response to Dominic of Grado, 49

Peter the Jailer: see Ananias the Priest

Pharantatus, Dionysius, owner, 18

Philadelphia, city in Asia Minor, MS from, 113, **77, 117b**

Philagrius, Ioannes(-Ioseph), scribe (A.D. 1361/1362), 128f., **85, 120b, 120c**

Philocales, monastery of, in Thessalonica, 60f. and note 145

philosophical MSS: see abbreviations; – script styles under "student-book cursive"

Philotheus, monastery of, on Mt. Athos, owner, 119f.

Photius, Bibliotheca, 42 note 99a

Φτέρη (Πτέρρη or Πτέρη), place connected with the monastery of Philotheus on Mt. Athos, 119f.

Pico della Mirandola, Giovanni, owner, 123

Pirkheimer, Bilibald, owner, 77 note 200

places and regions where MSS were written (or were presumably written): see Βαγενετία under Μικρὰ Βαγενετία (in Epirus); – Brindisi (Terra d'Otranto, South Italy); – Clarentza (Peloponnesus); – Constantinople; – Crete; – Cyprus; – Ephesus: see Mt. Galesion; – Epirus: see Βαγενετία under Μικρὰ Βαγενετία; Tzemernikos; – Italy or South Italy: see Brindisi; Messina; South Italy; – Macedonia: see Thessalonica; Zichnai; – Messina (Sicily, South Italy); – Μικρὰ Βαγενετία (in Epirus): see Βαγενετία under Μικρὰ Βαγενετία; – Mistra (Μυζιθρᾶς) near Sparta, in the Peloponnesus; – Mt. Galesion (or Galesios), near Ephesus in Asia Minor; – Mt. Sinai; – Paphos (Cyprus): see Cyprus; Encleistra, monastery, in Cyprus; – Peloponnesus: see Clarentza; Mistra; – Philadelphia, city in Asia Minor; – Sicily: see Messina; South Italy; – South Italy: see also Brindisi; Messina; – Sparta: see Mistra; – Terra d'Otranto: see also Brindisi; South Italy; – Thessalonica, in Macedonia; – Tzemernikos, in Epirus; – Zichnai, in Macedonia

Planudes, Manuel-Maximus, scribe and editor (circa A.D. 1290), 57–59, **41, 105c**; – Aratus, Phaenomena, edited and written by Planudes, vii, 57–59; – Augustine, St., De Trinitate, translated into Greek by Planudes, 42 note 99a, 107f., **75**; – Cleomedes, Circular Theory of the Stars, written in major part by Planudes, 57–59, **41**; – a note on the lunar eclipse of A.D. 1290, in the hand of Planudes, vii, 57, **105c**; – Nonnus, Paraphrase of the Gospel of John, written by Planudes, 58; – Planudean Anthology, written by Planudes, 58; – "Planudean" script style ("Fettaugenstil" or "Fettaugen-Mode"), 51, 53f. and note 123a, **32**, 57f., **41, 42**; – Planudean scriptorium in CP., 51, 54, 58

Plutarch, Parallel Lives, 116f., **79**, 129f., **87**; – tripartite recension of the Parallel Lives, 116f. and note 307a

poem, historical, in political verses, 45f.

Pontus: see St. Gregory of Nyssa, monastery and church of, in Trebizond; – St. Philip, church of, in Trebizond; – St. Savior, monastery of, of Chaldes, in Sürmene (near Trebizond); – Greek language under Dialects

Potter, John, abp. of Canterbury, 38

Praxapostolus: see Bible, New Testament under Acts of the Apostles and the Epistles

prayers, in Greek, 7, 28, 31, 49, 64; – see also invocations

prefixes: lesson prefixes in Gospel lectionaries and New Testament MSS adapted for liturgical use: in Gospel lessons, τῷ καιρῷ ἐκείνῳ, 43 note 100, 67, **46**, 81, **55**, 90, **59**, 94, **61**, 95, **63**, 96, **64**; – εἶπεν ὁ Κύριος κτλ., 18 and note 44, **6**, 43 and note 100, **26**, 95, **63**, 132, **89**; – in lessons from the Epistles, ἀδελφοί, 69, **47**, 73 and note 186, **50**; – prefix ἀρχ(ή) and end mark τέ(λος) or τέλ(ος) or τ(έ)λ(ος), marked for New Testament lessons in New Testament MSS adapted for liturgical use, 43 and note 101, **26**, 45, **27**, 67, **46**, 73, **50**, 81, **55**, 89, **59**, 91, **60**, 93, 94, **61**, 95, **63**, **64**, 104, **71**, 132, **89**, 146; – ἀρχ(ή) omitted by rubricator, 95, **63**; – ἑρμηνεία (in full or abbreviated form), prefix for comments, 13, 27, **14**; – ᾠδαί, εἱρμοί, τροπάρια, those commented upon marked by proper prefixes, 13; – see marginal marks; – Eusebian section and canon numbers in New Testament MSS; – pericopes, consecutive numbers of

Preveli (Πρέβελη), monastery of the B.V.M., in Crete, 68

Probus orthodoxus, Quaestiones ad Iacobitam, 49

Proclus Diadochus, On Platonic Theology (Books I–VI), 122–24, **82**; – Elements of Theology, 122f.

Prodromus, Theodore, Commentary on the Canons of Cosmas of Maïuma and St. John of Damascus, 126f., **84**; – Tetrastichs on the New Testament, 92 note 264

προηγούμενος, term probably used to designate an ex-abbot, 36 and note 90b

projection (ἔκθεσις) to the left of a letter or of the beginning of a line: to mark the beginning of a sentence or of a section either in the same line or in the preceding line or to emphasize a sentence in a prose text, 22 note 63, 30f., **19a**, **19b**, **20a**, **20b**, 63, **44**, 78, **53**, 97, **66**, 107, **74**, 119, **80a**, **80b**; in New Testament and lectionary texts, 20, **7**, 22, **10a**, **10b**, 45, **27**, 67, **46**, 73, **50**, 81, **55**, 83, **56**, 90, **59**, 105, **72**, 120, **81**, 132, **89**; – to mark the beginning of a lesson or of its initial line in New Testament and lectionary texts, 18, **6**, 91, **60**, 104, **71**; – in liturgical hymnbooks, capital initials of troparia projected to the left, 41 and note 99, **25**, **51**, 142 and note 366, **95**; – in Psalters, initials of στίχοι, 29, **17**, 32 and note 85, **21**, 100 and note 277, **68**, 143, **96**; initials of comments on single verses, 29, **17**; – in a subscription, a projected initial

capital overlooked by the rubricator, 93, **113a**, 104, **114c**; – see colors

προφητεία for προφητολόγιον, 40

Prophetologion (Old Testament lectionary): see Bible, Old Testament

prosody: see Greek language under Phonetics and Prosody; – versification

Psalter: see Bible, Old Testament under Psalms; – Biblical Writings, on Old Testament, under Psalms; – projection, in Psalters; – στιχηρῶς

Pseudo-Codinus, Πάτρια, 76 note 197; – Pseudo-Codinus, De officiis, 76 note 197

Pseudo-Nonnus, Histories of St. Gregory of Nazianzus, 28

ψυχικόν, meaning "commemorative donation to a church," 37

Πτέρρη (Πτέρη or Φτέρη), place-name known in reference to the monastery of Philotheus on Mt. Athos, 119f.

Pulumistrinus, Ioannes, sponsor, 44

punctuation signs: stop marks in the form of thick red dots, 143, **96**; – see τελεία (+) sign

quire: made of parchment and paper combined, 100 and note 278; – quinion composition, 83 and note 225, 87 note 245; – quire marks written in the lower righthand corner of the quire's last page, 53; – quire marks, replaced at time of revision, 93f.; quire marks as indication of lost quires, 101

quotation marks: see marginal marks

Rae, H. C., of Liverpool, commission merchant, 103 and note 285

Recanati, Giovan Battista, owner, 13 note 30

regional script styles: see Constantinople; – Cyprus; – Mt. Galesion; – South Italy; – Terra d'Otranto

religious texts, 100, 134; – see hagiographical texts; – homiletic texts; – liturgical books and texts

Resurrectional Canons: see Nicetas of Maroneia; – Zonaras, John

ῥαιφερενδάριος, ecclesiastical office, 141 and note 363

ῥακενδύτης + θύτης, to form θυτορακενδύτης, meaning "hieromonk," 120, cf. 137

Riemann, Othon, 19

Roe, Sir Thomas, owner, 25, 38, 55, 116

Romanus, monk, owner, 26 note 77

Romanus ⟨Chartophylax⟩, scribe: *see* ⟨Chartophylax⟩, Romanus

Rose, W. F., owner, 90

Rosenthal, A., bookseller, 74

Royal Library in Paris, acquisition of Colbert's MSS, 85 note 230

Royal Society of London, owner, 77f.

Saibante, Giovanni, owner, 41, 62, 71; – Saibante collection of Greek MSS, 41f. and note 99a

Saibante, Giulio, owner, 41, 62; – *see* preceding entry

St. Acacius (?), monastery of, 104

St. Catherine, monastery of, on Mt. Sinai, 80 and note 211; – owner, 92

St. Demetrius ὁ Μυροβλύτης, monastery of, location unknown, 91

St. George, church of, located at an unidentified site called τὸ Βαθύ, presumably in Cyprus, 98

St. Gregory of Nyssa, monastery and church of, in Trebizond, 145 and note 368d

St. Mark, church or monastery of, probably in Crete, owner, 140

St. Michael ἐν τῷ ᾿Ανάπλῳ, church or monastery of, on the Bosporus, 18

St. Philip, church of, in Trebizond, plundered by the Turks in A.D. 1665, 145 and note 368d

St. Sabas, monastery of (Mâr Sâbâ), southeast of Jerusalem, 22

St. Savior, monastery of, of Chaldes, in Sürmene (near Trebizond), 145

St. Savior, monastery of, de Lingua Phari, τοῦ ἀκρωτηρίου, in Messina, 25

Salento: *see* Terra d'Otranto

Salvi, C., bookseller, 41

San Antonio di Castello, monastery of, in Venice, owner, 123 and note 324

San Marco, Dominican monastery of, in Florence, owner, 121 and note 317

Sanctae Mariae de Popsi or de Ypopsi (Θεοτόκου τῆς ᾿Επόψης), monastery, in Calabria, 26 note 77

Saracinopulus, Georgius, lector, scribe (A.D. 1306/1307), 70, **48, 109c**; – family name in Byzantium, 70

Sauvan, Balthasar, French consul in Cyprus and buyer of MSS for Colbert, 84, 85 and notes 230, 236

Savile, Sir Henry, editor of St. John Chrysostom, 107 and note 297

Scholz, J. M. A., witness to the past location of a MS, 22

scribes of MSS represented in this work: *see* Andreas of Brindisi; – Basilius of Paphos, priest, teacher, notary; – Brizopulus, Demetrius, lector; – Charases, Constantinus, priest; – ⟨Chartophylax⟩, Romanus, lector; – Chrysocephalus, Michael-Macarius, metropolitan of Philadelphia; – Chumnus, Stelianus; – Constantinus of Adrianople; – Cucubistianus, Nilus, priest; – ⟨Damenus⟩, Nicolaus, lector at the Hours; – Darias, Georgius, lector; – Galaction, monk; – Gennadius, hieromonk; – Germanus, monk; – Gregorius, monk; – Hagiopetrites, Theodorus; – Iacobus, hieromonk; – Iacobus, hieromonk, on Mt. Sinai; – Ignatius; – Ioannes; – Ioasaph (?); – Ioasaph, of the monastery τῶν ᾿Οδηγῶν in Constantinople; – Ionas, monk; – Lulludes (Luludes), Michael, of Ephesus, priest; – Macarius; – Madaraces, Galaction, hieromonk; – Magedon, Constantinus, of Italy, priest and chartophylax; – Mantylides, Michael; – Marcus, hieromonk; – Mauromates, Manuel, of Zichnai; – Maurones, Nicetas; – Maximus, hieromonk; – Metaxares, priest; – Methodius, hieromonk; – Neophytus of Cyprus, monk, deacon; – Nicetas, priest; – Nicolaus of Clarentza; – Niphon, hieromonk; – Papadopulus, Michael, of Tzemernikos in Epirus; – Pastil, Constantinus, priest and notary; – Philagrius, Ioannes (-Ioseph); – Planudes, Manuel-Maximus; – Saracinopulus, Georgius, lector; – Sophus, Constantinus; – Sudarias, Georgius: *see* Darias, Georgius, lector; – Syropulus; – Theodosius; – Theophanes; – Theophilus, hieromonk; – Triclines (or Triclinius), Demetrius, of Thessalonica; – Tzycandyles, Manuel, of Constantinople

scribes of other MSS mentioned incidentally: *see* Gregorius, hieromonk, presumably of the monastery τῶν ᾿Οδηγῶν in CP.; – Hierotheus, priest; – Ionas of Mistra; – Neophytus the Recluse, St.; – Pancratius, Manuel; – Scutariotes, Ioannes Thettalus; – Serbopulus, Ioannes; – Spheneas, Manuel

scribes with two script styles: 21 (scribe A), **8a**, 53–55 (scribe B), **32, 36**, 92 (scribe B), 95, **113a, 62**, 98f., **113c, 67**; – *see also* ⟨Chartophylax⟩, Romanus; – Cucubistianus, Nilus; – ⟨Damenus⟩, Nicolaus; – Ioasaph, of the monastery τῶν Ὁδηγῶν in Constantinople; – Ionas, monk; – Nicolaus of Clarentza; – Niphon

script styles: majuscule script, 113, 106 (scriptura inferior); – minuscule scripts mixed in with conventional style in New Testament MSS, 93, **63, 64,** 96, **65;** – calligraphic script in a foundation typicon, 5, **1;** – script with abundant use of abbreviations in liturgical typica, 5; – conservative style in scriptural and liturgical MSS, viii, 26, 68, **46,** 83 and note 223, **56,** 93, **61, 62,** 99, **67;** – Cypriot calligraphy, 5 and note 5a, **1,** 68 and note 170, 82f., **112a, 56,** 98–100, **113c, 67;** – Cypriot "notarial" script, 85, 87f., **57, 58, 112b;** – Mt. Galesion script style, 24, **12,** 35, **24;** – τῶν Ὁδηγῶν, i.e., the monastery Θεοτόκου τῶν Ὁδηγῶν in Constantinople, script style of, 64, 119, **80a, 80b, 118a, 118b,** 120, **81, 119a,** 126, **83, 120a,** 132–34, **89, 90, 122b,** 142f., **96, 125,** 146–49, **96A, 126a, 126b;** – "Planudean" script style ("Fettaugenstil" or "Fettaugen-Mode"), 51, 53f. and note 123a, **32,** 57–59, **105c, 41, 42;** – Terra d'Otranto script style, 32f., **21, 102d, 102e;** – "student-book cursive" with many abbreviations, 26 and note 74, **13;** – see also regional script styles; – letter forms

Scrivener, F. H., note in MS, 81

Scutariotes, Ioannes Thettalus, scribe, 59

Selden, John, owner, 105, 106

ση(μείωσαι), marginal mark, meaning *nota bene,* 140 and note 362, **94**

Serbopulus, Ioannes, scribe of supplements to a MS, 105

Seripando, Antonio, owner, 118

Seripando, Cardinal Girolamo, owner, 118

Seven Soldiers in Phoenicia: see Ananias the Priest

⟨Severus⟩, Gabriel, metropolitan of Philadelphia, owner, 108

Sicily: see Messina; – South Italy

Sophianus, Manuel (A.D. 1537), reference in a MS, 149; – family, their MSS acquired by the Ambrosian Library in Milan, 149

Sophronius, St., patriarch of Jerusalem, Synodal Epistle to Sergius, patriarch of Constantinople, 49, 55, **39;** – Epitome of Synodal Epistle, 48

Sophronius, priest, note in MS, 104

Sophus, Constantinus, scribe (A.D. 1348),

115f., **78, 117c;** – family name in Byzantium, 115

South Italian: chronological practice (indication of the hour in subscriptions), 32 and note 82; – Greek language (the rare change of λ to ρ after a consonant), 91 note 262; – influence of South Italian writing manner on a MS written in the Peloponnesus, 101; – see colors; – initial capitals; – Brindisi; – Messina; – St. Savior, monastery of, de Lingua Phari, τοῦ ἀκρωτηρίου, in Messina; – Sanctae Mariae de Popsi or de Ypopsi (Θεοτόκου τῆς Ἐπόψης), monastery, in Calabria; – South Italy, MSS from; – Terra d'Otranto

South Italy, MSS from, 25f., **13, 101b,** 31f., **21, 102d, 102e,** 140 note 360; – see also Brindisi; – Messina; – Terra d'Otranto

Sparta: see Mistra (Μυζιθρᾶς)

Spheneas, Manuel, scribe, 35

sponsors of MSS (represented in this work and others mentioned incidentally): see Callinicus, hieromonk and archimandrite; – Contostephanus, Ioannes, of Constantinople; – Galaction the Blind of Mt. Galesion; – Georgius of Chandax; – Georgius ὁ Ἀγιασομματ(ί)τ(ης); – Gerasimus, monk, grand sceuophylax of the monastery τοῦ Φιλοκάλου in Thessalonica; – Gregorius, hieromonk, presumably of the monastery Θεοτόκου τῶν Ὁδηγῶν in CP.; – Hyalinas, Manuel; – Iacobus, monk; – Iacobus, monk, sceuophylax of the monastery of St. Savior de Lingua Phari in Messina; – Ioannes, monk and physician; – Maurozumes, Constantinus; – Pulumistrinus, Ioannes

Stelianus Chumnus: see Chumnus, Stelianus

Stephanus, Carolus, librarian of Johann Jakob Fugger, 124 note 330

Stethatus, Nicetas, Physicorum capitum centuria II, 140, **94**

στιχηρῶς, traditional manner of writing Psalters, 32, **21,** 100, **68;** – Psalter not written στιχηρῶς, 143, **96**

Strategopulina, widow of Constantine Strategopulus, 50f. and notes 120, 121

Στρηλίτζα(ς), Constantine, and his wife Constantina, reference in a MS, 96

Strumica: see Tiberiupolis

subscription commonplaces: χωρικός (referring to the scribe), 8, 101f.; – μὴ καταρᾶσθαι· ὅτι κτλ. (in a MS written in the Peloponnesus), 101f.; – metrical: dodecasyllabic, γόνυ – δέλτον, 125; ἔληξεν αὐχὴν δάκτυλοι τρεῖς καὶ γόνυ, 49 f.; ἔχοντι κ(αὶ) γράψαντι, σῶτερ μου σῶσον, 131; ἡ χεὶρ μὲν ἡ γράψασα κτλ., 15 and note 39, ἡ γὰρ χεὶρ ἡ γράψασα κτλ., 39 f.; Θ(εὸ)ν ἱλεούμενος τίμιε π(άτ)ερ, Θεοδώρου μέμνησο τοῦ καλλιγρά(φ)ου (characteristic of Theodorus Hagiopetrites), 60; τὸν δακτύλοις γράψαντα τὸν κεκτήμενον κτλ., 56 f.; ὥσπερ ξένοι χαίρουσιν ἰδεῖν πατρίδα κτλ., 8 and note 13, 38, 40, 117, 127; dodeca-syllabic note with the name of the scribe, 118; dodecasyllabic colophon with the name of the scribe, 120 f.; dodecasyllabic colophon with the name of the scribe, in a form characteristic of MSS from the scriptorium of the monastery Θεοτόκου τῶν Ὁδηγῶν in CP., Θεοῦ τὸ δῶρον κτλ. (characteristic of Ioasaph τῶν Ὁδηγῶν), 125 f., 132, 143, 148; –hexametric invocation, characteristic of MSS from the scriptorium of the monastery Θεοτόκου τῶν Ὁδηγῶν, Χριστέ – ἀρωγήν, 143, 148 and note 374; –iambic conclusion, τῷ συντελεστῇ τῶν καλῶν θ(ε)ῷ χάρις, 56, 122; two iambic trimeters stemming from St. Gregory of Nazianzus, θ(εο)ῦ διδόντος – ἰσχύει πόνος, 122

subscriptions, cryptographic: see cryptography

subscriptions decorated with leaf ornament: see ⟨Damenus⟩, Nicolaus

subscriptions, ownership entries, and scribal notes, metrical: dodecasyllabic, 4, 8, 15 f., 24, 28, 30, 38, 39, 40, 43, 49 f., 56, 60 and note 141, 65, 72, 84, 111, 113 f., 116, 117, 118, 120 f., 122, 125 f., 127, 131, 132, 143, 148; – iambic, 56, 122; – in political verse, 24, 65 f., 107; – in seven-syllable lines, 111; – see subscription commonplaces under metrical; – verses of scribes, owners, users

Sudarias, Georgius: see Darias, Georgius, lector, scribe

Surians (Σουριάνοι), Christians of Syrian background, 37 and note 91a

Sürmene (τὰ Σύρμενα or τὰ Σούρμενα), east of Trebizond, site of the monastery of St. Savior of Chaldes, 145

Symeon Metaphrastes, Menology, Life of St. Nicholas of Myra (BHG³ 1349), 109

Symeon the Old, Life of, 70, **48**

Synaxarion: tables of lessons from the New Testament (Menologion, here called Syn-

axarion), 148, **96A**; – in the meaning of "lives of saints," 29, **18**, 130 f. and note 334, **88**; – Synaxarion of Constantinople, 70, **48**

συνδρομή, meaning "contribution to the cost of producing a MS," 40; – see ἐπιδρομή

συνεργεῖν, meaning "to assist," "to provide the expenses," 147 f.; – συνεργία, meaning "(financial) assistance," 147 and note 372a

Syrmalenea, Michael, owner, 68

Syrmalenios, A., owner, perhaps abbot of the Preveli monastery in Crete, 68

Syropulus, scribe (A.D. 1279/1280), 27 f., **14, 16, 101c**

tables: of Eusebian canons, 92; – of Gospel lessons, 92; of New Testament lessons, 146, 148, **96A**; – paschal table, 142; – see Menologion; – Synaxarion

Tacuinus, Ioannes, de Tridino, Venetian printer, epigram on, by Victor Falchonius, 117

Tarasius, patriarch of Constantinople, Prayer at the opening of a church profaned by heretics, 49

Taronas, Vlach chieftain, 11 note 20

τελεία (+) sign, to mark a full stop in lectionaries, 11, **2**, 18 and note 45, **6**, 20, **7**, 23, **11**, 83, **56**

Terra d'Otranto (or Salento) in South Italy: see Brindisi; – MS from, 140 note 360; – script style, 31–33, **21, 102d, 102e**

τέτραδον (for τετράδιον or τετράς), meaning "quire," 119 and note 308

τετραυάγγελον, meaning "Four Gospels," 92 f. and note 265

Θηναία, district of Cephalonia, 18

Theodora Ducaena Palaeologina, wife of Emperor Michael VIII Palaeologus, 51 note 121

Theodore (Angelus) Ducas: see Ducas, Theodore Angelus

Theodore of Leucara, priest, invocation by, **4**

Theodore the Studite, St., Short Catecheses, 78 and note 203, **53**; – Testament, 78

Theodore Tiro, St.: see Nectarius*, patriarch of Constantinople

Theodorus Hagiopetrites, scribe: see Hagiopetrites, Theodorus

Theodosius, scribe (A.D. 1337/1338), 104, **72, 114c**

theological texts, 108; – theological and ascetic texts, 137; – see heresies

Theophanes, scribe (A.D. 1358), 125 f., **83, 120a**

Theophilus, hieromonk, scribe (A.D. 1285), 43, **26**, **103b**

Theophylact ⟨Hephaestus⟩, abp. of Bulgaria, Commentary on the Four Gospels, 12, **3**, 96, **65**

θεοφύλακτος, used in reference only to Constantinople, 40

θεόσωστος, used in reference to important cities, 40

Theotocarion, 73f., **51**

Θεοτόκου, monastery, on Mt. Galesion, near Ephesus, 33f. and note 90

Θεοτόκου τῆς Ἐπόψης, monastery, in Calabria: see Sanctae Mariae de Popsi or de Ypopsi

Θεοτόκου τῶν Ὁδηγῶν or τῆς Ὁδηγητρίας, monastery, in Constantinople: script style, 64, 119, **80a**, **80b**, **118a**, **118b**, 120, **81**, **119a**, 126, **83**, **120a**, 132–34, **89**, **90**, **122b**, 142f., **96**, **125**, 148f., **96A**, **126a**, **126b**; – scriptorium, 132, 143, 146; – typical form of subscription: see subscription commonplaces *under* metrical, dodecasyllabic colophon with the name of the scribe, in a form characteristic of MSS from the scriptorium of the monastery Θεοτόκου τῶν Ὁδηγῶν; – hexametric invocation, characteristic of, etc.; – *see also* colors, combinations, red and gold

Θεοτόκου Ὀμπλοῦ, monastery of the Presentation, southeast of Patras, owner, 79 and note 208

Θεοτόκου τῆς Παντανάσσης, church and convent, in Crete, 138 note 355

Θεοτόκου τῆς Σπηλαιωτίσσης, monastery, probably in Chios, 80

Θεοτόκου τῆς Σπηλαιωτίσσης, monastery of the Assumption, in Crete, μετόχιον of St. Catherine on Mt. Sinai, 80 note 211

Thessalonica, in Macedonia, MSS from, 60f. and note 146, **43**, **107a**, 71, **49**, **110a**; – scribe possibly from Thessalonica, 40

Thorpe, Thomas, bookseller, 90

θύτης, meaning "priest," 120, 137

θυτορακενδύτης, meaning "hieromonk," 120, cf. 137

Tiberiupolis (or Strumica), in Southern Serbia, origin of the scribe Galaction Madaraces, 111

τιθέναι, meaning "to donate" (a MS to a church or monastery), 98

τίτλοι of κεφάλαια (titles or summaries of Gospel chapters) in MSS of the New

Testament, 21, **9b**, 94, **61**, 95, **63**, **64**, 96, **65**, 104, **71**; – see colors

Tomasini, Iacopo Filippo, 124

Trebizond: the arrival there in 1335 of Basil I Comnenus and the Empress Irene, 45f.; – Metropolis of, seat transferred from St. Philip in Trebizond to the monastery of St. Gregory of Nyssa in A.D. 1665, 145; – see St. Gregory of Nyssa, monastery and church of; – St. Philip, church of

Triclines (or Triclinius), Demetrius, of Thessalonica, scribe (A.D. 1308) and scholar, 71f., **49**, **110a**; – change of name to Triclinius, 71 and note 182; – round breathing style, 71, **49**; – use of the Planudean edition of Aratus, a scholium possibly in Triclinius' hand, 59; – interest in astronomy, 59 note 136

Triclinius, Demetrius, scribe and scholar: see preceding entry

Trinity College, Cambridge, acquisition of MSS: see Bentley, Richard

Triodion, 38, 41, **25**

τριπλοἐχμαλλώτ(ου), meaning "thrice (i.e., utterly) unfortunate as αἰχμάλωτος (i.e., as a refugee)," 127

troparia, 41, **25**, 142 and note 366, **95**; – see colors; – projection

Tsemaratos: see Gennatas, Charalampos Tsemaratos

Tsitseles, E. A., 19

typica, liturgical (λειτουργικὰ τυπικά), with abundant use of abbreviations, 5 and note 5; – foundation typica (κτητορικὰ τυπικά), in calligraphic script without abundant use of abbreviations, 5, **1**

Typicon of the Encleistra monastery in Cyprus, a foundation typicon by St. Neophytus the Recluse, 3–7, **1**

τζακίζω, meaning "to steal," "to take away" in Cypriot Greek, 36f.

Tzemernikos (Τζεμέρνικος or Τζερμέρνικος, now called τὰ Τζουμέρκα), in Epirus, MS written by a scribe from this area of Epirus, 8–10, **2**, **98a**; – other places with this name, 10 note 20

Tzycandyles, Manuel, of Constantinople, scribe (A.D. 1362), 129f., **87**, **122a**, 147

Vainiá, in Crete: see Βαϊονέα

Vagenetia, in Epirus: see Βαγενετία

verses of scribes, owners, users (traditional and individual): dodecasyllabic, βίβλο(ς) πέφυκα, ζῶντο(ς) ὕδατος κρίνη, 84; γενοῦ βοηθὸς κἀμοὶ τῷ ξένῳ θύτα κτλ., 118; Θ(εὸ)ν ἱλεούμενος τίμιε π(άτ)ερ, Θεοδώρου μέμνησο τοῦ καλλιγρά(φ)ου, 60 and note 141; θύτης μοναστῆς, Γεννάδιος τῇ κλήσει, 118; καὶ βασάνων λύτρωσαι τῶν πικροτάτων κτλ., 72; Μακαρίου ταῦτ' ἐστι Φιλαδελφείας κτλ., 113; Μεθοδίου χείρ, τοῦ θυτορακενδύτου, 120f.; Νεοφύτου ἐγκλείστου τίσδε τῆς βίβλου κτλ., 4; οἱ π(ατέ)ρες μέμνησθε του Μ(ητ)ροφανους, 24, 55, 76, 77 and note 199, 116; πολλῶν πόνων ἔρανος ἠκριβωμένος κτλ., 113; σὺ βίβλε μακάριζε τὸν γράψαντά σε κτλ., 122; τέλος εἴληφε τὸ ποθούμενον ἔργον κτλ., 64; Τὸν συντεθέντα (συντιθ- legendum) Φιλαδελφείας πόθῳ κτλ., 113; Χρυσῶν ἐπῶν ἐνθάδε σωρεία, ἔργον, κτλ., 113; – in political verse, αὔτη ἡ βήβλος πέφηκε τῆς μονῆς Χορταΐτου· κτλ., 107; ἐτελειώθ(η) τοῦτο γε τῷ μη(νὶ) ἰουννίῳ. κτλ., 65f.; ἡ βίβλος αὔτη πέφυκε τῆς πὰντούργου τριάδος, κτλ., 24, 55, 76, 77 and note 199, 116; – see also subscription commonplaces, metrical. For longer metrical compositions, see subscriptions, ownership entries, and scribal notes, metrical

versification: accent influenced by meter, 65 and note 162; – faulty lines, 30, 65f. and note 164; – spelling and form influenced by meter, 66 and note 164a

Wake, William, abp. of Canterbury, owner, 79, 120, 136, 145

Warren, Frederick Edward, editor of the Typicon of the Encleistra in Cyprus, 3f., 7

watermarks: see paper (i.e., Western paper) under without watermarks

Williams, Theodore, owner, 90

Wise (Wyss), Albert von, German ambassador to Turkey, 77 and notes 198, 200

Yeni Mahalle (Yenimahalle), a quarter of Scutari, section of Constantinople on the Asian side, 46f. and note 110

Zichnai, in Macedonia, MS from, 134f., **91, 92, 123a–c**

Zigabenus, Euthymius, Commentary on the Psalms and Odes, 23f., **12**, 27, **14–16**, 28, **17**; – Panoplia dogmatica, 55 note 126; – recorded in a MS as Ioannes Zigabenus by mistake, 28

zodiac, list of the signs of, 117

Zonaras, John, Commentary on the Resurrectional Canons of the Octoechus, 126; – in its longer version, 13f., **4**

ζυγός, topographical term, 9 note 15

CORRIGENDUM to p. 17, lines 11–5 from bottom:

In the subscription of MS London, Brit. Mus., Additional 40754 (Pl. **100a**), line 4 is to be read τοῦ Δαρία: (*not* Σούδαρία:). Thus the MS was written by the lector Γεώργιος ὁ Δαρίας. Accordingly, in the listings of Pls. **6** and **100a** (on pp. xiii and xviii) and in the legends to Pls. **6** and **100a,** the scribe's family name is to be read Darias (*not* Sudarias).

The scribe's family name Δαρίας was probably derived from a place-name ἡ Δάρα, which is frequent on the Greek mainland. This toponym appears five times in the Peleponnesus (cf. Eleutheroudakes, Ἐγκυκλ.Λεξ., IV, p. 280); three of these toponyms are listed as masculines ὁ Δάρας in Λεξικὸν τῶν δήμων, p. 198. In the Byzantine East, there was the well-known fortress ἡ Δάρα (Ἀναστασιούπολις) in Upper Mesopotamia (cf. *RE*, IV, col. 2150, *s.v.* Dara 2; F. Dölger, Παρασπορά [Ettal (1961)], pp. 117 and note 41, 118). On the declension pattern of the name ὁ Δαρίας, τοῦ Δαρία, cf. Jannaris, *Historical Greek Grammar*, pp. 108f., §§ 277, 284.

PLATES

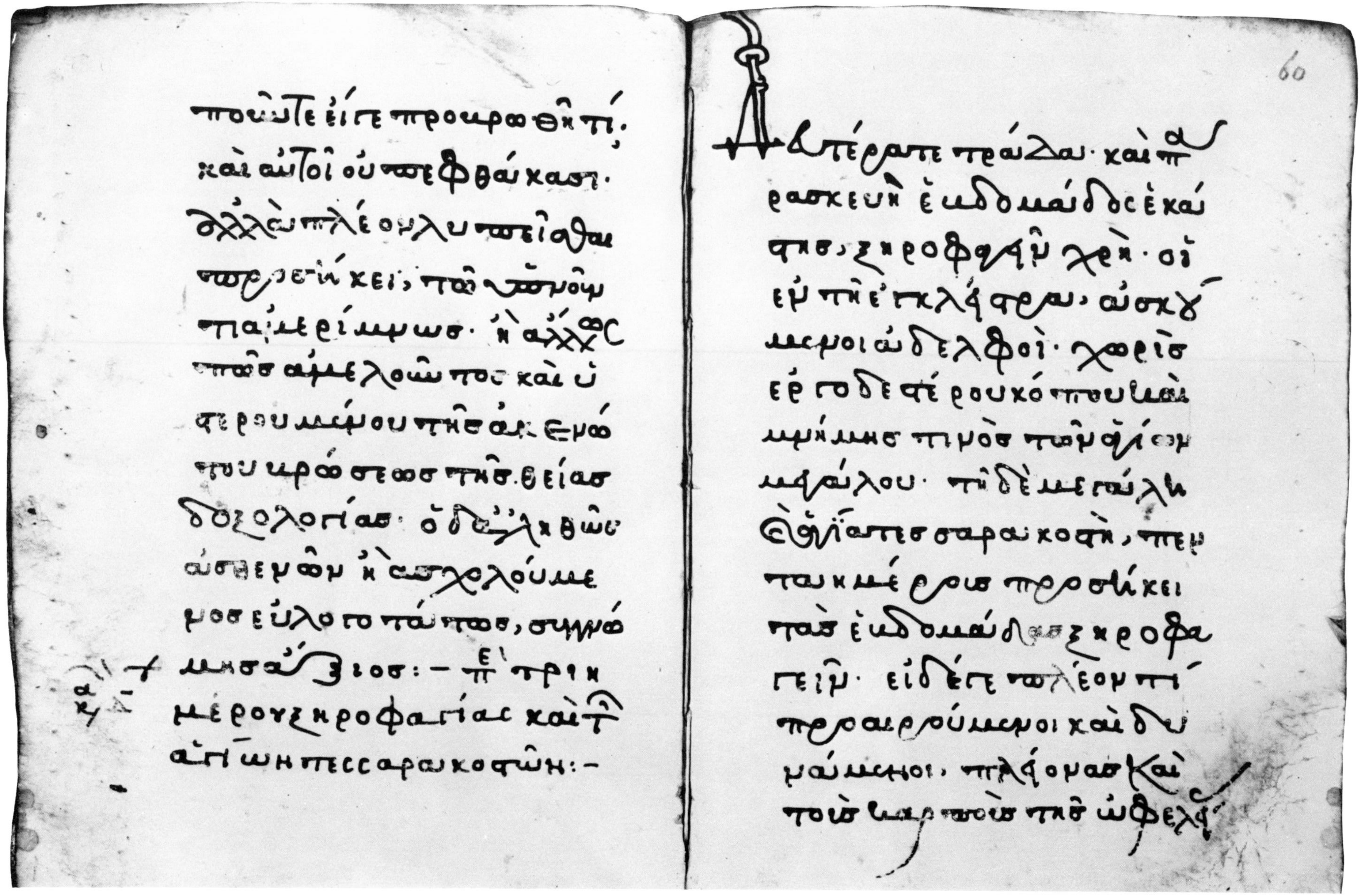

Plate 1

A.D. 1214: Written in Cyprus by the priest and notary Basilius of Paphos
St. Neophytus the Recluse, Typicon of the Encleistra monastery
Edinburgh, University Library, MS 224 (fols. 59v–60r)

Plate 2

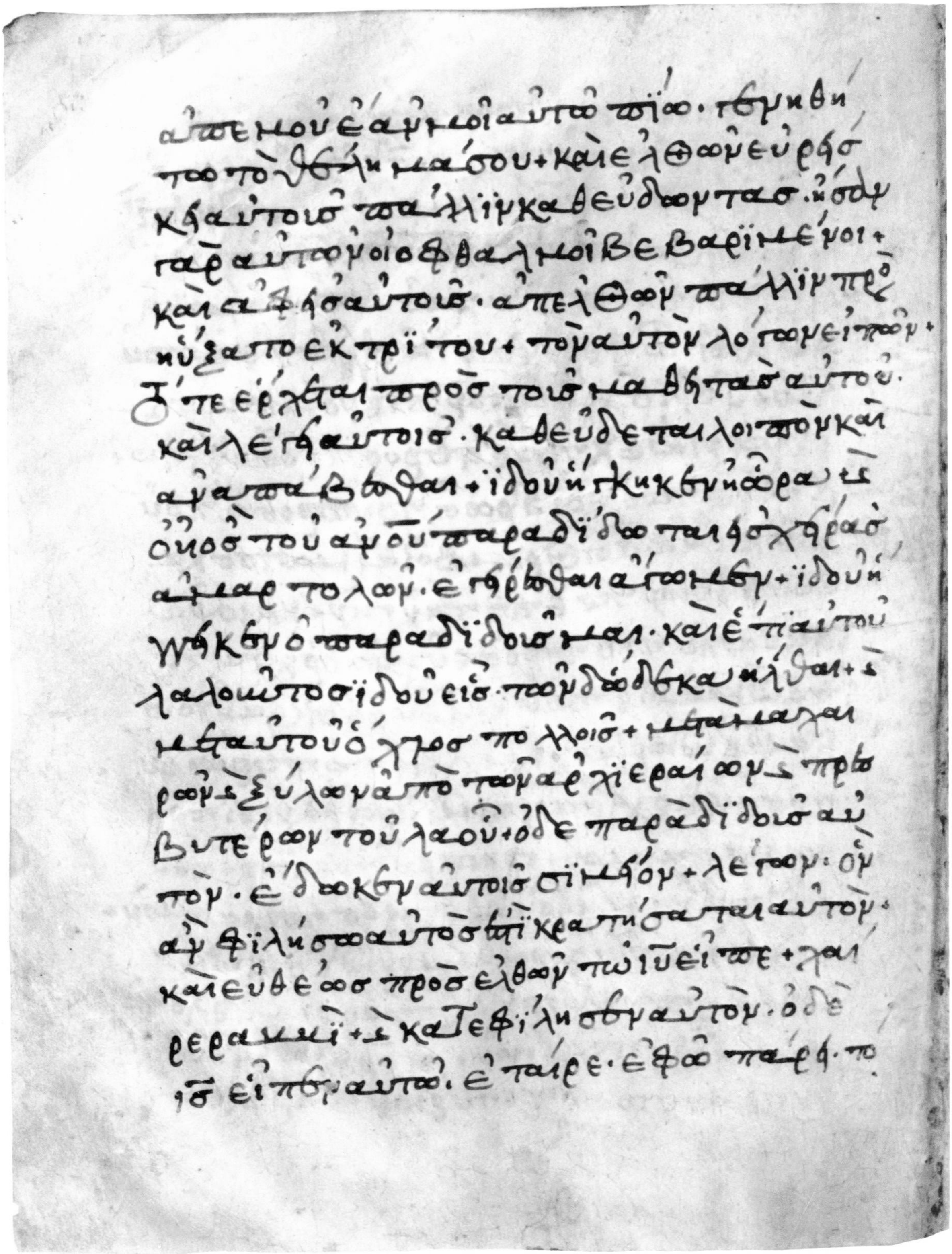

A.D. 1225: Written by the lector Michael Papadopulus of Tzemernikos in Epirus
Lessons from the New Testament
Oxford, Bodleian Library, MS Cromwell 11 (page 230)

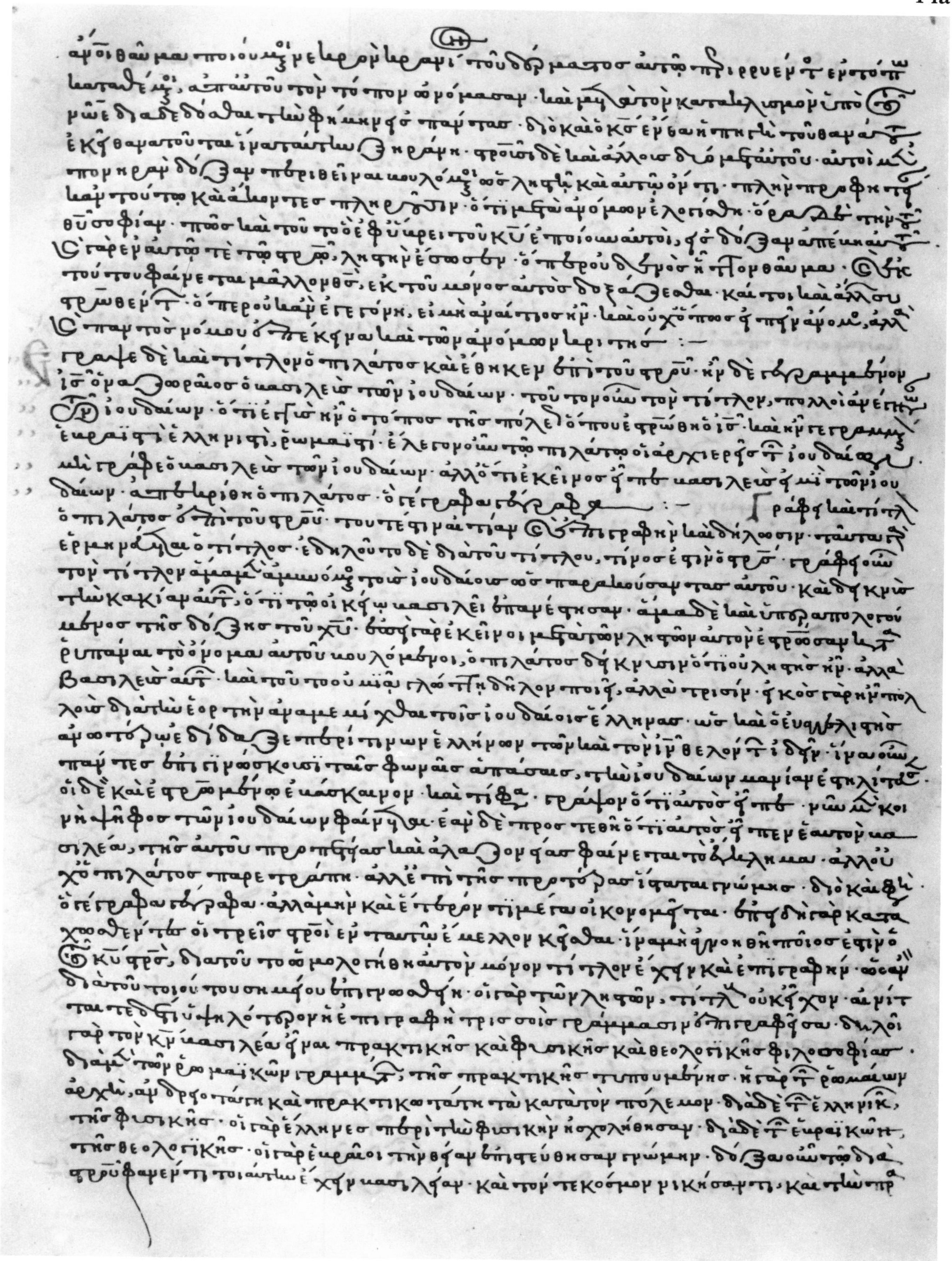

Plate 3

A.D. 1228: Written by the monk Gregorius
Theophylact, archbishop of Bulgaria, Commentary on the Four Gospels
Oxford, Bodleian Library, MS Holkham Greek 64 (fol. 291ᵛ)

Plate 4

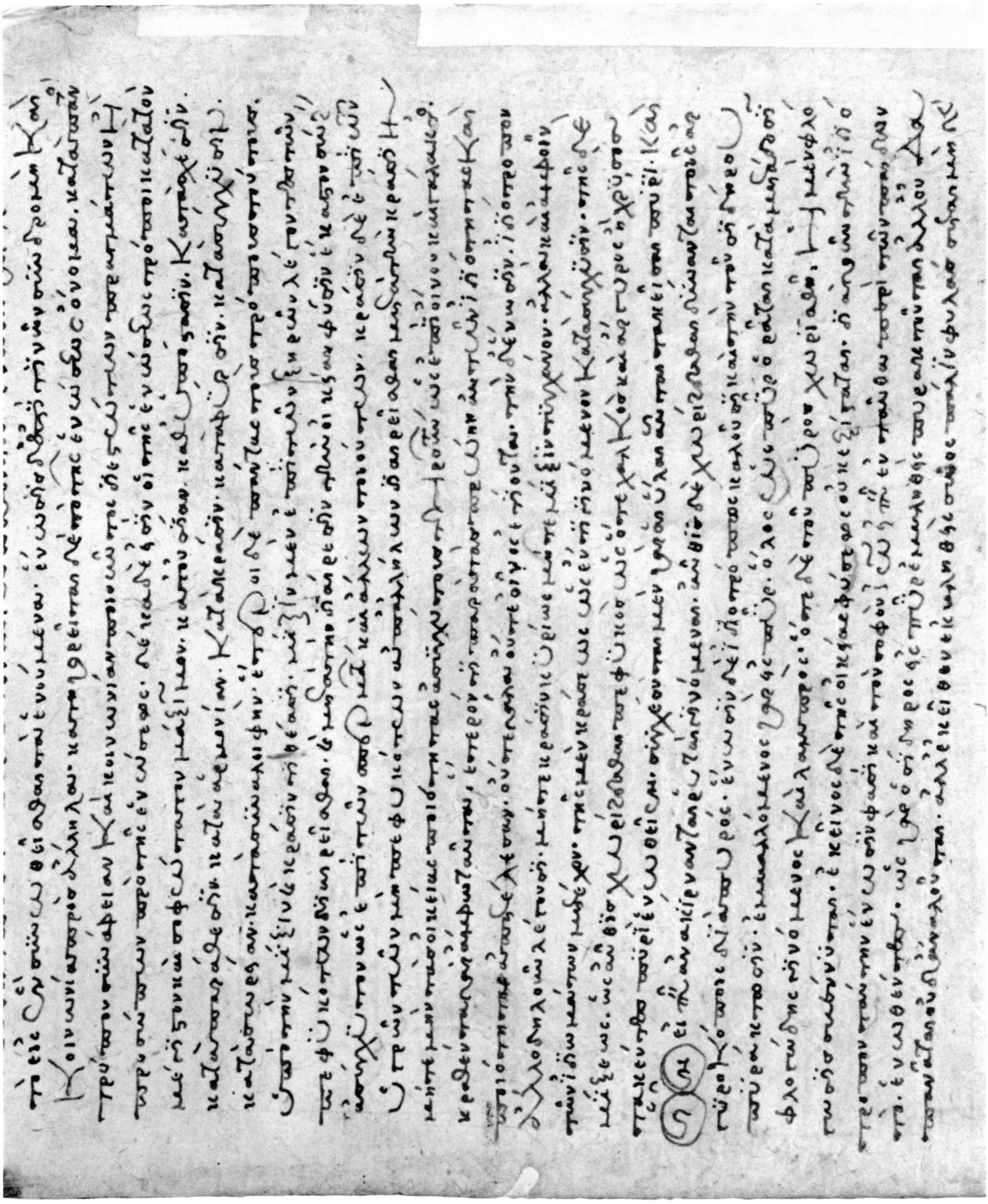

A.D. 1252

John Zonaras, Commentary on the Resurrectional Canons of the Octoechus
London, British Museum, MS Additional 27359 (fol. 126v, lower part)

Plate 5

μαθηταῖς· παρέδ(ωκεν)
τὸ ὄρη ρατου· λε
γετη μη(τρὶ) αὐτοῦ·
γύναι ἰδοὺ ὁ υ(ἱό)ς
σου· ἵτα λεγ(ε) τ(ῷ)
μαθητῇ· ἰδοὺ ἡ
μη(τη)ρ σου· καὶ ἀπ' ἐκε(ί)-
κ(αὶ) μ(ε)ν(ο)ς τῆς ὥρας
ἔλαβεν αὐτὴρ ὁ μ(α)-
θητης εἰς τα ϊ
δια· μ(ε)τὰ τοῦτο εἰδ(ὼς)
δ(ως) ὁ Ἰ(ησοῦ)ς ὅτι παν-
τα ἤδη τετέλε-
σται περι αὐτου·
κλίνας τὴν κεφα-
λὴν παρέδωκ(εν)
τὸ πν(εῦμ)α· Οἱ οὖν
ϊουδαῖοι ϊνα μη
μείνη ἐπὶ τοῦ σ(ταυ)-
ροῦ τὰ σώματα
ἐν τῷ σαββάτῳ· ·
ἐπεὶ π(α)ρασκ(ευὴ)
ἦν ἦρ· ἦν γὰρ

μεγάλη ἡ ἡμέρα
ἐκείνη τοῦ σαββά-
του· ἠρώτησαν τὸν
π(ιλ)ᾶτον ϊνα κα-
τεαγῶσιν αὐτῶν τ(ὰ)
σκέλη κ(αὶ) ἀρθῶσι(ν)·
ἦλθον οὖν οἱ στρατι-
ῶται καὶ τοῦ μ(ὲ)ν
πρώτου κατέαξ(αν)
τὰ σκέλη· καὶ τ(οῦ)
ἄλλου τοῦ συστ(αυ)ρω-
θέντος αὐτῷ· ἐ-
πι δὲ τὸν Ἰ(ησοῦ)ν ἐλθόν
τες· ὡς εἶδον αὐτὸν
ἤδη τεθνηκότα·
οὐ κατέαξαν αὐτ(οῦ)
τὰ σκέλη· ἀλλ' εἷς
τῶν στρατιωτῶν
λόγχη αὐτοῦ τὴν
πλευρὰν ἔνυξεν·
καὶ εὐθὺς ἐξῆλθεν
αἷμα καὶ ὕδωρ· καὶ
ὁ ἑωρακὼς μεμαρ-

A.D. 1253: Written by the lector Demetrius Brizopulus (presumably in Epirus)
Lectionary of the Gospels
Oxford, Bodleian Library, MS E. D. Clarke 8 (fol. 141ᵛ)

Plate 6

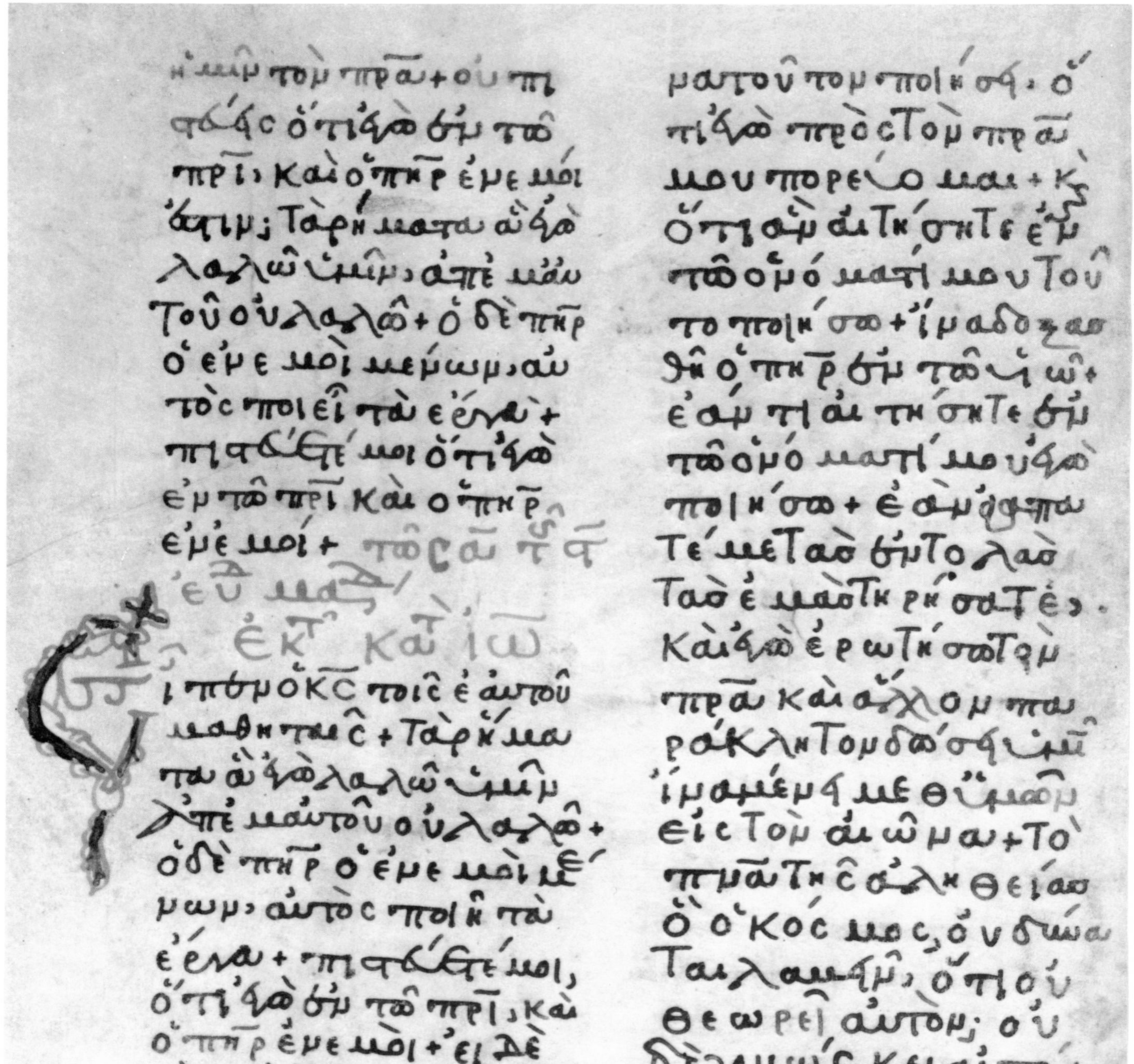

... μείζων τούτων ποιή+ ου πι
σεως ὅτι ἐγὼ ὑμ τω
πρι· καὶ ὁ πηρ ἐμε μοι
ἐστιν; Τὰ ρήματα ἃ ἐγὼ
λαλῶ ὑμῖν ἀπ' ἐμαυ
τοῦ οὐ λαλῶ+ ὁ δὲ πηρ
ὁ ἐμε μοι μενων αὐ
τὸς ποιεῖ τὰ ἔργα +
πιστεύετέ μοι ὅτι ἐγὼ
ἐν τῷ πρι· καὶ ὁ πηρ
ἐμε μοι +

ΤΩ ΣΑ ... ΕΥ ΜΑ
ΕΚ ΚΑ ΙΩ

ιπεν ὁ κς τοις ἑαυτοῦ
μαθηταις + Τὰ ρήμα
τα ἃ ἐγὼ λαλῶ ὑμῖν
ἀπ' ἐμαυτοῦ οὐ λαλῶ +
ὁ δὲ πηρ ὁ ἐμε μοι με
μων, αὐτὸς ποιῆ τὰ
ἔργα + πιστεύετέ μοι,
ὅτι ἐγὼ ἐν τῷ πρι, καὶ
ὁ πηρ ἐμε μοι + εἰ δὲ
μὴ διὰ τὰ ἔργα αὐτα
πιστεύετέ μοι + ἀμὴν
ἀμὴν λέγω ὑμῖν + ὁ πι
στεύων εἰς ἐμὲ τὰ ἔργα
ἃ ἐγὼ ποιῶ κἀκεῖνος
ποιήσει + καὶ μει βο

ματα τον ποι κ ος· ὁ
πι ἐγὼ πρὸς τὸν πρα
μου πορεύομαι + κ(αι)
ὅ τι ἂν αἰτήσητε ἐν
τῷ ὀνόματί μου του
το ποιήσω + ἵνα δοξα
σθῇ ὁ πηρ ἐν τῷ υἱ ῶ
ἐάν τι αἰτήσητε ἐν
τῷ ὀνόματί μου ἐγὼ
ποιήσω + ἐὰν ἀγαπα
τέ με τὰς ἐντολὰς
τὰς ἐμὰς τηρήσατε·
καὶ ἐγὼ ἐρωτήσω τὸν
πρα καὶ ἄλλον πα
ράκλητον δώσει ὑμῖν
ἵνα μένῃ μεθ' ὑμῶν
εἰς τὸν αἰῶνα + τὸ
πνα τῆς ἀληθείας
ὃ ὁ κόσμος, οὐ δύνα
ται λαβεῖν, ὅτι οὐ
θεωρεῖ αὐτόν; οὐ
δὲ γινώσκει αὐτο +
ὑμεῖς δὲ γινώσκετε
αὐτό· ὅτι παρ' ὑμῖν με
νει, καὶ ἐν ὑμῖν ἔσται +
οὐκ ἀφήσω ὑμᾶς ὀρ
φανούς + ἔρχομαι
πρὸς ὑμᾶς + ἔτι μι

A.D. 1255/1256: Written by the lector Georgius Sudarias
Lectionary of the Gospels
London, British Museum, MS Additional 40754 (fol. 25ᵛ)

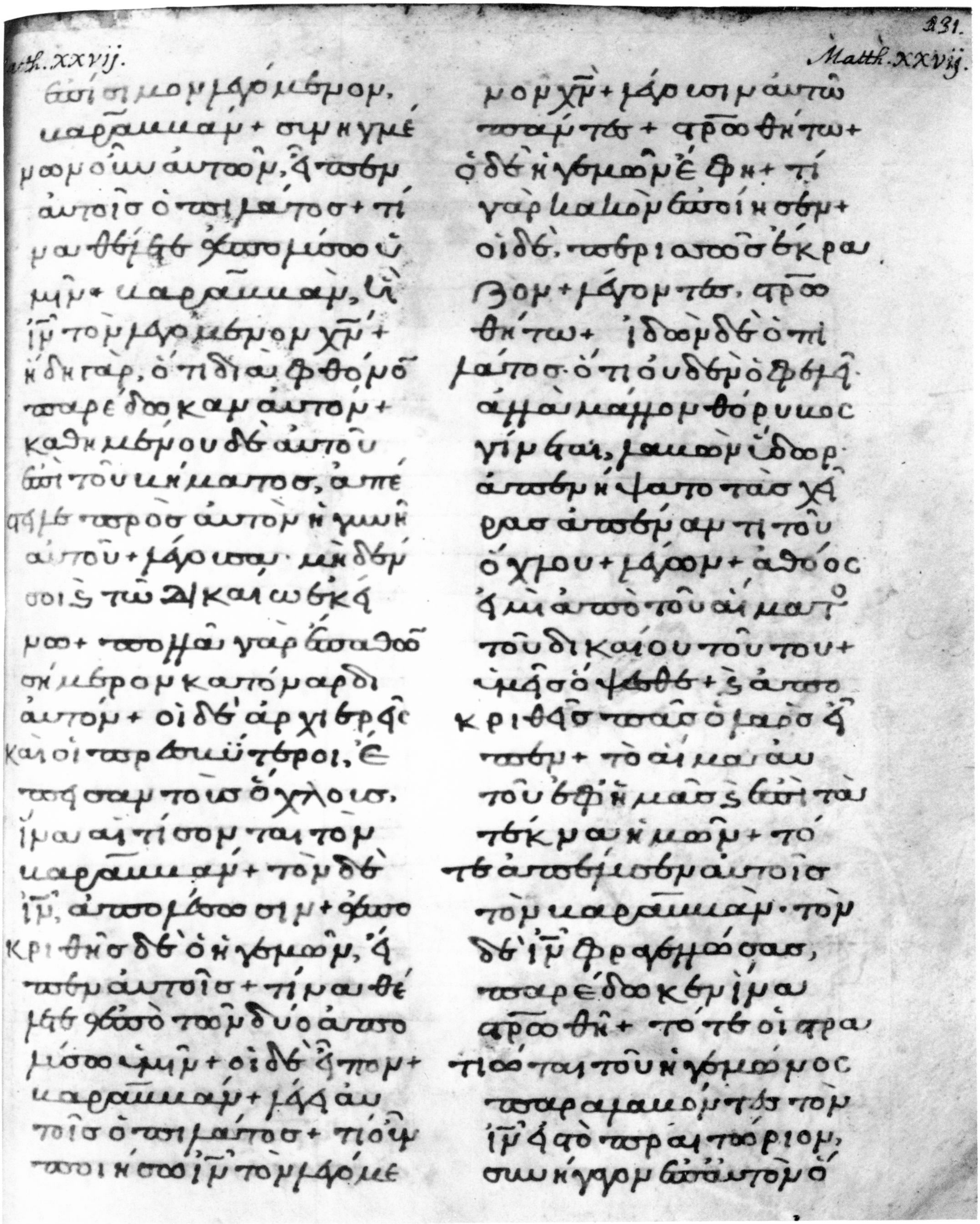

Plate 7

131.

A.D. 1258/1259
Lectionary of the Gospels
Glasgow, University Library, MS Hunter 440 (page 131)

Plate 8

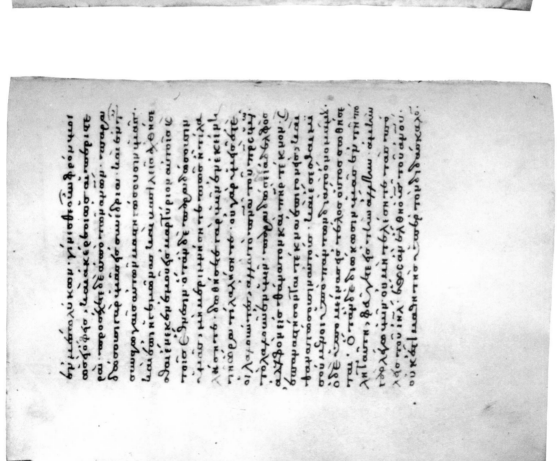

(b) A.D. 1271/1272
Four Gospels
London, British Museum, MS Additional 39597 (fol. 109r)

(a) A.D. 1271/1272
Four Gospels
London, British Museum, MS Additional 39597 (fol. 19v)

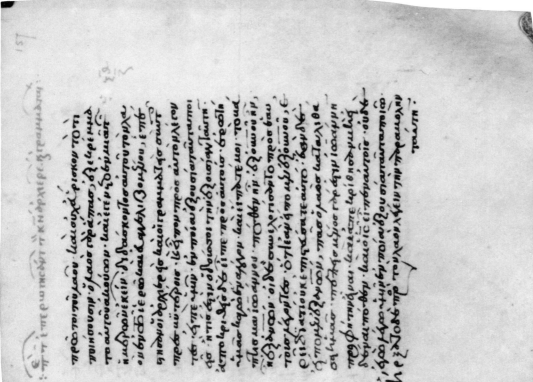

(b) A.D. 1271/1272
Four Gospels
London, British Museum, MS Additional 39597 (fol. 157r)

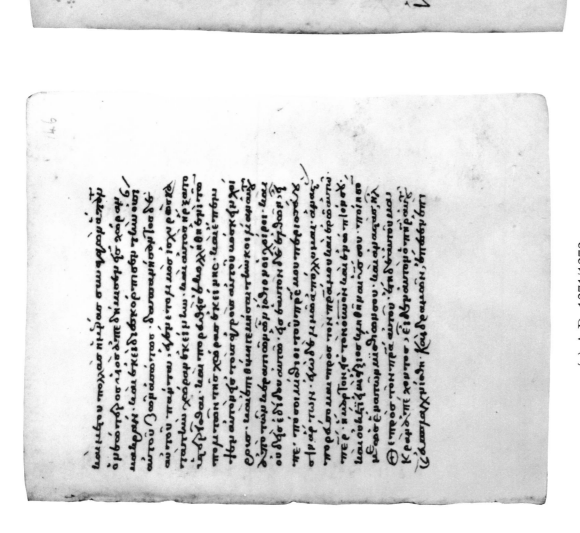

(a) A.D. 1271/1272
Four Gospels
London, British Museum, MS Additional 39597 (fol. 146r)

Plate 9

Plate 10

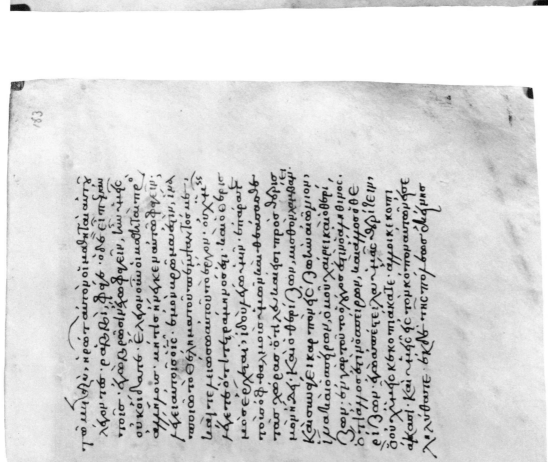

(b) A.D. 1271/1272
Four Gospels
London, British Museum, MS Additional 39597 (fol. 219v)

(a) A.D. 1271/1272
Four Gospels
London, British Museum, MS Additional 39597 (fol. 183r)

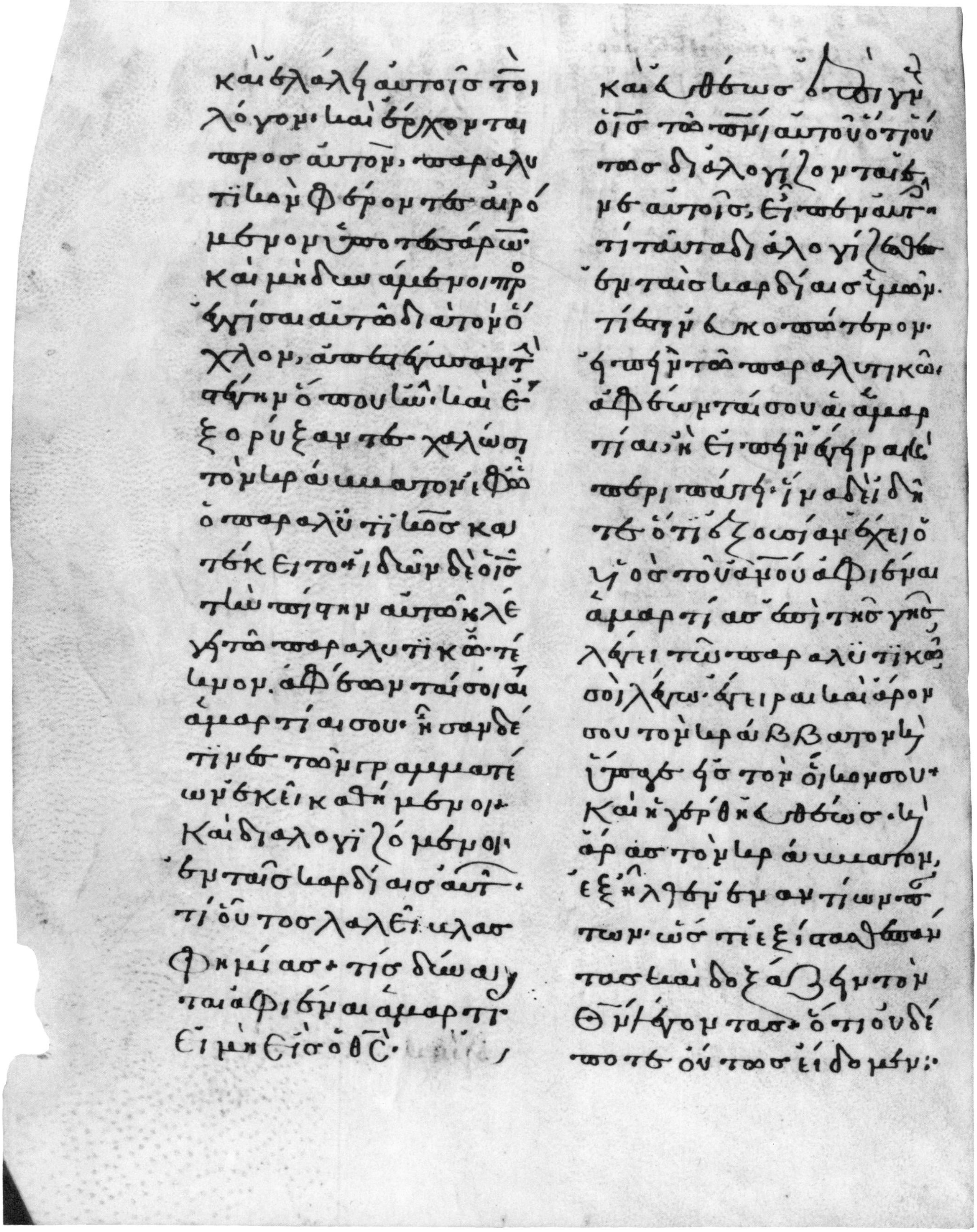

Plate 11

και ελαλει αυτοισ τον
λογον· και ερχονται
προσ αυτον· φεροντεσ παραλυ
τικον· φερομενον υπο
τεσσαρων·
και μη δυναμενοι προσ
εγγισαι αυτω δια τον ο
χλον· απεστεγασαν την
στεγην οπου ην· και εξ
ορυξαντεσ χαλωσι
τον κραββατον εφ ω
ο παραλυτικοσ κατεκει
το· ιδων δε ο ισ την
πιστιν αυτων λε
γει τω παραλυτικω· τε
κνον· αφεωνται σοι αι
αμαρτιαι σου· ησαν δε
τινεσ των γραμματε
ων εκει καθημενοι
και διαλογιζομενοι
εν ταισ καρδιαισ αυ
των· τι ουτοσ λαλει· βλασ
φημιασ· τισ δυναται
αφιεναι αμαρτιασ
ει μη εισ ο θσ·

και ευθεωσ επιγν[ουσ]
ο ισ τω πνι αυτου οτι ου
τωσ διαλογιζονται εν
εαυτοισ ειπεν αυτοισ
τι ταυτα διαλογιζεσθε
εν ταισ καρδιαισ υμων·
τι εστιν ευκοπωτερον·
ειπειν τω παραλυτικω·
αφεωνται σου αι αμαρ
τιαι· η ειπειν εγειραι·
και αρον τον κραββατον
σου και περιπατει· ινα δε ειδη
τε οτι εξουσιαν εχει ο
υσ του ανθρωπου αφιεναι
αμαρτιασ επι τησ γησ
λεγει τω παραλυτικω·
σοι λεγω εγειραι και αρον
σου τον κραββατον
και υπαγε εισ τον οικον σου·
και ηγερθη ευθεωσ· και
αρασ τον κραββατον·
εξηλθεν εναντιον παν
των· ωστε εξιστασθαι
παντασ και δοξαζειν τον
θν λεγοντασ· οτι ουδε
ποτε ουτωσ ειδομεν·

A.D. 1272: Written by the priest Metaxares
Lectionary of the Gospels
London, British Museum, MS Additional 28818 (fol. 33ᵛ)

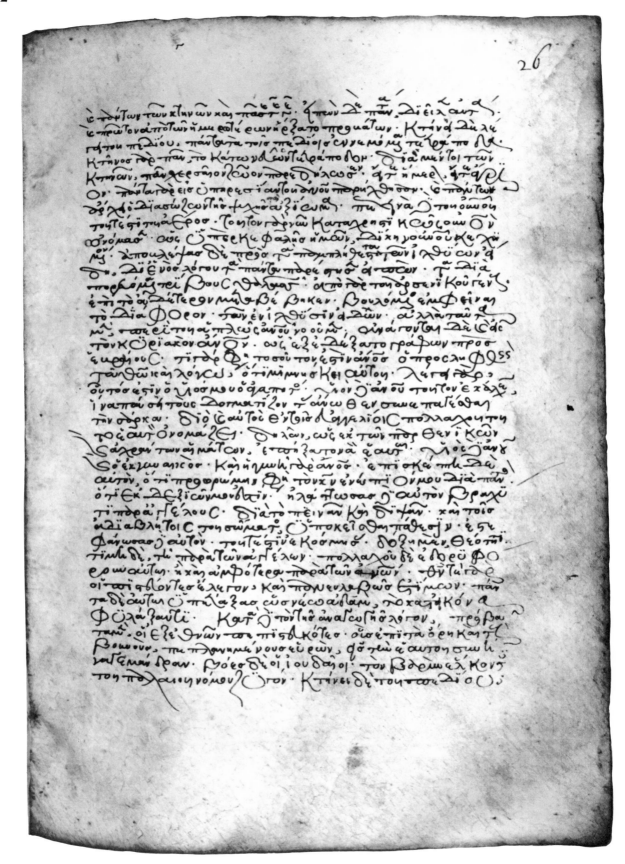

Plate 12

A.D. 1278/1279: Written by the monk Galaction
Euthymius Zigabenus, Commentary on the Psalms
Oxford, Bodleian Library, MS Roe 7 (fol. 26ʳ)

Plate 13

A.D. 1279: Written by the lector Nicolaus ⟨Damenus⟩ in Messina
Aristotle, Eudemian Ethics
Cambridge, University Library, MS Ii.5.44 (fol. 120ʳ)

Plate 14

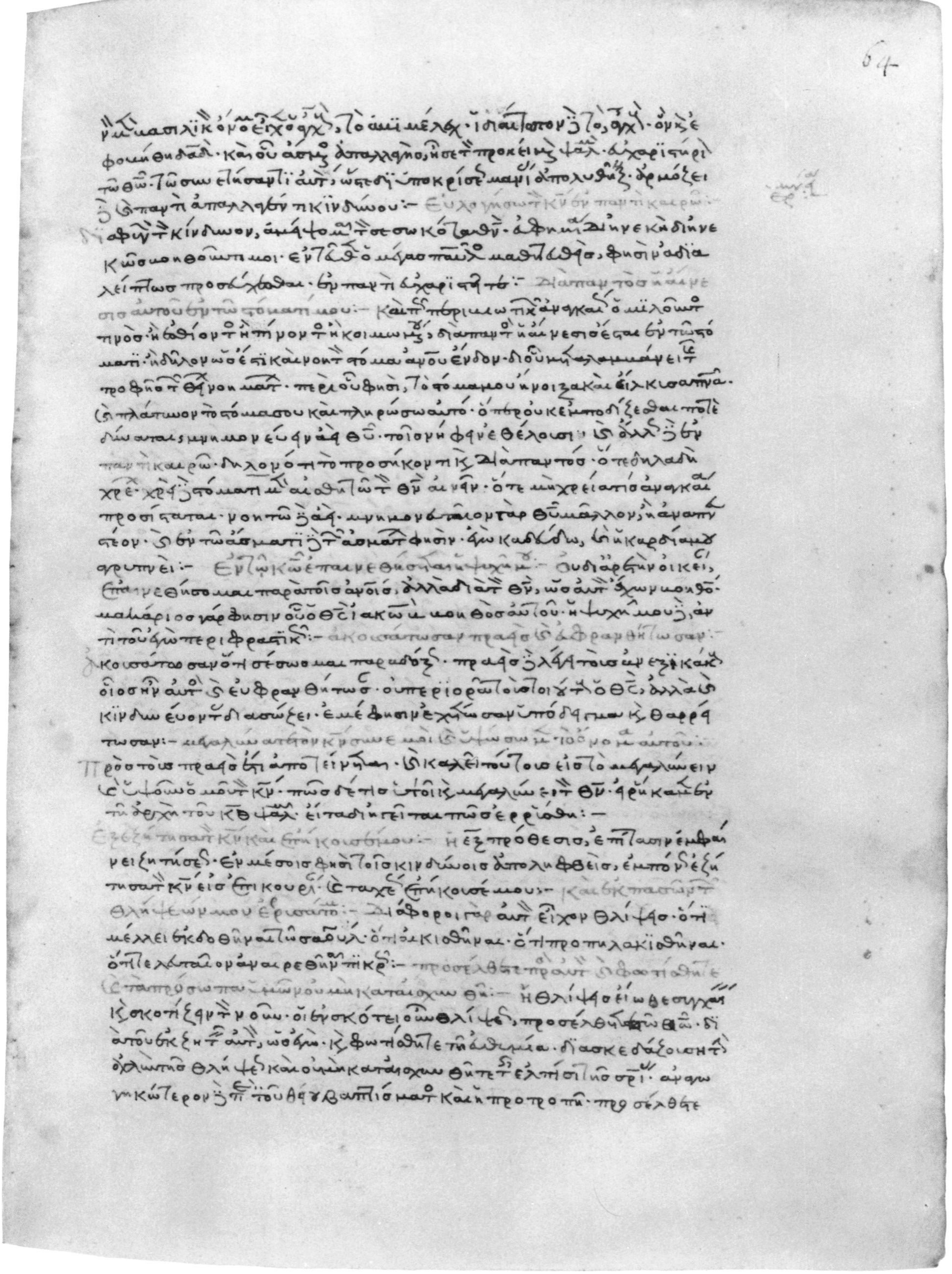

A.D. 1279/1280: Written by Syropulus
Euthymius Zigabenus, Commentary on the Psalms
Oxford, Bodleian Library, MS Barocci 122 (fol. 64r)

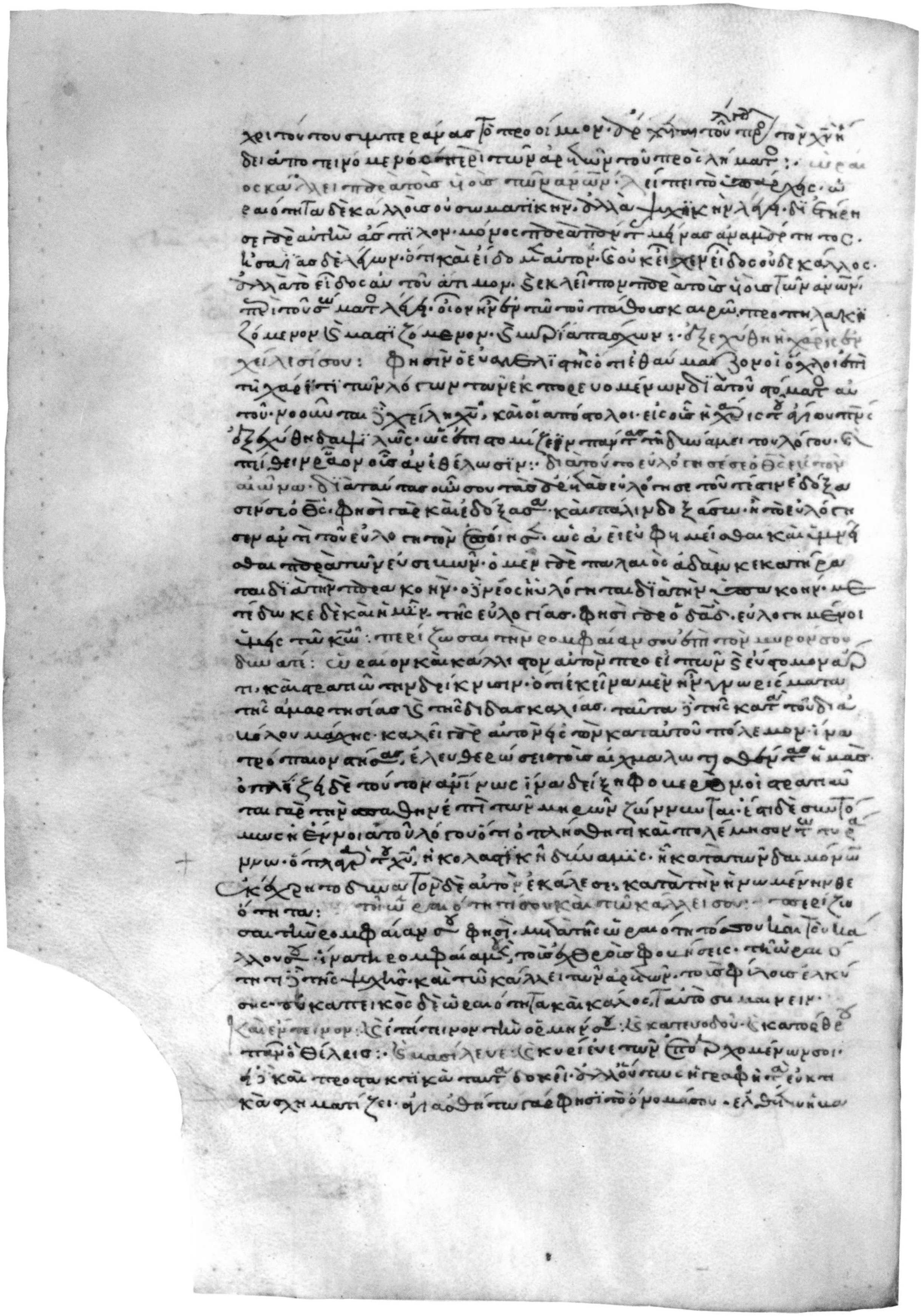

Plate 15

A.D. 1279/1280
Euthymius Zigabenus, Commentary on the Psalms
Oxford, Bodleian Library, MS Barocci 122 (fol. 82ᵛ)

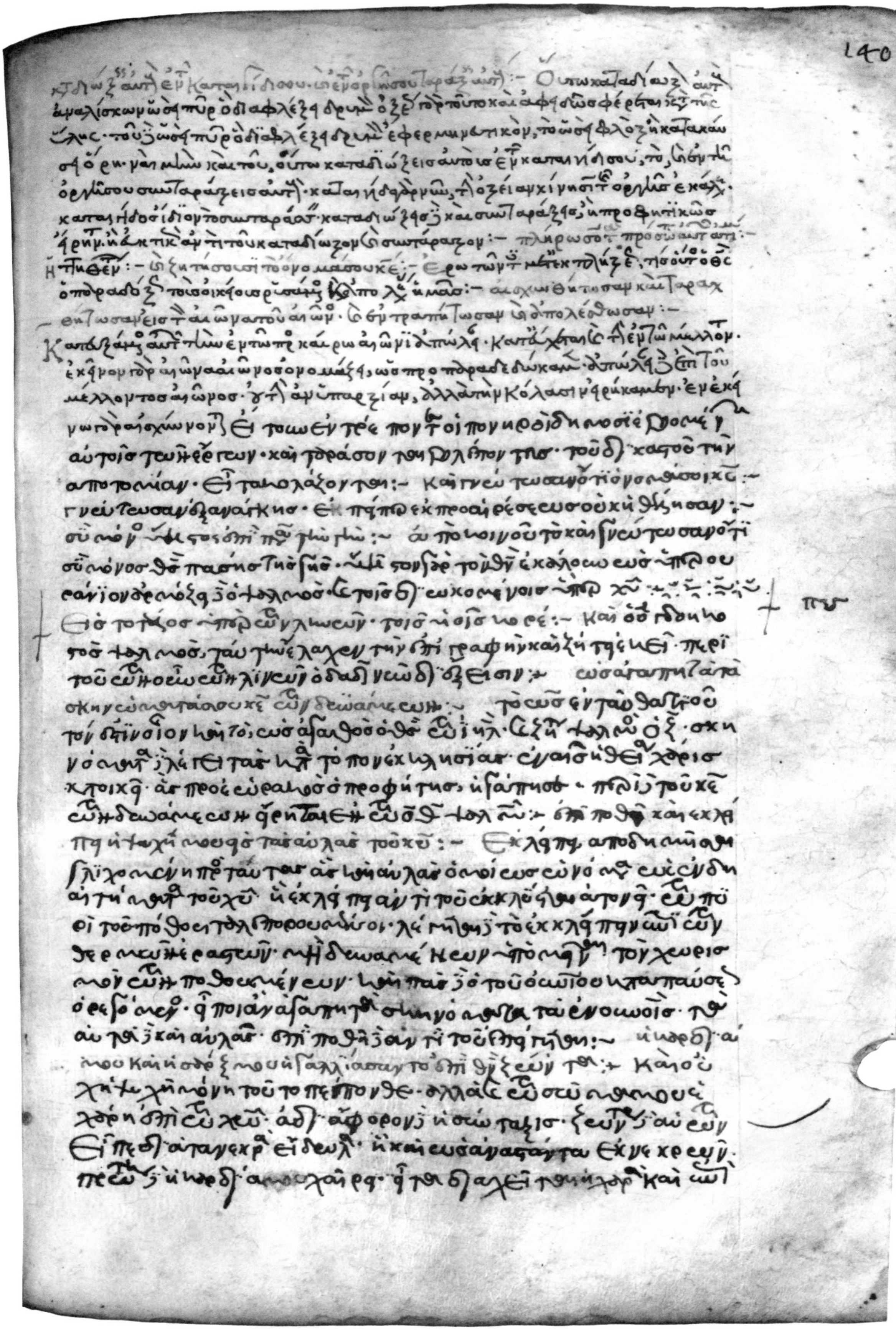

Plate 16

A.D. 1279/1280: Page written partly by Syropulus, partly by another scribe
Euthymius Zigabenus, Commentary on the Psalms
Oxford, Bodleian Library, MS Barocci 122 (fol. 140r)

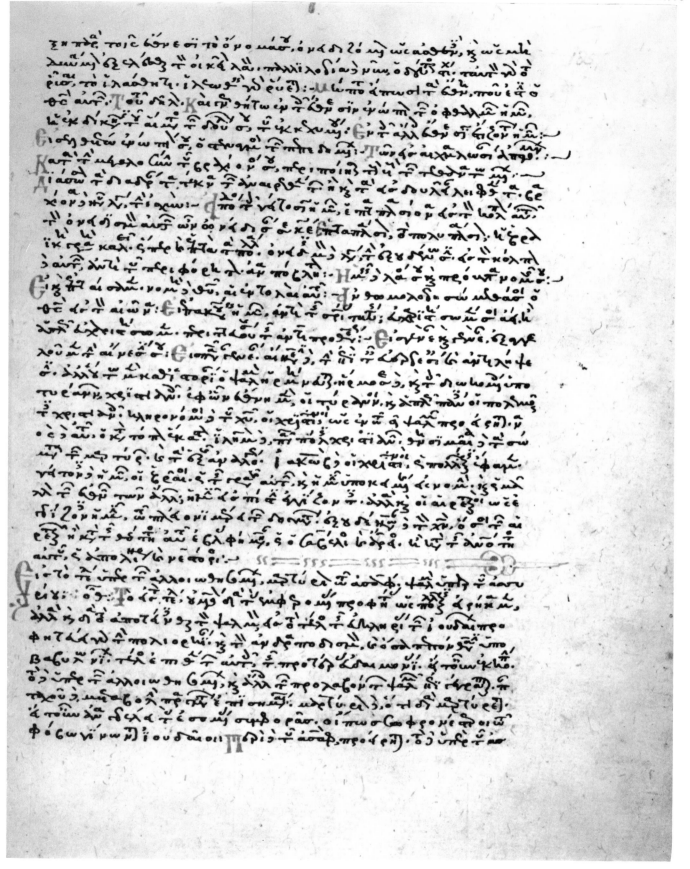

A.D. 1281: Written by the hieromonk Maximus
Euthymius Zigabenus, Commentary on the Psalms
London, British Museum, MS Harley 5575 (fol. 185ʳ)

Plate 18

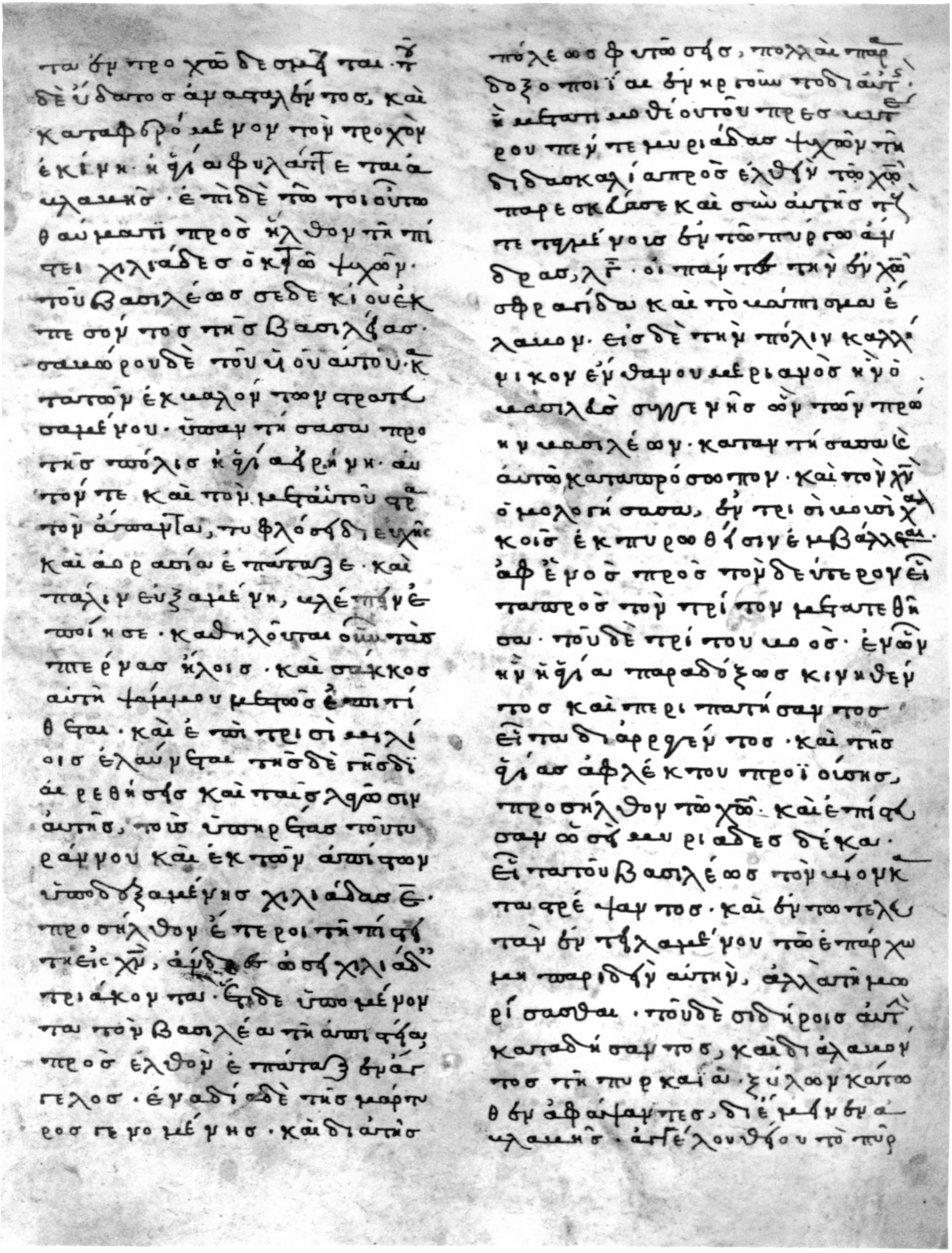

[Greek minuscule manuscript text, two columns]

A.D. 1281
Synaxarion (Lives of Saints)
Oxford, Bodleian Library, MS Auct.E.5.8 (fol. 62ʳ)

Plate 19

(*a*) A.D. 1282: Pages written by Ioasaph (?)
St. John Climacus, Ladder of Paradise
Manchester, John Rylands University Library, MS Rylands Gaster 1574 (fols. 344ᵛ–345ʳ)

(*b*) A.D. 1282
St. John Climacus, Ladder of Paradise
Manchester, John Rylands University Library, MS Rylands Gaster 1574 (fols. 181ᵛ–182ʳ)

Plate 20

(*a*) A.D. 1282
St. John Climacus, Ladder of Paradise
Manchester, John Rylands University Library, MS Rylands Gaster 1574 (fols. 343ᵛ–344ʳ)

(*b*) A.D. 1282
St. John Climacus, Ladder of Paradise
Manchester, John Rylands University Library, MS Rylands Gaster 1574 (fol. 87ʳ)

Plate 21

166

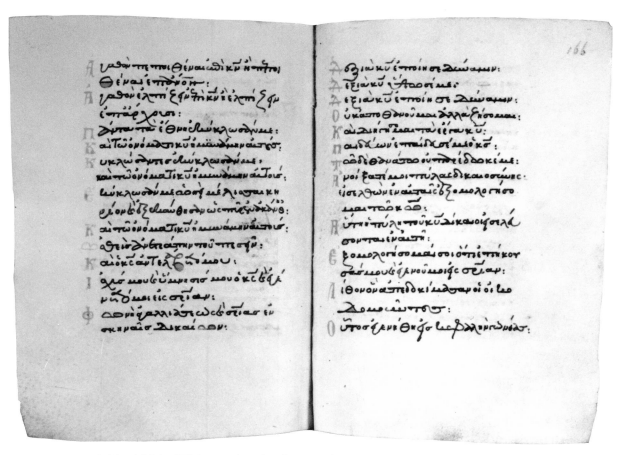

A.D. 1284: Written by Andreas of Brindisi (Terra d'Otranto)
Psalter
London, British Museum, MS Harley 5535 (fols. 165ᵛ–166ʳ)

Plate 22

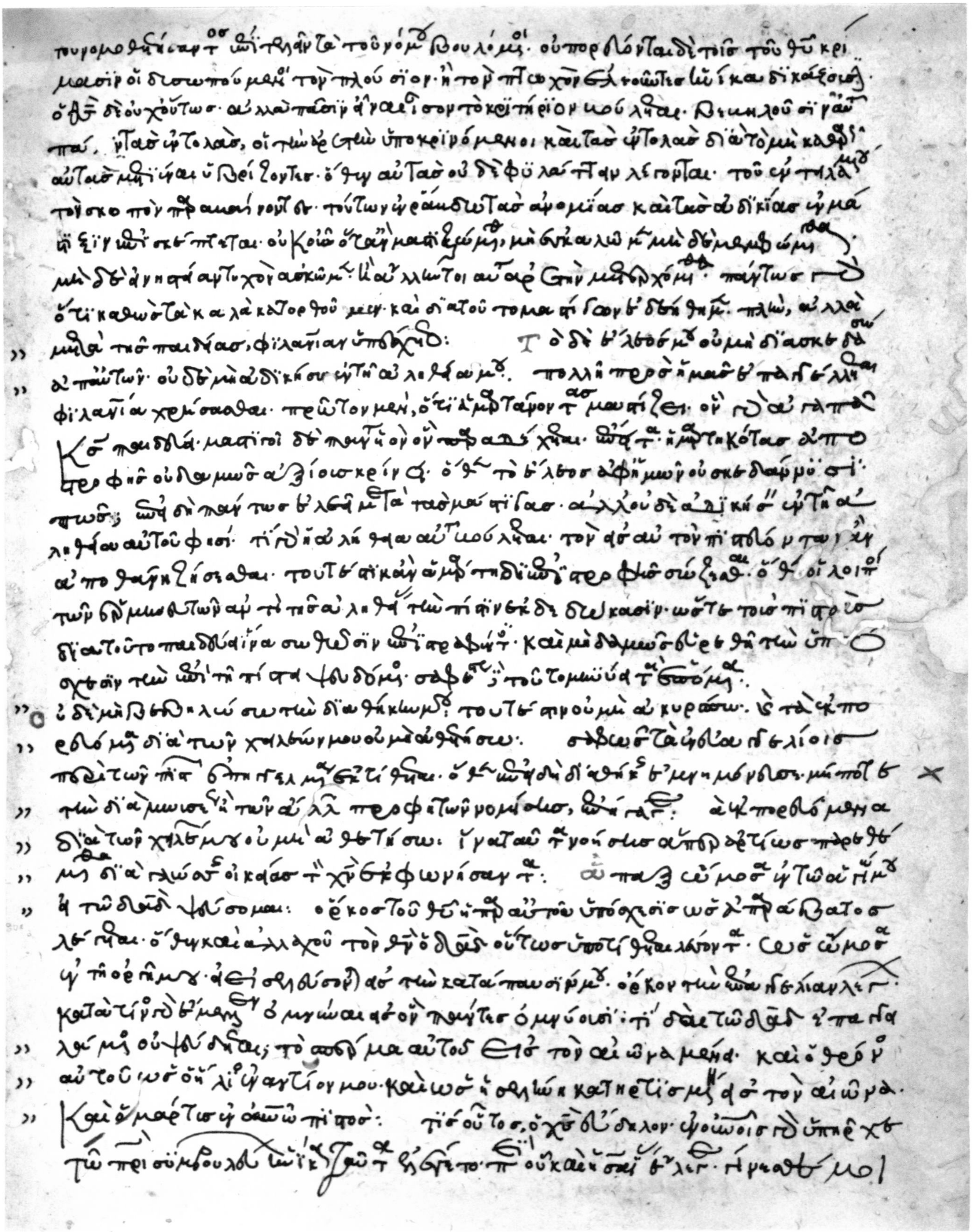

A.D. 1284/1285: Written on Mount Galesion (near Ephesus)
⟨Hesychius of Jerusalem⟩, (Third) Commentary on the Psalms
Oxford, Bodleian Library, MS Roe 13 (fol. 30ʳ)

καὶ ἡμ̅ καὶ ὁ λιμὸσ· καὶ ἡ ζωνία· καὶ ἔτι μ̅ καὶ ἀοίκητοσ
καὶ λιπὼν καὶ ἡ βαύ τησ· καὶ ξωι καὶ θάνατοσ καὶ παντᾱ τᾱ ἐρχ
μενα· τῷ μηδὲ αὐκεὶ βία αὐτὼ καὶ τωναν ⊕ ἀφου σιμ̅ καὶ ἀ πὲλιχει τι
οἱ βοήθειαι· τοῦτο τοῶ δηλῶν δ' αὐτί ὃ περφ̄τουὸ θ̅υ ἐλε̅ ἀπ̅τληε ποίασ
τι θ̅ι̅ο̅· καὶ τ̅ σρετα̅ αὐτοιὸ· εὐθ καὶ τ̅ σρετ̅απ̅ σὸ δῆ̅ καὶ ὁ̅ μοε εα
β' πω̅ τα̅ β αὐτοιῶ ἡ πυρ ώσ καὶ ἡ̅ ικ τ̅ δ ζω καὶ τὰ λιν δια̅ μ̅ ο ὺ
αἱ ἡ ἀργαι αὐτὸ ὲκ τ̅σ αἱ ς̅ λ̅π̅ καὶ β̅ ὅικου δ̅ουλίασ ἐλ̅ υ τερο̅ μ̅εν
αὐτοιὸ· δ̅ δ̅ λιε πο ίαν τα̅ τί μωείασ μὲν λαμ̅ βα̅π̅ οὕτω καὶ τὰ πρ
καὶ ὁ δ̅ καὶ ταῦτ̅ λι̅ ε ρι τοῦ τ̅ δ̅ιορθοῦ τ̅α· παιδ̅ βλόπ̅τα· παιδασ σωπτῶ̅τ
ψ̅ κό τοπ̅ τ̅ τ̅ λι̅ ν καὶ ειαρ έ τ̅η̅ ἀγαμ̅ε̅ δ̅ τα̅ μεα̅ λι̅ ς ρ̅ετ̅ οὗτο̅ ποιοῦ̅ οτι
τα̅ δι̅ μι̅ σοῦ̅ τ̅ο καὶ ἀ̅ π̅ τε τὸ̅ φ̅ με̅· ὁ δ̅ὲ θ̅υ φ̅ίλω̅ ποιᾱ παν̅ τα· οἱ ⊕
ἀ̅ ρ̅ετ̅ωτ̅ ε̅ θ̅υδ̅ ἱμ̅ τῶ̅ π̅ραδ̅δῶ̅ καὶ ἀ̅ λ̅εριτ̅ω̅ ε̅ ζ̅ε̅βα̅λ τοῦπ̅ραδ̅δο
ὲ̅ τε̅ η̅ τ̅ω̅ τον καλ̅ ακλιο̅ δέ ταδα̅ το̅· καὶ ἀ̅ ε̅ ρ̅ετ̅ω̅τ̅ τὸ π̅ τε̅ κ̅ α̅ ν̅ο τὸ δσ̅ο̅
δὲ̅ μ̅εν κα̅ τ̅ λ̅ω̅ τ̅ κ̅· καὶ ὁ̅ π̅ρ̅ α̅μ̅ δ̅π̅οι τι̅ σ τω̅ πρ̅ομ̅ε̅· ὲ̅ κ̅ αφ̅ρ̅ αδ̅ δ̅ι̅ε ετο̅σ̅α̅
ε̅ι̅ τε̅ η̅ τ̅ω̅τ̅ καὶ τ̅λω̅ τ̅ ε̅ ζ̅ρ̅η̅ τ̅ τ̅λ̅ λ̅ο̅· καὶ ἐκαδαι τω̅ δ̅ ο̅ι̅ π̅ερ̅ θ̅υ ο̅υ̅ δ̅ κ̅ αρ̅ντ̅ων̅
μ̅ ρον τα̅ παιδ̅ία· αὐ μα̅ καὶ τ̅ι̅ π̅ οντ̅σ̅· π̅ερ̅ δ̅ οι̅· κ̅ αι̅ ου̅ κ̅ λ̅α̅ εντοτ̅ι̅ τ̅π̅τον
ἡ̅ θ̅ρ̅ απλ̅ο̅ υ̅ιε̅· ου̅τ̅ω δ̅ καὶ ὁ̅ θ̅τ̅· δι̅ ὁ καὶ ὁ̅ παῦ̅ λ̅ε̅ λι̅· τι̅ ο̅ν̅ δ̅ ε̅ αὐ̅ρ̅ι̅ο̅ὸ·
οὐ̅ ὁ̅υ̅ παιδ̅σ̅ ε̅ ιπ̅ε̅· καὶ ὁ̅ σ̅ολομῶ̅· ο̅υ̅δ̅ α̅ π̅ τα̅ κ̅ π̅ αιδ̅δ̅α· μα̅ α̅ι̅ τ̅ οι̅ δ̅ὲ·
παν̅ τα̅ τ̅ υ̅ι̅ο̅υ̅ ο̅υ̅ π̅ραδ̅ δ̅ χ̅ θ̅αι· ἡ̅ δ̅ί κ̅ αιω̅ σ̅υ̅ νη̅ αὐτ̅ ου̅ μ̅ ενη̅ δ̅ τ̅ ορ̅ αι̅ ω̅ ρ̅ α̅·
τὸ̅ υ̅τ̅ ο̅ δ̅δ̅ κ̅ α̅ μ̅ α̅ι̅ υ̅τ̅ ε̅ι̅· ε̅ι̅ π̅ τ̅ δ̅ι̅ αι̅τ̅ οι̅ σ̅ κ̅ α̅ν̅δ̅ α̅λ̅ι̅ ζ̅ο̅μ̅ε̅ σ̅· π̅ ερ̅ο̅ τ̅ αι̅ σ̅υ̅μ̅ π̅ι̅ π̅ τοντ̅
δ̅ι̅ α̅χο̅ρ̅ η̅ τι̅ οι̅· π̅ρ̅ δ̅ λ̅ π̅ι̅ δ̅ασ· μ̅ο̅ γο̅γ̅ου̅χι̅ π̅ τ̅ α̅ι̅ γ̅ω̅ν̅ αὐτ̅ οι̅σ̅ καὶ λ̅ε̅ τ̅ω̅ η̅
μη̅ θ̅ οεν̅ β̅ου̅ ο̅υ̅κο̅ φα̅ ν̅ του̅ μ̅ε̅α̅νο̅ι̅σ̅ α̅γ̅ο̅ι̅ῶ̅ ὁ̅ ε̅ῶ̅ λ̅ω̅ έ̅ α̅ β̅ο̅μ̅η̅σ̅ π̅ερ̅ δ̅ η̅τ̅ιν̅
α̅ β̅ι̅ α̅γ̅κ̅ α̅κ̅ ω̅ π̅ αθ̅ χ̅ ο̅ν̅τ̅ α̅σ· μ̅η̅ γ̅ α̅ τ̅ ὸ̅ δ̅ι̅ κ̅ α̅ δ̅ η̅ ε̅ι̅ α̅ σ̅ δ̅ κ̅ αι̅ ον̅ μ̅ε̅ νη̅ σ̅ τ̅ φ̅
κ̅ αθ̅ δ̅ ε̅ τὸ̅ κ̅ α̅ τ̅ α̅· β̅ι̅ α̅ν̅ θ̅ κ̅ α̅· σ̅ω̅ τ̅ ω̅σ̅ τ̅ χο̅ι̅σ̅· ἡ̅ δ̅ὲ ρ̅ω̅ αὐ̅ τ̅ λω̅ ι̅ σ̅ ε̅ ν̅ τ̅ οι̅·
ὁ̅ ε̅ σ̅υ̅ μ̅η̅ κ̅ α̅ τ̅ α̅ σ̅ αυ̅τ̅ου̅ π̅ εω̅ τ̅ου̅ τ̅ λω̅ τ̅ α̅ φ̅· β̅ε̅ ε̅ γ̅ βᾱλ̅λ̅ο̅· δ̅ δ̅ὲ̅ μ̅ εμ̅ι̅ κ̅ αθ̅δ̅
κ̅ εα̅ ον̅ τ̅ α̅ υ̅ α̅ μ̅ε̅ τ̅ η̅μ̅ α̅τ̅· ὁ̅ γᾱ ι̅ μᾱ̅ τί̅ μ̅ ω̅ ρ̅ ε̅ι̅ α̅ν̅· καὶ ε̅ φ̅ι̅ κ̅ αιου̅ τ̅ λω̅ π̅ λη̅
μ̅ ε̅λ̅ ο̅υ̅ ν̅ τ̅ ω̅ν̅· τ̅ λω̅ δ̅ι̅ κ̅ αι̅ αρ̅ω̅ι̅· δ̅ φ̅ α̅ν̅ τ̅ δ̅φ̅ο̅ι̅σ̅· π̅ α̅ λ̅ αι̅ο̅υ̅σ̅ π̅ ερ̅ αγ̅ ν̅ε̅ π̅ α̅
τὸ̅ τ̅ σῶ̅ αι̅ω̅σ̅ σ̅ χ̅ ρ̅ο̅σ̅· καὶ τ̅ι̅ λ̅ι̅ π̅ οτ̅ σ̅ δ̅ α̅ν̅α̅ καὶ τ̅ ο̅υ̅ δ̅ ᾱπ̅ τ̅ ο̅υ̅ δ̅ κ̅ ο̅ε̅υ̅ φ̅ αι̅
τ̅ ου̅ ἡ̅ α̅γ̅ο̅ι̅σ̅ αὐ π̅ α̅ τ̅ δ̅ μ̅ ε̅ ὁ̅ σ̅ αι̅ τ̅ α̅ι̅· τοῦτο δ̅η̅ ε̅ ξ̅ αι̅ π̅ δ̅ ε̅ αι̅ σ̅ο̅ μᾱ̅· π̅ α̅υ̅ λ̅ο̅ν̅
ε̅ κ̅ α̅ ρον̅· τ̅ κ̅ η̅ ε̅ υ̅ κ̅ τ̅ π̅ τ̅σ̅ ὅι̅κου̅ μ̅ η̅σ̅· τ̅ον̅ δ̅ ᾱ· τ̅ ε̅ι̅ ὅι̅ μ̅ο̅ ρ̅ α̅σ̅ π̅ αδ̅ύ̅ τ̅· τ̅ αδ̅ ὁ̅
ᾱ σ̅ο̅ρ̅ αὐ̅ δ̅ κ̅ ο̅ σ̅· α̅ π̅ ε̅ν̅ ε̅χ̅ θ̅ υ̅ τ̅· το̅υ̅ τω̅ν̅ φ̅ ρ̅υ̅ κ̅ τ̅ω̅ν̅ κ̅ οι̅ν̅ω̅ρ̅ η̅ σ̅ αρ̅ τ̅ ι̅ μ̅ ε̅ι̅ δ̅ απ̅ ε̅σ̅ ⊙ο̅υ̅
τὸ̅ ὅκ̅λ̅η̅ σ̅ τ̅ λι̅ ὸ̅ ε̅ κ̅ λο̅ τ̅ π̅ ο̅σ̅· τ̅ ορ̅ρ̅ υ̅ μ̅ φ̅ α̅ το̅ τ̅ ο̅υ̅ χ̅υ̅· τ̅ ον̅ αὐ̅ δ̅ ε̅ λι̅ κ̅ λω̅ ω̅ι̅ σ̅ μ̅ ε̅α̅
μ̅ εν̅ ον̅ π̅ ολι̅ τ̅ σ̅ αν̅· τ̅ ορ̅ το̅ σ̅ αι̅ τ̅ λω̅ δ̅ ζ̅ ε̅ω̅ καὶ τ̅ ορ̅ η̅ω̅ σ̅ αρ̅ τ̅ α̅· ἀ̅ τὸ̅ δ̅ η̅ ε̅ β̅ δ̅ο̅υ̅
λ̅ ᾱ δ̅ η̅ μ̅ η̅ μ̅ αλ̅ ε̅ ρ̅ δ̅ υ̅ μ̅η̅ σ̅ αι̅ αὐ̅ τ̅ ω̅· μ̅η̅ δ̅ι̅ α̅ μ̅ αρ̅ χ̅ ε̅ δ̅ αι̅ αὐ̅τ̅ ου̅· ἀ̅ λ̅ λ̅ ω̅ σ̅ ι̅ κ̅ α̅
ἡ̅ μ̅ α̅ ε̅ τ̅ α̅ μ̅ε̅· καὶ δ̅ λ̅ α̅ σ̅ φ̅ η̅ μ̅η̅ καὶ δ̅ ε̅ σ̅ω̅ κ̅ η̅ κ̅ α̅ τ̅ α̅· π̅ ὸ̅ λ̅ ε̅ω̅ ι̅ π̅ αγ̅ αγ̅η̅ αὐ̅

A.D. 1284/1285: Written on Mount Galesion (near Ephesus)
St. John Chrysostom, Expositiones in Psalmos
Oxford, Bodleian Library, MS Roe 13 (fol. 103ᵛ)

Plate 24

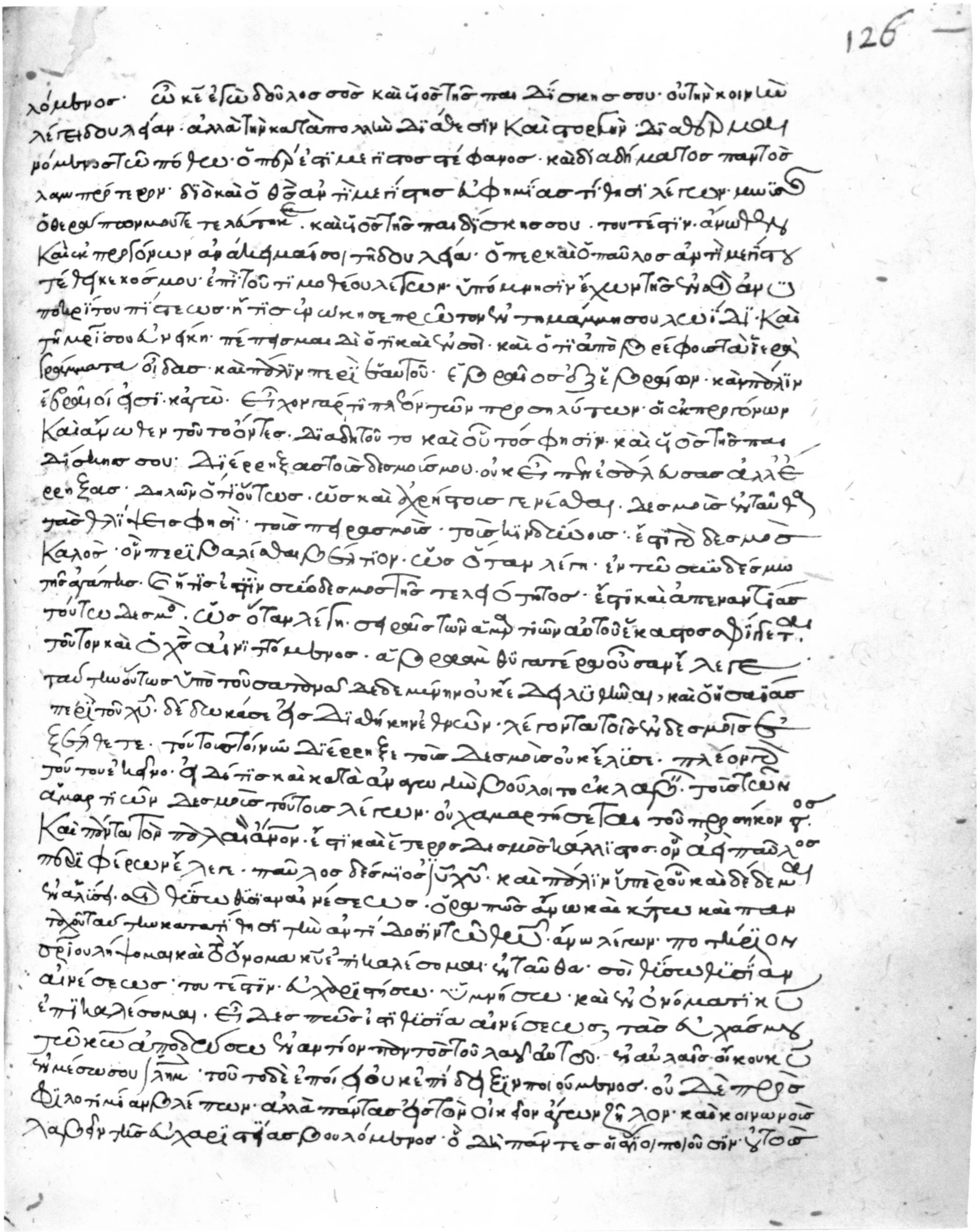

126

A.D. 1284/1285: Written on Mount Galesion (near Ephesus)
St. John Chrysostom, Expositiones in Psalmos
Oxford, Bodleian Library, MS Roe 13 (fol. 126ʳ)

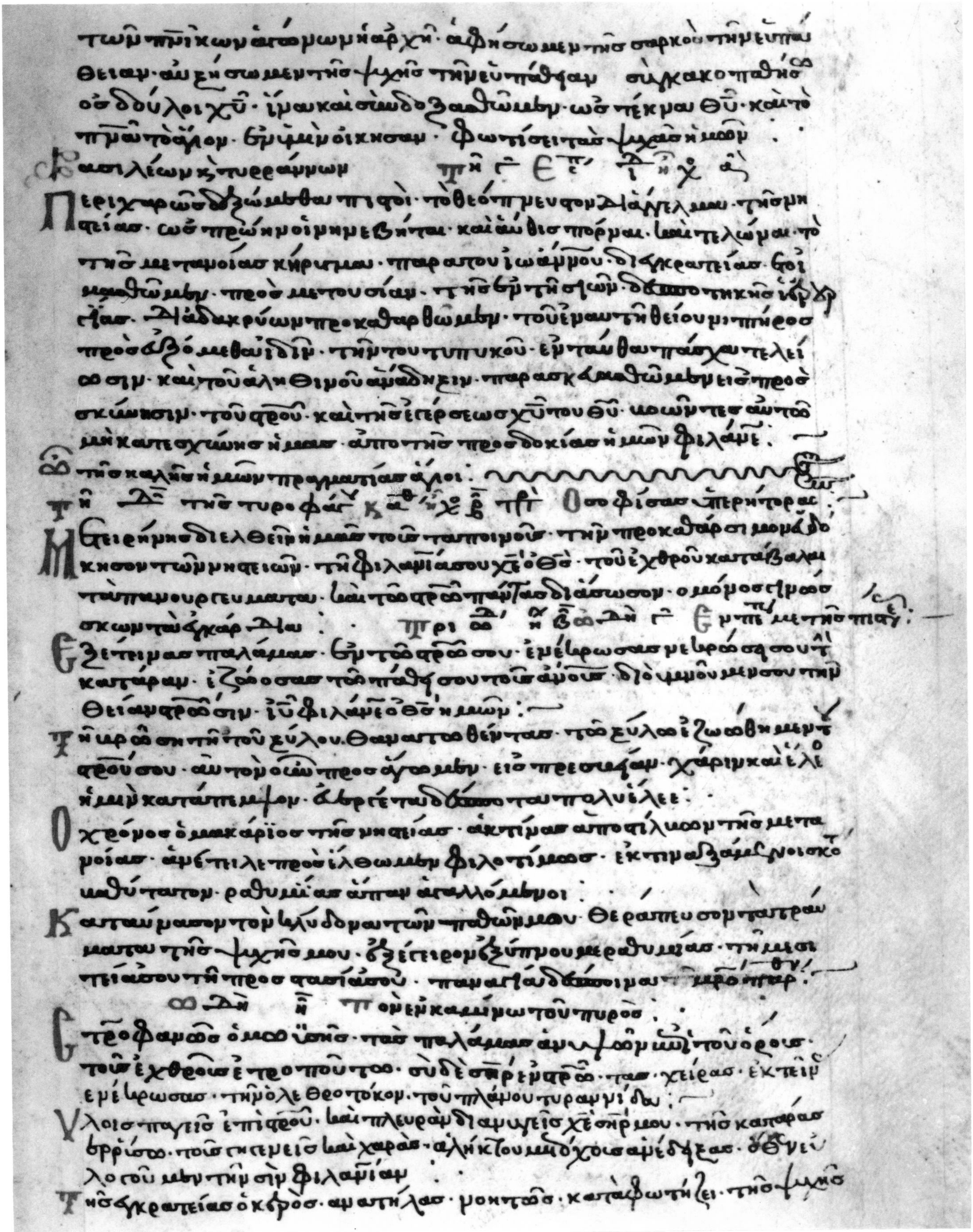

Plate 25

A.D. 1285: Written by the priest Nilus Cucubistianus
Triodion
Oxford, Bodleian Library, MS Auct.T.3.6 (fol. 12r)
(end of line 6 and lines 5-1 from the bottom are written by a different hand)

Plate 26

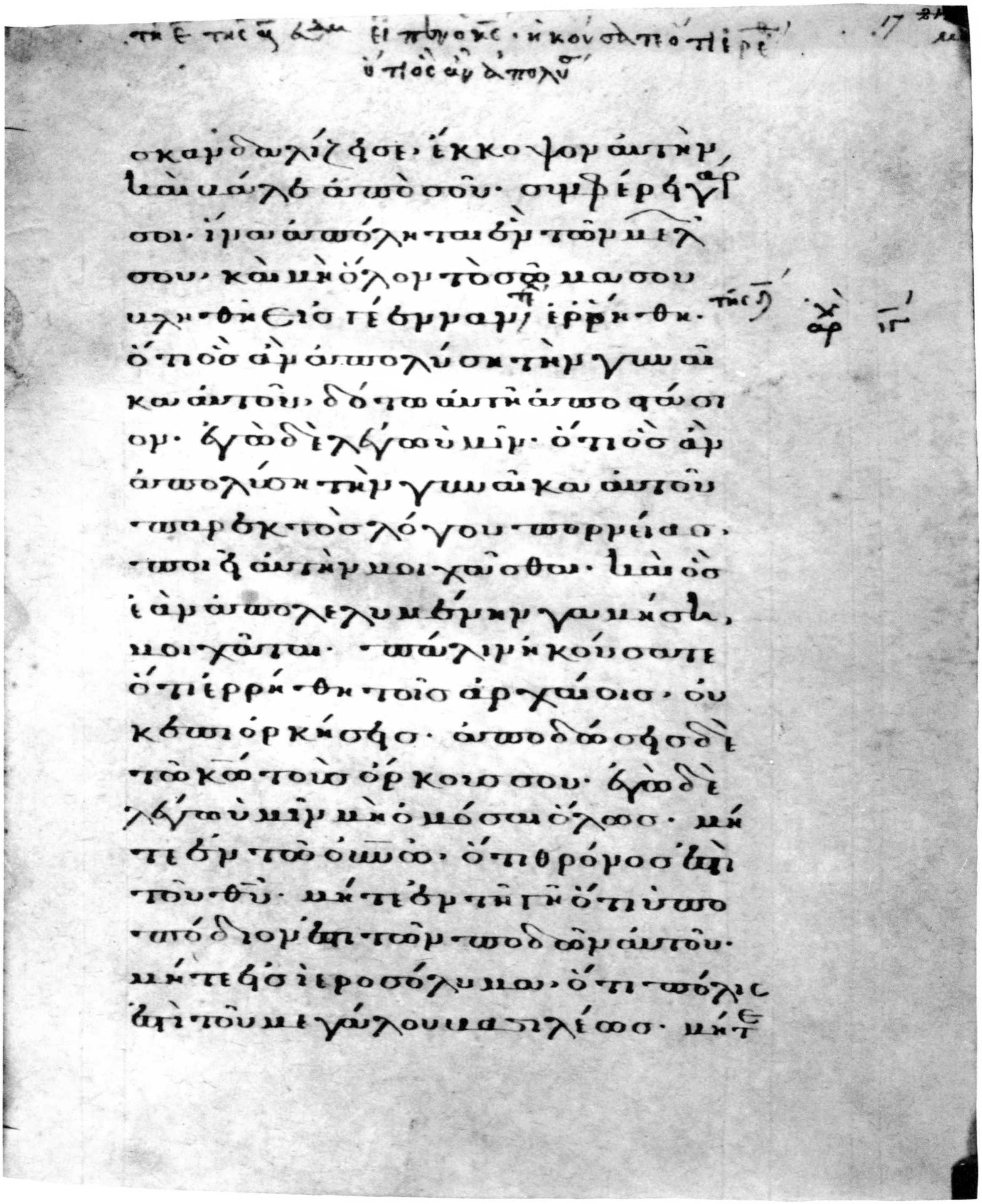

A.D. 1285: Written by the hieromonk Theophilus
Four Gospels
London, British Museum, MS Burney 20 (fol. 17ʳ)

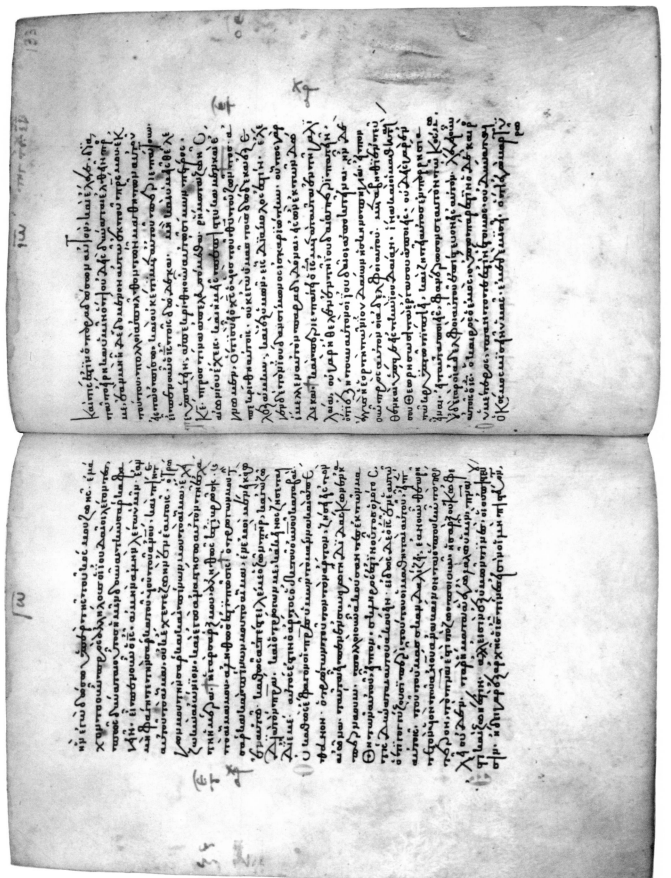

Plate 27

A.D. 1285/1286: Written by Nicetas Maurones
Four Gospels
Oxford, Bodleian Library, MS Laud Greek 3 (fols. 132v–133r)

Plate 28

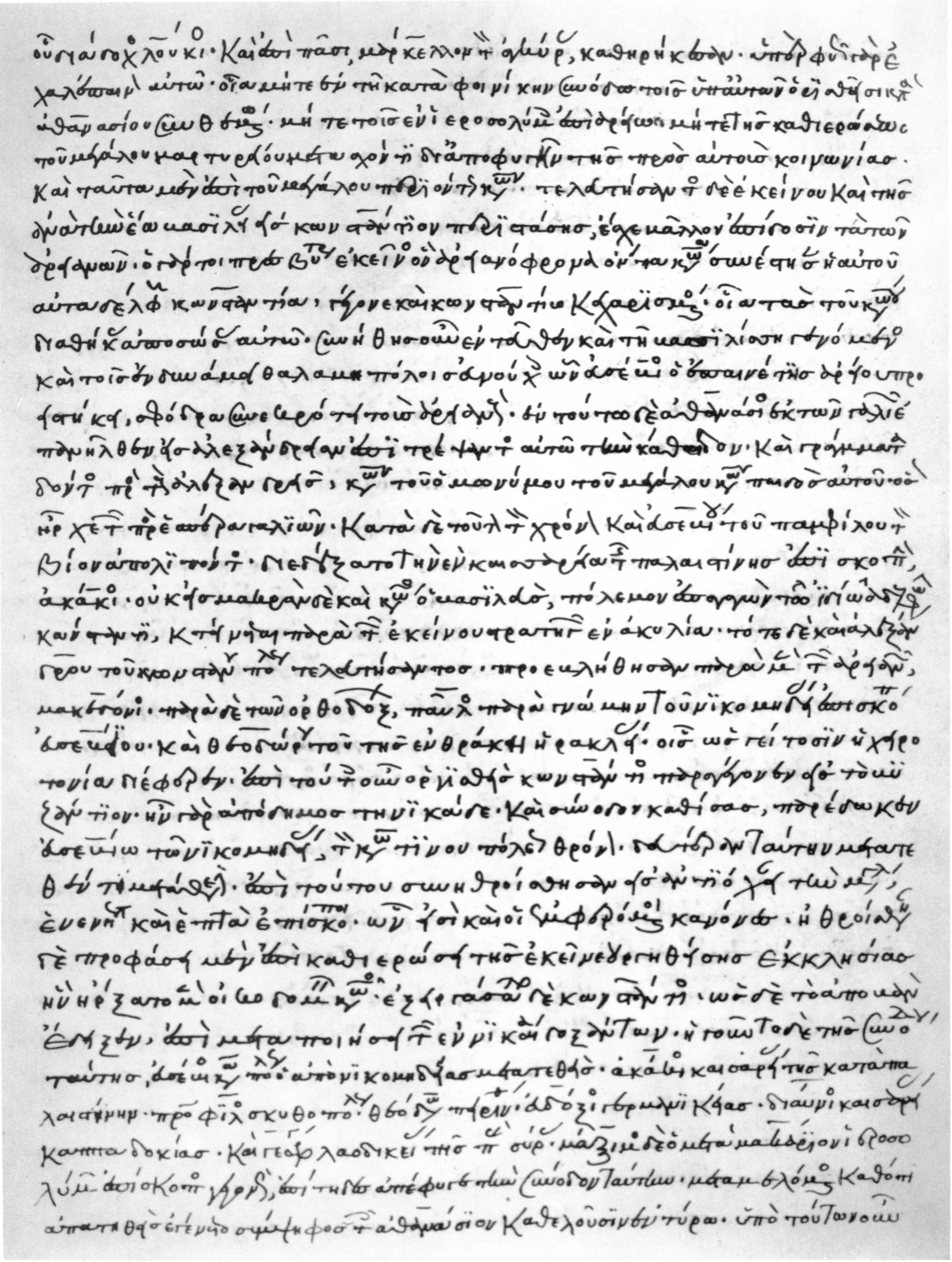

A.D. 1286: Written by the monk Ionas
Nicetas Choniates, Panoplia dogmatica (Thesaurus orthodoxiae)
Oxford, Bodleian Library, MS Roe 22 (fol. 146ᵛ)

Plate 29

A.D. 1286: Written by the monk Ionas
Nicetas Choniates, History
Oxford, Bodleian Library, MS Roe 22 (fol. 440ᵛ)

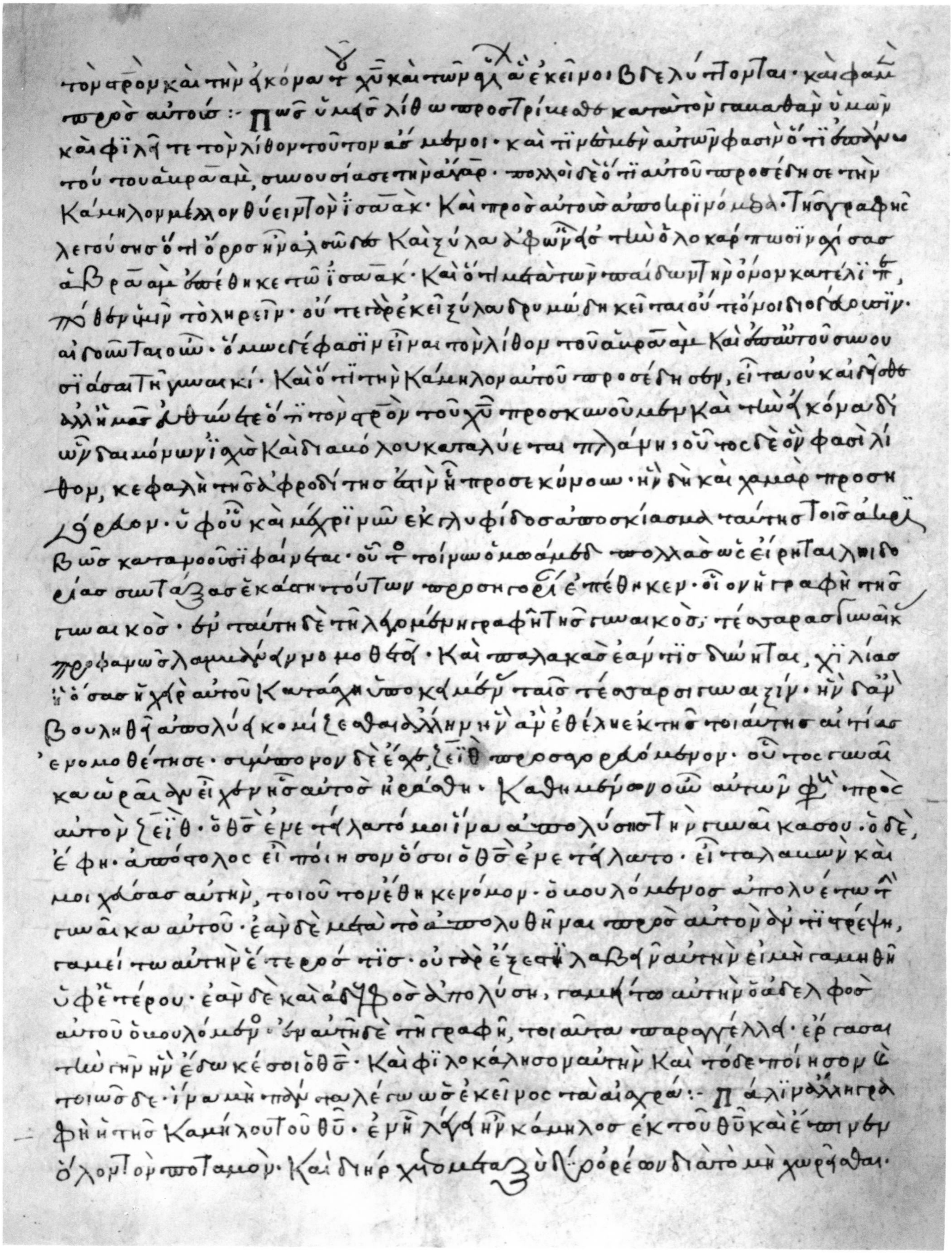

Plate 30

A.D. 1286: Written by the monk Ionas
Nicetas Choniates, Panoplia dogmatica (Thesaurus orthodoxiae)
Oxford, Bodleian Library, MS Roe 22 (fol. 290ᵛ)

Plate 31

A.D. 1286: Written by the monk Ionas
St. Anastasius Sinaita, Viae dux
Oxford, Bodleian Library, MS Roe 22 (fol. 507ʳ)

Plate 32

A.D. 1286: Page written by scribe B
Nicetas Choniates, Panoplia dogmatica (Thesaurus orthodoxiae)
Oxford, Bodleian Library, MS Roe 22 (fol. 195r)

Plate 33

A.D. 1286: Page written by scribe C
Nicetas Choniates, Panoplia dogmatica (Thesaurus orthodoxiae)
Oxford, Bodleian Library, MS Roe 22 (fol. 71ʳ)

A.D. 1286: Page written by scribe E
Nicetas Choniates, Panoplia dogmatica (Thesaurus orthodoxiae)
Oxford, Bodleian Library, MS Roe 22 (fol. 390ᵛ)

Plate 34

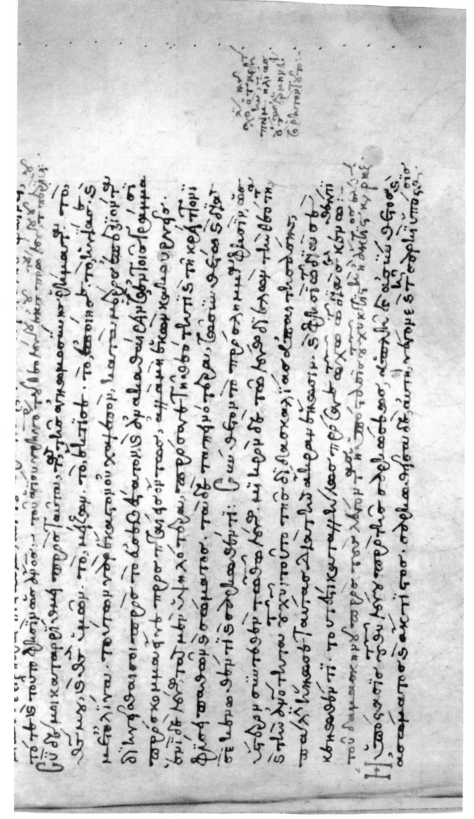

A.D. 1286: Page part written by scribe F

Nicetas Choniates, Panoplia dogmatica (Thesaurus orthodoxiae)

Oxford, Bodleian Library, MS Roe 22 (fol. 399r lines 18–33)

Plate 35

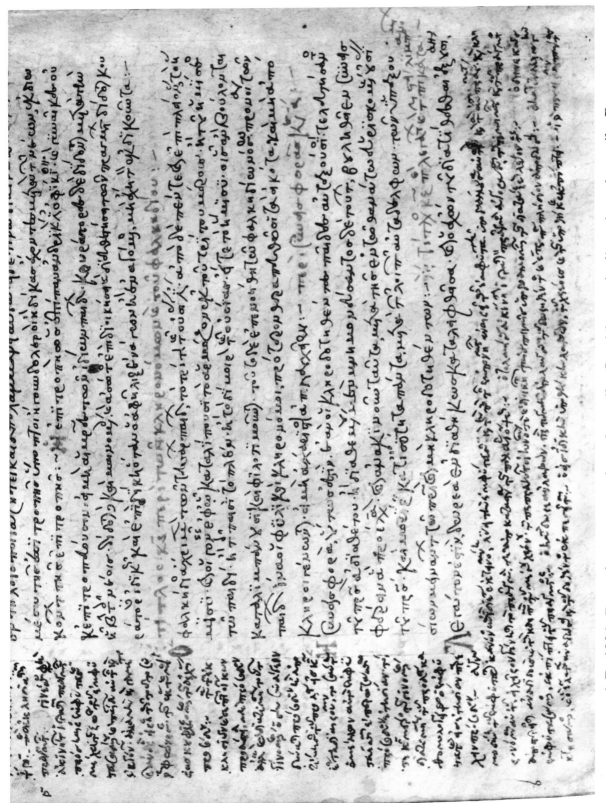

A.D. 1286: Part of text page written by scribe G, with marginalia written by scribe B
Michael Attaleiates, Law Treatise
(with marginal excerpts from the Collectio Constitutionum Ecclesiasticarum Tripartita)
Oxford, Bodleian Library, MS Roe 22 (fol. 460v, lower part)

A.D. 1286: Page written by scribes H (lines 1–6) and J (lines 6–33)
St. Anastasius Sinaita, Viae dux
Oxford, Bodleian Library, MS Roe 22 (fol. 501ᵛ)

Plate 37

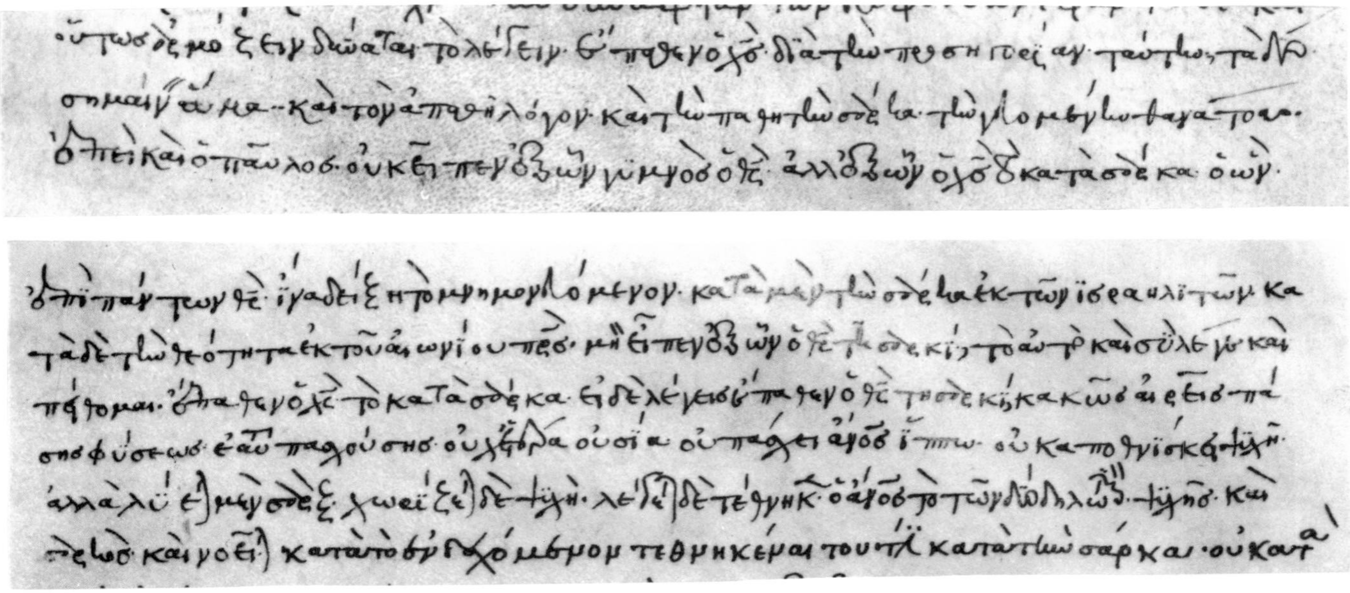

Plate 38

(*a*) A.D. 1286: Page parts written by scribe D
Nicetas Choniates, Panoplia dogmatica (Thesaurus orthodoxiae)
Oxford, Bodleian Library, MS Roe 22 (fols. 227ᵛ lines 31–33, 228ʳ lines 1–6)

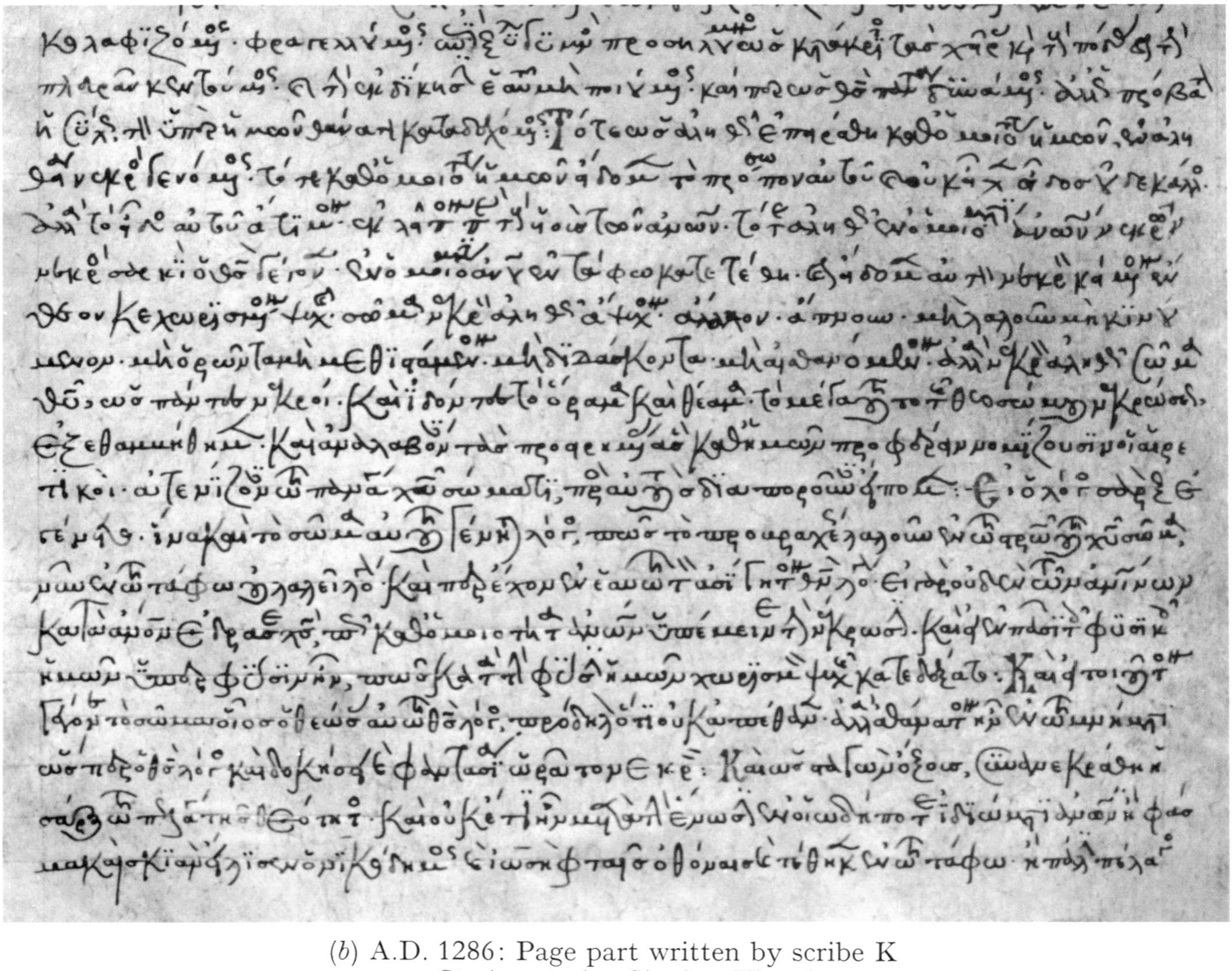

(*b*) A.D. 1286: Page part written by scribe K
St. Anastasius Sinaita, Viae dux
Oxford, Bodleian Library, MS Roe 22 (fol. 534ᵛ lines 15–33)

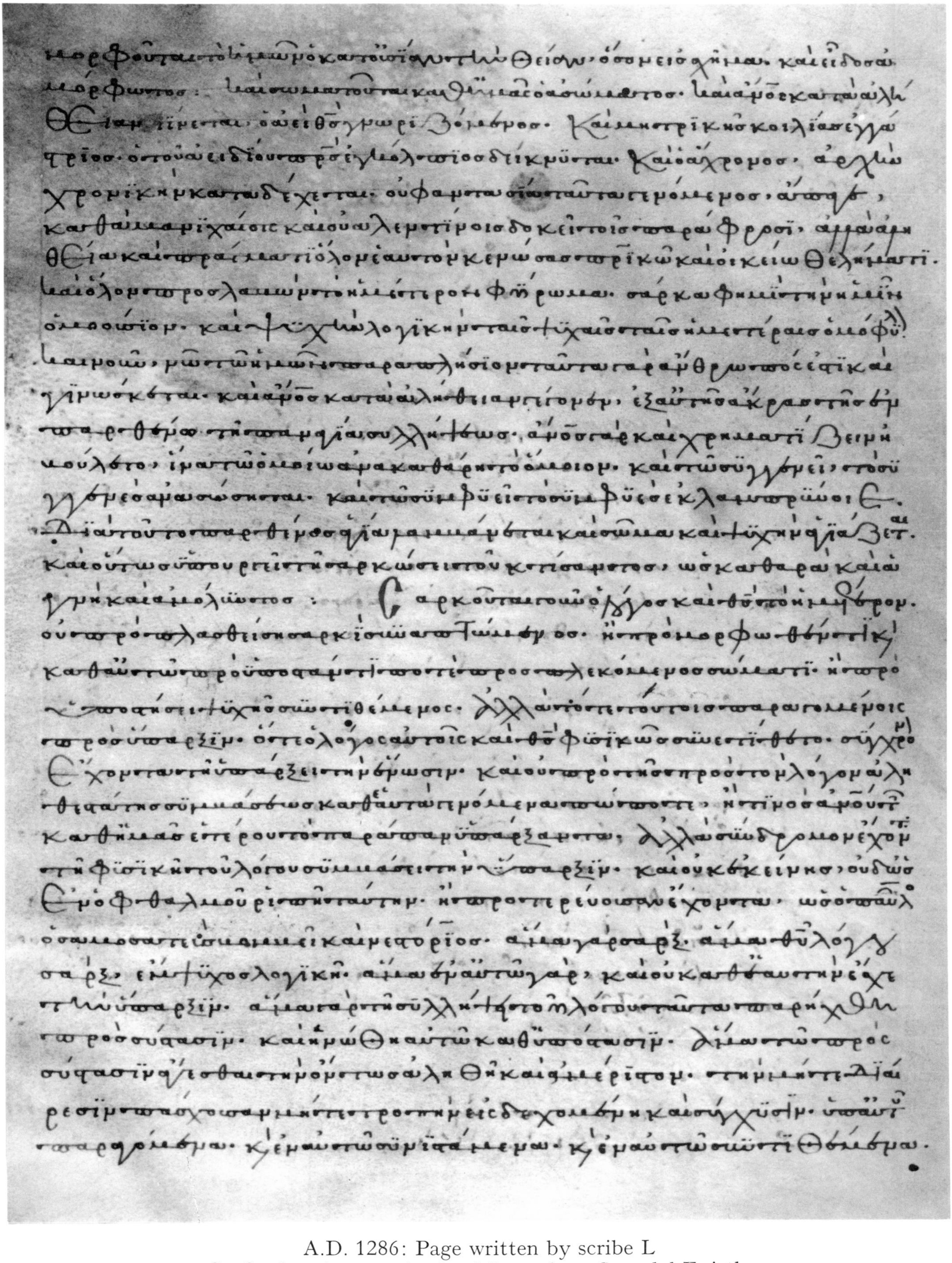

Plate 39

A.D. 1286: Page written by scribe L
St. Sophronius, patriarch of Jerusalem, Synodal Epistle
Oxford, Bodleian Library, MS Roe 22 (fol. 553ᵛ)

Plate 40

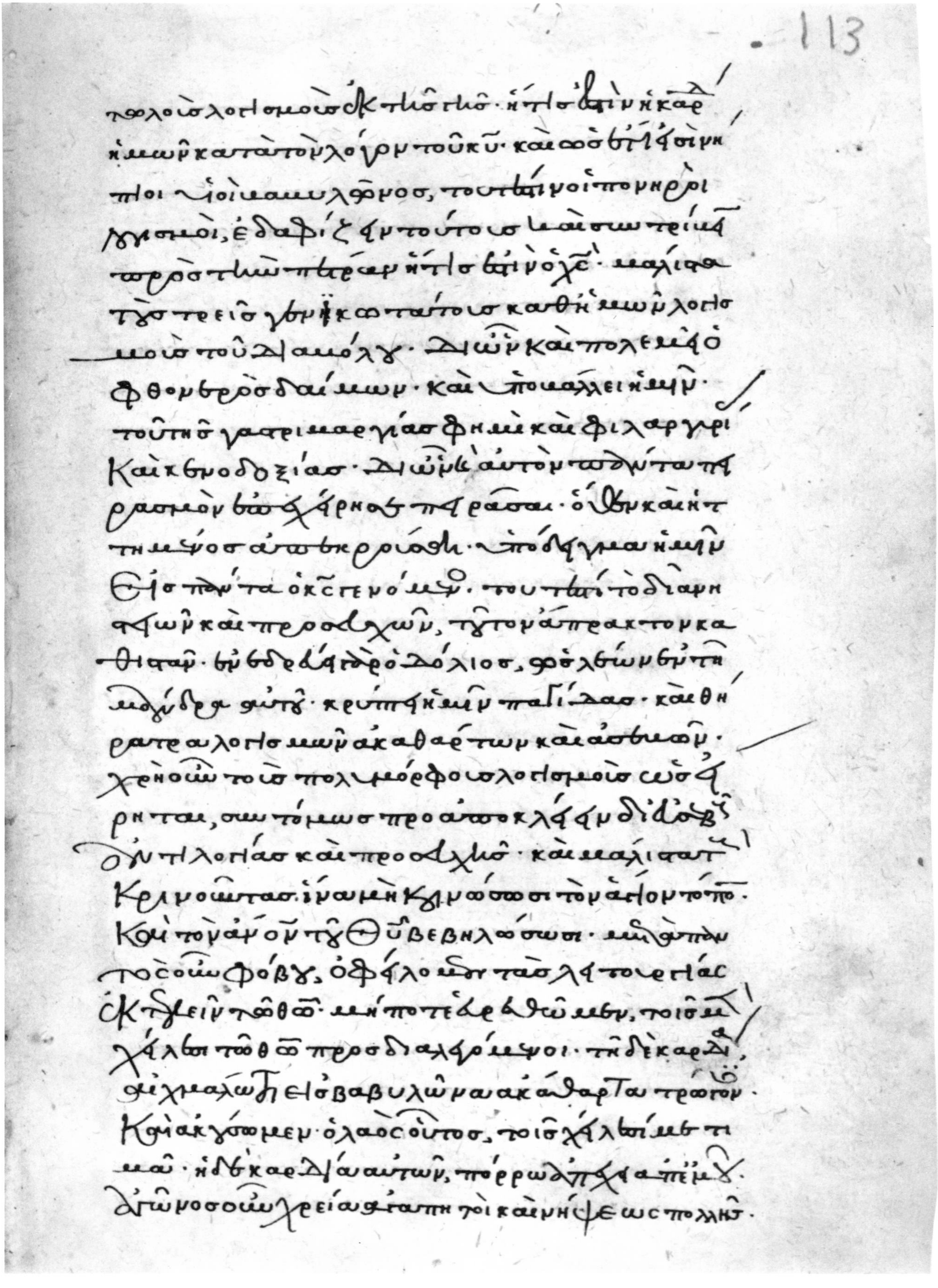

A.D. 1289/1290: Written by Macarius
Antiochus, monk of the Laura of St. Sabas, Pandectes Sacrae Scripturae
Oxford, Bodleian Library, MS Laud Greek 40 (fol. 113ʳ)

circa A.D. 1290: Written by Maximus Planudes, presumably in Constantinople
Cleomedes, Circular Theory of the Stars
Edinburgh, National Library of Scotland, MS Adv.18.7.15 (fol. 52ᵛ)

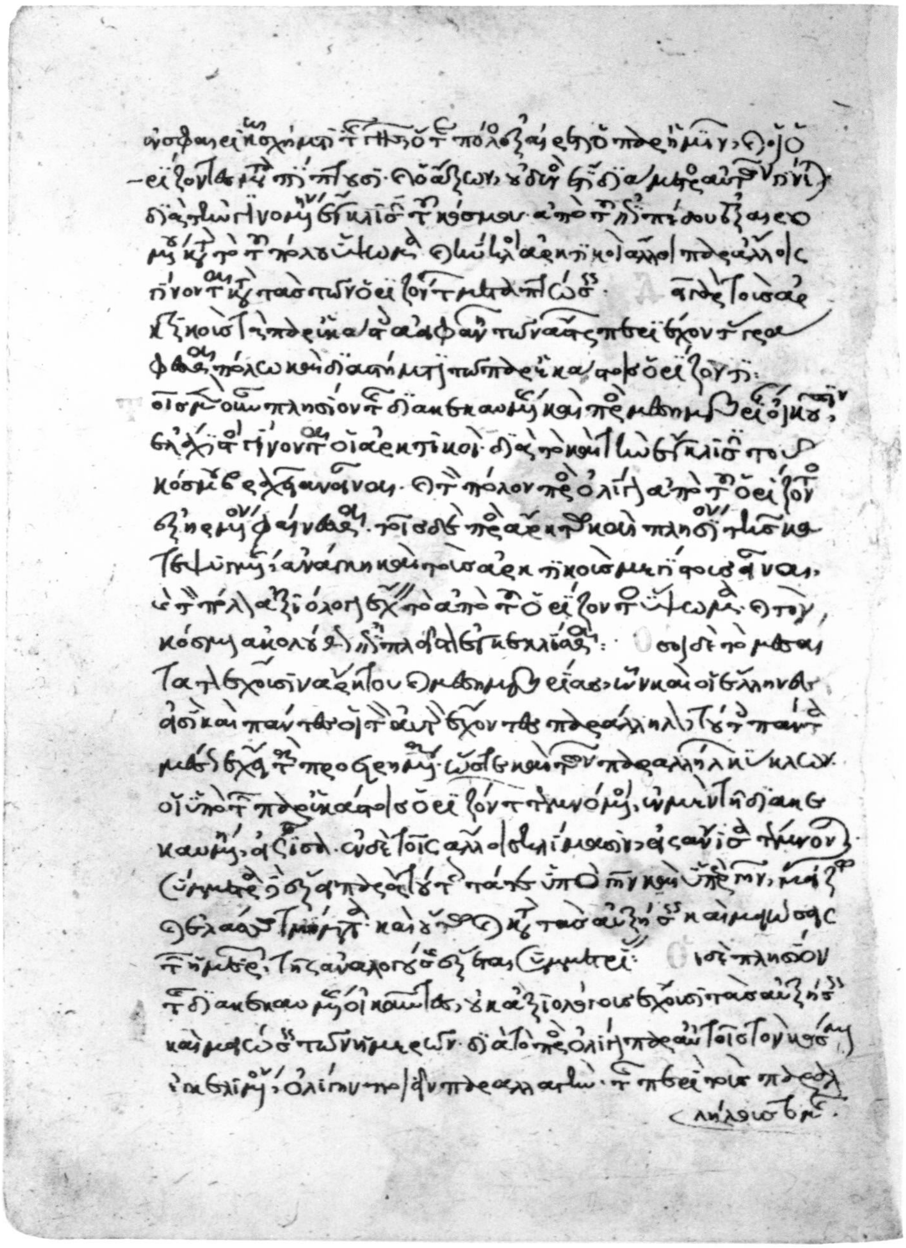

Plate 42

circa A.D. 1290: Written by an amanuensis of Maximus Planudes, presumably in Constantinople
Cleomedes, Circular Theory of the Stars
Edinburgh, National Library of Scotland, MS Adv.18.7.15 (fol. 12ᵛ)

Plate 43

καὶ λέγει αὐτοῖς· λάβετε πνεῦμα ἅγιον· ἄν τι
νων ἀφῆτε τὰς ἁμαρτίας, ἀφίενται
αὐτοῖς· ἄν τινων κρατῆτε, κεκράτην
ται. Θωμᾶς δὲ εἷς ἐκ τῶν δώδεκα ὁ
λεγόμενος Δίδυμος, οὐκ ἦν με
τ᾽ αὐτῶν ὅτε ἦλθεν ὁ Ἰησοῦς. ἔλεγον οὖν αὐ
τῷ οἱ ἄλλοι μαθηταί· ἑωράκαμεν τὸν
κύριον. ὁ δὲ εἶπεν αὐτοῖς· ἐὰν μὴ ἴδω ἐν
ταῖς χερσὶν αὐτοῦ τὸν τύπον τῶν ἥ
λων, καὶ βάλω τὸν δάκτυλόν μου εἰς
τὸν τύπον τῶν ἥλων, καὶ βάλω τὴν
χεῖρά μου εἰς τὴν πλευρὰν αὐτοῦ, οὐ μὴ
πιστεύσω. Καὶ μεθ᾽ ἡμέρας
ὀκτὼ, πάλιν ἦσαν ἔσω οἱ μαθηταὶ αὐ
τοῦ, καὶ Θωμᾶς μετ᾽ αὐτῶν· ἔρχεται ὁ
Ἰησοῦς τῶν θυρῶν κεκλεισμένων, καὶ ἔ
στη εἰς τὸ μέσον καὶ εἶπεν· εἰρήνη ὑμῖν·
εἶτα λέγει τῷ Θωμᾷ· φέρε τὸν δάκτυ
λόν σου ὧδε, καὶ ἴδε τὰς χεῖράς μου·
καὶ φέρε τὴν χεῖρά σου καὶ βάλε
εἰς τὴν πλευράν μου· καὶ μὴ γίνου
ἄπιστος, ἀλλὰ πιστός. καὶ ἀπεκρί
θη Θωμᾶς, καὶ εἶπεν αὐτῷ· ὁ κύριός
μου καὶ ὁ θεός μου· λέγει αὐτῷ ὁ Ἰησοῦς· ὅτι ἑώ

A.D. 1291/1292: Written by Theodorus Hagiopetrites
Four Gospels
London, British Museum, MS Burney 21 (fol. 249ᵛ)

Plate 44

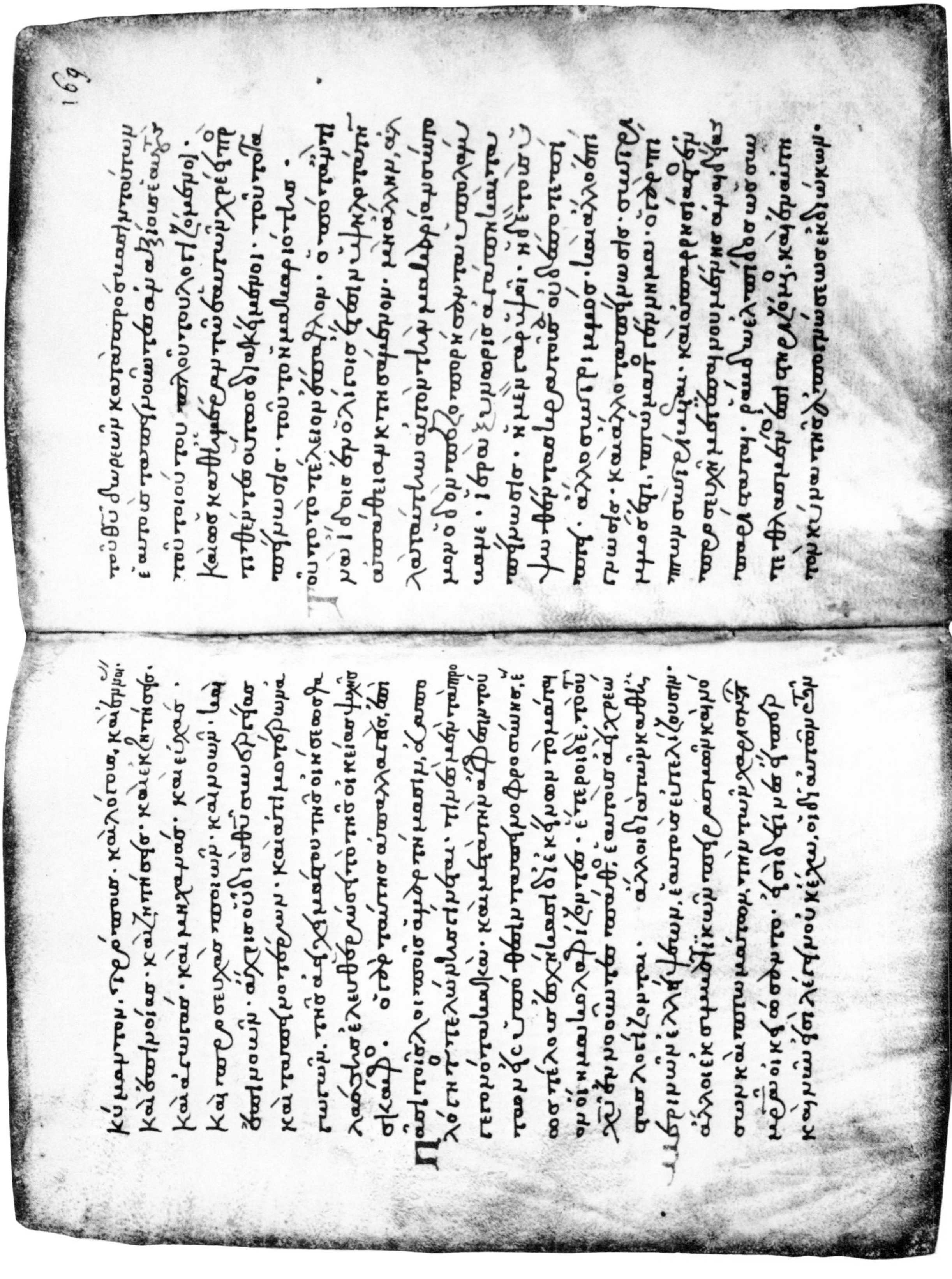

A.D. 1294
St. John Climacus, Ladder of Paradise
Oxford, Bodleian Library, MS Barocci 16 (fols. 168v–169r)

Plate 45

λέγει αὐτοῖς · ἀμὴν λέγω
μῖν ὅτι · καὶ ἐπὶ τοῦ ποτ' ἦλθο-
οἱ μαθηταὶ αὐτοῦ καὶ ἐθαύμα-
ζον ὅτι μετὰ γυναικὸς ἐλάλει ·
οὐδεὶς μὲν τοι εἶπεν τί ζητεῖς ·
ἢ τί λαλεῖς μετ' αὐτῆς · ἀφῆκεν
οὖν τὴν ὑδρίαν αὐτῆς ὁ ἢ τὴν
καὶ ἀπῆλθεν εἰς τὴν πόλιν
καὶ λέγει τοῖς ἀν(θρώπ)οις · δεῦτε ἴδε-
τε ἄν(θρωπ)ον, ὃς εἶπέ μοι πάντα
ὅσα ἐποίησα · μήτι οὗτός ἐ-
στιν ὁ Χ(ριστό)ς; ἐξῆλθον οὖν ἐκ τῆς
πόλεως καὶ ἤρχοντο πρὸς
αὐτόν · ἐν δὲ τῷ μεταξὺ ἠ-
τον αὐτὸν οἱ μαθηταὶ αὐτοῦ
λέγοντες · ῥαββὶ φάγε · ὁ δὲ
εἶπεν αὐτοῖς · ἐγὼ βρῶσιν
ἔχω φαγεῖν ἣν ὑμεῖς οὐκ οἴδατε · ἔλεγον οὖν οἱ μαθηταὶ
πρὸς ἀλλήλους, μήτις ἤνεγκεν
αὐτῷ φαγεῖν; λέγει αὐτοῖς ὁ
Ἰ(ησοῦ)ς · ἐμὸν βρῶμά ἐστιν ἵνα
ποιῶ τὸ θέλημα τοῦ πέμψαντός με, καὶ τελειώσω αὐτοῦ τὸ
ἔργον · οὐχ ὑμεῖς λέγετε ὅτι ἔτι
τετράμηνός ἐστι καὶ ὁ θερισ-

A.D. 1297: Written by Michael Mantylides
Four Gospels
Cambridge, University Library, MS Dd.9.69 (fol. 240ᵛ)

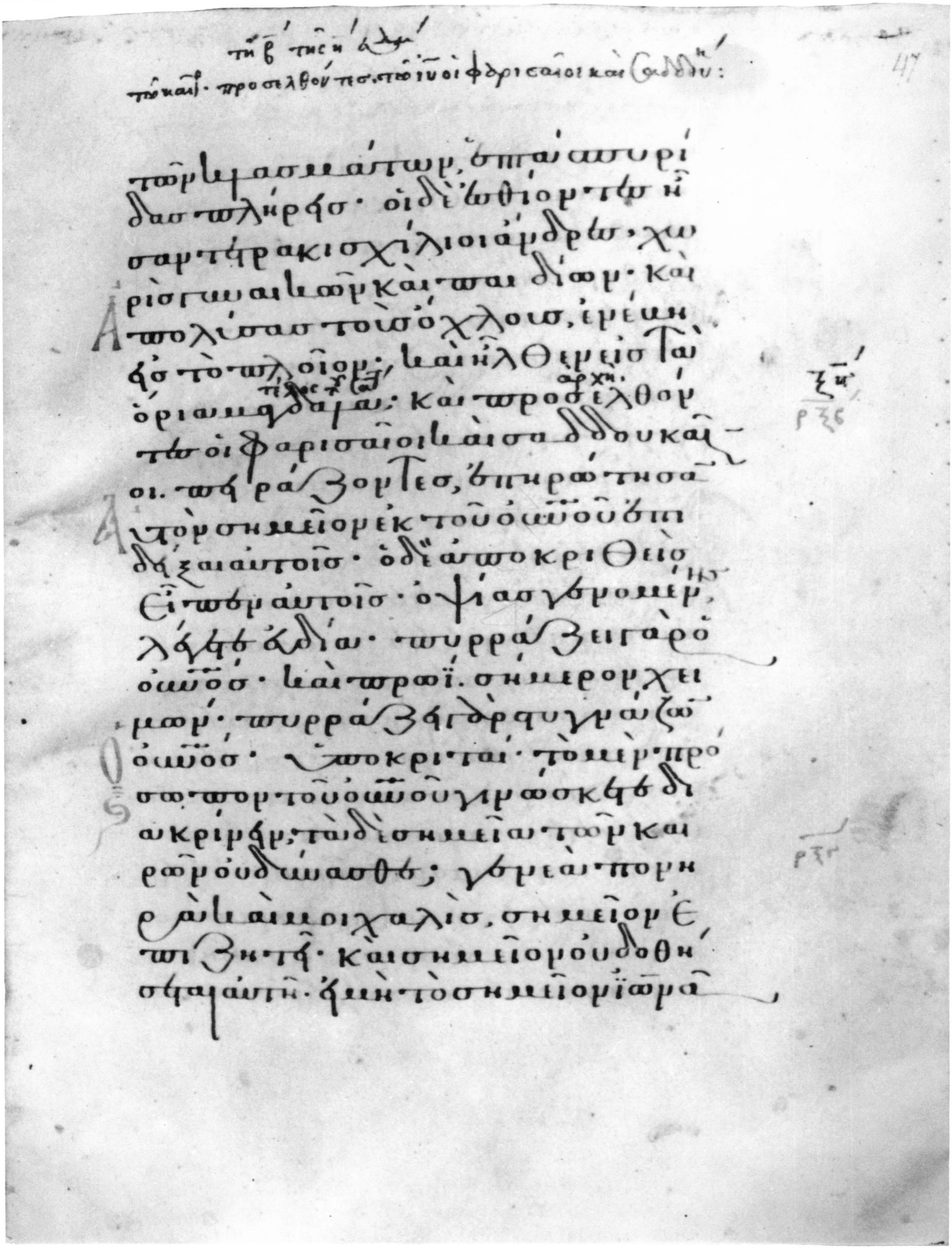

Plate 46

τῶν ἰχθύων, καὶ τῶν, ὅτι οἱ αἰσχύρι
δαο ωλιρέσο· οἱ δὲ ἐσθίοντω τω ἦ
σαρτ ἠρ ακιοχιλιοι αρ δρω· χω
ρισγυναικῶρ καὶ παι δίωρ· Καὶ
απολίσασ τοῦσ ὄχλουσ, ἐνέβη
εἰσ τὸ ω ̄ οἰορ· καὶ ἦλθεν εἰσ τὰ
ὅρια μαγδαλα· καὶ προσελθόν
τες οἱ φαρισαῖοι καὶ σαδδουκαῖ
οι. πειράζοντεσ, ἐπηρώτησα
αὐτὸν σημεῖον ἐκ τοῦ οὐ ̄ ̄ οῦ ὅτι
δειξαι αὐτοῖσ· ὁ δὲ ἀποκριθεισ
εἶπεν αὐτοῖσ· ὀψίασ γενομε̄,
λέγετε εὐδία· πυρράζει γὰρ ὁ
οὐ ̄ οσ· καὶ πρωΐ. σήμερον χει
μωρ· πυρράζει γὰρ στυγνάζω
ὁ οὐ ̄ οσ· ὑποκριταί. τὸ μὲν πρό
σωπον τοῦ οὐ ̄ οῦ γινώσκετε δι
ακρίνειρ· τὰ δὲ σημεῖα τῶν και
ρῶν οὐ δύνασθε; γενεὰ πονη
ρὰ καὶ μοιχαλίσ, σημεῖον ἐ
πιζητεῖ· καὶ σημεῖον οὐ δοθή
σεται αὐτῇ. εἰ μὴ τὸ σημεῖον ἰωνᾶ

A.D. 1304/1305: Written by the monk and deacon Neophytus of Cyprus
Four Gospels
London, British Museum, MS Additional 22506 (fol. 47r)

Plate 47

παγ ἀπὸ τῆς κοπῆς τῶν βασιλέων·
καὶ εὐλογήσας αὐτόν· ᾧ καὶ δεκάτην
ἀπὸ πάντων ἐμέρισεν ἀβραάμ· +
πρῶτον μὲν, ἑρμηνευόμενος βασιλεὺς δικαιοσύνης· ἔπειτα δὲ
καὶ βασιλεὺς σαλήμ· ὅ ἐστιν βασιλεὺς
εἰρήνης· ἀπάτωρ· ἀμήτωρ· ἀ-
γενεαλόγητος + μήτε ἀρχὴν ἡμερῶν, μήτε ζωῆς τέλος ἔχων·
ἀφωμοιωμένος δὲ τῷ υἱῷ τοῦ θῦ·
μένει ἱερεὺς εἰς τὸ διηνεκές· + θε-
ωρεῖτε δὲ πηλίκος οὗτος· ᾧ καὶ δεκάτην ἀβραὰμ ἔδωκεν ἐκ τῶν ἀκ-
ροθηνίων ὁ πατριάρχης· + καὶ οἱ
μὲν, ἐκ τῶν υἱῶν λευῒ τὴν ἱερατείαν
λαμβάνοντες· ἐντολὴν ἔχουσιν ἀπο-
δεκατοῦν τὸν λαὸν κατὰ τὸν νόμον·
τουτέστι τοὺς ἀδελφοὺς αὐτῶν· καί-
περ ἐξεληλυθότας ἐκ τῆς ὀσφύ-
ος ἀβραάμ + ὁ δὲ μὴ γενεαλογού-
μενος ἐξ αὐτῶν· δεδεκάτωκε τὸν
ἀβραάμ· καὶ τὸν ἔχοντα τὰς ἐπαγ-
γελίας εὐλόγηκε :~ τῇ αγ τῆς κθ :

: προς εβραιους :

ἀδελφοί· αἰσθήσει ἡρμένη πρὸ ὁδοῦ
σης ἐν τολῆς· διὰ τὸ αὐτῆς ἀσθε-
νὲς καὶ ἀνωφελὲς· οὐδὲν γὰρ ἐτε-
λείωσεν ὁ νόμος· ὁ ατ ὁσ αγω τῆς δε

A.D. 1305/1306: Written by Ignatius
Lectionary of the Acts and Epistles
London, British Museum, MS Additional 29714 (fol. 114ʳ)

Plate 48

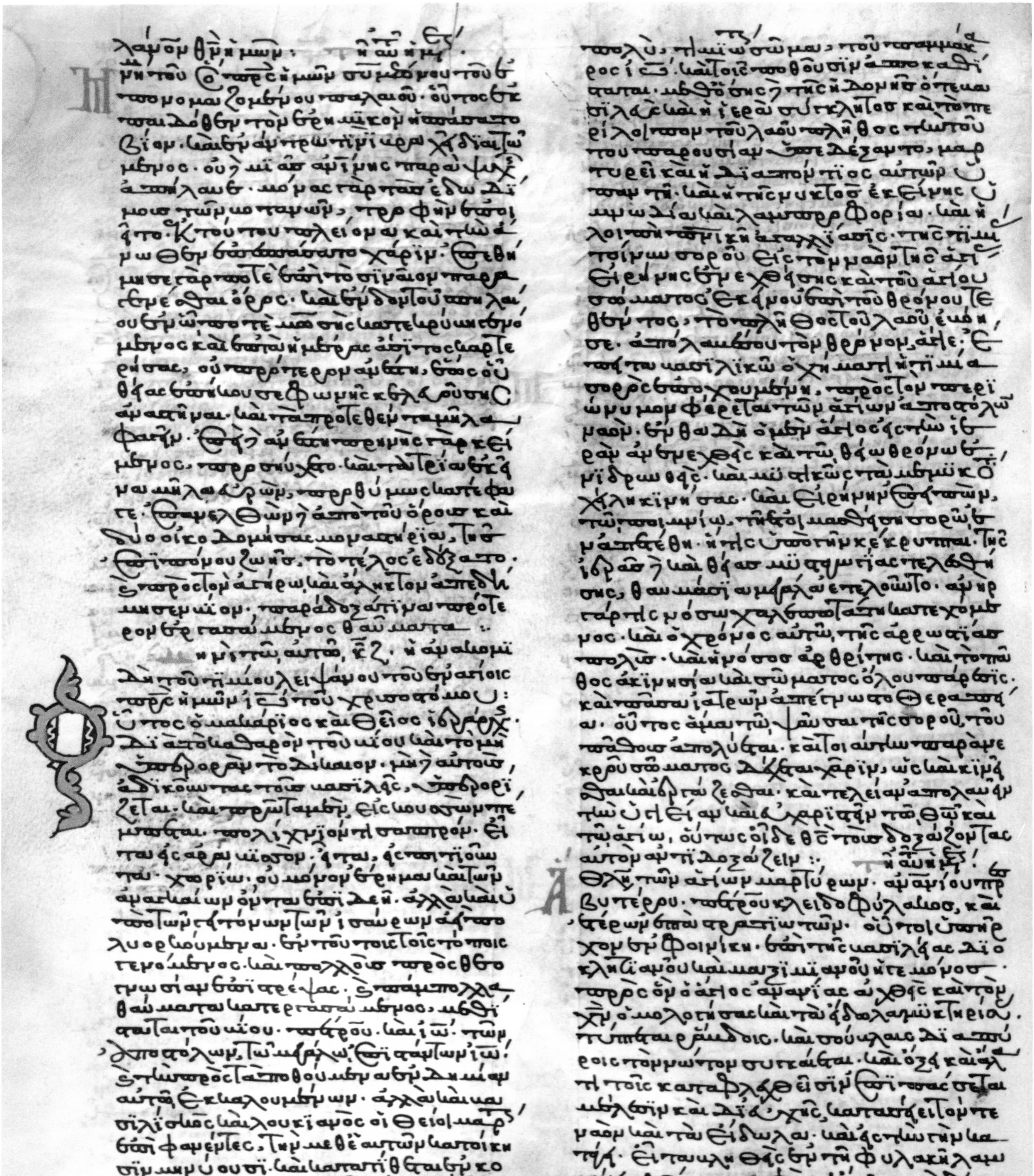

A.D. 1306/1307: Written by the lector Georgius Saracinopulus
Synaxarion (Lives of Saints) of Constantinople
Oxford, Bodleian Library, MS Auct.T.3.16 (fol. 45ᵛ)

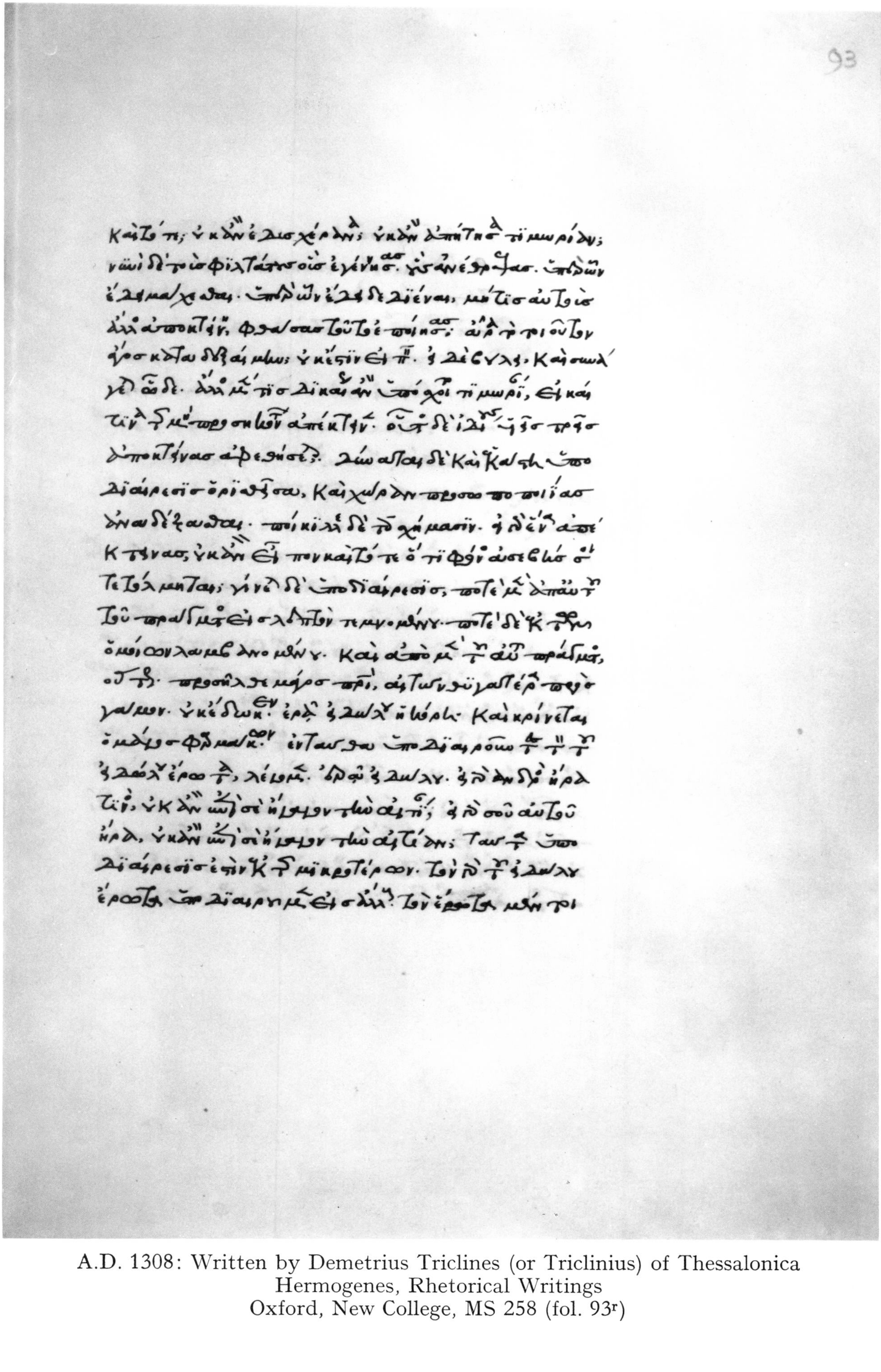

Plate 49

93

A.D. 1308: Written by Demetrius Triclines (or Triclinius) of Thessalonica
Hermogenes, Rhetorical Writings
Oxford, New College, MS 258 (fol. 93ʳ)

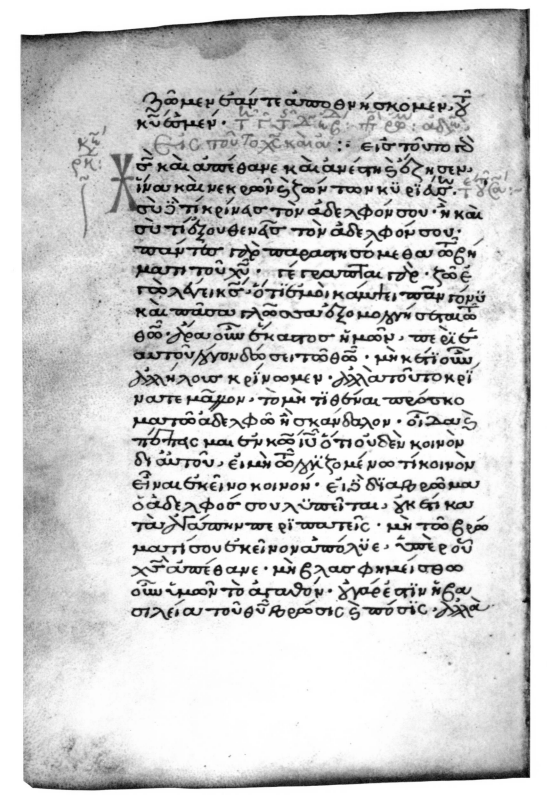

A.D. 1311/1312: Written by Ioannes
Acts of the Apostles and Epistles
London, British Museum, MS Additional 38538 (fol. 114ᵛ)

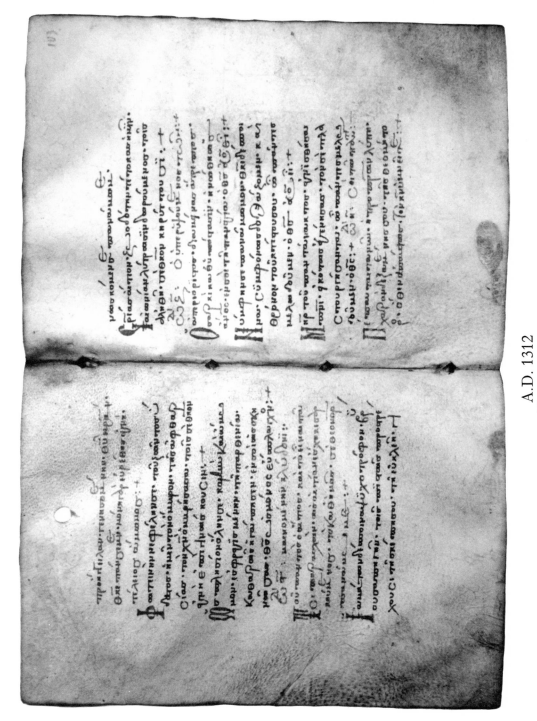

A.D. 1312
Theotocarion
Oxford, Bodleian Library, MS Lyell 94 (fols. 102^v–103^r)

Plate 51

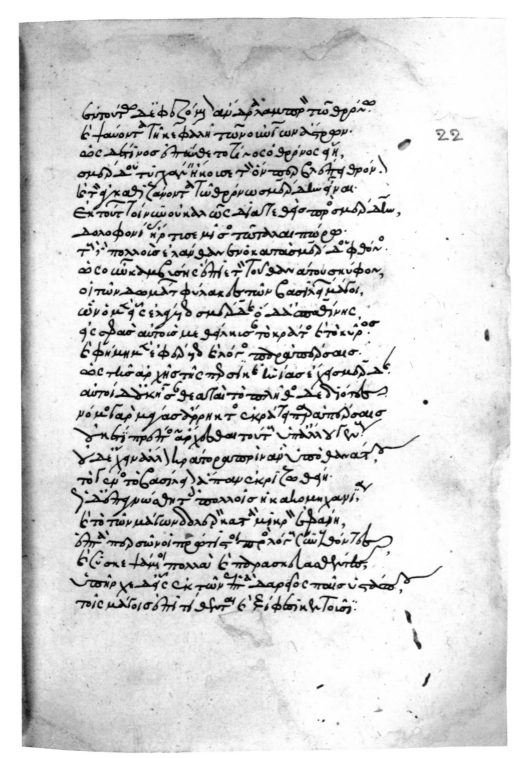

Plate 52

22

A.D. 1312/1313: Written in Crete by the priest Michael Lulludes of Ephesus
Constantine Manasses, Chronicle
London, British Museum, MS Arundel 523 (fol. 22ʳ)

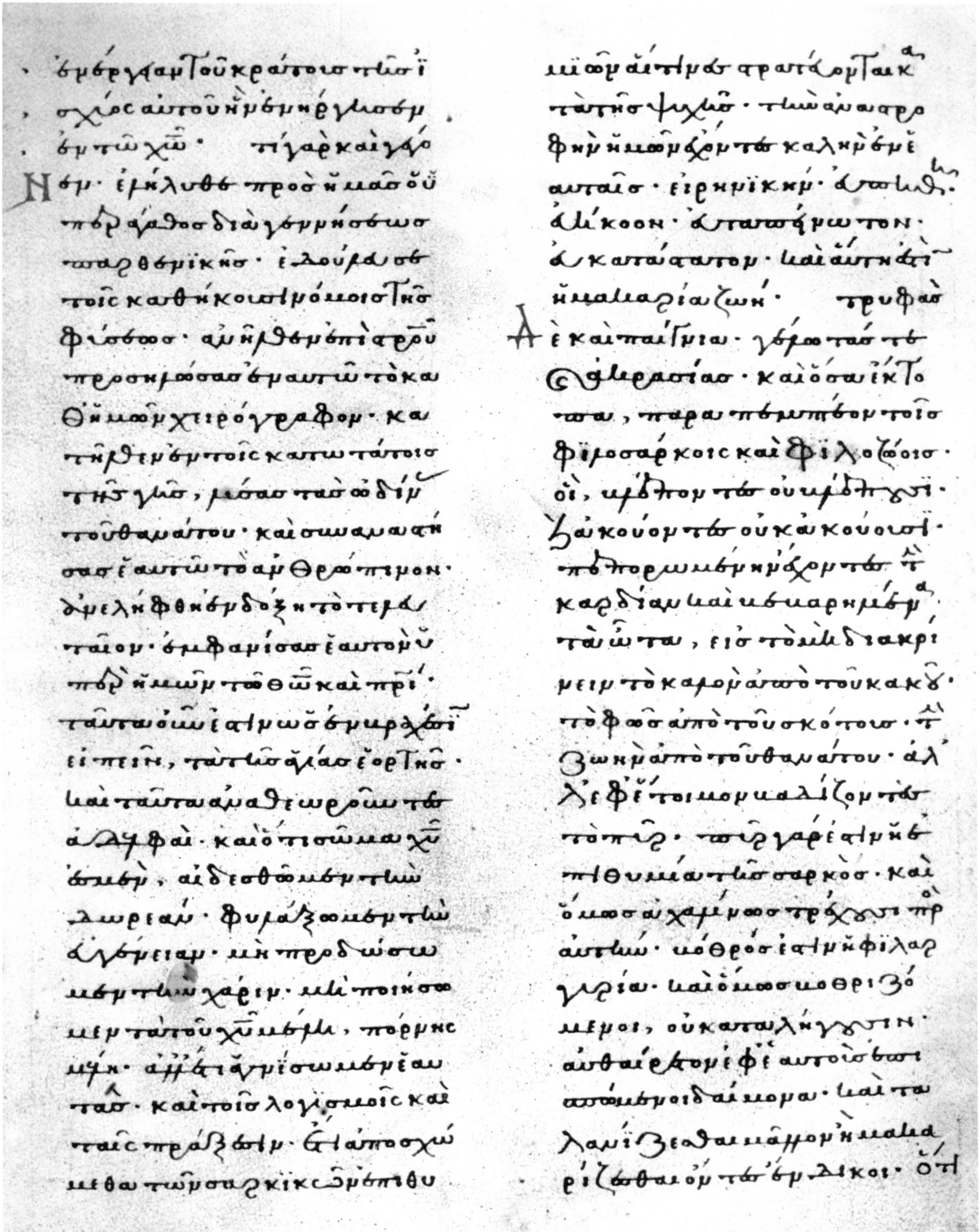

Plate 53

A.D. 1314/1315: Written by the hieromonk Marcus
St. Theodore the Studite, Short Catecheses
Oxford, Bodleian Library, MS Cromwell 22 (page 37)

τ̣ῆ̣ τὸ προφορᾷ καὶ τοῖς μονήμασι,
γυμέσθαι· ἀλλ' ἐ+τ̣άσθιὸ δ̣έλαιος· τ̣
ἀφρόμωρφαμ̣ᾶς ἀφρομέσθρος·
ὅη πολλοῖς μὲν, πλὴν καὶ ἐν τούτω·
φησὶ γὰρ· ὁ πλωὶκαδιαφόρων
βρωμάτων ὅπι θυμιᾷ ἢ μωρὴ ψυχὴ,
ἐν δὲ τω σπερμοιαθω και ὕδατι· ὅμοι
δ' τι πρρο τί τὰχ, τῶ ζ̄ ποίτι τῶ πα̣ι̣
δι, ὅη ι κήμαπ πάσαι ἀμ ὁιθ ζρ τὴι̣
κλίμακα· τοι ρωα αμ̣ατ̣ ἑβωοη τε σ̣αν̣
τομ ὅρομ ἡ μείς φη σω μὲν· ὁ πλωὶκ
διαφόρων κρωμάτων μ ἐπι θυμιᾷ ηει̣
λ ψυχὴ, φύσθως ει διορ τι ὅπιζη τει·
διο μη χαμ ἢ προς τὴω ταμμὴ χαμομ
χενσωμεθα· εἴωτερμὴ βαρ τατος
πόέετι πόλτμος· ἢ πτωμματος εὐθυ̣ψα̣
περικόψωμεμ τββος τὰ λί παιμομτ·
εἰ τωτ̣αὶ ἐκ λαιορτα· εἰ θ̣ὄ τωτὰ ἢ δύ
μορτω·

Plate 55

κ̄ν̄ α̅ τ̄ π̅ν̄ φλθ̅· τῶ καὶ ἐκ ϥ̄ π̄ ιωπ ο̄ι̅σ̄ ιδεν·

Εἰ π αυτοῖς ὅτι σ ἀμὴν ἀμὴν λέγω ὑμῖν πρὶν ἀβραὰμ
γενεσθαι ἐγώ εἰμι· ἦραν οὖν λίθους ἵνα βάλωσιν ἐπ
ἐπ αὐτόν· ἰ̅σ̅ δὲ ἐκρύβη καὶ ἐξῆλθεν ἐκ τοῦ ἱεροῦ δι
ελθῶν διὰ μέσου αὐτῶν καὶ παρῆγεν οὕτως· Ϛ π̅ε̅τ̅
παράγων εἶδεν ἄνον τυφλὸν ἐκ γενετῆς· καὶ ἠρώτη
σαν αὐτὸν οἱ μαθηταὶ αὐτοῦ λέγοντες· ῥαββὶ τίς ἥ
μαρτεν· οὗτος ἢ οἱ γονεῖς αὐτοῦ ἵνα τυφλὸς γεννη
θῆ· ἀπεκρίθη ἰ̅σ̅· οὔτε οὗτος ἥμαρτεν· οὔτε οἱ γονεῖς
αὐτοῦ· ἀλλ ἵνα φανερωθῇ τὰ ἔργα τοῦ θ̅υ̅ ἐν αὐτῷ·
ἐμὲ δεῖ ἐργάζεσθαι τὰ ἔργα τοῦ πέμψαντός με ἕ
ως ἡμέρα ἐστίν· ἔρχεται νὺξ· ὅτε οὐδεὶς δύναται
ἐργάζεσθαι· ὅταν ἐν τῶ κοσμω ὦ· φῶς εἰμι τοῦ
κόσμου· ταῦτα εἰπών ἔπτυσεν χαμαὶ καὶ ἐποίη
πηλὸν ἐκ τοῦ πτύσματος καὶ ἐπέχρισεν τὸν πηλὸν
ἐπὶ τοὺς ὀφθαλμοὺς τοῦ τυφλοῦ· καὶ εἶπεν αὐτῷ
ὕπαγε νίψαι εἰς τὴν κολυμβήθραν τοῦ σιλωάμ· ὃ
ἑρμηνεύεται ἀπεσταλμένος· ἀπῆλθεν οὖν καὶ ἐνί
ψατο· καὶ ἦλθεν βλέπων· οἱ οὖν γείτονες καὶ οἱ θε
ωροῦντες αὐτὸν τὸ πρότερον ὅτι τυφλὸς περι
σαι τὸν ἡμέραν· οὐχ οὗτός ἐστιν ὁ καθήμενος καὶ
προσαιτῶν· ἄλλοι ἔλεγον ὅτι οὗτός ἐστιν· ἄλλοι δε, ὃ
τι ὅμοιος αὐτῷ ἐστιν· ἐκεῖνος δὲ ἔλεγεν ὅτι ἐγώ εἰμι·
ἔλεγον οὖν αὐτῷ· πῶς ἀνεώχθησάν σου οἱ ὀφθαλ
μοί· ἀπεκρίθη ἐκεῖνος καὶ εἶπεν· ἄνθρωπος λεγόμενος
ἰ̅σ̅ πηλὸν ἐποίησεν καὶ ἐπέχρισέν μου τοὺς ὀφθαλ
μοὺς· καὶ εἶπέν μοι· ὕπαγε νίψαι εἰς τὴν κολυμβήθ
θραν τοῦ σιλωάμ· ἀπελθὼν καὶ νιψάμενος ἀ
νέβλεψα· εἶπον ... οὖν αὐτῷ· ποῦ ἐστιν ἐκεῖνος

A.D. 1315/1316: Written by the hieromonk Iacobus on Mount Sinai
Four Gospels
Cambridge, Trinity College, MS B.10.16 (fol. 141ᵛ)

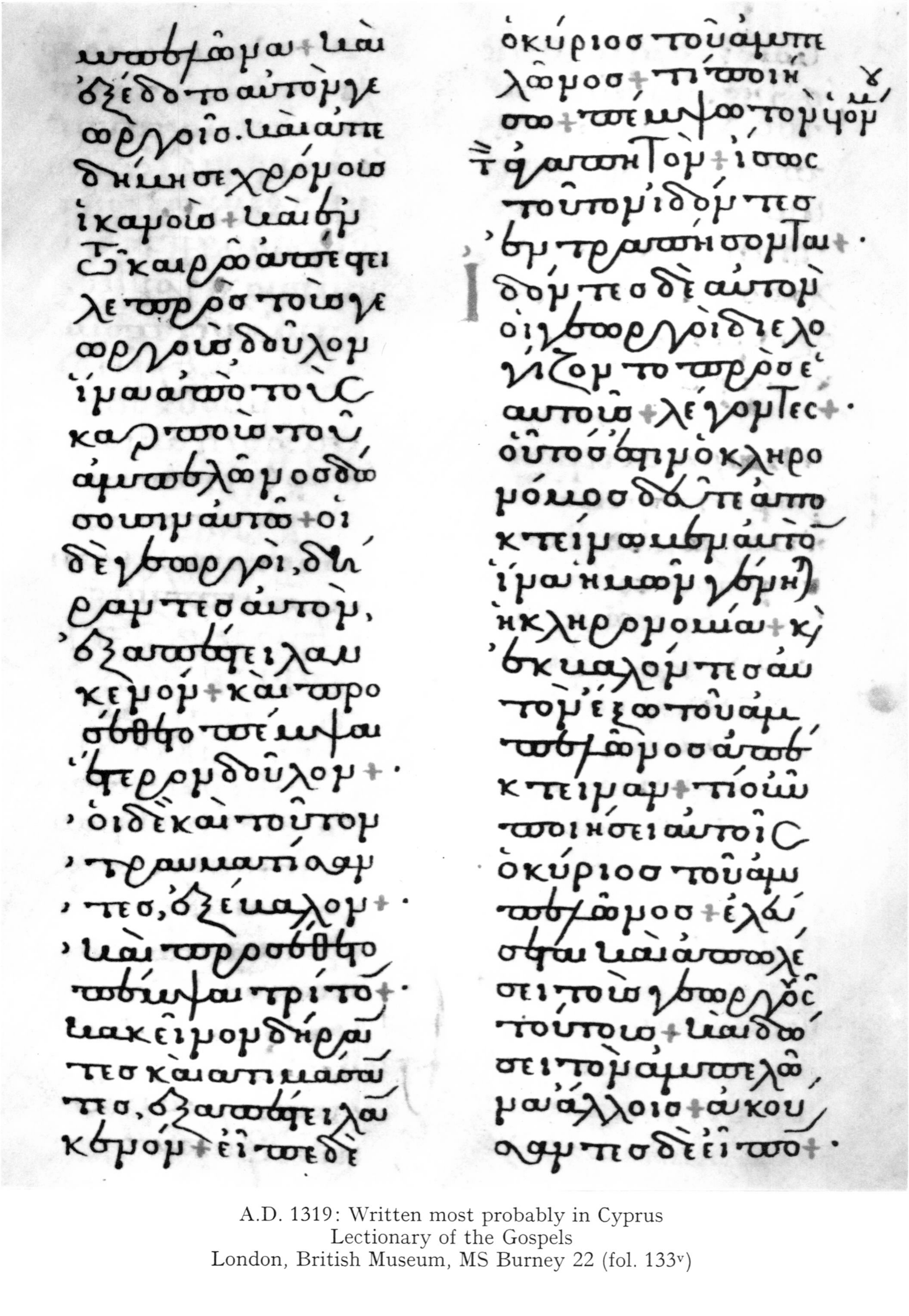

Plate 56

A.D. 1319: Written most probably in Cyprus
Lectionary of the Gospels
London, British Museum, MS Burney 22 (fol. 133ᵛ)

A.D. 1320/1321: Written by the lector Romanus ⟨Chartophylax⟩, most probably in Cyprus
St. Athanasius of Alexandria, Writings
London, British Museum, MS Harley 5579 (fol. 131ʳ)

Plate 58

A.D. 1320/1321: Written by the lector Romanus ⟨Chartophylax⟩, most probably in Cyprus
St. Athanasius of Alexandria, Writings
London, British Museum, MS Harley 5579 (fol. 209ᵛ)

δοκιμάσαι αὐτά· ἐρωτῶ σε ἔχε με παρῃτημέ-
νον· καὶ ἕτερος εἶπε· γυναῖκα ἔγημα, καὶ
διὰ τοῦτο οὐ δύναμαι ἐλθεῖν· καὶ παραγε-
νόμενος ὁ δοῦλος ὁ σκᾶμος, ἀπήγγειλε τῷ κυ-
ρίῳ αὐτοῦ ταῦτα· τότε ὀργισθεὶς ὁ οἰκοδε-
σπότης, εἶπε τῷ δούλῳ αὐτοῦ· ἔξελθε
ταχέως εἰς τὰς πλατείας καὶ ῥύμας τῆς
πόλεως· καὶ τοῖς πτωχοῖς· καὶ ἀναπήρους
καὶ τυφλοὺς καὶ χωλοὺς, εἰσάγαγε ὧδε· καὶ
εἶπεν ὁ δοῦλος· κύριε, γέγονεν ὡς ἐπέταξας·
καὶ ἔτι τόπος ἐστί· καὶ εἶπεν ὁ κύριος πρὸς
τὸν δοῦλον· ἔξελθε εἰς τὰς ὁδοὺς καὶ φραγμ-
οὺς καὶ ἀνάγκασον εἰσελθεῖν, ἵνα γεμισθῇ ὁ οἶκός
μου· λέγω γὰρ ὑμῖν, ὅτι οὐδεὶς τῶν ἀνδρῶν
ἐκείνων τῶν κεκλημένων, γεύσεταί μου τοῦ
δείπνου· τ· Συνεπορεύοντο δὲ αὐτῷ ὄχλοι
Πολλοί· καὶ στραφεὶς εἶπε πρὸς αὐτοῖς· εἴ τις
ἔρχεται πρός με· καὶ οὐ μισεῖ τὸν πρα αὐτοῦ
καὶ τὴν μρα· καὶ τὴν γυναῖκα· καὶ τὰ τέκνα·
καὶ τοῖς ἀδελφοῖς· καὶ τὰς ἀδελφάς· ἔτι δὲ

A.D. 1321/1322
Four Gospels
Oxford, Bodleian Library, MS Gr.bibl.d.1 (fol. 167ʳ)

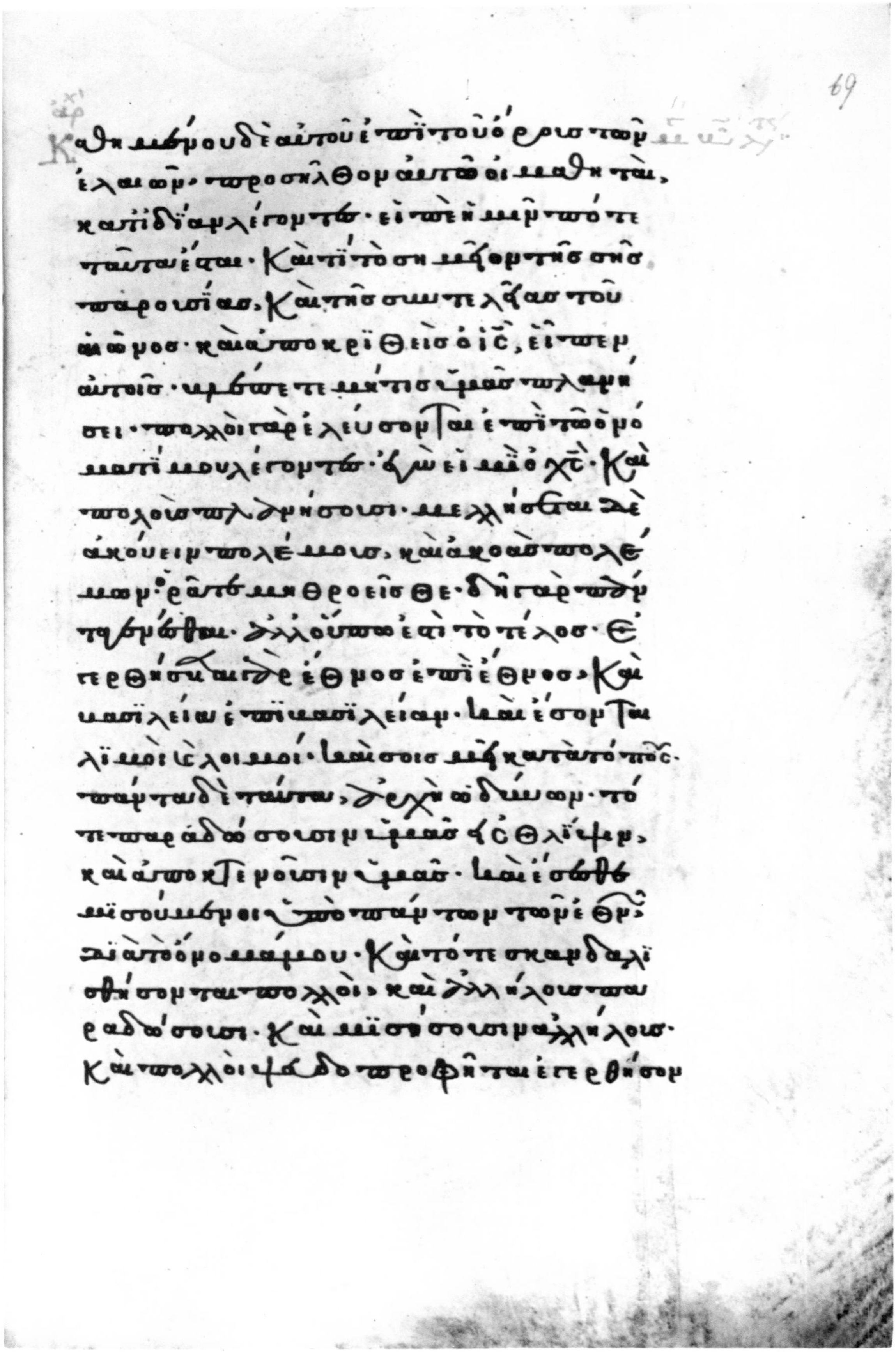

Plate 60

A.D. 1325/1326: Written by the priest and notary Constantinus Pastil
Four Gospels
London, British Museum, MS Additional 11838 (fol. 69r)

Plate 61

τὸ κοράσιον. ἡ ὅ ἐξῆλθεν ἡ φήμη αὕτη· εἰς
ὅλην τὴν γῆν ἐκείνην· καὶ παράγοντι
ἐκεῖθεν τῷ ἰ̅υ̅· ἠκολούθησαν αὐτῷ· δύο τυ-
φλοὶ κράζοντες καὶ λέγοντες· ἐλέησον ἡμᾶς
υἱὸς δα̅δ̅· ἐλθόντι δὲ εἰς τὴν οἰκίαν·
προσῆλθον αὐτῷ οἱ τυφλοί· καὶ λέγει αὐτοῖς
ὁ ι̅ς̅· πιστεύετε ὅτι δύναμαι τοῦτο ποιῆσαι·
λέγουσιν αὐτῷ ναὶ κ̅ε̅· τότε ἥψατο τῶν ὀφθαλ-
μῶν αὐτῶν λέγων· κατὰ τὴν πίστιν ὑμῶν
γενηθήτω ὑμῖν· καὶ ἀνεῴχθησαν αὐτῶν οἱ ὀ-
φθαλμοί· καὶ ἐνεβριμήσατο αὐτοῖς ὁ ι̅ς̅ λέγων·
ὁρᾶτε μηδεὶς γινωσκέτω· οἱ δὲ ἐξελθόντες·
διεφήμισαν αὐτὸν ἐν ὅλη τῇ γῇ ἐκείνῃ·
αὐτῶν δὲ ἐξερχομένων· ἰδοὺ προσήνεγκαν
αὐτῷ ἄνθρωπον· κωφὸν δαιμονιζόμενον· καὶ ἐκβλη-
θέντος τοῦ δαιμονίου· ἐλάλησεν ὁ κωφός·
καὶ ἐθαύμασαν οἱ ὄχλοι λέγοντες· οὐδέποτε
ἐφάνη οὕτως ἐν τῷ ἰ̅η̅λ̅· οἱ δὲ φαρισαῖοι ἔ-
λεγον· ἐν τῷ ἄρχοντι τῶν δαιμονίων· ἐκ-
βάλλει τὰ δαιμόνια· καὶ περιῆγεν ὁ ι̅ς̅ τὰς
πόλεις πάσας καὶ τὰς κώμας· διδάσκων ἐν
ταῖς συναγωγαῖς αὐτῶν· καὶ κηρύσσων τὸ ε̅υ̅-
αγγέλιον τῆς βασιλείας· καὶ θεραπεύων πᾶσαν νό-
σον καὶ πᾶσαν μαλακίαν ἐν τῷ λα̅ῷ̅·

A.D. 1326
Four Gospels
London, British Museum, MS Additional 5117 (fol. 40ᵛ)

A.D. 1326
Four Gospels
London, British Museum, MS Additional 5117 (fol. 158ᵛ)

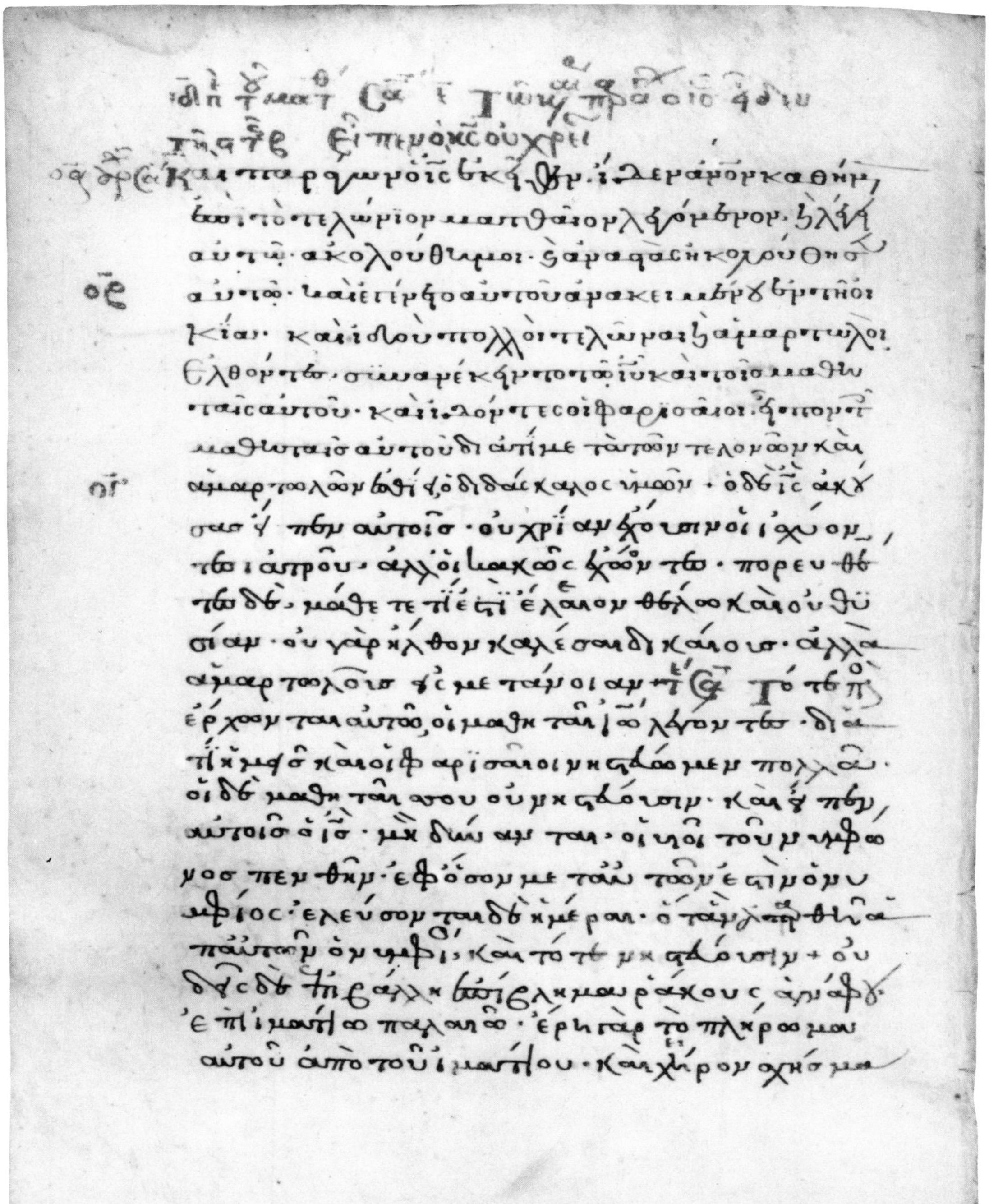

A.D. 1326
Four Gospels
London, British Museum, MS Additional 5117 (fol. 39v)

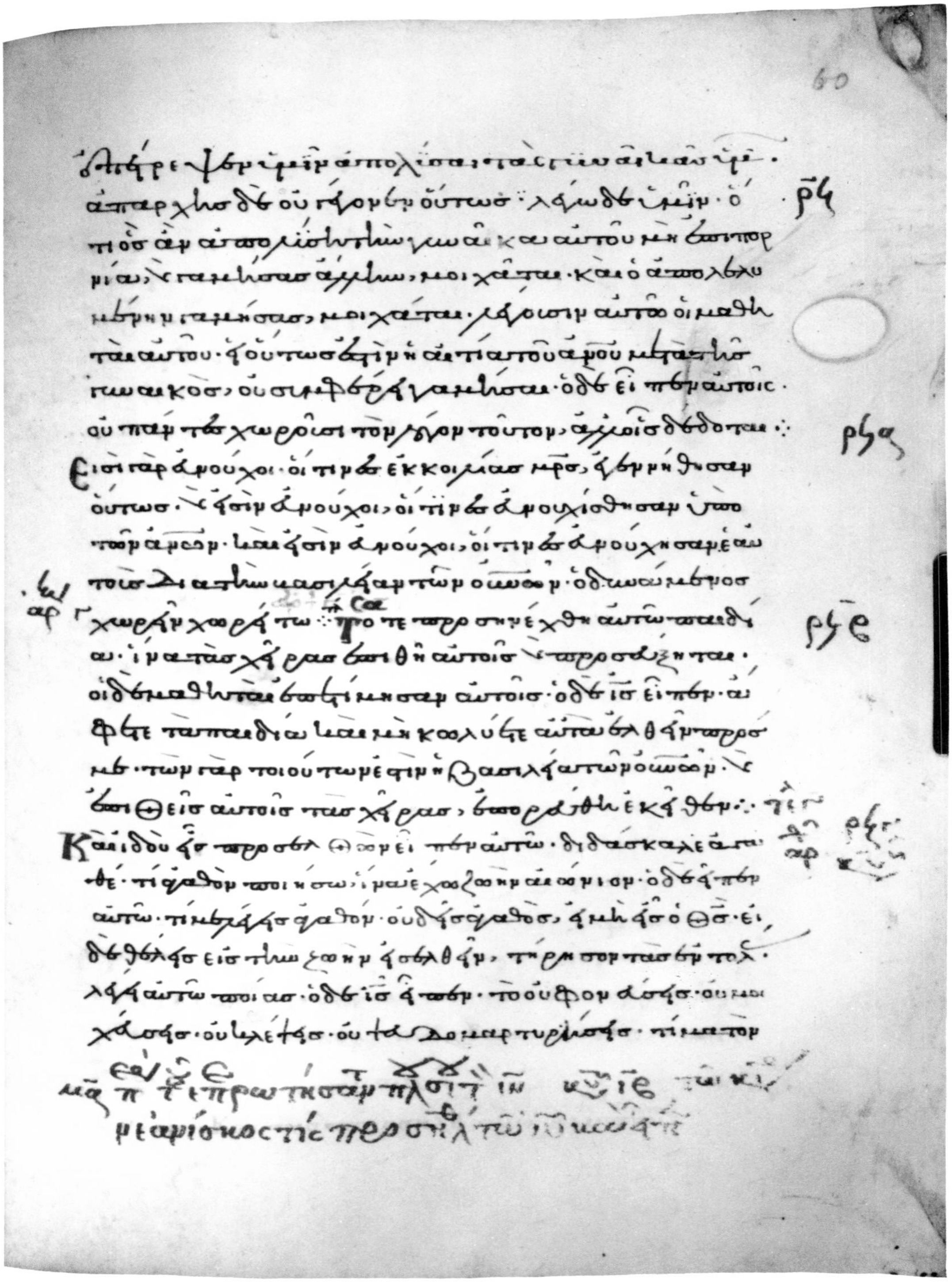

Plate 64

A.D. 1326
Four Gospels
London, British Museum, MS Additional 5117 (fol. 60r)

A.D. 1326
Hypothesis (end) and List of Chapters (beginning) to the Gospel of St. Mark
London, British Museum, MS Additional 5117 (fol. 83r)

Plate 66

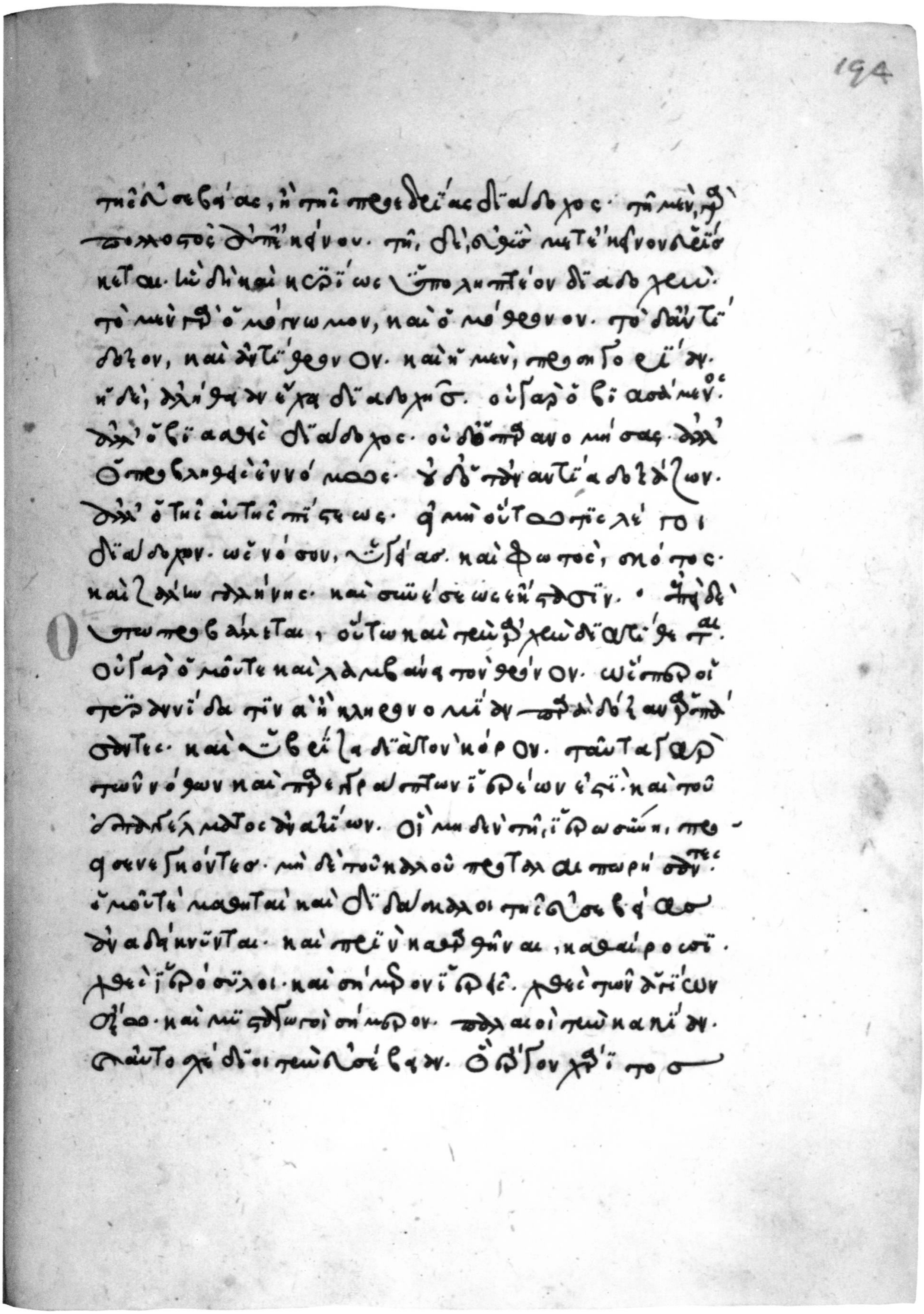

A.D. 1333
St. Gregory of Nazianzus, Orations
Oxford, Bodleian Library, MS Auct.T.5.28 (fol. 194ʳ)

Plate 67

κυρίου αὐτοῦ· μετὰ δὲ χρόνον
πολὺν· ἔρχεται ὁ κύριος τῶν
δούλων ἐκείνων καὶ συναίρει
μετ᾽ αὐτῶν λόγον· καὶ προσελθὼν
ὁ τὰ πέντε τάλαντα λαβὼν·
προσήνεγκαν ἄλλα πέντε τάλαν
τα· λέγων κε πέντε τάλαντά
μοι παρέδωκας· ἴδε ἄλλα πέντε
τάλαντα ἐκέρδησα ἐπ᾽ αὐτοῖς·
ἔφη αὐτῷ ὁ κύριος αὐτοῦ· εὖ δοῦλε
ἀγαθὲ καὶ πιστέ· ἐπὶ ὀλίγα ἦς πι
στὸς ἐπὶ πολλῶν σε καταστή σω·
εἴσελθε εἰς τὴν χαρὰν τοῦ κυρίου σου·
προσελθὼν δὲ καὶ ὁ τὰ δύο τάλαν
τα λαβὼν· εἶπεν· κύριε· δύο τά
λαντά μοι παρέδωκας· ἴδε ἄλλα
δύο τάλαντα ἐκέρδησα ἐπ᾽ αὐτοῖς·
ἔφη αὐτῷ ὁ κύριος αὐτοῦ· εὖ δοῦλε
ἀγαθὲ καὶ πιστέ· ἐπὶ ὀλίγα ἦς πιστὸς
ἐπὶ πολλῶν σε καταστή σω· εἴσελθε
εἰς τὴν χαρὰν τοῦ κυρίου σου· προσ
ελθὼν δὲ καὶ ὁ τὸ ἓν τάλαντον· εἰλη
φὼς εἶπεν· κύριε· ἔγνων σε ὅτι
σκληρὸς εἶ ἄνθρωπος· θερίζων ὅπου οὐ
κ ἔσπειρας· καὶ συνάγων ὅθεν οὐ

A.D. 1334/1335: Written probably in Cyprus
Lectionary of the Gospels
London, British Museum, MS Additional 19993 (fol. 131ᵛ)

143

τῶ μηρῶ σκὼλιᾶ τοῖσ πὸδασμου· ὁ
τσος ὁν φυλάξω τοῖσλόγοισ ἀ᾽:
δ᾽ τῶ τῶν κρῒμάτων σου οὐκ ὸξέκλιν. ὅτισοὺ
ἐνομοθέτησάσ μὲ· τῶ ἀλῦκὸτὰ τῶ λάρυ
ἦ μου τὼ λόγῒά σου. τῶ ὑμέλῒ τῶ τόματί μ᾽:
δ᾽ πὸ τῶν ὸντολῶν ὰ᾽ σύνῆκα. διὰ τοῦτο ἐμι
σῆ ὰ᾽ τὼ ὸδὸν ὸδὸν ὰδῒκῒάσ· λὺ χνῖ τοῖσ ποσῒ
μου ὁνόμος ὰ᾽ καὶ φῶσ Ταῖσ Ϛῒβοισ μου:
ὤ μος ὰ᾽ καὶ ἔ σχ ὰ᾽ τοῦ φὺλάξ ασθαι τὰ κρῖμά
τ᾽ τῆσ δῒκαιο σύνησ ὰ᾽· ὁ σπὼν ὁ θην ὁσω
σφό δρ ὰ᾽ κ᾽ ὸ ζῆν σου μὲ κὰ Ταῖ σὺν λόγον ὰ᾽:
τὰ ὸ κούσῖὰ τοῦ τό μάτός μου εὐ δόκησον
δὴ κ᾽ ὸ· καὶ τὰ κρῒμάτά σου δῖ δὲ ξονμὲ:
ἡ ψυχή μου ὸνταῖσ χὸρσί σου διὰ πὼν τὸσ· κ᾽
τοῦ νο μου σου οὐκ ὸσελαθ ὸμην· ὁ θὸν τὸ
διὰ ρ Ταολοῖ πῶ τῒ δ ὰ μοι καὶ ὸκ Τῶν ὁν τὸ
λῶν σου οὐκ ὸσελανθην:
ε᾽ κληρονὸμηκ ὰ᾽ τὼ μὸρ τῆρῒ ά σου δῖ σ᾽ τὸν αἰ
ῶν ὰ᾽. ὸτῒ ὸγὸλλῖ άμα τῆσ κ᾽ν δῖ δο μου ὁ σῖν:
ε᾽ κλιν ὰ τὴν κ ὸρ δῖ ὰν μου τοῦ ποιῆ σαι τ᾽ δῖκαι
ὸ μάτά σου ὰ᾽ ὸ Τὸν αἰῶν᾽ δῖ ὰν τὸμ ὰ ψιν:
π᾽ ὸρ ὸνόμουσ ὸ μῒ σησ ὰ᾽ τὸν δὲ νόμον σου ἠγὰ
τῶν ὰ᾽ μ ὸνθ όσ μου καὶ ὸν τί λήπ Τωρ μου
ὰ᾽ σὺ ὰ᾽ ὸ τοῖσ λόγοισ σου ὸπη τῶ ὰ᾽:

A.D. 1335/1336
Psalms
Oxford, Bodleian Library, MS Laud Greek 2 (fol. 157ʳ)

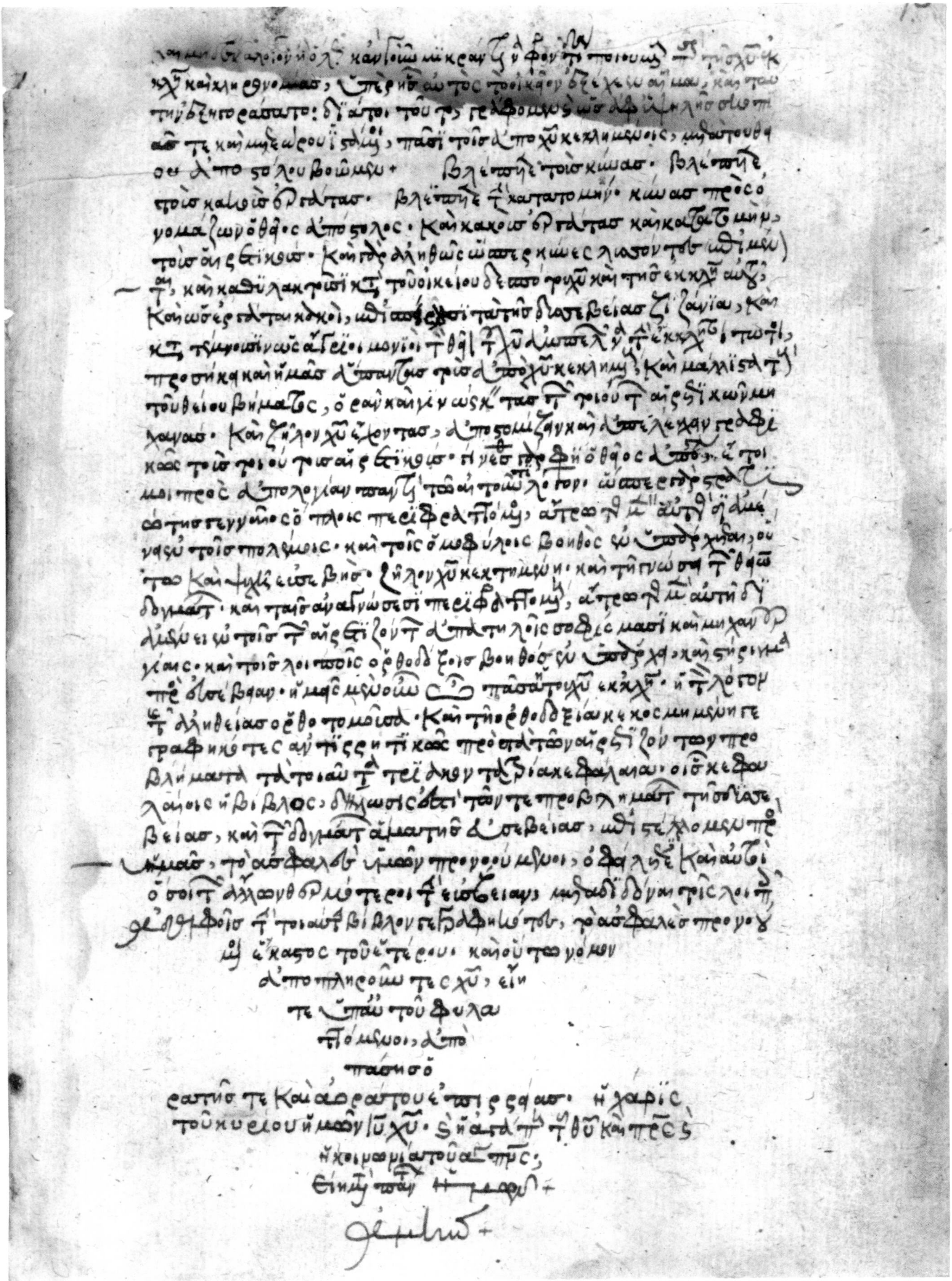

Plate 69

A.D. 1336: Written by Nicolaus of Clarentza (in the Peloponnesus)
George Moschampar, Capita antirrhetica contra Ioannis Becci dogmata et scripta
Cambridge, University Library, MS Additional 3049 (fol. 78r)

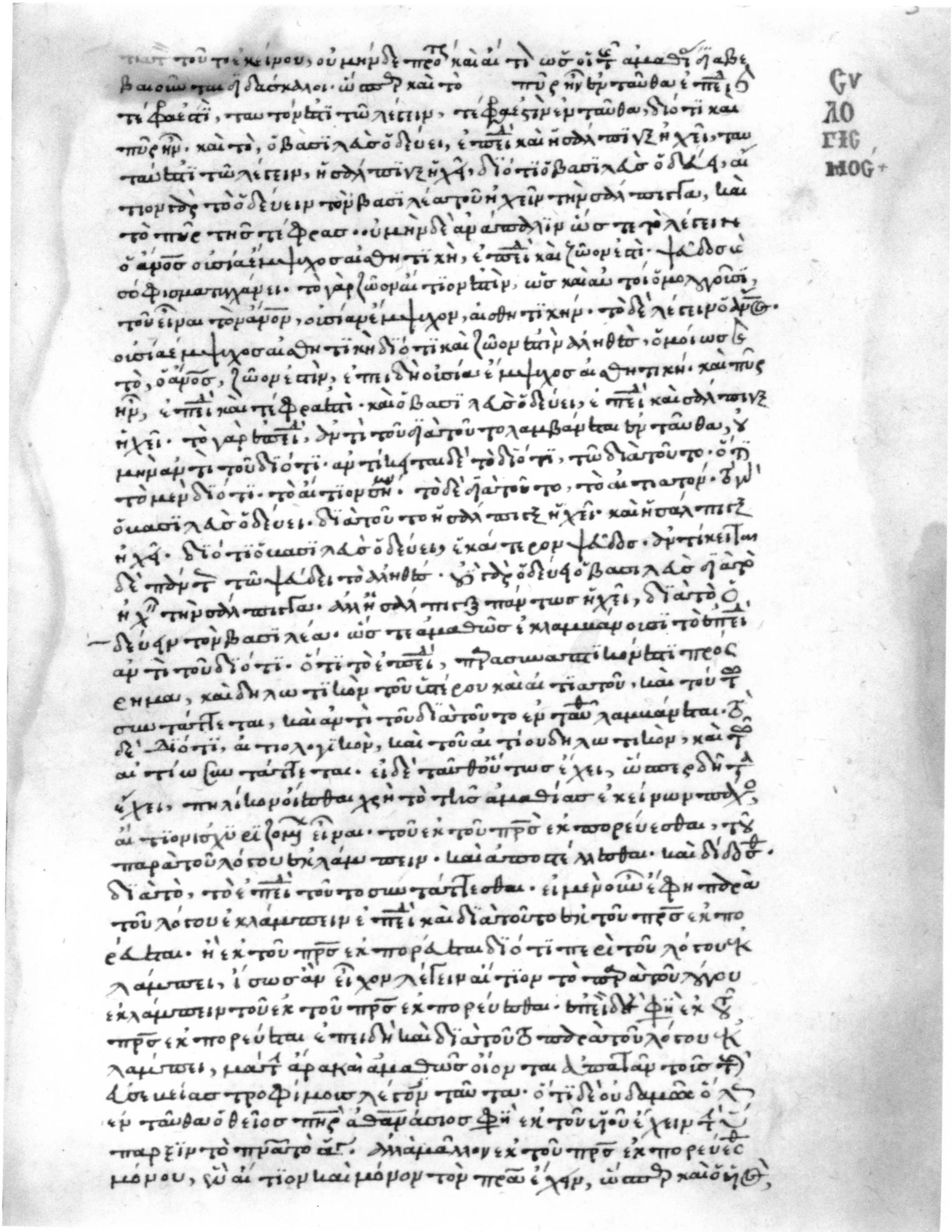

Plate 70

ΕΥ
ΛΟ
ΓΙC
ΜΟC +

A.D. 1336: Written in the Peloponnesus
George Moschampar, Capita antirrhetica contra Ioannis Becci dogmata et scripta
Cambridge, University Library, MS Additional 3049 (fol. 63ʳ)

Plate 71

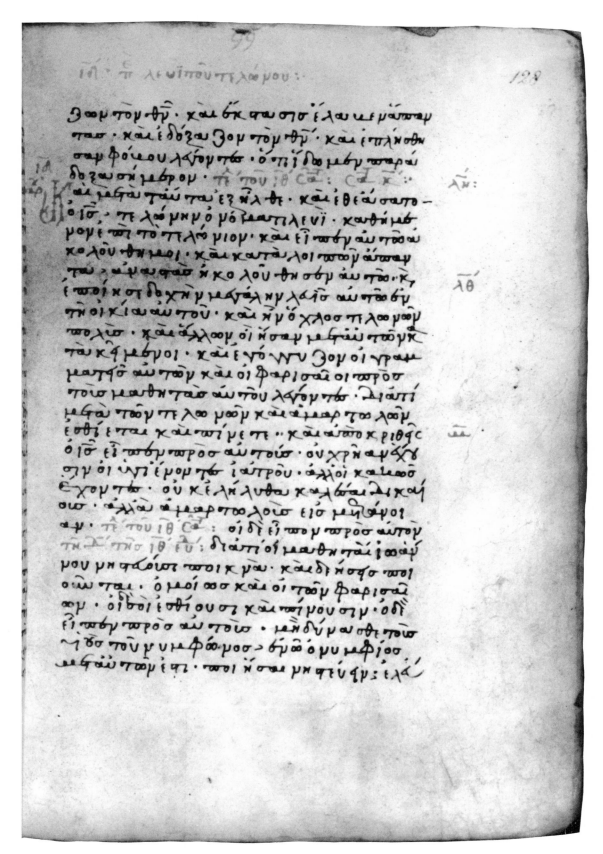

A.D. 1337: Written by Constantinus of Adrianople
Four Gospels
London, British Museum, MS Additional 5468 (fol. 129ʳ)

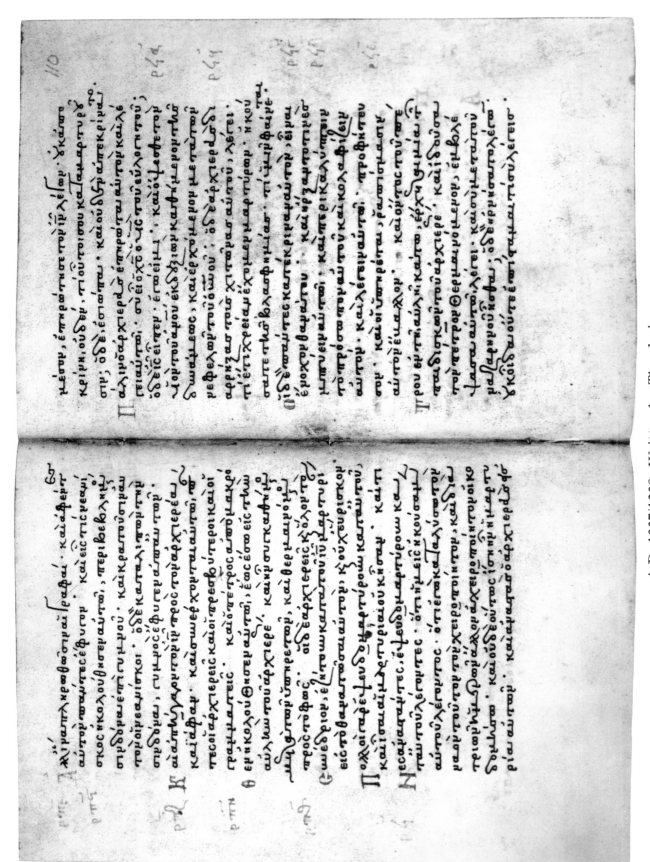

A.D. 1337/1338: Written by Theodosius
Four Gospels
Oxford, Bodleian Library, MS Selden Supra 29 (fols. 109v–110r)

Plate 72

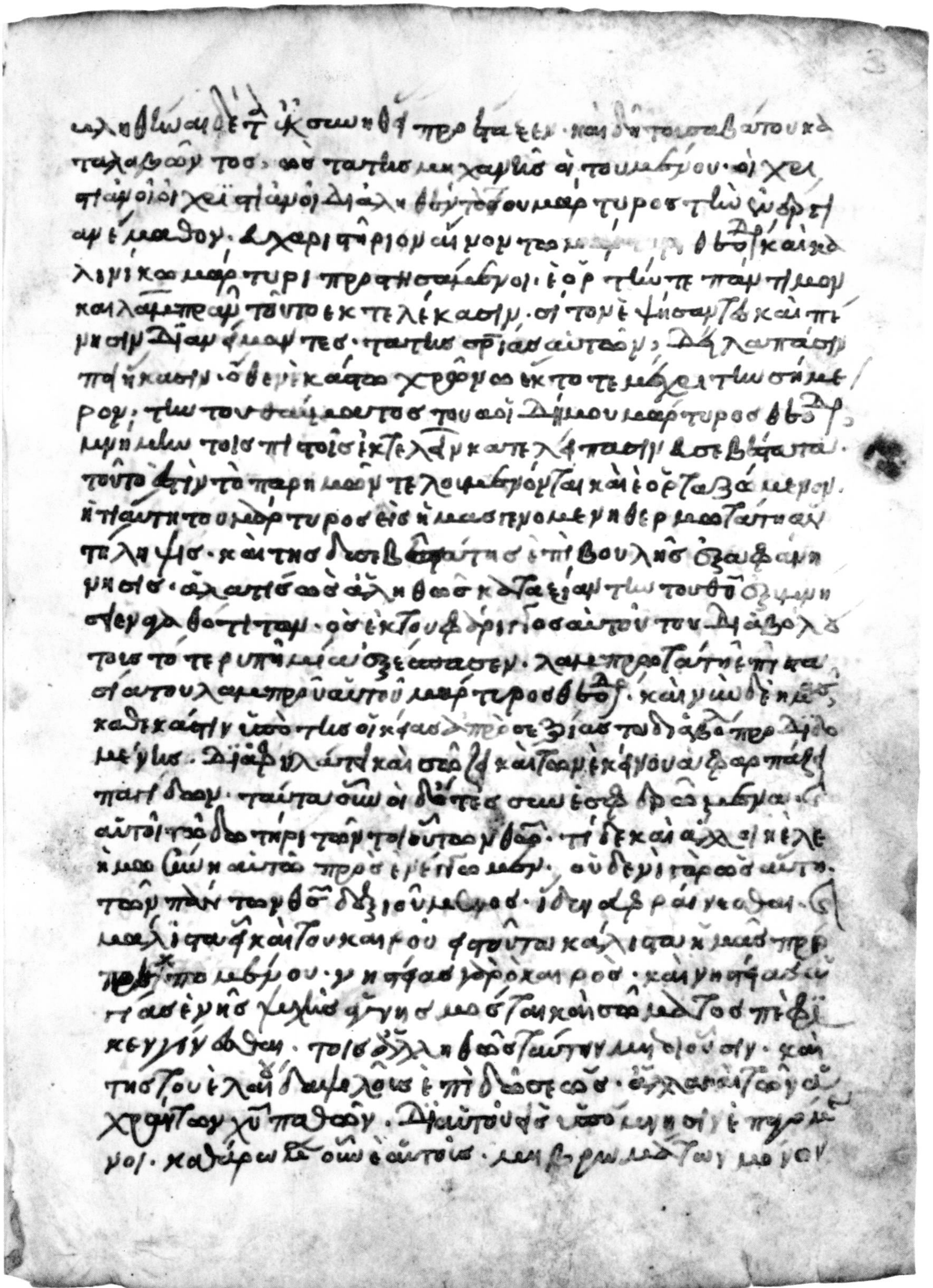

A.D. 1340: Written by the priest and chartophylax Constantinus Magedon of Italy
Panegyricon
Oxford, Bodleian Library, MS Selden Supra 9 (fol. 3r)

Plate 73

θερ΄τας, οὕτω πάλιν
τῆς μαστιλίας αἰστεθῇ,
τὸν αὐτὸν δὴ τε ὁ΄τωΝ
καὶ μῶ΄τι τὸ ὁζίας τὸ
σαρακοστὸ, τοῖς τῶν
δρόμον τὴν μῆστας
καταδοξαμένοιο, κα
θάπερ τα μοῖος κατα
γῶνει, ς ἐκ τας ς ἀη-
αροῖς καὶ λιμόν αο, τὰς
δύο ταύτας ἡμέρας
τῆς ἑβδομάδος ἱερα
χ ὑπὸ δι ἀναπαύ σεσθαι
κ χαρίται ὁ δε ἀπὸ της,
ἵνα ς τὸ σῶμα μικρὸν
ἀμεν τῶ ἀπὸ τῶν πον
τῆς μῆστας· καὶ τῶ
τυχῶ παραμυθσαι
μένοι, παμιν παρ εξ-
θο τῶ τῶν δύο του
τῶν ἡμερῶν, τῆς αὐτης
ὁδοῦ μεστα προθυμίας
ἀσωρίται, οἱ τῶ ἑαμην
ταύτην ς εσω φ εζη ὁδοι-

δὴ μετὰ ἀσφαλείας
φυλάπεσθαι, ἵνα
μικρὸν διαναπαῦσα σὺ΄
μενοι, τωάμη περ οσθη΄
κ ἐν ὁ βργαιον αδ΄ τοῖς
περαβόωσι, ς οὕτω κατ
μικρὸν ἡμῶ΄ την ὑπ
πορίαν ς αυτοῖς κατας
κα ὁ σαυτο, οὕτως δε΄
κυρίαμ ἡμέραν ἀσωαμτη
οη τό· καὶ τωο ἡμερας
μεμω ὑμῶν τῶ ὅλ καα
δα τῶ τωνι κῶ, ἐσ
λιμέμα τῆς φίλας βορ-
τῆς ὁ δοαρ η τό· ὡς
περ γὰρ τὰ παρὰ τοῦ δε
ἀπὸ του γβη ημετα δ΄
παντα· καθάπερ ὁ λο΄
γος ἀσωβ΄ ε κ αι ἡ ὧν
πραγμάτων διδασκα
μαρτυρία· λόγω τιμη
δε δημιουρ γη ται χε δαν
ἀναγκαίαν ἀσω πληρῦν
τα, οὕτως ς τὰ παρ ἡμ

A.D. 1340/1341
St. John Chrysostom, Homilies on Genesis
Oxford, Bodleian Library, MS Auct.E.1.14 (fol. 81ᵛ, upper part)

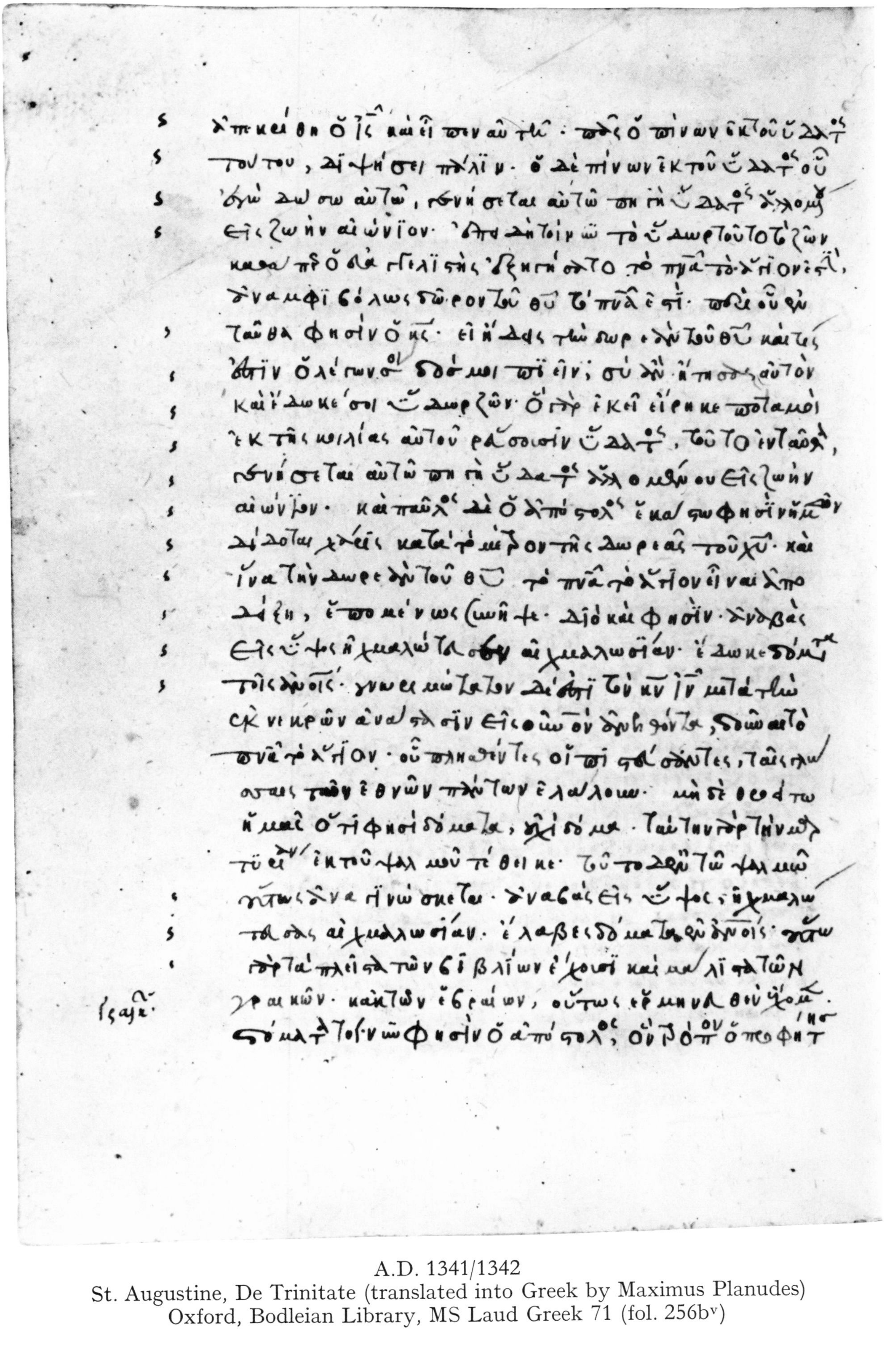

Plate 75

A.D. 1341/1342
St. Augustine, De Trinitate (translated into Greek by Maximus Planudes)
Oxford, Bodleian Library, MS Laud Greek 71 (fol. 256b^v)

Plate 76

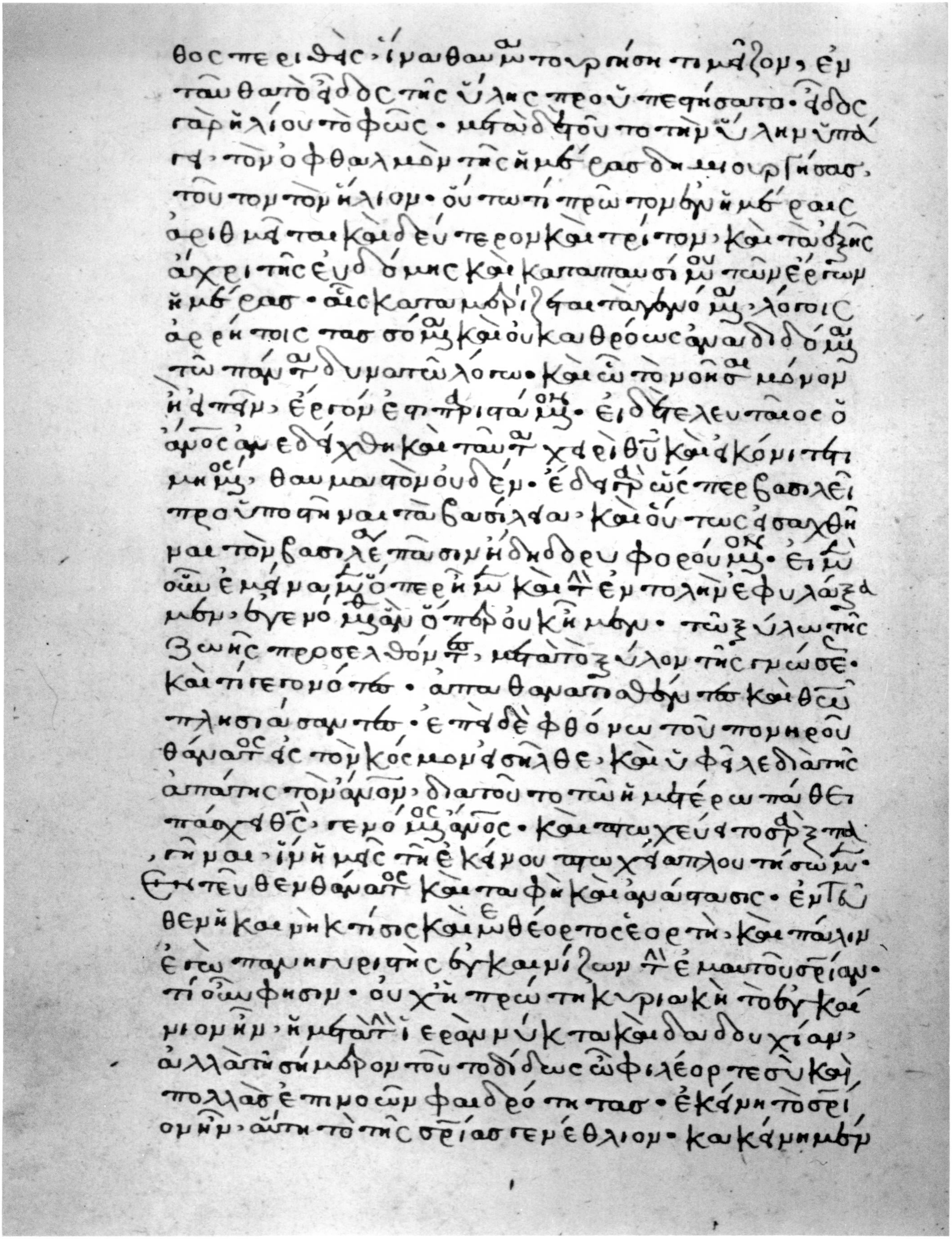

A.D. 1343: Written by the hieromonk Galaction Madaraces in Constantinople
St. Gregory of Nazianzus, Oration 44
Oxford, Bodleian Library, MS Barocci 197 (fol. 374ᵛ)

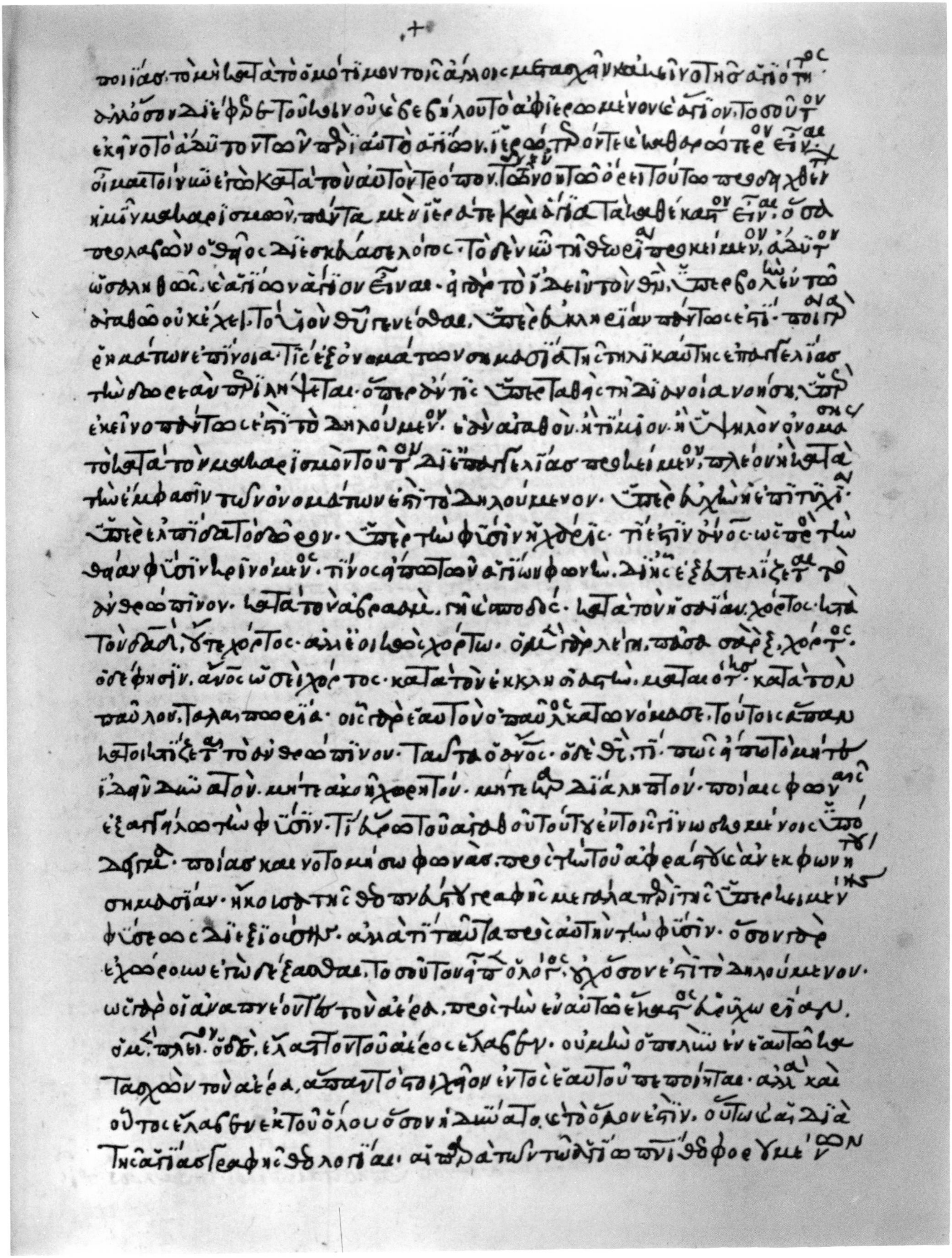

Plate 77

A.D. 1344: Written by Macarius Chrysocephalus, metropolitan of Philadelphia
Macarius Chrysocephalus, Catena on the Gospel of St. Matthew (Book I)
Oxford, Bodleian Library, MS Barocci 156 (fol. 177r)

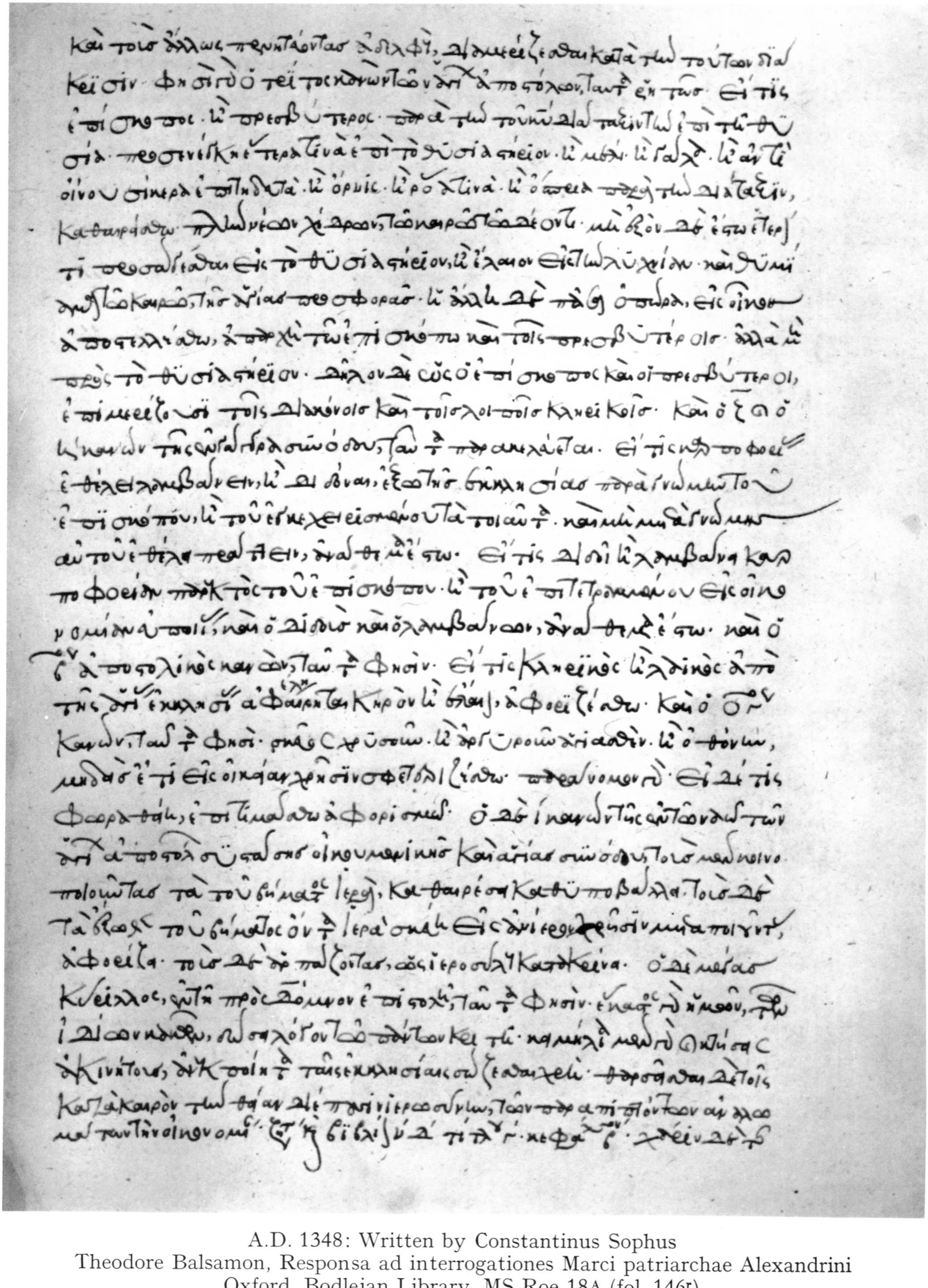

Plate 78

A.D. 1348: Written by Constantinus Sophus
Theodore Balsamon, Responsa ad interrogationes Marci patriarchae Alexandrini
Oxford, Bodleian Library, MS Roe 18ᴬ (fol. 146ʳ)

Plate 79

239

A.D. 1348
Plutarch, Parallel Lives
Glasgow, University Library, MS Hunter 424 (fol. 239r)

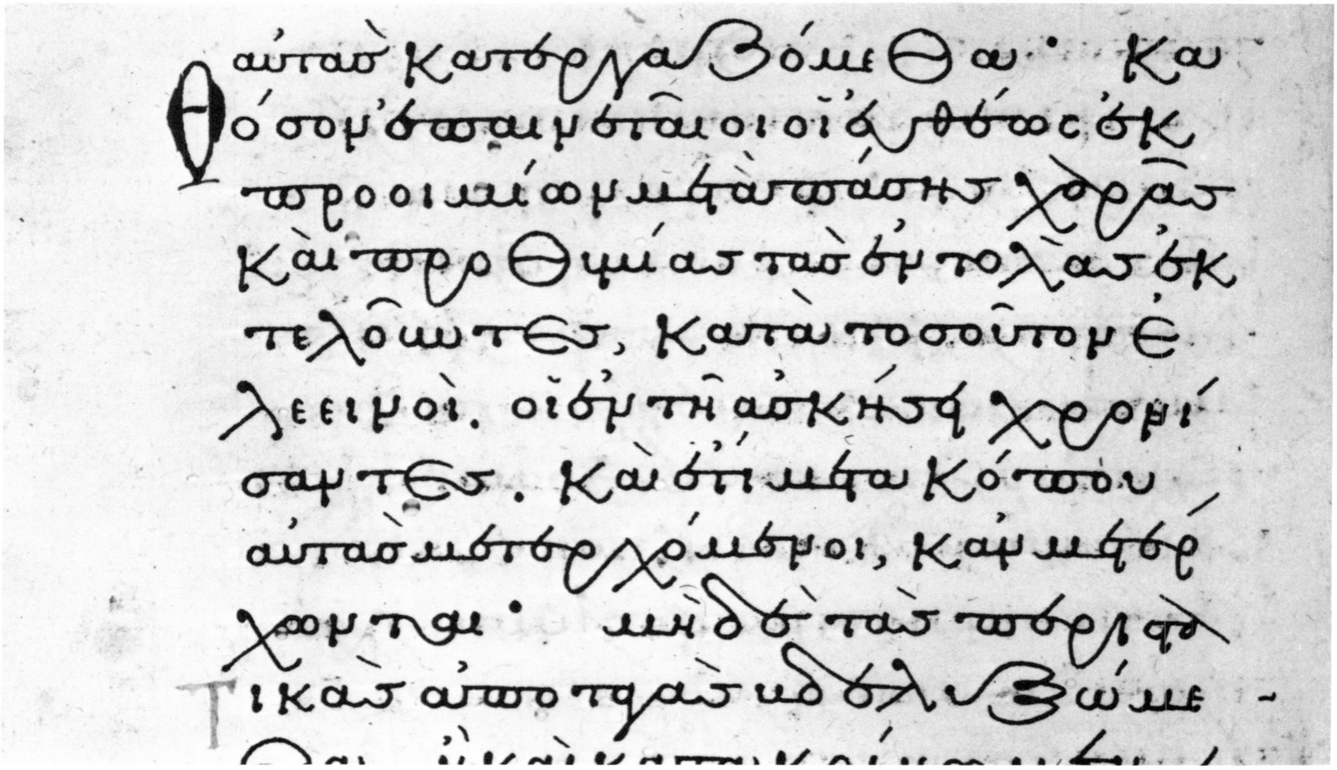

Plate 80

(*a*) A.D. 1355/1356: Written by the monk Germanus
St. John Climacus, Ladder of Paradise
Oxford, Christ Church, MS 63 (fol. 26ᵛ, upper part)

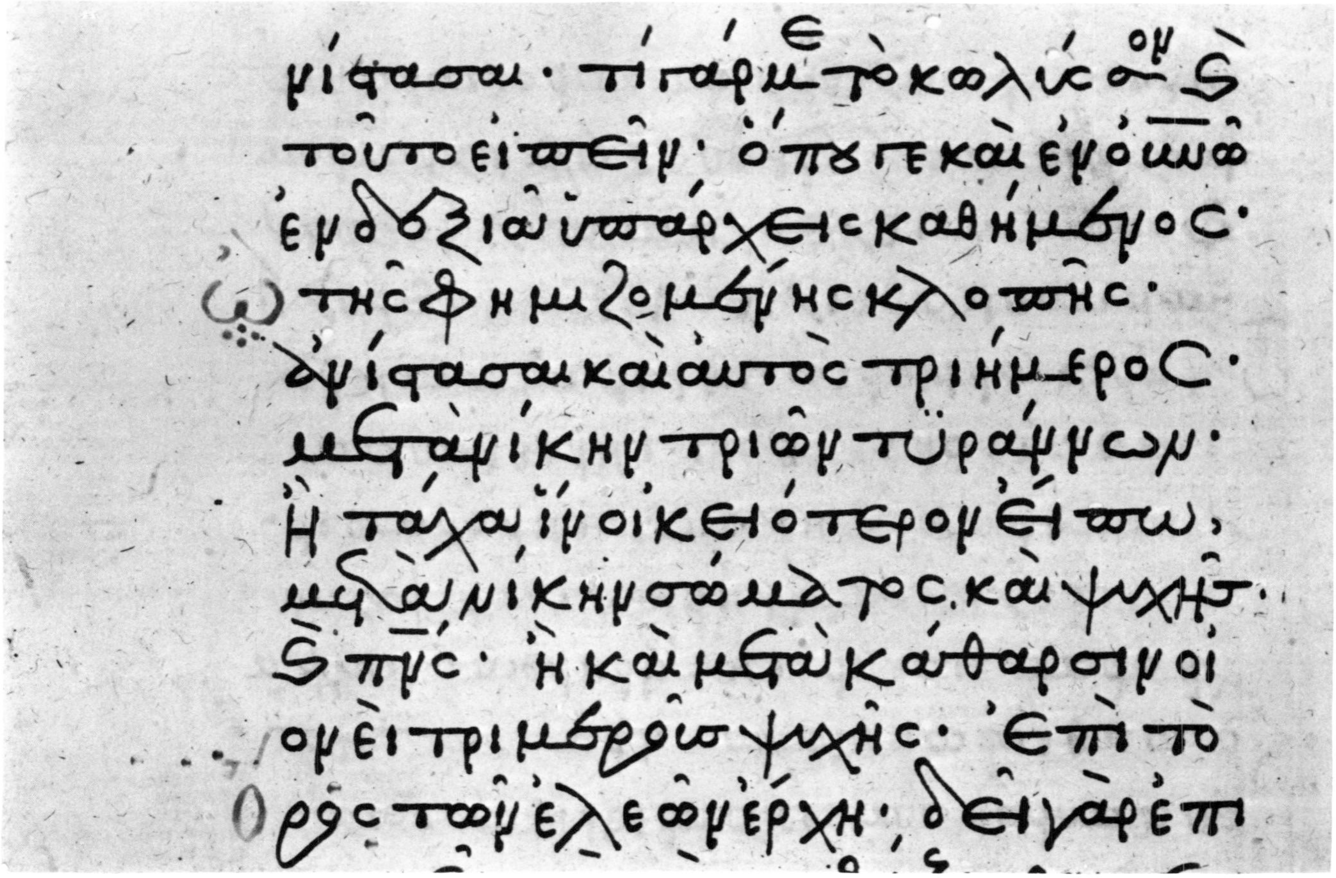

(*b*) A.D. 1355/1356: Written by the hieromonk Gennadius
St. John Climacus, Liber ad pastorem
Oxford, Christ Church, MS 63 (fol. 360ᵛ, upper part)

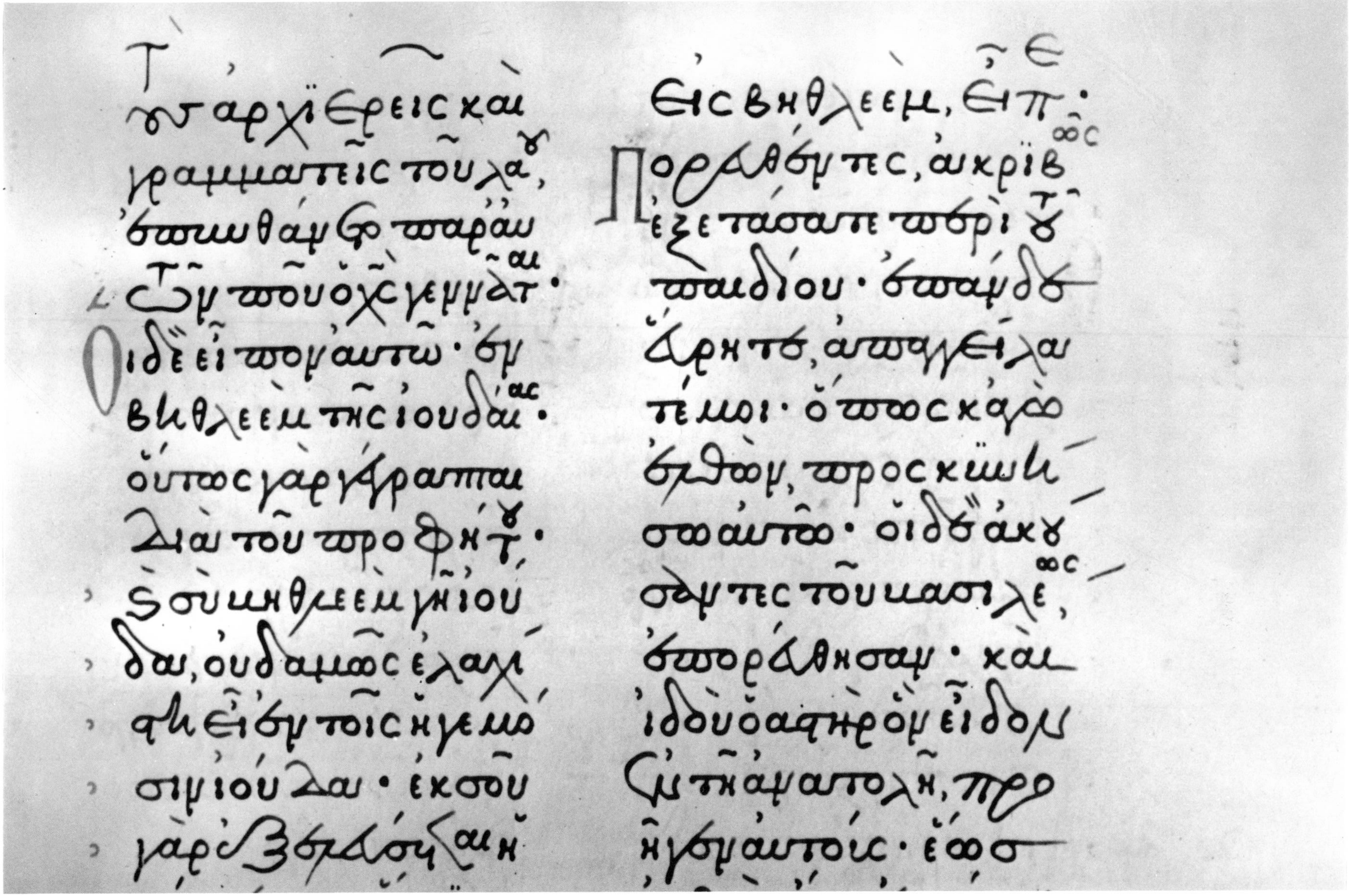

Plate 81

A.D. 1357: Written by the hieromonk Methodius (most probably in the monastery τῶν Ὁδηγῶν in Constantinople)

New Testament

London, British Museum, MS Additional 11837 (fol. 12r, upper part)

Plate 82

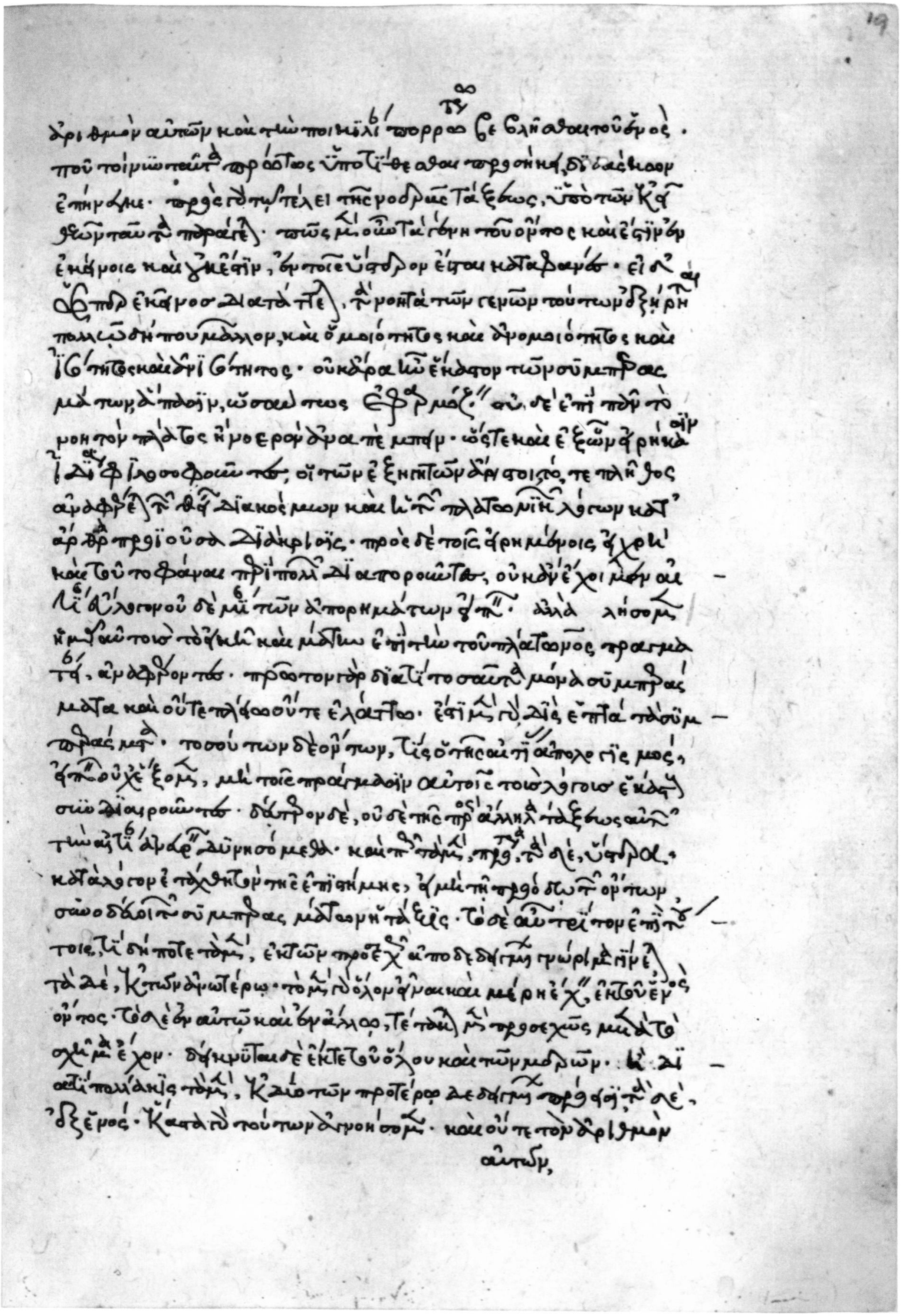

A.D. 1357/1358: Written by Stelianus Chumnus, probably in Constantinople
Proclus Diadochus, On Platonic Theology
Oxford, Bodleian Library, MS Laud Greek 18 (fol. 19r)

Plate 83

Καὶ λοιπὸν οὖν ἀδελφοί, καθὼς παρελάβε-
τε παρ' ἡμῶν, τὸ πῶς δεῖ ὑμᾶς περι-
πατεῖν καὶ ἀρέσκειν θ(ε)ῶ· ἵνα περισ-
σεύητε μᾶλλον· οἴδατε γὰρ τίνας πα-
ραγγελίας ἐδώκαμεν ὑμῖν διὰ τοῦ κυ-
ρίου Ἰ(ησο)ῦ· τοῦτο γάρ ἐστι θέλημα τοῦ θ(εο)ῦ, ὁ ἁγι-
ασμὸς ὑμῶν· ἀπέχεσθαι ὑμᾶς ἀπὸ
τῆς πορνείας· εἰδέναι ἕκαστον ὑμῶν
τὸ ἑαυτοῦ σκεῦος κτᾶσθαι ἐν ἁγιασμ(ῷ)
καὶ τιμῇ· μὴ ἐν πάθει ἐπιθυμίας·
καθάπερ καὶ τὰ ἔθνη τὰ μὴ εἰδότα τὸν
θ(εό)ν· τὸ μὴ ὑπερβαίνειν καὶ πλεονεκτεῖν
ἐν τῷ πράγματι τὸν ἀδελφὸν αὐτοῦ·
διότι ἔκδικος ὁ κ(ύριο)ς περὶ πάντων τούτων·
καθὼς καὶ προείπομεν ὑμῖν καὶ δι-
εμαρτυράμεθα· οὐ γὰρ ἐκάλεσεν ἡμᾶς
ὁ θ(εὸ)ς ἐπὶ ἀκαθαρσία· ἀλλ' ἐν ἁγιασμῷ·
τοιγαροῦν· ὁ ἀθετῶν, οὐκ ἄνθρωπον ἀθετεῖ·
ἀλλὰ τὸν θ(εό)ν· τὸν καὶ δόντα τὸ πν(εῦμ)α αὐτοῦ
τὸ ἅγιον εἰς ὑμᾶς· περὶ δὲ τῆς φιλαδελ-
φίας, οὐ χρείαν ἔχομεν γράφειν ὑμῖν·
αὐτοὶ γὰρ ὑμεῖς θεοδίδακτοί ἐστε τὸ
ἀγαπᾶν ἀλλήλους· καὶ γὰρ ποιεῖτε αὐτὸ
εἰς πάντας τοὺς ἀδελφοὺς τοὺς ἐν ὅλῃ
τῇ Μακεδονίᾳ· παρακαλοῦμεν
δὲ ὑμᾶς ἀδελφοί, περισσεύειν μᾶλ-
λον· καὶ φιλοτιμεῖσθαι ἡσυχάζειν

A.D. 1358: Written by Theophanes (most probably in the monastery τῶν Ὁδηγῶν in CP.)
Acts of the Apostles and Epistles
London, Lambeth Palace, MS 1183 (page 332)

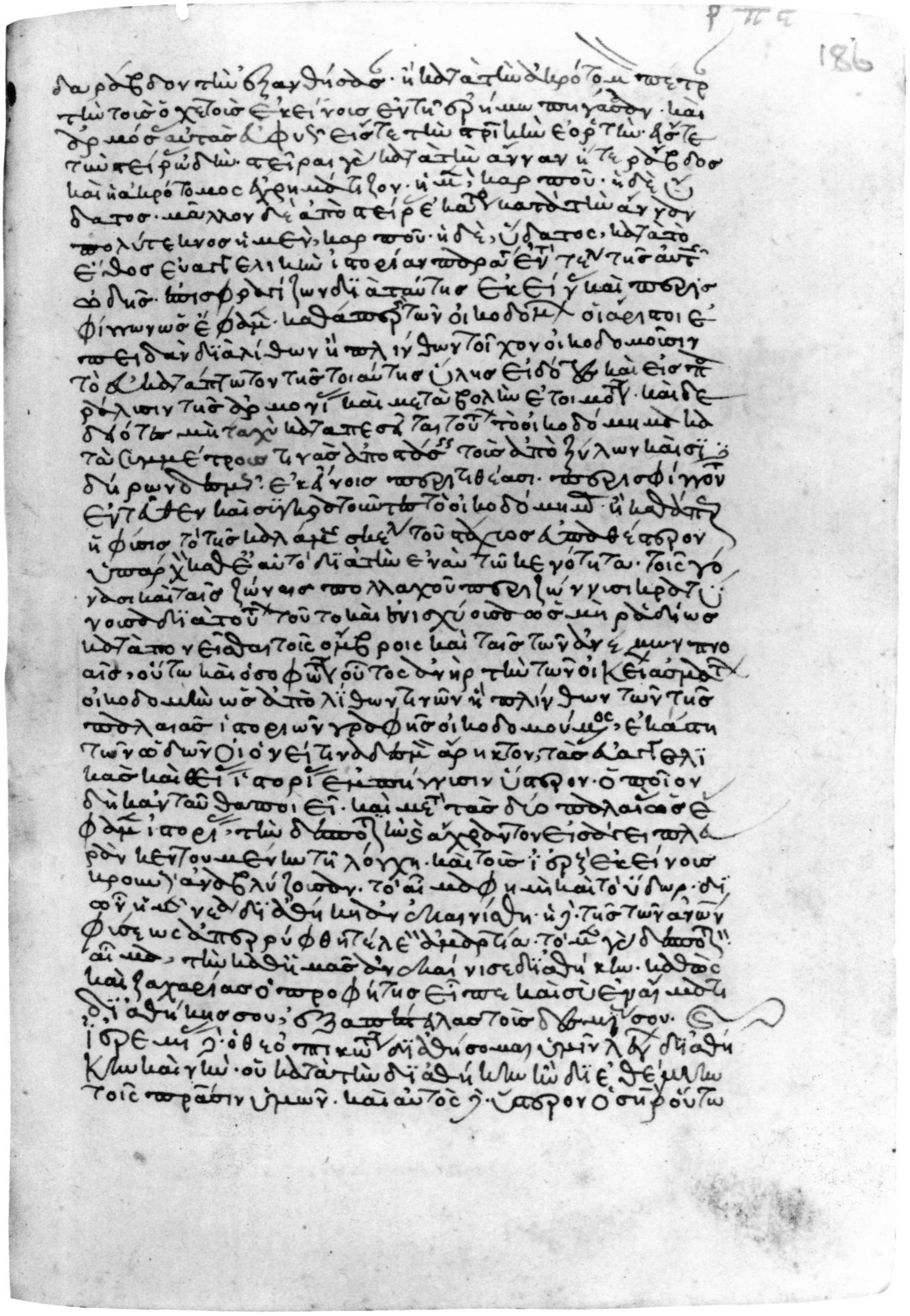

Plate 84

A.D. 1359/1360: Written by the priest Nicetas
Theodore Prodromus, Commentary on the Canons
of Cosmas of Maïuma and St. John of Damascus
Oxford, Bodleian Library, MS Barocci 110 (fol. 186ʳ)

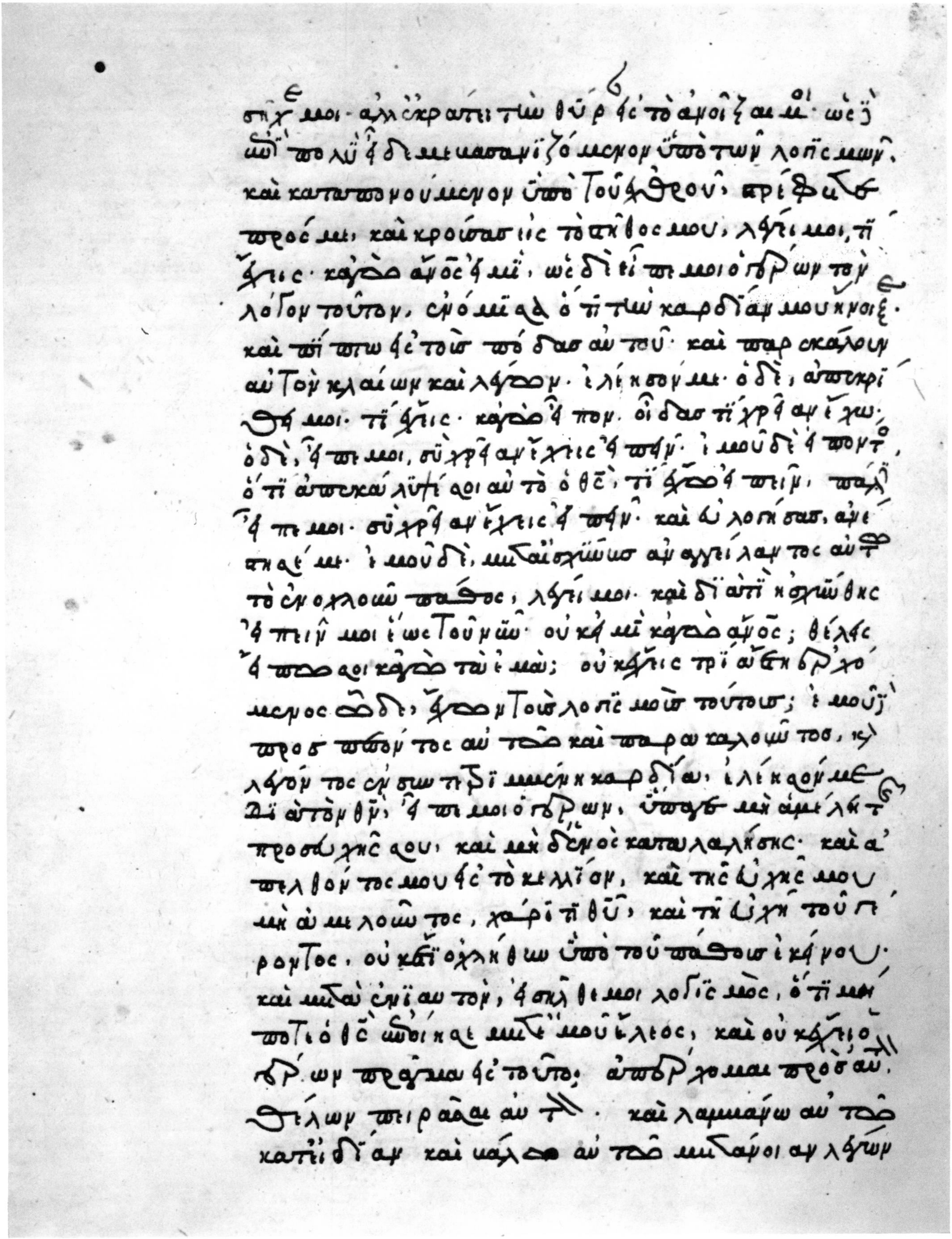

Plate 85

A.D. 1361/1362: Written by Ioannes(-Ioseph) Philagrius in Crete
Apophthegmata Patrum
London, British Museum, MS Burney 50 (part I, fol. 97ᵛ)

Plate 86

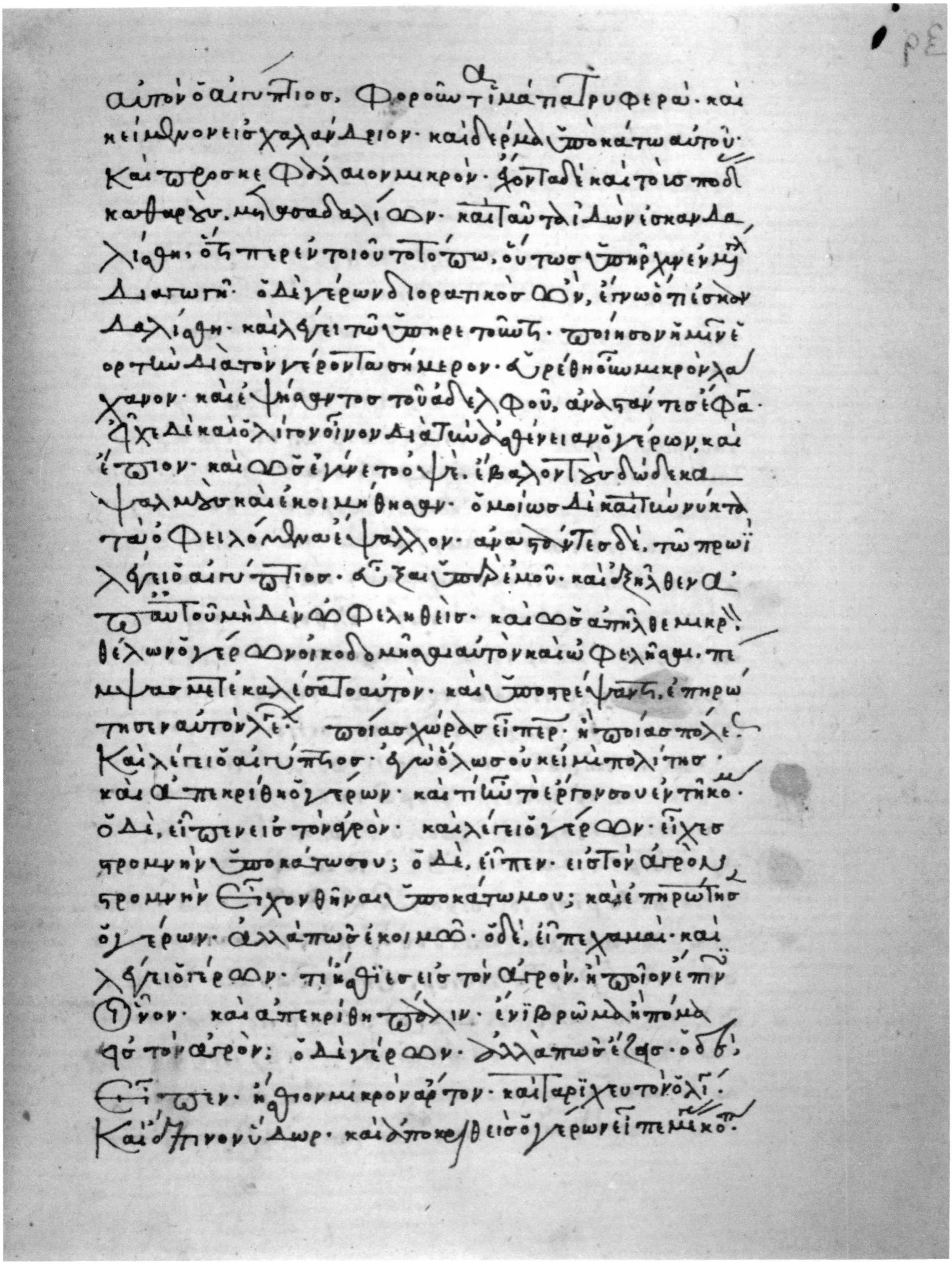

A.D. 1361/1362: Written in Crete
Apophthegmata Patrum
London, British Museum, MS Burney 50 (part I, fol. 163r)

Plate 87

A.D. 1362: Written by Manuel Tzycandyles in Mistra (near Sparta)

Plutarch, Parallel Lives

Oxford, Bodleian Library, MS Canonici Greek 93 (fol. 13r, middle part)

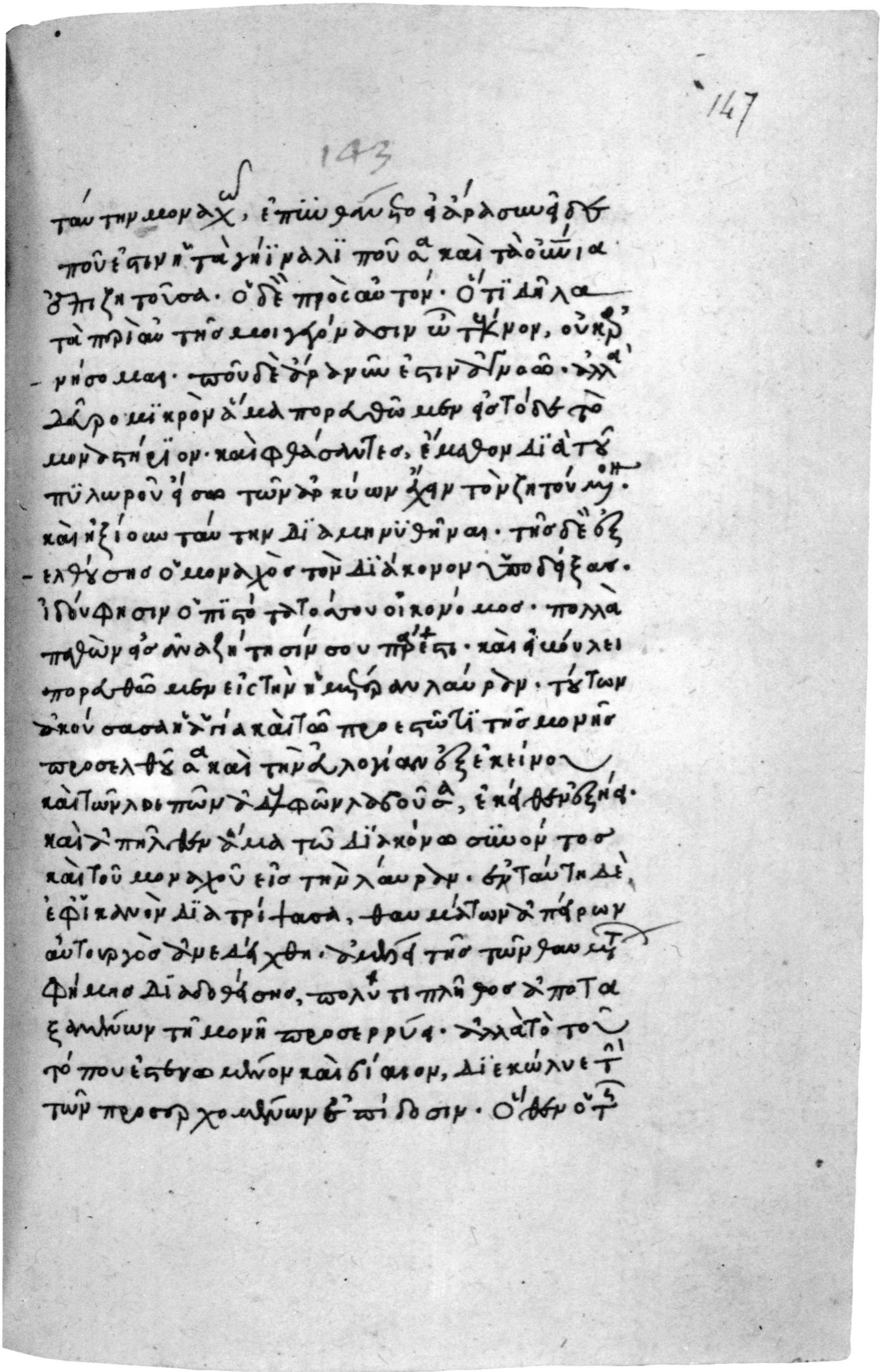

Plate 88

143

A.D. 1362/1363: Written by the hieromonk Iacobus
Synaxarion (Lives of Saints)
London, British Museum, MS Harley 5782 (fol. 147ʳ)

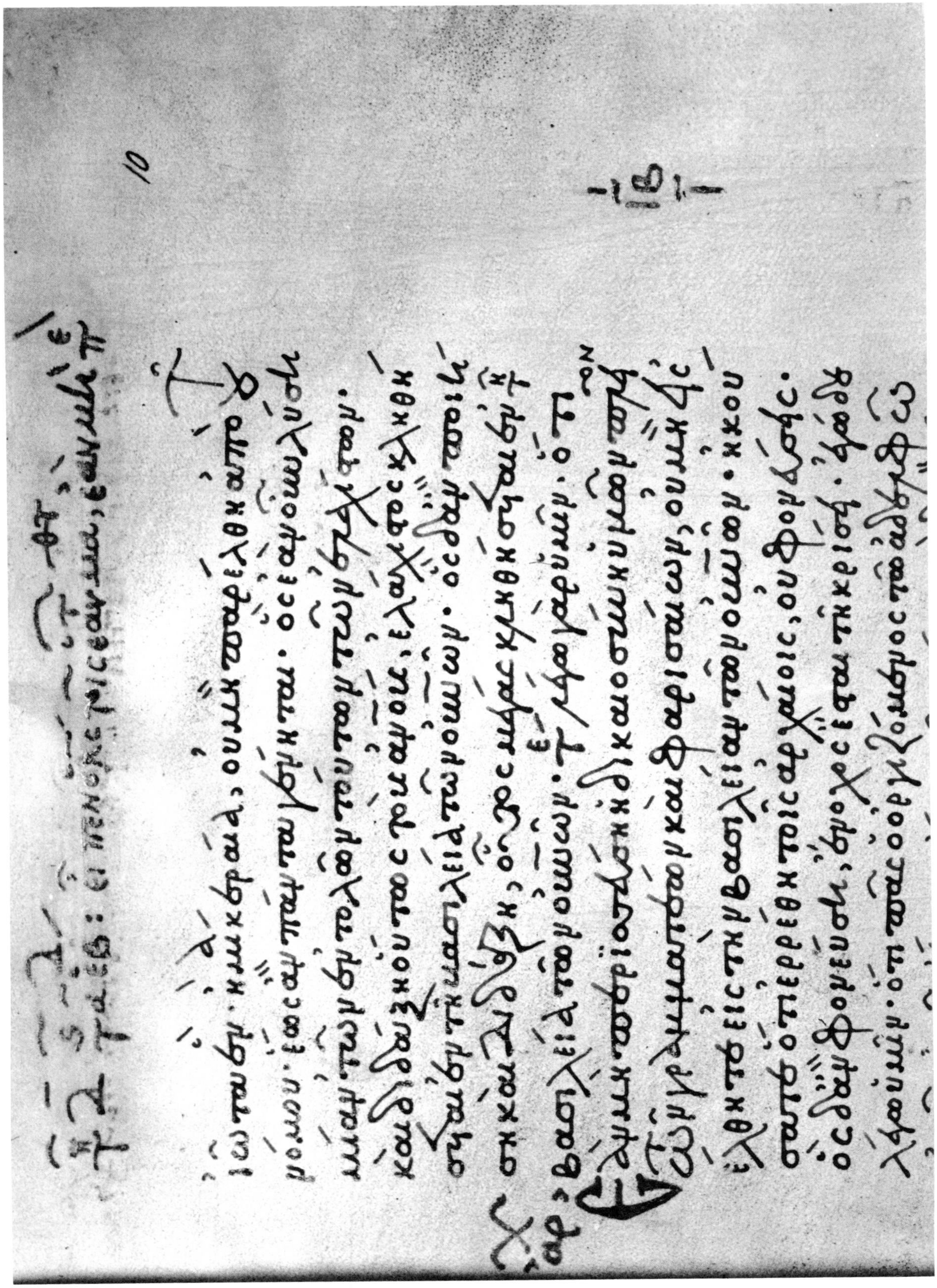

Plate 89

A.D. 1366: Written by Ioasaph (of the monastery τῶν Ὁδηγῶν in Constantinople)

Four Gospels

London, British Museum, MS Burney 18 (fol. 10r, upper part)

Plate 90

αὐτοῖς ἀπ' ἀλλήλων· ὡς πρόβατα ἀπὸ ἐρίφων· 247

τὰ πρόβατα ἀπὸ τῶν ἐρίφων· καὶ στήσει τὰ μὲν πρό-

βατα ἐκ δεξιῶν αὐτοῦ, τὰ δὲ ἐρίφια ἐξ εὐωνύμων·

τότε ἐρεῖ ὁ βασιλεὺς τοῖς ἐκ δεξιῶν αὐτοῦ· δεῦτε

οἱ εὐλογημένοι τοῦ πατρός μου, κληρονομήσατε τὴν

ἡτοιμασμένην ὑμῖν βασιλείαν ἀπὸ καταβολῆς

κόσμου· ἐπείνασα γὰρ καὶ ἐδώκατέ μοι φαγεῖν· ἐδί-

ψησα, καὶ ἐποτίσατέ με· ξένος ἤμην, καὶ συνηγά-

γετέ με· γυμνός, καὶ περιεβάλετέ με· ἠσθένησα,

καὶ ἐπεσκέψασθέ με· ἐν φυλακῇ ἤμην, καὶ ἤλθετε

πρός με· τότε ἀποκριθήσονται αὐτῷ οἱ δίκαιοι·

λέγοντες, κε· πότε σε εἴδομεν πεινῶντα καὶ

ἐθρέψαμεν; ἢ διψῶντα, καὶ ἐποτίσαμεν· πότε

δέ σε εἴδομεν ξένον, καὶ συνηγάγομεν· ἢ γυμνόν,

καὶ περιεβάλομεν· πότε δέ σε εἴδομεν ἀσθενῆ·

ἢ ἐν φυλακῇ, καὶ ἤλθομεν πρός σε· καὶ ἀποκριθεὶς

ὁ βασιλεὺς, ἐρεῖ αὐτοῖς· ἀμὴν λέγω ὑμῖν, ἐφ' ὅσον ἐποι-

ήσατε ἑνὶ τούτων τῶν ἀδελφῶν μου τῶν ἐλαχί-

στων, ἐμοὶ ἐποιήσατε· τότε ἐρεῖ καὶ τοῖς ἐξ εὐωνύμων·

πορεύεσθε ἀπ' ἐμοῦ οἱ κατηραμένοι, εἰς τὸ πῦρ

τὸ αἰώνιον· τὸ ἡτοιμασμένον τῷ διαβόλῳ καὶ τοῖς

ἀγγέλοις αὐτοῦ· ἐπείνασα γὰρ καὶ οὐκ ἐδώκατέ μοι φαγεῖν·

ἐδίψησα, καὶ οὐκ ἐποτίσατέ με· ξένος ἤμην, καὶ οὐ συνη-

A.D. 1366: Written by Ioasaph (of the monastery τῶν Ὁδηγῶν in Constantinople)
Four Gospels
London, British Museum, MS Burney 18 (fol. 53ʳ)

Plate 91

A.D. 1367: Written by Manuel Mauromates of Zichnai (in Macedonia)
Matthew Blastares, Syntagma
Oxford, Christ Church, MS 69 (fol. 44ʳ)

Plate 92

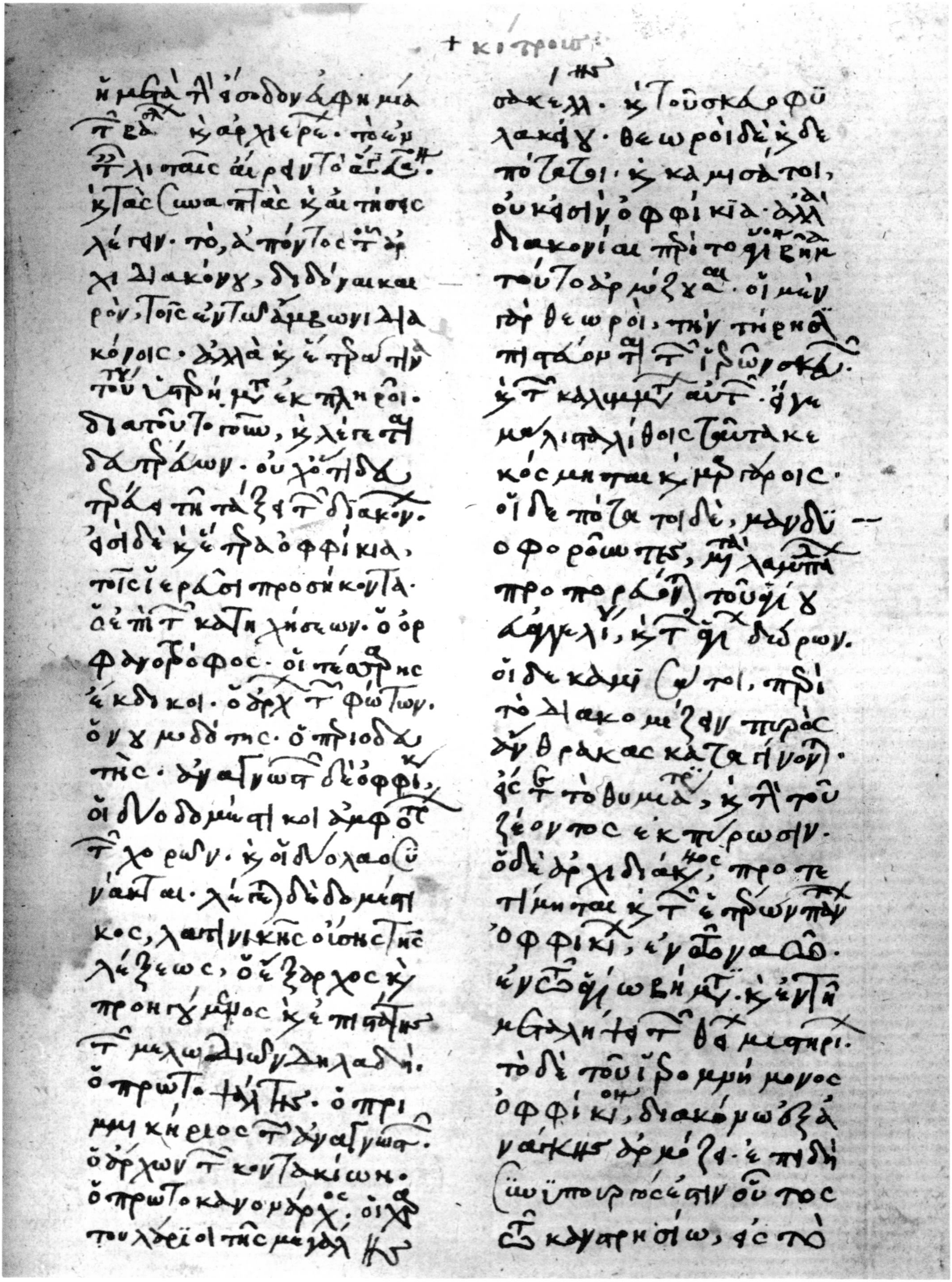

A.D. 1367: Written presumably in Zichnai (in Macedonia)
Matthew Blastares, Syntagma (Appendix)
Oxford, Christ Church, MS 69 (fol. 154ʳ)

A.D. 1378: Written by the hieromonk Niphon, presumably in Crete
Hesychius of Sinai, De temperantia et virtute
Oxford, Bodleian Library, MS Barocci 69 (fol. 261ᵛ)

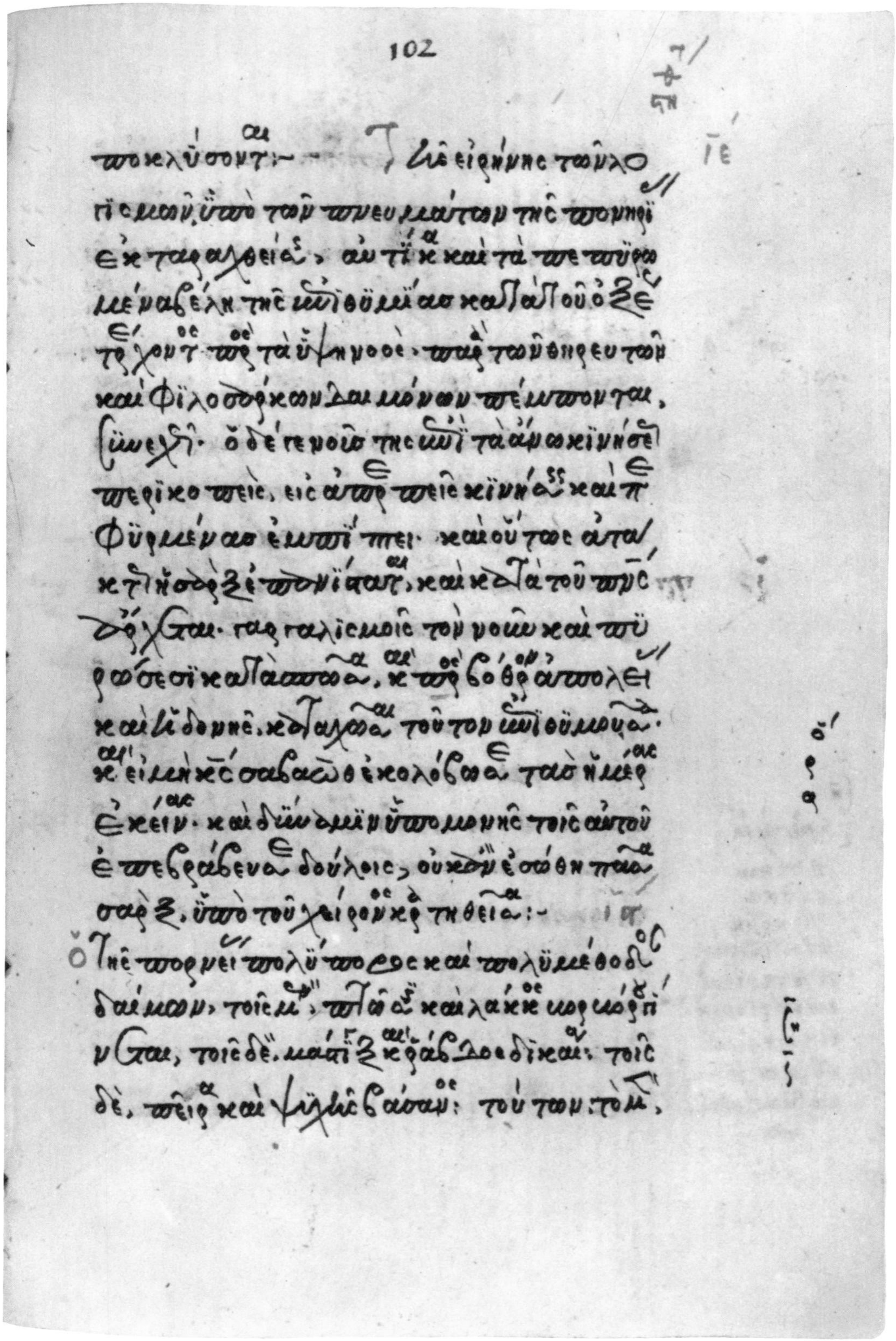

Plate 94

A.D. 1378: Written presumably in Crete
Nicetas Stethatus, Physicorum capitum centuria II
Oxford, Bodleian Library, MS Barocci 69 (fol. 102ʳ)

Plate 95

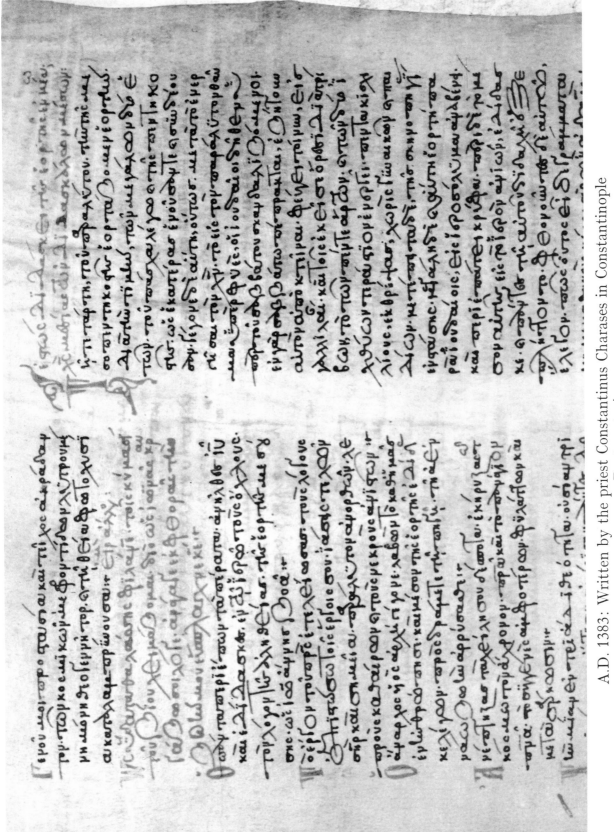

A.D. 1383: Written by the priest Constantinus Charases in Constantinople

Pentecostarion

Oxford, Bodleian Library, MS Canonici Greek 102 (fol. 30v, upper part)

Plate 96

αυτ· κυκλω τ σκηνωματ αυτ·
καιεφαγον καιενεπλησθησανσφο
δρα· ετηνεπιθυμιαναυτων, ημϗκ
αυτοις· ουκεστερηθησαναπο τῆς
επιθυμιαςαυτων· ετι της βρω
σεωςουσης εν τω στοματιαυτων,
οργη του θυ ανεβη επ αυτοις· εδ
το κτμενεν τοις πιοσιναυτ·
το τοις εκλεκτοις του ιηλ, συνεπο
δισεν· εμπασι τουτοις, ημαρτον
ετι· εουκ επιστευσανεν τοις
θαυμασιοις αυτου· εεξελιπ
εν ματαιοτητι ημεραι αυτων
εταιετη αυτων μετα σπουδης·
ταν απεκτενεν αυτοις, τοτε
εζητουναυτον· εεπεστρεφ
και ωρθριζον προς τον θν· εεμνη
σθησαν, οτι οθς βοηθος αυτων εστι·
εο θς ουψιστος, λυτρωτης αυτων εστι·
εηγαπησαναυτον εν τω στοματιαυτων·

A.D. 1391: Written by Ioasaph (of the monastery τῶν Ὁδηγῶν in Constantinople)
Psalter
Oxford, Christ Church, MS 61 (fol. 106ʳ)

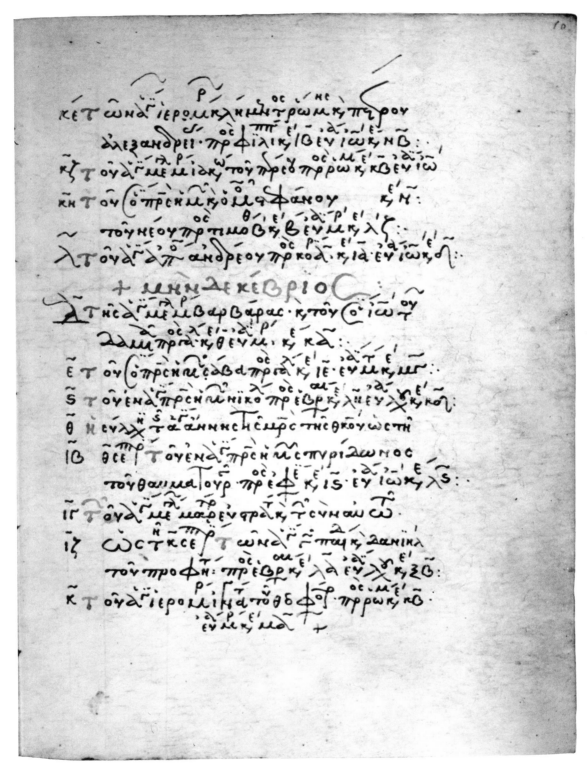

A.D. 1391: From an addition written by Ioasaph of the monastery τῶν Ὀδηγῶν in CP.
Synaxarion and Menologion (Tables of New Testament lessons)
Oxford, Bodleian Library, MS Auct.T.inf.1.10 (fol. 10ʳ)

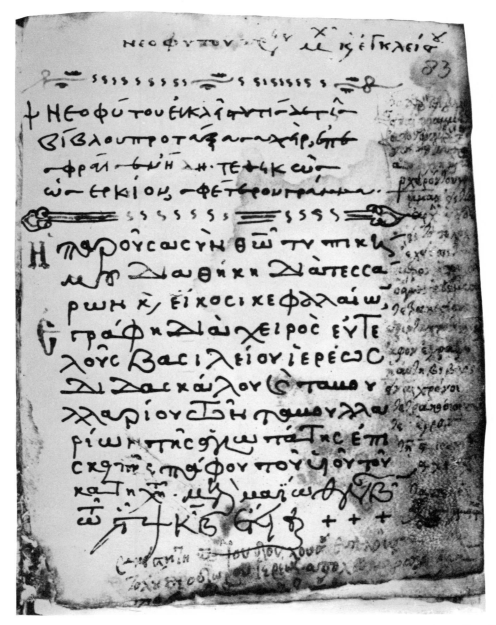

A.D. 1214: Subscription by the priest and notary Basilius of Paphos (in Cyprus)
preceded by an autographic note of St. Neophytus the Recluse
Edinburgh, University Library, MS 224 (fol. 83r)

Plate 98

(*a*) A.D. 1225: Subscription by the lector Michael Papadopulus of Tzemernikos in Epirus
Oxford, Bodleian Library, MS Cromwell 11 (page 416)

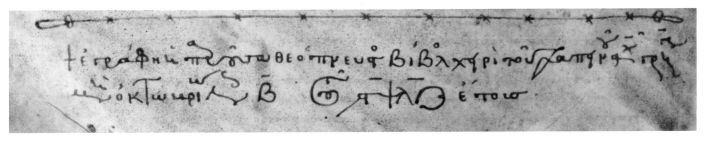

(*b*) A.D. 1228: Subscription by the monk Gregorius
Oxford, Bodleian Library, MS Holkham Greek 64 (fol. 300ᵛ)

Plate 99

(*a*) A.D. 1252, June 5: Subscription
London, British Museum, MS Additional 27359 (fol. 191ᵛ)

(*b*) A.D. 1252, July 6: Subscription
London, British Museum, MS Additional 27359 (fol. 239ᵛ)

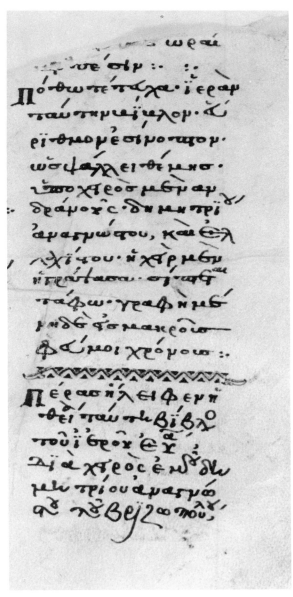

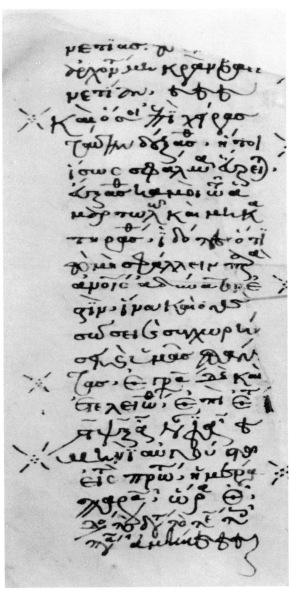

(*c*) A.D. 1253: Subscription by the lector Demetrius Brizopulus (presumably of Epirus)
Oxford, Bodleian Library, MS E. D. Clarke 8 (fol. 196ʳ right column – 196ᵛ left column)

Plate 100

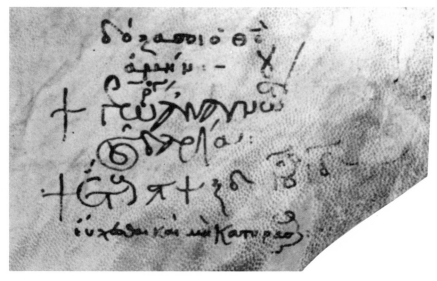

(*a*) A.D. 1255/1256: Subscription by the lector Georgius Sudarias
London, British Museum, MS Additional 40754 (fol. 151ʳ)

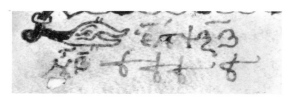

(*b*) A.D. 1258/1259: Subscription
Glasgow, University Library, MS Hunter 440 (page 224)

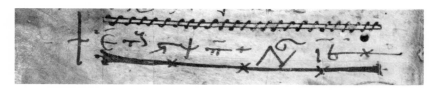

(*c*) A.D. 1271/1272: Subscription
London, British Museum, MS Additional 39597 (fol. 230ᵛ)

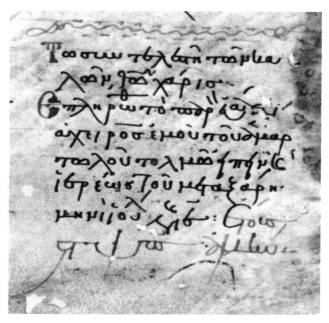

(*d*) A.D. 1272: Subscription by the priest Metaxares
London, British Museum, MS Additional 28818 (fol. 118ʳ)

Plate 101

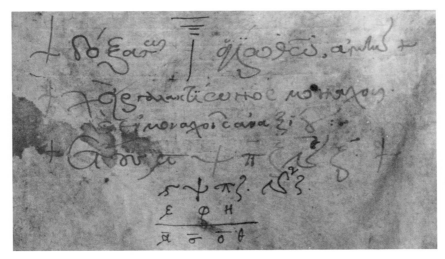

(*a*) A.D. 1278/1279: Subscription by the monk Galaction
Oxford, Bodleian Library, MS Roe 7 (fol. 331ᵛ)

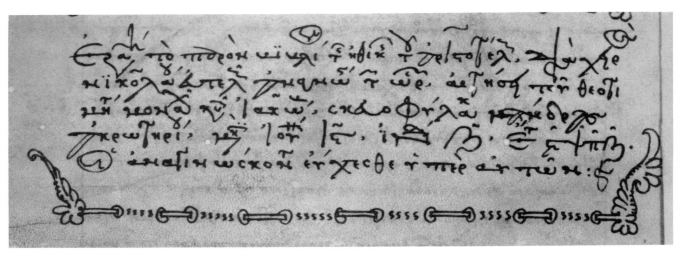

(*b*) A.D. 1279: Subscription by the lector Nicolaus ⟨Damenus⟩ written in Messina
Cambridge, University Library, MS Ii.5.44 (fol. 143ᵛ)

(*c*) A.D. 1279/1280: Subscription by Syropulus
Oxford, Bodleian Library, MS Barocci 122 (fol. 223ᵛ)

Plate 102

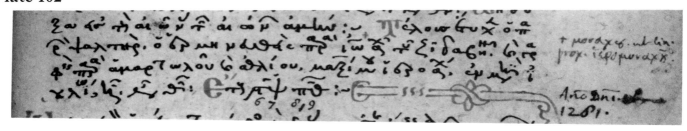

(*a*) A.D. 1281: Subscription by the hieromonk Maximus
London, British Museum, MS Harley 5575 (fol. 307ʳ)

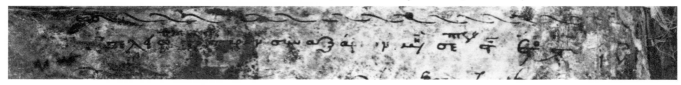

(*b*) A.D. 1281: Subscription
Oxford, Bodleian Library, MS Auct.E.5.8 (fol. 142ᵛ)

(*c*) A.D. 1282: Subscription (written by Ioasaph?)
Manchester, John Rylands University Library, MS Rylands Gaster 1574 (fols. 376ᵛ–377ʳ)

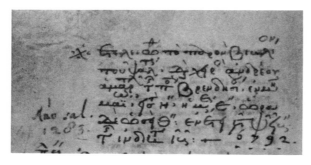

(*d*) A.D. 1284, May 8: Subscription by Andreas of Brindisi (Terra d'Otranto)
London, British Museum, MS Harley 5535 (fol. 221ᵛ)

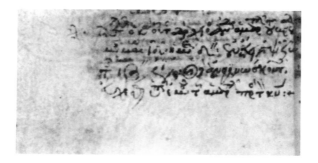

(*e*) A.D. 1284, May 14: Subscription by Andreas of Brindisi (Terra d'Otranto)
London, British Museum, MS Harley 5535 (fol. 260ᵛ)

Plate 103

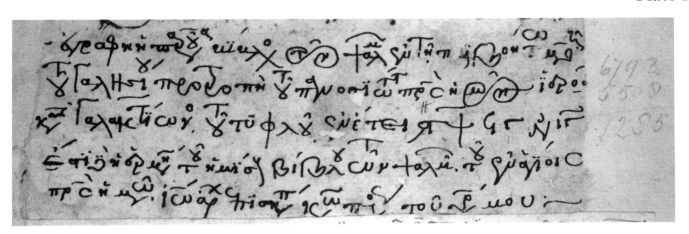

(*a*) A.D. 1284/1285: Subscription written on Mount Galesion (near Ephesus)
Oxford, Bodleian Library, MS Roe 13 (fol. 224ʳ)

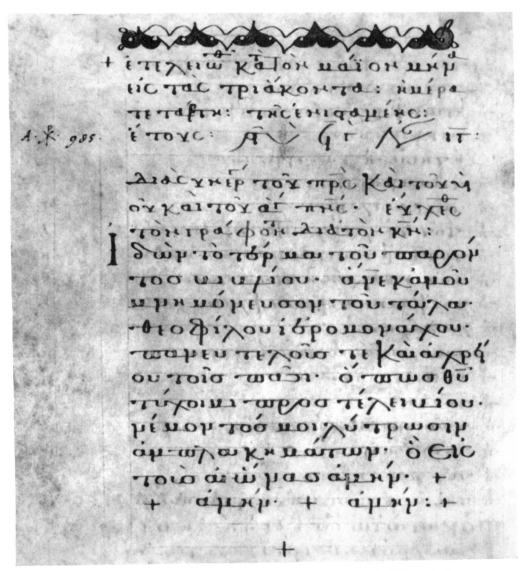

(*b*) A.D. 1285: Subscription by the hieromonk Theophilus
London, British Museum, MS Burney 20 (fol. 288ᵛ)

Plate 104

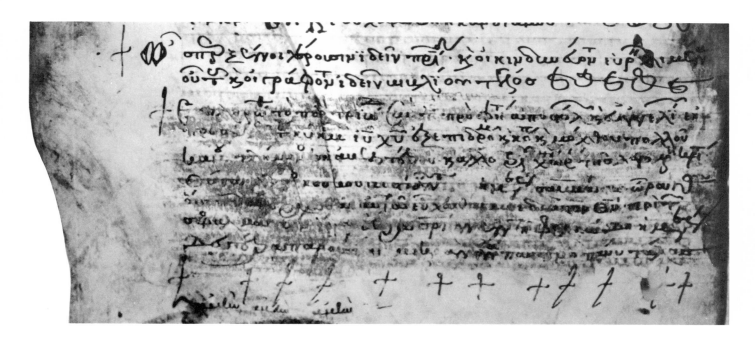

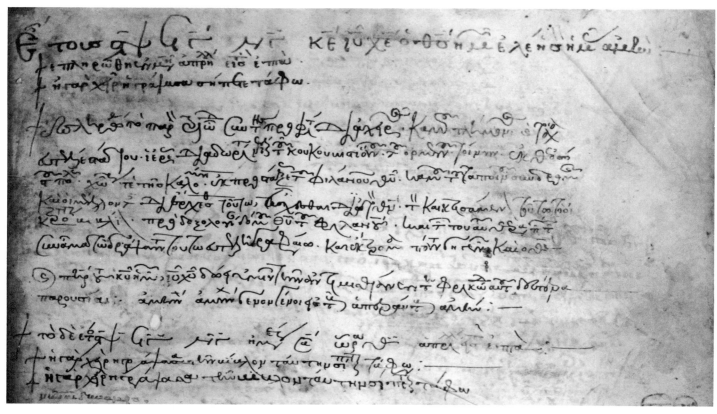

A.D. 1285: Two subscriptions by the priest Nilus Cucubistianus
Oxford, Bodleian Library, MS Auct.T.3.6 (fols. 201ᵛ–202ʳ)

Plate 105

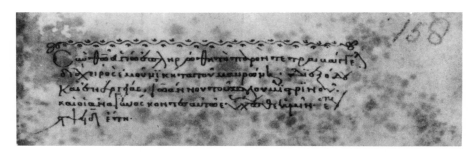

(*a*) A.D. 1285/1286: Subscription by Nicetas Maurones
Oxford, Bodleian Library, MS Laud Greek 3 (fol. 158ʳ)

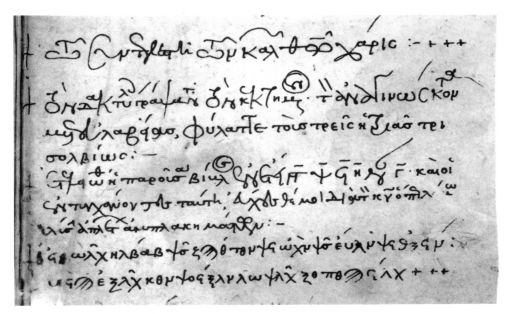

(*b*) A.D. 1289/1290: Subscription (partly cryptographic) by Macarius
Oxford, Bodleian Library, MS Laud Greek 40 (fol. 308ʳ)

(*c*) A.D. 1290: Note on lunar eclipse in the handwriting of Maximus Planudes
Edinburgh, National Library of Scotland, MS Adv.18.7.15 (fol. 54ᵛ)

Plate 106

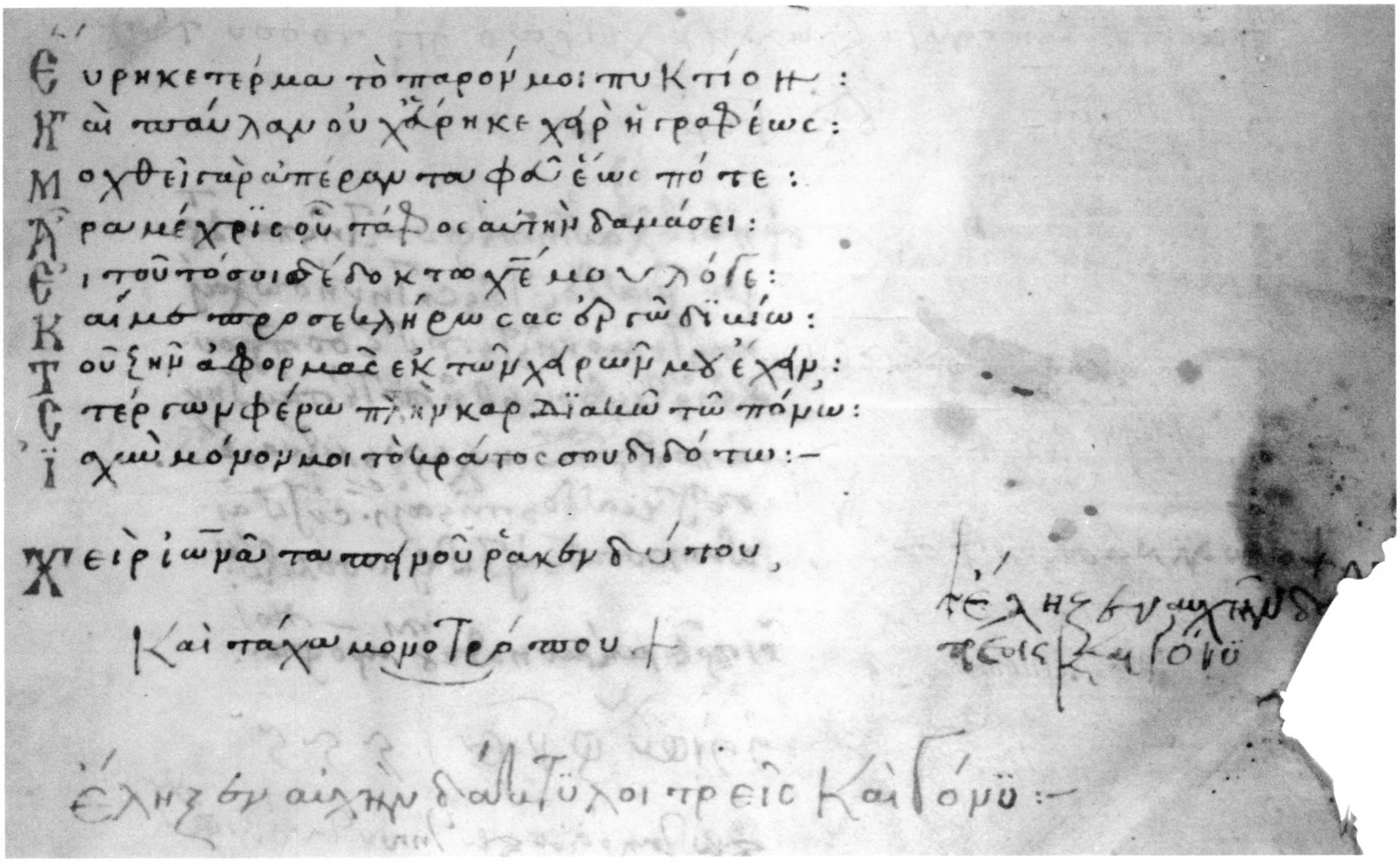

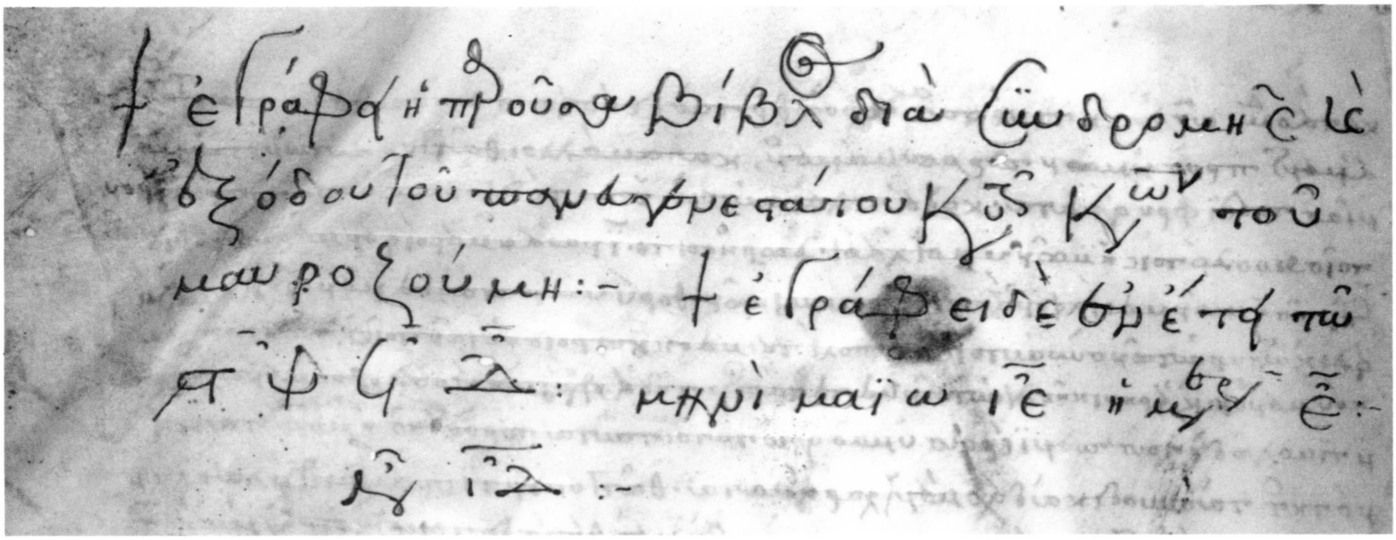

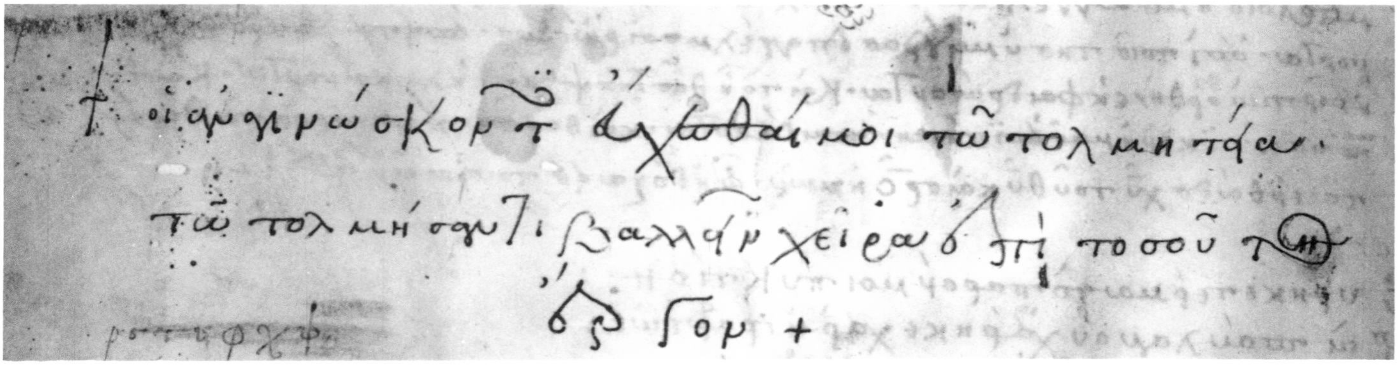

A.D. 1286: Subscription by the monk Ionas
Oxford, Bodleian Library, MS Roe 22 (fol. 560ʳ–560ᵛ)

Plate 107

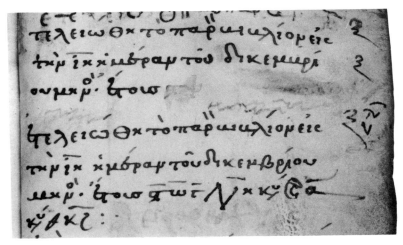

(a) A.D. 1291/1292: Subscription by Theodorus Hagiopetrites
London, British Museum, MS Burney 21 (fol. 258ʳ)

(b) A.D. 1294: Subscription
Oxford, Bodleian Library, MS Barocci 16 (fol. 283ʳ)

Plate 108

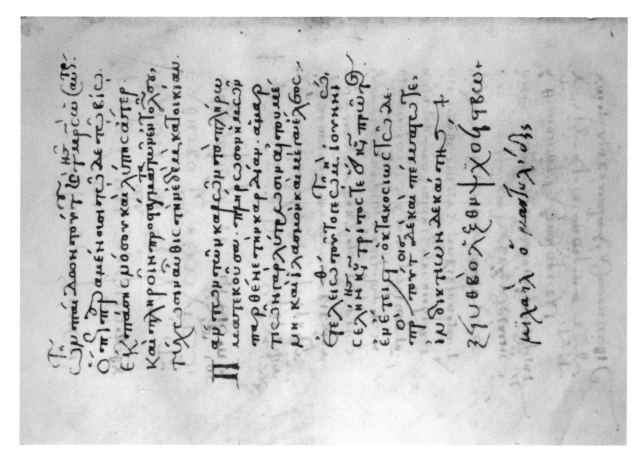

A.D. 1297: Subscription by Michael Mantylides
Cambridge, University Library, MS Dd.9.69 (fol. 293r–293v)

Plate 109

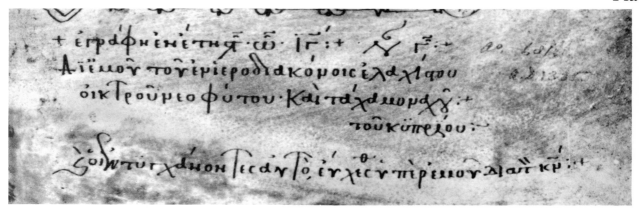

(*a*) A.D. 1304/1305: Subscription by the monk and deacon Neophytus of Cyprus
London, British Museum, MS Additional 22506 (fol. 219ʳ)

(*b*) A.D. 1305/1306: Subscription by Ignatius
London, British Museum, MS Additional 29714 (fol. 178ᵛ)

(*c*) A.D. 1306/1307: Subscription by the lector Georgius Saracinopulus
Oxford, Bodleian Library, MS Auct.T.3.16 (fol. 124ᵛ)

Plate 110

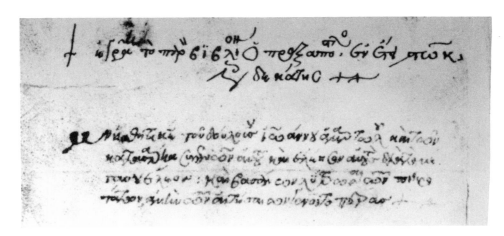

(*a*) A.D. 1308: Subscription by Demetrius Triclines (later Triclinius) (of Thessalonica)
Oxford, New College, MS 258 (fol. 250ᵛ)

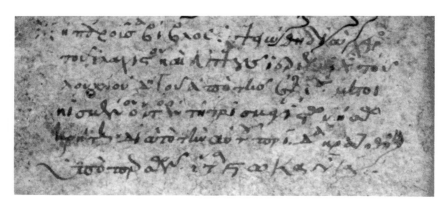

(*b*) A.D. 1311/1312: Subscription by Ioannes
London, British Museum, MS Additional 38538 (fol. 238ᵛ)

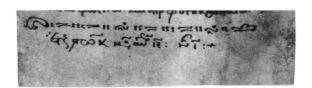

(*c*) A.D. 1312: Subscription
Oxford, Bodleian Library, MS Lyell 94 (fol. 189ʳ)

(*d*) A.D. 1312/1313: Subscription by the priest Michael Lulludes of Ephesus, written in Crete
London, British Museum, MS Arundel 523 (fol. 144ᵛ)

Plate 111

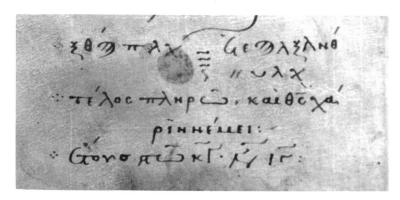

(*a*) A.D. 1314/1315: Subscription (partly cryptographic) by the hieromonk Marcus
Oxford, Bodleian Library, MS Cromwell 22 (page 450)

(*b*) A.D. 1315: Subscription
Oxford, Christ Church, MS 71 (fol. 342ᵛ)

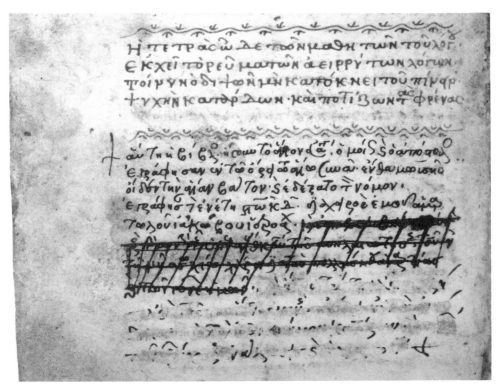

(*c*) A.D. 1315/1316: Subscription by the hieromonk Iacobus, written on Mount Sinai
Cambridge, Trinity College, MS B.10.16 (fol. 160ᵛ)

Plate 112

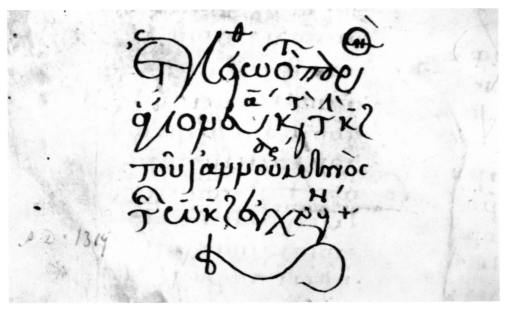

(*a*) A.D. 1319: Subscription written most probably in Cyprus
London, British Museum, MS Burney 22 (fol. 248ᵛ)

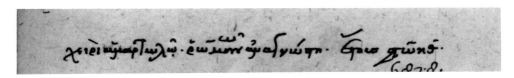

(*b*) A.D. 1320/1321: Subscription by the lector Romanus ⟨Chartophylax⟩,
written most probably in Cyprus
London, British Museum, MS Harley 5579 (fol. 210ʳ)

(*c*) A.D. 1321/1322: Subscription
Oxford, Bodleian Library, MS Gr.bibl.d.1 (fol. 271ʳ)

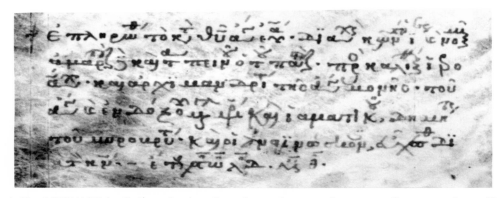

(*d*) A.D. 1325/1326: Subscription by the priest and notary Constantinus Pastil
London, British Museum, MS Additional 11838 (fol. 269ᵛ)

Plate 113

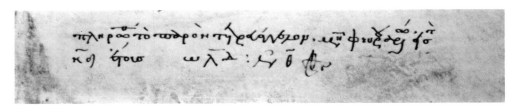

(*a*) A.D. 1326: Subscription
London, British Museum, MS Additional 5117 (fol. 224ʳ)

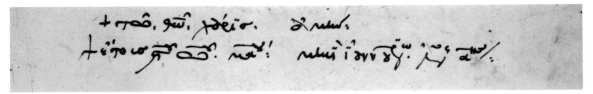

(*b*) A.D. 1333: Subscription
Oxford, Bodleian Library, MS Auct.T.5.28 (fol. 263ʳ)

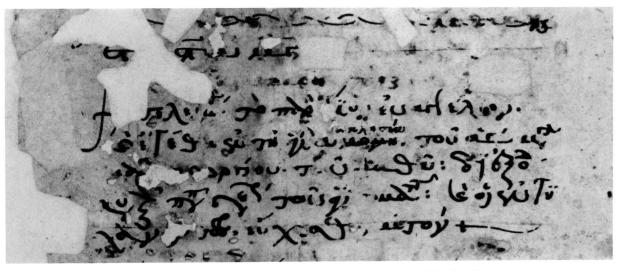

(*c*) A.D. 1334/1335: Subscription written probably in Cyprus
London, British Museum, MS Additional 19993 (fol. 281ᵛ)

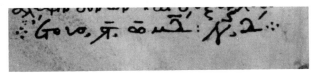

(*d*) A.D. 1335/1336: Subscription
Oxford, Bodleian Library, MS Laud Greek 2 (fol. 201ᵛ)

(*e*) A.D. 1348: Subscription
Glasgow, University Library, MS Hunter 424 (fol. 323ʳ)

Plate 114

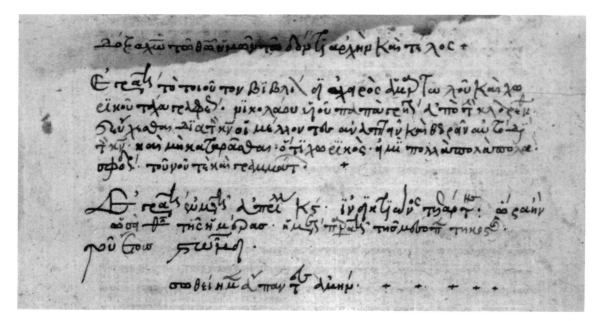

(*a*) A.D. 1336: Subscription by Nicolaus of Clarentza (in the Peloponnesus)
Cambridge, University Library, MS Additional 3049 (fol. 78ᵛ)

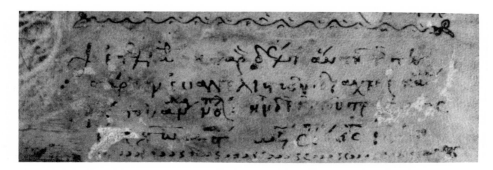

(*b*) A.D. 1337: Subscription by Constantinus of Adrianople
London, British Museum, MS Additional 5468 (fol. 225ᵛ)

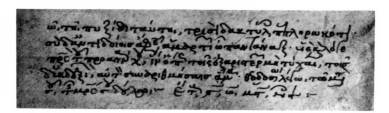

(*c*) A.D. 1337/1338: Subscription by Theodosius
Oxford, Bodleian Library, MS Selden Supra 29 (fol. 230ᵛ)

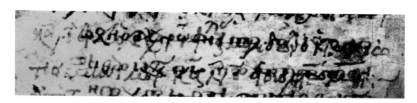

(*d*) A.D. 1340: Subscription by the priest and chartophylax Constantinus Magedon of Italy
Oxford, Bodleian Library, MS Selden Supra 9 (fol. 110ᵛ)

Plate 115

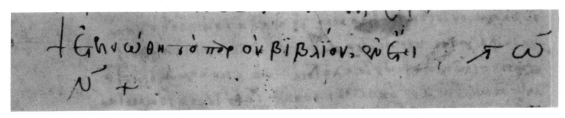

(*a*) A.D. 1340/1341: Subscription
Oxford, Bodleian Library, MS Auct.E.1.14 (fol. 296ᵛ)

(*b*) A.D. 1341/1342: Subscription
Oxford, Bodleian Library, MS Laud Greek 71 (fol. 270ᵛ)

(*c*) A.D. 1343, October 14: Note on an earthquake during the writing
(written by the hieromonk Galaction Madaraces in Constantinople)
Oxford, Bodleian Library, MS Barocci 197 (fol. 374ʳ)

(*d*) A.D. 1343, October 18–29: Note on an earthquake during the writing,
written by the hieromonk Galaction (Madaraces) in Constantinople
Oxford, Bodleian Library, MS Barocci 197 (fol. 380ᵛ)

(*e*) (A.D. 1343), November 20: Note on the time of the writing
(written by the hieromonk Galaction Madaraces in Constantinople)
Oxford, Bodleian Library, MS Barocci 197 (fol. 425ᵛ)

(*f*) (A.D. 1343), November 20: Note on an earthquake during the writing
(written by the hieromonk Galaction Madaraces in Constantinople)
Oxford, Bodleian Library, MS Barocci 197 (fol. 426ᵛ)

Plate 116

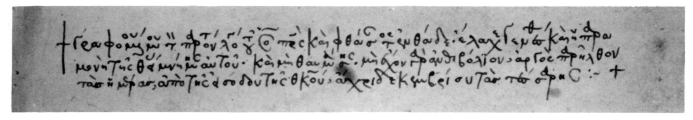

(*a*) (A.D. 1343), December 5: Note on the time of the writing
(written by the hieromonk Galaction Madaraces in Constantinople)
Oxford, Bodleian Library, MS Barocci 197 (fol. 434ʳ)

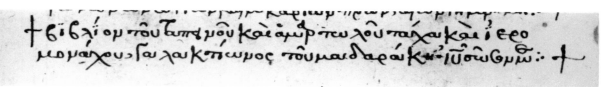

(*b*) (A.D. 1343): Personal reference by the scribe, hieromonk Galaction Madaraces
Oxford, Bodleian Library, MS Barocci 197 (fol. 277ᵛ)

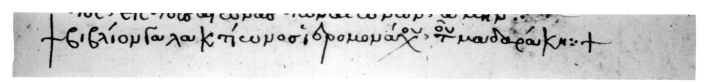

(*c*) (A.D. 1343): Personal reference by the scribe, hieromonk Galaction Madaraces
Oxford, Bodleian Library, MS Barocci 197 (fol. 344ʳ)

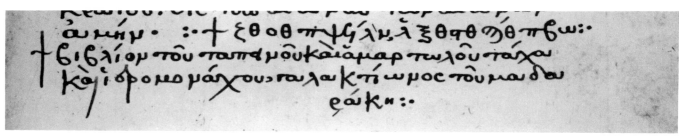

(*d*) (A.D. 1343): Personal reference by the scribe, hieromonk Galaction Madaraces
Oxford, Bodleian Library, MS Barocci 197 (fol. 460ʳ)

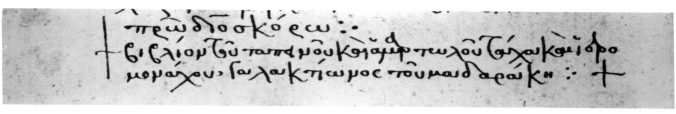

(*e*) (A.D. 1343): Personal reference by the scribe, hieromonk Galaction Madaraces
Oxford, Bodleian Library, MS Barocci 197 (fol. 630ᵛ)

Plate 117

(*a*) (transcribed shortly after A.D. 1343)
Transcript of the colophon of the hieromonk Galaction Madaraces
Oxford, Bodleian Library, MS Barocci 197 (fol. 669ʳ)

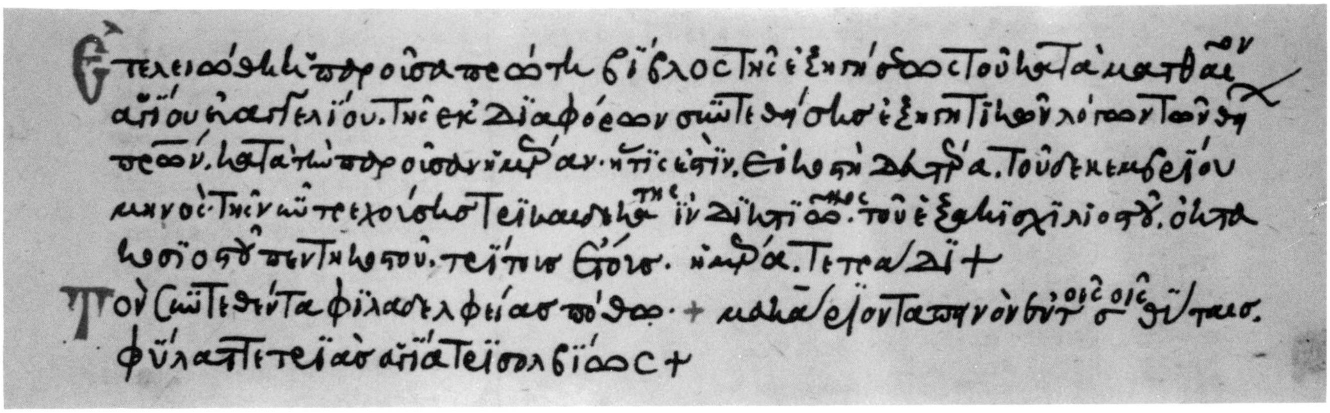

(*b*) A.D. 1344: Subscription by Macarius Chrysocephalus, metropolitan of Philadelphia
Oxford, Bodleian Library, MS Barocci 156 (fol. 360ᵛ)

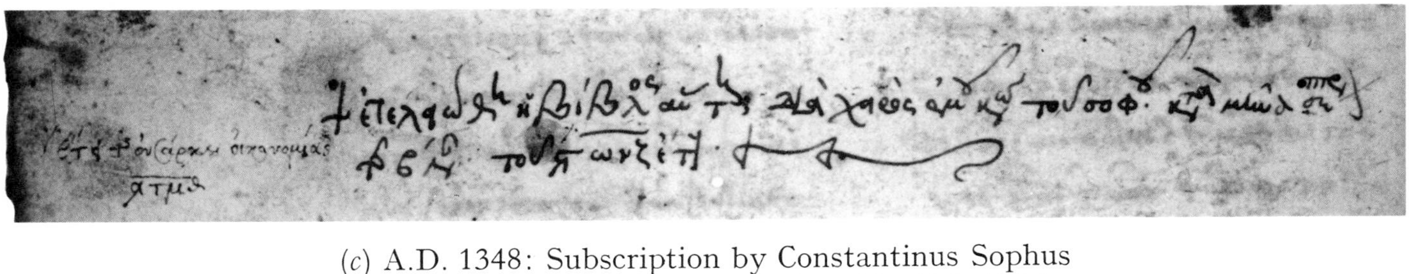

(*c*) A.D. 1348: Subscription by Constantinus Sophus
Oxford, Bodleian Library, MS Roe 18ᴮ (fol. 476ᵛ)

Plate 118

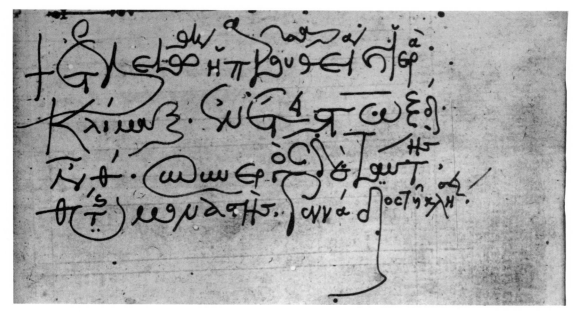

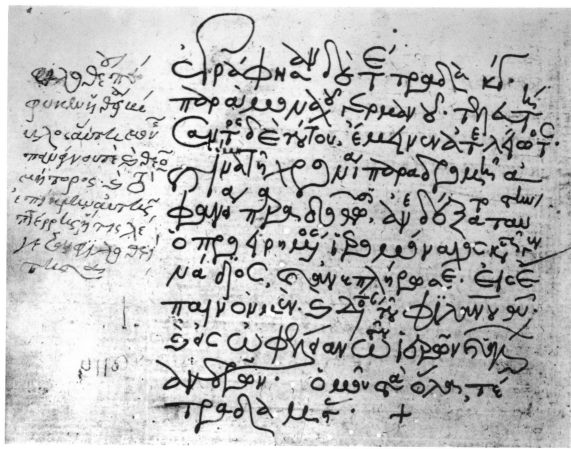

(*a*) A.D. 1355/1356: Subscription by the hieromonk Gennadius
Oxford, Christ Church, MS 63 (fol. 362ʳ–362ᵛ), 3/4 original size

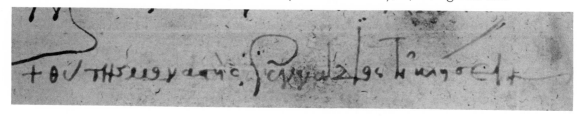

(*b*) (A.D. 1355/1356): Note by one of the scribes of the MS, the hieromonk Gennadius
Oxford, Christ Church, MS 63 (fol. 333ᵛ)

Plate 119

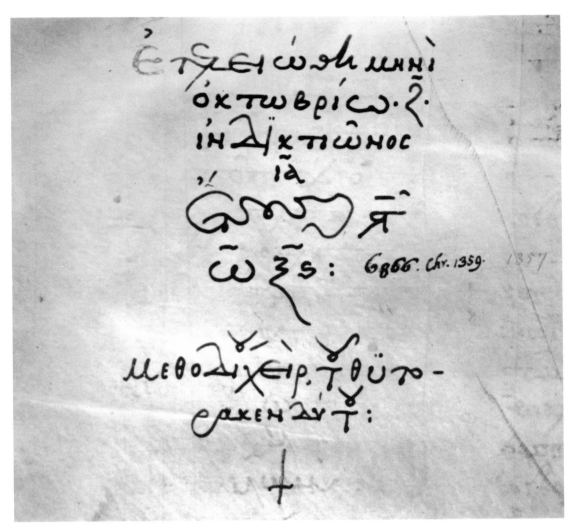

(*a*) A.D. 1357: Subscription by the hieromonk Methodius
(written most probably in the monastery τῶν Ὁδηγῶν in Constantinople)
London, British Museum, MS Additional 11837 (fol. 464ᵛ)

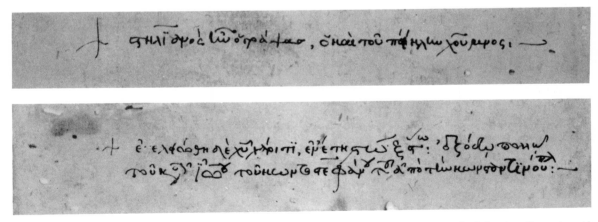

(*b*) A.D. 1357/1358: Subscription by Stelianus Chumnus, written probably in Constantinople
Oxford, Bodleian Library, MS Laud Greek 18 (parts of fol. 288ᵛ)

Plate 120

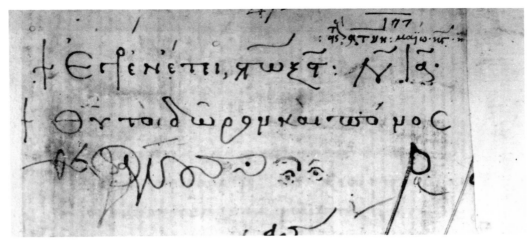

(*a*) A.D. 1358: Subscription by Theophanes
(written most probably in the monastery τῶν Ὁδηγῶν in Constantinople)
London, Lambeth Palace, MS 1183 (parts of page 472)

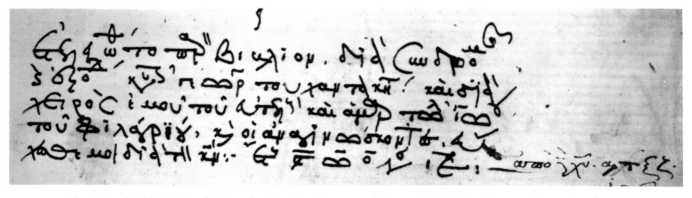

(*b*) A.D. 1361/1362: Subscription by Ioannes(-Ioseph) Philagrius, written in Crete
London, British Museum, MS Burney 50 (part II, fol. 179ʳ)

(*c*) (A.D. 1361/1362): Invocation by Ioannes(-Ioseph) Philagrius, written in Crete
London, British Museum, MS Burney 50 (part I, fol. 2ʳ)

Plate 121

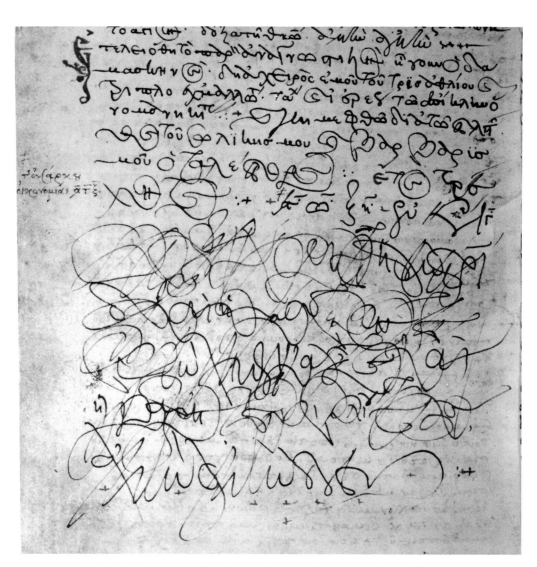

(a) A.D. 1359/1360: Subscription by the priest Nicetas
Oxford, Bodleian Library, MS Barocci 110 (fol. 362ᵛ)

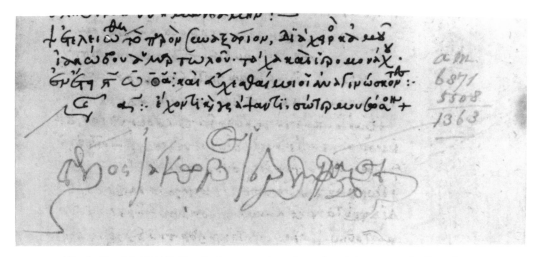

(b) A.D. 1362/1363: Subscription by the hieromonk Iacobus
London, British Museum, MS Harley 5782 (fol. 241ʳ)

Plate 122

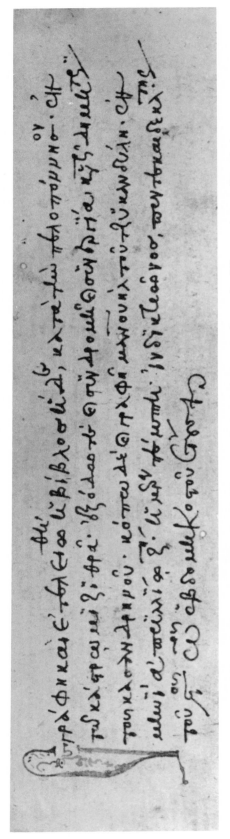

(a) A.D. 1362: Subscription by Manuel Tzycandyles, written in Mistra (near Sparta) at the conclusion of the once entire MS Oxford Canonici Greek 93 + Milan D 538 inf.
Milan, Biblioteca Ambrosiana, MS D 538 inf. (fol. 305v)

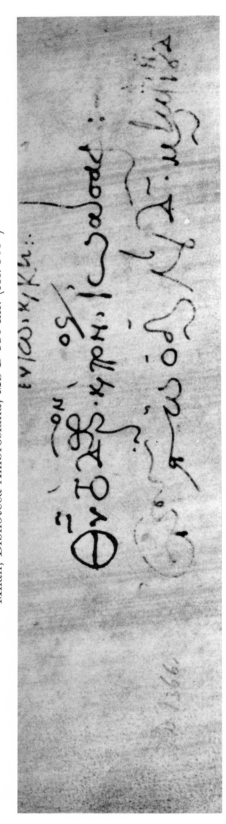

(b) A.D. 1366: Subscription by Ioasaph (of the monastery τῶν Ὁδηγῶν in Constantinople)
London, British Museum, MS Burney 18 (fol. 222v)

Plate 123

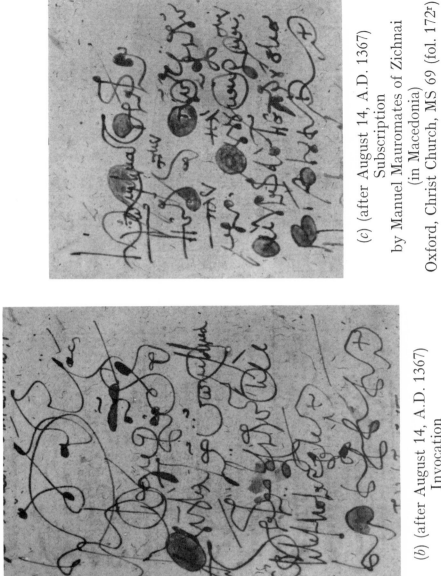

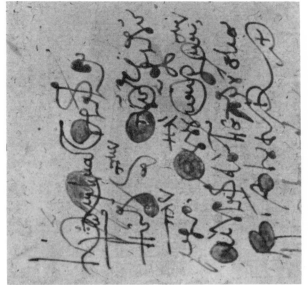

(a) August 14, A.D. 1367
Subscription
written presumably in Zichnai
(in Macedonia)
Oxford, Christ Church, MS 69 (fol. 156r)

(b) (after August 14, A.D. 1367)
Invocation
by Manuel (Mauromates) of Zichnai
(in Macedonia)
Oxford, Christ Church, MS 69 (fol. 171r)

(c) (after August 14, A.D. 1367)
Subscription
by Manuel Mauromates of Zichnai
(in Macedonia)
Oxford, Christ Church, MS 69 (fol. 172r)

Plate 124

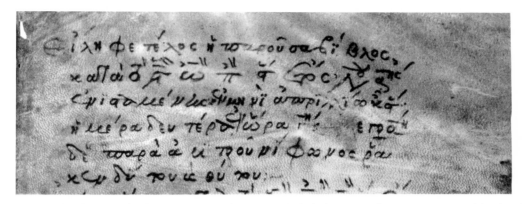

(*a*) A.D. 1378: Subscription by the hieromonk Niphon, written presumably in Crete
Oxford, Bodleian Library, MS Barocci 69 (fol. 280ʳ)

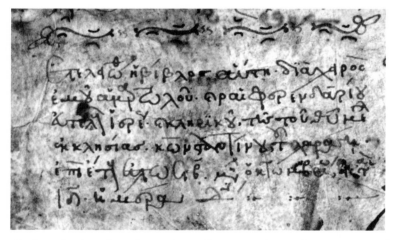

(*b*) A.D. 1383: Subscription by the priest Constantinus Charases of Constantinople
Oxford, Bodleian Library, MS Canonici Greek 102 (fol. 70ʳ)